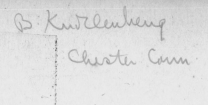

THE YALE EDITION

OF

HORACE WALPOLE'S

CORRESPONDENCE

EDITED BY W. S. LEWIS

VOLUME ONE

ADVISORY COMMITTEE

15-311-1

LIST OF SUBSCRIBERS

H. M. KING GEORGE VI

ALBERTUS MAGNUS COLLEGE LIBRARY, New Haven, Connecticut
RICHARD S. ALDRICH, Esq., Providence, Rhode Island
ALLEGHENY COLLEGE, THE REIS LIBRARY, Meadville, Pennsylvania
AMHERST COLLEGE, CONVERSE MEMORIAL LIBRARY, Amherst, Massachusetts
C. C. AUCHINCLOSS, Esq., New York, New York
Mrs HUGH D. AUCHINCLOSS, New York, New York
AVON OLD FARMS, Avon, Connecticut
JAMES T. BABB, Esq., New Haven, Connecticut
R. E. BALFOUR, Esq., Cambridge
Sir T. D. BARLOW, K.B.E., London
BAVARIAN STATE LIBRARY, Munich
BERKELEY COLLEGE LIBRARY, YALE UNIVERSITY, New Haven, Connecticut
THEODORE BESTERMAN, Esq., London
Messrs BICKERS AND SON, LTD., London
Mrs NORMAN H. BILTZ, Reno, Nevada
BIRMINGHAM PUBLIC LIBRARY, Birmingham
B. H. BLACKWELL, LTD., Oxford
R. K. BLAIR, Esq., Edinburgh
BOSTON ATHENAEUM, Boston, Massachusetts
BOSTON COLLEGE LIBRARY, Chestnut Hill, Massachusetts
BOSTON PUBLIC LIBRARY, Boston, Massachusetts
BOWDOIN COLLEGE LIBRARY, Brunswick, Maine
BROWN UNIVERSITY, JOHN HAY MEMORIAL LIBRARY, Providence, Rhode Island
BRYN MAWR COLLEGE LIBRARY, Bryn Mawr, Pennsylvania
JOHN N. BRYSON, Esq., Oxford
Messrs J. AND E. BUMPUS AND COMPANY, London
CHARLES EATON BURCH, Esq., Washington, D. C.

BUTLER UNIVERSITY LIBRARY, Indianapolis, Indiana
CALHOUN COLLEGE LIBRARY, YALE UNIVERSITY, New Haven, Connecticut
CALIFORNIA STATE LIBRARY, Sacramento, California
CARDIFF PUBLIC LIBRARY, Cardiff
The Countess of CARLISLE, London
LAURENCE R. CARTON, Esq., Towson, Maryland
CATHOLIC UNIVERSITY LIBRARY, Washington, D. C.
The Honorable Sir EVAN CHARTERIS, K.C., London
CICERO PUBLIC LIBRARY, Cicero, Illinois
HENRY E. COE, Esq., Syosset, Long Island, New York
COLUMBIA UNIVERSITY LIBRARY, New York, New York
CONNECTICUT COLLEGE, PALMER LIBRARY, New London, Connecticut
CONNECTICUT STATE LIBRARY, Hartford, Connecticut
REGINALD G. COOMBE, Esq., Greenwich, Connecticut
ROY COVENTRY, Esq., De Quetteville, Guernsey
THOMAS R. COWARD, Esq., New York, New York
DARTMOUTH COLLEGE, BAKER MEMORIAL LIBRARY, Hanover, New Hampshire
DAVENPORT COLLEGE LIBRARY, YALE UNIVERSITY, New Haven, Connecticut
DENVER PUBLIC LIBRARY, Denver, Colorado
DETROIT PUBLIC LIBRARY, Detroit, Michigan
Mrs ROBERT CLOUTMAN DEXTER, Belmont, Massachusetts
Mrs FRANK F. DODGE, New York, New York
DREW UNIVERSITY LIBRARY, Madison, New Jersey
DUKE UNIVERSITY LIBRARY, Durham, North Carolina
EDINBURGH PUBLIC LIBRARY, Edinburgh
EDINBURGH UNIVERSITY LIBRARY, Edinburgh
RODNEY R. ELLIS, Esq., Poultney, Vermont
EMORY UNIVERSITY LIBRARY, Emory University, Georgia
MAURICE FIRUSKI, Esq., Salisbury, Connecticut
Mrs MARGARET MITCHELL FLINT, Westport, Connecticut
FLORIDA STATE COLLEGE FOR WOMEN LIBRARY, Tallahassee, Florida
FORDHAM UNIVERSITY LIBRARY, New York, New York
FRANKLIN AND MARSHALL COLLEGE LIBRARY, Lancaster, Pennsylvania
FREE LIBRARY OF PHILADELPHIA, Philadelphia, Pennsylvania
DONALD T. GAMMONS, Esq., Boston, Massachusetts
GLASGOW UNIVERSITY LIBRARY, Glasgow

HOWARD L. GOODHART, Esq., New York, New York
Mrs WILLIAM GREENOUGH, Newport, Rhode Island
LAUDER GREENWAY, Esq., Greenwich, Connecticut
Mrs OCTAVIA GREGORY, Parkstone, Dorset
WILLIAM V. GRIFFIN, Esq., New York, New York
GROSVENOR LIBRARY, Buffalo, New York
SIDNEY LEWIS GULICK, Jr., Esq., Oakland, California
HACKLEY PUBLIC LIBRARY, Muskegon, Michigan
ALFRED E. HAMILL, Esq., Lake Forest, Illinois
ALLEN HAMILTON, Esq., M.D., Fort Wayne, Indiana
KENNETH E. HARTMAN, Esq., Des Moines, Iowa
HARVARD COLLEGE LIBRARY, Cambridge, Massachusetts
HAMILTON A. HIGBIE, Esq., Jamaica, New York
EDWIN L. HILDRETH, Esq., Brattleboro, Vermont
FREDERICK W. HILLES, Esq., New Haven, Connecticut
C. B. HOGAN, Esq., Woodbridge, Connecticut
WILLIAM S. HUNT, Esq., South Orange, New Jersey
HENRY E. HUNTINGTON LIBRARY AND ART GALLERY, San Marino,
    California
INDIANA STATE LIBRARY, Indianapolis, Indiana
INDIANA UNIVERSITY LIBRARY, Bloomington, Indiana
STUART W. JACKSON, Esq., Montclair, New Jersey
Miss ANNIE B. JENNINGS, Fairfield, Connecticut
JOHNS HOPKINS UNIVERSITY LIBRARY, Baltimore, Maryland
Mrs PERCY GAMBLE KAMMERER, Avon, Connecticut
The Lord KENYON, Whitchurch, Salop
KING'S COLLEGE LIBRARY, Cambridge
YALE KNEELAND, Jr., Esq., M.D., New York, New York
SEYMOUR H. KNOX, Esq., Buffalo, New York
LAFAYETTE COLLEGE LIBRARY, Easton, Pennsylvania
CLIFFORD LEAVENWORTH, Jr., Esq., Wallingford, Connecticut
LEEDS PUBLIC LIBRARIES, Leeds
A. N. LEWIS, Esq., San Francisco, California
LOUISIANA STATE UNIVERSITY LIBRARY, Baton Rouge, Louisiana
MANCHESTER PUBLIC LIBRARIES, Manchester
EDWARD MARTIN, Jr., Esq., New York, New York
C. L. McALEER, Esq., Brookline, Massachusetts
WILLIAM DAVIS MILLER, Esq., Wakefield, Rhode Island
MILLS COLLEGE LIBRARY, Oakland, California

UNIVERSITY OF BUFFALO, LOCKWOOD MEMORIAL LIBRARY, Buffalo, New York
UNIVERSITY OF CALIFORNIA LIBRARY, Berkeley, California
UNIVERSITY OF CHICAGO LIBRARIES, Chicago, Illinois
UNIVERSITY OF CINCINNATI LIBRARY, Cincinnati, Ohio
UNIVERSITY OF GEORGIA LIBRARIES, Athens, Georgia
UNIVERSITY OF KANSAS LIBRARY, Lawrence, Kansas
UNIVERSITY OF MICHIGAN LIBRARY, Ann Arbor, Michigan
UNIVERSITY OF MISSOURI LIBRARY, Columbia, Missouri
UNIVERSITY OF NEW MEXICO LIBRARY, Albuquerque, New Mexico
UNIVERSITY OF NORTH CAROLINA LIBRARY, Chapel Hill, North Carolina
UNIVERSITY OF NOTRE DAME LIBRARY, Notre Dame, Indiana
UNIVERSITY OF OREGON LIBRARY, Eugene, Oregon
UNIVERSITY OF PENNSYLVANIA LIBRARY, Philadelphia, Pennsylvania
UNIVERSITY OF PITTSBURGH LIBRARY, Pittsburgh, Pennsylvania
UNIVERSITY OF ROCHESTER LIBRARY, Rochester, New York
UNIVERSITY OF TEXAS LIBRARY, Austin, Texas
UNIVERSITY OF TORONTO LIBRARY, Toronto
UNIVERSITY OF UTAH LIBRARY, Salt Lake City, Utah
UNIVERSITY OF VIRGINIA LIBRARY, Charlottesville, Virginia
UNIVERSITY OF WISCONSIN LIBRARY, Madison, Wisconsin
THOMAS A. UNSWORTH, Esq., Burlington, Vermont
VASSAR COLLEGE LIBRARY, Poughkeepsie, New York
GEORGE WAHR, Esq., Ann Arbor, Michigan
M. E. WEATHERALL, Esq., North Clifton, Guernsey
WELLESLEY COLLEGE LIBRARY, Wellesley, Massachusetts
WELLS COLLEGE LIBRARY, Aurora, New York
WESLEYAN UNIVERSITY LIBRARY, Middletown, Connecticut
WALDEMAR WESTERGAARD, Esq., Los Angeles, California
WESTERN COLLEGE LIBRARY, Oxford, Ohio
WESTERN RESERVE UNIVERSITY LIBRARY, Cleveland, Ohio
HENRY WADE WHITE, Esq., Waterbury, Connecticut
WILLIAMS COLLEGE LIBRARY, Williamstown, Massachusetts
WORTHY PAPER COMPANY, West Springfield, Massachusetts
YALE CLUB LIBRARY, New York, New York
YALE UNIVERSITY LIBRARY, New Haven, Connecticut
MAURICE F. YORKE, Esq., Green Craig, Aberlady
INNIS YOUNG, Esq., New Haven, Connecticut

HORACE WALPOLE'S

CORRESPONDENCE

WITH

THE REV. WILLIAM COLE

I

EDITED BY W. S. LEWIS

AND

A. DAYLE WALLACE, Ph.D.

ASSOCIATE PROFESSOR OF ENGLISH IN THE
UNIVERSITY OF OMAHA

NEW HAVEN

YALE UNIVERSITY PRESS

LONDON : HUMPHREY MILFORD : OXFORD UNIVERSITY PRESS

1937

TO
A. B. L.

TABLE OF CONTENTS

VOLUME I

LIST OF ILLUSTRATIONS

VOLUME I

Grateful acknowledgment is made to the authorities of the Harvard College and New York Public Libraries for permission to reproduce the note and the drawing.

PREFACE

THERE are three good reasons for a new edition of Horace Walpole's correspondence: to give a correct text, to include for the first time the letters to him, and to annotate the whole with the fullness that the most informative record of the time deserves.

At the present time (June 1937) some six thousand letters to and from Walpole (out of an estimated seven thousand) have been located and have been secured for use in this edition by purchase of the originals, by photostating them, or by collating the Toynbee text with them. There have been discovered some three hundred unpublished letters of Walpole and several hundred more which the Toynbees did not see and which they had to print from the erratic text of earlier editors. Upwards of three thousand letters to Walpole will be given, two-thirds of them published for the first time in whole or in part.

Collation of the printed letters with the originals shows that the texts are frequently inaccurate. Many of the differences are trifling, but many are serious, involving dates, proper names and omitted passages. These far exceed the usual casualties of the press and are attributable, in part, to misplaced confidence in certain of the transcripts which were made by friendly owners with more goodwill than knowledge of Walpole's occasionally tricky handwriting. Furthermore, the final proofs could have been seldom, if ever, collated with the originals. But the 'editing' of the earlier editors was even more blameworthy. No letter which passed through the hands of Mary Berry remained the same. She inked out paragraphs, suppressed proper names, and wrote her notes wherever there was room for them. Her object was to improve the letters by deleting what she considered to be their less brilliant passages—the passages which are today, as often as not, of the greatest interest—for the Walpolian orchestra must play *fortissimo* or not at all. Hannah More was solely concerned

with her responsibility to the public morals, in case the letters to
her should ever be published; a responsibility she lived up to
with her pen, or, in great emergencies, with her scissors. She returned good for evil, however, and substituted words and phrases
which could enter the mind of innocence without danger. All
subsequent editors have suppressed passages, but this practice
has been abandoned in the present edition.

The advantages of including the letters to Walpole hardly
need to be stated. These letters answer innumerable questions
which cannot be answered in any other way and they bring Walpole's own letters into focus. As his side of several correspondences is missing, they make a large addition to his biography;
and many of the letters to him are of literary importance.

Walpole's letters have been often printed; they have never
been equipped with an adequate commentary. Cunningham and
Mrs Toynbee introduced biographical notes, but neither attempted complete clarification and illustration of the text. Yet
the need for this was stated in 1848 when the *Quarterly Review*
noticed the publication of Vernon Smith's edition of Walpole's
letters to Lady Ossory: 'Mr Smith, in his contempt of the humble duties of an annotator, mistakes we think the question. It is
not merely of the want of such illustration as may be collected
from registers or magazines that we complain—they may be obtained, as Mr Smith remarks, "by all who think it worth while
to pursue such inquiries," or, as we should rather have said, by
those who wish to be able to read his book without laying it
down an hundred times to consult an hundred others—but what
the reader most indispensably needs, and what registers and
magazines cannot supply, is the explanation of small events,
slight allusions, obscure anecdotes, traits of individual character,
the gossip of the circle, and all the little items and accidents of
domestic, social, and political life, which constitute in a most
peculiar degree the staple of Walpole's correspondence—the
most frequent occasions and chief objects of either his wit or his
sagacity, and without some knowledge of which his best letters
would be little more than a collection of riddles.' Something of

this the present edition attempts to do. Its primary intention is to facilitate the studies of scholars in the eighteenth century. Sooner or later, the eighteenth century scholar, be his subject what it may, must consult Walpole's correspondence. Politics, Society, Literature, and the Arts, these are the subjects which immediately come to mind when Horace Walpole is thought of, but there are as many more as there were divisions in eighteenth century life. This edition, through its index, hopes to lead the scholar, whether the subject of his search is Dr Johnson or ballooning, to whatever Walpole's correspondence may have to say about it.

We have had three advantages which previous editors have lacked: photography, which reduces the inevitable errors of the copyist, the use of a large collection of Walpoliana recently assembled, and the whole-hearted support of a University, with a great library especially strong in the period. It has been fortunate for this edition that Walpole has not been a general favourite with collectors. Although autograph collectors have wanted at least one of his letters and there have always been many good collections of the Strawberry Hill imprints, until recently no general Walpole collection was formed on a large scale. This lack of competition has enabled the present editor to make a wider collection than has previously existed, one which has been extended beyond the limits of Walpole's own books and the books from his Press, beyond the contents of Strawberry Hill,* to whatever might contribute to an understanding of Walpole's life and works. Much of this material is unpublished, and, taken in conjunction with the collections at Yale, it has been of great service in the elucidation of Walpole's text.

As publication will extend over many years, we shall be able, with the continued help of scholars, collectors, and librarians, to include additional material as the work progresses. Both sides of the Atlantic have already contributed so generously to the undertaking that it is to be hoped that readers of these first vol-

---

* The most important of these for this edition are the books, which Walpole, as often as not, annotated. Half the books in his library whose location is known today are now in the editor's possession.

umes will consider that they have a share in its success and will
communicate to the editor whatever corrections or additions
they can supply.

LETTER-WRITING was the natural vehicle of Horace Walpole's
mind. He tried all forms of writing: verse, pamphlets, essays,
catalogues raisonnés, history, biography, memoirs, a novel, a tragedy, a comedy. Many of these were pioneer works, the product
of a nervous and versatile mind stocked with curious learning
from four literatures. All were held to be successful by the eighteenth century, and they established for Walpole a solid contemporary reputation as an author. This declined, as Miss Hawkins
points out, after 1778, when a grossly unjust account of his dealings with Chatterton poisoned the public mind; but enough of
Walpole's reputation was left in the next century for Byron and
Scott to hail him in terms which today seem extravagant. 'It is
the fashion to underrate Horace Walpole,' wrote Byron in the
Preface to *Marino Faliero;* 'firstly, because he was a nobleman,
and secondly, because he was a gentleman; but to say nothing of
the composition of his incomparable letters, and of the Castle of
Otranto, he is the "Ultimus Romanorum," the author of the
Mysterious Mother, a tragedy of the highest order, and not a
puling love-play. He is the father of the first romance, and of the
last tragedy in our language, and surely worthy of a higher place
than any living writer, be he who he may.' *The Castle of Otranto*
has had some sixty editions since the first, five of them in the last
fifteen years; *The Mysterious Mother* maintains its eminence, a
dubious distinction in a period notable for bad tragedy. The
Catalogue of Royal and Noble Authors lingered on as a family
classic until Emerson swept it aside as frippery. The *Anecdotes
of Painting in England* is still the standard work on the subject,
although much buttressed by later editors. *Historic Doubts on
Richard III* attempted to 'debunk' history and exercised critics
for twenty-five years. The memoirs of the reigns of George II
and George III are still a chief source for professional historians.

But it is in none of these fields that Walpole stands today unchallenged.

Walpole was afraid of the public, especially that part of it which wrote reviews. This fear numbed his fingers, even while they 'wrote flying.' When writing the Memoirs he was afraid of posterity. He counted on us and believed in us, but, after all, he did not know us and, in spite of passionate appeals to us between chapters, he felt the awful weight of our ultimate judgment—'I sit down to resume a task, for which I fear posterity will condemn the author, at the same time that they feel their curiosity gratified.'

In his letters the weight is lifted. He chose his correspondents with care, each was the channel through which one particular interest chiefly flowed. The cardinal point with each was that he could be written to rapidly and easily, as if he were being talked to by the fireside in the evening at Strawberry Hill. Philip or Louis had brought in the candles, and beyond in the shadows of the room Walpole felt that posterity was eavesdropping.* This gave a sharpness and an excitement to what he was saying, but in that room, talking, as it were, to his carefully chosen friend, he was without fear.

Thus was built up in the half-light a special attitude, part professional, part informal, which stood to the formidable responsibilities of print as the private audiences at Holland House stood to the merciless public of Covent Garden. In this light, without fear of ridicule, Walpole could compose his great set-pieces—the execution of the Rebel Lords, the funeral of George II, the house-party at Stowe. This was history as a later age was to know it, but it was history written by an eager participant, brushing back lace ruffles from his wrist and dashing over the still-wet page the pounce that continues to glitter today.

For over sixty years Walpole kept it up, from Eton to his death. Throughout his life the graceful gesture, the slightly disillusioned smile, are too evident; they explain our refreshment in

* He retrieved many hundred letters and annotated them.

the directness of Boswell and Lady Mary Coke, Walpole's only rivals as journalists of the time. He has paid for his facile manner
in the false impression he has left with the casual reader. Four
thousand letters are a severe test for any man when he lets himself go as freely as Walpole does and when he makes capital out
of his weaknesses. The feminine element in his personality was
a strong one, as it has been in all great letter-writers, and this has
tended to minimize the effect of the many passages where he
shows deep feeling and unpremeditated kindness. Horace Walpole was a man of scrupulous honesty in an age when scrupulous
honesty was rare; and if he was a bitter enemy he was also a devoted friend; but we are not here concerned with Walpole as a
pattern for schoolboys. We are concerned with his passionate
ambition to be remembered as long as mankind should search the
memorials of the past. 'Monstrari digito praetereuntium,' Gilly
Williams wrote to Selwyn in the most penetrating remark on
Walpole ever made by an Englishman, 'For this he has wrote,
printed and built.' At an early age Walpole seems to have sensed
that his letters were what were most likely to insure for him the
finger of recognition, and that, therefore, they would justify
many thousand hours of unremitting labour. His job in life
was to accumulate and arrange the chronicles of his own time
and to present them in an entertaining way. If he could do this
posterity would point him out, but unless his facts were right he
would be rejected in the end. The 'gazettes' he prepared for his
friends and posterity would be as worthless as their broken seals
if when posterity did come to their minute examination it found
them false.

That time has now come, and Walpole stands the test. His
facts are right, he may be depended upon. The nightingales and
violins may still be enjoyed, but the daily hum of the eighteenth
century is equally audible. The ambition to reach the twentieth
century by recording the eighteenth has been fulfilled, and Walpole will be pointed out by the finger of those passing by as long
as interest in his age persists.

THE CORRESPONDENCE WITH COLE

EACH of Walpole's major correspondences may be given a particular classification, but in none is the subject so uniformly maintained as in the correspondence with Cole. The subject is English Antiquities.

William Cole was born 3 August 1714, three years before Walpole. The Eton List of 1728 shows him (a Colleger) and Walpole (an Oppidan) in the Third Form. He was admitted a sizar at Clare in 1732/3, but migrated to King's in 1735, where Walpole was a Fellow Commoner. They were close friends, but Cole was not of Walpole's innermost circle, although he corresponded with Richard West, was the life-long friend of Gray, and was called by them 'Tozhy.' Between 1736 and 1743 he made three trips abroad, spending six months of 1737 in Lisbon. He went into orders in 1744 and was given livings, due to the patronage of Lord Montfort and Browne Willis, that were just adequate to fill his house with prints and books and to populate, modestly, his farm yard. During the course of his correspondence with Walpole he had four livings, Bletchley, Waterbeach, Milton, and Burnham which he held while living at Milton. The first three places had the supreme merit of being near Cambridge. Cambridge is the capital of Cole's universe. While Walpole dreamed of being a fifteenth century monk at King's, Cole was living the life of one, brought up-to-date with his own house and an occasional visit to London. Against the many hard things said about the Universities of the eighteenth century, Cole's life should be counted. Cambridge is a shining place in his pages, filled with undoubted antiquities and, on the whole, agreeable men; a place of learning to which a man interested in the restoration and preservation of the past could dedicate himself.

Cole dedicated himself to the past, particularly to that part of it which belonged to Cambridge and Fenland. He had a passion for transcribing parish registers and cartularies and for reproducing coats of arms. Village churches were a particular excitement; he described their monuments and recorded their inscriptions. Cole is in the line of great English antiquaries from Bale and Stow to Hearne and Vertue. He is the Cambridge Anthony Wood, for his most important manuscript is his 'Collections for an Athenae Cantabrigienses.' Cole's manuscripts were used by many, often without acknowledgment, but he seldom complained of this treatment. Nothing mattered but the assemblage of ancient vital statistics and anecdotes in his folios. 'They are my only delight; they are my wife and children; they have been, in short, my whole employ and amusement for these twenty or thirty years.' He bequeathed them, 114 folio volumes, to the British Museum, and their usefulness is not yet exhausted.

The effect upon him of the appearance of the first two volumes of Walpole's *Anecdotes of Painting in England* in 1762 was so great that it drove him to write the detailed (and incredibly dull) letter which opens the correspondence. Nothing like the *Anecdotes* had ever appeared in England before. Walpole's *Catalogue of Royal and Noble Authors* four years earlier had been an exciting event in the antiquarian world, not only because it was a brilliant pioneer work, but because its author was himself a sprig of nobility. Cole, as he made his notes on it, must have been tempted to renew relations with his ingenious and Honourable schoolfellow. It is not clear how far these had been broken, for there are hints of invitations to Strawberry Hill before the correspondence begins;* but the enchantments of the *Anecdotes* were not to be resisted, and Cole wrote his professional welcome to the amateur. This must have been flattering to Walpole.

The correspondence covers twenty years, until Cole's death in 1782. During this time the two men seldom met. They were neighbours for a month in Paris in 1765, and they exchanged a few visits of a day or two which are red-letter occasions for Cole, but their correspondence was the life of their friendship. Although of opposite political and religious principles, which

---

* Cole also appears among the recipients of presentation copies of *Ædes Walpolianae*, 1747, in HW's MS list of them in his own copy (now Victoria and Albert Museum).

neither would abate, they prided themselves upon never quarrel-
ing. In his manuscripts, however, Cole relieved his feelings, as
may be seen in volume two, 372–3, and in his Comments on Walpole's disappointing 'Life of Thomas Baker.' Note 7 on page 184
of volume one shows another outburst which was probably echoed
elsewhere in Cole's marginalia,* but the glamour that had surrounded the Prime Minister's son at Eton was sustained by the
antiquarian glories of Strawberry Hill and the glitter of London.
Walpole was Cole's favourite contemporary author (who else
could write on dry subjects with such gusto?), and Cole was able
to rise above his private irritation. No irritation with Cole appears in Walpole's writing, in his letters, manuscripts, or marginalia. His attitude is genuinely affectionate throughout, if
faintly *de haut en bas*. Of the two, with all his crotchets and
quavers, Walpole was the 'easier.'

There is a secondary theme in this correspondence, the gout.
More subtle than Dean Milles, more heartless than Mr Masters, the gout is the remorseless enemy of Walpole and Cole. It
stretched them upon the rack, prevented their meetings, interrupted their studies and confused and mocked them by making
them believe that it was a specific against more serious enemies.
The object of their never-ending warfare against it was to keep
it on the ramparts, in the hands and feet, and out of the citadel,
the stomach and head, where once it was established all was lost.
The two friends were united in one form of defense, abstinence
from wine, otherwise they followed different schools. Walpole
trusted to the magic of Dr James's powders and the bootikins;
Cole to the bark and ever more clothes, which not only were to

---

* Cole's copy of *Historic Doubts* with
his notes was sold at Puttick and Simpson's, 24 June 1875, lot 194. The description reads: 'This volume was presented on
the 1st of Feb. 1768 by its author to the
Rev. William Cole . . . It was the knowledge of these notes probably that nettled
Walpole, and caused him three months
after Cole's death, Dec. 1782, to write, in a
letter to George Steevens, who had been
introduced to him by Cole himself only
the year before, a most disparaging character of Mr Cole, though he had been for

years on friendly terms with him. An extract of this letter is given on a fly-leaf,
but we do not remember to have seen it
in print.' The letter has not yet come to
light, nor the book located. Steevens fabri-
cated such notes in copies of his books, as
a practical joke upon posterity, and this
may well have been one of them. There is
no mention of Cole's notes in his copy of
Historic Doubts in White's catalogue of
Cole's library, 1784. The copy is lot 1149
in Steevens's sale, 1800, and was described
'with . . . copious MS notes by Mr Cole.'

defend him from the gout but from its allies, sore throats and fevers. When his horses ran away with him and he sat at the bottom of his chaise with his legs in the air, the loss of his hat worried Cole as much as the imminence of being broken to pieces. Walpole, on the other hand, prided himself on walking straight out into the cold and damp from a hot room without putting on his hat, and his fortress held out fifteen years after Cole's had surrendered.

Next to Cole's antiquities and gout came his High Church, Tory, principles. 'Cardinal Cole' he was called, and in middle life he seriously considered moving to France to savour more strongly the temptation to topple over to Rome, but he was dissuaded by Walpole, who pointed out that the King of France on Cole's death would have seized his manuscripts by the *droit d'aubaine* and that that would have been the end of them. His trip to France in 1765 extinguished any lingering desire to settle there, for he found that the French did not live in the English way and showed no signs of wishing to.

Cole's parishioners, it will be seen, were not one of his major concerns. If it were not for his diaries, we should not hear of them at all, but the diaries are as parochial as Parson Woodforde's: 'Jan. 25, 1766. Foggy. My beautiful parrot died at ten at night, without knowing the cause of his illness, he being very well last night . . . Feb. 1. Fine day and cold, Will Wood Junior carried three or four loads of dung into the clay-pit close. Baptized William the son of William Grace, blacksmith, who I married about six months before.' There is little in his diaries of the Cole we are concerned with in this correspondence, the Cole copying county history into his folios, 'a little diminutive dog, Busy,' in his lap. Michael Tyson found him at Milton in 1772: 'Cole has got two immense folios: the Leiger-books of Crowland and Spalding Monasteries, which he is busy transcribing . . .

> Amidst them all he in a chaire is sett,
>   Tossing and turning them withouten end;
> But for he was unable them to fett,
>   A little boy did on him still attend.

This admirable portrait of an antiquary one would think was drawn from the *very Milton Hearne* himself. His lameness, his employments, admirably answer.—Pray turn to your Spenser, book II, canto 9.'

And what was there in it for Walpole? He needed an antiquary among his correspondents, not only for his own researches, but as a medium through which he could express a dominant interest. The natural person for him to turn to was Gray, but Gray rather snubbed him as an antiquary. Henry Zouch preceded Cole as Walpole's antiquarian correspondent, but Cole's initial onslaught (of 16 May 1762) permitted of only one such correspondence, and Cole was an old friend, while Zouch was not. Cole was useful to him as a reference library that never failed, although Walpole used little of the material that Cole supplied. In Cole Walpole had a friend among the more professional antiquaries, one who was respected by all and one whose public loyalty and support never wavered through the controversies which rose out of the *Historic Doubts on Richard III* and the Chatterton affair. The friendship of the two men was useful and flattering to both; it overcame the differences of rank and training. Alexander Chalmers considered that their letters added 'little to the character of either, as men of sincerity or candour. Both were capable of writing polite and even flattering letters to gentlemen, whom in their mutual correspondence, perhaps by the same post, they treated with the utmost contempt and derision.' A less high-minded age is not bothered by a little duplicity and cynically doubts if there ever was a correspondence (including Chalmers's own) which has not contained similar insincerities.

Horace Walpole's interest in the past centered in three main fields: English portraiture (including prints), Gothic architecture, and county and family history, especially his own. Of the earlier English portraiture he was and still is the chief historian. He had the immense advantage of owning Vertue's manuscripts, and modern scholars have only admiration for his use of them. He was an expert editor and he had 'an eye' and a memory which, even if he had not been able to buy Vertue's manuscripts, would have made him a remarkable critic. His collection of English prints, to which Cole contributed, was possibly the finest and most extensive ever made. Walpole's claim to be the English Vasari is as secure, I believe, as is his claim to the primacy of English letter-writers.

Walpole's interest in 'Gothic' was, as I have suggested elsewhere,* pictorial, romantic and snobbish. Walpole's 'Gothic' outbid its rivals (Batty Langley's and Saunderson Miller's), in contemporary favour, and if not a letter of Walpole's had survived the introduction of a new era in taste would have been sufficient to ensure the lasting reputation he craved. His Gothic was an eclectic affair: Strawberry Hill was composed of admired Gothic details copied from the originals or prints of them in Dugdale and Dart. Walpole saw no impropriety in appropriating the gates of the choir at Rouen for a screen in a bedchamber, or in boiling down the north door of a cathedral to make a door in the Gallery. He knew he was right, for he had gone back to the originals. Stresses and strains were matters for journeymen builders; the great thing was to secure the 'effect' of past ages, and this is what, in the eyes of the eighteenth century, Strawberry Hill and *The Castle of Otranto* accomplished.

'Gothic' ceased to be a name of reproach; 'the rust of the Barons' Wars' became a beautiful unreality. The past was an elegant escape from the confusions and disappointments of the present—knights in armour, monks in chapels, ladies in distress, all set forth on a stage having doors with pointed arches and windows with lean saints, with machinery in the wings for supernatural employments; these were the elements which made 'Gothic' popular. Former ages, if one knelt before them, reached down and touched one on the shoulder; one lifted up intoxicated eyes and identified the actors present, William the Conqueror, William his son, Henry, Stephen, Henry, Richard and John—and, to make it personal, Ralph Walpole, Bishop of Ely, and Robert de Walpole, Clerk of the Pantry to Henry III. All

---

* In 'The Genesis of Strawberry Hill,' *Metropolitan Museum Studies*, New York, 1934, volume v, Part one, page 57.

these and a thousand more, fresh from the fields of Crécy, Agincourt and Bosworth, their visors up, their hands resting on their swords, their heads bowed in simple reverence to the eloquent benediction of a Church Father. 'The ages that do not disappoint.' One was safe in them because one created them oneself. Their men and women were as impersonal as the figures at Drury Lane, but they lived, talked, and dressed to one's own bidding, and when they came to die they laid themselves down in neat recumbent attitudes, with an interesting heraldic object at their heads and another at their feet, a sword on their bodies and a wife at their side, all under a stone canopy which was the inspiration for a chimney-piece at Strawberry Hill.

The third element in Walpole's enthusiasm for Gothic is the same that stimulated his interest in county history, family pride. The Grand Tour taught the importance of Race as well as the interest of ancient buildings and Race was a far livelier, more intimate thing, for when it was authenticated by the Heralds it afforded the delightful perquisite of recognized superiority to one's fellowmen. Walpole's emotions were deeply engaged here, for the Walpoles, though of ancient race, were relatively small beer compared to his Conway and Townshend cousins and most of his acquaintance. The new society which rose with the Revolution and waxed rich as the eighteenth century advanced, kept the College of Arms busy supplying ancestors who had 'arrived' before William III. Although Walpole insists that the Walpoles were nothing before Sir Robert, this did not lessen his desire to clamber back to ancestors who were something, in a laudable effort to acquire a leasehold in the ages which did not disappoint. Horace Walpole's 'position' in London society was never questioned. Even Lady Mary Coke at the height of her pique at him never suggests that his ancestry is dim, but like most newly-arrived he was preoccupied with the nuances of snobbery, the discrimination and cultivation of which have been a major contribution of the Anglo-Saxon peoples to civilization.

The Gothic Revival bore witness in 1750 to the same spirit which dotted American suburbs in 1920 with Colonial houses;

arrival in the *Mayflower* and *Arbella* is equivalent to departure
for the Crusades. It was not accident that Horace Walpole's first
full-dress work was *A Catalogue of Royal and Noble Authors*.
'I have recovered a barony in fee . . . and on my mother's side
it has mounted Lord knows whither, by the Philipps's to Henry
VIII, and has sucked in Dryden for a great-uncle; and by Lady
Philipps's mother, Darcy, to Edward III, and there I stop, for
brevity's sake—especially as Edward III is a second Adam . . .
I am the first antiquary of my race—people don't know how entertaining a study it is. Who begot whom is a most amusing kind
of hunting; one recovers a grandfather instead of breaking one's
own neck—and then one grows so pious to the memory of a thousand persons one never heard of before.'* In the Anglo-American
fellowship no element is more mutually recognizable than the
ambition to be identified with a wealthy and literate ancestry.

The past was the Land of Visions, but it should not float too
far above reality. The imagination would be more at ease in its
cloud-capp'd towers if it maintained some connection with the
earth; this basis of historical fidelity came from reading and from
Cole. In 1762 the first exuberance which conceived Strawberry
Hill had passed into a secondary phase. Walpole was still poring
over topographical folios in search of admired Gothic details to
apply to his new rooms, but the new rooms were on a scale com-
mensurate with his larger income and expanding knowledge.
The earlier rooms were small Georgian rooms 'gothicized' by
pointed windows and doors and chimney-pieces copied from
flamboyant tombs. The rooms of the middle period (1760–1776)
included the ceiling in the Gothic scheme, which aided the il-
lusion without establishing it. Towards the end of his life Walpole was to admit sadly that Strawberry was 'but a sketch by
beginners,' that he had not '*studied* the science,' but had hurried
impetuously ahead and produced what were 'more the works of
fancy than of imitation.' His friendship with Cole was a principal factor in this disillusionment, for however much he ap-
plauded Walpole's flights, Cole remained meritoriously upon the

* HW to Cole 5 June 1775.

ground. Cole's pedestrian way of life was a reassuring thing to
return to. It assisted Walpole in the conception of a great work
on English Gothic architecture which he and Cole, with Essex
and Tyson, were to produce under Royal patronage. There were
to be plates, Walpole wrote 12 August 1769, 'from the conclusion
of Saxon architecture, beginning with the round Roman arch'
down to Inigo Jones 'in his heaviest and worst style.' Essex was
to contribute 'observations on the art, proportions and method
of building, and the reasons observed by the Gothic architects
for what they did . . . The prices and the wages of workmen,
and the comparative value of money and provisions at the several
periods, should be stated, as far as it is possible to get materials.'
Tyson was to contribute the 'history of fashions and dresses . . .
as in elder times especially much must be depended on tombs
for dresses.' To Cole was to go the solid labour of ascertaining
'the chronologic period of each building—and not only of each
building, but of each tomb, that shall be exhibited.' Walpole
himself, in addition to getting the Royal assistance for so expensive a work, would add 'detached samples of the various patterns
of ornaments,' pinnacles and that parent of all the rest, the trefoil. There is no mention of the Church as a living organism, its
liturgical drama or its music, and although we were to have the
people's dresses, there was no interest in their speech, but the
scheme is perhaps as comprehensive as anyone in the eighteenth
century could have devised and it was actually carried out in
part (with full quotation of Walpole's letter) by Richard Gough's
Sepulchral Monuments seventeen years later.

Doubtless the solidity of these studies penetrated Strawberry
Hill and *The Castle of Otranto* more than is apparent, and gave
to those works the vitality which upwards of two centuries have
shown them to possess, although now none but can 'brook tears,
at the thought of those enchantments cold.' Cole has not, I think,
been given credit for contributing to the Romantic Movement,
but it was not chance that led Walpole to describe the writing
of *Otranto* to him, alone among his English correspondents, or
to embed in his manuscripts (which Walpole knew were destined

for posterity), the concluding sentence of the second passage. 'You will laugh at my earnestness [Cole would not, but posterity might]: but if I have amused you, by retracing with any fidelity, the manners of ancient days, I am content, and give you leave to think me as idle as you please.'

METHOD

THE first decision in editing this work was to publish the letters by correspondences and not chronologically. The Advisory Committee, I believe, are now unanimous that this decision is the right one, since most of the major correspondences and many of the minor ones have a predominant subject. It is my belief that Walpole selected his correspondents with a subject more or less in his mind and that when the correspondence ended, through death or 'coolness,' he immediately chose another correspondent to whom he could write on the same themes. As we have seen, Cole followed Zouch; Lort and Pinkerton followed Cole. Mason followed Gray and was succeeded by Hannah More. Lady Ossory followed Montagu, and so on. A chronological arrangement would have destroyed this unity, and would have hampered the reader concerned with a specific subject. To take an example at random, the following letters are at present known for February 1764: Cole to Walpole, Walpole to Hertford, Walpole to Cole, Cole to Walpole, Drumgold to Walpole, Walpole to Hertford, Hertford to Walpole, Mann to Walpole, Walpole to Mann, Walpole to Anne Pitt, Walpole to Cole, Walpole to Dalrymple, Walpole to Hertford, Hertford to Walpole, Walpole to Grosvenor Bedford. Such an arrangement lacks the simplicity of a single correspondence and becomes a maze of unrelated subjects. Walpole's letters gain greatly in interest by being restored to his correspondent's. They can now be read for the first time, as they were written and answered, with 'ease and opportunity,' in Stevenson's phrase.

A much more difficult decision, and one in which the Advisory Committee are by no means unanimous, was what to do about 'normalization.' The decision was to retain Walpole's punctuation and spelling of proper names, but to normalize other spellings and capitalization. A list of Walpole's obsolete spellings is given on page xliii. It is often not possible to tell whether Walpole intended a capital, and the extra labour and expense of printing it (incorrectly, no doubt, in many cases), have not seemed to justify the securing of something which, to many, is relatively unimportant. As we shall have to edit several hundred letters from nineteenth century texts, uniformity would be lost in any event. What is amusing and 'flavoursome' in small doses becomes wearisome in large, and it imparts an air of quaintness to a text which was not apparent to the correspondents themselves. There is, finally, a considerable gain in readability and appearance.

The text has been transcribed from photostats of Walpole's letters, now British Museum Additional Manuscripts 5952, 5953, and from photostats of Cole's letters, now Victoria and Albert Museum, Foster Manuscript 110. Cole's copies of many of his letters to Walpole and of Walpole's letters to him are scattered through the manuscript volumes which Cole bequeathed to the British Museum. The transcription has been made by Dr Wallace, who also collated the proofs with the photostats.

The letters which went through the post are the ones printed wherever possible. Walpole seems to have made few drafts, although he frequently made notes on the back of letters for his replies. These are given in the introduction to the letters they apply to. Cole copied many of his letters into his manuscript volumes, but as both the copies and the letters which went through the post are remarkably free from deletion and correction, it is possible that both are copies of a draft subsequently destroyed. The inadvertent omissions and blunders of many of Cole's letters that Walpole received and the suppression of chatty and satirical comment which the slightly formal tone of the correspondence tended to discourage, do suggest, however, that some of Cole's letters which went through the post may have been copied from his folios, although the absence from them of many letters shows that Cole did not habitually copy his letters into his volumes first. Cole's letters are published here for the first time. Additional information from his copies is given in the notes.

All biographical notes without reference are from the *Dictionary of National Biography* or *The Complete Peerage*.

All books named are printed in London, unless otherwise stated.

Square brackets indicate editorial emendation; angular brackets, the restoration of the manuscript where it is mutilated.

The compilation of the notes is largely the work of Dr Wallace, but they have been revised by me, and the final responsibility is mine. In writing them we have been exceedingly fortunate in receiving the active help of many scholars whose names and contributions are listed under Acknowledgments.

W. S. LEWIS

Farmington, Connecticut
  June 1937.

ACKNOWLEDGMENTS

THE satisfaction of acknowledging much of the help which I have already received must be deferred to the volumes where it will appear, for the list of those to whom I am indebted has become, in Walpole's phrase, 'a bede-roll' of kindness, and proper acknowledgment of it here would run to so many pages that the ends of acknowledgment would be defeated. I do not wish, however, to miss this opportunity of thanking the many friends and acquaintances abroad and at home whose active interest has contributed to the usefulness of the work and whose friendliness has made it a pleasure.

My first acknowledgment is due to my friends at Yale who recommended that the University sponsor a project conducted by one at that time outside the academic fold. Without their help this edition would have lacked the authority which the University conferred upon it, and it would not have been attempted. These friends, in particular, are Professors Keogh, Pottle, Tinker and Karl Young, Dean Furniss, and Provost (now President) Seymour.

The Delegates of the Clarendon Press have generously placed at my disposal all the materials bequeathed them by the late Dr Paget Toynbee for a future edition of Walpole's letters, together with the correspondence of Mrs Toynbee and Dr Toynbee relating to their edition and covering thirty years.

The Trustees of the British Museum and of the Victoria and Albert kindly granted me permission to have photostats made of the letters in their possession and to edit from them. At the British Museum I am particularly indebted to Dr Flower for constant assistance and to Mr A. J. Watson of the Department of Manuscripts for hours of research carefully and cheerfully performed. I am also indebted to the Earl of Derby, K.G., for permission to print Walpole's unsent letter of 26 March 1780 (ii. 363); and to Mrs Alvin Scheuer of New York for permission to print (for the first time correctly) Walpole's letter of 19 August 1762.

The richness of Yale's collections in Walpole's period is so great that it can only be realized by one who has actually worked in the Library. An undertaking like the present requires the use of thousands of volumes, many, perhaps most, of which stir rarely from the shelves. The comparatively few which we have lacked have been bought immediately by the University whenever it was able to do so, and for this prompt and generous help I wish to thank the Head of the Purchasing Department, Mr Carl L. Cannon. The helpfulness of the Yale Library Staff is proverbial, and for their unfailing patience and resourcefulness I cannot be too grateful.

No project of this sort can ever have been more fortunate in its Advisory Committee. Each one of these gentlemen has responded at once to all the many appeals for help which I have made to them, and no problem has been too difficult or too time-consuming for them. They have not been willing merely to lend their names, but they have given with all possible generosity of their knowledge and experience. The proofs have been read entirely through by Messrs R. W. Chapman, R. W. Ketton-Cremer, F. A. Pottle, and Leonard Whibley. Mr Ketton-Cremer has been particularly helpful with matters relating to Norfolk and Mr Whibley with those relating to Gray and Cambridge.

Professor Karl Young and Mr K. B. McFarlane of Magdalen College, Oxford, in particular, have read the Latin passages and saved us from many *voces nihili*. Professor Angelo Lipari of Yale has rendered similar service with the Italian. Professor Namier has given us the benefit of his unrivalled knowledge of the early Parliaments of George III. Mr William A. Jackson of New York has helped solve various bibliographical difficulties.

The Marchioness of Cholmondeley kindly sent the Russian inscription under the portrait of Catherine the Great at Houghton; and the Earl of Ilchester, the photograph of Walpole's wax medallion of Benedict XIV.

To Constable and Co., Ltd (through the kind offices of Mr

Michael Sadleir), I am indebted for the use of proofs of Cole's unpublished *Waterbeach Diary*.

The class at the University of Illinois Library School under Miss Rose B. Phelps identified several persons who had eluded us. Dr Hale Sturges assisted in the reading of the proof and in preparing the Appendices; Dr John P. Kirby rendered invaluable service in the final stages of printing.

For help with the many questions of editorial method I am indebted to Professor Notestein, to M. Seymour de Ricci, and the Printer to Yale University, Mr C. P. Rollins. Above all, I am indebted to Dr Chapman and to Professor Pottle, not only for help at every point of the present undertaking, but for their friendly Walpolian interest during the years which preceded it.

Further, I wish to express my thanks to the following: Dr J. Q. Adams, the Folger Shakespeare Library, Washington, D. C.; Professor A. R. Bellinger of Yale; the late Mr Richard Bentley; the Rev. H. E. D. Blakiston, President of Trinity College, Oxford; Dr Benjamin Boyce of the Municipal University at Omaha; Mr S. G. Campbell, the Bursar of Christ's College, Cambridge; Sir Sydney Cockerell, Director of the Fitzwilliam Museum, Cambridge; Professor R. S. Crane of the University of Chicago; Dr Harvey Cushing; Mr W. D. Davies, the Librarian of the National Library of Wales; Dr J. F. Fulton; Mr J. T. Gerould, the Librarian of the Princeton College Library; Mr Blake-More Godwin, Director of the Toledo Museum of Art, Toledo, Ohio; Mr J. W. Goodison of the Fitzwilliam; Miss Ruth Granniss, the Librarian of the Grolier Club, New York City; Mr George Hayward, the City Librarian of Norwich; the Rt Rev. Bernard Francis Oliver Heywood, Bishop of Ely; Professor Raymond T. Hill of Yale; Dr John Johnson, Printer to the University of Oxford; Mr C. H. Kemp, the Town Clerk of Cambridge; Mr H. S. Kingsford of the Society of Antiquaries; the Rev. J. Leonard, C.M., St. Mary's College, Strawberry Hill; Mr H. M. Lydenberg, the Librarian of the New York Public Library; Sir Eric Maclagan, Director of the Victoria and Albert Museum; Major Henry Milner, Librarian to Lord Derby, Knowsley Hall; Professor D.

Nichol Smith of Oxford; the Editors of *Notes and Queries;* Mr Charles Noyes of the Yale School of Medicine; Mr E. S. Peck of Cambridge; Mr Graham Pollard; Mr A. C. Potter, Librarian of the Harvard College Library; the Rev. T. L. Riggs of New Haven; Mr John Saltmarsh of King's College, Cambridge; Mr Romney Sedgwick; Sir Wathen A. Waller, Bt, Woodcote, Warwick; Mrs Walpole and Miss Pamela Walpole of Wolterton Park, Norwich; Dr G. P. Winship of the Harvard College Library.

Finally, I wish to express my great indebtedness to Mrs Nicholas Moseley of Meriden, Connecticut, for the Index which has been entrusted to her experienced care.

WALPOLE'S SPELLING

The following are a selection of Walpole's spellings which differ from modern usage.

artfull, beautifull, etc.
aspin (aspen)
atchieved
chace
chearfull
cieling
cloaths
compleat
confident (confidant)
coud
crouded
devysed
doat (dote)

fancyfull
gardiner
litterature
meer
numpskulls
oeconomy
origine
pacquet
pannel
passtimes
plaister
plie (ply)
red (read)

rejoyce
relicks
satten
scite (site)
seperate
style (stile)
swoln
teaze
wainscotts
wastecoat
wave (waive)

CUE TITLES AND ABBREVIATIONS

Add MS . . .	Additional Manuscript, British Museum.
Aedes, Works ii. . .	Horace Walpole, *Ædes Walpolianae: or, A Description of the Collection of Pictures at Houghton Hall in Norfolk, the Seat of . . . Sir Robert Walpole;* in vol. ii of *The Works of Horatio Walpole, Earl of Orford,* 5 vols, 1798.
Alumni Cantab. . .	*Alumni Cantabrigienses,* comp. by John Venn and J. A. Venn, Cambridge, 4 vols, 1922–7.
Alumni Oxon. . .	Joseph Foster, *Alumni Oxonienses: The Members of the University of Oxford, 1500–1714,* Oxford, 4 vols, 1891–2; *1715–1886,* London, 4 vols, 1887–8.
Anecdotes[1] . . .	Horace Walpole, *Anecdotes of Painting in England,* Strawberry Hill; vols i and ii, 1762; vol. iii, 1763; vol. iv, 1771.
Anecdotes[2] . . .	Horace Walpole, *Anecdotes of Painting in England,* second edn, Strawberry Hill, vols i, ii and iii, 1765.
Anecdotes, ed. Dallaway	Horace Walpole, *Anecdotes of Painting in England,* ed. Rev. James Dallaway, 5 vols, 1828.
Anecdotes, ed. Wornum, 1876 . . .	Horace Walpole, *Anecdotes of Painting in England,* ed. Ralph N. Wornum, 3 vols, 1876.
Baker, *History of St John's College* . .	Thomas Baker, *History of the College of St John the Evangelist, Cambridge,* ed. John E. B. Mayor, Cambridge, 2 vols, 1869.
Bentham, *Ely*[2] .	James Bentham, *The History and Antiquities of the Conventual & Cathedral Church of Ely,* Norwich, 1812.
Betham, *Baronetage* .	William Betham, *The Baronetage of England,* 5 vols, 1801–5.
Blecheley Diary . .	*The Blecheley Diary of the Rev. William Cole . . . 1765–67,* ed. Francis Griffin Stokes, 1931.
Blomefield, *Norfolk*[2] .	Francis Blomefield, and Charles Parkin, *An Essay towards a Topographical History of the County of Norfolk,* 11 vols, 1805–10.
BM	British Museum.

Boswell, *Johnson* . . *Boswell's Life of Johnson,* ed. George Birkbeck Hill, revised by L. F. Powell, Oxford, 6 vols, 1934–.

Brydges, *Restituta* . Sir Egerton Brydges, *Restituta; or, Titles, Extracts, and Characters of Old Books in English Literature, Revived,* 4 vols, 1814–16.

Burke, *Commoners* . John Burke, *History of the Commoners of Great Britain and Ireland,* 4 vols, 1833–8.

Burnet, *Hist. of His Own Times* . . . Gilbert Burnet, *History of His Own Times,* 2 vols, 1723–34.

Camden, *Britannia*[2] . William Camden, *Britannia,* revised by Edmund Gibson, 2 vols, 1722.

Cole, *Jour. to Paris* . William Cole, *A Journal of My Journey to Paris in the Year 1765,* ed. Francis Griffin Stokes, 1931.

Collins, *Peerage,* 1812 . *Collins's Peerage of England,* ed. Sir Egerton Brydges, 9 vols, 1812.

Cooper, *Annals* . . Charles Henry Cooper, *Annals of Cambridge,* Cambridge, 4 vols, 1842–52; vol. 5, ed. John William Cooper, Cambridge, 1908.

Cooper, *Memorials* . Charles Henry Cooper, *Memorials of Cambridge,* Cambridge, 3 vols, 1860–66.

Country Seats . . *Horace Walpole's Journals of Visits to Country Seats, &c.,* in *The Walpole Society,* Oxford, vol. xvi, 1928.

Cunningham . . Peter Cunningham (ed.), *The Letters of Horace Walpole, Earl of Orford,* 9 vols, 1857–9.

Description of SH . . Horace Walpole, *A Description of the Villa of Mr Horace Walpole, at Strawberry Hill near Twickenham,* in vol. ii of *The Works of Horatio Walpole, Earl of Orford,* 5 vols, 1798.

Dictionary of English Church History . . Sidney Leslie Ollard (ed.), *A Dictionary of English Church History,* London, Oxford, and Milwaukee, second edn, [1919].

DNB . . . . *Dictionary of National Biography.*

Dugdale, *Baronage* . Sir William Dugdale, *The Baronage of England,* 3 vols in 2, 1675–6.

EBP . . . . Freeman O'Donoghue and Henry M. Hake, *Catalogue of Engraved British Portraits . . . in the British Museum,* 6 vols, 1908–25.

Engravers, Works . . Horace Walpole, *A Catalogue of Engravers,* in vol. iv of *The Works of Horatio Walpole, Earl of Orford*, 5 vols, 1798.

Engravers² . . . Horace Walpole, *A Catalogue of Engravers*, second edn, Strawberry Hill, 1765.

Eton Coll. Reg. 1698– 1752 . . . Richard Arthur Austen-Leigh (ed.), *The Eton College Register 1698–1752*, Eton, 1927.

Eton Coll. Reg. 1753– 1790 . . . Richard Arthur Austen-Leigh (ed.), *The Eton College Register 1753–1790*, Eton, 1921.

Fugitive Verses . . . W. S. Lewis (ed.), *Horace Walpole's Fugitive Verses*, New York and Oxford, 1931.

GEC . . . . G. E. Cokayne, *The Complete Peerage*, revised by Vicary Gibbs, *et al.*, 1910–.

'Genesis of SH' . . W. S. Lewis, 'The Genesis of Strawberry Hill,' *Metropolitan Museum Studies*, New York, vol. v, pt i, June, 1934.

GM . . . . *The Gentleman's Magazine.*

Gough, *British Topography²* . . . Richard Gough, *British Topography*, second edn, 2 vols, 1780.

Gough, *Sepulchral Monuments* . . . Richard Gough, *Sepulchral Monuments in Great Britain*, 2 vols in 5, 1786–96.

Granger¹ . . . James Granger, *A Biographical History of England*, 2 vols, 1769 (with *Supplement*, 1774).

Granger⁵ . . . James Granger, *A Biographical History of England*, fifth edn, 6 vols, 1824.

Granger, *Correspondence* *Letters between the Rev. James Granger . . . and . . . Eminent Literary Men of His Time*, ed. J. P. Malcolm, 1805.

Gray's Corr. . . . *Correspondence of Thomas Gray*, ed. Paget Toynbee and Leonard Whibley, Oxford, 3 vols, 1935.

Hardwicke, *State Papers* Philip Yorke, 2d Earl of Hardwicke, *Miscellaneous State Papers*, 2 vols, 1778.

Historic Doubts¹ . Horace Walpole, *Historic Doubts on the Life and Reign of King Richard the Third*, 1768.

HW . . . . Horace Walpole.

Jour. Print. Off. . . Horace Walpole, *Journal of the Printing-Office at Strawberry Hill*, ed. Paget Toynbee, 1923.

LA . . . . John Nichols, *Literary Anecdotes of the Eighteenth Century*, 9 vols, 1812–15.

Last Journals . . Horace Walpole, *The Last Journals of Horace Walpole during the Reign of George III from 1771–1783*, ed. A. Francis Steuart, 2 vols, 1910.

Le Neve, *Knights* .   .   George W. Marshall (ed.), *Le Neve's Pedigrees of the Knights* (*Publications of the Harleian Society*, vol. viii), 1873.

LI   .   .   .   .   John Nichols, *Illustrations of the Literary History of the Eighteenth Century*, 8 vols, 1817–58.

Lysons, *Mag. Brit.*   .   Daniel and Samuel Lysons, *Magna Britannia*, vol. ii containing *Cambridgeshire*, 1808; vol. iii containing *Cambridgeshire and . . . Chester*, 1810.

Mason, *Gray*[1]   .   .   William Mason, *The Poems of Mr Gray*, York, 1775.

Masters, *History of CCCC*, 1831   .   Robert Masters, *History of the College of Corpus Christi and the Blessed Virgin Mary in the University of Cambridge*, 1831.

Mem. of the Reign of George II .   .   Horace Walpole, *Memoirs of the Reign of King George the Second*, ed. Henry R. V. Fox, Lord Holland, 3 vols, 1847.

Mem. of the Reign of George III   .   Horace Walpole, *Memoirs of the Reign of King George the Third*, ed. G. F. Russell Barker, 4 vols, 1894.

Meyerstein, *Chatterton*   E. H. W. Meyerstein, *A Life of Thomas Chatterton*, New York, 1930.

MS Cat.   .   .   .   Horace Walpole, 'Catalogue of the Library of Mr Horace Walpole at Strawberry Hill, 1763.' Unpublished MS, in possession (1937) of Lord Walpole, Wolterton Park, Norwich. The letters and numbers which follow are the shelf-marks in the books mentioned as shown in this catalogue: e.g., MS Cat. F. 9. 10 means that these shelf-marks occur opposite the title of the book in the manuscript catalogue. The shelf-marks were written above the book-plate, or verso of first fly-leaf, if the end-paper was marbled. F. 9. 10 (Blount's *Art of Making Devices*, 1650) was kept in the library at SH in press F, the ninth shelf from the bottom, the tenth book from the left.

Musgrave, *Obituary*   .   *Obituary Prior to 1800 . . . Compiled by Sir William Musgrave*, ed. Sir George J. Armytage, 6 vols, 1899–1901.

N&Q   .   .   .   .   *Notes and Queries.*

OED . . . . *A New English Dictionary on Historical Principles.*

Palmer, *Monumental Inscriptions* . . . William M. Palmer (ed.), *Monumental Inscriptions and Coats of Arms from Cambridgeshire,* Cambridge, 1932.

Palmer, *William Cole* . William M. Palmer, *William Cole of Milton,* Cambridge, 1935.

Paris Jour. . . . Horace Walpole, *Paris Journals* (see App. 1, du Deffand Corr.).

Peck, *Desid. Cur.*[1] . . Francis Peck, *Desiderata Curiosa,* 2 vols in 1, 1779.

Pennant, *Tour in Scotland . . . 1769* . . Thomas Pennant, *A Tour in Scotland; MDCCLXIX* (3d edn; 1st in quarto), Warrington, 1774.

Pennant, *Tour in Scotland . . . 1772* . . Thomas Pennant, *A Tour in Scotland, and Voyage to the Hebrides; MDCCLXXII,* Chester, 1774.

Redgrave, *Dict. of Artists* Samuel Redgrave, *A Dictionary of Artists of the English School,* 1878.

Reminiscences . . Paget Toynbee (ed.), *Reminiscences Written by Mr Horace Walpole in 1788,* Oxford, 1924.

Roy. & Nob. Authors, Works i . . . Horace Walpole, *A Catalogue of the Royal and Noble Authors,* in vol. i of *The Works of Horatio Walpole, Earl of Orford,* 5 vols, 1798.

SH . . . . Strawberry Hill.

SH Accounts . . Paget Toynbee (ed.), *Strawberry Hill Accounts . . . Kept by Mr Horace Walpole from 1747 to 1795,* Oxford, 1927.

'Short Notes' . . Horace Walpole, 'Short Notes of My Life.' First published in *Letters of Horace Walpole to Sir Horace Mann* (4 vols, 1843), iv. 335–358; reprinted by Cunningham (i. *lxi–lxxvii*) and by Toynbee (i. *xxxiv–lvi*).

Sold London . . *A Catalogue of the Collection of Scarce Prints, Removed from Strawberry Hill,* 13–23 June, 1842. The number following 'Sold London' is the lot number in the sale. As the lots were numbered continuously throughout the sale, the day is not given.

Sold SH . . . *A Catalogue of the Classic Contents of Strawberry Hill Collected by Horace Walpole* 25 April–21 May, 1842. The roman and arabic numerals which follow these entries indicate the day and lot number: e.g., sold SH vi. 2 = sold at the Strawberry Hill sale, sixth day, lot 2.

Times Lit. Supp. . . . *The Times Literary Supplement*, London.

Toynbee . . . *The Letters of Horace Walpole, Fourth Earl of Orford*, ed. Mrs Paget Toynbee, Oxford, 16 vols, 1903–5; *Supplement*, 3 vols, 1918–25.

Vetusta Monumenta . Society of Antiquaries of London, *Vetusta Monumenta: quae ad rerum britannicarum memoriam conservandam*, 7 vols, 1747, 1906.

Walpoliana . . . [John Pinkerton], *Walpoliana*, 2 vols [1799].

Warton, *An Enquiry* . Thomas Warton, *An Enquiry into the Authenticity of the Poems Attributed to Thomas Rowley*, 1782.

Warton, *Hist. of English Poetry* . . . Thomas Warton, *History of English Poetry*, 3 vols, 1774–81.

Waterbeach Diary . William Cole, *Waterbeach Diary;* proof sheets of the forthcoming edition edited by Miss Helen Waddell and Francis Griffin Stokes. As the last portion of Cole's MS has not been set up at the time of going to press, it is referred to as Add MS 5835.

Works . . . Horace Walpole, *The Works of Horatio Walpole, Earl of Orford*, 5 vols, 1798.

WSL . . . . W. S. Lewis. 'Now WSL' = 'now in the possession of.'

BIBLIOGRAPHICAL NOTE ON THE COLE CORRESPONDENCE

COLE'S manuscripts arrived at the British Museum in 1783 and were not opened, under the terms of his will, until 1803.* Walpole's letters to him were first printed in quarto in 1818 'for Rodwell and Martin, Bond Street and Henry Colburn, Conduit Street.' The editor (who did little more than print the letters) was almost certainly John Martin, the bibliographer, who brought out Walpole's letters to Montagu in this same year. In 1822 John Murray (who had apparently bought the unsold sheets of both correspondences), brought them out together, with an additional title-page, as volume six of Lord Orford's *Works*. The first five letters in the Cole correspondence are not to Cole, but to Thomas Birch (the first two letters are not by Walpole, but by his Uncle Horace). Walpole's letters are 178 in number, including one not sent, which is published now for the first time.

They have been printed in five editions before the present one:

PRIVATE CORRESPONDENCE OF HORACE WALPOLE, EARL OF ORFORD. Now first collected. London: printed for Rodwell and

---

* They are now:

Add MSS 5798 A and B–5887 (except 5818 which never came to the Museum)

	90 vols
Add MSS 5952–5962	11 vols
Add MSS 5992–5994	3 vols
Add MSS 6034, 6057, 6151	3 vols
Add MSS 6396–6402	7 vols

(6399 is listed as A and B, two separate volumes, in the *Catalogue of Additions, 1783–1835*, but 6399B was presented to the BM in 1801 by George Chalmers and is not part of the Cole bequest).

Total	114 vols

Add MSS 6035 is listed under Cole in the index of the above *Catalogue*, but it was purchased by the BM at the Richard Gough Sale, April 1810, lot 4208.

The following are catalogued as having belonged to Cole, although they did not form part of his bequest:

Add MSS 6411. Speeches, etc., in the Parliament of 1640.

Add MSS 27866. Psalter, ca 1300.

Add MSS Miscellaneous Papers, 16th–19th centuries, many of which belonged to Cole.

Add MSS 38715. Certificates of Penance, 1670–1772. The Phillipps folio catalogue, 1837, p. 363, states this to have been one of Cole's MSS.

(Information from Mr A. J. Watson.)

Martin, Bond Street; and Colburn and Co., Conduit Street. 1820. 8vo. 4 vols. Four letters are missing.

A second edition of this in three volumes 'with numerous il-lustrative notes, now first added.' Henry Colburn, 1837. The text of this edition is identical with the preceding, except that it has been Bowdlerized. Four letters are missing.

THE LETTERS OF HORACE WALPOLE, EARL OF ORFORD: in-cluding numerous letters now first published from the original Manuscripts. Richard Bentley. 1840. 8vo. 6 vols. Edited by John Wright, who states (i. i), that 'the letters to the Rev. William Cole have been carefully examined with the originals, and many explanatory notes added, from the manuscript collections of that indefatigable antiquary, deposited in the British Museum.' Eleven letters are missing.

THE LETTERS OF HORACE WALPOLE . . . edited by Peter Cunningham. Bentley. 1857. 9 vols. Ten letters are missing. Re-printed three times, 1861–1866, 1877, 1891, and twice in New York, 1876, 1879.

THE LETTERS OF HORACE WALPOLE . . . edited by Mrs Paget Toynbee. Oxford. 1903–5. 16 vols and supplements i–iii, edited by Paget Toynbee, 1918–25. 'The letters to the Rev. William Cole have been collated with the originals in the British Mu-seum' (i. xviii).

Cole's letters to Walpole remained at Strawberry Hill until the Sale of 1842, when they were sold, Sixth Day, lot 135. They are 186 in number, including two not sent. They were bought by Henry Colburn, the publisher, for £33.12s., presumably with the intention of publishing them.

Cunningham printed a few extracts from them, but the most extensive use of these letters until now was made in Warburton's *Memoirs of Horace Walpole,* 1851, Chapter VIII of the second volume, pp. 359–443, where some fifty letters appear, many of them virtually complete.

LIST OF LETTERS IN
COLE CORRESPONDENCE

The letters from Cole are printed in italics

		YALE	TOYNBEE	CUNNINGHAM
1762	*16 May*	i. 1		
	20 May	i. 11	v. 204	iii. 506
	29 July	i. 14	v. 220	iv. 4
	31 July	i. 14		
	5 Aug.	i. 21	v. 229	iv. 11
	Robert Masters to			
	HW	i. 22		
	19 Aug.	i. 24	v. 235	iv. 14
	Notes on Gothurst	i. 26		
	30 Sept.	i. 28	v. 254	iv. 29
	19 Oct.	i. 29		
	3 Nov.	i. 30		
	13 Nov.	i. 32	v. 274	iv. 44
	23 Dec.	i. 32	v. 286	iv. 54
1763	16 May	i. 33	v. 326	iv. 81
	19 May	i. 34		
	1 July	i. 36	v. 348	iv. 97
	3 July	i. 37		
	12 July	i. 41	v. 350	iv. 98
	[16 July]	i. 41	v. 351	iv. 98
	31 July	i. 42		
	8 Aug.	i. 43	v. 356	iv. 102
	27 Aug.	i. 44		
	30 Sept.	i. 45		
	8 Oct.	i. 46	v. 376	iv. 117
	13 Oct.	i. 47		
	1 Dec.	i. 48		
	6 Dec.	i. 51	v. 405	iv. 141
1764	31 Jan.	i. 53	v. 447	iv. 176
	2 Feb.	i. 53		
	7 Feb.	i. 56	v. 172*	iii. 483*

* Misplaced in 1762.

		YALE	TOYNBEE	CUNNINGHAM
	13 May	i. 115	vi. 459	iv. 499
	[17 May]	i. 116	vi. 459	Missing
	20 May	i. 117		
	16 Sept.	i. 118		
	18 Sept.	i. 118	vii. 39	v. 11
	21 Sept.	i. 119		
1767	24 Oct.	i. 120	vii. 140	v. 69
	29 Oct.	i. 121		
	19 Dec.	i. 123	vii. 152	v. 76
	27 Dec.	i. 125		
1768	1 Feb.	i. 127	vii. 159	v. 81
	16 Feb.	i. 128		
	16 April	i. 132	vii. 182	v. 96
	14 May	i. 135		
	15 May	i. 143 (missing)		
	6 June	i. 143	vii. 189	v. 101
	20 July	i. 145		
	20 Aug.	i. 150	vii. 221	v. 125 (misdated 30 Aug.)
	5 Oct.	i. 152		
1769	27 May	i. 156	vii. 282	v. 166
	29 May	i. 157		
	6 June	i. 159		
	14 June	i. 163	vii. 283	v. 167
	17–21 June	i. 166		
	26 June	i. 176	vii. 290	v. 172
	15 July	i. 178	vii. 294	v. 176
	3 Aug.	i. 184		
	12 [11] Aug.	i. 189	vii. 302	v. 179
	14 Dec.	i. 192	vii. 341	Missing
	18 Dec.	i. 192		
	21 Dec.	i. 195	vii. 341	v. 208
1770	5 Jan.	i. 197		
	15 Nov.	i. 198	vii. 421	v. 267
	15 Nov.	i. 199		
	20 Nov.	i. 200	vii. 422	v. 267
	28 Nov.	i. 201		
	15 Dec.	i. 203		

		YALE	TOYNBEE	CUNNINGHAM
	20 Dec.	i. 205	vii. 426	v. 270
1771	3 Jan.	i. 208		
	10 Jan.	i. 211	vii. 435	v. 277
	18 April	i. 212		
	29 May	i. 214	viii. 34	v. 298
	30 May	i. 217		
	9 June	i. 217		
	11 June	i. 218	viii. 40	v. 302
	16 June	i. 219		
	18 June	i. 225		
	22 June	i. 225	viii. 48	v. 308
	24 June	i. 227	viii. 51	v. 310
	12 Aug.	i. 228	viii. 72	v. 326
	21 Aug.	i. 230		
	24 Aug.	i. 232		
	10 Sept.	i. 235	viii. 86	v. 337
	16 Sept.	i. 237		
	12 Oct.	i. 240	viii. 93	v. 343
	19 Oct.	i. 241		
	23 Oct.	i. 243	viii. 97	v. 345
	3 Nov.	i. 245		
1772	17 Jan.	i. 246		
	28 Jan.	i. 247	viii. 140	v. 371
	9 June	i. 248	viii. 171	v. 390
	11 June	i. 250		
	17 June	i. 254	viii. 173	v. 392
	21 June	i. 256		
	22 June	i. 260		
	28 June	i. 264	viii. 177	Missing
	7 July	i. 264	viii. 181	Missing
	9 July	i. 266		
	28 July	i. 270	viii. 187	v. 401
	30 July	i. 272		
	6 Aug.	i. 274		
	25 Aug.	i. 274	viii. 197	v. 406
	25 Aug.	i. 276		
	28 Aug.	i. 279	viii. 198	v. 408
	3 Oct.	i. 280		

		YALE	TOYNBEE	CUNNINGHAM
	24 Oct.	i. 284		
	7 Nov.	i. 285	viii. 212	v. 417
	20 Nov.	i. 286		
	[15 Dec.]	i. 289	viii. 217	v. 418
1773	6 Jan.	i. 289		
	8 Jan.	i. 292	viii. 223	v. 424
	13 Jan.	i. 295		
	12 Feb.	i. 297		
	18 Feb.	i. 300	viii. 241	v. 439
	19 March	i. 302		
	7 April	i. 304	viii. 264	v. 454
	16 April	i. 306		
	24 April	i. 307		
	27 April	i. 308	viii. 267	v. 457
	3 May	i. 310		
	4 May	i. 315	viii. 274	v. 460
	13 May	i. 317		
	29 May	i. 318	viii. 281	v. 469
	13 June	i. 319		
1774	4 May	i. 324	viii. 451	vi. 81
	19 May	i. 326		
	28 May	i. 328	ix. 1	vi. 85
	2 June	i. 331		
	18 July	i. 335		
	21 July	i. 336	ix. 18	vi. 93
				(misdated 21 June)
	25 July	i. 338		
	15 Aug.	i. 340	ix. 28	vi. 104
	5 Oct.	i. 346		
	11 Oct.	i. 347	ix. 65	vi. 131
	18 Nov.	i. 348		
1775	9 Jan.	i. 351	ix. 124	vi. 166
	9 April	i. 352		
	11 April	i. 355	ix. 176	vi. 198
	[20] April	i. 358		
	25 April	i. 366	ix. 187	vi. 205
	29 April	i. 369		
	2 June	i. 371		

		YALE	TOYNBEE	CUNNINGHAM
	5 June	i. 373	ix. 205	vi. 220
	9 June	i. 376		
	10 Dec.	i. 378	ix. 292	vi. 289
	12 Dec.	i. 380		
	14 Dec.	i. 383	ix. 294	vi. 291
	24 Dec.	i. 385		
1776	26 Jan.	ii. 1	ix. 318	vi. 303
	30 Jan.	ii. 3		
	1 March	ii. 7	ix. 335	vi. 314
	26 March	ii. 7		
	16 April	ii. 9	ix. 347	vi. 325
	30 May	ii. 10		
	1 June	ii. 12	ix. 371	vi. 344
	9 June	ii. 13		
	11 June	ii. 15	ix. 375	vi. 348
	17 July	ii. 15		
	[23 July]	ii. 17	ix. 394	vi. 360
	24 July	ii. 17	ix. 394	vi. 360
	28 July	ii. 19		
	19 Aug.	ii. 21	ix. 404	vi. 367
	22 Aug.	ii. 22		
	9 Sept.	ii. 24	ix. 411	vi. 371
	19 Sept.	ii. 26		
	9 Dec.	ii. 27	ix. 447	vi. 396
	15 Dec.	ii. 29		
1777	20 Feb.	ii. 30	x. 16	vi. 413
	21 Feb.	ii. 34		
	23 Feb.	ii. 35		
	27 Feb.	ii. 40	x. 19	vi. 415
	2 March	ii. 41		
	18 May	ii. 43		
	22 May	ii. 45	x. 52	vi. 441
	28 May	ii. 47	x. 54	Missing
	1 June	ii. 48		
	15 June	ii. 50		
	19 June	ii. 51	x. 67	vi. 447
	28 Aug.	ii. 53		
	31 Aug.	ii. 54	x. 100	vi. 471

		YALE	TOYNBEE	CUNNINGHAM
	12 Sept.	ii. 56		
	16 Sept.	ii. 58	x. 106	vi. 477
	22 Sept.	ii. 59	x. 117	vi. 486
	2 Oct.	ii. 62	x. 124	Missing
	4 Oct.	ii. 63		
	7 Oct.	ii. 65		
	15 Oct.	ii. 66	x. 135	vi. 502
				(misdated 19 Oct.)
	30 Oct.	ii. 68		
1778	*29 March*	ii. 71		
	31 March	ii. 73	x. 213	vii. 48
	16 April	ii. 73		
	23 April	ii. 74	x. 227	vii. 57
	10 May	ii. 76		
	21 May	ii. 79	x. 241	vii. 69
	23 May	ii. 81		
	28 May	ii. 339 Not sent		
	3 June	ii. 83	x. 259	vii. 76
	7 June	ii. 85		
	10 June	ii. 88	x. 262	vii. 78
	14 June	ii. 91		
	2 July	ii. 94		
	4 July	ii. 97		
	12 July	ii. 98	x. 278	vii. 92
	19 July	ii. 100		
	24 July	ii. 102	x. 287	vii. 99
	4 Aug.	ii. 103		
	15 Aug.	ii. 105	x. 297	vii. 108
	17 Aug.	ii. 106		
	22 Aug.	ii. 109	x. 300	vii. 110
	29 Aug.	ii. 112		
	1 Sept.	ii. 115	x. 311	vii. 122
	3 Sept.	ii. 118		
	10 Sept.	ii. 120	x. 314	vii. 129
				(misdated 18 Sept.)
	14 Oct.	ii. 123	x. 335	vii. 141
	18 Oct.	ii. 126		
	26 Oct.	ii. 129	x. 338	vii. 144

		YALE	TOYNBEE	CUNNINGHAM
	1 Nov.	ii. 131		
	4 Nov.	ii. 137	x. 343	vii. 147
	8 Nov.	ii. 133		
1779	3 Jan.	ii. 134	x. 355	vii. 158
	3 Jan.	ii. 136		
	11 Jan.	ii. 137		
	15 Jan.	ii. 138	x. 364	vii. 165
	26 Jan.	ii. 139		
	28 Jan.	ii. 141	x. 365	vii. 166
	29 Jan.	ii. 356 Not sent		
	30 Jan.	ii. 142		
	4 Feb.	ii. 143	x. 374	vii. 173
	7 Feb.	ii. 144		
	18 Feb.	ii. 146	x. 380	vii. 177
	18 Feb.	ii. 147		
	2 March	ii. 147		
	28 March	ii. 149	x. 393	vii. 187
	7 April	ii. 151		
	12 April	ii. 155	x. 399	vii. 192
	20 April	ii. 156	x. 403	vii. 194
	20 April	ii. 157		
	23 April	ii. 158	x. 403	vii. 195
	27 April	ii. 158		
	21 May	ii. 159	x. 410	vii. 200
	25 May	ii. 161		
	2 June	ii. 163	x. 415	vii. 203
	9 June	ii. 165		
	12 July	ii. 168	x. 448	vii. 227
	24 July	ii. 171		
	12 Aug.	ii. 173	xi. 12	vii. 239
	14 Nov.	ii. 173		
	16 Nov.	ii. 176	xi. 60	vii. 279
	27 Dec.	ii. 178	xi. 85	vii. 298
	30 Dec.	ii. 179		
1780	5 Jan.	ii. 183	xi. 95	vii. 305
	5 Feb.	ii. 186	xi. 122	vii. 326
	12 Feb.	ii. 190		
	27 Feb.	ii. 193	xi. 131	vii. 333

		YALE	TOYNBEE	CUNNINGHAM
	1 March	ii. 195		
	6 March	ii. 198	xi. 136	vii. 336
	10 March	ii. 200		
	13 March	ii. 203	xi. 138	vii. 337
	26 March	ii. 361	Not sent. Now first published	
	27 March	ii. 206		
	30 March	ii. 209	xi. 148	vii. 345
	1 April	ii. 209		
	11 May	ii. 211	xi. 166	vii. 363
	14 May	ii. 212		
	19 May	ii. 216	xi. 175	vii. 366
	24 May	ii. 218		
	30 May	ii. 219	xi. 183	vii. 372
	1 June	ii. 221		
	15 June	ii. 223	xi. 224	vii. 402
	2 July	ii. 225		
	4 July	ii. 229	xi. 239	vii. 413
	8 July	ii. 230		
	27 Sept.	ii. 233	xi. 285	vii. 445
	30 Sept.	ii. 234		
	3 Oct.	ii. 236	xi. 288	vii. 446
	11 Nov.	ii. 237	xi. 313	vii. 459
	13 Nov.	ii. 241		
	24 Nov.	ii. 244	xi. 320	vii. 464
	27 Nov.	ii. 246		
	30 Nov.	ii. 248	xi. 327	vii. 467
	17 Dec.	ii. 250		
	19 Dec.	ii. 253	xi. 341	vii. 477
1781	*3 Feb.*	ii. 254		
	7 Feb.	ii. 256	xi. 387	viii. 1
	9 Feb.	ii. 257	xi. 388	viii. 1
	12 Feb.	ii. 259		
	2 March	ii. 260	xi. 407	viii. 14
	4 March	ii. 261		
	5 March	ii. 262	xi. 411	viii. 17
	7 March	ii. 263		
	29 March	ii. 265	xi. 418	viii. 20
	30 March	ii. 266		

		YALE	TOYNBEE	CUNNINGHAM
	3 April	ii. 267	xi. 426	viii. 25
	4 May	ii. 268	xi. 436	viii. 33
	7 May	ii. 270		
	16 May [16 June]	ii. 272	xi. 451	viii. 54
	30 June	ii. 276		
	23 July	ii. 278		
	26 July	ii. 279	xii. 32	viii. 69
	5 Aug.	ii. 280		
	7 July [7 Aug.]	ii. 282	xii. 36	viii. 63
	22 Dec.	ii. 284		
	30 Dec.	ii. 286	xii. 135	viii. 135
1782	4 Jan.	ii. 290		
	27 Jan.	ii. 292	xii. 150	viii. 146
	7 Feb.	ii. 293		
	11 Feb.	ii. 295		
	14 Feb.	ii. 297	xii. 162	viii. 153
	15 Feb.	ii. 300	xii. 168	viii. 157
	17 Feb.	ii. 303		
	22 Feb.	ii. 305	xii. 173	viii. 160
	24 Feb.	ii. 306		
	5 March	ii. 308		
	9 March	ii. 309	xii. 189	viii. 174
	12 April	ii. 310		
	13 April	ii. 313	xii. 228	viii. 205
	13 May	ii. 315		
	14 May	ii. 317	xii. 248	Missing
	16 May	ii. 317		
	24 May	ii. 318	xii. 253	viii. 223
	27 May	ii. 320		
	1 June	ii. 322	xii. 257	viii. 226
	18 June	ii. 325		
	21 June	ii. 327	xii. 268	viii. 233
	29 June	ii. 329		
	23 July	ii. 331	xii. 302	viii. 259
	25 July	ii. 333		
	30 Oct.	ii. 334		
	5 Nov.	ii. 336	xii. 360	viii. 299
	7 Nov.	ii. 338		

From COLE, Sunday 16 May 1762

COLE's copy, Add MS 5831, ff. 222–4. The original is missing.

Cole prefixed the following note to the letter: 'In the course of my reading Mr Walpole's book lately published on *Painting in England,* I made a few observations which I sent to him in the following letter, and as I had not put together the account of Sir Horatio Palavicini, and as two or three other things in it were not entered in any of my volumes, particularly concerning the executioner of King Charles I, I will e'en transcribe the whole as I sent it.'

Address: For the Honourable Horace Walpole, Esq., in Arlington Street, London.

Blecheley,[1] May 16, 1762.

Dear Sir,

THE extreme pleasure and entertainment I have received from your two late volumes on *Painting in England*[2] call for my most grateful acknowledgments. Indeed it was a continual feast from one end to the other, and it is no small satisfaction to think that we are to be favoured with another volume before the entertainment is to be over.

After having said thus much, which truth and gratitude force from me, I must apologize for the present trouble and inform you that in the course of my reading your book I met with two or three errata, or false printings, which I hope you will excuse me for pointing out, if you have not done it already, which is more probable. With these I have put down two or three trifling observations of another sort, which perhaps might as well have been let alone. Yet, such as they are, I submit them to your candour, where I well know I am safe, and so shall put them down without further ceremony.

Vol. 1, p. 148. In the article of Petruccio Ubaldini,[3] one of his

1. Bucks. The modern spelling is Bletchley. 'In 1753, he [Cole] was presented by his early friend and patron Browne Willis, Esq., to the rectory of Bletchley in Buckinghamshire; which he resigned, March 20, 1768, in favour of his patron's grandson' (LA i. 658).

2. *Anecdotes of Painting in England; with some account of the principal artists; and incidental notes on other arts; collected by the late Mr. George Vertue; and now digested and published from his original MSS. By Mr. Horace Walpole* . . . Strawberry Hill, 1762. 'The two first volumes were published February 15, 1762' (*Jour. Print. Off.* 10).

3. (1524?–1600?), illuminator and scholar; first visited England in 1545, and resided there at intervals; employed by Henry VIII and Edward VI. The book mentioned by Cole is not the one mentioned by HW in *Anecdotes* (see DNB *sub* Ubaldini).

books is there thus entitled: *Le Vite ed i fatti di sei donne illustri.*
Perhaps this may be a different book from one in my possession
which is thus entitled at large, and is in quarto:

*Le Vite delle Donne illustri del Regno d'Inghilterra & del Regno di
Scotia, & di quelle, che d'altri paesi ne i due detti Regni sono stato mari-
tate.* [. . .] *Scritte in lingua Italiana da Petruccio Ubaldino, Cittadin
Fiorentino. Londra. Appreso Giovanni Volfio. 1591.*

If this is a different book from that which you have given us the title
of, my observation is impertinent, as I was apt to suppose it might be
the same. However, to make the best apology for it, whether right or
wrong, if you have not the book already, I shall think myself much
obliged if you will give it a place in your library, and at the same
time will do myself the further pleasure of bringing it and staying
a day or two with you at Strawberry Hill some time before the summer is concluded: a pleasure I should long ago have embraced, as you
have been so obliging more than once to invite me,[4] was it not for a
fear of coming unopportunely: and therefore shall take it as a very
particular favour, if you would be pleased any time when you are
most at leisure, to let me know it, as the distance between us[5] will
easily allow me to reach you in one day, and my time always my own.

P. 160, vol. 1. You seem to mention Horatio Palavicini[6] as a person
concerned in the tapestry manufacture, and possibly he might be
so. However, the constant tradition that prevails about him at the
place where he lived, and where I was born,[7] is, that he was collector
of the Pope's dues in England in Queen Mary's time, and on her

---

4. The dates of these invitations are not known.

5. The distance between Bletchley and SH, via Aylesbury and Uxbridge, was about 45 miles.

6. Sir Horatio Palavicini (d. 1600), architect and financial agent, was born at Genoa, but took up residence in England and was knighted in 1587. Cole's account, which agrees substantially with that in DNB, was adopted in part by HW in *Anecdotes*[2] i. 172 n. Cole wrote to Richard Gough 24 Dec. 1775: 'After Mr Walpole had published his *Anecdotes on Painting*, I sent him, in 1762, an account of the Palavicini family as an illustration of what he had said about Horace Palavi-

cini. I will transcribe my account just as I sent it to him' (LA i. 676). Gough inserted Cole's notes, without acknowledgment, almost *verbatim* in his enlarged edition of William Camden's *Britannia*, 3 vols, 1789, ii. 138. He also used the account in his *Short Genealogical View of the Family of Oliver Cromwell*, 1785, Appendix vi, 44–5 (this work forms No. 31 of John Nichols's *Bibliotheca Topographica Britannica*). DNB spells his name Palavicino.

7. Babraham, near Gog Magog Hills, Cambs. Cole refers to Babraham as 'my native parish, though I was born in Little Abington just by' (LA viii. 382). See also Palmer, *Monumental Inscriptions, passim.*

death and sister's accession, he took the liberty of detaining his master's money and staying in a country where, at that time, such a piece of knavery and dishonesty would be sure to meet with the public applause, and not be looked upon in the light it deserved. Thus much is certain, that he was owner of the estate and house at Baberham,[8] about five or six miles from Cambridge, where in the hall, on a noble chimney-piece, adorned with the history of Mutius Scaevola,[9] are his arms still remaining, as they were also over the portal of the door of the manor-house at Little Shelford,[10] built by him in the Italian style, with a large piazza or gallery with pillars on the second storey, which house at Shelford was pulled down about twelve years ago and a new one erected in the same delightful situation on the banks of a pretty trout stream, by Mr Finch,[11] an opulent ironmonger of Cambridge, who purchased the estate. The family were all buried at Baberham, as appears by the following entries in the parish register of that village:

Toby son of Sir Horatio Palavicini born 20 May and baptized the same day 1593.

Baptina, daughter of Sir Horace Palavicini[12] baptized 22 Sept. 1594.

Horace Palavicini son of Toby Palavicini and Jane his wife baptized 1 Sept. 1611.

Tobias son of Toby Palavicini July 14, 1612, baptized.

James son of Toby Palavicini baptized 3 Dec. 1620.

Sir Horace Palavicini died 6 July 1600; his body was buried the 17th, and his funeral kept Aug. 4, 1600.

Tobias Palavicini buried 19 Nov. 1612.

Elizabeth daughter of Toby Palavicini buried 23 May 1620.

Mr Oliver Cromwell[13] and the Lady Anne Palavicini[13a] married July 7, 1601.

8. 'Mr. W. should have said that Baberham [sic] in Cambridgeshire was the first specimen of the pure Italian style, built by Sir H. Palavicini. Little Shelford, which he quotes, was built in imitation of it, by his son, Tobias Palavicini' (*Anecdotes*, ed. Dallaway, 1828, ii. 160).

9. A legendary Roman who, being threatened with death, laid his right hand on an altar of burning coals to prove his fortitude.

10. About four miles SE of Cambridge.

11. William Finch (d. 28 Jan. 1762. See Cooper, *Memorials* iii. 310). Elsewhere Cole says Finch erected in place of Palavicini's

house 'a small neat box, now occupied, 1782, by his great-nephew William Ingle Finch' (LA v. 256 n).

12. Cole writes 'Palivicini' in the remainder of this list, doubtless following the original spelling in the register.

13. Sir Oliver Cromwell (1562–1655), of Hinchinbrooke, Hunts, great-uncle to the Protector. (For further connections between the Palavicini and Cromwell families, see DNB, *sub* Palavicino; Mark Noble, *Protectoral House of Cromwell*, 2d edn, 2 vols, Birmingham, 1787, i. 49–60, 173–80.)

13a. (d. 1626), dau. of Egidius Hoostman, of Antwerp (op. cit. i. 46).

By the last entry it appears that Sir Horace's widow paid him that respect as not to marry again till a full year after the death of her husband, but one can't help observing that it was the very first day after the year was complete. When I was in Cheshire about two or three years ago with my friend Mr John Allen,[14] Fellow of Trinity College in Cambridge, who had in his custody all the papers of Sir John Crew of Utkinton[15] in the parish of Torporley, a great antiquary and herald, I met with the following MS epitaph upon Sir Horace in one of his books, which for the oddity of it, and as it confirms what I have said before of him concerning his honesty and integrity, and more especially as it is not very long, I will transcribe:[16]

Here lyes Horatio Palavazene,
Who robb'd the Pope to lend the Queene.
He was a theife. A Theife! Thow lyest.
For whie? Hee robb'd but Antichrist.
Him Death wyth Besome swept from Babram
Into the Bosome of ould Abraham:
But then came Hercules wyth his Clubb
And struck him downe to Belzebub.

14. Rev. John Allen (1699–1778), antiquary and herald; rector of Tarporley, Cheshire, 1752–78, and Senior Fellow of Trinity College, Cambridge, at the time of his death. The date of this visit is not known, but Cole visited Allen in 1755 (see Lysons, *Mag. Brit.* iii. 791). In 1755 Cole wrote of him: 'He is an exceeding good historian, and an excellent antiquary and herald; and as such has made collections towards an history of his native county of Stafford.' (John Nichols, *History and Antiquities of the County of Leicester*, 4 vols, 1795–1815, iii, pt 2, 1128). See also *Blecheley Diary, passim,* and Thomas Pennant, *Journey from Chester to London,* 1782, p. 9. Cole's correspondence with Allen is in Add MSS 5824, 5836, 6400.

15. Sir John Crew or Crewe (1640–1711), knighted 1673, is buried in Tarporley Church. He had a valuable library at Utkinton Hall (see Lysons, loc. cit.; Pennant, loc. cit.). Utkinton is about 12 miles from Chester. HW printed the name *Uthington* in *Anecdotes*[2] i. 172, and it is erroneously called *Ushington* in DNB (*sub* Palavicini).

16. The following notes, added by Cole after he sent his letter to HW, appear in the margins of the MS: 'In the *Acta Regia,* p. 503, is this: "A Patent for the Denization of Horace Palavicini, a Genoese. Dated Nov. 2, 1586 at Westminster. The King makes Denizens, & the Parliament naturalizes. Horace Palavicini was employed by the Queen in her negotiations with the German Princes." In the *Acta Regia,* p. 504, it appears that he was employed by the Queen to William Landgrave of Hesse in 1590.' These notes were included in Cole to Gough 24 Dec. 1775, and the latter quoted them, together with the epitaph and the rest of the paragraph, almost *verbatim* and without acknowledgment in his edition of Camden's *Britannia,* 3 vols, 1789, ii. 139. HW quoted the epitaph in *Anecdotes*[2] and used some of Cole's information, without acknowledgment. This epitaph appears in *Recreations for ingenious Headpieces, or a pleasant Grove for their Wits to walk in,* 1667 (see LA v. 256 n).

If we had not the aforesaid authorities from the registers for Sir Horace's living in Cambridgeshire, we were sufficiently informed of that circumstance by that very ridiculous fellow, Tom Coryat, whom you have done justice to in your late performance,[17] who tells us, pp. 255, 259, of his *Crudities*,[18] that he met at Mezolt one John Curtabatus of Chiavenna, who spoke pretty good English, having served Sir Horace Palavicini many years in Cambridgeshire. How long before 1593 Sir Horace settled himself at Baberham I know not, but suppose only for a short time. That he was in some repute at court about 1596 is evident, I think, from Lord Arundel of Wardour,[19] as he was afterwards created, his referring his case (on his accepting the title of Count of the Empire, for which he was put into confinement by the Queen) to him, among others, in these words, in his letter to one of the principal lords of Queen Elizabeth's court: "Neither doe I thinke England to be so unfurnished of experienced men, but that either Horatio Pallavicino, Sir Robert Sidney,[20] Mr Dyer,[21] or some other, can witness a truth therein." This is printed in Peck's *Desiderata Curiosa*, vol. 2, p. 52, lib. 7.

But I have swelled this article out to an immense length: and indeed, when I first sat down to write, could I have thought that I should have wrote more in the whole than I have done in these two articles, I would not have thought to have troubled you with so much stuff, but antiquaries, as you have somewhere observed,[22] love not to omit the smallest details, which are important with them.

Vol. 2, p. 21. Sir Francis Crane.[23] About three years ago in my

17. In his account of Inigo Jones, HW says: 'Jones had dabbled in poetry himself: there is a copy of verses by him prefixed to Coryat's *Crudities*, among many others by the wits of that age, who all affected to turn Coryat's book into ridicule, but which at least is not so foolish as their verses' (*Anecdotes*[1] ii. 148). Cf. *Roy. & Nob. Authors, Works* i. 465.

18. A slip for pp. 355, 359. Mr William A. Jackson points out that the variations in copies of *Crudities*[1] (1611) are confined to the preliminaries.

19. Thomas Arundel (1560?–1639), 1st Bn Arundel of Wardour Castle, Wilts. He was created a Count of the Holy Roman Empire by Emperor Rudolph II, 14 Dec. 1595, and was imprisoned by Queen Elizabeth for accepting a foreign honour without her permission. The date of his letter, which Peck suggests may be addressed to Lord Burghley, is c. 5 Aug. 1596 (Peck, *Desid. Cur.*[1], ii. Lib. vii, 51).

20. (1563–1626), cr. (1618) E. of Leicester.

21. Sir Edward Dyer (d. 1607), poet and courtier, friend of Sir Philip Sidney. He was knighted in 1596.

22. 'From the antiquarian I expect greater thanks; he is more cheaply pleased than a common reader: the one demands to be diverted, at least instructed—the other requires only to be informed' (*Anecdotes*[1] i. p. vi).

23. (d. 1636), director of the tapestry works established by James I at Mortlake, Surrey. HW adopted, in condensed form, Cole's notes in *Anecdotes*[2] ii. 24, without acknowledgment.

parish was an excellent half-length portrait of him in tapestry, with the collar of St George about his neck, as worn in the time of King Charles I. It is in the possession of a descendant of his, or at least relation, Mrs Markham,[24] a Roman Catholic lady, whose maiden name was Crane. She is now removed out of this parish to a place called Somerby near Grantham[25] in Lincolnshire, and has also an exceeding good picture, if it may be so called, in tapestry, of St George killing the dragon. I suppose them both to be capital works of his manufactory.[26]

Vol. 2, p. 29. Lady Danvers's tomb at Stow with the Nine Churches[27] in Northamptonshire. Being at Chester a few years ago,[28] and calling upon the present bishop,[29] his Lordship, knowing my passion for antiquity, desired me to look into this church of Stow in my return home, as it was not a mile out of my road, and indeed it amply rewarded me for the trouble of going to see this charming piece of sculpture, which was designed for the Lady Elizabeth Neville,[30] daughter and coheir of John Lord Latimer, by Lady Lucy Somerset,[31] daughter of Henry Earl of Worcester: which Elizabeth Neville was first married to Sir John Danvers of Dauntesey,[32] and afterwards to Sir Edmund Carey,[33] third son of Henry Lord Huns-

24. Mary Crane (d. 1768) of Gedney, Lincs, m. Thomas Markham (1698–1743), 4th son of Thomas Markham of Ollerton, Notts, and Claxby, Lincs (see *Markham Memorials,* ed. Sir Clements R. Markham, 2 vols, 1913, i. 114–5). According to a letter from Father Bedingfield to Cole in 1768, there quoted, Mrs Markham left the two tapestry pictures first to her sister, Mrs Watkins, and then to her niece by marriage, Lady Arundell (Mary Christina Conquest, m. 1763, Henry Arundell, 8th Bn Arundell of Wardour). (Information from Mr H. J. B. Clements through Mr William A. Jackson.)

25. Somerby Hall (see J to P 20–1).

26. Cole's note: 'Sir Robert Crane, *vide* vol. 28 [of Cole's MSS Add MS 5827] p. 115.' He apparently did not include this note in his letter to HW.

27. Stowe Nine Churches, or Church Stowe, six miles SE of Daventry. HW condensed this information, without acknowledgment to Cole, in a note on Lady Danvers, *Anecdotes*[2] ii. 31 n. Lady Danvers's tomb is in the Church of St Michael, and is fully described in *The Note-Book and*

Account Book of Nicholas Stone, ed. Walter Lewis Spiers, *Walpole Society* vii (1919). 46–7. Part of Cole's description is there quoted, and a plate (IX) of the monument appears opp. p. 47.

28. In 1757 (see *Walpole Society,* loc. cit.).

29. Edmund Keene (1714–81), Bp of Chester 1752–71, and of Ely 1771–81.

30. (1550?–1630), 4th dau. of John Neville, 4th Bn Latimer (1520?–77). As she was 27 years of age at her father's death in 1577 she would be 81, not 84, as Cole says, at her death in 1630.

31. (1524?–83), 2d dau. of Henry Somerset (1495?–1549), E. of Worcester.

32. (1540–94), Kt of Dauntsey, Wilts. He had ten children, three sons and seven daughters, by Elizabeth Neville (see *Walpole Society* vii. 47).

33. (fl. 1580–1600), m. Lady Elizabeth Danvers as his 2d wife. He had no issue by her. According to John Aubrey (*Brief Lives,* ed. Andrew Clark, 2 vols, Oxford, 1898, i. 193), Lady Elizabeth married him 'to obtain pardon for her sonnes . . . but kept him to hard meate.'

don.[34] She died in 1630, aged 84 years. The lady lies in an half-reclining posture, with her head on a cushion and her hands in the most natural and easy position imaginable, with the utmost composure and serenity in her face, as though she was asleep. Her head is dressed in a sort of veil, and she has a robe or mantle over her shoulders in as light and loose and airy a manner as possible: in short, I want words to express half the beauties of this elegant monument, so very unlike all I have ever seen, and so much out of the taste of works of this sort. I know of but one in the same style, and which I always concluded was done by the same artist, till I saw by your book[35] that Nicholas Stone[36] died in 1647, the very year that this which I allude to was placed in Bassingbourn[37] Church in Cambridgeshire, by the Lady Dingley for her brother Mr Henry Butler:[38] which is a most elegant and neat piece of sculpture, and very probably executed by Mr Stone's son.[39] If ever you should pass this way, I dare venture to say you would be greatly pleased with this monument at Stow Nine Churches, and I should think myself happy to wait on you to see it.[40] It is not far[41] from Towcester; and if I knew any one of that lady's family, a plate of her tomb for the edition of the *History of Northamptonshire* which is now publishing[42] would do credit to the donor and much adorn that book, though I much question whether any engraver would do it justice. Two or three years ago I wrote to the editor[43] to give a particular account of its singular beauty, but it was too late, that part relating to Stow having been printed off. The reason Mr Vertue calls her by the name of Davers, is, as I suppose, from his not observing the dash over Dāvers, according to the usage of that time.

34. Henry Carey (1526–96), 1st Bn Hunsdon.

35. *Anecdotes*[1] ii. 30.

36. (1586–1647), the elder; mason, statuary and architect, best known for his monuments of Sir Thomas Bodley at Oxford and of John Donne in St Paul's (see *Walpole Society* vol. vii).

37. About two miles NW of Royston. Cole visited the church and copied the inscriptions, etc. 24 April 1747 (see Palmer, *Monumental Inscriptions* 10–12).

38. Cole's full description of the monument appears ibid. 10. Henry Butler d. 2 Sept. 1647.

39. Stone had three sons, Henry (1616–53), Nicholas (1618–47), and John (1620–

67), but there is no evidence to support Cole's attribution of the monument to any of them (see *Walpole Society* vii. 20–30).

40. The visit was never made.

41. About eight miles.

42. *The History and Antiquities of Northamptonshire. Compiled from the manuscript Collections of the late learned Antiquary, John Bridges, Esq. By the Rev. Peter Whalley, late Fellow of St John's College, Oxford,* 2 vols, Oxford, 1791. 'The first volume appeared in 1762, and the first part of the second in 1769,' but the work was not completed until 1791 (LA ii. 107–8 nn).

43. Peter Whalley.

P. 34, vol. 2. Saffron Walden is in Essex.[44] The house built by the Earl of Suffolk,[45] I suppose, occasioned the oversight.

P. 63, vol. 2. It was not in the Cathedral of Salisbury, but in the parish church of St Edmund in that city, that Sherfield the recorder[46] broke down with his staff a window of painted glass, for which he was fined in the Star Chamber. See Heylin's *History of Archbishop Laud*,[47] p. 217.

To the very curious anecdote in the same page relating to my Lord Grey's being concerned in rewarding the executioner of King Charles,[48] give me leave to add what I have noted in one of my books concerning that affair:

At a meeting of the Society of Antiquaries in London, February 6, 1745-6, James West,[49] Esq., produced a curious and authentic account of the beheading of the Royal Martyr. The executioner's name was Richard Brandon:[50] his attendant, a ragman of Rosemary Lane. The villain received £30 for the hellish job, and refused 20s. for the orange stuck with cloves which he found in the King's pocket on the scaffold, but took 10s. for it in his way home. These particulars I received by letter from Dr Morell,[51] a member of the Society, the day after.[52]

44. HW had said it was in Suffolk. He corrected the passage in *Anecdotes*[2] ii. 37 n.

45. Thomas Howard (1561–1626), 1st E. of Suffolk; Lord High Treasurer (1614–9) under James I.

46. Henry Sherfield (d. 1634), recorder of Salisbury. Although Cole's note is correct, HW allowed the error to stand in *Anecdotes*[2] ii. 68, and in later editions.

47. *Cyprianus Anglicus, or the History of the Life and Death of the most reverend and renowned Prelate William . . . Lord Archbishop of Canterbury*, 1668, by Peter Heylyn (1600–62), chaplain to Charles I and II.

48. Thomas Grey (1623?–57), Bn Grey of Groby, one of the judges of Charles I. HW believed that an order for £100, given the day after the King's execution, to be used as Lord Grey thought fit, was intended as a reward for the executioner. HW adopted part of Cole's note in *Anecdotes*[2] ii. 69 n.

49. (1704?–72), politician and antiquary, well known for his collections of MSS, books, prints, coins and pictures, which were dispersed by auction after his death (see *post* 12, 18 Feb. and 7 April 1773).

50. (d. 1649), son of Gregory Brandon, common hangman of London. It is now generally believed, in spite of the claims of several other candidates, that he was the executioner of Charles I (see DNB).

51. Thomas Morell (1703–84), D.D., of King's College, Cambridge; rector of Buckland in Herefordshire. Cole wrote of him in 1777 as 'my old acquaintance,' who 'let himself down' 'by keeping low company, especially of the musical tribe, and writing [the libretti of] their operas [Handel's among them], and mixing much with them.' He was, however, 'a very ingenious, good-tempered man, and a good scholar: but always in debt, and needy, so as frequently to be obliged to abscond' (Brydges, *Restituta* i. 464). Boswell was much pleased with a sermon which he heard Morell preach 3 Sept. 1769 (see *Private Papers of James Boswell from Malahide Castle*, ed. Geoffrey Scott and Frederick A. Pottle, 18 vols, 1928–34, viii. 89), and records a ridiculous story of Morell and Handel (op. cit. xv. 171).

52. In the margins of the MS are additional references to the King's execution, made by Cole at later dates: '*Vide* [White]

P. 94, vol. 2. There are at Mr Wright's[53] at Gothurst[54] in this neighbourhood, a seat formerly belonging to Sir Kenelm Digby, several full-length portraits of that family, but of whom particularly, or of what merit and value, I am no judge: yet there is a most elegant bust in brass or copper of the Lady Venetia Digby,[55] with a long inscription on the pediment, which I will copy out the first opportunity. These were left here when Sir Nathan Wright[56] made the purchase of the estate. It is probable the bust is the same with that destroyed in the Fire of London.[57]

P. 121, vol. 2. Dr Michael Honeywood[58] was Dean of Lincoln, and a great benefactor to the library there. In his printed epitaph it is said that his grandmother (not his mother) lived to see 367 (not 365) persons descended from her. As to the number, it must be accurate, as the several persons of each generation being cast up make all together 367, else I should not so readily have depended upon my authority.

P. 156, vol. 2. Walker's[59] picture of Oliver[60] is still at Horseth[61] (not Horsey) Hall in Cambridgeshire. It was given to the late Lord Montfort[62] by Mr Commissary Greaves,[63] who met with it in some ordinary ale-house or inn in the country.

Kennett's *Register and Chronicle*, [1728] p. 282. See William Lilly's *Life* by himself, edit. 2, 1725, p. 90, etc. *Vide Memoirs of Thomas Hollis, Esq.*, vol. i, pp. 131–2. London, 2 vols, 4to, 1780. University Library.' 'One William Walker [1621–1700], who died at Sheffield, was the executioner. *Vide Gentleman's Magazine* for November 1767, pp. 548–9, and January 1768, pp. 10[–11].'

53. George Wright (ca 1703–66), grandson of Sir Nathan Wright; Cole's 'friend and neighbour,' and M.P. for Leicester 1727–66 (*Alumni Cantab.; Blecheley Diary* 10).

54. Gothurst or Gayhurst House, near Newport Pagnell, Bucks. Cole later sent HW some notes on the pictures and busts there, and in July 1763 they visited the place together (see *post* Sept. 1762; *Country Seats* 52).

55. Venetia Stanley (1600–33), dau. of Sir Edward Stanley of Tonge Castle, Salop; m. (1625) Sir Kenelm Digby.

56. (1654–1721), Lord Keeper of the Great Seal. Cole gives an account of him in *Blecheley Diary* 10–11.

57. Cole added, apparently in 1779, the following note on this passage: 'See *Mélanges d'Histoire et de Litterature* par Vigneul Merveille ou Dom Bonaventure d'Argogne, Chartreux. Tome 3, p. 252.' Cf. *post* 21 May 1779 (introductory note) and 14 Nov. 1779. For 'tome 3' in Cole's citation, read 'tome 1' (2d edn, Rotterdam, 1702, i. 202).

58. Michael Honywood (1597–1681), Dean of Lincoln, 1660–81; grandson of Mrs Mary Honywood (1527–1620), whose lineal descendants numbered 367 in her lifetime (see DNB). Both mistakes stand in *Anecdotes*[2] ii. 137 and in later editions.

59. Robert Walker (d. 1658?), portrait-painter.

60. Cromwell.

61. Horseheath Hall (which Cole usually spells *Horseth* or *Horsheth*), the seat of the Bromley family until 1765, when it was sold by Thomas Bromley, 2d Bn Montfort. HW altered the passage in *Anecdotes*[2] ii. 180.

62. Henry Bromley (1705–55), 1st Bn Montfort, who committed suicide as a result of gambling losses (see HW to Bent-

As you are pleased at p. 112 of your first volume to lament that we have none of our ancient architects whose names are transmitted to posterity, it may probably be some satisfaction to you to meet with one who was concerned in building the most elegant and noble Gothic church in England: I mean the Cathedral of Lincoln, for such it is pronounced to be, according to an original letter now by me,[64] by the late Earl of Burlington[65] and Mr Kent[66] upon their viewing it in their return from York, which cathedral they esteemed to be inferior to it. The architect's name, or at least of some part of the fabric, was Richard de Gaynisbourgh,[67] but the exact time of his death is uncertain, as that part of the inscription is obliterated. It was but lately cleared from the dirt in order to come at the inscription, by the late Mr Sympson,[68] an industrious antiquary of Lincoln, who had collected materials for an history of that place. The gravestone lies in the Cathedral Church of Lincoln, with the following inscription cut in Saxon letters, as he calls them in his letter now before me, and was never printed. It is as follows:

Hic jacet Ricardus de Gaynisbourgh olym Cementarius istius Ecclesie qui obiit duodecim Kalendarum Junii Anno Domini M.C.C.C....

At p. 146, vol. 1, you seem to say that the tapestry hangings representing the destruction of the Armada were put up in the House of Lords in Oliver's administration, when that House was made use of for Committees of the Commons: at least I understand you so. If so, how can we account for a print by Hollar, representing Arch-

ley 9 Jan. 1755; [Wm B. Boulton,] *The History of White's*, 2 vols, [1892], i. 105–7). Cole, distantly related and intimate with him and his son, repeatedly defends his reputation in his MSS.

63. William Greaves (d. 1787), of Fulbourn, Cambs; Commissary of Cambridge University 1726–79, and steward of the estates of Trinity College. He married a daughter of Beaupré Bell, of Upwell and Outwell, Norfolk; when he inherited the estates he changed his name to William Greaves Beaupré Bell (see GM, March 1787, lvii. 277b).

64. The letter, dated 9 July 1740, was from Thomas Sympson of Lincoln to 'Mr. Precentor Trimnel.' James Essex quoted part of it ('From the Rev. Mr. Cole's MS Collections') in a paper, 'Some Observa-

tions on Lincoln Cathedral,' which he contributed to *Archaeologia* iv (1777). 149–59. Cole's copy of the letter is in Add MS 5841, f. 57. HW made no use of this part of Cole's information.

65. Richard Boyle (1695–1753), 3d E. of Burlington; statesman and patron of literature and the arts.

66. William Kent (1684–1748), painter, architect, and landscape-gardener, much admired by HW (see *On Modern Gardening, Works* ii. 536).

67. Of whom HW inserted an account in *Anecdotes²* i. 119.

68. Thomas Sympson (fl. 1740–50), Master of the Works of Lincoln Cathedral; member of the Gentlemen's Society at Spalding (see LA vi. 114).

bishop Laud's trial in the House of Lords in 1645, where those very hangings are represented by references of the letter *T* as being the hangings of '88? This print is the frontispiece of one of Prynne's books called *Hidden Works of Darkenesse brought to publicke Light, or a necessary Introduction to the History of the Archbishop of Canterbury's Tryal.* Folio. London, 1645.[69]

Dear Sir, I once more beg pardon for so much impertinence, and beg leave to subscribe myself, Sir,

Your most obedient and obliged humble servant,

WM. COLE

To COLE, Thursday 20 May 1762

Add MS 5952, ff. 3–4.

Address and Postmark: Missing from original, but the following note in Cole's hand precedes his copy (Add MS 5831, f. 224v) of the letter: 'On Friday, May 21, 1762, I received the following answer from Mr Walpole: To the Reverend Mr Cole at Blecheley near Fenny Stratford, Buckinghamshire. Free Hor. Walpole. Postmark MA 20. Isleworth. Seal of red wax, a cupid with a large mask of a monkey's face. An antique. Oval.' Cole's drawing of the seal is in the margin.

Strawberry Hill, May 20, 1762.

Dear Sir,

YOU have sent me the most kind and obliging letter in the world, and I cannot sufficiently thank you for it; but I shall be very glad to have an opportunity of acknowledging it in person, by accepting the agreeable visit you are so good as to offer me, and for which I have long been impatient. I should name the earliest day possible; but besides having some visits to make, I think it will be more pleasant to you a few weeks hence (I mean any time in July) when the works with which I am finishing my house[1] will be more

---

69. COLE has a similar note in his copy (now wsl) of George Vertue, *A Description of the Works of . . . Wenceslaus Hollar,* 1745, at p. 10.

1. The chief of these 'works' were the Gallery and Cabinet (later called Chapel and Tribune). Because of strikes (see HW to Mann 1 July 1762) they were delayed.

advanced, and the noisy part, as laying floors, and fixing wainscots, at an end, and which now make me in a deplorable litter. As you give me leave, I will send you notice.

I am glad my books[2] amused you—yet you, who are so much deeper an antiquarian, must have found more faults and omissions, I fear, than your politeness suffers you to reprehend. Yet you will, I trust, be a little more severe. We both labour, I will not say for the public, for the public troubles its head very little about our labours, but for the few of posterity that shall be curious, and therefore for their sakes you must assist me in making my work as complete as possible. This sounds ungrateful, after all the trouble you have given yourself: but I say it, to prove my gratitude, and to show you how fond I am of being corrected.

For the faults of impression, they were owing to the knavery of a printer, who when I had corrected the sheets, amused me with revised proofs, and never printed off the whole number, and then ran away[3]—This accounts too for the difference of the ink in various sheets,[4] and for some other blemishes; though there are still enough of my own which I must not charge on others.

Ubaldini's book I have not,[5] and shall be pleased to see it, but I cannot think of robbing your collection; and am amply obliged by the offer.

The anecdotes of Horatio Palavicini are extremely entertaining. In an Itinerary of the late Mr Smart Lethuillier[6] I met the very tomb

The Cabinet was not completed until April 1763 (see HW to Montagu 14 April 1763), and the Gallery not until August 1763 (see *post* 8 Aug. 1763). The main building at SH was not finished until the Beauclerc Tower was added in 1776 (see 'Genesis of SH' 82).

2. *Anecdotes*[1] i. and ii.

3. Thomas Farmer, printer at SH from 16 July 1759 to 2 Dec. 1761 (see *Jour. Print. Off.* 9–10). 'Just when I thought my book finished, my printer ran away, and had left eighteen [cf. *Jour. Print. Off.* 10, where HW says 'nineteen'] sheets in the middle of the book untouched, having amused me with sending proofs. He had got into debt, and two girls with child—being two, he could not marry both Hannahs' (HW to Montagu 23 Dec. 1761). For HW's fuller account

of Farmer's disappearance, see *Jour. Print. Off.* 81–2.

4. It is not known which sheets Farmer did not print off. The ink varies considerably from sheet to sheet.

5. It appears from MS Cat. that he had a copy of the book before 1763, with pressmark L.3.28. It was sold SH iv. 88. HW introduced a note on it in *Anecdotes*[2] i. 159 n.

6. Smart Lethieullier (1701–60), of Aldersbrook House, Essex; antiquary (C. H. Iyan Chown, 'The Lethieullier Family of Aldersbrook House,' 2 parts, *Essex Review*, Colchester, xxxv (1926). 203–20; xxxvi (1927). 1–21). His library was sold at auction by Samuel Baker, York Street, Covent Garden, 23 Feb. 1761 and six days following. A priced copy of the catalogue is in

of Gainsborough this winter that you mention, and to be secure, sent to Lincoln for an exact draught of it.[7] But what vexed me then and does still, is, that by the defect at the end of the inscription, one cannot be certain whether he lived in CCC, or CCCC; as another C might have been there. Have you any corroborating circumstance, Sir, to affix his existence to 1300, more than to 1400?[8] Besides, I don't know any proof of his having been architect of the church; his epitaph only calls him *Caementarius,* which, I suppose, means *mason.*

I have observed, since my book was published, what you mention of the tapestry in Laud's trial; yet as the journals[9] were my authority, and certainly cannot be mistaken, I have concluded that Hollar engraved his print after the Restoration. Mr Wight,[10] clerk of the House of Lords, says, that Oliver placed them in the House of Commons—I don't know on what grounds he says so.

I am, Sir, with great gratitude, Your most obliged humble servant,

HOR. WALPOLE

the British Museum. The 'Itinerary' was part of a larger work in three folio volumes, described in the London Sale Catalogue, lot 1260, as 'containing upwards of 280 drawings, etc. . . . The following note is entered by Lord Orford, at the commencement of the first volume: "These three volumes of ancient buildings were drawn by Smart Lethuillier, Esq. . . . and by Charles Frederick, Esq., afterwards Knight of the Bath. I bought them for three score pounds, in 1761, after the death of Mr. Lethuillier.—Horace Walpole." ' See also *post* 11 Nov. 1780. The three volumes are now Add MSS 27348–50.

Cole made the following note on his copy of this letter: 'See a letter of Mr Sympson in my vol. 40, p. 112, in which he says he showed Mr Lethuillier the inscription on Richard de Gaynisbourgh' (Add MS 5831, f. 225). The passage to which Cole refers is Add MS 5841, f. 57v, where Sympson says he showed some tombs to 'two gentlemen, travellers . . . one of them called Lethiulier, the other's

name I forget, but as neat a draughtsman as I ever saw.'

7. It is not known to whom HW applied for the draught of the tomb.

8. 'In 1306 the Dean and Chapter contracted with Richard of Stow, mason—"cementarius"—to superintend the new work—"novum opus"—and to employ other masons under him. The plain work was to be done by measure, and the fine carved work and images by the day' (Rev. Edmund Venables, 'The Architectural History of Lincoln Cathedral,' *The Archaeological Journal*, 1883, xl. 404).

9. 'See *Journals of the Commons*, January 1, 1650[–1]' (HW's note in *Anecdotes*[1] i. 146).

10. Joseph Wight, an officer in the House of Lords for 'forty years and upwards.' He served as Reading Clerk and Clerk of the Private Committees until 30 Jan. 1753, and as Clerk Assistant from that time until 1765, when he resigned because of ill health (see *Journals of the House of Lords*, 27, 29 May 1732; 31 Jan. 1753; 13, 20 May 1765).

To Cole, Thursday 29 July 1762

Add MS 5952, f. 5.

Strawberry Hill, July 29, 1762.

Sir,

I FEAR you will have thought me neglectful of the visit you was so good as to offer me for a day or two at this place: the truth is I have been in Somersetshire on a visit which was protracted much longer than I intended.[1] I am now returned, and shall be glad to see you as soon as you please, Sunday or Monday next if you like either, or any other day you will name. I cannot defer the pleasure of seeing you any longer, though to my mortification you will find Strawberry Hill with its worst looks—not a blade of grass. My workmen too have disappointed me; they have been in the association for forcing their masters to raise their wages, and but two are yet returned—so you must excuse litter and shavings.[2]

I am, Sir, Your obedient servant,

Hor. Walpole

From Cole, Saturday 31 July 1762

Cole's copy, Add MS 5831, ff. 225v–227v.

Cole wrote at the top of the page: 'My letter to Mr Walpole on his book on painting.'

Blecheley, July 31, 1762.

Dear Sir,

THE favour of yours of the 29th instant I received yesterday, and as our post goes not out till tomorrow, though I write my answer now, it won't go forward till then.

I am sorry to hear Strawberry Hill is in the same state with us in this part of the country, where there is not a blade of grass to be

1. HW had just returned from a visit of about a fortnight to the Earl of Ilchester at Redlynch House, near Bruton, Somerset. Lord Ilchester accompanied HW on a tour to several country seats in Dorset and Wiltshire (HW to Ilchester 29 July 1762; *Country Seats* 41–8).

2. See also HW to Mann 1 July 1762, and to Strafford 5 Aug. 1762.

seen, and hardly any water for the cattle. We have been daily tantalized with rain, but not a drop has fallen here to any purpose these three months: though, by accounts, other places have had very plentiful showers.

I am concerned that particular business prevents my waiting upon you so soon as you mention. I am detained here next week, and am obliged to be in Cambridgeshire on the beginning of the following, where I am informed that one of my tenants is going to break, which I am afraid will be the case with many this year. However, I propose myself the pleasure of being with you about the 11th or 12th of next month, if that time should be agreeable to you, and not interfere with any of your engagements. In case it should, a line will find me here all next week, and at Mr Newcome's at Hackney[1] about the 9th or 10th of August.

On a second perusal of your book on *Painting in England,* I have made a few farther observations which I am emboldened to communicate, as I have your express orders for it: not that they are of consequence any farther than as they serve to illustrate a subject which has received no small honour by your condescending to treat of.

Vol. 1, p. 2. St Wolstan,[2] the famous bishop of Worcester in 1062, is recorded by his historian and biographer, William of Malmsbury[3] (who wrote his life in three books), as a proficient in the art of limning, long before the Conquest. His master's name is also transmitted to us by the same historian, which was Ervenius, or Erwen. This life is published by Mr Wharton[4] in *Anglia Sacra,* vol. 2, pp. 241[-70], and as it is possible that you may not have the book, I will transcribe what he says on the subject.

Habebat [Wulstanus][5] tunc Magistrum Ervenium nomine, in scribendo et quidlibet coloribus effingendo peritum. Is libros scriptos, Sacramen-

1. Henry Newcome (fl. 1750–80), son of Dr Henry Newcome, a well-known schoolmaster of Hackney, whom he succeeded as master of the school. He m. (1759) Cole's niece, Mary Mawdesley (d. 1782), dau. of Hector Mawdesley, a wholesale cheesemonger of London, by Mary Cole (Joseph Hunter, *Familiae Minorum Gentium,* ed. John W. Clay, *Harleian Society's Publications,* 1895, xxxix. 1045; GM, July 1782, lii. 357b).

2. St Wulfstan (1012?–95), Bp of Worcester 1062–95.

3. (d. 1143?), author of *Gesta Regum Anglorum,* 1125, and *Gesta Pontificum Anglorum,* 1125.

4. Henry Wharton (1664–95), divine and author of *Anglia Sacra,* 2 vols, 1691.

5. The brackets are Cole's.

tarium et Psalterium, quorum principales literas auro effigiaverit, puero W[u]lstano delegandos curavit. Ille preciosorum apicum captus miraculo, dum pulchritudinem intentis oculis rimatur, et scientiam literarum internis hausit medullis. Verum doctor ad sæculi spectans commodum, spe majoris præmii, Sacramentarium Regi tunc temporis Cnutoni, Psalterium Emmæ Reginæ contribuit. Perculit puerilem animum facti dispendium; et ex imo pectore alta traxit suspiria.[6]

If this does not absolutely determine St Wolstan to be himself a proficient in limning, yet it is quite clear for his Saxon master Erwen. Dr Patrick,[7] in his quotation of this passage in his supplement to Mr Gunton's *History of Peterborough,*[8] p. 259, has made two or three considerable blunders. He calls the author of this MS life of St Wolstan, *Bravonius,* which is no other than the old name of the city of Worcester. He was led into this mistake by the MS in Sir John Cotton's Library,[9] having *Senatus Bravonius* wrote on it in a modern hand. Now *Senatus Bravonius,* or *Senatus Wigorniensis* as Bale[10] calls him, Cent. 3, No. X, was Prior of the Church of Worcester from A.D. 1189 to 1196. But that William of Malmsbury was the real and true author of this MS Mr Wharton has evidently shown in his preface to *Anglia Sacra,* vol. 2, p. xv. Neither did Eruentus, as Dr Patrick calls him by mistake for Ervenius, make St Wolstan write the sacramentary and psalter: he only sent them to him for his perusal and amusement, or lent them to him before he sent them to court, Ervenius himself being the illuminator or limner of the drawings, as is evident from the quotation above.

Vol. 1, p. 45.[11] In the Golden Register of all the benefactors to

6. *Anglia Sacra* ii. 244. See also *The Vita Wulfstani of William of Malmsbury,* ed. R. R. Darlington, Camden Society, 3d series, vol. XL, 1928, p. 5. Note 2 suggests that Erwinus was subsequently Abbot of Peterborough. HW quoted this passage and added a note on St Wulfstan and Ervenius in *Anecdotes*[2] i. 2.

7. Simon Patrick (1626–1707), Bp of Chichester 1689–91, and of Ely 1691–1707.

8. The collections of Simon Gunton (1609–76), vicar of Peterborough 1660–6, were edited by Patrick under the title, *The History of Peterborough,* 1686. Patrick's supplement was included in this edition of the *History.* The original MS of the supplement is now Add MS 22,666.

Cole's copy of this work is now in the Bodleian.

9. Sir John Cotton (1621–1701), 3d Bt, grandson of Sir Robert Bruce Cotton (1571–1631), 1st Bt and original owner of the Cottonian Library, transferred to the nation in 1702 by Sir John Cotton (1679–1731), 4th Bt.

10. John Bale (1495–1563), Bp of Ossory. Cole apparently refers to the second edition of his *Illustrium Maioris Britanniae scriptorum summarium,* which was published at Basle, 1557–9, as *Scriptorum Illustrium Maioris Britanniae.*

11. This note (which HW did not use) is not upon HW's text, but is a continuation of his introduction to Chapter III.

the Abbey of St Albans, Alan Strayler, their painter or limner, is commemorated as remitting to the Abbey 3s. 4d. owing to him for colours, in this manner:

> Nomen Pictoris Alanus Strayler habetur
> Qui sine fine choris celestibus associetur.[12]

This is recorded in Weever's *Funeral Monuments*, p. 578, and I observe that you have mentioned him as a limner at p. 16 of your first volume, so probably you took it from the same authority.[13]

Vol. 1, p. 99.[14] In the archives of Caius College in Cambridge, formerly communicated to me by my worthy friend the present Master of that College, Sir James Burrough, Knight,[15] is the following particular relating to the architect of King's College Chapel:

> To alle Christen People this p[re]sent Writyng endented seeng, redyng or heryng, John Wulrich, Maistr Mason of the Werkes of the Kyng's College Roial of Our Lady & Seynt Nicholas of Cambrigge, John Bell, Mason Wardeyn in the same Werkes, Richard Adam, & Rob. Dogett, Carpenters, Arbitrours indifferently chosen by the reverent Fader in God, Edward, by the Grace of God, Byshopp of Karlyle,[16] Mr. or Wardeyn of the Hous or College of St. Michael of Cambr. & the Scolers of the same, on the oon part; & Maist. Henry Cossey, Warden of the College or Hall of the Annuntiation or Gonville Hall, & the Fellowes & Scolers of the same, on the other Part, Of & upon the Evesdroppe into the Garden of Ffysshwyke Hostle, belonging to Gonville Halle &c.—Written at Cambr. 17 Aug. 1476. 16 Edw. 4.—Ex Archivis Gonv. & Caii.

In Hearne's preface to the *History of Glastonbury*,[17] p. lxv, is this farther account of another architect of that most stately and elegant structure:

The book is now BM MS Cotton. Nero D vii. It was done about 1380.

12. Ibid., folio 108.

13. HW was a careful reader of Weever and probably did get his note on Strayler from him.

14. The following quotation, with a paraphrase of Cole's introduction, was quoted in *Anecdotes*[2] i. 107 n, without acknowledgment.

15. (1691–1764), an amateur architect who did much to introduce the classical style of architecture into the University. Cole's eulogistic account of him, Add MS

5832, f. 83, is quoted in *Biographical History of Gonville and Caius College*, compiled by John Venn, 3 vols, 1897–1901, iii. 127. See also Robert Willis, *Architectural History of the University of Cambridge*, 4 vols, 1886, i. 165 ff.

16. Edward Story (d. 1503), Bp of Carlisle, 1468–77, and of Chichester, 1477–1503.

17. *The History and Antiquities of Glastonbury* [by Richard Rawlinson] . . . *To all which pieces (never before printed) a preface is prefix'd and an appendix subjoin'd by* . . . *T. Hearne*, Oxford, 1722.

All that see[18] King's College Chapel in Cambridge are struck with Admiration, & most are mighty desirous of knowing the Architect's Name. Yet few can tell it. It appears, however, from their Books at King's College (as I am informed by my Friend Mr. Baker,[19] the learned Antiquary of Cambridge) that one Mr. Cloos, (Father of Nicholas Cloos,[20] one of the first Fellows of that College, & afterwards Bishop of Litchfield) was the Architect of this Chapel, (though Godwin[21] says, the Bishop himself was Master of the King's Works here) as far as Henry the 6th's share reacheth, and Contriver or Designer of the Whole, afterwards finished by Henry 7th & further beautified by Henry the 8.

In a MS account of all the members of King's College, a copy of which is in my possession, Bishop Nicholas Close is mentioned as a person in whose 'capacity King Henry 6, (who had placed him in Fellow A. D. 1443) had such Confidence, that he appointed him Overseer & Manager of all his intended Buildings & Designs for this College.' And in the same MS historiette of King's College, John Canterbury,[22] a native of Tewksbury, and fellow of the college in 1451, is said to have been Clerk of the Works for the building of the same.[23]

Vol. 1, p. 112. In St Michael's Church at St Albans are, or were in Weever's time, the following inscriptions[24] for two architects of the same age:

18. HW added this passage to *Anecdotes*[2] i. 105 n.

19. Thomas Baker (1656–1740), antiquary and ejected fellow of St John's College, Cambridge, who left in MS numerous collections relating to the University, of which the first 23 vols are now in the Harleian Collection in the British Museum and vols 24–42 are in the University Library, Cambridge. In 1778 HW, at Cole's suggestion, wrote a 'Life of Baker,' which was first published in *Works* ii. 339–62.

20. Nicholas Close (d. 1452), Bp of Carlisle, 1450, and of Lichfield, 1452; Chancellor of Cambridge.

21. Francis Godwin (1562–1633), Bp of Llandaff, 1601, and of Hereford, 1617; author of *Catalogue of the Bishops of England*, 1601, which was edited and continued by William Richardson, 1643.

22. (fl. 1450–70) also has the distinction of being the first (so termed) Esquire Bedell of the University (see *Alumni Cantab.*).

23. HW makes use of this paragraph in the following manner: 'In a MS account of all the members of King's College, a copy of which is in the possession of the Rev. Mr Cole of Blecheley, to whom the public and I are obliged for this and several other curious particulars, Bishop Nicholas Close is mentioned as a person in whose capacity King Henry VI (who had appointed him fellow in 1443) had such confidence, that he made him overseer and manager of all his intended buildings and designs for that college: In the same MS John Canterbury, a native of Tewksbury and fellow of the college in 1451, is said to have been clerk of the works there' (*Anecdotes*[2] i. 105–6 n). This is the only passage in which Cole is mentioned by name in *Anecdotes*[2].

24. HW quoted both inscriptions and the sentence from John Weever, *Ancient Funerall Monuments*, 1631, in *Anecdotes*[2] i. 120. Cole's transcription is *verbatim et literatim*.

Hic jacet Thomas Wolvey (or Wolven)[24a] Latomus in Arte, necnon Armiger illustrissimi Principis Ric. secundi quondam Regis Anglie, qui obiit Anno Dom. MCCCCXXX in vigilia Sancti Thome Martyris. Cujus anime propitietur Deus. Amen.

'This Man, as far as I understand by this Inscription (says Weever, p. 582) was the Master Mason, or Surveior of the King's stone-works: as also Esquire to the King's Person.'

Hic jacet Richardus Wolven (or Wolvey) Lathonius [sic], filius Johannis Wolven, cum Uxoribus suis Agnete et Agnete, et cum octo filiis et decem Filiabus suis, qui Richardus obiit....Ann. 1490. Quorum animabus, &c.

Vol. 2, p. 18.[25] It is very probable that an half-length portrait of Bishop Felton,[26] with his arms impaled by those of the see of Ely, and ensigned with a mitre, and which I made a present of to the late Sir Thomas Gooch, Baronet,[27] Lord Bishop of Ely, for the use of him and his successors, to be hung up in the gallery of the Palace at Ely, is by this Edward Norgate.[28] The head is excellently well finished, and full of life; but the lawn sleeves and drapery stiff. It formerly belonged to Sclater Bacon, Esquire, Member for the town of Cambridge,[29] and I bought it with some other pictures out of his collection at the sale of his goods at Catley in Cambridgeshire.[30] There is a picture of Bishop Felton in the library of Pembroke Hall, not comparable to this.

Vol. 2, p. 22.[31] I was lately told (June 2, 1762) by the Rev. Father Charles Bedingfield[32] of the Order of St Francis, a recollet and a friend of mine, that Sir Francis Crane was buried at a village near

---

24a. Wolvey is the correct form (see *Calendar of Close Rolls, 1396–1399*, p. 239).

25. HW did not use this note.

26. Nicholas Felton (1556–1626), Bp of Bristol 1617–9, and of Ely 1619–26.

27. (1674–1754), 2d Bt; Master of Caius, 1716–54; Bp of Bristol 1737–8, of Norwich 1738–48, and of Ely 1748–54. Cole's brilliant description of him, Add MS 5832, f. 139, is quoted in *Biographical History of Gonville and Caius College*, compiled by John Venn, 3 vols, 1897–1901, iii. 118–9.

28. (d. 1650), art connoisseur and herald. 'He was brought up by Nicholas Felton Bishop of Ely who married his mother' (*Anecdotes*[1] ii. 18).

29. Thomas Sclater, who later took the name of Bacon (1664–1736), was F.R.S. 1721, M.P. for Cambridge 1722–36, and left a fortune of £200,000 (see Cooper, *Annals* iv. 126–37; Musgrave, *Obituary* 329). HW had a portrait of 'a young man, by Sir Godfrey Kneller,' from Bacon's collection. It was in the Gallery at SH (*Description of SH, Works* ii. 464).

30. This sale was possibly on 19 July 1749, when Cole records that he bought a picture 'at the auction of the goods late Robert King's of Catley, near Linton, Esq., one of the heirs of Tho. Sclater Bacon Esq.' (Palmer, *Monumental Inscriptions* 267).

31. HW did not use this note.

32. Father Charles Bonaventure Beding-

Norwich,[33] and not far from Mr Gurdon's of Letton,[34] but he could not recollect the name of it.

Vol. 2, p. 17.[35] The observation of Mr Edmund Chishull, B. D. and Chaplain to the English factory at Smyrna,[36] is very ingenious with regard to the art of staining glass. It is in his *Travels in Turkey*,[37] at p. 6, where he observes that this art was flourishing in that country in this manner:

It seemed strange to us to observe several pieces of painted glass in the windows of our *effendi's* house, inscribed in Turkish characters with the name of the proprietor, together with some religious sentences of Mahometan devotion. But we were much more surprized, when we were informed, that it was the manufacture of this place [Magnesia];[38] for it is stained with a beautiful, as well as deep and durable colour, and comes up to the perfection of the best we have seen in England. This gave us occasion to reflect on the different fortune of arts and sciences, which, like men, seem to take delight in shifting their station; for while other arts have now left these places, and travelled westward, this alone in exchange for all the rest, seems to have retired into this, and is deplored as lost in Christendom.

And at p. 8 he observes:

The windows [of their mosques] are furnished with excellent painted glass, full of flower work, and religious inscriptions . . .

But as their religion forbids the making of representations of men, so by that injunction, the chief beauty of that art is of no benefit to them; inasmuch as it deprives them of the use of history-painting; the most excellent of all in that art!

In 1746, being at Glocester, the then worthy Bishop, Dr Martin Benson,[39] showed me his elegant and small chapel in his palace, neatly fitted up by himself and wainscoted with cedar, but that

---

field, chaplain to Mrs Markham of Somerby Hall near Grantham, Lincolnshire, and one of Cole's correspondents (see *Blecheley Diary, passim;* Cole, *Jour. to Paris* 20).

33. Sir Francis Crane died at Paris, 26 June 1636, but 'his body was brought to England and buried at Woodrising in Norfolk, 10 July 1636, a gravestone to his memory being placed in the chancel of the church' (DNB: W. P. Courtney).

34. Thornhagh Gurdon (d. 1783) (Burke,

Commoners i. 396). Letton is five miles SW of East Dereham.

35. HW did not use these notes.

36. Rev. Edmund Chishull (1671–1733), chaplain at Smyrna 1698–1702.

37. *Travels in Turkey, and back to England,* 1747. It was published by Chishull's son, with a preface by Dr Mead.

38. Cole's brackets.

39. (1689–1752), rector of Bletchley 1727; Bp of Gloucester 1735–52.

which struck me most was a beautiful east window of painted glass, representing our Lord's ascension, which cost the Bishop 150 pounds, and was probably done by Price,[40] but of this I am not certain.

See an account of several painted windows in the chapels of the two universities and at Fairford, in Dr Wilson's *Ornaments of Churches Considered*,[41] printed in 1761, in quarto, Appendix No. X, p. 32, as also the postscript to it, printed in 1762, p. 6, where he intimates a design of publishing an account of all the painted glass windows of any esteem now remaining in England and Ireland.

Vol. 2, p. 133. Query if *Raphael de Rouvigny*[42] should not be *Rachael*.

Dear Sir, I hope you'll excuse all this scribble. I'm sure if I don't tire you, I have myself, as this very hot weather disagrees with my constitution, and therefore will put an end to it by assuring you of my most sincere and unfeigned regard, and am, Sir,

Your most faithful servant,

Wm Cole

To Cole, Thursday 5 August 1762

Add MS 5952, f. 6.

Strawberry Hill, Aug. 5, 1762.

Sir,

AS I had been dilatory in accepting your kind offer of coming hither, I proposed it as soon as I returned.[1] As we are so burnt, and as my workmen have disappointed me, I am not quite sorry that

40. William Price (d. 1765), the younger, painted windows in Westminster Abbey, Winchester and New College. HW wrote to Bentley Sept. 1753: 'The Bishop's house [at Gloucester] is pretty, and restored to the Gothic by the last Bishop [Benson]. Price has painted a large chapel window ['The Resurrection'] for him, which is scarce inferior for colours, and is a much better picture than any of the old glass.' HW employed him extensively at SH (*SH Accounts*).

41. *The Ornaments of Churches Considered, with a particular View to the late Decoration of the Parish Church of St. Margaret Westminster* [by W. Hole], *to which is subjoined, an Appendix, containing the History of the said Church* [by Thomas Wilson], Oxford, 1761, edited, with an introduction and a postscript, 1762, by Wilson.

42. HW corrected this mistake in *Anecdotes*[2] ii. 151. Rachel de Ruvigny (1603–40) m., as his first wife, Thomas Wriothesley (1607–67), 4th E. of Southampton.

1. From Somerset (see *ante* 29 July).

I had not the pleasure of seeing you this week. Next week I am obliged to be in town on business.[2] If you please therefore, we will postpone our meeting till the first of September, by which time I flatter myself we shall be green, and I shall be able to show you my additional apartment[3] to more advantage. Unless you forbid me, I will expect you, Sir, the very beginning of next month. In the meantime I will only thank you for the obliging and curious notes you have sent me, which will make a great figure in my second edition.

I am, Sir, Your much obliged humble servant,

HOR. WALPOLE

The Rev. ROBERT MASTERS to HW, August 1762

Cole's reply to HW's letter, 5 Aug. 1762, is missing, but it was probably merely a note with the following communication to HW from Robert Masters (1713–98), Fellow of Corpus Christi Coll., Cambridge, 1736–50; rector of Landbeach, 1756, and of Waterbeach, 1759; author of *History of the College of Corpus Christi*, 1753. As HW's next letter to Cole is almost entirely in answer to it, this indirect letter of Masters's is inserted here. The whereabouts of the original is not known. The text is that of LA iii. 482.

[August 1762.]

MR MASTERS has perused Mr Walpole's *Anecdotes of Painting* (which Mr Cole was so obliging as to lend him) with great pleasure; and finds he has by him one of the miniatures of Henry VII described in vol. i, p. 46,[1] being 14 inches by 10½, undoubtedly a picture of that time, and in its original frame, which, if worth Mr Walpole's acceptance as a collector of such curiosities, is much at his service.

There must surely be a mistake in the sum paid for the tapestry in p. 145, since at 10*l*. 1s. per ell it amounts to 7,115*l*. 8s.[2]

2. This business was no doubt connected with HW's place at the Exchequer. He was in London 12 Aug. 1762 (HW to Mann, that date).

3. Either the Gallery or the Tribune (Chapel, Cabinet) (see *ante* 20 May 1762 n. 1).

1. 'Two miniatures of Henry VII each in a black cap, and one of them with a rose in his hand are mentioned in a MS in the Harleian collection' (*Anecdotes*[1] i. 46 n).

2. 'This error (which remains uncorrected in the Quarto Edition of Lord Orford's *Works*, vol. III. p. 124) is probably not in the sum total, but in the 10*l*. 1s. which is likely to be intended for "10 rix dollars and 1 guilder."' (Nichols's note, LA iii. 482 n.)

Mr Walpole speaks of a monument and bust, p. 164, erected to the memory of Sir Nathaniel Bacon[3] in the Church of Culford; which, if true, there must have been two, since there is certainly one at Stiffkey in Norfolk, where he built the hall, and was interred, as his epitaph sets forth. (See Masters's *Hist. of Bene't Coll.* App. p. 85.)

P. 102. The Kings in Chichester Cathedral were repainted by Tremayne[4] at the expense of Bishop Mawson.[5]

Mr Walpole, in vol. ii, p. 58, speaks of the first lecture of geography read at Sir Balthazar Gerbier's[6] Academy at Bednal Green, which yet he had not seen; now, although this might be the first lecture, on that subject, yet I presume it was not the first read there, since I have by me 'The Art of Well Speaking, being a Lecture read gratis at Sir Balthazar Gerbier's Academy,' dated 6 Jan. 1649 [i.e., 1650, N.S.], which, in the dedication to the Parliament of England, he styles his *first lecture*. I have a print of him different both in person and dress from that in the book;[7] which has the motto, *Heureux qui in Dieu se confie,* and round the oval, *D. Balthazar Gerbierius, Eques auratus,* but no C. R. 1653, on the medal hanging on his left side, as in p. 60. Mr Masters apprehends that the person who dedicated his book *to the right high and supreme Power of this Nation, the Parliament of England,* etc., in 1649, could scarce be so much in favour with the King as to have a medal given him in 1653: the date is therefore probably wrong.

Mr Masters has part of a collection of the heads of painters, etc., the last number of which is 116, by different hands, but chiefly engraved by Pet. de Jode,[8] and printed by Jo. Meyssens,[9] which does not seem to correspond to either of the collections spoken of in p. 90.

3. (fl. 1640), painter, was the 7th son of Sir Nicholas Bacon, 1st Bt. HW confounds this Sir Nathaniel with his uncle of the same name, of Stiffkey, Norfolk, who was the eldest son of the Lord Keeper. HW calls the painter 'the younger son of the keeper.' HW added a note in *Anecdotes*[2] i. 177, embodying the information furnished by Masters and referring to Masters's *History of the College of Corpus Christi,* Cambridge, 1753–5.

4. HW refers to him as 'one Tremaine,' who repainted the pictures of the kings in 1747. Apparently nothing further is known of him.

5. Matthias Mawson (1683–1770), Bp of Llandaff 1738–40, of Chichester 1740–54, and of Ely 1754–70.

6. (1591?–1667), painter, architect and courtier, established an academy at Bethnal Green. HW had written, 'In 1649 he published the first lecture of geography,' etc. HW used part of the information furnished by Masters in *Anecdotes*[2] ii. 63 n. with acknowledgment.

7. Mentioned in *Anecdotes*[1] ii. 58. HW did not use this part of Masters's note.

8. Peter de Jode (1606–74?), the younger, a Belgian artist who engraved after Van Dyck and other artists (see *Allgemeines Lexikon der Bildenden Künstler,* Leipzig, 1907–).

9. Joannes Meyssens (1612–70), painter, draughtsman, engraver and publisher (op. cit.).

Hen. Van der Borcht, mentioned p. 73, is the 89th in your collection.[10]

P. 116. Nic. Laniere[11] is said to have died in 1646; and yet to have been a purchaser of pictures in the sale of the King's goods, which could not have been begun before 1648: see p. 64.

Mr Masters has a good picture of the Duchess of Richmond mentioned p. 132, half-length, with this inscription on the frame: 'Frances Dutchesse of Richmond and Lenox, daughter of Thomas Lord Howard of Bindon,[12] who was second son to Thomas Duke of Norfolke, whose mother was the Lady Elizabeth Stafford, eldest daughter of Edward Duke of Buckingham. Her Grace was born 27 July 1577. London, 1633.' She is drawn in black, with a very fine lawn ruff and handkerchief, and many strings of pearls; on her left side hangs a miniature, probably of her husband, exceedingly well done; her right hand is supported by her fan, and on a small table on the other side is placed her coronet. This may probably be the picture of Petitot Vertue speaks of.[13]

To COLE, Thursday 19 August 1762

Edited from a photostat of the original in possession (June 1934) of Mrs. Alwin Scheuer of New York, by whose permission it is printed here.

Mrs. Toynbee states that she edited this letter 'after collation with original in

10. Read 'that collection.' Cole must have misread *yt* for *yr*. Henry van der Borcht, father and son, painters of Brussels. The latter was employed by Charles II in England, but died at Antwerp.

11. Nichols erroneously reads 'Nic. Lanicre' (LA iii. 483). Nicholas Laniere (1588–1666), musician and amateur of art, is the person who purchased pictures at the sale of the King's goods. Another person of the same name (1568–1646?), probably a cousin, was an etcher. Masters was unaware of the difference. HW's account of Laniere remained unchanged in later editions.

12. Frances Howard (ca 1573–1639), dau. of Thomas Howard (1520?–82), 1st Vct Howard of Bindon, m. (1621) as her 3d husband Ludovic Stuart (1574–1624), 2d D. of Lennox and Richmond. HW added the following note to *Engravers*[2] p. 27: 'Mr. Masters, author of the History of C. C. C.

Cambridge, has another of these' [i.e., portraits of the Duchess of Richmond]. Cole wrote on this passage in his copy of the work (now WSL): 'This I have often seen at Landbeche in Cambridgeshire, where he is rector: it is but a very moderate piece, as I think; that at Mr Walpole's in his beautiful Gothic gallery at Strawberry Hill is quite another thing, much larger, being below the knees, and a most elegant picture. This mentioned here, which Mr Masters offered to Mr Walpole, is not above half as big and poorly executed, and unworthy of any place but a parsonage house: how it came to be offered is extraordinary.'

13. 'I have found a short note in one of Vertue's MSS that Petitot certainly drew the Duchess of Richmond here in the time of Charles I' (*Anecdotes*[1] ii. 132 n).

possession of Mrs. Alfred Morrison,' but the Morrison 'original' was actually a
copy of the letter in an unknown late eighteenth-century hand, as appears from
the facsimile of it in the *Morrison Catalogue* v. 50. The Morrison copy follows the
incorrect text as given in LA iii. 483–4, where the sentence 'Petitot never painted
but in enamel' was transferred to a footnote to which was added: 'The miniature
might notwithstanding be copied from him. W.C.' The Morrison copy has this
note, but lacks Cole's initials, and the note thus became erroneously incorporated
into the letter as a postscript.

Strawberry Hill, August 19, 1762.

Sir,

I AM very sensible of the obligations I have to you and to Mr Masters, and ought to make separate obligations to both; but not
knowing how to direct to him, I must hope that you will kindly be
once more the channel of our correspondence, and that you will be so
good as to convey to him, an answer to what you communicated from
him to me, and in particular my thanks for the most obliging offer he
has made me of a picture of Henry VII, of which I will by no means
rob him. My view in publishing the *Anecdotes* was to assist gentlemen in discovering the hands of pictures they possess, and I am sufficiently rewarded when that purpose is answered.

If there is another edition the mistake in the calculation of the tapestry shall be rectified,[1] and any others which any gentleman will be
so good as to point out. With regard to the monument of Sir Nathaniel Bacon, Vertue certainly describes it as at Culford; and in looking
into the place to which I am referred, in Mr Masters's *History of
C.C.C.C.* I think he himself allows in the note that there is such a
monument at Culford.[2]

Of Sir Balthazar Gerbier there are several different prints.[3]

Nich. Laniere purchasing pictures at the King's sale is undoubtedly
a mistake for one of his brothers. I cannot tell now whether Vertue's
mistake or my own.

At Longleate[4] is a whole-length of Frances Duchess of Richmond
exactly such as Mr Masters describes, but in oil. Petitot never painted
but in enamel. I have another whole-length of the same Duchess, I

1. But see n. 2 of preceding letter.
2. 'There is a monument erected to his
[Sir Nathaniel Bacon's] memory . . . on
the north wall of the chancel of Culford'
(Robert Masters, *History of the College of
Corpus Christi*, Cambridge, 1753, App.
85 n).

3. EBP gives three, one of them from
Anecdotes, and all copied from the same
portrait by Van Dyck.
4. Longleat, in Wilts, the seat of Lord
Weymouth. HW saw the picture of the
Duchess of Richmond in July 1762 (*Country Seats* 45).

believe, by Mytens,[5] but younger than that at Longleate. But the best picture of her is in Wilson's *Life of King James*,[6] and very diverting indeed.

I will not trouble you, Sir, or Mr Masters with any more at present, but repeating my thanks to both, will assure you that I am, Sir,

Your obliged humble servant,

Hor. Walpole

Cole's notes on Gothurst sent to HW with a letter, now missing, ca 25 September 1762

Edited from photostat of Cole's copy of the notes, Add MS 5831, ff. 227v, 228. The approximate date is determined by HW's reply, 30 Sept. 1762.

[Bletchley, September 1762.]

DINING at Mr Wright's at Gothurst near Newport Pagnell in Buckinghamshire, Sept. 14, 1762, I took the following notes. *Vide* vol. 33, p. 41.[1]

When Mr Wright's grandfather, Sir Nathan Wright, purchased this estate of the Digbys, there were left a great number of family pictures and other furniture of the house. Among the rest I observed one, now put over the chimney-piece of a very fine salon newly fitted up abovestairs, the half-length picture of a beautiful lady sitting, and on each side of her a youth of about six or seven years of age, most probably her sons; in her right hand is a serpent, which rests on her knees, and her other hand is playing with a pair of doves. This probably may be an original or copy[2] by Van Dyke, as it is in his manner,

---

5. HW ascribes this picture to Mark Garrard in *Description of SH* (*Works* ii. 466), and notes that it came from Easton Neston, the seat of the Earl of Pomfret.

6. *History of Great Britain, being the Life and Reign of King James the First*, 1653, by Arthur Wilson (1595–1652), historian and dramatist. The word-picture of the Duchess of Richmond appears at pp. 257–9. The passage is quoted in *Walpoliana* ii. 118–24, where it is introduced by HW's observation: 'That curious whole-length of Frances, Duchess of Richmond and Lennox, came from Easton-Neston,

the seat of the Earl of Pomfret. We shall sit down here before her, and read the equally curious portrait of her by Wilson, in his *Reign of James I*. One feature he does not mention—that her eyes, as you see, bear some resemblance to those of a cat.' HW's copy of Wilson's *History* (F.2.29) was sold SH ii. 163.

---

1. Cole's MS volume, now Add MS 5834.

2. HW, on his visit to Gothurst in July 1763, refers to it as a copy (*Country Seats* 52).

and no doubt represents Lady Venetia Digby, as the emblems about it, with her two sons, correspond exactly with the two pictures of her mentioned by Mr Walpole in his 2nd vol. of *Anecdotes of Painting in England,* p. 94.

In a lower room are four full-length pictures of the same family, one supposed to be of Sir Kenelm Digby himself, and another of his father: both in black; a third is of a young gentleman in the strait and close habit of Queen Elizabeth's time, and of a mixture of red and white: in one corner of this picture is the representation in miniature of a lady offering a great purse of gold to a young gentleman who seems to fly from her researches and to avoid her, and by it is wrote, *His Majora.* Whatever it might allude to, there is now no trace of any tradition whereby to discover the history of it. I take it the fourth is a companion to this, and is the lady of the aforesaid gentleman: she is dressed in black, with black hair, and in the habit of Queen Elizabeth's reign.[3] Mr Wright supposed it might be Lady Venetia Digby, but I could not discover the features of her in it, as represented in that by Van Dyke, no more than in two very fine busts of copper gilt, or brass, standing in Mr Wright's study, on two elegant pedestals of black and white marble. It is by no means improbable but the bust put up for this lady by her husband Sir Kenelm in Christ Church without Newgate in London was cast in the same mould with one of these: that bust and monument were destroyed in the Fire of London. One of these busts[4] is dressed in a loose and light habit, but in a fine taste, and with her hair rather more flowing than the other, which is frizzled out and curled, and ribbons behind; the figure is larger and fatter, and is habited after the Van Dyke manner with a large laced handkerchief. At the back of this last are the following arms cut on a piece of white marble on the pedestal: Party per pale, baron and femme, first quartering of four: first, on a bend three stags' heads caboshed, and a crescent in the sinister chief, for Stanley; second, three legs conjoined in triangle, for the Isle of Man; third, on a chief indented, three plates, for Latham; fourth, a fret, for Vernon

3. HW identified the first two figures in the picture as Sir Kenelm Digby's father, Sir Everard (1578–1606), executed for the Gunpowder Plot, and Sir Kenelm's brother John (incorrectly described by HW as his uncle), 'killed in the service of Charles I.' HW identified the young man fleeing from temptation as Sir Kenelm's grandfather, Everard (d. 1592), and agreed with Cole that the fourth figure was his wife, Mary Neale (loc. cit.).

4. This bust was engraved for Thomas Pennant's *Journey from Chester to London,* 1782, Plate XXI, opp. p. 337. Cf. *post* 2 March 1777.

of Derbyshire: impaling quartering of four: first quartering, first and fourth, a lion rampant; second and third, three lucies hauriant, these two for Piercy; second, two bars undy ermine for . . .; third, France and England quartering within a bordure gobony for Beaufort; fourth, a fess inter six cross crosslets, for Beauchamp. Under these arms, which are those of the lady's father and mother, on a rim of the marble is this inscription engraved in gold capitals: *Uxorem vivam amare, voluptas est, defunctam religio.* From the turn of this inscription I should conclude that this was the cast of the same bust which was put up for her monument in Christ Church. The inscriptions on white marble on the pedestals of both these fine busts are the same, and as follows:

Venetia,
Kenelmi Digby Eq. Aur.
Conjux,
Edwardi Stanley Eq. Balnei
Filii Thomæ (Edwardi Comi-
tis Derbiæ Filii) Filia et
Cohæres, ex Lucia Thomæ
Comitis Northumbriæ Filia
et Cohærede.

To COLE, Thursday 30 September 1762

Add MS 5952, f. 7.

Strawberry Hill, Sept. 30, 1762.

IT gives me great satisfaction that Strawberry Hill pleased you enough to make it a second visit.[1] I could name the time instantly, but you threaten me with coming so loaded with presents,[2] that it will look mercenary not friendly to accept your visit. If your chaise is empty, to be sure I shall rejoice to hear it at my gate about the 22d of this next month: if it is crammed, though I have built a convent, I have not so much of the monk in me as not to blush—nor can content myself with praying to our Lady of Strawberries to reward you.

1. The first visit was of three days in the first week in September 1762, as Cole records 3 Sept. 1762 (Add MS 5841, f. 76), and the second took place 29 Oct. 1762 (Add MS 5841, f. 78v). During his visits Cole made notes on 'Some of the Antiquities at Strawberry Hill' (Add MS 5841, f. 149). See Appendix 5.

2. Not identified.

STRAWBERRY HILL. SOUTH FRONT.
BY EDWARD EDWARDS, 1781 OR 1783

I am greatly obliged to you for the accounts from Gothurst. What treasures there are still in private seats if one knew where to hunt them! The emblematic picture of Lady Digby is like that at Windsor, and the fine small one at Mr Skinner's.[3] I should be curious to see the portrait of Sir Kenelm's father; was not he the remarkable Everard Digby? How singular too is the picture of young Joseph and Madam Potiphar![4] *His majora*—one has heard of Josephs that did not find the lady's purse any hindrance to majora.

You are exceedingly obliging to make an index to my prints, Sir; but that would be a sad way of entertaining you. I am antiquary and virtuoso enough myself not to dislike such employment, but could never think it charming enough to trouble anybody else with it. Whenever you do me the favour of coming hither, you will find yourself entirely at liberty to choose your own amusement—if you choose a bad one, and in truth there is not very good, you must blame yourself; while you know I hope that it would be my wish that you did not repent your favours to,

Sir, Your most obliged humble servant,

Hor. Walpole

From Cole, Tuesday 19 October 1762

VA, Forster MS 110, f. 1. Cole kept no copy.

Blecheley, Oct. 19, 1762.

Dear Sir,

I ALMOST begin to think that some fatality or evil genius throws itself in the way against waiting upon you at your appointments. When both my coach-horses were in a manner recovered from their lamenesses, which had been upon them a fortnight, and I was assured that I might set out on Thursday, in order to reach Strawberry Hill on the 22d, yesterday as I was going to sit down to dinner with some of my neighbours, my servant[1] had a return of his tertian ague: so

3. Both are mentioned in *Anecdotes*[1] ii. 94.

4. HW refers to the picture of Everard Digby (see preceding letter).

1. Thomas Wood (b. 1745), who entered Cole's service about 1760. He survived his master and acted as one of his executors (see *Blecheley Diary, passim*; Palmer, *Wil-*

that it will be impossible for me to go out with him, however my horses may be able to perform their journey, till I see whether he has another attack of it, which will be on Thursday. This, therefore, is to return thanks for your last favour, and to acquaint you with my distresses; and also of my design to be with you on the beginning of next week,[2] if a letter by Sunday's post don't tell me that it is inconvenient to you at that time. At all events I have enclosed the print of the Duchess of Orleans,[3] and will send the rubbish I mentioned by a parcel, if I don't have the pleasure of bringing them myself.

I am, dear Sir,

Your most obliged humble servant,

WM COLE

From COLE, Wednesday 3 November 1762

VA, Forster MS 110, f. 2. Cole kept no copy.

Dear Sir,   Cambridge, Nov. 3, 1762.

I GOT here last night with good weather and good roads, but today threatens more floods and bad weather, insomuch that I wish myself at home. I did not forget your commission about the piece of painted glass in old King's Hall, which the Society lately removed for better security into the Hall of Trinity College. I was to see it this morning, but found it not to my purpose, as it is a very ancient piece of painting, with *Richardus Dux* wrote under a small figure in armour of about a foot and half in length.[1] As the title is unfortunately

liam Cole 29). A passage in Cole's last will describes him: 'I give and devise unto my honest, sober, faithful servant, Thomas Wood, who has lived with me from a boy, going on 40 years, to him his heirs and assigns all my freehold and copyhold lands and tenements in Milton and Impington. . . . also I give him £50, and mourning, and all my wearing apparel . . . except 16 shirts . . . and also the bed and furniture on which he lies; he has been a faithful trusty servant to me, never gave me occasion to find fault, never knew him drunk, never told me a falsity, and is guilty of no vice that I know of, might have gotten better service and has a bad constitution, and

I think it my duty to provide for his maintenance.' Cole also left him £150 if he survived his sister, Jane Cole (ibid. 67).

2. Cole probably reached SH Friday 29 Oct.

3. Probably Princess Henrietta Anne (1644–70), youngest daughter of Charles I, who married Philip Duke of Orleans. Twenty-three prints of her are listed in EBP.

———

1. The glass is now (1934) in the oriel window in the Hall of Trinity College (information from the Dean of King's College, the Rev. Eric Milner-White). King's

lost, I imagined it would not answer your purpose, and consequently did not order the draft of it: neither are there any notices about it, as arms, etc., to determine it to any particular person. I suppose it to have been done, from the sort of glass, painting, letters and manner, about Edward III's time. If you choose to have it copied, I can easily procure it for you, as I am going to employ the man[2] to engrave me an old conventual seal. I went the same morning to refresh my memory with some old painting in glass in a vestry of Christ's College Chapel, which are more worth preserving than any I have seen a long time. There are seven figures, very well painted, of men and women: certainly two of Henry VII, and two of the Countess of Richmond,[3] as her name is under one, and very beautifully finished; one man, royally crowned, holds a ring in his hand. These figures are about Henry VII's time, and are about two feet high.[4]

I here send you a very curious copy for the Ely History[5] of a piece of painted glass lately taken by the Bishop of Ely[6] from Ely House in Holbourn and by him carried to Ely and put up in a window of the Palace there,[7] where he thought it safer. It is a full-length picture of St Etheldreda,[8] the royal foundress of the religious house at Ely, and is the exact bigness of the original.[9] It is not yet finished, but I thought it would gratify you, and therefore I send it, and am, dear Sir,

Yours most sincerely, etc., in a hurry,

WM COLE

Hall, founded by Edward III in 1337, was incorporated into Trinity College on its foundation in 1546.

2. Not identified.

3. Margaret Beaufort (1443–1509), Countess of Richmond; mother of Henry VII.

4. Mr S. G. Campbell, Bursar of Christ's College, reports (1936) 'that the old glass . . . is still in Christ's College Chapel, with the exception of one of the figures. The glass is now placed in the windows of the north side of the Chapel, not in a Vestry. The figures remaining are:

(1) *Perhaps* a representation of Henry VI.

(2) Figure of St Gregory.

(3) Kneeling figure of crowned king.

(4) Kneeling figure of Henry VII.

(5) Edward the Confessor holding in his right hand a ring and in his left a sceptre.

(6) Kneeling figure of the Countess of Richmond.'

5. James Bentham's *History of Ely Cathedral*, which was not published until 1771.

6. Matthias Mawson.

7. The painted glass was later (before 1812) placed 'in the middle of the three lowest lancet windows at the east end of the Cathedral' (Bentham, *Ely*[2] p. 290 n). The present (1934) Bishop of Ely (the Right Rev. Bernard Francis Oliver Heywood), states that there is a small figure of St Etheldreda in the westernmost window of the north choir.

8. A print of this painted-glass portrait appears in Bentham's *Ely*[2], opp. p. 45. A full account of St Etheldreda (630?–79) may be seen in the same work, pp. 45–59, and in DNB. Ely Cathedral was erected over her tomb.

9. That is, the copy was the same size as the painted-glass portrait, not the latter life-size.

To Cole, Saturday 13 November 1762

Add MS 5952, ff. 8–9.
Address: To the Reverend Mr Cole at Blecheley near Fenny Stratford, Bucks.
Free Hor Walpole. *Postmark:* Isleworth 13 NO.

Strawberry Hill, Nov. 13, 1762.

Dear Sir,

YOU will easily guess that my delay in answering your obliging letter was solely owing to my not knowing whither to direct to you. I waited till I thought you may be returned home. Thank you for all the trouble you have given and do give yourself for me; it is vastly more than I deserve.

Duke Richard's portrait I willingly waive, at least for the present, till one can find out who he is. I have more curiosity about the figures of Henry VII at Christ's College; I shall be glad sometime or other to visit them,[1] to see how far either of them agree with his portrait in my picture of his marriage.[2] St Ethelreda[3] was mighty welcome.

We have had variety of bad weather since I saw [you], but I fear none of the patterns made your journey more agreeable.

I am, Sir, Your much obliged humble servant,

HOR. WALPOLE

To Cole, Thursday 23 December 1762

Add MS 5952, f. 10. Cole's letter to which this is a reply is missing.

Arlington Street, Dec. 23, 1762.

Dear Sir,

YOU are always abundantly kind to me, and pass my power of thanking you. You do nothing but give yourself trouble, and me presents. My cousin Calthorp[1] is a great rarity, and I think I ought

1. HW visited Cambridge in the following year and saw pictures in Trinity, Queen's and St John's, but he does not mention a visit to Christ's (*Country Seats* 59).
2. Painted by John Mabuse. It is described (and engraved by Grignon) in *Anecdotes*[1] i. 50. HW bought it for £84 at Lord Pomfret's sale, and it remained one of his favourite pictures. It was sold SH

xxi. 52 to John Dent, Esq., of Sudeley Castle, Winchcombe, Glos, for £178.10s, and is now at Sudeley *penes* Major J. H. Dent Brocklehurst. It is reproduced in Emma Dent, *Annals of Winchcombe and Sudeley*, 1877, p. 132.
3. So in MS.

1. That is, a print of James Calthorpe (1604–52) of East Barsham, Norfolk, en-

therefore to return him to you, but that would not be treating him like a relation or you like a friend: my ancestor's epitaph[2] too was very agreeable to me.

I have not been at Strawberry Hill these three weeks. My maid is ill there, and I have not been well myself, with the same flying gout in my stomach and breast, of which you heard me complain a little in the summer. I am much persuaded to go to a warmer climate,[3] which often disperses these unsettled complaints. I do not care for it, nor can determine till I see I grow worse: if I do go, I hope it will not be for long; and you shall certainly hear again before I set out.

Yours most sincerely,

Hor. Walpole

To Cole, Monday 16 May 1763

Add MS 5952, f. 11.

Strawberry Hill, May 16, 1763.

Dear Sir,

I PROMISED you should hear from me if I did not go abroad, and I flatter myself that you will not be sorry to know that I am much better in health than I was at the beginning of the winter. My jour-

---

graved by Faithorne. Blomefield records that there is a monument to him in the Church of East Barsham with the inscription, 'In memory of James Calthorpe, Esq; late of East-Barsham; here interred, who died April 19, 1652, aged 48' (Blomefield, *Norfolk*[2] vii. 63). A copy of the print appears in the same work, vii. opp. p. 57. HW's copy of the original print, 'a brilliant impression,' was sold London ii. 239.

In a printed 'Pedigree of Walpole to explain the Portraits and Coats of Arms at Strawberry Hill, Anno 1776,' which HW pasted into his 1784 *Description of SH* (now wsl, the only copy of the pedigree located, although another was sold in Kirgate's Collection, 14 Dec. 1810, lot 182), are the arms of Calthorpe which were brought into the Walpole family by Margery, daughter and heiress of —— Harsick of Southacre, Norfolk, who married Henry

Walpole (fl. 1475). The city librarian of Norwich (Mr George Hayward) points out an earlier connection between the two families: 'in [Anthony] Norris's *Pedigrees* . . ., page 1194 [Rye MS 4], it is recorded that Sir William de Calthorpe was a trustee of Henry de Walpole, 9 Henry IV.' Mr Hayward also calls attention to a passage (ibid. 339) stating that Susan Crane (1632–67), dau. of Sir Robert Crane (d. 1643), m., in 1649, Sir Edward Walpole of Houghton (see Burke, *Landed Gentry*, 1851).

2. Possibly the epitaph of his 'cousin Calthorp.'

3. 'I am thinking seriously of a journey to Italy in March' (HW to Mann 20 Dec. 1762). A severe frost in January, however, almost cured him of the gout, and he dismissed the thought of an Italian journey (HW to Mann 28 Jan. 1763).

ney is quite laid aside, at least for this year; though as Lord Hertford[1] goes Embassador to Paris, I propose to make him a visit there early next spring.[2]

As I shall be a good deal here this summer, I hope you did not take a surfeit of Strawberry Hill, but will bestow a visit on it while its beauty lasts; the gallery advances fast now, and I think in a few weeks will make a figure worth your looking at.

I am, Dear Sir, Your obedient humble servant,

HOR. WALPOLE

From COLE, Thursday 19 May 1763

VA, Forster MS 110, ff. 3–4. Cole kept no copy.

Blecheley, May 19, 1763.

Dear Sir,

YOUR very obliging favour I received yesterday, and am sincerely glad that your health is such as not to require a change of climate, which may possibly be found better in other parts. Beauties of every kind you will be difficulted to meet with wherever you shift the scene to: of this I have been, as far as I am able to judge, an ocular witness, though both times saw your paradise to disadvantage, in great inundations. With your leave I will endeavour to see the difference, though at some distance, as I am going a long journey into Cheshire the week after next to see a friend[1] who has promised to go with me a little way into the finest part of North Wales. I purpose being gone from hence about three weeks at farthest, but when I return shall have my hands full, I hope, of haymaking, and then follows my little harvest: so that, except I can get a few days between, I am afraid I must defer the pleasure of seeing you till these things are over. However, I am not quite clear of my Cheshire journey, for except I am better in respect to my old lameness[2] than I have been for these

---

1. Francis Seymour Conway (1719–94), 1st E. of Hertford, cr. (1793) M. of Hertford, HW's 1st cousin and correspondent and brother of Hon. Henry Seymour Conway. He was ambassador to Paris, Oct. 1763–June 1765.

2. He did not go to Paris until Sept. 1765 (*Paris Jour.*).

1. John Allen.

2. In 1755 Cole broke one of his legs, which afterwards caused him no little pain. He wrote Joseph Bentham, from Litchfield, 4 Oct. 1755: 'It may be proper to tell you . . . that although I am very well, and my leg is well joined together, yet it is very crooked: but the fault is my

ten days I shall not be fit to go out of the parish. I heartily congratulate you on your health. This spring has been the most trying one to me I ever experienced, having first had a nervous fever, which went off after a long time, with, what I never had before, an ague, and that not quite left me as to its consequences yet. But too much of oneself.

I will now beg leave to enclose to you the conjecture of an ingenious though very conceited gentleman[3] to whom I lent your books on painting, which he returned with the enclosed scrap of paper, and so leave it to you to judge of the worth of it.

I have been twice disappointed within this month of visiting Dr Apthorp[4] at Burnham, by a return of my illness. Last week I heard from him to let me know that Payne the bookbinder[5] had sent some books, which I had sent to him for binding, to his house at Burnham for me, with his bill. Among other articles the Lucan you was so kind to give me was one: this the Doctor informs me is charged at a guinea and half for binding. I long to see the book, as it must be a curiosity.[6] The other books are in proportion.

I shan't presume to come to you without giving you notice beforehand that, if it should not be convenient to you, I may defer my visit. In the meantime I am, dear Sir,

Your most faithful and obliged servant,

WM COLE

own; for the surgeon would have remedied it, had I been consenting, after it had been set a fortnight; but I considered that it was very little significant, whether a person who generally wears petticoats, and is no dancer at assemblies, had a straight or crooked leg, so it served the purpose of conveying him from place to place; so as it would have put me to some pain, to which I was always a great enemy, I rather chose to have it as it is' (LA ix. 391).

3. That is, 'R. E.,' the author of Cole's enclosure (see below).

4. Stephen Apthorpe (1708?–90), D.D., Cole's half-brother; son of Charles Apthorpe by Catherine Tuer (Cole's mother); Eton and King's; fellow of Eton 1758; rector of Monxton, Hants, 1749; vicar of Burnham, Bucks, 1759–74; rector of Worplesdon, Surrey, 1774–90 (*Eton Coll. Reg. 1698–1752*). Cole's MS volumes are filled with references to Burnham and Apthorpe.

Many of them have been transcribed by John G. Nichols in *Collectanea, Topographica et Genealogica* iv. 265–304.

5. Probably Roger Payne (1739–97), who was with Pote, the Eton bookseller, at this time.

6. This was the edition of Lucan, with notes by Richard Bentley (1662–1742), printed in quarto at SH, 1760 (see *Jour. Print. Off.* 9, 38–9). What made it a curiosity was doubtless the binding, which was expensive for the time. Cole gave his copy to Lord Montfort (Palmer, *William Cole* 72). It later came into the possession of William Beckford, and was sold at Sotheby's in the Hamilton Palace Libraries sale, 20 Dec. 1882 (2d portion, 9th day, lot 1927), to Bain for £5.17.6. It is described in the catalogue as 'calf extra, covered with gold tooling, gilt and marble edges, presentation copy from H. Walpole to Cole.'

[Enclosure.]

Compare the term *vidimus* in this page 100, with *verimas*,[7] page 3 and its note at the bottom of that page. Query, whether both words do not mean the same thing, viz., a *pattern* or *design*.

R. E.[8]

May 10, 1763.

[Cole's note, added to the slip of paper.] The same word occurs also in the last page[9] of the Appendix, etc., viz., *vidimus* for *pattern*.

To Cole, Friday 1 July 1763

Add MS 5952, f. 12.

Address: [From Cole's copy, Add MS 5831, f. 228v.] To the Rev. Mr Cole at Blecheley near Fenny Stratford, Bucks. Free Hor Walpole.

Dear Sir,   Strawberry Hill, July 1, 1763.

As you have given me leave,[1] I propose to pass a day with you on my way to Mr Montagu's.[2] If you have no engagement, I will be with you on the 16th of this month, and if it is not inconvenient, and you will tell me truly whether it is or not, I shall bring my friend Mr Chute[3] with me, who is destined to the same place. I will beg you too

---

7. In his note on this word (*Anecdotes*[1] i. 3 n.) HW calls it 'a barbarous word, not to be found even in Dufresne's glossary.' Dallaway adds: 'The word *verimas* is not barbarous only, but unknown. The transcriber from the Close Rolls was not aware that the word is really *venestras* or *fenestras*, by which no one will be puzzled' (*Anecdotes* ed. Dallaway, 1828, i. 6 n). HW allowed *vidimus* and *verimas* to stand. OED, quoting no authority but HW, defines *vidimus* as a 'design for a painted or stained-glass window.' *Verimas* may be a mistake for *verinés* or *verrinés*, O.F. forms meaning 'garnis de verrières' (Frédéric Godefroy, *Dictionnaire de L'Ancienne Langue Française*, 1895). See also in this connection, LA iv. 505 n. Samuel Pegge argues that *verimas* should read *verrinas*, meaning glass windows (*Anonymiana*, 1818, p. 189).

8. Rev. Richard Eyre (d. 1778), D.D., vicar of Whaddon, Bucks, and rector of Brightwalton, Berks; son-in-law of Browne Willis; F.R.S. and F.S.A. (1767) (*Alumni Oxon;* LA vi. 195; LI viii. 549).

9. A slip by Cole for 'next to the last page' (*Anecdotes*[1] i. sig. Zz).

---

1. When Cole and HW met accidentally in Twickenham (see following letter).

2. George Montagu (1713?–80), eldest son of Brigadier-General Edward Montagu by Arabella Trevor, and one of HW's chief correspondents, was living at this time in a house which he had hired, Greatworth, near Brackley, Northants, where HW had visited him twice before (*Country Seats* 51). HW's friendship with him began at Eton, and lasted until ten years before Montagu's death (see *post* 11 May 1780).

3. John Chute (1701–76), 10th and youngest son of Edward and Katharine Chute, friend and correspondent of HW, whose intimacy with him began in Florence in 1740 and continued until Chute's death (*Eton Coll. Reg. 1698–1752*).

to let me know how far it is to Blecheley, and what road I must take.
That is, how far from London, or how far from Twickenham, and
the road from each, as I am uncertain yet from which I shall set out.
If any part of this proposal does not suit you, I trust you will own it,
and I will take some other opportunity of calling on you, being most
truly, Dear Sir, Your much obliged and obedient servant,

HOR. WALPOLE

From COLE, Sunday 3 July 1763

VA, Forster MS 110, ff. 5–8. COLE's copy, Add MS 5831, ff. 228v, 229, 230.
Address: For the Honourable Horace Walpole Esq. at Strawberry Hill in
Twickenham, Middlesex. *Postmark:* F. Stratford.

Dear Sir,   Blecheley, July 3, 1763.

I THIS moment received the favour of yours, informing me of your
obliging design of being here on the 16th, and staying a day with
me. I had a design of writing myself immediately on my getting home
after meeting with you in Twickenham, to put you in mind of your
kind promise, but I judged it best not to do so, as my importunacy
might have obliged your civility to have taken a route not altogether
convenient to you. I am entirely free of all engagements, and can
promise you and Mr Chute aired beds, as also for your servants, etc.
I was in hopes of your longer stay, and that you would have made a
little antiquary excursion to Peterborough or Ely, as I think you once
mentioned.[1] If this would be agreeable I would, after your stay at Mr
Mountague's, meet you for such a ramble, as I hope my hay will be
all got in by that time. After being sadly burnt up, we had a fine rain
on Thursday, which will do great service to the backward grass of
this country.

As I have spare room I shall, according to my scribbling genius, fill
up the opposite side with two or three observations I made in reading over some of your books, most of which probably you have observed before me; however, I shall put them down as I made them.

The road from Twickenham to this place is through Uxbridge,
Amersham, Missenden, Wendover, Aylesbury: thus far exceeding
good turnpike road; from Aylesbury to me fifteen measured and ten

1. Apparently in conversation.

computed miles, horridly bad in the winter, but very well for this country now. I went that way t'other day to Eton:[2] it is a difficult way to find, but if you'll be so kind as to give me a line which way you determine your route, I will send my boy[3] to Aylesbury to meet you, who will direct you a very safe and good way. The way from London is through Barnet, St Albans, Dunstable, and Fenny Stratford, from which last place I am a mile and half. From London to F. Stratford is exactly forty-five measured miles on the great Chester Road.

I am, dear Sir, in an hurry to save the post,

Your most obliged and faithful servant,

WM COLE

Noble Authors, vol. 2, p. 172.[4]

You mention the mother of the famous Countess of Dorset, Pembroke and Montgomery,[5] Margaret Russel Countess of Cumberland,[6] though not as an author, which yet, if being a poetess and writing an epitaph would give her admittance into that list, according to my poor judgment in poetry, she has a good title. For in the Church of Hornsey in Middlesex, where I was sometime rector,[7] is an exceeding well-fancied monument erected against the wall, being an obelisk or pyramid, on the base of which is this epitaph[8] in the style of Spenser and, as I suppose, of her Ladyship's own composition; for above it, on the pyramid, under the Clifford crest of a goat[9] and earl's coronet above it, is wrote

Promised & made by Margaret
Countess of Cōberland 1601.

An Epitaph upon the Death of the worshipfull &

2. To visit his half-brother, Stephen Apthorpe.

3. James or 'Jem' Wood, younger brother of Cole's servant, Thomas Wood. He was chiefly employed on errands for Cole and later acted as groom and coachman (cf. *post* 13 Jan. 1773).

4. These references are to the first edition.

5. Anne Clifford (1590–1676), an account of whom appears in *Roy. & Nob. Authors* (*Works* i. 485–6). See also DNB.

6. Margaret Russell (1560–1616), dau. of

Francis Russell, 2d E. of Bedford; m. (1577) George Clifford (1558–1605), 3d E. of Cumberland. HW did not include her in his revised edition (1787) which was reprinted in *Works*.

7. He was rector of Hornsey, 25 Nov. 1749 to 9 Jan. 1751.

8. It is printed in Daniel Lysons, *Environs of London* iii (1795). 54.

9. Cole is mistaken: the crest is that of Bedford, 'on a wreath, a goat passant, argent, armed, or' (Collins, *Peerage*, 1812, i. 301; cf. Lysons, loc. cit.).

rarely accomplished Master Richard Candish[10] of
Suffolk Esqr.

Candish deriv'd from noble Parentage,
Adorn'd with virtuous and heroicke Partes,
Most learned, bountifull, devout & sage,
Grac'd with the Graces, Muses & the Artes:
Deer to his Prince, in English Court adïr'd
Belov'd of great & honourable Peeres;
Of all esteem'd, embraced & desir'd,
'Till Death cutt off his well-employed yeares;
Within this Earth, his Earth entombed lyes:
Whose heavenly Parte surmounted hath the Skyes.

The arms are Argent three Piles wavy Gules, for Candish.

Noble Authors.

I have seen a little book in 12mo with a print before it of the
Countess, containing receipts in physic, etc., by a Countess of Kent,
but I forget the title, though I have the print.[11] Very probably you
have seen the book I mean, but did not think it worth mentioning.

Hentzner,[12] p. 25.

Margaret Countess of Richmond died not in 1463, but 1509, on 29
of June. The occasion of the mistake in Hentzner, as I presume, was
his copying in an hurry the epitaph on the tomb, which is wrote in
Roman capitals: first, by not observing exactly the number of C's;
secondly, mistaking the letter L for an I; and lastly, by placing the III
of the calends of July too near the date of the year: as may easily be
seen by casting your eye on Hentzner.[13]

10. Richard Cavendish (d. 1601?), politician and author.

11. Elizabeth Talbot (1581–1651), 2d dau. of Gilbert Talbot, 7th E. of Shrewsbury; m. (1601) Henry Grey (1583?–1639), 8th E. of Kent, after whose death she is said to have married John Selden, to whom she left her property. The title of the book is *A Choice Manuall, or Rare and Select Secrets in Physick and Chyrurgery*, 1653; 19th edn, 1687. Cole sent the print (a small oval, which varies in different editions) to HW in 1769 (see *post* 3 Aug. 1769; EBP). HW did not add Lady Kent to *Roy. & Nob. Authors*.

12. *A Journey into England . . . in the Year 1598*, SH 1757, by Paul Hentzner (1558–1625). (*Jour. Print. Off.* 3, 26.)

13. That is, the inscription reads MCCC-CCIX III Cal. Julii, which Hentzner (or Richard Bentley who prepared the book for the press) misread MCCCCLXIII. Cal. Julii.

Mr Spence's *Life of Mr Hill*,[14] p. 53.

In the note it is said that the Bishop[15] lived with Sir Thomas Throckmorton. If it means the Roman Catholic family of that name, and I know no other in Buckinghamshire, it must be Sir Robert Throckmorton, the present and late Baronet being of that name,[16] and none of the name of Thomas for some generations. This is not worth observing, but I know you love to be exact in your books, or those under your inspection. I shall just mention another trifle in your

Fugitive Pieces,[17] p. 5.

The epitaph in the note, mentioned to be in King's College Chapel, and in the *Spectator*, vol. 7, No. 518, though extremely fine, yet, in my opinion, wants a great deal to come up to the nobleness and loftiness of that really in one of the side chapels of King's College Chapel, on Mr Tho. Crouch,[18] who died 1679, and is without his name to it.

> Aperiet Deus Tumulos et educet
> Nos de Sepulchris:
> Qualis eram Dies isthæc cum
> Venerit, scies.

The former part of which epitaph has something so grand, solemn and sublime in it, that it is impossible to read it and not be much affected by it: which capital beauty is wanting in that quoted by Mr Addi<son, and> has only the last turn of thought: which, though <extre>mely beautiful, would not singly and separately have been taken notice of, to the neglect of the former, had so judicious a person ever seen it. From whence I conclude that the epitaph he mentions must have been in some other place than King's Chapel.

14. *A Parallel in the Manner of Plutarch: between a most celebrated Man of Florence and one scarce ever heard of in England.* By the Rev. Mr Spence. SH 1758. Joseph Spence (1699–1768) was the friend of Pope and occasional correspondent of HW. The celebrated man of Florence was Antonio Magliabechi (1633–1714); the unknown Englishman, Robert Hill (1699–1777), a self-educated tailor of Buckingham. The book was sold by Dodsley for the benefit of Hill (*Jour. Print. Off.* 7, 33).

15. An unidentified priest, 'supposed to be a bishop.'

16. That is, Spence made a mistake in the first name. The 'present' Baronet was Sir Robert Throckmorton (1702–91), 4th Bt; the 'late' Baronet was Sir Robert Throckmorton (1662–1721).

17. HW's *Fugitive Pieces in Verse and Prose*, SH 1758. Cole's copy was given him by HW in 1762, as appears from Cole's MS statement on the verso of p. 219. Cole has written the note on the epitaph in King's College, with a few minor changes, on p. 5. The book is now in the Harvard College Library, the gift of Mrs Percival Merritt of Boston, Mass.

18. Thomas Crouch (1610?–79), M.P. for the University 1660–79 (*Alumni Cantab.*).

To Cole, Tuesday 12 July 1763

Add MS 5952, f. 13.

Dear Sir,   Strawberry Hill, July 12, 1763.

UPON consulting maps and roads and the knowing, I find it will
be my best way to call on Mr Montagu first, before I come to
you, or I must go the same road twice. This will make it a few days
later than I intended, before I wait on you, and will leave you time
to complete your hay-harvest, as I gladly embrace your offer of bearing me company on the tour I meditate to Burleigh, Drayton, Peterborough, Ely and twenty other places,[1] of all which you shall take as
much or as little as you please. It will I think be Wednesday, or Thursday sennight before I wait on you, that is the 20th or 21st, and I fear
I shall come alone, for Mr Chute is confined with the gout; but you
shall hear again before I set out. Remember I am to see Sir Kenelm
Digby's.[2]

Thank you much for your informations; the Countess of Cumberland is an acquisition, and quite new to me. With the Countess of
Kent I am acquainted since my last edition.

Addison certainly changed *scies* in the epitaph to *indicabit* to avoid
the jingle with *dies:* though it is possible that the thought may have
been borrowed elsewhere.

Adieu! Sir, Yours ever,

H. WALPOLE

To Cole, Saturday 16 July 1763

Add MS 5952, ff. 14–5. The letter is dated by the postmark.

Address: To the Reverend Mr Cole at Blecheley near Fenny Stratford, Bucks.
Free Hor Walpole. *Postmark:* Isleworth 16 IY.

Dear Sir,   Satu<rda>y [July 16, 1763.]

WEDNESDAY[1] is the day I propose waiting on you; what time
of it the Lord and the roads know; so don't wait for me any

---

1. HW's accounts of this tour, which
HW and Cole made together, may be seen
in *Country Seats* 52–9, and in HW to
Montagu 23, 25 July 1763.

2. That is, Gothurst.

---

1. 20 July.

part of it. If I should be violently pressed to stay a day longer at Mr Montagu's, I hope it will be no disappointment to you; but I love to be uncertain, rather than make myself expected and fail.

Yours ever,

H. Walpole

From Cole, Sunday 31 July 1763

VA, Forster MS 110, f. 9. Cole kept no copy.
Address: For the Honourable Horace Walpole Esq. at Strawberry Hill in Twickenham, Middlesex. *Postmark:* 1 AV.

Blecheley, July 31, 1763.

Dear Sir,

I CAN'T begin my letter to you, about an account of the Master of Pembroke,[1] which I promised to send you, without returning you a million of thanks for the great pleasure you gave me in my late journey, which I shall ever recollect with infinite satisfaction. I hope, after all the fatigues and inconveniences of it, the beauties of Strawberry Hill appear, if possible, with greater lustre. To be master of such an enchanting place may be looked upon in some measure as a misfortune, as no place can make you amends for what you quit for it.

I stayed only one day at Hackney,[2] and got safely home on Wednesday afternoon,[3] and had the pleasure of meeting my last load of hay coming into the yard. I immediately looked for Robert Shorter, Master of St John's and Pembroke, but found it was a mistake of the new Cambridge book.[4] My accounts all call him Shirton or Shorton, and none I can meet with give him the name of Shorter.[5] Mr Baker in his little book of Bishop Fisher's Funeral Sermon on the Countess of

1. Robert Shorton (d. 1535), first Master of St John's, Cambridge, 1511–6; Master of Pembroke, Cambridge, 1518–34.
2. Where Cole's sister, Catherine, and his niece, Mrs Henry Newcome, lived. He had probably gone as far as Hackney with HW on the latter's return to SH.
3. 27 July.
4. *Cantabrigia Depicta. A Concise and*

Accurate Description of the University and Town of Cambridge and its Environs, Cambridge, [1763]. At p. 35 in a list of benefactors of Pembroke appears, 'Robert Shorter, D.D., Master of St John's College, and afterwards of Pembroke.' (Information from Mr Leonard Whibley.)
5. The surname of HW's mother.

Richmond,[6] mentions him at pp. 33, 35, 38, 48, 51, 52, etc.: in all which places he is called Shorton, and his authority, who was so well acquainted with the names of all of his own Society, will be sufficient to ascertain it to be the true one. I have a very long account of him,[7] which I will readily transcribe for you, and think it no sort of trouble, but I fancy from what I have said, you will have no further curiosity about him. If I should be mistaken, you will please to let me know.

I thought you had dropped some of your collectanea Cantabrigiensia at this house, and wish you have not elsewhere. I picked up the enclosed two leaves[8] on my return.

I have only time to thank you once more for your repeated civilities, the man staying for the letter, and to subscribe myself, dear Sir,

Your most obliged and faithful servant,

WM COLE

To Cole, Monday 8 August 1763

Add MS 5952, ff. 16–7.

Address: To the Reverend Mr Cole at Blecheley near Fenny Stratford, Bucks. Free Hor Walpole. *Postmark:* Isleworth 9 AV.

Strawberry Hill, Aug. 8, 1763.

Dear Sir,

YOU judge rightly, I am very indifferent about Dr Shorton, since he is not Dr Shorter.

It has done nothing but rain, since my return; whoever wants hay, must fish for it; it is all drowned, or swimming about the country. I am glad our tour gave you so much pleasure; you was so very obliging, as you have always been to me, that I should have been grieved not to have had it give you satisfaction. I hope your servant is quite recovered.

6. *The Funeral Sermon of Margaret Countess of Richmond and Derby, Mother to King Henry VII,* by Bishop John Fisher, edited, with a biographical introduction, by Thomas Baker, 1708. Cole refers to the introduction, the pagination of which is in Roman numerals.

7. 'See a long account of Dr Shorton's life composed by me at Blecheley . . . in my vol. 19' [Add MS 5820] (Cole's note on Baker's life of Shorton, in Baker's *History of St John's College,* ed. John E. B. Mayor, 1869, p. 564).

8. Not identified.

The painters and gilders quit my gallery this week, but I have not got a chair or a table for it yet; however I hope it will have all its clothes on by the time you have promised me a visit.

I am, Dear Sir, Your much obliged humble servant,

Hor. Walpole

From Cole, Saturday 27 August 1763

VA, Forster MS 110, f. 10. Cole kept no copy.
Address: For the Honourable Horace Walpole Esq. at Strawberry Hill in Twickenham, Middlesex.

Blecheley, Aug. 27, 1763.

Dear Sir,

I HOPE you'll excuse the liberty I take in begging a favour of you: my niece Mrs Newcome and her husband, Mr Newcome, of Hackney, leaving me this day and going on Tuesday next on a party with two of their relations to see Mr Hamilton's,[1] Woburn Farm,[2] Lord Lincoln's,[3] Claremont[4] and some other houses, are desirous, before their return home, to see the beauties of your enchanting castle of Strawberry Hill. If you will give them that pleasure you will add to the many obligations already conferred upon, dear Sir,

Your most obliged and faithful servant,

Wm Cole

I shall give you a line sometime in October before I wait upon you, to know whether my visit will be seasonable.

1. Painshill, near Cobham, Surrey, the seat of the Hon. Charles Hamilton (1704–87), 9th and youngest son of James Hamilton, 6th E. of Abercorn. See HW's account of Painshill in 1761 in *Country Seats* 36–7. In *Modern Gardening* he praised Painshill as a perfect example of 'the forest or savage garden' (*Works* ii. 541).

2. The seat of Philip Southcote, at Chertsey, Surrey. It was 'one of the first places improved according to the princi-

ples of modern gardening, and laid the foundation of a taste which is admired by all true lovers of that science' (LA ix. 629). HW credits Southcote with inventing the 'ferme ornée' (*Works* ii. 541).

3. Oatlands, near Weybridge, Surrey, the seat of Henry Fiennes Clinton (1720–94), 9th E. of Lincoln and 2d D. of Newcastle.

4. Near Esher, Surrey, the seat of Thomas Pelham-Holles (1693–1768), 1st D. of Newcastle.

From COLE, Friday 30 September 1763

VA, Forster MS 110, f. 11. Cole kept no copy.

Blecheley, Sept. 30, 1763.

Dear Sir,

I LATELY sent for a book from London which is published but just now, yet it is probable it may not fall under your notice, as the author of it bears no reputation among the learned. In it were some few things which I thought might fall in with your design of giving some account of English engravers,[1] and therefore I marked them down as I ran over the book, for your use. The book is, in my opinion, not worth the six shillings it cost me, and therefore if you choose I should be more explicit and larger in my account of the following persons, I will gladly be so: but if you send for it yourself there will be no occasion. It is called *The Origin and Progress of Letters* (viz., alphabetical letters), etc., by William Massey, schoolmaster. London, 8vo., 1763. Printed by J. Johnson opposite the Monument.

Part 2, p. 16. Mention of one John Mellis[2] of Norwich, 1594, who had a natural genius for drawing of proportions, maps, buildings, etc.

Part 2, p. 52. Edward Cocker[3] was an indefatigable performer both with the pen and burin: an ingenious artist in figures, etc., born in 1631.

Pp. 88–9. George Bickham[4] the engraver. Some account of him under the name of George Johnson.

1. This 'design' of printing *A Catalogue of Engravers who have been born or resided in England* at SH had presumably been communicated by HW to Cole on their tour in July. As a matter of fact, the book had been completed in May (*Jour. Print. Off.* 11) except for 'some of the plates' (see following letter). It is not clear why HW withheld the knowledge of its having been printed from the friend perhaps most interested in it, but doubtless it was the result of mood and a too lively interest on Cole's part which, if encouraged, might have led to an extensive and unwelcome revision of the book. HW did not use any of the notes Cole sent in this letter, although he implied that he would in the following letter.

2. Teacher of writing, arithmetic and drawing (see Sir Ambrose Heal, *The English Writing Masters . . . 1570–1800,* Cambridge, 1931, p. 75).

3. (1631–76), the elder, 'writing-master, engraver of calligraphy and arithmetician'; reputed author of *Cocker's Arithmetick,* of which at least 65 editions were published 1678–1787 (ibid. 33–6). See also *The Philobiblion, A Monthly Bibliographical Journal,* New York, April, 1862, p. 115.

4. (1684?–1758?), the elder, engraver of calligraphy, whose 'monumental work, *The Universal Penman* . . . appeared in 52 parts between 1733 and 1741.' He used occasionally the pen-name of George Johnson (Sir Ambrose Heal, op. cit. 14–6, 65). Cf. *Engravers, Works* iv. 104.

P. 97. John Langton,[5] a painter on glass at Stamford in Lincolnshire. The same person has a curious piece of writing framed and glazed at Burghley,[6] and which, if you remember, my Lord Exeter[7] showed you, hanging, I think, in the same room where those two fine old painted earthen vases or vessels[8] were, near the door.

P. 159. Caleb Williams,[9] a self-taught engraver, but when he lived, or where, is not said.

I am afraid if you buy the book you will be not well pleased with me for giving you so much trouble as the reading of it will occasion. However, I was willing that you should know of it, and make what use or unuse you pleased of it.

  I am, dear Sir,

Your ever obliged servant,

Wm Cole

To Cole, Saturday 8 October 1763

Add MS 5952, ff. 20–1.

Address: To the Reverend Mr Cole at Blecheley near Fenny Stratford, Bucks. Free Hor Walpole. *Postmark:* IW [Isleworth] 9 [OC].

Strawberry Hill, Oct. 8, 1763.

Dear Sir,

YOU are always obliging to me and always thinking of me kindly; yet for once you have forgotten the way of obliging me most. You do not mention any thought of coming hither, which you had given me cause to hope would be about this time. I flatter myself nothing has intervened to deprive me of that visit. Lord Hertford goes to France the end of next week; I shall be in town to take leave of him; but after the 15th, that is, this day sennight I shall be quite

---

5. (1671–1724), teacher of writing and arithmetic, who is noticed ibid. 68–9. Tyson's account of him (*post* 21 June 1769) adds several details to his biography.

6. The seat of Lord Exeter, which HW and Cole visited on their tour (*Country Seats* 58). HW does not mention Langton's 'writing.'

7. Brownlow Cecil (1725–93), 9th E. of Exeter.

8. 'Two large and fine flat vessels of the Raphael faience, bought by this Lord at Mr Hampden's sale, who had them from Jarvis's widow. They cost my Lord £38' (loc. cit.).

9. (fl. 1693?), author of *Nuncius Oris: A Round-hand Coppy Book* (Sir Ambrose Heal, op. cit. 116–7).

unengaged, and the sooner I see you after the 15th the better, for I should be sorry to drag you 'cross the country in the badness of November roads.

I shall treasure up your notices against my second edition;[1] for the volume of *Engravers* is printed off and has been some time; I only wait for some of the plates. The book you mention[2] I have not seen, nor do you encourage me to buy it. Sometime or other however I will get you to let me turn it over.

As I will trust that you will let me know soon when I shall have the pleasure of seeing you here, I will make this a very short letter; indeed, I know nothing new or old worth telling you.

Your obedient and obliged humble servant,

Hor. Walpole

From Cole, Thursday 13 October 1763

VA, Forster MS 110, f. 12. Cole kept no copy.
Address: For the Honourable Horatio Walpole Esq. at Strawberry Hill in Twickenham, Middlesex. *Postmark:* F Stratford 14 OC.

Blecheley, Oct. 13, 1763.

Dear Sir,

YOUR most obliging letter of the 8th reached me the next day, but by reason of our Archdeacon's[1] visitation, which always used to be about the middle of this month, and of which I have as yet heard nothing, made me desirous of knowing whether I could attend him before I sat out [on] my expeditions. If I hear nothing this week I will defer it no longer, and at all events will do myself the great pleasure of waiting upon you for two days on Monday, 24th of this month, though upon looking upon the almanac I see two red-letter days immediately follow the 24th,[2] when it may possibly be incon-

1. An habitual form of evasion with HW.
2. *The Origin and Progress of Letters,* by William Massey (see preceding letter). It does not appear in MS Cat.

1. John Taylor (1704–66), of St John's, Cambridge; F.R.S. and F.S.A. 1759; Arch-

deacon of Buckingham 1753–66. In April 1766 Cole referred to him as 'my late deservedly worthy friend' (*Blecheley Diary* 32).

2. The anniversaries of the days on which George III succeeded to the throne and was proclaimed King.

venient, as you may be in town. If it should, would put off my visit till the latter end of that week, but if I hear nothing to the contrary, will wait on you the Monday aforesaid.

I have not forgot my commission about my Lady Allington's tomb.[3] It is most probable I shall look after it myself, as I have had two letters from Mrs Cadogan[4] to desire me to see her at her brother's on the 17th of this month, where she will stay a fortnight or three weeks, but as I am not fond of staying over-long with his frolicsome Lordship,[5] shall probably go down just before she leaves Horsheth, and there stay two or three days only. I shall then be able to give you a better account of the state of the tomb and the expense it may require to repair it. If it should be more than I expect it will, I will give you notice before anything is done to it, and will give you a better draught of it. In the meantime I am, dear Sir,

Your ever most obliged servant,

WM COLE

From COLE, Thursday 1 December 1763

COLE's copy, Add MS 5831, f. 230. The original is missing.

Address: For the Honourable Horace Walpole in Arlington Street, Westminster.

Blecheley, Dec. 1, 1763.[1]

Dear Sir,

AFTER I left Strawberry Hill[2] I stayed in Cambridgeshire near three weeks, and though I have been returned near as long to this place, yet I could not prevail with myself to sit down close to my

3. See following letter.
4. Hon. Frances Bromley (d. 1768), dau. of Henry Bromley, 1st Bn Montfort, by Frances Wyndham, dau. of Thomas Wyndham of Trent; m. (1747) Hon. Charles Sloane Cadogan (1728–1807), who in 1776 succeeded to the peerage as 3d Bn Cadogan of Oakley, and in 1800 was cr. Vct Chelsea and E. Cadogan.
5. Her brother was Thomas Bromley (1733–99), 2d Bn Montfort, whose seat was at Horseheath Hall, Cambs. Montfort 'owned a celebrated menagerie. References

to his high-spirited and riotous behaviour can be found in the Hardwicke MSS in the British Museum' (Palmer, *William Cole* 59; see also pp. 60, 63, 64). Throughout Cole's life Cole acted as Montfort's affectionate mentor.

1. The first four paragraphs of this letter are printed in *Collectanea Topographica et Genealogica*, ed. John G. Nichols, 8 vols, 1834–43, iv. 37–40.
2. 26 or 27 Oct. (see preceding letter).

business[3] till now, from an indolence of disposition and an enjoyment of myself and fireside after so long a ramble.

The first thing I did when I got to Horsheth was to go to the
church and take as exact a draught[4] of the monument of your great-
grandmother[5] as I could: the which I have now copied out on this
paper from my rough awkward notes. However, such as it is, it will
serve to give you some idea of the monument, which I was glad to
find wanted no reparation, the late Lord Montfort, at my repeated
request, having, just before his death, ordered it to be repaired. I will
now give you a very minute description of it.

On the north side of the chancel of Horseth Church, on the steps
of the altar, is erected against the wall a very noble monument of
various-coloured marble and alabaster. On the altar part lie two complete figures in alabaster, of a knight in armour nearest the wall, with
a stiffened collar about his neck, his head on a cushion, and a talbot
at his feet: his lady has a ruff about her neck, her hair nicely dressed
out, and her head lying on two cushions, with the Cecil crest of a garb
between two lions rampant at her feet. Her clothes are painted black,
and his armour painted and gilt, and both figures in a recumbent,
supplicant posture, very well executed for the age they were done in.
On the side and ends of the tomb are the statues of ten children in
marble on their knees, painted and gilt. At the head are two females,
full grown, and a child: on the front are six, three men and three
women: the first son in armour, and a Death's head by him:[6] the two
others in short cloaks, and the three ladies in stiffened collars, hair
dressed out, with farthingales: at the foot is a child with a Death's
head in its hands: a female. All the children's habits are painted
black. Above this tomb is erected against the wall a sort of canopy,
supported by two black marble Corinthian pillars: the whole richly
painted, carved and gilt. On the top, under a Death's head with
gilded wings, and between two pyramidal obelisks of white marble, is
a round figure which surrounds a shield of six quarters for Allington;
on the helmet above it is placed the crest, viz., a talbot passant, ermine. Immediately under this coat on a frieze is another plain shield
having the six coats of Allington impaling the single coat of Cecil.
On the said frieze, and on each side of the first round coat of Alling-

3. Not his parochial duties, but his antiquarian pleasures.

4. This is missing.

5. Lady Dorothy Allington (see below).
HW was her great-great-grandson.

6. 'In his hands' (loc. cit. 38 n).

ton, near the two obelisks, are also two other coats in ornamented
shields: that on the right hand has the six quarters of Allington singly; and the other the six quarters of Cecil Earl of Exeter. Under this
canopy is a marble arch, and under that in the wall is fixed a table of
black marble, within a frame of white marble, with this inscription.

Here resteth in assured Hope to rise in Christ, Sir Giles Allington[7] of
Horsheath, Knight, accompanied with Lady Dorothy his Wife, Daughter
of Thomas Earle of Excester,[8] Baron Burghley, & who having made him a
joyfull father of tenne Children, viz: Elizabeth, Thomas, Giles, James,
Dorothy, Suzan, Anne, Catherine, William & Mary, ended this transitory
Lyfe the 10th of November 1613. To whose deare Memory her sorrowfull
Husband, mindfull of his own Mortality, erected this Monument.[9]

I shall send under another cover the pedigree of Allington,[10] according to promise: and when I was at Horsheth I took an exact catalogue of all the pictures there, as well as this Lord[11] could inform me;
for he told me the hands, most of which I had forgot. This catalogue[12]
shall come under the same cover.

I mentioned to you a painter, a great-uncle of mine, one Herbert
Tuer, of whom you desired me to send you more particulars. All I
know of him is that he, with my grandfather Theophilus Tuer, were
grandsons of one Mr Abdias Tuer,[13] who was vicar of Sabridgeworth
in Hertfordshire about the latter end of Queen Elizabeth's time. Both
he and my grandfather were born in England, but in the troublesome times following the beheading of King Charles they went into
Flanders in the military way, as appears by the dress of my grandfather, who is habited as an officer. Here my Uncle Herbert married
a daughter[14] of one Van Gameren, procureur, as he is styled, of
Utrecht, and was a painter of some merit and esteem, as is evident

7. (1572–1638), Kt (see Arthur Hervey,
'Horseheath and the Alingtons,' *Suffolk Institute of Archaeology and Natural History*, 1874, iv. 114, 121).

8. Thomas Cecil (1542–1622), 2d Bn
Burghley and 1st E. of Exeter. (Collins,
Peerage, 1812, ii. 602.)

9. Nichols gives a long note on Sir Giles
(*Collectanea Topographica* iv. 39).

10. Cole's copy of it is Add MS 5807, ff.
71–4; 5812, ff. 192v–193 (*Index to the Additional Manuscripts . . . in the British Mu-

seum . . . 1783–1835,* 1849). The pedigree
that Cole sent is missing.

11. Montfort.

12. Cole's copy is Add MS 5808, ff. 223–5
(op. cit.). The account he sent to HW is
missing.

13. Abdias or Abdy Tuer (d. 1627?), of St
Mary Hall (B.A. 1590) and Christ Church;
vicar of Sawbridgeworth, Herts, 1609–27
(*Alumni Oxon*).

14. Mary (see *post* 2 Sept. 1764).

from some pictures of the family now remaining with it, on board and copper. He left a son, John Tuer, by his Dutch wife, who was settled at Nimeguen about 1680. In a Dutch letter of my grandfather's there is mention of an head-piece, very curiously painted, to be seen in the Painter's Hall at Utrecht, which was the work of his brother Herbert Tuer. This is all I know of him.

My grandfather Theophilus Tuer was a very worthy, honest and industrious man, but as such he falls not under your immediate notice. The only reason I have to mention him to you is from a memorandum of his in a book, which I shall give you in his own words, after having first observed that on his return into England after the Restoration, he settled with his relations at your borough town of King's Lynn,[15] where his wife's father, Robert Dix, was a woollen draper, then for a little time at Downham in Norfolk, and soon after at Cambridge: 'The said Theophilus Tuer was married to Mary his Wife at Houghton Church in Norfolke, by Mr Nesling,[16] Robert Walpole Esqr.[17] his Chaplaine, on Friday July 12, 1678.'

After begging pardon for all this stuff, which I was accidentally led into by looking for Mr Herbert Tuer, I must hasten to a conclusion, the paper not allowing me to say more than that I am, dear Sir,

Your ever obliged servant,

WM COLE

To COLE, Tuesday 6 December 1763

Add MS 5952, f. 18.

Arlington Street, Dec. 6, 1763.

Dear Sir,

ACCORDING to custom I am excessively obliged to you: you are continually giving me proofs of your kindness. I have now three

15. HW was at this time M.P. for King's Lynn, which the Walpoles had represented for generations.

16. Probably Richard Nesling (d. 1724) of Emmanuel (B.A. 1668–9); ordained priest at Norwich, 1673; vicar of Beyton, Suffolk, 1681–1724 (*Alumni Cantab.*). The chaplaincy at Houghton supplies a part missing in his biography.

17. (1650–1700), HW's grandfather.

packets[1] to thank you for, full of information, and have only to lament the trouble you have given yourself.

I am glad for the tomb's sake and my own that Sir Giles Allington's monument is restored. The draught you have sent is very perfect. The account of your ancestor Tuer shall not be forgotten in my next edition.[2] The pedigree of Allington I had from Collins[3] before his death, but I think not so perfect as yours. You have made one little slip in it; my mother[4] was grand-daughter, not daughter of Sir John Shorter,[5] and was not an heiress, having three brothers,[6] who all died after her, and we only quarter the arms of Shorter, which I fancy occasioned the mistake, by their leaving no children. The verses by Sir Edward Walpole[7] and the translation by Bland[8] are published in my *Description of Houghton*.[9]

I am come late from the House of Lords,[10] and am just going to the opera, so you will excuse my saying more, than that I have a print of Archbishop Hutton[11] for you (it is Dr Ducarel's)[12] and a little plate of

1. The preceding letter, the pedigree of Allington, and the catalogue of the pictures at Horseheath Hall.

2. HW included the account in *Anecdotes*[2] iii. 63.

3. Arthur Collins (1690?–1760), author of *The Peerage of England*. No letters between Collins and HW have been located.

4. Catherine Shorter (1682–1737), 1st wife of Sir Robert Walpole, was the dau. of John Shorter (b. 1660), a timber merchant, of Bybrook, Kent, by Elizabeth Phillips (fl. 1628), dau. of Sir Erasmus Phillips, Bt, of Picton Castle, Pembroke (Le Neve, *Knights* 302).

5. (1624–88), Kt, Lord Mayor of London (Musgrave, *Obituary*).

6. John, the eldest son, who succeeded to the estate; Erasmus and Arthur (d. 1753). It appears that either John or Erasmus died in 1734 (GM, Nov. 1734, iv. 627b), which does not agree with HW's statement that they all died after 1737 (Le Neve, *Knights* 302).

7. (1621–68), HW's great-grandfather, 'created Knight of the Bath at the coronation of King Charles II, and made a great figure in Parliament' (*Aedes, Works* ii. 238). He was M.P. for Lynn (Walter Rye, *Norfolk Families*, Norwich, 1913, p. 978).

8. Henry Bland (d. 1746), D.D., Dean of

Durham 1727–46; headmaster (1720–8) and provost (1733–46) of Eton; friend of Sir Robert Walpole (*Eton Coll. Reg. 1698–1752* p. xx; LA iii. 661).

9. See *Aedes, Works* ii. 238.

10. Where inquiry was made into the causes of the riots of 3 Dec., when the *North Briton* was burned at the Royal Exchange. See HW to Hertford, 9 Dec. 1763, and to Mann, 12 Dec. 1763.

11. Matthew Hutton (1693–1758), Abp of York 1747–57, and of Canterbury 1757–8. The print HW mentions was probably 'a mezzotinto engraving of the Archbishop, twelve inches by ten, *T. Hudson pinxit* [in 1754], *J. Faber fecit*,' etc., which Ducarel prefixed to his MS *Memoirs of the Hutton Family*, first printed in 1843 in *The Publications of the Surtees Society* xvii. 7–49 (see especially, p. 44 n). Cole reminded Ducarel, 22 Dec. 1781, that 'you was so kind, many years ago, to give me a private print of Archbishop Hutton' (LA viii. 219 n). Apparently this print was later sold by Faber at the price of two shillings, and after 1757 the inscription was changed to include Hutton's new title (EBP).

12. Andrew Coltee Ducarel (1713–85), antiquary, and correspondent of HW and Cole.

Strawberry,[13] but I do not send them by the post as it would crease them; if you will tell me how to convey them otherwise, I will. I repeat many thanks to you and am,

Dear Sir, Yours most sincerely,

H. WALPOLE

To Cole, Tuesday 31 January 1764

Add MS 5952, ff. 21–2.

Address: To the Reverend Mr Cole at Blecheley near Fenny Stratford, Bucks. Free Hor Walpole. *Postmark:* 31 IA.

Arlington Street, Jan. 31, 1764.

Dear Sir,

SEVERAL weeks ago I begged you to tell me how to convey to you a print of Strawberry Hill, and another of Archbishop Hutton. I must now repeat the same request for two more volumes of my *Anecdotes of Painting*, which are on the point of being published.[1] I hope no illness prevented my hearing from you.

Yours ever,

H. WALPOLE

From Cole, Thursday 2 February 1764

VA, Forster MS 110, ff. 13–4. Cole kept no copy.

Blecheley, Feb. 2, 1764.

Dear Sir,

YOUR most obliging letter I received yesterday, and am greatly obliged to you for your kind remembrance of me, for your two new volumes of the *Anecdotes on Painting*, as also for the two prints you mention in this and your former letter, which I should have answered had it not been for the sole motive of giving you trouble. I

---

13. Presumably the vignette on the title of *Life of Lord Herbert of Cherbury*.

1. *Anecdotes*[1] iii, and *A Catalogue of Engravers*. They were published 6 Feb. 1764, but both volumes bore the date 1763 on the title-pages (*Jour. Print. Off.* 12, 44). *The London Chronicle* evidently had an advance copy of vol. iii, for it published long extracts from it, 4–18 Feb.

know how your time is always taken up, and I know as well your natural civility and politeness in answering your letters; therefore I was unwilling to give you that trouble till I had a fresh opportunity of writing to you. If you ever send so far as Ludgate Street, I shall be obliged to you if the things are left at Mr Cartwright's,[1] a lace merchant in that street, who is a neighbour of mine, and every week sends down a hamper to this parish; he will take care of them for me.

If you have not observed it already, which I think very probable, in your first volume of *Anecdotes* at p. 128, note †, there is a very minute mistake in calling Dr Wilson, Sir Thomas Wilson.[2] Although he was a layman, yet he was Dean of Durham and one of Queen Elizabeth's Secretaries of State: I know he was never knighted, being only LL.D. I know you will pardon me this freedom, because I think you would be accurate in your own copy: otherways it is hardly worth dwelling upon.

You are so kind as to mention my health as an excuse why I answered not your last kind letter. Thank God, notwithstanding the misery of the last four months, which have totally confined me to my parlour, not even stirring into the garden, it has been so wet and dirty, yet I have enjoyed a fireside as much as if it was better weather, nor have had the least complaint till about a fortnight ago, when I had a pretty sharp fit of the gravel, as they tell me it is, being a very violent pain across my loins, so as to disable me to sit or stand upright, and not to turn myself in my bed. However, I am much better, and if I should tell you how I have employed the last week in my convalescence, you would be surprised at anyone else, though not at me, who have done something like it at Strawberry Hill: in short, looking over my own collection of prints, I found it would be very useful to have an easy alphabetical index to Mr Ames's *Catalogue of English Heads*[3] to recur to, for though his is alphabetical, it is done in so slovenly and bad a method that it is endless to look for any particular print in it; nay, may go from one end to the other before you

1. There were two brothers, James and Nathaniel Cartwright, who divided their time between their shop in Ludgate Street and Bletchley. They executed commissions for Cole, frequently dined with him, etc. (see *Blecheley Diary, passim*).

2. Thomas Wilson (1525?–81), Eton and King's, author of *Discourse Upon Usury*, 1572; LL.D. Ferrara, 1559; Secretary of State, 1577; lay Dean of Durham, 1580. HW did not correct the mistake, and it stands in later editions. Cole mentioned it again, *post* 4 Nov. 1764.

3. *A Catalogue of English Heads: or an Account of about two Thousand Prints*, 1748, by Joseph Ames (1689–1759), biographer and antiquary, and the author of *Typographical Antiquities*, 1749. In his

find it, as some persons are put down in it by their titles of honour or dignity, and some by their proper names. This chaos I have reduced to a regular alphabet, but had I known the trouble of it before I sat about it, I believe it would have been undone. Now it is done, if you would have a copy of it, and think it worth your having, to see what you have already and what you want that is in that catalogue, I will readily send it you, for now it is only sheer writing, whereas I had twenty different papers to a single letter to reduce them to order.

Dr Ducarel this very day sent me as a present by Mr Cartwright a small quarto pamphlet called *Descriptio Angliae et Descriptio Londini*,[4] two poems in Latin verse, supposed to be wrote in the fifteenth century. By the glimpse I have had of them, they seem to be no great matter. I suppose the Doctor is the publisher,[5] though he says nothing of it himself. Shall I presume to beg the favour of letting your servant put a line of thanks to him into the Penny Post?[6]

But I will trouble you no more at present, than only saying that I have not forgot the promise of the volume I mentioned in which I

'Book of Materials, 1759,' now in the Folger Library, HW wrote (p. 67*bis*): 'Joseph Ames, Secretary of the Society of Antiquaries, and author of the *Lives of English Printers*, 4to, and of a *Catalogue of English Heads*, was originally a ship-chandler in Wapping. He took to the study of antiquities late in his life, and was very illiterate, but very laborious, and a quiet good man. He died in 1759. His library and prints were sold by auction in May 1760. His daughter was married during that sale.' Cole wrote on the verso of the title-page of his copy of Ames's *Typographical Antiquities*, 1749, *penes* the Grolier Club, New York City: 'The author, Mr Ames, I was well acquainted with, having been several times to see him, in order to look over his curious prints, of which he had no small collection, especially of the heads of Englishmen, many of which, at different times, I bought of him, to add to my collection of the same sort: he lived in a strange alley or lane in Wapping, and was a patten-maker, and an Anabaptist, with a spice of Deism mixed with it. I have often thought it no small reproach to the Antiquary Society to have so ignorant a person their secretary: he could not even spell, much more write English: I have several of his letters by me

at this time which show it: nor was it at all proper for such a person to be in a station which required his reading aloud at the meetings of the Society several papers, of which he was used to make miserable work. He was a little friendly and good-tempered man, and one of great industry and application in collecting curious old printed books, old prints and other curiosities in the natural as well as artificial way: and this it was which recommended him to the Society. He must have got someone to have perused his book for him: the printers would correct the false English and spelling.'

4. *Descriptio Angliae, et Descriptio Londini: being two poems in Latin verse, supposed to be written in the XVth* [XVI] *century*, 1763. The verses were by George Coryate (d. 1607), rector of Odcombe, Somerset, father of Thomas Coryate the traveller. Richard Gough dates the verses before 1571. Their editor was James Lumley Kingston of Dorchester, F.S.A. (Gough, *British Topography*[2] i. 34).

5. It is said on the title-page that the pamphlet is published 'at the request of several learned gentlemen, lovers of antiquity,' of whom Ducarel probably was one.

6. Cole's letter to Ducarel is missing.

have entered several miscellaneous pieces of poetry, etc.;[7] the truth is, among the rest there are two severe epigrams upon your father, which I could not cut out, and was not willing to send the volume with those two offensive pieces in it. In good truth, I put down in that volume all the old and new MSS that I found last year in my drawers, of what sort soever, and so if you will excuse and overlook that which I meant not as any injury to my Lord Orford,[8] for whose memory and services no one has a greater value and esteem, I will send it, and am in the meantime, dear Sir,

Your ever obliged and most faithful servant,

WM COLE

To COLE, Tuesday 7 February 1764

Add MS 5952, f. 1.

Misdated 1762 in previous editions.

[Arlington Street,] Tuesday, Feb. 7, [1764].

Dear Sir,

THE little leisure I have today will, I trust, excuse my saying very few words in answer to your obliging letter, of which no part touches me more than what concerns your health, which however I rejoice to hear is re-establishing itself.

I am sorry I did not save your trouble of cataloguing Ames's *Heads,* by telling you that another person has actually done it and designs to publish a new edition ranged in a different method.[1] I don't know

7. Cole probably mentioned the volume when he was at SH in Oct. 1763. Later references show that the volume is Add MS 5832, sometimes called Cole's 'Commonplace Book,' which contained, among other things, an index to Thomas Baker's MSS (see *post* 11 Feb. 1764).

8. HW's father, Sir Robert Walpole (1676–1745); cr. (1742) E. of Orford.

1. Rev. James Granger (1723–76), vicar of Shiplake, Oxfordshire. The 'new edition' was *A Biographical History of England, from Egbert the Great to the Revolution,* 2 vols (in 4 parts), 1769. It was dedicated to HW, to whom Granger later acknowledged

his indebtedness 'for the first hint of the plan of this work, communicated to me by a gentleman [Sir William Musgrave] who had seen the fine collection of heads at Strawberry Hill' (*Granger*[5] i. p. xxi n). In his 'Book of Materials, 1771,' now in the Folger Library, HW wrote (pp. 1–2): 'I had been thirty years collecting English heads, and ranged mine according to the several reigns. Mr Granger of Shiplake, who had begun a collection, took the hint, and after ranging Sir William Musgrave's collection in that method, and making a catalogue from thence and from mine and Mr West's collections, published a biographic list down to the Revolution.'

the gentleman's name, but he is a friend of Sir William Musgrave,[2] from whom I had this information some months ago.

You will oblige me much by the sight of the volume you mention. Don't mind the epigrams you transcribed on my father. I have been inured to abuse on him from my birth. It is not a quarter of an hour ago since cutting the leaves of a new dab called *Anecdotes of Polite Literature*,[3] I found myself abused for having defended my father. I don't know the author[4] and suppose I never shall, for I find Glover's *Leonidas*[5] is one of the things he admires—and so I leave them to be forgotten together, *fortunati ambo!*

I sent your letter to Ducarel, who has promised me those poems[6]—I accepted the promise to get rid of him t'other day, when he would have talked me to death. Adieu! Dear Sir,

Yours very sincerely,

H. Walpole

From Cole, Saturday 11 February 1764

VA, Forster MS 110, ff. 15–6. Cole kept no copy.

Blecheley, Feb. 11, 1764.

Dear Sir,

I RECEIVED yours of Feb. 7 yesterday, but can't have the pleasure of reading your book[1] till next week, as I sent up one of the two former volumes in order to have your last kind favour in the same

---

2. (1735–1800), 6th Bt, compiler of the work generally known as *Musgrave's Obituary;* antiquary and collector of prints. 'This information' was repeated in Musgrave to HW 3 April 1764.

3. After attacking Sir Robert Walpole for paying money to authors and printers of newspapers, whose panegyrics 'on their patron are now buried in oblivion,' the anonymous author continues: 'What could induce Mr Walpole to introduce strokes of party politics into his *Catalogue of Royal and Noble Authors,* I cannot conceive: they are unpardonable in a mere literary book; but particularly so, when they transgress the bounds of truth. "It is not proper nor

necessary," says he, "for me to touch his [Sir Robert's] character here.—Sixteen unfortunate and inglorious years since his removal have already written his eulogium." ' [*Roy. & Nob. Authors* ii. 138.] (*Anecdotes of Polite Literature,* 5 vols, 1764, ii. part 1. 164. For the entire passage see pp. 162–7.)

4. The author is not known. It is incorrectly assigned to HW by Charles Stonehill, *Anonyma and Pseudonyma,* 1927. See N&Q 10 S. vi. 201–3; John C. Bryce, *Times Lit. Supp.* 18 April 1936.

5. Richard Glover (1712–85), poet and politician; opposed to Sir Robert Walpole. His *Leonidas* appeared in 1737. HW's copy

binding.[2] It was with difficulty that I deferred my curiosity, for I long extremely to have them, as everything that comes from under your hands gives me more than ordinary pleasure. I will say no more, and could not help saying so much.

I shall send the volume in question to Mr Cartwright's, where it will be on Wednesday morning, and he will send it to you in a day or two, if you have no opportunity of calling for it in the meantime. I ought to make a thousand apologies to you for letting such a mess of stuff go out of my hands: of all my numerous collections I have not one that I am so deservedly ashamed of, as few of the others have any poetry or modernity in them. The way how this came to be so stuffed with them was this: Last year I had a mind to bind up my loose pamphlets and papers, and looking over every drawer and box I have in the world, I burnt about 1000 letters and infinite papers which have been collecting and laying by me near thirty years, some few of which, for some reason or no reason, I had a mind to save, among the rest the two or three I have already mentioned; some exceeding stupid verses, superstitiously preserved by me for the author's or giver's sake.

Among the titles of Mr Baker's MSS I have here and there added zealously, in my way of writing, very foolish things that no one should see, and I know, and am sure, that none will see but yourself, and I am very easy about it, as I know your candour and good nature. At p. 194 is the inventory of jewels given by Prince Charles to the Infanta,[3] which occasioned the mention of this volume, and at p. 204 is the very severe satire on Bishop Fletcher of London.[4] When I tran-

---

was sold SH iii. 104. The author of *Anecdotes of Polite Literature* devotes fourteen pages of eulogy to him, beginning: 'Mr Glover, though not one of the greatest epic poets, deserves to be ranked among them for his *Leonidas*' (i. 139).

6. George Coryate's *Descriptio Angliae et Descriptio Londini*, a copy of which Ducarel had also sent to Cole.

1. Cole meant books, *Anecdotes*[1] iii, and *Engravers*[1] (see *ante* 31 Jan. and *post* 23 Feb. 1764).

2. Cole's London binder is not known. HW, in accordance with Cole's instruc-

tions, sent the books to Cartwright, who sent them to the binder. Both volumes were issued in blue-grey wrappers.

3. Prince Charles, afterwards Charles I, visited Madrid in 1623 with the intention of completing negotiations for his marriage with the Infanta Maria, daughter of Philip III of Spain (secret negotiations began as early as 1614). The affair was broken off shortly thereafter. The inventory is in Add MS 5832.

4. Richard Fletcher (d. 1596), Bp of Bristol 1589, of Worcester 1593, and of London 1594, was chaplain to Elizabeth, but later lost her favour. The satire is in Add MS 5832.

scribe anything, I usually burn it: however, a few of these MSS which I had from out of Cheshire are preserved, and I send them to you, as useless to me. When the book itself is looked over, be pleased to return it to Mr Cartwright in Ludgate Street, lace merchant, and he will send it to me. I don't say this to hurry you, for I assure you I am in no hurry to have it again, only that you may know what to do with it when you have satisfied your curiosity. Anything in it, or that I have, is entirely at your service to transcribe if you think it worth it.

I met with a book, indeed it was given to me in November, which if you have not, I beg your acceptance of, as I have one of the same sort already: it is an *History of Sir Robert Walpole,* by Mr Musgrave.[5]

Thank God, I have got rid of my complaint, but these deluges have occasioned me great losses in my estate. One of my tenants has not an acre of dry ground to put his cattle into, and the water is in his house and barns so that they can hardly stir about. Without an abatement of full a half-year's rent he won't stay: this I have granted with pleasure, and think myself very happy that the rest of my land lies on an hill, and that I have only neighbours face below it,[6] but what makes me think myself in Fortune's favour, if nothing worse happens, is that an £100 prize in the last lottery will, I hope, bear me through my losses for this year, and if worse follows another year, I must e'en be contented. But I will trouble you no longer, and wishing you the full enjoyment of your health, with many thanks for all your kind favours, I am, dear Sir,

Your ever obliged and faithful servant,

WM COLE

May I presume to beg the favour of you to frank the enclosed two letters, which may go to the postoffice whenever your servant carries your own, for it is not necessary to send on purpose, as they will keep this week or two.

---

5. *A Brief and True History of Sir Robert Walpole,* 1738, by William Musgrave. Cole had two copies, one of which he sent to HW (see *post* 4 March 1764). The other, bound with nine other pamphlets relating to Sir Robert, is now WSL.

6. That is, none of Cole's tenants except the one mentioned above lived on the low land opposite his hill.

To Cole, Thursday 23 February 1764

Add MS 5952, f. 23.

Dated by Cole's endorsement: 'Received February 24, St Matthias, 1764.' Cole usually received HW's letters at Bletchley the day after they were posted.

[Arlington Street, 23 Feb. 1764.]

Dear Sir,

I AM impatient for your manuscript,[1] but have not yet received it. You may depend on my keeping it to myself, and returning it safely.

I do not know that history of my father, which you mention, by the name of Musgrave.[2] If it is the *Critical History of his Administration*,[3] I have it: if not, I shall be obliged to you for it.

Your kindness to your tenants is like yourself and most humane. I am glad your prize rewards you, and wish your fortune had been as good as mine, who with a single ticket in this last lottery got five hundred pounds.

I have nothing new, that is, nothing old, to tell you. You care not about the present world, and are the only real philosopher I know.

I this winter met with a very large lot of English heads, chiefly of the reign of James I, which very nearly perfects my collection. There were several which I had in vain hunted for these ten years. I have bought too some very scarce, but more modern, ones out of Sir Charles Cotterel's collection.[4] Except a few of Faithorne,[5] there are scarce any now that I much wish for.

---

1. Add MS 5832.

2. HW apparently had forgotten the book, as it is listed in MS Cat. This copy, with HW's youthful signature, was sold SH vi. 64, with the *Critical History of the Administration of Sir Robert Walpole,* and is now WSL.

3. 'By a Gentleman of the Middle-Temple' [James Ralph (1705?–62), pamphleteer and miscellaneous writer], 1743. See n. 2.

4. Sir Charles Cottrell-Dormer (d. 1779), Kt, of Rousham, Oxon; Master of the Ceremonies at Court. The collection was made by his father's cousin, Lt-Gen. James Dormer (1679–1741) and his father, Sir Clement Cottrell-Dormer (1685–1758), and was sold by auction, 20 Feb. 1764 and the nine-

teen days following. The prints purchased by HW were in Thuanus's *Historiarum,* 7 vols bound in 14, large paper, 1733 (lot 2590 in the Cottrell sale). HW notes in MS Cat: 'N.B. This magnificent set of books belonged to Sir Clement Cotterel Dormer, and is adorned with a great variety of the finest and most scarce prints of the principal personages. When Sir Charles Cotterel sold his father's library by auction in 1764, Mr Walpole bought this edition of Thuanus there, and gave fifty guineas for it.' The SH pressmark was L.8. 1–14. The most important prints are listed in the London Sale Catalogue viii. 1099. The lot was sold to Tiffin for £40.

5. William Faithorne (1616–91), the

With my *Anecdotes* I packed up for you the head of Archbishop Hutton, and a new little print of Strawberry. If the volumes, as I understand by your letter, stay in town to be bound, I hope your bookseller will take care not to lose those trifles.

I am, Dear Sir, Your ever obliged humble servant,

Hor. Walpole

To Cole, Saturday 3 March 1764

Add MS 5952, f. 24.

Arlington Street, March 3, 1764.

Dear Sir,

JUST as I was going to the opera, I received your MS and would not defer telling you so, that you may know it is safe. But I have additional reason to write to you immediately, for on opening the book, the first thing I saw was a new obligation to you, the charming Faithorne of Sir Orlando Bridgman,[1] which according to your constantly obliging manner you have sent me, and I almost fear you think I begged it; but I can disculpate myself, for I had discovered that it belongs to Dugdale's *Origines Judiciales*,[2] and had ordered my bookseller to try to get me that book, which when I accomplish, you shall command your own print again, for it is too fine an impression to rob you of.

I have been so entertained with your book, that I have stayed at home on purpose and gone through three parts of it. It makes me wish earnestly sometime or other to go through all your collections,

elder. For a list of prints by Faithorne which HW lacked, see *post* 15 July 1769; for the complete collection (possibly the finest of Faithorne ever made), see London Sale Catalogue vi. 737–805. Lot 806 formed a collection of 32 of the 43 mezzotints by William Faithorne (1656–1701?), the younger.

1. 'Orlandus Bridgeman [1606?–74] Miles et Baronettus, Custos Magni Sigilli Angliae.' 1st Bt. This was London Sale vi. 743,

'extra fine,' and was bought by the British Museum.

2. HW printed the title so in *Engravers*[2] 68n, but corrected *Judiciales* to *Juridiciales* in *Works* iv. 52. The print of Sir Orlando Bridgeman first appeared in Sir William Dugdale's *Origines Juridiciales, or Historical Memorials of the English Laws, Courts of Justice*, 2d edn, 1671 (*Granger*[1] ii. 258; William Upcott, *English Topography* ii. 760). There is no record that HW acquired another copy of the print.

for I have already found twenty things of great moment to me. One is particularly satisfactory to me; it is in Mr Baker's MSS at Cambridge, the title of Eglesham's book against the Duke of Bucks,[3] mentioned by me in the account of Gerbier,[4] from Vertue, who fished out everything, and always proves in the right. This piece I must get transcribed by Mr Gray's[5] assistance. I fear I shall detain your MS prisoner a little, for the notices I have found, but I will take infinite care of it as it deserves.

I have got among my *new* old prints a most curious one of one Toole.[6] It seems to be a burlesque. He lived in temp. Jac. I and appears to have been an adventurer like Sir Ant. Shirley:[7] can you tell me anything of him?

I must repeat how infinitely I think myself obliged to you both for the print and the use of your MS which is of the greatest use and entertainment to me—but you frighten me about Mr Baker's MSS from the neglect of them.[8] I should lose all patience if yours were to be treated so. Bind them in iron, and leave them in a chest of cedar. They are I am sure most valuable, from what I have found already. Adieu! Dear Sir,

Your very much obliged humble servant,

Hor. Walpole

3. George Eglisham (fl. 1612–42), physician to James I, and poet, published in 1626 his *Prodromus Vindictae*, in which he accused George Villiers (1592–1628), 1st D. of Buckingham, of having caused by poisoning the deaths of James I and of James Hamilton (1589–1625), 2d M. of Hamilton. The pamphlet was translated into English and published as *The Forerunners of Revenge*, 1642. HW added a note on this book in *Anecdotes*[2] ii. 61.

4. HW refers to *Anecdotes*[1] ii. 56.

5. See Gray to HW Sunday — March 1764.

6. Arthur O'Toole (1538–1622?), soldier of fortune. HW described the print (by Francis Delaram): 'Arthurus Severus Toole Nonesuch, aetatis 80, 1618. An old man with a large beard, a sceptre in his hand with eleven crowns upon it. Eight English burlesque verses. Seems to be the effigies of some adventurer' (*Engravers*[2] p. 19). The

name is printed *O'Toole* in *Works* iv. 15. Granger comments on the print: 'I never saw it but in the collection of the Honourable Horace Walpole; and that gentleman told me that he never saw any print of this person besides his own' (*Granger*[1] i. 273). In *Granger*[5] ii. 100–1, O'Toole is identified as a boasting adventurer who in 1622 was living in Westminster. He was the object of John Taylor the Water-Poet's ironical panegyric, *To the Honour of the Noble Captaine O'Toole*, 1622, to which, Granger was informed, the print was prefixed. HW's copy was London Sale i. 146.

7. Sir Anthony Shirley (1565–1635?), Kt, traveller and diplomatist (HW to Conway, 14 Aug. 1757).

8. For Cole's remarks on this neglect, dated 7 Feb. 1772, see LA v. 117. The remark to which HW refers is probably similar.

From Cole, Sunday 4 March 1764

VA, Forster MS 110, ff. 17–8. Cole kept no copy.

Address: For the Honourable Horace Walpole Esq. in Arlington Street, Westminster. *Postmark:* F. Stratford 5 MR.

Blecheley, March 4, 1764.

Dear Sir,

I AM glad the MS volume I sent is of any use. I am sure I shall esteem them the more for what you say of them, and I wish you don't inspire me with a vanity I assure you I hitherto have been free from, of thinking them of any moment. But no more of that: so long as they have amused you or been useful,[1] it is much more than I ever thought they were capable of attaining. It is so far lucky that at least they give me, or you give me, an opportunity of repaying some part of the infinite pleasure I have received from your spirited manner of treating a subject[2] which many people would have thought dry without it. I had selected particular passages which most struck me, but they occur so frequently that I can't have time to specify them. I never was more entertained in my life than in reading the volumes, and only wished they would not so soon conclude.

I am ashamed of my indolence that I did not write in answer to your last, and was surprised that my friend had been so negligent in sending the volume, as he had it a full fortnight by him.

I know and am satisfied you did not beg the print of Sir O. Bridgeman, for I offered it and you refused it,[3] but as I then told you truth, so I now confirm it, that I had no particular value for it, and therefore the obligation was trifling. I have no good collection: all I aim at is as large a quantity of English heads, good or bad, as I can come at; therefore I beg you would not trouble yourself about sending it, for I really did not know it was particularly valuable till you told me so. I know nothing of Toole, having never seen the print or read of such a person.

Was the *Life of the Earl of Orford*[4] new to you? It seems to me to be a bookseller's work. I have another of them.

1. See *post* 9 Mar. 1765, the conclusion of HW's first paragraph, for an echo of this.
2. Of painting and engraving in England.

3. Apparently in conversation at SH.
4. Cole evidently had sent a copy of Musgrave's work to HW with the MS, but HW did not acknowledge it.

You are welcome to keep the MS as long as you please, and to command as many more of them as you think proper. I wish you would send in the book, at its return, another print of yourself,[5] if I am not unreasonable, as I should be glad of having one among my collection: that you was so kind as to give me before being otherways disposed of.[6] But I can neither tire you any longer or write myself, having just time to subscribe myself, dear Sir,

Your ever obliged and faithful servant,

WM COLE

To Cole, Thursday 12 April 1764

Add MS 5952, ff. 25–6.
Address: To the Reverend Mr Cole at Blecheley near Fenny Stratford, Bucks. Free Hor Walpole. *Postmark:* IW [Isleworth] 12 AP.

Arlington Street, April 12, 1764.

Dear Sir,

I SHALL send your MS volume this week to Mr Cartwright; and with a thousand thanks. I ought to beg your pardon for having detained it so long. The truth is, I had not time till last week to copy two or three little things at most. Do not let this delay discourage you from lending me more. If I have them in summer, I shall keep them much less time than in winter. I do not send my print with it as you ordered me, because I find it is too large to lie within the volume;[1] and doubling a mezzotinto you know spoils it. You shall have one or more if you please whenever I see you.

5. The print engraved by James Mc-Ardell (1729?–65) after the portrait by Reynolds (see HW to Grosvenor Bedford, 9 Nov. 1757). 'Mr Walpole's picture . . . from which there is a mezzotinto print in 1757, by Mac-Ardal, standing in a pensive posture, by a table, in which is his fine antique eagle in a print, is very like him, except that it is a little too plump for him' (Cole, *Jour. to Paris* 55–6).

6. Cole had framed it (see *post* 18 July 1764), and later gave it to be hung in the parlour of King's College (see *post* 18 July 1774).

1. The print is 12¼ by 9⅞ inches (see Gordon Goodwin, *James McArdell*, 1903, p. 57). Cole's MS volume is in folio, but slightly smaller.

J. Reynolds pinx.t   J. M.c Ardell fecit 1757

Horace Walpole

Youngest Son of S.r Rob.t Walpole Earl of Orford.

I have lately made a few curious additions to my collections[2] of various sorts, and shall hope to show them to you at Strawberry Hill. Adieu! Dear Sir,

Your much obliged,

Hor. Walpole

From Cole, Thursday 19 April 1764

VA, Forster MS 110, f. 19. Cole kept no copy.
Address: For the Honourable Horace Walpole Esq. in Arlington Street, London.
Postmark: 20 AP.

Blecheley, April 19, 1764.

Dear Sir,

THIS is to advertise you of the safe arrival of my book, which I thought you might be uneasy about till you heard that I had it, as also to thank you for your last kind letter and invitation to Strawberry Hill, which I shall gladly accept of for two or three days when I know that I shall be least troublesome and you most at leisure. I long to review your collections of various sorts, and the improvements of them, and if from that miserable specimen of my MSS your curiosity should lead you to look into any more, they are quite at your service. In the meantime, I beg leave to subscribe myself, dear Sir,

Your most obliged servant,

Wm Cole

I could but admire at the impudence of the Critical Reviewers about two months since, who to make their performance sell, wisely and politicly retailed out of your last volumes on painting about twenty pages of sorry criticism:[1] without such assistance no one would buy their book.

2. Among these were some 'Norman tiles' sent him by his brother-in-law, Charles Churchill (see HW to Churchill 27 March 1764). He doubtless also had in mind the prints bought at Sir Charles Cottrell's sale.

1. *The Critical Review*, Feb. 1764, xvii. 113–29, had reviews of *Anecdotes*[1] vol. 3, and *Engravers*[1]. The reviews were largely extracts and paraphrases, presented in the tone assumed by the Tory *Critical Review* when noticing Whig authors.

To Cole, Monday 16 July 1764

Add MS 5952, ff. 27–8.
Address: To the Reverend Mr Cole at Blecheley near Fenny Stratford, Bucks.
Free Hor Walpole. *Postmark:* Isleworth 17 IY.

Strawberry Hill, July 16, 1764.

Dear Sir,

YOU must think me a brute to have been so long without taking any notice of your obliging offer of coming hither. The truth is, I have not been at all settled here for three days together; nay, nor do I know when I shall be. I go tomorrow into Sussex;[1] in August into Yorkshire,[2] and in September—into France.[3] If in any interval of these jaunts, I can be sure of remaining here a week, which I literally have not been this whole summer, I will certainly let you know, and will claim your promise.

Another reason for my writing now, is, I want to know how I may send you Lord Herbert's *Life*,[4] which I have just printed. Did I remember the favour you did me of asking for my own print? If I did not, it shall accompany this book. Adieu! Dear Sir,

Yours most faithfully,

HOR. WALPOLE

From Cole, Wednesday 18 July 1764

VA, Forster MS 110, ff. 20–1. Cole kept no copy.

Blecheley, July 18, 1764.

Dear Sir,

MANY thanks for your most obliging letter of the 16th, and though I know of your journey into Sussex yesterday, yet I can't forbear acknowledging the receipt of it immediately, not only for your very kind remembrance of me at all (amidst the multiplicity

1. Probably to Goodwood (see HW to Montagu 10 June 1765).
2. To visit Lord Strafford at Wentworth Castle, near Barnsley, as well as the Duke of Devonshire at Chatsworth Hall in Derbyshire. The journey was laid aside because of the illness of the Duke of Devon-

shire (see HW to Mann 27 July 1764; to Hertford 3 Aug. 1764; and to Montagu 16 Aug. 1764).
3. He did not go to France until Sept. 1765 (*Paris Jour.*).
4. *The Life of Edward Lord Herbert of Cherbury*, written by himself, the printing

of your avocations of pleasure and necessity, for surely the beauties of
your own villa must make you regret to leave it so often), but also
for your most obliging design of sending me Lord Herbert's *Life:* a
performance I have long wished to look into, from what you was
pleased to say to me about it last summer.[1] I can't help, on this account, to wish your Sussex journey and visit may be short, as I am apprehensive I may not have that pleasure gratified till your return: for
as to that other of waiting upon you in the intervals of your journeys
into Yorkshire and France, I know too well the value of your time to
think of interrupting it, and will rather defer my visit to Strawberry
Hill till after your return. Even *I* know the comfort of a retreat by
myself after a visiting journey: you, who have so many of them, and
have full employ on your hands at home, in so sweet a place, both
without and in your study, etc., are not to be broke in upon without
a crime.

I shall be much obliged for the print you mention,[2] which I never
received, except one I framed: the other is for my book of prints. At
the same time, if it could with any conveniency, I should be much
obliged to you for a few orange flowers, if possible to be sent in a
small box or basket, with the book and print, or else a handful or two
of small green oranges that drop off and fall under the trees. You will
wonder perhaps at this request, but having occasion to send last week
to Cambridge, I wrote to Mr Gray and begged his receipt to make a
potpourri,[3] and the above are part of the ingredients.

I was in London about three weeks since, and calling upon Mr
White,[4] a virtuoso in Newgate Street, to whom I made a present of a
curious gold medal of British coin, in return he this week sent me by
Mr Cartwright about twenty of his duplicates, among which the enclosed one of Edward the Confessor was one, which I beg your acceptance of, if you think it worth it and have it not already, for I
think you have some collection of English coins, or at least like them.
If you should ever call at this Mr White's, he has the most curious

of which was completed 27 Jan. 1764 (*Jour.
Print. Off.* 12). For unexplained reasons
HW did not distribute copies to his friends
until July (see HW to Montagu 16 July
1764).

———

1. On their tour into Northamptonshire
in July 1763. For HW's opinion of Lord
Herbert's *Life,* see HW to Montagu 16
July 1764.

2. McArdell's print of HW.

3. Apparently neither Cole's letter nor
Gray's receipt has survived. The first use
of 'potpourri' (in this sense) in OED is in
1749.

4. John White (d. 1787), hatter, 'celebrated collector (and supposed fabricator)
of ancient coins' (LI v. 187 n).

and valuable collection of British, Saxon, Norman and English coins perhaps anywhere to be met with. I was quite amazed to see so many British and Saxon pieces, much superior to those after the Conquest. I am sure you would be much entertained, and the more so as the gentleman is a very civil, modest and not a conceited man.

I heartily wish you the enjoyment of your health in your intended journeys: to beg to hear from you in France would be unreasonable, as your correspondence must be so large, yet I can't help saying I should be glad to hear from you, if it was only to say I am well. However, thus much I hope, that on your return I may know it, when I will most willingly wait on you at Strawberry Hill. May I also beg of you, if in any of your rambles and excursions at a good distance from Paris you should hear or see any little snug country retirement,[5] in cheap part and pleasant situation, that would accommodate my small fortunes, that you would make a memorandum of it, and of which I may have the pleasure of talking on your return. But I will detain you no longer, and once more wishing you all earthly enjoyments, I am, dear Sir,

Your ever faithful and most obliged servant,

Wm Cole

The parcel may be directed to be left for me at Mr Rowley's,[6] linen-draper, at the Anchor, in Ludgate Street, where my neighbour Mr Cartwright will take it up for me.

To Cole, Saturday 21 July 1764

Add MS 5952, ff. 29–30.

Address: To the Reverend Mr Cole at Blecheley near Fenny Stratford, Bucks, Free Hor Walpole. *Postmark:* IW [Isleworth] 21 IY.

Arlington Street, July 21, 1764.

Dear Sir,

I MUST never send you trifles, for you always make me real presents in return. The beauty of the coin[1] surprises me. Mr White

---

5. Cole's desire to retire to France, 'either in Flanders, Artois, or Normandy,' was cooled by his visit to Paris in 1765 (see Cole, *Jour. to Paris* 1, and *passim*).

6. John Rowley, whom Cole knew through Rowley's lodgers, James and Nathaniel Cartwright (*Blecheley Diary* 228; Cole, *Jour. to Paris* 3).

1. Of Edward the Confessor, a present to

must be rich, when such are his duplicates. I am acquainted with him, and have often intended to visit his collection, but it is one of those things one never does, because one always may. I give you a thousand thanks in return, and what are not worth more, my own print, Lord Herbert's Life (this is curious, though it costs me little[2]) and some orange flowers. I wish you had mentioned the latter sooner; I have had an amazing profusion this year, and given them away to the right and left by handfuls. These are all I could collect today, as I was coming to town, but you shall have more if you want them.

I consign these things as you ordered. I wish the print may arrive without being rumpled; it is difficult to convey mezzotintos, but if this is spoiled, you shall have another.

If I make any stay in France, which I do not think I shall above six weeks at most, you shall certainly hear from me—but I am a bad commissioner for searching you out a hermitage. It is too much against my interest, and I had much rather find you one in the neighbourhood of Strawberry. Adieu! Dear Sir,

Yours most sincerely,

H. Walpole

From Cole, Thursday 2 August 1764

VA, Forster MS 110, ff. 22–3. Cole's copy, Add MS 5831, ff. 231v, 232.
Address: [From Cole's copy.] For the Honourable Horace Walpole at Strawberry Hill in Twickenham, Middlesex.

Blecheley, Aug. 2, 1764.

Dear Sir,

MANY thanks for your kind remembrance of me, for your book, your print[1] and the orange flowers. The last, through neglect of the rascally carrier, who detained it in London ten days, so that I

Cole from John White. It was sold SH ix. 106, where it was described as having been coined at York.

2. It was printed at SH from the MS in the possession of Lord Herbert's descendant Henry Arthur Herbert, 1st E. of Powis. HW and Lord Powis divided the 200 copies between themselves. It is possible from HW's 'though it costs me little'

that Lord Powis shared the expense of printing, although that was against HW's practice.

———

1. This was the second print of himself by McArdell after Reynolds which HW sent Cole. Cole pasted it into a book of prints, only to have it begged from him by a friend (see *post* 27 Dec. 1767).

received the box on Monday night last, were quite putrified and black and all matted together. The book delighted me excessively as well as surprised me: who could have believed that the philosophic author of *De Veritate*[2] could have lived and acted the part of Don Quixote in reality? Yet give me leave to speak truth, as I know you love it, both from habit and lately from many expressions in the said book—I say, give me leave to speak my mind freely and without a grain of flattery, that however delighted I was in general with the *Life,* yet I could heartily have wished that many parts in it had been shorter, so that your own preface or advertisement had been longer.[3] I won't dwell longer on this subject, as it may give offense, and will just mention an observation or two that occurred to me in the reading it.

In the pedigree,[4] through oversight of the engraver, Sir *John* Bromley is put for *Thomas.*

At p. 9, lines 11 and 24, *Woollen beads,* I apprehend should be *wooden beads.*[5] Wooden beads are put in contradistinction to any other of more precious materials of metal, stone or jewels, and are commonly used by the poorer people to this day, as no doubt they were then. As to beads made of wool or woolen cloth, I don't conceive they can be useful for the purpose they are intended, of slipping quick by a string for devotion. But this you will determine according to your better judgment.

P. 12. Mr George Herbert died in 1635[6] and lies buried under a marble gravestone without any inscription under the altar of Bemerton Church. He was my great-great-uncle, Theophilus Tuer, my great-grandfather, marrying a niece of his, but by which of his brothers or sisters I am ignorant:[7] their eldest son Herbert Tuer was the painter I formerly mentioned to you, as his second brother Theophilus was a soldier. We had an original small picture of Mr George

---

2. Lord Herbert's chief philosophical treatise, *De Veritate, prout distinguitur a Revelatione, a Verisimili, a Possibili, et a Falso,* Paris, 1624.

3. HW's advertisement covers 5½ pages, the *Life* 171.

4. It is usually missing, having been suppressed by HW because of its inaccuracy.

5. Cole's reasonable conjecture has not been adopted in any later edition of the *Life,* and the passage still reads 'woollen beads.' The extant MS copy of the *Life* (in

possession of the Earl of Powis at Powis Castle, Welshpool) is incomplete and does not include this portion (information from the Librarian of the National Library of Wales, Mr W. D. Davies).

6. Cole is mistaken: Herbert died in 1633, and was buried beneath the altar of Bemerton Church, 3 March 1633.

7. Cole's grandfather, Theophilus Tuer, was the son of Theophilus Tuer by Catharine Vaughan, 'the third and youngest daughter of Owen Vaughan, of Llwydiart;

Herbert in the family, painted on copper in oval. I have only the old black frame of it, the picture itself being stole out of my chambers when at college. When my relations, I being a boy, used often to talk of our Cousin Herbert, the divine poet, they were, I suppose, totally ignorant of his extraction, as well as myself. The only part of his character they prided themselves in was his virtue and good name.

P. 13. Thomas the seventh son was the author of that excellent book of travels printed in 1634, entitled *A Relation of Some Yeares Travaile begunne Anno 1626 into Afrique, Asia,* etc.,[8] and dedicated to Philip Earl of Pembroke and Montgomerie.[9] I have the book. It is rather scarce and printed in a thin folio, with excellently engraved prints by William Marshall,[10] better and softer executed than I have seen usually of his doing.

I hope you'll excuse the above observations. I was led to talk of my relationship to Mr George Herbert from a MS note of the late Mr Browne Willis[11] concerning his death and place of burial: in his printed account of Lincoln Cathedral[12] he says he died in 1636, but this is corrected by himself in another place to 1635.

From what has been said, I hope you'll think me less impertinent when I am so bold as to beg the favour, sometime or other when I have the honour of waiting on you at Strawberry Hill on your return from France,[13] to give me a print of Lord Herbert.[14] I wish you had

which Owen Vaughan married Margaret, second sister of Mr George Herbert the poet, fifth son of Richard Herbert, of Montgomery, by Magdalen his wife, daughter of Sir Richard Newport by Margaret his wife, daughter and sole heir of Sir Thomas Bromley, of the Privy Council to Henry VIII' (LA i. 657).

8. Cole is again mistaken: Thomas Herbert (1597–1642?), although an author, did not write it. Doubtless Cole means Sir Thomas Herbert (1606–82), son of Christopher Herbert, author of *A Description of the Persian Monarchy now beinge: the Orientall Indyes Iles and other parts of the Greater Asia and Africk,* 1634, reprinted with additions (1638, 1665, etc.) under the title *Some Yeares Travels into divers Parts of Asia and Afrique.*

9. Philip Herbert (1584–1650), 4th E. of Pembroke and 1st E. of Montgomery.

10. (fl. 1630–50). He is noticed in *Engravers, Works* iv. 32–3. (See Mrs Arundell Esdaile, *Times Lit. Supp.,* 30 Jan. 1937.)

The mention of Marshall's name at this time, when HW was finishing *The Castle of Otranto,* may have resulted in his name being used as the 'translator' of that story.

11. (1682–1760), antiquary, friend and patron of Cole. He presented Cole to the living of Bletchley on condition that Cole resign in favour of Willis's grandson when the latter was fitted to succeed him (see *Blecheley Diary* 106).

12. That is, in *A Survey of the Cathedrals,* 3 vols, 1727–30 (issued with new title-pages, 1742), ii. 207. Cole's copy of the 1742 issue, with copious MS notes and extracts by Cole from notes in Willis's copy, is in the British Museum.

13. 'where I could have wished that you would have observed some private retreat for me about a year or two hence' (addition in Cole's copy).

14. The frontispiece to Lord Herbert's *Life* ('Ja. Oliver pinx. Ant. Walker sculp.'), showing Lord Herbert reclining under a tree.

given us some little history of that print, which from its manner, shield and ornaments, seems to be as romantic as the *Life* itself.

I will detain you no longer, but with wishing you every earthly enjoyment I remain, dear Sir,

Your ever obliged and most faithful servant,

WM COLE

To COLE, Wednesday 29 August 1764

Add MS 5952, ff. 31–2.
Address: To the Reverend Mr Cole at Blecheley near Fenny Stratford, Bucks. Free Hor Walpole. *Postmark:* Isleworth 30 AV.

Strawberry Hill, Aug. 29, 1764.

Dear Sir,

AMONG the multitude of my papers I have mislaid, though not lost, [is] the account you was so good as to give me of your ancestor Tuer, as a painter.[1] I have been hunting for it, to insert in the new edition of my *Anecdotes*.[2] It is not very reasonable to save myself trouble at the expense of yours, but perhaps you can much sooner turn to your notes, than I find your letter. Will you be so good as to send me soon all the particulars you recollect of him? I have a print of Sir Lionel Jenkins from his painting.[3]

I did not send you any more orange flowers as you desired, for the continual rains rotted all the latter blow; but I had made a vast potpourri, from whence you shall have as much as you please, when I have the pleasure of seeing you here, which I should be glad might be in the beginning of October, if it suits your convenience. At the same time you shall have a print of Lord Herbert, which I think I did not send you.[4]

I am, Most truly yours,

HOR. WALPOLE

PS. I trust you will bring me a volume or two of your MSS of which I am most thirsty.

1. See *ante* 1 Dec. 1763.
2. HW inserted an account of Tuer in *Anecdotes*[2] iii. 63.
3. The print was engraved by Gerard Van der Gucht (1696–1776) in 1723

(*Granger*[1] ii. 250). Sir Lionel (or Leoline) Jenkins (1623–85).
4. That is, an extra print, separate from the book.

From Cole, Sunday 2 September 1764

VA, Forster MS 110, ff. 24–5. Cole's copy, Add MS 5831, f. 232.
Address: For the Honourable Horace Walpole Esq. at Strawberry Hill in Twickenham, Middlesex. *Postmark:* F. Stratford 3 SE.

Blecheley, Sept. 2, 1764.

Dear Sir,

I HAD made a memorandum[1] of the account of my great-uncle Herbert Tuer, which I drew up from my grandfather's papers,[2] and is as follows.

Herbert Tuer, the second son[2a] of Theophilus Tuer by Catherine his wife, a niece of Mr George Herbert the poet (from whence he derived his Christian name of Herbert) was a painter of some eminence, though perhaps little known in England, of which however he was a native, his grandfather[3] and great-grandfather[4] being, the first[5] vicar of Elsenham in Essex, the other of Sabridgeworth in Hertfordshire about the latter end of the reign of Queen Elizabeth; yet by quitting[6] the kingdom together with his third brother Theophilus Tuer (my grandfather) in the troubles consequent on the beheading of Charles I, they both went into Flanders in a military capacity, at least my grandfather, who is dressed in his picture in the habit of an officer, with a great belt across his shoulders: by which means the works of my Uncle Herbert Tuer, who settled in Flanders, where he died, are probably little known in England: for marrying Mary, the daughter of one Van Gameren, procureur of Utrecht, as he is styled in a letter of my \<gr\>andfather (probably a counsellor, attorney or some profession of the law), he had by her one son, John Tuer, who survived him and was settled at Nimeguen in 1680, with his mother-in-law,[7] Elizabeth Van Heymenbergh, my Uncle Herbert's second wife and widow, of the same country: but whether he had any children by her,

---

1. Cole probably refers to *ante* 1 Dec. 1763, of which he had kept a copy. HW compressed this account in *Anecdotes*[2], without acknowledgment.

2. Theophilus Tuer's MSS and Cole's notes on the Tuer family are now in Add MS 5819.

2a. But see *ante* 2 Aug., where Cole calls him the eldest.

3. Abdias Tuer, vicar of Sawbridgeworth, Herts, 1699.

4. John Tuer (1567–1621), vicar of Elsenham, Essex, 1592–1621 (*Alumni Oxon*). Cole has reversed the preferments of Abdias and John Tuer.

5. That is, the grandfather (see preceding note).

6. Cole's copy reads 'by his being obliged to quit.'

7. That is, his stepmother.

or when or where he died, I am ignorant: most likely the last at Utrecht. It is very probable that on his first going over into Flanders that he was put under some painter, in which art after a time he became a tolerable proficient, as is evident from some small family pictures of his hand, still remaining in the family, on board and copper, one of which is a picture of himself. In a Dutch letter of my grandfather The<ophi>lus Tuer, who returned into England after the <Resto>ration, there is mention <of> an head, very curiously painted, to be seen in <the P>ainter's Hall at Utrecht, which was the performance of his brother Herbert Tuer. I shall be extremely glad to see the print of Sir Lionel Jenkins from a painting of his, which you mention, and when I wait on you at the beginning of October I will endeavour to bring his picture and some of his works with me, as they are small. I shall think you do both me and my uncle a singular honour, if you think him deserving of it, to give him a corner of a plate, in the same manner as you have done Isaac Becket, etc.[8] But of this you will be a better judge, both as to propriety and convenience.

I can't finish this letter without mentioning an anecdote relating to my grandfather, both as it is an instance of his great accuracy, and as it in some degree connects me to a family for whom all my family, on Father and Mother's side, have ever had the greatest veneration and, as appears by the following note, formerly also (probably by some dependence on it), had the same sentiments. This grandfather of mine, Theophilus Tuer, brother to the said Herbert Tuer, after his return into England, settled at first with his relations (some of the principal people there) at your borough town of King's Lynn, where his wife's father, Robert Dix, was a woollen-draper. He afterwards lived for a time at Downham in Norfolk, and lastly at Cambridge, where he was a merchant, and being a very worthy, honest and industrious man, brought up a large family very reputably. He constantly kept a sort of journal of occurrences, and in one of his books is this entry, for which I refer you to the truth of it to your own parish register at Houghton, and which is the reason for my troubling you with all this nonsense about him: 'The said Theophilus Tuer was married to Mary his wife at Houghton Church in Norfolke,

8. The print of Isaac Becket and three others appears in the corners of the print of Robert White, *Engravers*[1] opp. p. 92.

The print of Tuer was similarly inserted in the print of Sevonyans, *Anecdotes*[2] iii. opp. p. 136.

by Mr Nesling, Robert Walpole Esquire his chaplaine, on Friday, July 12, 1678.' As Mr Blomefield's book does not take in Houghton,[9] I can't be positive whether Mr Nesling was parson there.[10] If he was not, it is probable that he lived in your family as chaplain, as was common at that time.

I shall be much obliged to you for the print of Lord Herbert, as also for a little part of your potpourri, and I won't forget the MSS, though I wonder, considering the little time you have to spare from your necessary visits and books, that you will throw away any of what is so precious on what is held in low estimation even by, dear Sir,

Your ever obliged and most faithful servant,

WM COLE

From COLE, Sunday 23 September 1764

VA, Forster MS 110, f. 26. Cole kept no copy.

Address: For the Honourable Horatio Walpole Esq. at Strawberry Hill in Twickenham, Middlesex. *Postmark:* F. Stratford 24 SE.

Blecheley, Sept. 23, 1764.

Dear Sir,

THE time drawing near that you was so good to appoint to me to wait on you at Strawberry Hill, viz., the beginning of October, this is to beg the favour of you to know if more towards the middle of the month or third week in October would find you unengaged there. If not, I will wait on you for two or three days in the first week, though not quite so convenient to, dear Sir,

Your ever obliged and faithful servant,

WM COLE

9. *The History of Norfolk,* by Francis Blomefield, 5 vols, Fersfield, Norwich and Lynn, 1739–75. At this time only volumes i, ii, iii (to p. 678) had been published. The account of Houghton appeared in the continuation of vol. 3 by Charles Parkin (1769), iii. 796–801. Only the first three volumes were in HW's library (E.2.13–5). They were sold SH ii. 84.

10. Nesling's name does not appear in the list of rectors at Houghton printed in Blomefield, *Norfolk*[2], vi. 131–3. Nesling was probably Richard Nesling (see *ante* 1 Dec. 1763, n. 16).

To Cole, Tuesday 25 September 1764

Add MS 5952, ff. 33–4.
Address: To the Reverend Mr Cole at Blecheley near Fenny Stratford, Bucks.
Free Hor Walpole. *Postmark:* Isleworth 25 SE.

Strawberry Hill, Sept. 25, 1764.

Dear Sir,

THE third week in October will be just as convenient to me as any other time, and as you choose it, more agreeable, because when you are so obliging to take the trouble of coming so far, I should not be easy, if it laid you under any difficulty. Shall we therefore settle it for the twenty-second or twenty-third of October?

Your ever obliged humble servant,

Hor. Walpole

From Cole, Thursday 18 October 1764

VA, Forster MS 110, f. 27. Cole kept no copy.
Address: For the Honourable Horace Walpole Esq. at Strawberry Hill in Twickenham, Middlesex. *Postmark:* F. Stratford 20 [OC].

Blecheley, Oct. 18, 1764.

Dear Sir,

TO prevent my appearing ruder than my intention, this comes to inform you that it seems to me very doubtful whether I shall be able to fulfil my engagement of waiting on you next week, as a very troublesome sore throat has seized me ever since last Sunday, and though I am a little better today and design to be blooded tomorrow, yet if on Saturday it should not be clear gone, I shall be afraid to venture from home, as I am very apt to catch cold. If I am so lucky to get rid of this ill complaint, I purpose being at Strawberry Hill by three o'clock on Tuesday[1] for two or three days, if I shall not incom-

---

1. 23 Oct. Cole did not make the journey (see the following letters).

mode you, and purpose bringing one of my MS volumes with me, and am in the meantime, dear Sir,

Your ever obedient and most faithful obliged servant,

WM COLE

To COLE, Saturday 20 October 1764

Add MS 5952, f. 36.

Dated on the supposition that HW answered Cole's letter the same day he received it.

[Strawberry Hill, 20 Oct. 1764.]

Dear Sir,

I AM heartily concerned for my disappointment and more for the cause of it. Take care of yourself, and by no means venture catching cold. I shall be equally glad to see you on Tuesday; but I beg you not to come even then, if your throat is not perfectly cured.

Yours most sincerely,

HOR. WALPOLE

To COLE, Saturday 27 October 1764

Add MS 5952, f. 35.

Strawberry Hill, Oct. 27, 1764.

Dear Sir,

THOUGH I am much concerned at not seeing you, I am more so at not hearing from you, as I fear your sore throat has proved more troublesome than you apprehended. Pray write me one line to tell me how you are.

I will not trouble you with more now, but to inclose a sheet,[1] by

1. Not with the MS. It contained HW's account of Cole's ancestor, Herbert Tuer (see following letter).

which I hope you will approve the manner in which I have obeyed you.

Yours most faithfully,

Hor. Walpole

From Cole, Sunday 28 October 1764

VA, Forster MS 110, f. 28. Cole's copy, Add MS 5831, ff. 232v, 233.
Address: For the Honourable Horace Walpole Esq. at Strawberry Hill in Twickenham, Middlesex. *Postmark:* F. Stratford 28 OC.

Blecheley, Oct. 28, 1764.

Dear Sir,

I AM under so many ties and obligations to you that I know not well which to acknowledge first: your kind concern for my health in your two last calls for my sincerest thanks, as your immortalizing my Uncle Herbert Tuer in your volume has gratified both my vanity and parental piety in a very singular degree. Indeed I am greatly obliged to you for giving him so honourable a place in a book which will last as long as taste shall be cultivated among us. Your putting it together is exactly what I could have wished, and the only exception I can find in it is in the equivocal word *procurer,*[1] which in our language bears another meaning from what you intend, and *advocate* perhaps might supply its place if the sheet is not already printed off; if it is, those who understand French will know what it means.

Indeed I have had a very severe trial of my patience in as bad a sore throat as ever I experienced. Thank God, I am now well, but not in a capacity of stirring, as my servant is so much out of order that it would be cruelty to make him ride on horseback; otherwise should have been at Dr Apthorp's at Burnham this week, as one of my sisters, who lives at Bath,[2] is now with him, and leaves him, as I apprehend, in a few days. Yet if she is there next week, and my servant better, I purpose setting out on Monday, 5 November, and stay two or three days with him, and if you'll give me leave, take a dinner

1. HW had written 'Mary Van Gameren, daughter of a procurer of Utrecht.' From HW's reply it would appear that this was a proof sheet, doubtless *Additional Lives to the First Edition of Anecdotes of Painting in England,* 1–4. The fact that there is no MS with HW's letter lends support to this assumption. The printing of the sheet is not mentioned in *Jour. Print. Off.*

2. Jane Cole (1719?–ca 1790), Cole's youngest sister.

with you at Strawberry Hill about Thursday, as I shall be obliged to go through London and be here again on Saturday, and if I should call and not find you at home, I will just give a peep into your gallery and leave a volume of my MSS.

I will just mention an observation I made in my second reading of my Lord Herbert's *Life,* p. 60, where in a note you observe the absurdity of retaining the old usages of the Knighthood of the Bath. In 1552 the ceremonies of the Order of the Garter, being thought superstitious, were revised and altered and a new form prescribed, which was translated out of English into Latin by King Edward himself. The account, which is curious, may be seen in Burnet's *History of the Reformation,*[3] vol. 2, pp. 205–6, and the young King's performance in the appendix, p. 73, of my first edition of that book.

I hope you'll excuse the scrawl, as I am in the greatest hurry, or I should have sent you two or three other remarks on the first volume of *Anecdotes,* but I write in company which came in before I had half wrote my letter, and I am, dear Sir,

Your ever affectionate and most obliged servant,

WM COLE

To COLE, Tuesday 30 October 1764

Add MS 5952, f. 37.

Strawberry Hill, Oct. 30, 1764.

Dear Sir,

I AM rejoiced to hear you are well, but horridly vexed at my own negligence and oversight. Assure yourself I never wrote *procurer,* but procure*ur,* leaving the original term, as I think one seldom gives a just idea by translating titles. If I *castrate* the whole half-sheet, I will not leave it *procurer.*[1]

I am obliged to go to London on Saturday for two or three days,[2]

3. 3 vols, 1679–1715.

———

1. Nevertheless, *procurer* remains in *Anecdotes*[2] and in all later editions, and HW's use of it in this place is quoted by OED, where it appears as the last example of the word's original meaning, advocate.

As the *Additional Lives* were printed in quarto in half sheets these four pages constitute a gathering.

2. HW was in London on Saturday, 3 Nov., to meet Conway (HW to Conway 29 Oct., and to Hertford 1 Nov. 1764).

but have no doubt of being back here before Thursday 8th, and if I am, hope to see you for longer than a dinner. Thank you for your notices; I am sure, say what you will, I am still in your debt for a thousand obliging instances of friendship—and in truth, am willing to be more so, for the communication of your MSS.

Yours most sincerely,

H. WALPOLE

PS. The enclosed trifle[3] is only to fill up the packet.

From COLE, Sunday 4 November 1764

VA, Forster MS 110, ff. 29–30. COLE's copy, Add MS 5831, f. 233.

Blecheley, Nov. 4, 1764.

Dear Sir,

I FIND I must give up my excursion of this season, as my servant is in no condition to be taken out, and I can't well do without him. It is a great mortification to me not to bless my eyes with Strawberry Hill, which used to compose me for the winter in this dreary quarter. I thought it best to mention this, that I might not give the trouble of any waiting for me.

I heartily thank you for that elegant pretty piece of poetry you was so kind to send me in your last. Bonaventure des Periers[1] will be obliged to you for introducing him to so much advantage into our language. Your introduction is elegant beyond expression, and the tale is told in words the most natural and numbers the most harmonious, easy and spirited that can be conceived. I shall never see a magpie but I shall think of

Go, cater where you list.[2]

I am really sorry you should, through your printer's oversight, have

3. *The Magpie and Her Brood, A Fable, from the Tales of Bonaventure des Periers, Valet de Chambre to the Queen of Navarre; Addressed to Miss Hotham.* See following letter. HW wrote the fable 15 Oct., and two days later he printed 200 copies at SH (*Jour. Print. Off.* 13, 46). It was reprinted in *Works* i. 34.

1. Bonaventure Despériers (ca 1490–ca 1544), French satirist, author of *Les nouvelles récréations et joyeux devis*, first printed at Lyons, 1558, from which HW took the fable, *The Magpie and Her Brood*. HW's copy, Lyons, 1561 (K.2.33, changed to I.3) was sold SH iii. 105.
2. The closing line of *The Magpie and Her Brood*.

so much trouble on my account, and yet I can't but say that I am
very glad the word *procurer* will be altered. If it is not already done,
and you still determine to do [it], I should be further obliged to you
to add only that his brother Theophilus, or indeed any of his family,
settled at Cambridge.[3] This is out of my infinite regard and value for
that place. But this is a thing of so little consequence, that if it is already altered, or if not, if you think it better without it, I am and
shall be always equally obliged to you for what is already said and
done.

I will now take the liberty of putting down the three or four notices that I mentioned in a former letter that I observed on a second
perusal of your first volume of *Anecdotes,* though they are of that
little importance that was I not writing and had room, they don't
seem to be worth acquainting you with.

Pp. 12 and 28, Note * *The edition of Matthew Paris in miniatures,* etc. As it is a *MS* you mention, query whether the word *edition*
is proper, though no doubt as a *MS* is put out into the world as a
printed book, for use, it may be very proper, yet as the word *edition*
is in a manner confined to *printed books,* whether the word *copy* is
not more in use.[4]

P. 56. *A° 30 Hen. 8, 1583.* A fault of the printer for *1538.*[5]

P. 75. *Latter* at line 15. Query, if it should not be former,[6] for there
is now at the Archbishop's Palace at Lambeth an excellent original
picture of Archbishop Warham, which I have seen there, a copy of
which is printed by Mr Vertue among the *Illustrious Men's Heads,*
and said to be taken from Holbein's original picture there;[7] also another from the same picture in Dr Knight's *Life of Erasmus,* pp. 82
and 309.[8]

P. 97. *King Henry's religion.*[9] If Torrigiano died in 1522, it was be-

3. HW did not add this (see following
letter).

4. HW changed the first passage to read
'The original copy' (*Anecdotes*[2] i. 13), but
the second (p. 28 note *) remains unchanged in all later editions. The alteration was made independently of Cole's suggestion (see following letter).

5. The mistake stands in *Anecdotes*[2] i.
59, and in *Works* iii. 54. James Dallaway,
in his edition, 5 vols, 1828, i. 108, changed
the date to 1543, an error which has been
followed in later editions.

6. HW changed *latter* to *former* in *Anecdotes*[2] i. 79.

7. See *The Heads of Illustrious Persons
of Great Britain,* by Thomas Birch, 2 vols,
1743–52, i. 7. The portrait was engraved by
Vertue.

8. *The Life of Erasmus,* Cambridge,
1726, by Samuel Knight (1675–1746). Vertue also engraved the portrait of Archbishop Warham for this work (opp. p. 82).

9. Cole's note was occasioned by HW's
account of Pietro Torrigiano, who, after
his visit to England and return to Spain,

fore King Henry had any religious qualms of conscience. They did not appear till 1527, when he was determined to part with Queen Catherine for Anne Bolein, and even long after this he was a good Catholic, till the opposition from Rome made him otherwise.

I hope you'll both excuse these crude observations and a very bad pen from, Sir,

Your most obliged and ever faithful servant,

Wm Cole

I think I mentioned in a former letter[10] that at p. 128, note †, *Sir Thomas Wilson,* though Dean of Durham, was a layman, Doctor of Laws, Secretary of State, yet never *knighted.*

To Cole, Thursday 8 November 1764

Add MS 5952, ff. 38–9.

Address: To the Reverend Mr Cole at Blecheley near Fenny Stratford, Bucks. Free Hor Walpole. *Postmark:* Isleworth 8 NO.

Strawberry Hill, Nov. 8, 1764.

I AM much disappointed, I own, dear Sir, at not seeing you: more so, as I fear it will be long before I shall, for I think of going to Paris early in February.[1] I ought indeed to go directly, as the winter does not agree with me here. Without being positively ill, I am positively not well: about this time of year I have little fevers every night and pains in my breast and stomach, which bid me repair to a more flannel climate. These little complaints are already begun, and as soon as affairs will permit me, I mean to transport them southward.

I am sorry it is out of my power to make the addition you wish to Mr Tuer's article: many of the following sheets are printed off, and there is no inserting anything now, without shoving the whole text forwards, which you see is impossible. You promised to bring me a portrait of him; as I shall have four or five new plates, I can get his

was accused, tried and condemned for heresy. He obtained a respite, but became mad and 'starved himself to death at Seville in 1522.' HW then observed that 'Torreggiano, it seems, with Henry's turbulence of temper, had adopted his religion.' The passage remains unchanged in later editions.

10. See *ante* 2 Feb. 1764.

1. He did not leave for Paris until 9 Sept. 1765 (see *Paris Jour.*).

head into one of them;[2] will you send it as soon as you can possibly to my house in Arlington Street; I will take great care of it, and return it to you safe.

Thank you much for your corrections, though they are too late for my next edition; it is printed to past the middle of the third volume.

Yours most sincerely,

Hor. Walpole

From Cole, Sunday 18 November 1764

VA, Forster MS 110, f. 31. Cole kept no copy.
Address: For the Honourable Horace Walpole Esq. at Strawberry Hill in Twickenham, Middlesex. *Postmark:* F. Stratford 19 NO.

Blecheley, Nov. 18, 1764.

Dear Sir,

HEARING from one of my sisters today that Dr Cock, equally related to Herbert Tuer as myself,[1] had sent you his picture, which I had wrote to her to procure for me of him, I am now to return you my hearty thanks for your last kind letter, intimating your purpose of giving a small head of him, for which I can never think myself sufficiently grateful. The alteration[2] was not material, and it was only love to my old Alma Mater that made me desirous of having it mentioned that he bore any the least relation to her.

I should have wrote before, but waited for this answer, and was unwilling to trouble you continually with my letters. I am vastly concerned at your complaint, and wish you the utmost success a warmer clime may be able to effect. If that does not altogether answer your purpose in respect to the feverish complaint, I am satisfied a season at Bristol[3] would do you infinite service. I speak this experimentally: I

2. See *ante* 2 Sept. 1764 n. 8.

1. John Cock (1715–96), D.D., son of Joseph Cock, a merchant of Cambridge, by Anne Tuer (sister of Cole's mother, Catherine Tuer); rector of Debden, Essex, 1745–96, and of Great Horkesley, Essex, 1761–96 (*Eton Coll. Reg. 1698–1752; Blecheley Diary, passim*).

2. In HW's account of Tuer.

3. The Hot Wells at Bristol were in high repute as a watering place until the last decade of the eighteenth century, when they lost favour because of the exorbitant prices charged (see John Latimer, *The Annals of Bristol in the Eighteenth Century*, privately printed, 1893, pp. 489–90, *et passim*). The scene of part of Fanny Burney's *Evelina* (1778) is laid there.

had a slow hectic fever lurking about me for six or seven years; I drank gallons of Bristol water at Cambridge, but when I came to take them on the spot I immediately found the difference, and on my return was perfectly cured.

I have had a very uneasy affair on my hands this last week which has given me much concern and made me very uneasy. A neighbouring clergyman,[4] to whom I was enabled to give a small chapel as rector of this parish, has taken such liberties and been so abusive, though I never see him or have the least acquaintance with him,[5] that I have been obliged, greatly against my nature and inclination, to have recourse to the Bishop[6] to bring him to some order. But how the matter will turn out, as the Bishop must hear both sides, I know not. I only know that could I have anyways avoided applying to him, I certainly should. But I beg pardon for giving you this trouble: what is uppermost will be intruding itself, though to little purpose, and making this my excuse, I remain, dear Sir,

Your ever obliged and most faithful humble servant,

Wm Cole

To Cole, Thursday 28 February 1765

Add MS 5952, f. 40.

Address: [From Cole's copy, Add MS 5831, f. 210v.] To the Rev. Mr Cole at Blecheley near Fenny Stratford, Bucks. Free Hor Walpole.

Strawberry Hill, Feb. 28, 1765.

Dear Sir,

AS you do not deal with newspapers, nor trouble yourself with the occurrences of modern times, you may perhaps conclude from what I told you and from my silence, that I am in France. This will

4. Ralph Leicester or Leycester (1738–1803) of White Place, Berks; Exeter College, Oxford (B.A. 1759); curate of Simpson, Bucks, before Cole appointed him curate of Fenny Stratford, 1761 (see *Eton Coll. Reg. 1698–1752;* George Lipscomb, *The History and Antiquities of the County of Buckingham,* 4 vols, 1847, iv. 37). Cole gives an account of his difficulties with Leycester in *Blecheley Diary* 100–1, *et passim.*

5. Cole presented Leycester to the curacy against his own judgment 'out of regard and friendship to his [Leycester's] wife's relations' (*Blecheley Diary* 101). Leycester's wife was Susanna Hanmer, sister of Sir Walden Hanmer, 1st Bt.

6. John Green (1706?–79), Bp of Lincoln 1761–79. It appears from *Blecheley Diary* that Cole had a poor opinion of him.

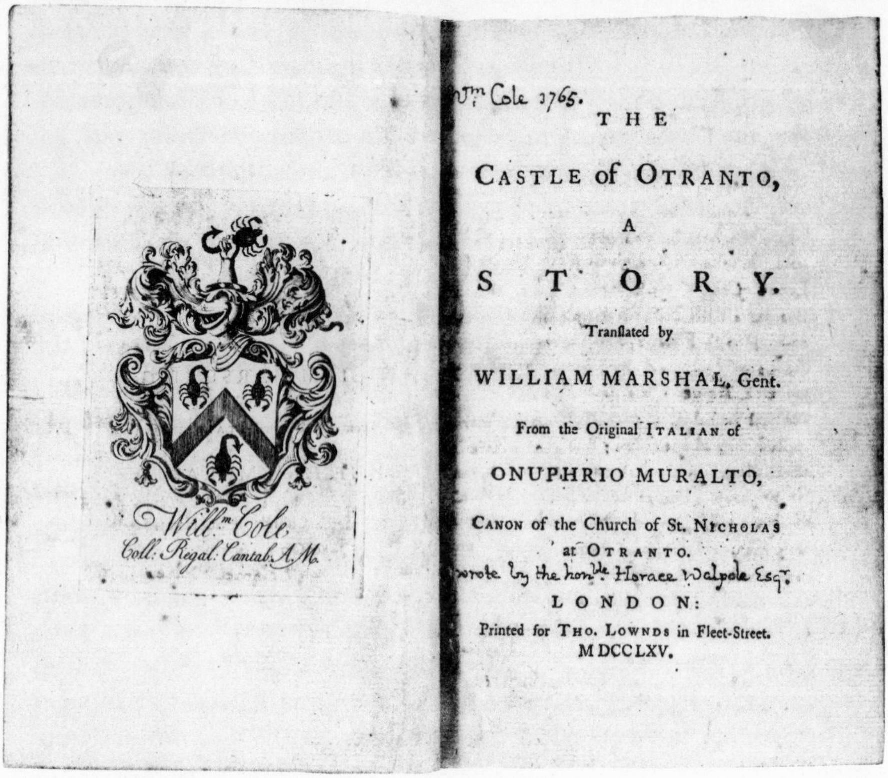

Will.m Cole
Coll: Regal: Cantab: A.M.

Wm Cole 1765.

THE
CASTLE of OTRANTO,
A
STORY.
Translated by
WILLIAM MARSHAL, Gent.
From the Original ITALIAN of
ONUPHRIO MURALTO,
CANON of the Church of St. NICHOLAS
at OTRANTO.
wrote by the honble Horace Walpole Esqr.
LONDON:
Printed for THO. LOWNDS in Fleet-Street.
MDCCLXV.

COLE'S COPY OF "THE CASTLE OF OTRANTO"

tell you that I am not, though I have been long thinking of it and still intend it, though not exactly yet. My silence I must lay upon this uncertainty, and from having been much out of order above a month with a very bad cold and cough, for which I am come hither to try change of air. Your brother Apthorpe, who was so good as to call on me about a fortnight ago in town, found me too hoarse almost to speak to him. We both asked one another the same question, news of you? You have I hope got rid of all trouble from your impertinent neighbour, and reverted to the tranquillity you love.

I have for some time had the pictures from Dr Cock, and shall have the one engraved that I conclude your ancestor, though there seem to be no very accurate marks to specify it.

I have lately had an accession to my territory here, by the death of good old Frankland[1] to whom I had given for his life the lease of the cottage and garden 'cross the road. Besides a little pleasure in planting and in crowding it with flowers, I intend to make what I am sure you are antiquarian enough to approve, a bower,[2] though your friends the abbots did not indulge in such retreats, at least not under that appellation; but though we love the same ages, you must excuse worldly me for preferring the romantic scenes of antiquity. If you will tell me how to send it, and are partial enough to me to read a profane work in the style of former centuries, I shall convey to you a little story-book, which I published some time ago, though not boldly with my own name; but it has succeeded so well, that I do not any longer entirely keep the secret: does the title, *The Castle of Otranto*,[3] tempt you?

I shall be glad to hear you are well and happy, and am

Ever yours,

H. WALPOLE

Pray direct your answer to Arlington Street.

1. Richard Francklin, printer of *The Craftsman,* the opposition paper to Sir Robert Walpole. He became HW's tenant about 1753 (see HW to Mann 27 April 1753). He died 1 Feb. 1765 (Musgrave, *Obituary*).

2. The 'Bower' was a two-room brick cottage which was erected on the site of the old one, formerly occupied by Francklin. It was not entirely completed until

1776 (*SH Accounts* 11, 130–1; 'Genesis of SH' 87–8).

3. The first and second editions (500 copies each) were published 24 Dec. 1764 and 11 April 1765 ('Short Notes'). Cole's copy of the first edition (the one mentioned here) is now wsl. Cole transcribed upon the flyleaves this part of HW's letter and that part of the succeeding one, 9 March 1765, which relates to the story.

From COLE, Sunday 3 March 1765

VA, Forster MS 110, f. 32. COLE's copy, Add MS 5831, ff. 210v, 211v.

Address: For the Honourable Horace Walpole Esq. in Arlington Street, Westminster. *Postmark:* F. Stratford 4 MR.

Blecheley, March 3, 1765.

Dearest Sir,

THE favour of yours of February 28 I received on Friday, and had the post gone out sooner than today, should have thanked you for the contents of it, so great is my impatience to see the enchantments of *The Castle of Otranto.* I have wrote by this day's post to a friend in town[1] to send a porter to your house in Arlington Street for the packet, and hope by the latter end of the week to be among my admired friends of the twelfth or thirteenth century. Indeed you judge very right concerning my indifference about what is going forward in the world, where I live in it as though I was no way concerned about it except in paying, with my contemporaries, the usual taxes and impositions. In good truth I am very indifferent about my Lord Bute or Mr Pitt, as I have long been convinced and satisfied in my own mind that all oppositions are from the ins and the outs,[2] and that power and wealth and dignity are the things struggled for, not the good of the whole. You led me to this declaration, and I hope what I have said will not be offensive.

I am sincerely sorry to hear of your cough and cold, and hope by this time care, warmth and change of air have set you to rights again. I hope you know me too well to think that I could be so self-interested even to wish you a pain in your little finger that I might be benefited by it: yet if change of air would be of use to you, I know none better than this place enjoys. How happy would it make me to see you here for one, two or three days! You have been pleased to say you have been entertained with my rubbish: here are forty volumes all at your service, and no one's else in the world. Would not a retreat for two or three days in Lent, according to the custom of the venerable as well as romantic inhabitants of those ages we both are in love with, be of service? Here is nothing to tempt you to such a retreat but what I have mentioned, a well-aired bed, warm fires, no company and a most hearty welcome.

1. Probably James or Nathaniel Cartwright.

2. 'and never more than in the present case' (addition in Cole's copy).

I have been so busied in writing and reading all this winter, in my way, that I have not had time to examine a budget of old MSS sent me out of Cheshire[3] some months ago. Indeed the bad hand they are wrote in discouraged me. There is a very long account of the trial of Queen Elizabeth's Earl of Essex: if it is not printed in the *State Trials*,[4] which I know nothing of, it may be worth your perusal, and if you can inform me whether it is there or not and whether you would choose to see it, I will transcribe it for you or send you the original, which is very long.

I am glad you are going to amuse yourself in your bower, which I can easily conceive will be perfect in its kind, though I have not fancy or taste enough to form the plan of it. This will, however, be a means of keeping you in England, and will both amuse and do you good. I hope for the pleasure of visiting it sometime in the summer when you are most at leisure.

I ardently long for a retreat in some of the cheap and colder provinces of France, and only dread the trouble of a removal, and search after one. I had thoughts of going into France for a month this summer on that errand, and may probably still put them in execution. I heartily wish you a good journey to Paris whenever you set forward, and as safe a return. I am going a long journey as soon as Easter is over into Cheshire and to visit a few places in North Wales with the gentleman I am going to into Cheshire, who has long expected me and whom I have often disappointed.[5]

The picture which Dr Cock had of my ancestors I hardly remember, but I think my great-uncle Herbert Tuer is a small picture with a flowing robe about him, whereas my great-grandfather and his wife[6] are in the dress of their times, he in a soldier's coat and buff scarf over his shoulders, and she in a little black hood: this I mention as you say you can't well distinguish them.

But I will tire you no further, and wishing you every contentment, I am, dear Sir,

Your ever affectionate and faithful servant,

WM COLE

3. Probably by John Allen.
4. It had been printed there (see following letter).
5. Cole's plans did not materialize (see *post* 3 Sept. 1765). 'The gentleman' was John Allen. At this time Cole also had

plans of going to France in the winter of this year (*Blecheley Diary* 25, 47).
6. Theophilus Tuer (fl. 1625) and his wife Catherine (fl. 1625). See *ante* 2 Sept. 1764.

To Cole, Saturday 9 March 1765

Add MS 5952, ff. 41–2.
Address: [From Cole's copy, Add MS 5831, f. 211v.] To the Rev. Mr Cole at Blecheley near Fenny Stratford, Bucks. Free Hor Walpole.

Strawberry Hill, March 9, 1765.

Dear Sir,

I HAD time to write but a short note[1] with *The Castle of Otranto*, as your messenger called on me at four o'clock as I was going to dine abroad. Your partiality to me and Strawberry have I hope inclined you to excuse the wildness of the story. You will even have found some traits to put you in mind of this place. When you read of the picture quitting its panel,[2] did not you recollect the portrait of Lord Falkland[3] all in white in my gallery? Shall I even confess to you what was the origin of this romance? I waked one morning in the beginning of last June from a dream, of which all I could recover was, that I had thought myself in an ancient castle (a very natural dream for a head filled like mine with Gothic story) and that on the uppermost bannister of a great staircase I saw a gigantic hand in armour. In the evening I sat down and began to write, without knowing in the least what I intended to say or relate. The work grew on my hands, and I grew fond of it—add that I was very glad to think of anything rather than politics—In short I was so engrossed with my tale, which I completed in less than two months, that one evening I wrote from the time I had drunk my tea, about six o'clock, till half an hour after one in the morning, when my hand and fingers were so weary, that I could not hold the pen to finish the sentence, but left Matilda and Isabella talking, in the middle of a paragraph. You will laugh at my earnestness, but if I have amused you by retracing with any fidelity the manners of ancient days, I am content, and give you leave to think me as idle as you please.

You are, as you have long been to me, exceedingly kind, and I

1. Missing.
2. See *The Castle of Otranto*, Ch. I (*Works* ii. 21).
3. Sir Henry Cary (d. 1633), 1st Vct Falkland, Lord Deputy of Ireland 1622–9. The portrait, by VanSomer, is mentioned in *Description of SH, Works* ii. 466, where HW says that 'the idea of the picture walking out of its frame in *The Castle of Otranto*, was suggested by this portrait.' It was sold SH xxi. 99 to J. Tollemache, Esq., of Helmingham Hall, Suffolk, and was drawn by G. P. Harding and engraved by J. Brown for *Ancient Historical Pictures*, 1844.

should with great satisfaction embrace your offer of visiting the solitude of Blecheley, though my cold is in a manner gone and my cough quite, if I was at liberty: but as I am preparing for my French journey, I have forty businesses upon my hands, and can only now and then purloin a day or half a day to come hither. You know I am not cordially disposed to *your* French journey, which is much more serious, as it is to be much more lasting. However, though I may suffer by your absence, I would not dissuade what may suit your inclination and circumstances. One thing however has struck me which I must mention, though it would depend on a circumstance that would give me the most real concern. It was suggested to me by that great fondness I have for your MSS for your kindness about which I feel the utmost gratitude. You would not, I think, leave them behind you; and are you aware of the danger they would run if you settled entirely in France? Do you know that the King of France is heir to all strangers who die in his dominions, by what they call the *droit d'aubaine?*[4] Sometimes by great interest and favour persons have obtained a remission of this right in their lifetime; and yet that, even that, has not secured their effects from being embezzled. Old Lady Sandwich[5] had obtained this remission, and yet, though she left everything to the present Lord,[6] her grandson, a man for whose rank one should have thought they would have had regard, the King's officers forced themselves into her house, after her death, and plundered. You see, if you go, I shall expect to have your MSS deposited with me—seriously, you must leave them in safe custody behind you.

Lord Essex's trial is printed with the *State Trials.*[7] In return for your obliging offer, I can acquaint you with a delightful publication of this winter, a collection of old ballads and poetry in three volumes,[8] many from Pepys's collection at Cambridge. There were three

4. *'Vide* Sir Leoline Jenkins's *Life,* vol. 2, pp. 663–4, for *droit d'aubaine'* (Cole's note on his copy of HW's letter, Add MS 5831, f. 212v). A right claimed by French kings, in default of treaty to the contrary, to the property of any alien who died in their country. It was abolished in 1790, re-established by Napoleon I, and finally annulled in 1819.

5. Elizabeth Wilmot, m. (c. 1689) Edward Montagu (1670?–1729), 3d E. of Sandwich, after whose death she resided in Paris, where she died 2 July 1757 in the Rue Vaugirard.

6. John Montagu (1718–92), 4th E. of Sandwich; 'Jemmy Twitcher.'

7. The trial of the Earl of Essex appears in *A Complete Collection of State Trials,* 4 vols, 1719, i. 164–73. HW's edition, 7 vols 8vo, 1720 (I.6.11–17), was sold SH iii. 86. It is now WSL. Essex's trial is at i. 99–106.

8. Percy's *Reliques of Ancient English Poetry,* 1765. HW's copy was sold SH v. 141, and another edition, 3 vols, 1767 (I.8), was sold SH v. 240. The latter is now WSL.

such published between thirty and forty years ago,[9] but very care-
lessly, and wanting many in this set: indeed there were others, of a
looser sort, which the present editor, who is a clergyman,[10] thought it
decent to omit.

When you go into Cheshire and upon your ramble, may I trouble
you with a commission, but about which you must promise me not to
go a step out of your way. Mr Bateman[11] has a cloister at Old Windsor furnished with ancient wooden chairs, most of them triangular,
but all of various patterns, and carved or turned in the most uncouth
and whimsical forms. He picked them up one by one, for two, three,
five or six shillings apiece from different farmhouses in Herefordshire.[12] I have long envied and coveted them.[13] There may be such in
poor cottages in so neighbouring a county as Cheshire. I should not
grudge any expense for purchase or carriage; and should be glad even
of a couple such for my cloister here. When you are copying inscriptions in a churchyard in any village, think of me, and step into the
first cottage you see—but don't take farther trouble than that. I long
to know what your bundle of MSS from Cheshire contains.

My bower is determined, but not at all what it is to be. Though I
write romances, I cannot tell how to build all that belongs to them.
Madame Danois[14] in the fairy tales used to tapestry them with jonquils, but as that furniture will not last above a fortnight in the year,
I shall prefer something more huckaback. I have decided that the outside shall be treillage, which however I shall not commence, till I
have again seen some of old Louis's old-fashioned *galanteries* at Ver-

9. *A Collection of Old Ballads, corrected
from the best and most ancient copies extant.* [Collected by Ambrose Philips.] 3
vols, 1723–5; 2d edn 1726–38.

10. Thomas Percy (1729–1811), Bp of
Dromore, 1782–1811.

11. Richard Bateman (ca 1705–73), 3d son
of Sir James Bateman, Kt, and brother of
William, 1st Vct Bateman (Le Neve,
Knights 463). HW boasted that he 'converted Dicky Bateman from a Chinese to
a Goth. Though he was the founder of the
Sharawadgi taste in England, I preached so
effectually that his every pagoda took the
veil' (HW to Strafford 13 June 1781). For
an account of Bateman's house and collection, see Thomas Eustace Harwood, *Windsor Old and New*, 1929, pp. 313–34.

12. Cf. HW to Montagu 20 Aug. 1761.
Apparently neither Cole nor Montagu succeeded in the search.

13. Ten years later HW bought at Bateman's sale, 'eight very ancient Welsh
chairs, turned, and four stands' (*Description of SH, Works* ii. 506; HW to Lady Ossory 3 Aug. 1775). Four of these chairs and
one of the stands were sold SH xvii. 114.
Two other chairs purchased at Bateman's
sale were in the Star Chamber, but they
were of a different style. HW apparently
paid £31.10.7 for the ten chairs (*SH Accounts* 15, 162–3). [See illustration.]

14. Marie-Catherine-Jumelle de Berne-
ville (d. 1705), Comtesse d'Aulnoy. HW's
copy of her *Tales of the Fairies*, 3 vols,
1721 (I.9.7–9), was sold SH iii. 73.

BATEMAN'S CHAIRS IN THE GREAT CLOISTER
STRAWBERRY HILL

sailles.[15] Rosamond's bower,[16] you and I and Tom Hearne know was a labyrinth, but as my territory will admit of a very short clue, I lay aside all thoughts of a mazy habitation; though a bower is very different from an arbour, and must have more chambers than one. In short, I both know and don't know what it should be. I am almost afraid I must go and read Spenser, and wade through his allegories and drawling stanzas to get at a picture—but goodnight; you see how one gossips, when one is alone and at quiet on one's own dunghill!— Well! it may be trifling, yet it is such trifling as Ambition never is happy enough to know! Ambition orders palaces, but it is Content that chats for a page or two over a bower.

Yours ever,

H. Walpole

From Cole, Sunday 17 March 1765

VA, Forster MS 110, ff. 33–4. Cole's copy, Add MS 5831, ff. 213v, 214v.
Address: For the Honourable Horace Walpole Esq. in Arlington Street, Westminster. *Postmark:* F. Stratford.

Blecheley, March 17, 1765.

Dear Sir,

I AM to thank you for a double favour: first, in sending me your book,[1] and then for your kind letter which soon followed it; for both the one and the other you have my heartiest thanks, and though your book gave me the utmost entertainment and called many pleasing scenes at Strawberry Hill to my remembrance,[2] yet your letter was so warmly expressive of the kindest sentiments in respect to my welfare, that I can't express half my gratitude.

I was aware of the inconvenience you mention, but apprehend that

---

15. HW did not use treillage (see illustration *Works* ii. opp. 509).

16. Rosamund Clifford (d. 1176?), mistress of Henry II, lived in 'an howse of a wonder workynge, so that noo creature, man nor woman, myght wyn to her, but if he were instructe by the kynge, or suche as were ryght secret wt hym, touchynge yt mater. This house, after some wryters, was named, labor intus [Labyrinthus], or Deladus [Dedalus] werke, or howse, which is to mean, after moost exposytours, an howse wrought lyke unto a knot in a garden, called a mase [maze]' (Robert Fabyan, *New Chronicles of England and France,* ed. Henry Ellis, 1811, p. 277).

---

1. *The Castle of Otranto.*

2. SH was the setting of much of *The Castle of Otranto* (see HW to du Deffand 27 Jan. 1775).

purchasing a little farm or retreat would take away the horrid and inhospitable law, and make the *droit d'aubaine* of no effect, as by that means you become an inhabitant and no stranger. I should be glad to be certainly informed about that circumstance, for I am sure I would never think of living there on any other condition: for though you are so kind as to speak of my MSS with more kindness than they deserve, yet few, I suppose, would treat them with that indulgence. As to myself, they are my only delight; they are my wife and children; they have been, in short, my whole employ and amusement for these twenty or thirty years, and though I really and sincerely think the greatest part of them stuff and trash, and deserve no other treatment than the fire, yet the collections which I have made towards an history of Cambridgeshire, the chief point in view of them, with an oblique or transient view of an *Athenae Cantabrigienses,* will be of singular use to anyone who will have more patience and perseverance than I am master of, to put the materials together. These therefore I should be much concerned should fall into the hands of the French King's officers, and from your kind hint shall give myself some trouble to find out whether, on my removal to any part of his dominions, my children will be in safety after my decease. Excuse all this long scribble about so uninteresting a subject.

I, who know your facility and ease in composing, am not so much surprised at the shortness of the time you completed your volume in, as at the insight you have expressed in the nature and language, both of the male and female domestics. Their dialogues, especially the latter, are inimitable and very Nature itself.[3]

I am [glad] Lord Essex's trial is printed, because the MS is so long and so wretchedly wrote. If you have the least desire to see the other Cheshire MSS which came with it, which are wrote as badly, I will send them and you may return them at your leisure. A great deal is poetry of the time of King Charles I. From what you have said of the late three volumes of old ballads, I shall send for them: that called 'The Lye'[4] is among the old MSS out of Cheshire.

3. Cole, desiring to please, probably took his cue from a paragraph of HW's Preface in which he defends the use of the domestics, but Cole was forthright in criticism and his praise was doubtless sincere. His letter must have reached HW as HW was writing his 'Preface to the Second Edition' and may well have encouraged him to enlarge upon the conduct of the domestics and to bring in Shakespeare as his model. 'My rule was nature,' he wrote; 'That great master of nature, *Shakespeare,* was the model I copied.'

4. By Sir Walter Raleigh (1552?–1618). It was included in Percy's *Reliques,* 1765 (ed. H. B. Wheatley, 1876, ii. 297–300).

You may depend upon my best endeavours after the chairs you mention. I know the sort that will please you, as I have seen those at Mr Bateman's and much admired them. I will be as inquisitive as I can, and wish I may be as successful. I suppose, as your bower is to contain more rooms than one, other old furniture would be agreeable: I remember in this parish, having occasion some seven or eight years ago, to visit a sick person, I took particular notice of a very old-fashioned wooden chest in which the family kept their provisions, a sort of original buffet with folding doors, about four or five feet high. I don't know whether the man would part with it, as he has some property, but if he would, and it would come cheap, I think it would be very suitable to your design. Here are many old oaken chairs of a very clumsy, heavy fashion, but that sort I don't think would please you. The sort at Old Windsor are light, whimsical and sufficiently old-fashioned, and I wish I may be lucky enough to meet with any. But I am obliged by the bell[5] to finish this long epistle, and if I hear not from you before you leave England, I heartily wish you a most agreeable and happy journey and return, and am, dear Sir,

Your ever obliged servant,

WM COLE

Shall I beg the favour of you to frank me the two enclosed letters. My sister's is sealed with my coat of arms.

To Mr Phillips at Spetchley near Worcester.[6]

To Mrs Cole[7] at Mrs Ansty's in Stall Street, Bath.

From COLE, Tuesday 3 September 1765

VA, Forster MS 110, ff. 35–6. COLE's copy, Add MS 5831, ff. 214v, 215v.

Address: For the Honourable Horace Walpole Esq. at Strawberry Hill in Twickenham, Middlesex. *Postmark:* [F. Stratford.] 4 SE.

Blecheley, Sept. 3, 1765.

Dear Sir,

I SEE so few people who are conversant in the world, and know so little what is going forward in it, that was it not for a weekly coun-

5. The church bell. Cole wrote many of his letters on Sunday.

6. Cole's copy reads, 'To Mr Tho. Phil-

lips at Mr Berkeley's at Spetchley near Worcester.'

7. Cole's copy reads, 'Mrs Jane Cole.'

try newspaper[1] I should be totally ignorant of its concerns. Some weeks ago I was alarmed by one of them of your having a dangerous fit of the gout,[2] and had it not been for that, I should have concluded that you had spent some part of this summer in France, according to your design in the spring. I was loath to add to your trouble anything which would increase it, for I concluded that your innate goodness of heart and great civility would force you to answer my letter, though it might be inconvenient and uneasy to you: but an article in my last Cambridge paper, that you was setting out for the south of France for the recovery of your health[3] obliges me to give you this trouble in wishing you from my heart the utmost that a good air can do for you, if it is in fact that you are in quest of it, for the common prints are so stuffed with falsities that I don't much regard them, and I pray God this may be one of that sort.

I had an opportunity about a month ago to see at a clergyman's house in Bedfordshire a very ancient and noble piece of furniture which I think would[4] suit you. It is a large cabinet of ebony, almost wholly plated over both withinside and out with embossed silver; the drawers in the inside are painted with stories from Ovid's *Metamorphosis,* and is in pretty good preservation considering that it is an old family relic of many generations. I hope, after your return from France, that you will either give a look at it yourself or commission me to purchase it for you.[5]

Various accidents have prevented my going into Cheshire[6] this year. I was to have set out on Saturday was sevennight, when one of my horses fell ill the evening before, and is yet very ill.

I am almost determined myself to set out for Paris, which I never saw, and have a great curiosity to see it, about October 16 and 18[7] and

---

1. *The Cambridge Chronicle* (see *Blecheley Diary, passim*).

2. 'The Hon. Horatio Walpole lies dangerously ill of the gout, at his house in Arlington Street, St. James's' (*The London Chronicle* 4–6 July 1765). Evidently this notice, or a similar one, was copied into *The Cambridge Chronicle,* probably for the following week.

3. 'We hear that the Hon. Horatio Walpole will speedily set out for the South of France for the recovery of his health' (*The London Chronicle* 24–7 Aug. 1765; *Lloyd's Evening Post* 26–8 Aug. 1765). The notice

in *The Cambridge Chronicle* was probably in the same words.

4. 'not disgrace your Bishop's chamber' (addition in Cole's copy). Cole refers to the Holbein Chamber, which was furnished with ebony chairs and tables.

5. 'for it would as well become your elegant house as it is ill suited to its present situation' (addition in Cole's copy).

6. Cole's copy reads: 'Various accidents have prevented my journey three times this year into Cheshire.'

7. That is, probably, to leave Bletchley the 16th, and Dover the 18th.

to stay about a month. If you should happen to be there at that time I should think myself fortunate, but I will trouble you no more at present, but with wishing you a most prosperous journey and every circumstance that can contribute to your health and felicity, I remain, dear Sir,

Your ever affectionate, faithful and most obliged servant,

WM COLE

To COLE, Thursday 5 September 1765

Add MS 5952, f. 43.

Address: [From COLE's copy, Add MS 5831, f. 215v.] To the Rev. Mr Cole at Blecheley near Fenny Stratford, Bucks. Free Hor Walpole.
Postmark: [From COLE's copy.] Isleworth 6 SE.

Strawberry Hill, Sept. 5, 1765.

Dear Sir,

YOU cannot think how agreeable your letter was to me, and how luckily it was timed. I thought you in Cheshire and did not know how to direct; I now sit down to answer it instantly.

I have been extremely ill indeed with the gout all over, in head, stomach, both feet, both wrists and both shoulders. I kept my bed a fortnight in the most sultry part of this summer, and for nine weeks could not say I was recovered. Though I am still weak and very soon tired with the least walk, I am in other respects quite well. However to promote my entire re-establishment, I shall set out for Paris next Monday.[1] Thus your letter came luckily. To hear you talk of going thither too, made it most agreeable. Why should not you advance your journey? Why defer it till the winter is coming on? It would make me quite happy to visit churches and convents with you; but they are not comfortable in cold weather. Do, I beseech you, follow me as soon as possible. The thought of your being there at the same time makes me much more pleased with my journey; you will not I hope like it the less; and if our meeting there should tempt you to stay longer, it will make me still more happy. If in the meantime I

1. He left London for Paris as he planned, Monday 9 Sept. ('Short Notes'; *Paris Jour.*).

can be of any use to you, I shall be glad, either in taking a lodging for you, or anything else. Let me know, and direct to me in Arlington Street, whence my servant[2] will convey it to me. Tell me above all things that you will set out sooner.

If I have any money left when I return, and can find a place for it, I shall be very glad to purchase the ebony cabinet you mention,[3] and will make it a visit with you next summer if you please—but first let us go to Paris. I don't give up my passion for ebony; but since the destruction of the Jesuits,[4] I hear one can pick up so many of their spoils, that I am impatient for the opportunity.

I must finish, as I have so much business before I set out; but I must repeat how lucky the arrival of your letter was, how glad I was to hear of your intended journey, and how much I wish it may take place directly. I will only add, that the court goes to Fontainbleau the last week in September, or first in October, and therefore it is the season in the world for seeing *all* Versailles quietly and at one's ease, Adieu! Dear Sir.

Yours most cordially,

HOR. WALPOLE

From COLE, Wednesday 11 September 1765

VA, Forster MS 110, ff. 37–8. COLE's copy, Add MS 5831, ff. 216v, 217v.

Address: For the Honourable Horace Walpole Esq. in Arlington Street, London.
Postmark: [F. Stratford.] 13 SE.

Blecheley, Sept. 11, 1765.

Dear Sir,

AFTER my most hearty thanks for the most kind and obliging letter in the world, I hope I may now congratulate you upon your safe arrival at Paris after an agreeable and pleasant journey, for the weather was as favourable as possible, and it mortifies me not a little

---

2. Favre, HW's Swiss servant, who was left in charge of the house in Arlington Street during HW's absence (HW to Grosvenor Bedford 5 Sept. 1765).

3. Apparently HW did not purchase it. HW notes in his 'Book of Materials, 1759' (now Folger Library), p. 230: 'Mr Willet at Brentford Butts told me, Sept. 5, 1765, of an old gent. there that has two ebony

chairs and a table that he would sell; Mr Cole, of an ebony cabinet in Bedfordshire to be sold.'

4. The French Parliament (6 Aug. 1762) decreed the abolition of the Society of Jesus, secularized its members and confiscated its property, and a royal edict (26 Nov. 1764) confirmed the suppression.

to think that it may [be] totally altered by the time I shall be enabled to set forward, which, as I am so exceeding fortunate to hope to find you there, will be in about three weeks. Sooner I certainly would come, for many reasons, was it possible: the chief bar to my journey is that one of my tenants who owes me two years' rent is now selling an estate to pay me and some other creditors. Though I went into the Isle of Ely about six weeks ago upon this affair, and was then assured it was upon the point of being finished,[1] yet the two last Cambridge papers have had advertisements that it is still upon sale. I wrote to the lawyer a post before I had your most obliging letter to put him in mind of his promise on my not troubling his client some months before, and hope to have his answer and see this affair finished in some way or <other> in a very short time.

As you are so good as to offer me your assistance in getting me a lodging, etc., at Paris, I will beg the favour of you to know if it is convenient for you to let me deposit an hundred pounds in your banker's hands in London and receive it at Paris, as I shall allow myself that sum for my journey and a few things I may purchase. If this would be agreeable, I shall be much obliged to you to let me know as much, and where it is I may find him, as also your dwelling in Paris when I get there. I think I had not better trouble you to provide me lodgings, as I shall come to some English hotel, and finding you out, may either take lodgings or continue at the inn,[2] as shall be convenient, for I am afraid of the expense of too elegant lodgings, and shall be sorry to be at a distance from you. I look upon it as the most lucky circumstance that could have happened that your going to Paris should tally so fortunately with my journey thither, and am chagrined to the greatest degree that this affair, which was promised to be finished four months ago, should be so unluckily protracted to this time.

A short letter to me to tell me that you have a good and safe journey, that you continue well, and that you remove not from Paris before I get there, will be adding to the numberless obligations you have conferred upon and give the greatest satisfaction to, dear Sir,

Your most faithful and most obliged servant,

WM COLE

1. 'by another of my tenants making the purchase' (addition in Cole's copy).

2. See *post* 31 Oct. 1765.

To Cole, Wednesday 18 September 1765

Add MS 5952, f. 44.

Cole dated the letter in full in his copy, Add MS 5831, ff. 217v, 218v.

Address: [From Cole's copy.] To the Rev. Mr Cole at Blecheley near Fenny Stratford, Bucks. Free Hor Walpole.

Postmark: [From Cole's copy.] P. 24 SE.

Paris, Wednesday, Sept. 18, [1765.]

Dear Sir,

I HAVE this moment received your letter, and as a courier is just setting out, I had rather take the opportunity of writing you a short letter, than defer it for a longer.

I had a very good passage and pleasant journey, and find myself surprisingly recovered for the time. Thank you for the good news you tell me of your coming: it gives me great joy. To the end of this week I shall be in Lord Hertford's house, so have not yet got lodging: but when I do, you will easily find me. I have no banker,[1] but credit on a merchant[2] who is a private friend of Lord Hertford, consequently I cannot give you credit on him; but you shall have the use of my credit, which will be the same thing, and we can settle our accounts together. I brought about £100 with me as I would advise you to do. Guineas you may change into louis or French crowns at Calais and Boulogne, and even small bank-bills will be taken here. In any shape I will assist you. Be careful on the road. My portmanteau with part of my linen was stolen from before my chaise at noon while I went to see Chantilly.[3] If you stir out of your room, lock the door of it in the inn, or leave your man in it.

If you arrive near the time you propose, you will find me here and I hope much longer.

Yours ever,

Hor. Walpole

1. But HW calls Robert Ralph Foley (1727?–82), Bt cr. 1767, the English banker at Paris (see *Letters of Laurence Sterne,* ed. L. P. Curtis, Oxford, 1935, p. 153, n. 16) 'my banker' (HW to Mann 27 Aug. 1765, and to Brand 19 Oct. 1765), and received letters through him (HW to Lady Suffolk 20 Sept. 1765).

2. It is probable that HW refers to Foley; 'merchant' and 'banker' were loosely used in the eighteenth century.

3. 'Here the Prince of Condé has a most magnificent palace, gardens and stables: but as Mr Walpole in going to Paris, while he went to look at these things had his portmanteau taken off from before his

From Cole, Thursday 31 October 1765

VA, Forster MS 110, f. 39. Cole kept no copy.

Cole reached Paris 24 Oct. 1765, and obtained lodgings at the Hôtel d'Orléans in the Rue des Petits Augustins, near the Hôtel du Parc Royal (in the Rue de Colombier), where HW lodged after he left Lord Hertford's. Their hotels were 'so contiguous, that I could see into the courtyard of his hotel, and see when his coach was going out with him, from a back window of my own' (Cole, *Jour. to Paris* 53). They frequently dined and visited places of interest together.

Cole records that on 31 Oct. there was a 'Great Fog.' He wrote several letters, had his measure taken for a French peruke, and was solicited for alms by a Capuchin friar. 'I excused myself from dining with Mr Walpole this day; and enjoyed myself by not stirring out anywhere' (Cole, *Jour. to Paris* 145–6).

Address: For the Honourable Mr Walpole.

[Paris,] October 31, 1765.

MR COLE presents his compliments to Mr Walpole, and begs the favour of him to excuse Mr Cole's waiting on him today, as he finds himself indisposed to go out, but will wait on him either tomorrow or Saturday. Mr Cole has sent the paper,[1] and if Mr Walpole has anything else of the same sort to employ him about, Mr Cole will readily undertake it, as he don't purpose stirring out.

From Cole, Sunday 5 January 1766

VA, Forster MS 110, ff. 40–1. Cole's copy, Add MS 5831, ff. 218v, 197v, 198v.

Although Cole's copy of this letter shows the address as given below, it is probable that Cole addressed the original to Arlington Street, and that Favre forwarded it to HW at Paris (see *post* 11 Feb. 1766).

Address: [From Cole's copy.] A Monsieur Monsieur Walpole à l'Hotel du Parc Royal, Rue Colombier, Fauxbourg St Germaine à Paris.

Blecheley, Jan. 5, 1766.

Dear Sir,

NO doubt you will wonder that you receive not a letter from me before this, both as you was so kind as to desire me to write, as in acknowledgment for the many civilities I received at your hands

chaise, with all his linen and wearing apparel in it . . . I determined not to go there at all' (Cole, *Jour. to Paris* 328).

---

1. Probably an 'inflammatory speech,'

'Extrait d'un discours de Monsieur de Castillon, avocat général du parlement d'Aix, prononcé pour la rentrée du Parlement le 1er Octobre 1765,' which HW lent to Cole 26 Oct. 1765 in order that Cole

while I stayed at Paris. The truth is, I was loath to give you that pain
and uneasiness I know I should have occasioned you had I wrote to
you sooner, for in getting out of the ship in the dark in a very rough
sea into the long-boat, which was to convey about thirty or forty of
us ashore, about a league at sea to Dover, the boat dashed against one
of my feet[1] and gave me such a jar as took away the use of my leg
when I landed on the shore, where with the utmost difficulty and
pain, and with two people to help me, I got to near the town; but
then falling down and almost fainting, I wrenched my knee to such a
degree that I was forced to be carried to the inn in a chair and put to
bed, where I laid, without being able to get out of it or turn myself
in it, just three weeks, at the end of which I was able to get up for
two or three hours in a day, and after just a month's confinement at
Dover I hired a post-coach and four horses and reached home in five
days very easily and comfortably, and can now walk without a crutch
tolerably well: so that I hope in a few weeks, with patience and
warmer weather, I shall be as well as before.

After this long detail, I will give you an account of your commissions. As you told me that you would be glad to have your letters put
into your servant's hands[2] as soon as possible, I thought it best, as I
foresaw I should be detained at Dover for some time, and as the
packet was too big for the post, to beg the favour of my Lord St
George,[3] who came over in the same ship with me, to put it into the
Penny Post when he came to London or to let his servant deliver it to
yours in Arlington Street. Accordingly I wrote a line to his Lordship
the next morning and sent it by my servant, whom he very obligingly
assured that he would take all due care of them, which I hope he did
accordingly. I thought it best to beg such a favour of him than to
trust the packet with I knew not who. After I had been at Dover near
a fortnight, and saw no prospect even then of getting away very soon,

---

might copy it. The letter 'made great noise
among the clergy and people: the gentry
and magistracy seeming all to be running
into infidelity.' Monsieur de Castillon
afterwards denied having spoken the address (see Cole's note and his copy of the
speech, Add MS 5824, f. 186v ff.).

1. Cole gives the details of his accident
in *Jour. to Paris* 363–91. He was injured at
Dover, 2 Dec., left there 28 Dec. 1765, and,

travelling in easy stages, reached his parsonage at Bletchley, 1 Jan. 1766 (see
Blecheley Diary 1–3).

2. That is, Favre's.

3. St George St George (formerly Usher)
(ca 1715–75), 1st Bn St George of Hatley St
George. Cole calls him 'a well-looking,
well-behaved man' who 'very kindly undertook' to convey the letters to London (Cole,
Jour. to Paris 360, 369).

I thought it possible that you had given intelligence to my Lady Hervey[4] and my Lady Littleton[5] that you had sent them each a small parcel by me, and that their Ladyships might be uneasy at hearing no news of them: so I wrote to your servant Mr Fevre to let him know that your snuff-box, etc., were safe, and that I would pack them up all in a basket and send them by the coach to my friend Mr Cartwright in London, to whom I directed them, and begged he would employ a trusty porter to convey them to your house. This he has done, as I find since I came home about two days ago.[6] Had I known they had been delivered, I should have wrote sooner, for Mr Cartwright neglected to give me notice of it, though I desired it, and made me rather uneasy about it.

When you come over you will find no difficulty in getting the mate of the ship to take as many things as you please into his custody, and he will bring them to you by little and little at a time on shore. I gave him a guinea,[7] and he brought me everything I wanted, so that you need be in no concern about sending over little parcels by anyone else. At Dover they are strict at the custom-house in searching for laced clothes, and rummage the boxes quite to the bottom, and at Dartford, they told me, the officers were very exact after run goods, and search very narrowly, though I passed through the town and saw nothing of them.

I never was more pleased in my life with a Gothic building than with the Cathedral of Amiens:[8] everything so light and elegant, and the doors so richly ornamented with figures. I was sorry I was rather too much in the evening to see the inside to perfection. At Montreille,[9] if you come after the gates are shut, you need only call to the sentinels, who will be very glad to let you in, with the Commandant's leave, which is never refused, and most frequently practised. I know it was so three times the night I was there. I got in about seven, an-

4. Mary (the celebrated 'Molly') Lepell (1700–68), m. (1720) Hon. John Hervey (Pope's 'Sporus') (1696–1743), cr. (1733) Bn Hervey of Ickworth.

5. Elizabeth Rich (1716–95) m., as his 2d wife (1749), George Lyttelton (1709–73), 1st Bn Lyttelton of Hagley, Worcestershire. Both were correspondents of HW.

6. It appears from Lady Hervey to HW 19 Dec. 1765, that she received the parcel 18 Dec. It contained two work-bags from

Mme Geoffrin (see HW to Lady Hervey 21, 28 Nov. 1765).

7. It was customary to tip the officers of the ship after a crossing (see *Paris Jour.*).

8. 'It is the most airy, lightsome, elegant and pleasing Gothic structure that can be seen' (Cole, *Jour. to Paris* 334). Cole saw it 27 Nov. 1765.

9. Cole had some unpleasant moments before he obtained his lodgings there (op. cit. 339–47).

other company came to the same inn at nine, and a third set of English at twelve. If it had not been practicable, I know not what I should have done, for the suburbs on that side towards Paris are nothing but huts: the other side where you lodged is a good town in respect to that. The inn is the Cour de France, and a very good one.

The weather here is set in very severe, so that ever since last Saturday, the day I set out from Dover, the roads and ground have been as hard as a stone: any moving I dreaded excessively in my condition, but travelling upon a pavement so many miles was dreadful. However, I bore my journey with vast ease, and had no other complaint than a disorder in my stomach, occasioned, probably, by lying so long in bed and then being put into a continual motion. However, even that, I hope, is removed. But I will fatigue you no longer, and wishing you a perfect enjoyment of your limbs and health, I am, with the greatest esteem, dear Sir,

Your ever obliged servant,

WM COLE

Be so kind as to let Louis[10] know that his packet was safely delivered to Mr Fevre, and that I should be much obliged to him, on his return, to bring me half a pound or a pound of pastilles,[11] those that I had with me being chiefly bruised and crumbled to dust by bad packing up.

To COLE, Saturday 18 January 1766

Add MS 5952, ff. 45–6.

HW sent the letter to Cole, 20 Jan., by Dr Gatti (*Paris Jour.*), who did not post it until 31 Jan. (see postmark below). Cole received it Wednesday 5 Feb. (*Blecheley Diary* 14).

Address: [From COLE's copy, Add MS 5831, f. 198v.] To the Rev. Mr Cole at Blecheley near Fenny Stratford, Bucks. Free Hor Walpole.

Postmark: [From COLE's copy.] GC 31 IA.

Paris, Jan. 18, 1766.

Dear Sir,

I HAD extreme satisfaction in receiving your letter, having been in great pain about you, and not knowing whither to direct a letter.

10. HW's Swiss servant who accompanied him to Paris. He died early in 1767 (see HW to Montagu 13 Jan. 1767).

11. 'Incense or *pastilles à bruler;* which they [the French] use in their churches, and are very agreeable to burn, a little at a

Favre told me you had had an accident, did not say what it was, but that you was not come to town.[1] He received all the letters and parcels safe, for which I give you many thanks, and a thousand more for your kindness in thinking of them when you was suffering so much. It was a dreadful conclusion of your travels, but I trust will leave no consequences behind it. The weather is by no means favorable for a recovery, if it is as severe in England[2] as at Paris. We have had two or three days of fog rather than thaw, but the frost is set in again as sharp as ever. I persisted in going about to churches and convents till I thought I should have lost my nose and fingers. I have submitted at last to the season, and lie abed all the morning; but I hope in February and March to recover the time I have lost. I shall not return to England before the end of March,[3] being determined not to hazard anything. I continue perfectly well, and few things could tempt me to risk five months more of gout.

I will certainly bring you some pastilles, and have them better packed if it is possible. You know how happy I should be if you would send me any other commission.

As you say nothing of the Eton living,[4] I fear that prospect has failed you, which gives me great regret, as it would give me very sensible pleasure to have you fixed somewhere (and not far from me) to your ease and satisfaction.

I am glad the Cathedral of Amiens answered your expectation. So has the Sainte Chapelle mine[5]—you did not tell me what charming enamels I should find in the ante-chapel. I have seen another vast piece and very fine of the Constable Montmorenci[6] at the Maréchale Duchesse de Luxembourg's.[7]

time, in one's parlour, immediately after dinner is removed, to take away the scent of the victuals: and is a piece of luxury I learned with him [HW] at Paris' (*Blecheley Diary* 23). See also HW to Mann 12 Dec. 1761, where HW asks Mann to send him some pastilles 'in the first person's pocket that is returning.'

1. Neither side of the HW-Favre correspondence appears to have survived.
2. For an account of the weather in England at this time, see *Blecheley Diary*.
3. He arrived in London 22 April 1766 ('Short Notes'; *Paris Jour.*).

4. The living of Burnham, Bucks (see Cole, *Jour. to Paris* 56). Cole did not become (non-resident) vicar of Burnham until 1774.
5. In the Palais de Justice. For HW's account of it, see *Paris Jour.* 28 Nov. 1765; HW to Conway 29 Oct. 1774.
6. Anne de Montmorency (1492–1567), Constable of France. HW mentions the enamel of him in *Paris Jour.* 12 Dec. 1765.
7. Madeleine-Angélique de Neufville (1707–87), Duchesse de Luxembourg. She was a friend of Mme du Deffand, and is often mentioned in her letters to HW, and in the latter's *Paris Journals*.

Rousseau is gone to England with Mr. Hume.[8] You will very probably see a letter to Rousseau in the name of the King of Prussia,[9] writ to laugh at his affectations. It has made excessive noise here, and I believe quite ruined the author with many of the philosophers. When I tell you I was the author, it is telling you how cheap I hold their anger. If it does not reach you, you shall see it at Strawberry, where I flatter myself I shall see you this summer, and quite well. Adieu! dear Sir.

Your ever obliged and faithful servant,

Hor. Walpole

From Cole, Tuesday 11 February 1766

VA, Forster MS 110, ff. 42–4. Cole's copy, Add MS 5831, ff. 199v, 200v, 201v. 5824, f. 186v.

Cole's copy is addressed: 'A Monsieur Monsieur Walpole, à l'Hotel du Parc Royal, Rue Colombier, Fauxbourg St Germain, à Paris.' The original, however, is addressed as below.

Address: For the Honourable Horace Walpole in Arlington Street, Westminster. *Postmark:* F. Stratford 12 FE.

Blecheley, Feb. 11, 1766.

Dear Sir,

AS nothing in this world could afford me greater pleasure (except the account you give of your health in the former part) than the news you tell me in the latter concerning Rousseau, give me leave to begin my answer at the wrong end. My impatience to see what you say[1] will not permit me to stay till I have the pleasure of seeing you at Strawberry Hill, for if it is to be had in London I will have it before the end of this week, or as soon as I can. My zeal against such impolitic philosophy (to call it by no other name), which only tends to unhinge what on all sides is allowed to have a good tendency on the government of the world and on people's morals (even supposing it to have no other), and at the same time to give us no other system in its room, is such as, if you remember it, made me say a thing at your

8. They set out for England 4 Jan. 1766 (HW to Lady Mary Coke 4 Jan. 1766).

9. The famous letter which caused the quarrel between Rousseau and Hume. (For the text, see *post* 25 Feb. 1766).

1. In the letter to Rousseau.

hotel one evening[2] which I was almost ashamed of, for fear you should think it a gross compliment, and was in truth my real sentiments. It was when the Chevalier Lorenzi[3] and Mr Dromgould[4] were with you, at which time you exerted yourself[5] against the absurd conduct of the French philosophers. I said, when they were gone, that was it only for that evening's conversation, my journey to Paris was well worth the trouble of it. I remember when, another time, I could not help lamenting the fate of the Jesuits, after having been to see their great church, now stripped and left naked, you could not help rallying me on my old attachment to popery, which I can't help thinking will suffer[6] by the disgrace of these Fathers, let their failings be what they will: yet I can't help making this reflection, that had they had among them as good an advocate for their cause as good sense and reason has found in you, it is my real opinion they might have been in possession of their churches, as I hope reasonable Christianity will be in our island. How much then are we obliged to gentlemen of quality and learning when they will vouchsafe to draw the pen against such disturbers of civil society? But I will say no more; perhaps your modesty will think I have said too much, but my zeal was intemperate, and I could not stop my pen. Yet one word more before I finish on this head. Since Mr Rousseau's happy arrival in England, we have had in every paper two or three articles[7] on his account. We seem to think we have a mighty acquisition in what his own country has justly rejected. If the Emperor had paid us a visit the nation could not be more stunned with his arrival. In short, there is nothing now in our

2. Saturday 26 Oct. 1765. Cole's account of the conversation of the evening (with many digressions) is in Cole, *Jour. to Paris* 62–80, the most pertinent passage occurring at p. 68.

3. Probably Jacques Roland (d. 1784), Comte de Lorenzi, Chevalier and brother of Count Lorenzi, French minister at Florence (see *Journal de Paris*, 1784, i. 438; Cole, *Jour. to Paris* 62). He visited England in 1749 and dined with HW at SH (HW to Mann 12 Sept. 1749). His social blunders, which were proverbial, are often mentioned in HW's letters.

4. Jean Dromgould (Dromgold, Dromgoole) (1720–81), a member of an Irish Jacobite family of Danish extraction, settled at Paris; author of several poems and critical works. He went to England in 1762 as secretary to the Duc de Nivernois, and

in 1775 he entertained Johnson at Paris (Boswell, *Johnson* ii. 401–2, 526–7). Cole described him in 1765 as 'Knight of the Order of St Lewis, a very pretty gentleman [between forty and fifty years of age] . . . dressed in a military habit: he was thin and well shaped' (Cole, *Jour. to Paris* 63). HW frequently mentions him in *Paris Jour.*

5. Cole's copy reads 'at which time you, with the latter gentlemen, exerted yourselves.'

6. 'together with our common Christianity' (addition in Cole's copy).

7. 'concerning his different motions from Dover to London; and when he arrived there, his lodgings, when he went to the play, where he was seated, with his design of retiring into Herefordshire to spend the remainder of his life' (addition in Cole's copy).

papers but some article about[8] Mr Rousseau, the Prince and Princess of Brunswic[9] and their new-born son, who came into the world last Friday.[10]

I am most sincerely glad you are in perfect health. I hope you will run no risks, but keep so, and that for many years. Thank God, I am now got as well as if no accident had happened to me. We have had a very severe winter, but rather pleasant, as there was no snow, and the ground underfoot as good to walk on as in summer. Yesterday a quick thaw succeeded a very severe frost. I hope it is gone, as the farmers want to get their beans into the ground.

I am so unfortunate as to have missed the living of Burnham, for, as I foretold to my brother before I left England, I thought some of his seniors would not let so good a benefice as Worplesdon[11] pass by without taking it. Accordingly Dr Burton quitted his old one[12] for it, by which means Dr Apthorp is left at his own.[13] It is the more sensible to me, as the situation would have brought me within distance of Strawberry Hill, not to mention the awkward situation I am in at present,[14] with a prospect of leaving this at the end of next year, and having no other retreat than what I can find for myself. But thank God, I have a competency and can be content, though a little more added to my own property would make me much easier.

8. 'The American Stamp Act, Mr Rousseau' (addition in Cole's copy).

9. Charles William Ferdinand (1735–1806), Hereditary Prince, and afterwards (1780–1806) Duke, of Brunswick-Wolfenbüttel; nephew of Frederick the Great. He m. (1764) Princess Augusta (1737–1813), eld. dau. of Frederick Prince of Wales, and sister of George III.

10. Prince Charles George Augustus, their eldest son, who is said to have been 'well-nigh imbecile' (Lord Edmond Fitzmaurice, *Charles William Ferdinand, Duke of Brunswick*, 1901, p. 16). He died 20 Sept. 1806, and his father was mortally wounded at Auerstadt 14 Oct. following. The date usually given for his birth is Saturday 8 Feb.

11. 'Void by the death of Dr Stephen Sleech, the late Provost [of Eton] and rector of Worplesdon near Guilford in Surrey, a living [worth] about 400 pounds per annum' (Cole, *Jour. to Paris* 56).

12. John Burton (1696–1771), Vice-Provost (1752–71) of Eton; vicar of Mapledurham, Oxon, 1734–66, and rector of Worplesdon 1766–71.

13. 'for, although he might, if he pleased, succeed to Maple-Durham, voided by Dr Burton, which is about an £100 per annum better than Burnham, yet he does not choose to do so, as he quitted two livings in Hampshire when he took Burnham, about £100 per annum inferior to it, merely for the situation, as bringing him within a long walk or short ride of his fellowship in the college. My brother would have procured Maple-Durham for me, if the Society had not then entered into a new method of disposing of their livings, by which each Fellow is to take his turn as they fall' (addition in Cole's copy).

14. The obligation to resign the living of Bletchley to the patron's grandson, Thomas Willis (1743–90), in two years (see George Lipscomb, *The History and Antiquities of the County of Buckingham*, 4 vols, 1847, iv. 25).

My cousin Dr Cock, by the misfortune of poor Dr Birch's death by a fall from his horse,[15] has added greatly to his preferment, for they had exchanged livings about four years ago: by Dr Birch's death, Dr Cock enters of course into his former living of above £300 per annum, he being the patron of it himself,[16] so that it is a bad wind indeed that blows no good to anyone.

At Cambridge they seem to be going mad. Last week a grace was actually prepared in the Senate House[17] in order to petition the Parliament for leave that the Fellows of colleges might marry: you may easily conceive that it was promoted by the junior part of the University. How it will proceed I know not, but they are in earnest.[18] I hope the several overseers of the poor of the different parishes in Cambridge will prepare a petition also at the same time, requesting that a way may be found out that the wives, children and servants (if they can keep any) may not become burdensome to their respective parishes to which they may belong. For surely this scheme must not only end in misery and beggary to the Fellows themselves, but greatly to the discredit of the University, where, upon this plan, each college will become a sort of hospital.[19]

Though I have been thus tedious, I wish the last part of my letter may not be still more so, as I know you neither love long letters nor commissions. Yet as you was so kind as to say you would execute any for me, I have taken the liberty to beg of you to complete my set of St Cloud or Seve china. When I had the honour of attending you to

15. Thomas Birch (1705–66), antiquary and HW's occasional correspondent. 'Whilst riding in the Hampstead Road he fell from his horse, it is believed in an apoplectic fit, and died on 9 Jan. 1766' (DNB: W. P. Courtney).

16. Birch received the living of Great Horksley, Essex, from Lord Hardwicke, who allowed him to exchange in 1761 with Cock for Debden, Essex. Birch wished to be nearer London, where he had other preferments, and Cock had 'taken a disgust to the place [Debden], from having been robbed and gagged and confined in his cellar, by a gang of smugglers' (Cole, quoted in LA ix. 799; see also ibid. v. 285–6).

17. 'though not read, by reason one Mr Ashby, who had undertaken to present it, at the time refused to do so' (addition in Cole's copy). 'Mr Ashby' was George Ashby

(1724–1808), antiquary; president of St John's College, 1769–75. Cole later became acquainted with him. Cole received his information from the Rev. Edward Betham, Fellow and Bursar of King's, in a letter of 31 Jan. 1766 (see Cooper, Annals iv. 340–1). Nothing came of the attempt.

18. 'though many people thought they were only in jest at their first stirring about it some four months ago' (addition in Cole's copy).

19. 'It is to be hoped that if they are so utterly absurd themselves, that the wisdom of Parliament will take care that a set of foolish and idle Fellows by their own ill judgment may not be the occasion of ruining what was not meant to gratify themselves only, but to be a nursery of learning for future generations' (addition in Cole's copy).

Madame du Lac's, I bought two coffee cups and saucers of her of eight or nine livres the cup and saucer: one cup and saucer of blue and white, the other of red and white, with gold edges.[20] They are so admired here that everyone laments I did not bring a set of six. If it would not be too much trouble when you went that way, I should be obliged to you to buy me four more, and let them come with your own china to England. I am in no hurry for them, nor do I want them all of a sort: I had rather have them all different, if you approve of it, for I bought one of the same price at Monsieur Poirier's which was enamelled,[21] but I leave this to you to do as you please, and if I have them not at all, I am and shall be quite easy about it, so that the pastilles and you come safe, and wishing you a good journey, pleasant and safe passage and full health, I beg leave to subscribe myself, dear Sir,

Your most obliged and faithful servant,

WM COLE

We are now in the height of a dispute between Bishop Warburton[22] and Dr Lowth:[23] the latter has attacked, after some provocation from the Bishop, his *Divine Legation* with uncommon spirit, and I think with an inveteracy[24] and sharpness equal to anything in the Bishop's own style.

20. They visited Mme du Lac's shop Wednesday 13 Nov. 1765, 'where the mistress was as tempting as the things she sold, and where a younger man than myself would run great risk of losing what is of more value than money, except he was much upon his guard' (Cole, *Jour. to Paris* 233–4).

21. The following day (Thursday 14 Nov.) Cole accompanied HW to M. Poirier's shop, where 'the china and toys and fine cabinets were rather richer and in greater abundance' than at Mme du Lac's, and where Cole paid twelve livres for 'a single coffee cup and saucer of the enamelled Chantilly manufactured china' (ibid. 245).

22. William Warburton (1698–1779), Bp of Gloucester; friend and editor of Pope. In *The Divine Legation of Moses*, 2 parts, 1737–41, he maintained the law of Moses to be of divine origin, a view which plunged him into a controversy that lasted

for thirty years (see A[rthur] W[illiam] Evans, *Warburton and the Warburtonians*, Oxford, 1932).

23. Robert Lowth (1710–87), Bp of Oxford 1766–77 and of London 1777–87. His dispute with Warburton grew out of a slight disagreement in 1756, augmented by Warburton's attack on him in an appendix to the sixth book of *The Divine Legation*. Lowth replied in 'a pamphlet full of amusing sarcasm,' his *Letter to the ... Author of 'The Divine Legation' in Answer by a late Professor of Oxford*, 1765, in which he published his correspondence with Warburton in 1756. After Warburton's rejoinder, Lowth replied with the scathing *Second Part of a Literary Correspondence between the Bishop of Gloucester and a late Professor of Oxford*, 1766, the pamphlet to which Cole refers. It was generally believed that Lowth had the better part of the argument (A. W. Evans, op. cit. 250–5).

24. 'acrimony, peevishness and ill man-

To COLE, Tuesday 25 February 1766

Add MS 5952, ff. 49–50.

Although HW (and Cole in his copy, Add MS 5824, ff. 192v, 193v) dates this letter *Feb. 28,* the date probably should be *Feb. 25,* as under that date HW records in *Paris Jour.,* 'Went to the plaine de Sablon to see the race between Count Lauragais and Lord Forbes, which was won by the latter;' and in this letter HW says that he saw the race 'today.'

HW sent the letter to England by Major Bruce, 1 March (which he misdates *29 February* in *Paris Jour.*), and Cole received it 7 March (*Blecheley Diary* 23).

Address: [From COLE's copy.] To the Reverend Mr Cole at Blecheley near Fenny Stratford, Bucks. Free Hor Walpole.

Postmark: [From COLE's copy.] PW 6 MR.

Paris, Feb. 28 [25], 1766.

Dear Sir,

AS you cannot, I believe, get a copy of the letter to Rousseau, and are impatient for it, I send it you, though the brevity of it will not answer your expectation. It is no answer to any of his works, and is only a laugh at his affectations. I hear he does not succeed in England, where singularities are no curiosity. Yet he must stay there, or give up all his pretensions. To quit a country where he may live at ease and unpersecuted, will be owning that tranquillity is not what he seeks. If he again seeks persecution, who will pity him? I should think even bigots would let him alone, out of contempt.

I have executed your commission in a way that I hope will please you. As you tell me you have a blue cup and saucer, and a red one, and would have them completed to six, without being all alike, I have bought one other blue, one other red, and two sprigged, in the same manner, with colours; so you will have just three pair, which seems preferable to six odd ones, and which indeed at nineteen livres apiece[1] I think I could not have found.

I shall keep pretty near to the time I proposed returning, though I am a little tempted to wait for the appearance of leaves. As I may never come hither again, I am disposed to see a little of their villas and gardens, though it will vex me to lose spring and lilac-tide at Strawberry. The weather has been so bad and continues so cold, that I have not yet seen all I intend in Paris. Today I have been to the

ners equal, if not superior, to anything in the Bishop's own style' (addition in Cole's copy).

1. HW's mistake for 'nine livres apiece' (see *post* 17 May 1766).

plaine de Sablon, by the Bois de Boulogne, to see a horse-race, rid in person by Count Lauragais[2] and Lord Forbes.[3] All Paris was in motion by nine o'clock this morning, and the coaches and crowds were innumerable at so novel a sight—Would you believe it, that there was an Englishman to whom it was quite as new? That Englishman was I. Though I live within two miles of Hounslow,[4] have been fifty times in my life at Newmarket, and have passed through it at the time of the races, I never before saw a complete one. I once went from Cambridge on purpose, saw the beginning, was tired and went away. If there was to be a *review* in Lapland,[5] perhaps I might see a review too, which yet I have never seen. Lauragais was distanced at the second circuit. What added to the singularity was, that at the same instant his brother[6] was gone to church to be married; but as Lauragais is at variance with his father and wife, he chose this expedient to show he was not at the wedding. Adieu! dear Sir.

Yours ever,

H. WALPOLE

[Enclosure.][7]

Le Roi de Prusse à Monsieur Rousseau.

Mon cher Jean Jacques,

Vous avez renoncé à Geneve, votre Patrie; vous vous etes fait chasser de

2. Louis-Léon-Félicité de Brancas (1733–1824), Comte de Lauraguais, afterwards Duc de Brancas; son of Louis de Villars-Brancas (1714–ca 1780), Duc de Lauraguais. 'Ami et protecteur des lettres et des sciences, littérateur et savant lui-même, il s'est rendu célèbre par ses bonmots, ses écrits piquants, ses excentricités et son esprit frondeur qui lui valut quatre emprisonnements et cinq exils.' He was the author of two tragedies, *Clytemnestre*, 1761, and *Socrate*, 1781 (Ludovic Lalanne, *Dict. Hist. de la France*, 1872; *Paris Jour.*, *passim*). (See also Cole's note 8 to this letter, and, for its unhappy sequel, HW to Anne Pitt 1 March 1766, and to Hertford 10 March 1766.)

3. James Forbes (1725?–1804), 17th Bn Forbes. He was noted as a gentleman-jockey.

4. 'A village 12 miles north of London, on the edge of the heath of the same name, which is equally famous for horse-races and robberies' (*London and Its Environs Described*, 6 vols, 1761, iii. 204).

5. That is, Paris, where it was excessively cold during the winter of 1765–6. HW wrote Chute 7 Jan. 1766, 'Lapland is the torrid zone in comparison of Paris.'

6. Bufile-Antoine-Léon de Brancas (b. 1735), Comte de Brancas, 2d son of the Duc de Lauraguais; m. (by contract signed 23 Feb. 1766) Marie-Louise de Lowendal (1746–1834), dau. of Woldemar, Comte de Lowendal, Maréchal de France (see La Chenaye-Desbois and Badier, *Dict. de la Noblesse*, 3d edn, 1863–76).

7. The following letter is printed *verbatim et literatim* from HW's MS.

la Suisse, paÿs tant vanté dans vos Écrits; la France vous a decreté: venez
donc chez moi: j'admire vos talents, je m'amuse de vos reveries; qui (soit
dit en passant) vous occupent trop et trop longtems. Il faut à la fin etre
sage et heureux. Vous avez fait assez parler de vous par des singularités
peu convenables à un veritable grand Homme. Demontrez à vos Ennemis,
que vous pouvez avoir quelquefois le sens commun. Cela les fachera, sans
vous faire tort. Mes Etats vous offrent une retraite paisible; je vous veux
de bien, & je vous en ferai, si vous la trouvez bon; mais si vous vous obsti-
nez à rejetter mon secours, attendez vous que je ne le dirai à personne. Si
vous persistez à vous creuser l'esprit pour trouver de nouveaux malheurs,
choisissez les tels que vous voudrez; je suis Roi, je puis vous en procurer
au gré de vos Souhaits: & ce qui surement ne vous arrivera pas vis à vis de
vos Ennemis, je cesserai de vous persecuter, quand vous cesserez de mettre
votre gloire à l'etre.

Votre bon Ami,

FREDERIC[8]

To COLE, Saturday 10 May 1766

Add MS 5952, ff. 51–2.
Cole received the letter Sunday, 11 May (*Blecheley Diary* 48).
Address: To the Reverend Mr Cole at Blecheley near Fenny Stratford, Bucks.
Free Hor Walpole. *Postmark:* PW 10 MA.

Arlington Street, May 10, 1766.

AT last I am come back,[1] dear Sir, and in good health. I have
brought you four cups and saucers, one red and white, one blue
and white, and two coloured; and a little box of pastilles. Tell me
whether and how I shall convey them to you, or whether you will, as
I hope, come to Strawberry this summer, and fetch them yourself.
But if you are in the least hurry, I will send them.

8. Cole wrote the following observations
on HW's letter, at the end of his copy of it,
Add MS 5824, ff. 193v, 194v, 195v: 'Mr
Walpole made a great mistake in buying
me four cups and saucers at nineteen livres
the cup and saucer: I only mentioned in
my letter eight or nine, which I thought a
great price, but as I had three already, was

willing to complete my set. When I was at
Paris in October and November 1765, I remember to have heard talk of an horse-
race at that time at Fountainbleau, which
was looked upon as a great curiosity, and
was rode, I think, by this Lord Forbes. I
saw the Count Lauragais several times at
Paris, who was very fond of English horses,

I flatter myself that you have quite recovered your accident, and have no remains of lameness. The spring is very wet and cold, but Strawberry alone contains more verdure than all France.

I scrambled very well through the custom-house at Dover, and have got all my china safe from that here in town.[2] You will see the fruits when you come to Strawberry Hill. Adieu!

Yours ever,

H. Walpole

and had a large stud of them: he is son to the Duke de Brancas. One ought to be better acquainted with the private character of Rousseau and his singularities than I am, to enter into the spirit and finesse of Mr Walpole's letter. However, from the general turn of it, one may easily conceive what he would ridicule. One of his artifices I heard at Mr Walpole's one afternoon when I was there with other company: and that was, that he would not receive presents that were offered him. This gained him great credit and a reputation of vast disinterestedness, for his free-thinking principles had made many proselytes among the French noblesse and gentry, who were all forward to contribute to a martyr for infidelity, and persecuted from one country to another for his opinions: just in the same manner as Gordon got a good estate left him by one of his way of thinking for his writings against the religion of his country, and as the famous Mr Pitt got £10,000 from the old Duchess of Marlborough and a noble estate from Sir William Pynsent, by which means he disinherited his nephew, for his patriotism: though this great patriot at this time, in full height of his popularity, enjoys most meanly a pension of £3000 per annum from the government and has a title for his wife, to descend to his son: so inconsistent are both himself and his adorers! By this art Rousseau thought, probably, he might gain some very ample benefaction, though he might lose smaller presents. Accordingly, the Duchess of Luxembourg, a great patron of his, for his infidel writings, bethought herself of some stratagem to make him accept of a large sum of money: which, though the thing was the same, yet he framed to himself some way to accept it. I shall give a trans-

lation of Mr Walpole's letter to Rousseau under the name of the King of Prussia here.' The translation follows in the MS.

'In the *Gentleman's Magazine* for February 1766, p. 53, are anecdotes relating to the persecution of this Mr Rousseau, where it is said that the King of Prussia took him under his protection.

'In the *Cambridge Chronicle* of April 5, 1766, is a translation of the abovesaid letter, but not well done in many expressions, and one material and capital paragraph quite left out.

'In the *Cambridge Chronicle* of April 19, 1766, is the following article and angry letter from Rousseau.

' "The letter said to be written by the King of Prussia to Mr Rousseau, and which had been handed about in manuscript for some time, has occasioned a letter from that gentleman, who is now at Wootton, to the printer of the paper in which it first appeared; and the following is a translation of it. [A translation of Rousseau's letter to the 'Author of the *St James's Chronicle*,' 7 April 1766, follows in the MS. The letter appeared in the *St James's Chronicle*, 8–10 April 1766 (see *Oeuvres Complètes de Rousseau*, 13 vols, Paris, 1871–7, xi. 327; *Letters of David Hume*, ed. J. Y. T. Greig, 2 vols, Oxford, 1932, ii. 402–3)]."

It is a sure sign the letter pinched him in a tender part when he winces so much at it.'

---

1. He reached London 22 April (*Paris Jour.*).

2. He brought back five large cases (containing 37 small cases) of china (mostly Sèvres), and left another large case with the Duke of Richmond (ibid.).

From COLE, Sunday 11 May 1766

VA, Forster MS 110, ff. 45–6. COLE's copy, Add MS 5824, ff. 195v, 196v.
Address: For the Honourable Horace Walpole Esq. in Arlington Street, Westminster. *Postmark:* F. Stratford 12 MA.

Blecheley, May 11, 1766.

Dear Sir,

I HOPE I may by this time[1] congratulate you on your safe arrival in England, and that you are even in good time to enjoy the delights of the banks of the Thames in lilac-tide: a season thrown away, in my opinion, in that kennel of a place, Paris, in comparison to the beauties, natural and artificial, of the environs of London.[2] I hope the time you have mortified there will be amply made up to you in the full enjoyment of your health to riot in the delights of Strawberry Hill.

To say how much obliged [I am] to you for the communication of your short letter to Rousseau is beyond the limits of this letter. Perhaps the conciseness of such an epistle may be esteemed one of its great merits, yet I am so singular as to wish it had been as many pages as there are letters. The sneer is so cutting that the gentleman is very visibly hurt by it, as appears by a short letter of his dated from Wootton, April 7, published in the public prints. A sad and miserable translation into English of your spirited letter was published in the *Cambridge Chronicle* of April 5. The letter from Wootton was also in the same paper, possibly both taken from London papers.[3] I assure you, upon my faith and honour, that your letter was never out of my own hands, nor did I ever give a copy of it to any soul alive or dead. [This] I mention for fear you should be tempted to think, as it appeared in the Cambridge paper, that I might by some means or other be accessory to its publication. I saw in the last magazine a very ingenious extract of a letter from Voltaire to Rousseau,[4] upon the same

1. 'though I have not seen it in any of the papers' (addition in Cole's copy).
2. 'How doubly enchanting must the Thames appear after a residence of seven or eight months upon the banks of the filthy River Seine! a river which at Paris will always give one an idea of the ancient state of Fleet Ditch before its modern alteration and appearance' (addition in Cole's copy).

3. See *ante* 25 Feb. 1766.
4. GM for April 1766 (xxxvi. 192–3; Cole's copy of which is in the Yale University Library), contains a review of *A Letter from M. Voltaire to M. Jean-Jacques Rousseau,* the first edition of which was published in London 8 April (see *London Chronicle* 3–5, 5–8, 17–9 April 1766). The French title (the French text and the English translation were printed on opp. pages) was *Lettre*

plan of ridiculing his affectations. When I first read it I was apt to suspect that Voltaire was not the real name.[5]

In reading over your *Fugitive Pieces* t'other day, and what had escaped me two or three times before, you observe at p. 204, in a note, that you can make no sense of the word *noĩe,* and take it for a redundancy of the carver or a repetition of the three last syllables of *Desmoniae. Noĩe* is a common abbreviation in old writings and inscriptions for *nomine,* and so it stands very properly in its place.[6]

Lately purchasing Sir Leoline Jenkins's *Life,*[7] I find my uncle Tuer very honourably mentioned by him as an English painter at pp. 682 and 683 of vol. 2, under the name of Tuart, a misnomer in French for Tuer. I remember my grandfather at Cambridge, by the common people, was generally called Stuart.

Pray excuse the length of this letter, for its late addressing you. I should have wrote sooner but from the uncertainty of your arrival, and know you'll excuse, dear and honoured Sir,

Your ever faithful and obliged servant,

WM COLE

May I presume to beg the favour of your writing the following direction to the enclosed letter to my sister:

For Mrs J. Cole in Stall Street, Bath.

From COLE, Sunday 11 May 1766 *bis*

VA, Forster MS 110, f. 47. Cole kept no copy.

Address: For the Honourable Horace Walpole Esq. in Arlington Street, Westminster. *Postmark:* [F. Stratford.] 12 MA.

Blecheley, May 11, 1766.

SINCE I sent to the post for letters, when my boy carried that for you which I wrote first, he brought me in return your very kind

de M. de Voltaire au Docteur J.-J. Pansophe. The question of its authorship has not been settled, but it is believed that Voltaire or his friend Charles de Borde wrote it (see Georges Bengesco, *Voltaire: Bibliographie de ses oeuvres,* 4 vols, Paris, 1882–90, ii. 179–83; *Oeuvres complètes de Voltaire,* 52 vols, Paris, 1877–85, xxvi. 17–27).

5. That is, Cole suspects HW is author of the letter, as its style is similar to that

of HW's letter to Rousseau in the name of the King of Prussia.

6. HW deleted the note in the copy of *Fugitive Pieces* which he corrected for *Works* (now in the Fitzwilliam Museum, Cambridge), and wrote 'Abbreviated for *nomine.*' This appears in *Works* i. 211 n.

7. *The Life of Sir Leoline Jenkins,* by William Wynne, 2 vols, 1724.

letter, which gave me no small joy on account of the news of your safe arrival and good health. I could not resist acknowledging your favour, and at the same time, though I am in no manner of hurry to have the china which you have been so kind to buy for me and the pastilles, and though I have a full and settled purpose of waiting upon you sometime this summer at Strawberry Hill, at your most convenient time, yet to disencumber you of my parcel I will get my neighbour Mr Cartwright to call for them sometime this week, who will have an opportunity of bringing them down to me soon after. The price I will pay when I have the honour of seeing you, though I apprehend you made a mistake[1] in your letter to me from Paris, which told me that you paid nineteen livres each cup and saucer, which I suppose you wrote in an hurry for nine livres, that being the price I begged you to give, and what I gave myself at Madame <du> Lac's. However, if it should be re<ally> nineteen, I suppose they are finer than those I have already and shall be very well satisfied with whatever they are, which, with my wishes for your health and every good, I am, in no small hurry,

Your ever faithful and obliged servant,

WM COLE

I am ashamed to be so troublesome, but beg you will excuse my troubling you to direct the enclosed to a gentleman who does some business for me, and who loves not to pay for my letters if he can avoid it:

For the Rev. Mr Masters at Landbeche near Cambridge.

To COLE, Tuesday 13 May 1766

Add MS 5952, f. 53.
Cole received the letter 14 May *(Blecheley Diary* 50).

Arlington Street, May 13, 1766.

Dear Sir,

I AM forced to do a very awkward thing and send you back one of your letters,[1] and what is still worse, opened. The case was this: I

---

1. HW paid only nine livres (see *post* 17 May 1766).

1. Cole's letter to his sister, Jane Cole, which he had requested HW to frank (see *ante* 11 May 1766, first letter).

received your two at dinner, opened one and laid the other in my lap; but forgetting that I had taken one out of the first, I took up the wrong, and broke it open, without perceiving my mistake, till I saw the words, *Dear Sister*. I give you my honour I read no farther, but had torn it too much to send it away. Pray excuse me; and another time I beg you will put an envelope, for you write just where the seal comes;[2] and besides, place the seals so together, that though I did not quite open the fourth letter,[3] yet it stuck so to the outer seal, that I could not help tearing it a little.[4]

Your things[5] shall be ready whenever they are called for. Adieu!

Yours ever,

H. W.

To Cole, Saturday 17 May 1766

Add MS 5952, ff. 47–8.

The letter is dated by the postmark. Cole received it 18 May (*Blecheley Diary* 50).

Address: To the Reverend Mr Cole at Blecheley near Fenny Stratford, Bucks. Free Hor Walpole. *Postmark:* JO 17 MA.

[Arlington Street, 17 May 1766.]

Dear Sir,

IF you wonder you have not received the china and pastilles, I must tell you the reason. They were sent for late in the evening when I was not at home. The servant desired they might be ready by eight next morning, but did not come for them, but afterwards left word they were to go by the wagon. I knew that was not safe for the china, and would reduce the pastilles to powder, and therefore did not send them. When you send for them, be so good as to let me have a day or

2. The seal, of course, was on the outside of the letter, on the fourth side of the folded quarto sheet. Cole habitually wrote entirely across the third side. In breaking the seal to open the letter, therefore, it was difficult not to carry away some of the MS.

3. That is, Cole's letter to Masters (see *ante* the second letter of 11 May). HW received four letters from Cole in two covers on this day. The first cover contained the letter to Mrs Cole, the second, the letter to Masters.

4. That is, Cole had laid the sealed letter to Masters inside his own letter with the seal upwards, so that it stuck to the seal which Cole put on his covering letter to HW.

5. The china and pastilles.

two of notice, because I am never at home in an evening, and often out of town.

The cups certainly cost but nine livres apiece, and nineteen was a mistake.

Yours ever,

H. W.

From Cole, Tuesday 20 May 1766

VA, Forster MS 110, f. 48. Cole kept no copy.
Address: For the Honourable Horace Walpole Esq., in Arlington Street, Westminster. *Postmark:* F. Stratford 21 MA.

Blecheley, May 20, 1766.

Dear Sir,

I AM vastly concerned that I should give you so much trouble, and will endeavour to make amends for it by the shortness of this. I well know how your time is taken up, and therefore can't think of three letters from you within these ten days without blushing. I will beg the favour of you to keep the china and pastilles with you till I have the honour of waiting on you sometime this summer, but must thank you again for your great care in not suffering them to go by the wagon, which I know by my own would have powdered all the pastilles and probably broken the china. The person I sent to,[1] in order to bring them to me, was a near neighbour who I knew was setting out of town at the time with his own equipage, and I thought they would be safe under his care.

I am, dear Sir,

Your most faithful and obliged servant,

Wm Cole

If I should have any other fair opportunity of getting them down to me by a friend, I will give you notice beforehand.

1. Rev. Philip Barton (1717–86), Cole's 'most worthy and much esteemed schoolfellow,' rector of Sherington, Bucks, 1743–81 (see *Blecheley Diary* 49–50; George Lipscomb, *History and Antiquities of the County of Buckingham*, 4 vols, 1847, iv. 81, 336, 362; *Eton Coll. Reg. 1698–1752*).

From COLE, Tuesday 16 September 1766

VA, Forster MS 110, f. 49. Cole kept no copy.

Address: For the Honourable Horace Walpole in Arlington Street, Westminster. *Postmark:* [F. Stratford.] 17 SE.

Blecheley, Sept. 16, 1766.

Dear Sir,

IT was with infinite concern that I read an article in my last newspaper,[1] and shall be greatly rejoiced to find that it was exaggerated. A line from your servant to inform me that you was better would give me great pleasure. However, I thought it became me, who lie under so many obligations to your friendship, to offer you my best services in case your papers should want sorting or putting in order, or to execute any other thing in the poor abilities of, dear and honoured Sir,

Your ever faithful and obliged servant,

WM COLE

To COLE, Thursday 18 September 1766

Add MS 5952, ff. 54–5.

Cole received the letter 19 Sept. *(Blecheley Diary 123–4).*

Address: To the Reverend Mr Cole at Blecheley near Fenny Stratford, Bucks. Free Hor Walpole. *Postmark:* IW [Isleworth] 18 SE.

Arlington Street, Sept. 18, 1766.

Dear Sir,

I AM exceedingly obliged to you for your very friendly letter, and hurt at the absurdity of the newspapers that occasioned the alarm. Sure I am not of consequence enough to be lied about! It is true I am ill, have been extremely so, and have been ill long, but with nothing like paralytic as they have reported me. It has been this long dis-

---

1. 'Thursday [11 Sept.] the Hon. Horace Walpole, Esq., was seized with a paralytic disorder at his house in Arlington Street, and continues very ill' *(Whitehall Evening Post* 11–13 Sept. 1766). Cole read the account in this newspaper, Sunday 14 Sept.

(Blecheley Diary 120). HW's illness was described as 'a paralytic gout' in *Lloyd's Evening Post* 12–5 Sept. 1766. See also *Gray's Corr.* iii. 936 and Gray to HW 24 Sept. 1766.

order alone that has prevented my profiting of your company at
Strawberry, according to the leave you gave me of asking it. I have
lived upon the road between that place and this, never settled there,
and uncertain whether I should go to Bath or abroad. Yesterday sennight I grew exceedingly ill indeed, with what they[1] say has been the
gout in my stomach, bowels, back, and kidneys. The worst seems over,
and I have been to take the air today for the first time, but bore it so
ill, that I don't know how soon I shall be able to set out for Bath,[2]
whither they want me to go immediately. As that journey makes it
very uncertain when I shall be at Strawberry again, and as you must
want your cups and pastilles, will you tell me if I can convey them to
you any way safely?

Excuse my saying more today, as I am so faint and weak, but it was
impossible not to acknowledge your kindness the first minute I was
able. Adieu! Dear Sir.

Yours ever,

Hor. Walpole

From Cole, Sunday 21 September 1766

VA, Forster MS 110, f. 50. Cole kept no copy.
Address: For the Honourable Horace Walpole in Arlington Street, London.
Postmark: 22 SE.

Blecheley, Sept. 21, 1766.

Dear Sir,

YOUR own handwriting on the outside of the letter gave me great
joy, and though the contents of it in the ill account of your
health was a great abatement to it, yet surely nothing is so deplorable
as to be a living inanimate statue, especially to one who makes so
good use of his fingers as yourself, so that, although I cannot congratulate you on the enjoyment of your health, the best of blessings,
yet I am sincerely glad it was not such as the newspapers represented

1. Lord Hertford and Conway called in
Sir John Pringle (1707–82), to attend HW
(see HW to Mann 25 Sept. 1766, to Lady
Mary Coke 17 Sept. 1766).

2. 'Saturday [27 Sept.] the Hon. Horatio
Walpole set out for Park Place, the seat
of the Right Hon. Henry Seymour Con-

way, Esq., and from thence will set out
from [for] Bath' (*Whitehall Evening Post*
27–30 Sept. 1766). He reached Bath 1 Oct.
(see HW to Conway 2 Oct. 1766), and returned to SH about 22 Oct. (HW to Montagu 22 Oct. 1766).

it. I hope the Bath waters will restore you to your former state, and the sooner they are recurred to the better. I was pleasing myself with the hopes of waiting on you in about two or three weeks when I saw the account in the papers. I hope still to have that pleasure when you are returned, and if those waters, in which I have great faith, don't do all the good your friends wish, a warmer climate will set you up.

I will send a neighbour's servant for the china and pastilles and will remember that I have not paid for them the first time I have the honour <of s>eeing you, which I hope and pray will not be long off, and wishing you a perfect re-establishment of your health, with many thanks for your letter, I remain, dear Sir,

Your ever obliged and faithful servant,

WM COLE

To COLE, Saturday 24 October 1767

COLE's copy, Add MS 5824, f. 173v. The original is missing.
Cole received the letter Sunday, 25 Oct. (*Blecheley Diary* 280).

Address: [From COLE's copy.] To the Rev. Mr Cole at Blecheley near Fenny Stratford, Bucks. Free Hor Walpole.

Arlington Street, Oct. 24, 1767.

Dear Sir,

IT is an age since we have had any correspondence. My long and dangerous illness last year, with my journey to Bath: my long attendance in Parliament all winter, spring, and to the beginning of summer;[1] and my journey to France since, from whence I returned but last week,[2] prevented my asking the pleasure of seeing you at Strawberry Hill.

I wish to hear that you have enjoyed your health, and shall be glad of any news of you. The season is too late, and the Parliament too near opening,[3] for me to propose a winter journey to you. If you

---

1. Parliament met 11 Nov. 1766, and 'rose on the 2nd of July, after one of the longest sessions that was almost ever known' (*Mem. of the Reign of George III*, iii. 44).

2. HW left for Paris 20 Aug. 1767, and returned 12 Oct. (*Paris Jour.*).
3. It met 24 Nov.

should happen to think at all of London, I trust you would do me the favour to call on me. In short, this is only a letter of inquiry after you, and to show you that I am always,

Most truly yours,

Hor. Walpole

From Cole, Thursday 29 October 1767

VA, Forster MS 110, ff. 51–2. Cole's copy, Add MS 5824, ff. 173v, 174v.

Cole's entry in *Blecheley Diary* (p. 281) for Wednesday, 28 Oct., shows that he wrote the letter on that day.

Address: For the Honourable Horace Walpole in Arlington Street, London. *Postmark:* F. Stratford 30 OC.

Blecheley, Oct. 29, 1767.

Dear Sir,

YOUR very kind letter gave me no small pleasure, both as it assured me of your health and the continuance of your remembrance of me. Your return from France was quite news to me, as I had not the least idea of your being out of the island, for I have not seen any one person these twelve months that could give me any account of your motions, and indeed have been so little from this place that I may venture to say, except one journey for three or four days to look at the house I am removing to,[1] that I have not lain one night from home for the same space of time. I am glad you left England this summer, in hopes that you found better weather than we were blessed with. Altogether, from Christmas to this time, surely never was remembered such a succession of vile weather! and what makes it more grievous to me in particular was the damage I sustained in the beginning of it, and the inconvenience I am like to prove by its perseverance. On the melting of the great snow in January, I had a farm of near £100 per annum covered four feet under water by the breaking of the banks of the Bedford Level River,[2] from which I expect to receive nothing for some time, especially as the summer has been so

1. For this journey, 15–20 June 1767, see *Blecheley Diary* 228–32. Cole went to London, then to Cambridge, where he agreed with the Rev. Robert Masters to take the vicarage of Waterbeach.

2. Cole received a letter 10 Feb. from Joseph Bentham of Cambridge 'to inform me that Mr Masters called on him to tell him that the river banks near Over broke down and overflowed all the low grounds,

wet and continues in the same style; and now I am removing from
this place, the continual rains have made the roads across the country
so very bad that I shall with difficulty be able to get carriages to undertake the removal of my goods. I am obliged to be from this place
by Christmas, and, as ill luck would have it, could not procure myself a convenient retreat before now, on account of the difficulty of
getting workmen in harvest time. The place is now ready to receive
me, as I had notice by this day's post.[3] It is at a place called Waterbeche, within five miles of Cambridge and ten of Ely, on a fine turnpike road, which is the only good thing about it, for the village is a
wretched one, and the house still more deplorable, with hardly any
common tolerable conveniences about it. I made all possible inquiries
for a suitable place on the other side the county, and indeed in
other counties, but all to no purpose,[4] so I was drove at last to take up
with what I don't at all approve of. But it is time to leave off to give
so bad an account of myself and situation. However, as you was so
good as to inquire about me, I am obliged to tell the truth, though
the subject may not be so pleasant either to you or myself, and therefore I will dwell no longer upon it.

In your next, which will probably meet me at Waterbeche (as I
think of sending my goods next week if I can, and following them
soon after, as soon as some can be put up for my reception), I shall be
much obliged to you to inform me of the state of your health, and
whether it was that wh<ich oc>casioned your French journey, how
you was amused there, and whether you think it probable that the old
Popish religion with the abbeys will be able to keep its footing in that
kingdom or not. I hope I have not asked too many questions. If I
have, I beg to be resolved only in those which concern only yourself.

I long to show you a work that has taken up all my time for these
four months. When I was last in Cambridgeshire[5] I was at a person's
house[6] whom I am under obligations to, and who had met with fif-

and that my tenant, Mr Huckle, was forced
to remove all his stock and goods to Wil-
lingham from Frog Hall Farm [Cole's
farm], . . . his wheat stack being five foot
under water' (*Blecheley Diary* 184).

3. Cole wrote in *Blecheley Diary* for
Wednesday, 28 Oct.: 'L[ette]r from Mr
Masters, who was amazed exceedingly at
my silence, as the house is ready for me' (p.
281).

4. Cole's search for a suitable house figures largely in *Blecheley Diary*.

5. 'to look at the house I am now removing to' (addition in Cole's copy). On
this journey Cole left Blecheley 11 Aug.
and returned 15 Aug. (*Blecheley Diary*
247–50).

6. The Rev. Robert Masters's at Landbeach.

teen large maps of a parish which were taken in 1601, and where he
has large property under a college.[7] These he wanted copies of, and
knew not how to get them. A man at Cambridge undertook to do
them for six guineas, which he did not care to part with for them.
Laborious and little entertaining as the work seemed to be, I undertook it, and with the help of a little man in my parish,[8] I have not
only copied each exactly, field, acre and rood, but with my brushes
and paint[9] have ornamented with arms of the old proprietors and
other embellishments every corner and vacant space, that I am quite
enamoured with my own performances, and stand amazed at my own
ingenuity.[10] Thus day by day time passes under me, and happy I think
myself that I can so amuse myself with such trifles, as to be unconcerned with what is going forward in the world. But I will tire your
patience no longer, and wishing you every blessing this world can afford, among which health I reckon the most valuable, I am, dear Sir,

Your ever faithful and obliged servant,

WM COLE

To COLE, Saturday 19 December 1767

Add MS 5952, f. 56.

Cole received the letter 26 Dec. (*Blecheley Diary* 304).

Address: [From COLE's copy, Add MS 5824, f. 174v.] To the Rev. Mr Cole at
Waterbeche near Cambridge. Free Hor Walpole.

Strawberry Hill, Dec. 19, 1767.

YOU are now I reckon settled in your new habitation:[1] I would
not interrupt you in your journeyings, dear Sir, but am not at
all pleased that you are seated so little to your mind—and yet I think

---

7. '15 or 16 large maps of the parish of
Gamlingay, belonging to Merton College,
and done extremely well in 1601, by one
Tho. Langdon; they were lent privately to
Mr Masters, who holds an estate in that
parish, under that College, by Mr Joseph
Kilner, Fellow of the same . . . . I undertook it in order to oblige Mr Masters, who
is at some trouble on my account in preparing an house for me at Waterbeche'
(ibid. 251).

8. Edward Wells, formerly the schoolmaster of Water Eaton, Bucks. Apparently
he drew the outlines of the maps, which
Cole then filled in and coloured. He
worked 17 Aug.–26 Sept. (ibid. 251–67).

9. 'which I never used before in my life'
(addition in Cole's copy).

10. 'This has led me, since I sent for
brushes and colours in shells from London
for this work, to blazon in their proper
colours all the heraldry in my numerous

you will stay there; Cambridge and Ely are neighbourhoods to your taste, and if you do not again shift your quarters, I shall make you and them a visit: Ely I have never seen. I could have wished that you had preferred this part of the world, and yet I trust I shall see you here oftener than I have done of late. This to my great satisfaction is my last session of Parliament, to which and to politics I shall forever bid adieu!

I did not go to Paris for my health, though I found the journey and the sea-sickness, which I had never experienced before, contributed to it greatly. I have not been so well for some years as I am at present; and if I continue to plump up as I do at present, I do not know but by the time we meet whether you may not discover—with a microscope, that I am really fatter. I went to make a visit to my dear old blind woman,[2] and to see some things I could not see in winter.

For the Catholic religion, I think it very consumptive—with a little patience, if Whitfield, Wesley, my Lady Huntingdon[3] and that rogue Madan[4] live, I do not doubt but we shall have something very like it here, and yet I had rather live at the end of a tawdry religion than at the beginning, which is always more stern and hypocritic.

I shall be very glad to see your laborious work of the maps: you are indefatigable, I know; I think mapping would try my patience more than anything.

My *Richard III* will go to the press this week, and you shall have one of the first copies which I think will be in about a month, if you will tell me how to convey it.[5] Direct to Arlington Street.

Mr Gray went to Cambridge yesterday sennight; I wait for some papers from him for my purpose.[6]

MS volumes, so that at least they will have the merit of finery to recommend them' (addition in Cole's copy).

1. At Waterbeach, where Cole 'went to reside' 1 Dec. (*Blecheley Diary* 295).
2. Mme du Deffand.
3. Selina Shirley (1707–91), m. (1728) Theophilus Hastings (1696–1746), 9th E. of Huntingdon. She was the foundress of 'Lady Huntingdon's Connection,' a sect of Calvinistic Methodists opposed to Wesley.
4. The Rev. Martin Madam (1726–90), follower and correspondent of John Wesley, and friend of Lady Huntingdon. HW's 'rogue' was doubtless provoked by Madan's

stand in 'the Aldwinkle affair' of this year, for which see DNB and Falconer Madan, *The Madan Family*, Oxford, 1933, pp. 281–4.
5. *Historic Doubts on the Life and Reign of King Richard the Third.* It was published by J. Dodsley 1 Feb. 1768. 'I had begun it in the winter of 1767; continued it in the summer, and finished it after my return from Paris. Twelve hundred copies were printed, and sold so very fast that a new edition was undertaken the next day of 1,000 more, and published the next week' ('Short Notes').
6. Gray to HW 24 Dec. 1767 sent information concerning Richard III's letter

I grieve for your sufferings by the inundation, but you are not only a hermit, but what is better, a real philosopher. Let me hear from you soon.

Yours ever,

H. W.

From COLE, Sunday 27 December 1767

VA, Forster MS 110, f. 53. COLE's copy, Add MS 5824, ff. 174v, 175v.
HW wrote on the cover: '3d & 4th Anecd[otes]

Herbert Tuer
Books bound
Bp Newton
Ld Balt 2d Edit.
Patagonians 2.'

He used some of these notes in his reply of 1 Feb. 1768.
    Address: For the Honourable Mr Horace Walpole in Arlington Street, London.
    Postmark: Cambridge 30 DE.

Waterbeche, Dec. 27, 1767.

Dear Sir,

ONE has need of a good share of real philosophy and patience, or such a friendly and kind remembrance of me as I received from you yesterday (though dated the 19th of this instant), to keep up one's spirits in such a smoky house as I have got into.[1] Had it been free from that trying fault I should have made no complaints about the wretchedness of its situation and conveniences about it, and I assure you, was it still more inconvenient than it really is, I would stay in it was it only to claim the promise of seeing you here, where I hope in the summer that I shall be able to provide you a warm and clean bed, if you will excuse the paltriness of the place. That can be no point with you, who will doubly enjoy the sweets and elegances of Strawberry Hill after seeing the rusticity of a true fen town.

I have been here just a month, but have neither been to see or have seen anyone here from Cambridge since my arrival. I longed

---

on Jane Shore (printed in *Historic Doubts* pp. 118–9), and another letter presumably from Richard III to his mother. See also HW to Gray 18 Feb. 1768.

1. Cole fully describes his house and poor situation in his letter to Mrs Barton, Christmas Day 1767, printed in *Blecheley Diary* 307–12.

after an hermitage, and I believe I have found the very spot where it was designed to be built, but I could have liked to have been placed where were fewer religious brawls than in this parish, where above half the people assemble in a barn, being the disciples of one Berridge whom you may remember at Clare Hall, a gloomy me<lan>-cholic kind of man, and whose principles are the same you mention in your letter. This man, though now in a college living, yet keeps up a party all over this county and alternately preaches Methodism among them.[2]

The account you give me of your health is the most agreeable part of your kind letter: may you grow as fat and jolly as your worthy father was, if you like it and feel no inconvenience from it! For my part, though not unwieldily fat,[3] yet I had rather be as lean as yourself than bear such an encumbrance continually about me. Few are contented with their own size and condition, yet I suppose the inconveniences of one and the other are by no means to [be] put in competition.

Many thanks for your kind purpose of sending me your *Richard III,* which I am impatient to see. If you will be so good as to send it to my late parishioner, Mr Cartwright, who is a laceman in Ludgate Street, he will convey it to me. I wish you mayn't think me troublesome and impertinent if I ask you for your Patagonian book,[4] which I have <not> yet seen, no more than the last volume of your *Paint-*

2. John Berridge (1716–93), evangelical clergyman and author, contemporary with HW and Cole at Cambridge; vicar of Everton, Bedfordshire, 1755, the 'college living' in the gift of Clare Hall, which Cole mentions. He met Wesley and Whitefield in 1758, and became an enthusiastic Methodist. Cole later wrote: 'He has now the honour to be head of a sect called "Berridges" in the neighbourhood of Cambridge, and at Waterbeche used frequently to preach in a barn, where he to this day contributes to the support of many labourers, gardeners, collar-makers, tailors, etc., as preachers, who go from thence on Sundays to neighbouring villages to preach' (quoted in Thompson Cooper, *A New Biographical Dictionary,* New York, 1874). See also *Blecheley Diary* 249, 310–11.

3. For Cole's weight at various periods between 1758 and 1775, see LA i. 698. About eight months after the date of this letter (23 Aug. 1768) he weighed '14 stone 2 pounds' (198 pounds), which in 1775 had increased to '15 stone' (210 pounds).

4. *An Account of the Giants lately Discovered,* written by HW 28–9 June 1766, and published 25 Aug. following ('Short Notes'). It was reprinted in *Works* ii. 91–102. HW satirizes the extravagant newspaper accounts of the Patagonians, as reported by Hon. John Byron (1723–86), captain of the 'Dolphin,' which returned 9 May 1766 from a voyage of discovery. *A Voyage round the World, in his Majesty's Ship the Dolphin . . . By an Officer on Board the said Ship* was not published until 1767; part of this account was reprinted in *Terra Australis Cognita* [*Callander's Voyages*], 3 vols, Edinburgh, 1766–8, iii. 673–714. HW's essay, one of his best, is on the doubtful benefits of civilization.

ers,[5] and if you gave any <pr>int of my uncle Herbert Tuer,[6] shall
be much obliged to you for a few copies to give to each of my sisters
and one or two others, as also one for myself and another for my book
of prints, and at the same time another print of yourself in mezzotinto: you was so kind to give me two formerly: one is framed and I
had the other in my said book of prints, where it was seen by a friend
to whom I could not deny it on his begging it of me.

As I generally take notes in my reading of anything which I think
may be curious to my friends as well as myself, I lately met with an
account of a learned society or *accademia* at Florence which had one
of your ancestors, as I conceive, for its president or protector between
1650 and 1660. I met with it in the *Mescolanze* of Menage, wrote in
Italian.[7] If you have not the book, or have not made the remark yourself, I will transcribe the whole passage and send it you. He is called
'Il Signor Walpoole, Inglese.'

I will tire you no more at present, but with wishing you a long
continuance of that health and good spirits you seem to enjoy, and
am, dear Sir,

Your ever obliged and most faithful servant,

WM COLE

To COLE, Monday 1 February 1768

Add MS 5952, ff. 57–8.

Cole wrote on the cover, 'Petruccio Ubaldini's print.' He received the letter
6 Feb. (*Waterbeach Diary* 12).

Address: To the Reverend Mr Cole at Waterbeche near Cambridge. Free Hor
Walpole. *Postmark:* [?] O 1 FE.

Arlington Street, Feb. 1, 1768.

Dear Sir,

I HAVE waited for the impression of my *Richard,* to send you the
whole parcel together. This moment I have conveyed to Mr Cartwright a large bundle for you, containing *Richard III,* the four volumes of the new edition of the *Anecdotes,*[1] and six prints of your re-

5. *Anecdotes*[1] iv. It was not published
until 9 Oct. 1780.

6. The print of Tuer was inserted on the
plate with Sevonyans, *Anecdotes*[2] iii. opp.
p. 136.

7. See *post* 16 Feb. 1768.

———

1. *Anecdotes of Painting*[2], 3 vols, 1765,
and *A Catalogue of Engravers*[2], 1765. Cole's
copy of the *Engravers*, now WSL, contains

lation Tuer. You will find his head very small, but the original was too inconsiderable to allow it to be larger. I have sent you no Patagonians, for they are out of print, I have only my own copy and could not get another. Pray tell me how or what you heard of it, and tell me sincerely, for I did not know it had made any noise.

I shall be much obliged to you for the extract relating to the academy of which a Walpole was president. I doubt if he was of our branch, and rather think he was of the younger and Roman Catholic branch.

Are you reconciled to your new habitation?² Don't you find it too damp? And if you do, don't deceive yourself, and try to surmount it; but remove immediately. Health is the most important of all considerations. Adieu! Dear Sir.

Yours ever,

H. WALPOLE

From COLE, Tuesday 16 February 1768

VA, Forster MS 110, ff. 54–7. COLE's copy, Add MS 5824, ff. 175v, 176v.
Address: For the honourable Horace Walpole Esq. in Arlington Street, London.
Postmark: Cambridge 18 FE. [Cole gave the letter to 'Capt. Wiles' to post (*Waterbeach Diary* 16).]

Waterbeche near Cambridge, Feb. 16, 1768.

Dear Sir,

A MOST violent cold attended with a fever has been the occasion of my not answering your last kind letter and most valuable present before. The latter, particularly the new piece,¹ came most opportunely to amuse me when nothing else could. It has pleased me beyond measure and thoroughly convinced me that if Richard was no saint, yet he was not the sinner that he has been represented. It will be no easy task to refute the arguments you have so masterly drawn up in his favour. That this is spoke out of mere conviction and thor-

numerous notes in Cole's hand. Immediately preceding the index, p. 20 of 'List of Vertue's Works,' is his inscription: 'Wm. Cole. Ex Donis honorab: Auctoris Febr: 1. 1768.'

2. Waterbeach.

———

1. *Historic Doubts.* Cole did not receive the bundle until 11 Feb. (*Waterbeach Diary* 14).

ough persuasion of its truth you may be assured when I ingenuously tell you that I began to read it with no small prepossession against the writer who had treated my good friends the monks so harshly in the preface,[2] so that I could scarce forbear wishing you wrote more like other people. Such a pen as yours will do them and their cause more mischief in such a volume as yours is, than in all the laboured writings against them since their destruction.

My thanks, I am sure, are more than due for your obliging mention of my name[3] in a work that will last when no traces will be found that such an one as myself ever existed. I never knew that you had done me that honour, or that a new edition of your *Anecdotes* had passed the press till you were so kind as to send it to me. I only thought that you had given the remaining volume of *Painters*, which is still wanting, but may it be not long so, for I never had more eagerness or curiosity for any books than for those from Strawberry Hill. The print of my uncle Herbert Tuer is very neat, and I can never enough thank you for placing him in your Temple of Fame, where he will never more be forgotten.

Sorry I am you could not favour me with a Patagonian, as I never yet saw the book or any extract from it. The first notice I had of it was from a particular friend of mine in Cheshire, Mr John Allen, who wrote me word how entertained he had been with it. <Soon> after I met with one Captain Mansell,[4] a gentleman of Northamptonshire, who was in raptures about it. He had read it at the Duke of Grafton's at Wakefield Lodge in Wittlebury Forest,[5] where it was the only subject of conversation for a time. And this is all, I am sorry,

2. HW accused the monks of falsifying history: they 'wrote with so little judgment, and committed such palpable forgeries, that if we cannot discover what really happened in those ages, we can at least be very sure what did not. . . . Yet how long were these imposters the only persons who attempted to write history!' (*Historic Doubts*[1] p. vii). 'Mr Walpole's preface to *Richard III* very severe on the monks and too sceptical' (*Waterbeach Diary* 15).

3. HW mentions 'a MS account of all the members of King's College, a copy of which is in the possession of the Rev. Mr Cole of Blecheley, to whom the public and I are obliged for this and several other curious particulars' (*Anecdotes*[2] i. 105–6 nn). When he adopts Cole's other notes, it is without acknowledgment.

4. 'of Cosgrove in Northamptonshire' (addition in Cole's copy). John Mansel (d. 1794), afterwards Lt-Col of the Third Dragoon Guards and Major-General in the army, was 'a highly distinguished and gallant officer' who was killed at the Battle of Coteau, 2 April 1794 (Burke, *Landed Gentry*, 2 vols, 1851, i. 828).

5. Wakefield Lodge in Whittlebury Forest, 'an elegant house . . . originally built by Mr Claypole, son-in-law to Oliver Cromwell' (see Thomas Pennant, *Journey from Chester to London*, 1782, p. 204).

I can say of it, though I make no doubt, when I get out of this dirt and get to Cambridge, I shall be able to meet with it somewhere or other. Bishop Joseph Hall,[6] in an odd quaint book which I have got, called a *Discovery of a New World in the South Indies,* printed before he was a bishop, mentions the Patagonians.[7] This was in James or Charles I's time, for my edition is not dated.

Have you a print of Petruccio Ubaldini? I have a good one which I value not at all.

I shall transcribe the whole letter relating to the academy whereof Il Signor Walpole was president. It puts me in mind of something like it which you have mentioned in your ingenious account of Sir Balthazar Gerbier.[8] Is not this Signor Walpole the same person who patronized Sir William Dugdale and his works? as I think I remember a plate or two[9] inscribed with your arms in some of his books. In the new edition of the *Menagiana* at Paris, 1729, in four volumes, is this testimony, however, of the author of the letter.[10]

M. Coltellini étoit du nombre des amis que j'ai eus, & que j'ai encore à Florence. Il avoit beaucoup de mérite, il etoit Avocat de Florence, Garde des Archives de la Ville, Chef de l'Academie des Apathistes, membre de celle de la Crusca, & grand ami de Nicolas Heinsius. Il étoit aussi grand Juriconsulte, & il a fait imprimer quelques poësies Italiennes, & quelques discours de dévotion en prose.

The following note is added to this article:

Voiez dans les *Mescolanze* de M. Ménage deux lettres que ce Coltellini lui écrit, dans la premiere desquelles il est parlé des *Apathistes,* c'est-à-dire, hommes sans passions, surnom qu'au rapport de Coltellini, leur donna le fameux *Udeno Nisieli,* autrement Benedetto Fioretti, dont nous avons *Proginnasmi Poëtici* en 5. volumes *in* 4°. Augustin Coltellini mourut à Florence âgé de 81. ans le 26. d'Août 1693.

6. (1574–1656), Bishop of Exeter and Norwich, and satirist.

7. *The Discovery of a New World* was first published in Latin as *Mundus alter et idem,* Frankfort, 1605; the English translation by John Healey appeared in London about 1608 or 1609. The work is a prose satire, with numerous gibes at the Roman Catholic Church (see DNB, *sub* Joseph Hall).

8. Sir Balthazar Gerbier founded (1648) and became president of an academy 'for foreign languages and all noble sciences and exercises' (*Anecdotes, Works* iii. 191).

9. Plate 166 in Dugdale's *St Paul's* is dedicated 'Johannem Walpoole de Pinchbeck in Com. Linc. Militem.' It is inscribed with the Walpole arms, differenced with a canton, sable, bearing a lion passant. The crest is that of the Lincolnshire branch of the Walpole family.

10. The following quotation and note appear in Gilles de Ménage (1613–92), *Menagiana,* new edn, Paris, 1729, iii. 137–8.

Lettera del S. Agostino Coltellini al Signor Egidio Menagio.[11]

E proprio di Persone grandi l'esser conosciuto anche da coloro i quali talvolta non conoscono: e chi da Opere alla Stampa, non si dee maravigliare, se il suo Nome, reso celebre, pervenga all'altrui Notizia. Questo è avvenuto a me: che udendo più volte far Menzione nell'Academia della Crusca (dove ancor'io son descritto, e tra' Deputati del Vocabolario, ancorchè immeritamente, annoverato) di V. Illustrissima e del S. Capellano: e vedendo di più le loro ingegnose ed erudite Opere, mi sono invogliato di dedicarmi all'uno e all'altro parzial Servitore: e dando loro qualche sommaria Notizia di me medesimo, far' ad essi ancor Parte di quel poco che sin quì anno reso i miei sterili Talenti. Ma cominciando a venir a' Particulari, dirò, che applicato nella mia Fanciullezza a gli Studi, nel Progresso de gli Anni cominciai a regunar Conversazione de' miei Eguali; e appoco appoco andò crescendo in Guisa, col divino Aiuto, che oggi sotto Nome d'*Università* abbraccia tutte le Nazioni che ci concorrono: ed è libero l'operare in tutte le Lingue, ed il trattar di tutte le Scienze ed Arti: e l'onorano con i loro Nomi i primi Principi, si Ecclesiastici, come Secolari, di varie Parti del Mondo: ed i più celebri Letterati e Cavalieri che vadano attorno: come potrà vedere dalla Lettera del S. Einsio scritta al S. Carlo Dati, uno de' chiari Lumi, non meno di essa, che dell'altre Academie, e della Nobilità erudita di questa Patria. E perchè a Principio ebbi Intenzione, che l'Adunanza fosse non meno una Scola di Scienze, e d'Arti, che del Governo civile ancora, subalternai a questo Genere un'Accademia, denominata *de gl'Apatisti,* da quel celebre Udeno Nisieli, di cui avrà veduti gli eruditissimi Proginnasmi; perchè avendola egli in Astratto, per usar questi Termini Scolastici, lo invitai nella mia Casa, mettendola in Concreto, con farle l'Impresa che vedrà, e ordinarla in quel miglior Modo, che si giudicò opportuno. Il Capo dell'Università, quando è Gentiluomo, si chiama *Gran Priore;* quando è Principe, *Protettore;* si come fù già l'Eminentissimo Signor Cardinale Giovan-Carlo, ed oggi il Serenissimo Granduca, nostro Signore: per cui, come Luogotenenti, riseggono, o il Signor Marchese Coppoli, Maestro di Camera, o il Signor Desiderio Montemagni, Segretario di Stato. Il *Presidente* dell'Accademia, che per Eccelenza si chiama *l'Apatista Reggente,* è sempre qualche Cavaliere, o Letterato celebre, nostrale, o forestiero: come furono il Signor Walpoole, Inglese, e il S. Einsio, secondo che si porge l'Occasione. Questi propone un Dubbio a suo Arbitrio, da risolversi nella futura Sessione: se è Teologo, di Teologia; se Giurisconsulto, di Giurisprudenza, &c. e dopo, per Corona dell'Accademia, si leggono Poesie in quella Lingua, che a essa più

---

11. This letter appears in *Mescolanze d'Egidio Menagio,* Venice, 1736, pp. 171–3. Cole's transcript has been followed *verbatim et literatim.*

aggrada. Si lodano annualmente diversi Santi, nostri Protettori; e particolarmente San Luigi, Rè di Francia; di cui il Signor Abbate Strozzi già celebrò le Lodi: ed ultimamente à riseduto come Apatista, dando Saggi corrispondenti al suo nobile e gentile Ingegno. Si vanno giornalmente aggregando nuovi Suggetti: tra' quali ultimamente con dovuto Applauso di tutti questi miei Signori, sono stati descritti, e V. S. Illustrissima, ed il Signor Capellano: sperando che l'uno e l'altro sia per gradire questa Dimostrazione d'una particulare Stima, e d'un reverente Affetto verso la Singularità de' loro Meriti: ed appreso onorar l'Accademia con le loro nobilissime Composizioni. Io poi nel Resto me la passo impiegato, per lo più da sua Altezza, in qualchuno de' primi Magistrati di questa Città. O' date in Luce più Opere in Versi ed in Prosa; le quali, quando mi si porga comoda Occasione, manderò a lor Signorie: e se m'accennasse a chi devo consegnarle, lo farò prontamente: non perchè Io le giudichi degne di loro, ma per dar' quel ch'io posso, già che non posso quel che dovrei. E quì, pregando V. S. illustrissima a perdonarmi della Lunghezza, ossequiosamente la riverisco. Firenze 16 Ottob: 1659.

I beg that I may have the advantage of Signor Coltellini's conclusion of his long letter, because I can't make a conciser apology for all this scrawl, yet I chose not to curtail the letter, as you might have a curiosity to see the whole.

I am, dear Sir,

Your ever faithful and obliged servant,

WM COLE

To COLE, Saturday 16 April 1768

Add MS 5952, ff. 59–60.

Cole wrote on the cover for his reply, 14 May 1768:

'Martin Droeshout sculpsit London. Wm Shakespeare quarto print. [See Granger, *Biographical History*[1] i. 285.]

'Sir Francis Crane was commissioned with Francis Earl of Bedford and others, 1634, to see after the draining the fens in the counties of Cambridge, Huntingdon, Northampton, Lincoln, Norfolk, Suffolk and Isle of Ely: by means of which noble and beneficial undertaking, as I suppose, the estate at Cov[eney?] came into his family. Dugdale's *History of Imbanking and Drayning of Divers Fens and Marshes*, p. 410.

'Geoffrey Hudson the Dwarf. Wright's *Rutland*, p. 105.' [Cole has marked through this note.]

Cole did not use the first note in the copy of his reply (from which the letter is edited), but he may have done so in the letter he sent.

Cole received this letter 18 April (*Waterbeach Diary* 40).

Address: To the Reverend Mr Cole at Waterbeche near Cambridge.

Postmark: Isleworth 16 AP. Cambridge Of. 299 [In a circle within a circle].

John Black 667 [Within a circle. The meaning of these stamps is not clear].

Strawberry Hill, April 16, 1768.

WELL, dear Sir, does your new habitation improve as the spring advances? There has been dry weather and east wind enough to drain and parch the fens. We find that the severe beginning of this last winter has made terrible havoc among the evergreens, though of old standing. Half my cypresses have been bewitched and turned into brooms, and the laurustinus is perished everywhere. I am Goth enough to choose now and then to believe in prognostics, and I hope this destruction imports that though foreigners should take root here, they cannot last in this climate. I would fain persuade myself that we are to be our own empire to eternity.

The Duke of Manchester[1] has lent me an invaluable curiosity, I mean, invaluable to us antiquaries—but I perhaps have already mentioned it to you,[2] I forget whether I have or not. It is the original roll of the Earls of Warwick, as long as my gallery, and drawn by John Rous himself[3]—ay, and what is more, there are portraits of Richard III, his Queen and son, the two former corresponding almost exactly with my print,[4] and a panegyric on the virtues of Richard,[5] and a satire upwards and downwards, on the illegal marriage of Edward IV and on the extortions of Henry VII. I have had these and seven other portraits copied, and shall sometime or other give plates of them— but I wait for an excuse;[6] I mean till Mr Hume shall publish a few

1. George Montagu (1737–88), 4th D. of Manchester, from whom Sandwich borrowed the roll for HW (see HW to Gray 26 Feb. 1768; 'Supplement to the Historic Doubts,' *Works* ii. 216).

2. HW is thinking of his letter to Gray 26 Feb. 1768.

3. HW describes the roll in his letter to Gray 26 Feb. 1768, and in *Works* ii. 216–7. John Rous (1411?–91), antiquary of Warwick, drew up two versions of the roll, the earlier (which HW saw) commended Richard III, the later (prepared after 1485) was strongly Lancastrian in tone. The earlier was privately printed (100 copies) in 1845,

but it was not published until 1859 (with an introduction by William Courthope) under the title *This rol was laburd & finished by Master John Rows of Warrewyk* (see DNB). The copy HW saw 'is seven yards and a half long' (*Works,* loc. cit.), twenty feet shorter than the Long Gallery at SH.

4. A print of Richard III and Queen Anne in *Historic Doubts*[1], opp. p. 103.

5. Which HW quoted in 'Supplement to the Historic Doubts,' *Works* ii. 217.

6. Before 1790 HW 'had some of the portraits not only copied but engraved for a second [i.e., third] edition of my *Historic Doubts,* though I have been too indolent

remarks he has made on my book[7]—they are very far from substantial, yet still better than any other trash that has been written against it, nothing of which deserves an answer.

I have long had thoughts of drawing up something for London like St Foix's *Rues de Paris*,[8] and have made some collections.[9] I wish you would be so good in the course of your reading to mark down any passages to that end; as where any great houses of the nobility were situated, or in what street any memorable event happened. I fear the subject will not furnish much till later times, as our princes kept their courts up and down the country in such a vagrant manner.

I expect Mr Gray and Mr Mason to pass the day with me here tomorrow. When I am more settled here, I shall put you in mind of your promise to bestow more than one day on me.

I hope the Methodist your neighbour[10] does not like his patriarch Whitfield encourage the people to forge, murder, etc., in order to have the benefit of being converted at the gallows. That arch-rogue preached lately a funeral sermon[11] on one Gibson hanged for forgery,[12] and told his audience that he could assure them Gibson was

to put my intention in practice' (to George Nicol [?], 6 July 1790). The ten prints were first included in *Historic Doubts, Works* ii. between pp. 166 and 167, on two large folding plates.

7. Hume's observations were first published in French as notes (pp. 26–35) to Gibbon's review of *Historic Doubts* (pp. 1–25) in *Mémoires littéraires de la Grande Bretagne pour l'an 1768*, London, 1769. HW intemperately replied to Hume and other critics in 'Supplement to the Historic Doubts,' which he showed to Hume in MS, but his reply was not published until 1798, in *Works* ii. 185–220. Cf. 'Short Notes' for 1769.

8. Germain François Poullain de St Foix (1698–1776) was the author of *Essais historiques sur Paris*, first published in Paris, 5 vols, 1754–7. The first part contains an historical account of the streets of Paris. It appears from MS Cat. that HW had only one volume of the work, London, 1755 (G.6.35), which was sold SH iv. 29. He slightingly refers to a later edition under the title 'Les Anecdotes des rues de Paris' in *Engravers, Works* iv. 8.

9. HW devoted one section of a MS 'Book of Materials,' which he began in

Sept. 1759, to 'Anecdotes of the Streets of London and other places,' and in another, which he began in 1771, to 'The Streets of London.' Both books, formerly in the Waller Collection, are now in the Folger Library.

10. John Berridge.

11. Apparently nothing further is known of this sermon.

12. James Gibson, an attorney about 45 years of age, who forged receipts enabling him to embezzle more than £900 and was hanged at Tyburn 23 March 1768. On the morning of his execution he received the sacrament from Whitefield in Newgate (*Whitehall Evening Post* 22–4 March 1768). It was reported that Whitefield had previously converted Gibson from Catholicism (*London Chronicle* 24–6 March 1768). For an account of the affair, see *The London Magazine*, Ser. I, vol. 35 (1766), pp. 51, 132–3 and vol. 37 (1768), pp. 53, 164; Gibson's own account, *The Case of James Gibson, Attorney at Law, faithfully and impartially stated*, 1768, a pamphlet of 40 pages, which is noticed in *The London Chronicle* 20–3 Feb. 1768; *The Complete Newgate Calendar*, ed. J. L. Rayner and G. T. Crook, privately printed for the Navarre Society, 5

now in heaven, and that another fellow,[13] executed at the same time, had the happiness of touching Gibson's coat, as he was turned off. As little as you and I agree about an hundred years ago, I don't desire a reign of fanatics. Oxford has begun with these rascals, and I hope Cambridge will wake—I don't mean that I would have them persecuted, which is what they wish—but I would have the clergy fight them and ridicule them. Adieu! dear Sir,

Yours ever,

H. W.

From Cole, Saturday 14 May 1768

Cole's copy, Add MS 5824, ff. 177v–180v. The original is missing.

Address: [From Cole's copy.] For the Honourable Horace Walpole at Strawberry Hill in Twickenham, Middlesex.

Waterbeche, May 14, 1768.

Dear Sir,

YOUR most entertaining and obliging letter of April 16th deserved a much earlier answer. You would have had one also, but for two or three reasons: the most material is, I am desired by an old acquaintance[1] who undertook twenty years ago to write an *History of the Cathedral of Ely* to help him to forward this long-expected work into the world;[2] and if I do not, I am much afraid it will never be done at all. About two months ago he begged that I would write the lives of Bishop West[3] and his successors to this time: Bishop West lived in Henry VIII's reign; since which he has again desired me to

---

vols, 1926, iv. 58–9; and *Mem. of the Reign of George III*, iii. 132. James Boswell found the hanging, on the whole, the best he ever saw (*Private Papers of James Boswell* vii. 164).

13. Benjamin Payne, a footpad, about 19 years of age, servant to a carpenter, and lodged in Islington. He was captured 22 Jan. 1768 after robbing a post-chariot, committed to Clerkenwell Bridewell, and hanged at Tyburn 23 March 1768. Gibson requested that Payne be allowed to accompany him in his mourning-coach, instead of being carried in a cart, but the sheriff refused (*Private Papers of James*

Boswell, loc. cit.; *The Complete Newgate Calendar*, loc. cit.; *The Whitehall Evening Post* 23–6 Jan. 1768).

1. James Bentham.
2. Cole's extensive contributions to this work are indicated below and in Bentham's *Ely* itself. Cole's caustic notes in his own copy of *Ely* are printed in William Davis's *Olio of Bibliographical and Literary Anecdotes and Memoranda*, 1814, pp. 109–26.
3. Nicolas West (1461–1533), Bp of Ely 1515–33 (Bentham, *Ely*[2] pp. 187–9).

begin so early as Bishop Lewis de Luxemberg's[4] time, under Henry VI. All before this are already printed off; so that I have been very busy, having nothing else to do, in composing some of these lives, and I foresee, if I do not go on with the whole, as priors, deans, archdeacons, prebendaries, the book will never come out, which would be a great pity, for there are already very neatly engraved about fifty plates of views of the church, tombs, old Saxon and Gothic doors and windows, with other antiquities. I know you will be much pleased with this part of the work when it is published, and therefore, on that presumption, I take the liberty to beg your assistance particularly in the life of Cardinal Lewis de Luxemburgh, who had been Archbishop of Rouen, and on King Henry's loss of France, as a partisan of his, was forced to follow him into England, who gave him the See of Ely to hold as Perpetual Administrator. It is probable you may have some good modern history, or ancient, of Normandy, in which the lives of the archbishops of Rouen are wrote. If you have, I shall be obliged for a short abstract concerning him, his family, preferments, arms, cause of his banishment, or any enlivening circumstance you know so well how to relate.

I have drawn up, and finished this very day, a long account of Cardinal Morton,[5] in which I have taken the liberty, not to mention your name, but to hint at your last performance in these very words: which, if you object to, I shall readily blot out and take no sort of notice of what you have said about him. You know my veneration to anything that ever had any relation to a mitre.

Historic Doubts on the Life of Richard III, p. 18.   A most ingenious[6] writer has lately obliquely accused our bishop of violation of his allegiance to Richard III. But can there be any violation of allegiance to a person to whom no allegiance was due, or for aught that appears, was ever made? As the bishop was clapped up in prison before Richard III was crowned, and never after at liberty till he attained it by his own flight, it is most probable he never swore any allegiance to him at all.

Perhaps you may give me cause to alter this.

In this *Life* of Bishop Morton is a curious account of his installa-

---

4. Cardinal Louis de Luxembourg St Pol (d. 1443), Abp of Rouen and Bp of Ely 1438–43 (ibid. 168–72).

5. Bentham, *Ely*[2] 179–81. John Morton

(1420?–1500), Abp of Canterbury and Cardinal, was Bishop of Ely 1478–86.

6. This passage, with minor changes, appears ibid. 180 n.

tion dinner, with old English verses, mixed with French, on every course.[7] Some of the words I can make nothing of; I know, if you saw them, you could much help me. Over every course is wrote in this manner.

Un sotalte de lyon blanke rehersal. Or,
Un sotelte le glede Ely rehersall. Or,
Un sotalte de Dieu Schepard etc.— Or,
Un sotelte de le eglesure letonne rehersall. etc.

I want to know the meaning of the word *sotalte* or *sotelte*.[8] If you can inform me I shall be obliged to you. I would send the whole *Life,* if I knew how.

Another reason I wrote not before, was, I was desirous to see St Foix's book on the *Rues de Paris*. I never saw it, but by the argument of it, I know it would please me, and I have sent for it, but it is not yet come.[9] I wish I may be able to assist you: I am sure no one will do it with more pleasure. I have met with one observation, however, to your purpose, which is the more curious as it takes notice of the public stews at the same time, so often mentioned by our historians, as allowed by the Bishop of Winchester.[10] It is in that curious and scarce book of Sir William Dugdale, on the *Imbanking and Draining the Fens,* published at London in folio, 1662, at pp. 66–67,[11] where it ascertains the mansion of the ancestors of the great Dukes of Norfolk. I will transcribe the whole account.

In 26 E. III. (1352) Will Thorpe, James Husee, and Will. de Fifhide were appointed to view and repair the banks at the Stewes, and in other places adjacent, by the breach whereof divers grounds and meadows lay then totally drowned. And in 37 E. III. Edmund Chelreye, Thomas Mor-

---

7. This account, 'copied from an old book in the Herald's Office, wanting the title-page, printed in the old black character,' is printed ibid. Appendix No. XXX, pp. *35–*36.

8. *Sotelte,* an obsolete form of *subtlety,* in cookery, 'a highly ornamental device, wholly or chiefly made of sugar, sometimes eaten, sometimes used as a table decoration' (OED). See also William Edward Mead, *The English Medieval Feast,* [1931], p. 165 ff.

9. Cole's edition was an English translation, *Essays upon Paris,* 3 vols, 1767 (see Cole, *Jour. to Paris* 118).

10. 'A number of brothels anciently situated on the Bankside, Southwark, and licensed by the Bishop of Winchester. There were at first eighteen of these houses, but afterwards only twelve were allowed.' They were governed by strict regulations, confirmed by Act of Parliament in the reign of Henry II, but were 'put down by order of Henry VIII in the year 1546' (*London and its Environs Described,* 6 vols, 1761, vi. 73–5).

11. *History of Imbanking and Draining of Divers Fens and Marshes.*

ice, and Michael Skillyng, had the like appointment for those banks near the said Stewes, which were opposite to the manor house of John de Moubray. Before which commissioners, divers presentments were then made touching those banks and sewers near the same Stewes; where divers persons, being found faulty, paid fines to the king; others acknowledged that they ought to repair them by the perch; and others had made good what belonged to them to do; whereof the prior of St. John of Jerusalem was one; who had two mills there, and other lands, to the value of xl. *per annum*. The like was certified of Sir John de Moubray knight, and Elizabeth, his wife, daughter and heir of John de Segrave.

I take it for granted that Southwark, as a suburb, is within the limits of your design, which I shall be the better judge of when I see St Foix's book.

When I was last at Cambridge I saw one of the oldest register books, called Alpha, that belongs to the University.[12] It is in the custody of the Vice-Chancellor. In turning it over I accidentally spied two letters, one in Latin, the other in English, from the University to Richard III: one while Protector, the first when just crowned. I was in hopes they had been more curious, and got leave to transcribe them, in order to transmit them to you, though I gave not the least distant hint that such was my design, for fear of meeting any obstruction. I find the whole is to intercede with him for the enlargement of their chancellor, Archbishop Rotheram,[13] then in custody. If you have any curiosity to have them, pray let me know it, and I will send them. They may be curious for their style, and as they show Richard to have been a great patron and friend to the University before his accession to the Crown: and they tell that before his royal dignity, and while he was only Duke of Gloucester, they had granted him a favour which they had never granted before to any mortal living.

I am vastly pleased with the account you give me of your acquisition from the Duke of Manchester, and long to see the effects of it. The prints you propose to give the public will be great curiosities: and really you have done more in the way of Father Montfaucon's

---

12. *Grace Book A containing the Proctors' Accounts and other Records of the University of Cambridge for the Years 1454–1488*, ed. Stanley M. Leathes, Cambridge, 1897. The letters described by Cole are printed at pp. 171–2.

13. Thomas Rotherham (1423–1500), Abp of York, four times Chancellor of Cambridge between 1469 and 1500.

Antiquitez de la Monarchie Francoise than all the English world beside. That is a work I long to see some wealthy, great and noble-spirited person set on foot.[14] As to what Mr Hume will say in his answer to some parts of your late book, I can be no judge, but I conceive his Scotch spirit will not remain easy without a reply. I make no doubt but that your answer will be sufficient. What an impudent pack of scoundrels are the Critical Reviewers! The month before your *Historic Doubts* appeared, you was highly in their favour for giving a print and speaking well of a Scotch painter, one Jameson;[15] the very next month, I think, showed their nationality, if I may use the expression. Then you was everything that was bad for not naming a Scotch writer, Guthrie, preferable to Mr Carte.[16] They forget the compliment you very justly paid their nation in your *Noble Authors*.[17] I believe you vex and fret them more by your neglect, and taking no kind of notice of them, than if you exposed them in the most poignant manner, which they well deserve and you know how to perform. Writing against them would do them too much credit: they are like the Methodists: they want to be noticed.

No one can be more dull than Impartialis.[18]

14. In response to a suggestion from Bute (then Secretary of State), HW began, 21 Feb. 1762, to outline the chapters for 'A History of the Manners, Customs, Habits, Fashions, Ceremonies, &c. &c. &c. of England' (see Bute to HW 13 Feb. 1762; HW to Bute 15 Feb. 1762; *Works* v. 400–2). Unfortunately, the work was not pursued. Cole first heard of this plan several years later (see *post* 24 Feb. 1782).

15. In *The Critical Review* for Jan. 1768 (Ser. i, vol. 25, pp. 57–8) is a review of *Additional Lives to the First Edition of Anecdotes of Painting in England*, which consists chiefly of quotations from HW's account of Jamesone.

16. William Guthrie (1708–70), Scottish historian and miscellaneous writer, was the author of the abusive review of *Historic Doubts* in *The Critical Review* for Feb. 1768 (Ser. i, vol. 25, pp. 116–26) (see HW to Montagu 12 March 1768). He was angry because HW did not mention his *General History of England*, 3 vols, 1744–51, from which, Guthrie claimed, Thomas Carte (1686–1754) had borrowed for his *History of England*, 4 vols, 1747–55, a work to

which HW acknowledged his indebtedness. HW replied to him in 'Supplement to the Historic Doubts,' *Works* ii. 187–91.

17. In the introduction to his account of Scots authors, HW says: 'It is not my purpose to give an exact account of the royal and noble authors of Scotland: I am not enough versed in them to do justice to writers of the most accomplished nation in Europe; the nation to which, if any one country is endowed with a superior partition of sense, I should be inclined to give the preference in that particular' (*Works* i. 492).

18. The anonymous author of a series of six letters printed in *The London Chronicle* between 10–12 March and 28–31 May 1768, criticizing *Historic Doubts*. Within that period three additional letters on the same subject were printed: (1) 17–19 March, signed 'Sceptic,' supporting HW; (2) 29–31 March, Impartialis's answer to Sceptic; (3) 23–26 April, unsigned letter from Kent, supporting Impartialis. HW replied to Impartialis in 'Supplement to the Historic Doubts,' *Works* ii. 192. See also the following letter.

This letter is to be one of criticisms, and I know you'll excuse me.

In your *Noble Authors,* vol. 1, p. 20,[19] you make a mistake, I think, in the account of the pedigree of Sir Henry Capel.[20] I have one which was given to me by a descendant of that family many years ago; it is thus in that pedigree:

The wife of Henry Capel was Catherine, daughter of Thomas Lord Roos, Earl of Rutland, by his wife Eleanor, daughter of Sir William Paston of Norfolk: which Thomas Earl of Rutland was son of Sir George Manners, Lord Roos, by his wife Anne, daughter of Sir Thomas St Leger, by his wife Anne Plantagenet, Duchess of Exeter,[21] and sister to King Edward IV.

Page 46 of *Noble Authors,* vol. 1: No such place as Everton[22] in Cambridgeshire; it means Eversden, as I suppose, where the Tiptofts[23] had property.

Page 6 of ditto: Query, if the person in a black gown, on his knees, by Earl Rivers be Caxton? because he is shorn as a priest, and I don't know that Caxton was such.[24]

P. 105 of ditto: Typographical[25] etc.

You somewhere[26] say that you know not when the distinction of coronets was introduced. Leland, in his *Itinerary,* vol. 1, p. 36,[27] says that in Doncaster Whitefriers was buried Margaret Cobham, Countess of Westmorland: but as her coronet is made, says he, it should be for a Duchess. This shows a long distinction. In his second volume, p. 71, he has this observation also on the same subject: 'In the north part of this [Dunster in Somersetshire][28] was buried undre an arche by

19. First edition.

20. HW, quoting John Strype, *Ecclesiastical Memorials,* 3 vols, 1721–33, iii. 468, had said Lady Capel was 'Anne, daughter of George Manners, Lord Roos, whose wife Anne was daughter of the Duchess of Exeter, sister of Edward the Fourth.'

21. Cole's pedigree is correct. HW did not adopt it.

22. The passage stands in *Roy. & Nob. Authors, Works* i. 281. HW took his information from John Leland, *De Scriptoribus Britannicis,* Oxford, 2 vols, 1709, ii. 475.

23. The Barons de Tibetot or Tiptoft, who flourished in the fifteenth century.

24. The print of Lord Rivers presenting Caxton and his book to Edward IV usually appears as the frontispiece to *Roy. & Nob. Authors,* vol. 1. This portrait of Caxton 'is,

in all probability, a spurious one' (Joseph Ames, *Typographical Antiquities,* ed. T. F. Dibdin, 4 vols, 1810–9, i. p. cxxix). It is reproduced in *Works* i. opp. 243. There is no authentic portrait of Caxton (see DNB); for a discussion of an 'Engraving of an author, possibly Caxton . . . prefixed to the Chatsworth copy of the *Recuyell,*' see Alfred W. Pollard, *Fine Books* [1912], pp. 272–3.

25. The text of *Roy. & Nob. Authors* (loc. cit.) reads 'topographical.' HW corrected this in *Works* i. 311.

26. In *Roy. & Nob. Authors, Works* i. 300. HW did not use Cole's note.

27. John Leland's *Itinerary*[2], 9 vols, Oxford, 1744–5, to which Cole was a subscriber.

28. Cole's brackets.

the high altare, one of the Luterelles, or, as I rather thynke, of the Moions [Mohuns, perhaps][28] for he hath a garland about his helmet, and so were lordes of old tymes usid to be buried.'

I don't know whether you ever saw it, but there is a very curious account of Geoffrey Hudson, the dwarf,[29] in Wright's *History of Rutland*,[30] p. 105.

I was lately at Ely, where I saw in Dr Gooch's[31] prebendal house a most excellent landscape, done by one Browne,[32] formerly a coalheaver at Norwich, where he now practises painting in oil. He is a great natural genius. The picture I saw was done for Sir Thomas Gooch,[33] the Doctor's brother, and cost seventeen guineas. If you have not yet heard of this painter, I thought this mention of him would be agreeable to you. I went into Bishop West's chapel,[34] when at Ely, and was struck with amazement and horror at the excessive nice and elegant work in it, which is as much defaced with axes and hammers as any place I ever yet saw. Fanaticism seems to have a particular spite against the most curious performances. You would be much pleased to see the nice work and vast variety in this little chapel, where there are hundreds of niches with Gothic ornaments, and hardly one like another. In the house where I now am I cannot possibly offer you a bed to rest you between Cambridge and Ely, for there is no conveniencies of any sort. I hope soon to be better accommodated, and then I shall be glad to attend you in a pilgrimage to Ely.

I don't know whether you have taken notice of a namesake of mine, one James Cole,[35] among your engravers. He has some excellent

29. Jeffery Hudson (1619–82), who was eighteen inches high until he was thirty years old, but later reached the height of three feet six or nine inches. HW gives an account of him in *Anecdotes*[1] ii. 8–10.

30. *The History and Antiquities of the County of Rutland*, 1684, by James Wright (1643–1713). HW referred to this work in his account of Jeffery Hudson, *Anecdotes*[1] ii. 8 n.

31. John Gooch (1730?–1804), younger son of Sir Thomas Gooch (1675–1754), 2d Bt and Bp of Ely; Prebendary of Ely, 1753–1804. 'With the gravity of a clergyman Dr. Gooch united the easy manner of a gentleman. He was a cheerful and pleasant companion; his disposition and habits were friendly and hospitable' (Bentham, *Ely*[2] Addenda, p. 18; see also ibid. 252).

32. Possibly John Browne (1741–1801), landscape engraver, who was educated at Norwich, though there is no record that he was ever a coal-heaver or that he painted in oil (see Redgrave, *Dict. of Artists*).

33. (1720–81), 3d Bt.

34. Nicholas West (1461–1533), Bp of Ely 1515–33. 'According to his appointment, he was buried in the Chapel which he had built for that purpose, at the east end of the south aisle of the presbytery of his Cathedral:—a work whose singular elegance and exquisite workmanship still appears, notwithstanding the outrageous violences which it has suffered from the fanaticism of enthusiastic reformers' (Bentham, *Ely*[2] p. 189). The passage was undoubtedly written by Cole.

35. James Cole (fl. 1726), who engraved

prints, particularly one of Dean Bargrave,[36] equal to any of our best hands, in Dart's *Antiquities of Canterbury*.

We have a young gentleman of Benet College, one Mr Tyson,[37] with whom I hope soon to be acquainted, who has an excellent turn for drawing; he also engraves on copper. He has taken a plate of Jane Shore from the picture in our Provost's lodge.[38] I have two copies of it:[39] one is reserved for you. He has an admirable turn for caricature drawing, and has taken several remarkable persons most exactly: among the rest, Dr George Baker[40] of our College, Jacob Butler,[41] late of Barnwell, etc.

I am now going to be a beggar. I hope at last I am in a way to be settled for life, for I give up all pretensions to preferment, and shall be contented with my own humble fortunes. I have had three small livings offered me since I came here, but a small one shall not tempt me to leave the neighbourhood of Cambridge, and quiet, to engage myself in a profession I have no great turn for. Where people can't bustle for their dues, they must be contented to be cheated, and that is not pleasant. I have fixed on a most deplorable downfall[en] old cottage or small farm-house belonging to our College, at Milton,[42] one mile nearer Cambridge than where I am at present. The temptation is a most admirable gravel road close up to the door, and about a stone's cast from an excellent turnpike from Ely to Cambridge. As I shall be obliged totally to make it a new house in every respect ex-

all the plates for John Dart's *History and Antiquities of the Cathedral Church of Canterbury*, 1726. HW merely records his name at the conclusion of *Engravers* in a list of those 'of whom the notices are so slight, that it is not worth while to endeavour finding proper places for them' (*Works* iv. 115).

36. Isaac Bargrave (1586–1643), Dean of Canterbury 1625–43. James Cole's print of him appears in Dart's *Canterbury* 58.

37. Michael Tyson (1740–80), antiquary and artist, at this time Fellow of Corpus. Cole, and later HW, became acquainted with him, and frequently mentioned him in their letters. Cole's interesting and personal account of him is in Brydges, *Restituta* iv. 236–9. See also DNB and LA vi. 209 *et passim*.

38. The picture etched by Tyson was from an oil painting on a panel, 'bust, to left, naked, with necklace' (EBP). Accord-

ing to EBP the subject is probably Diane de Poitiers.

39. Cole received one from Lort, 26 March 1768 (*Waterbeach Diary 32*).

40. (1722–1809), M.D. 1756; physician to the King and Queen; cr. Bt 1776. 'No man, perhaps, ever followed the career of physic, and the elegant paths of the Greek or Roman muses, for the space of several years, with more success than Sir George Baker' (LA iii. 71 n).

41. (1681–1765), 'of Barnwell near Cambridge . . . a noisy, busy, troublesome lawyer, of no practice in his profession, but a great party man, and half-crazed' (Cole, quoted in Brydges, *Restituta* iv. 379). For a curious account of him and his eccentricities, see Cooper, *Annals* iv. 336–9, and the references there cited. See also EBP.

42. Cole moved to Milton early in the year 1770, and lived there until his death.

cept pulling it down, I would fain, especially for my own room or two below stairs, make it as Gothic as I can. If you have any offcast old casements, any old Gothic ornaments that would do for a chimney, or old wainscot that would work up into a Gothic sort of furniture, particularly old window frames with pointed Gothic arches, I should be much obliged to you for them and would willingly be at the expense of their carriage; and if you have any bits of painted glass which you know not where to dispose of, I should be greatly obliged to you for them and would work them up into a window.

If I have not tired *you,* I am sure I have my own fingers, which can hardly hold the pen to subscribe myself, dear Sir,

Your most obliged servant,

WM COLE

From COLE, Sunday 15 May 1768

Missing. 'Sund. 15 . . . Wrote to Mr Walpole and sent it by Mr Furlow of the Rose Tavern'[1] (*Waterbeach Diary* 50). It is possible that HW did not receive it, for his next letter is in answer to 14 May 1768.

To COLE, Monday 6 June 1768

Add MS 5952, ff. 61–2.

Cole received this letter 9 June (*Waterbeach Diary* 57).

Address: To the Reverend Mr Cole at Waterbeach near Cambridge.
Postmark: Isleworth 7 IV.

Strawberry Hill, June 6, 1768.

YOU have told me what makes me both sorry and glad: long have I expected the appearance of Ely, and thought it on the eve of coming forth! Now you tell me it is not half written—but then I am rejoiced that you are to write it. Pray do; the author is very much in the right to make you author for him. I cannot say you have addressed yourself quite so judiciously as he has. I never heard of Cardinal Lewis of Luxembourg in my days, nor have a scrap of the history of

1. The Rose and Crown Inn, commonly referred to as The Rose, faced the Market Place in Cambridge at the site of the pres- ent Rose Crescent (Thomas D. Atkinson, *Cambridge Described & Illustrated,* 1897, p. 72).

Normandy, but Ducarel's tour to the Conqueror's kitchen.[1] But your best way will be to come and rummage my library yourself; not to set me to writing the lives of prelates; I shall strip them stark, and you will have them to re-consecrate. Cardinal Morton is at your service; pray, say *for* him and *of* me, what you please. I have very slender opinion of his integrity, but as I am not spiteful, it would be hard to exact from you a less favourable account of him, than I conclude your piety will bestow on all his predecessors and successors. Seriously you know how little I take contradiction to heart, and beg you will have no scruples about defending Morton. When I bestow but a momentary smile on the abuse of my answerers, I am not likely to stint a friend in a fair and obliging remark. The man whom you mention that calls himself *Impartialis,* is I suppose some hackney historian, I shall never inquire whom, angry at being censured in the lump, and not named. I foretold he would drop his criticisms before he entered on Perkin Warbeck, which I knew he could not answer, and so it happened[2]— good night to him!

Unfortunately I am no culinary antiquary: the Bishop of Carlisle,[3] who is, I have oft heard talk of a *sotelte,*[4] as an ancient dish. He is rambling between London, Hagley,[5] and Carlisle, that I do not know where to consult him; but if the book is not printed before winter, I am sure he could translate your bill of fare into modern phrase. As I trust I shall see you here some time this summer, you might bring your papers with you, and we will try what we can make of them. Tell me, do, when it will be most convenient to you to come from now to the end of October. At the same time I will beg to see the letters of the University to King Richard: and shall be still more obliged to you for the print of Jane Shore. I have a very bad mezzotinto of her, either from the picture at Cambridge or Eton.[6]

1. *Anglo-Norman Antiquities Considered, in a Tour through Part of Normandy,* 1767, by Andrew Coltee Ducarel, who presented a copy to HW (see HW to Ducarel 25 April 1767).

2. In his last letter in *The London Chronicle* 28–31 May 1768, Impartialis wrote: 'To follow our Author [Walpole] through a long circumstantial train of arguments, that endeavour to prove Perkin Warbeck to be the real Duke of York, and son to Edward IV would not be consistent with the plan of a periodical publication.' Then he confesses that in response to many requests from his friends he may enlarge and revise his remarks and publish them in book form. He did not do so.

3. Charles Lyttelton (1714–68), Bp of Carlisle 1762–8; P.S.A. 1765–8; friend and correspondent of HW. He died 22 Dec. 1768.

4. MS reads *sotelle.*

5. Hagley Park, Worcs, the seat of the Lytteltons, near Stourbridge (for HW's description of it, see HW to Bentley Sept. 1753).

6. The first print HW mentions is by Tyson (see preceding letter), the second by

I wish I could return these favours by contributing to the decoration of your *new old* house; but as you know, I erected an old house, not demolished one, I had no windows or frames for windows but what I bespoke on purpose for the places where they are. My painted glass was so exhausted, before I had got through my design, that I was forced to have the windows in the gallery painted on purpose by Pecket.[7] What scraps I have remaining are so bad, I cannot make you pay for the carriage of them, as I think there is not one whole piece, but you shall see them when you come hither, and I will search if I can find anything for your purpose—I am sure I owe it you. Adieu!

Yours ever,
H. Walpole

From Cole, Wednesday 20 July 1768

Cole's copy, Add MS 5824, ff. 181v–183v.

Address: [From Cole's copy.] To the Honourable Mr Walpole at Strawberry Hill in Twickenham, Middlesex.

Waterbeche, July 20, 1768.

Dear Sir,

I FORESEE I shall write you a long letter, and therefore have taken paper accordingly. I am greatly obliged to you for your kind invitation, but my present unfixed situation makes it not convenient stirring. When I shall be fully settled I shall be more my own master: nay, even this summer, if I can find leisure, I will embrace it and pay my respects to you at Strawberry Hill, on many accounts. I long to see yourself; I long to see your gallery, which was not finished when I was last with you;[1] in short, to see many things at Strawberry Hill which are to be seen nowhere else.

John Faber from the picture at Eton. HW acquired another copy of the latter, which was described as 'extra fine and rare' in the London Sale Catalogue, i. 12.

7. William Peckitt (1731–95), glass-painter, originally a carver and gilder of York (see J. A. Knowles, 'William Peckitt, Glass-Painter,' *Walpole Society*, 1929, xvii. 45–60). HW records that on 15 May 1762 he paid Peckitt £34.14.0 'for the five

painted tops of the gallery windows and the yellow star in the ceiling of the Cabinet' (*SH Accounts* 9). HW again employed him in 1773 (ibid. 13, 113–4).

1. Cole's latest visit to SH was in Oct. 1763 (see Cole to HW 13 Oct. and 1 Dec. 1763). He did not visit SH until the following year (see *post* 26 June 1769).

I am upon the eve of fixing either at Milton or Ely. I go tomorrow with Dr Gooch for two or three days to the last place, to look at a little dwelling in the College, offered to me by the Dean,[2] which the Dean of Salisbury[3] much presses me to take. However, my mind is more for Milton, as it lies so convenient for Cambridge, only three miles and an half on a delightful turnpike road, and where I can keep two or three cows and employ my horses in a few acres of plowing, which I much like. Ely would, nevertheless, afford me great entertainment at present, where they are going forthwith to rummage among the old tombs and antiquities, and are going to do great things. The Bishop has lately offered the Chapter £1000 to ornament their Cathedral, upon condition that they will give as much for the same purpose: this is complied with, and now they are going to remove their choir from under the great lantern or cupola, and lay that part quite open, and place the choir beyond it, in a part of the church called the presbytery. They talk of employing Pecket[4] in their east window, and placing their organ immediately under it, just above their altar-piece, as it is in the Royal Chapel at Versailles.

If you should not already from the Bishop of Carlisle [have] heard an account of what they have lately done at Exeter in that way, it may be acceptable to you. Mr Betham,[5] whom you may remember, Fellow of our College, was lately there as bursar, and sent me from thence this account.[6]

I forget whether you have ever been at Exeter. The Cathedral there is greatly ornamented: the choir all paved; the stalls too all new, and the organ. The west window within these two years has been decorated with painted glass by Mr Pecket of York, so as to be greatly admired. It con-

2. Hugh Thomas (1707–80), Dean of Ely 1758–80; Master of Christ's College, 1754–80; a noted pluralist. According to Cole, he was 'always esteemed a very worthy man' (John Peile, *Biographical Register of Christ's College 1505–1905*, 2 vols, Cambridge, 1910–3, ii. 208–9).

3. Thomas Greene (d. 1780), Dean of Salisbury 1757–80 (see DNB, *sub* Thomas Green (1658–1738); Bentham, *Ely*² p. 249; Addenda, p. 18). Cole describes him as 'a finical man always taking snuff up his nose' (Add MS 5873, f. 82).

4. 'The figure of St Peter in the last window of the northern nave triforium and some heraldic work [in Ely Cathedral] are probably by Peckitt' (J. A. Knowles, 'William Peckitt, Glass-Painter,' *Walpole Society*, 1929, xvii. 58).

5. Edward Betham (1709–83), Fellow of King's 1731–71, and Bursar for many years; friend and correspondent of Cole, though the latter called him 'a covetous old bachelor'; benefactor of Eton and the Botanical Garden at Cambridge (see Brydges, *Restituta* iv. 429; *Eton Coll. Reg. 1698–1752*).

6. '*Vide* my vol. 24, p. 99' (Cole's note). The quotation from Betham's letter, of 6 June 1768, is taken from Add MS 5825, f. 100v, to which Cole's reference corresponds.

tains seven of the Apostles at full length: St Peter, St Matthew, Mark, Luke, John, St Paul and St Andrew. The rest of the window is filled with the arms of the King, Archbishop of Canterbury, Bishop of Exeter, the Dean, City, nobility and principal families in Devonshire. It cost a large sum of money. Though the arms were given by the several persons, it is said to have cost the chapter little less than £400. It makes a very grand appearance, and by connoisseurs the whole is thought to be well executed: the arms more especially. In the figures, as a painter, Mr Pecket, to me seems not to come up to our chapel. The colours are very bright and vivid, but occasion, I think, rather too great a glare, so as to be somewhat painful to the eye. The window on the outside is strongly secured with wire. Dr Milles, the Dean, a brother of yours of the Antiquary Society, has had this work much at heart, and been very zealous in the execution of it every way.

I now send you the two letters from our University to King Richard III which, although in different languages, I presume were sent at the same time, notwithstanding the different style in them both.[7]

Here follow a few scraps which I have picked up in your way since I wrote last.

I suppose the roll belonging to the Duke of Manchester is the same that is mentioned in the preface to *Johannis Rossi Historia*, published by Hearne, at p. xxx, with a picture of John Rous.[8] The roll [is] there said[9] to be then in the possession of Robert Arden de Parkhall, Esq.[10]

Helias de Berham (or Derham, as in another authority)[11] *Canon Sarum qui a prima fundatione rector fuit novæ fabricæ eccliæ' Sarum 25 annis. Nova fabrica Sarum dedicata A° Dñi 1258.*—Leland's *Itinerary*,[12] vol. 3, pp. 80, 81.

Bishop Alcock,[13] a great favourite of King Henry VII, who ap-

7. '*Vide* my vol. 19, p. 180' (Cole's note). See *ante* 14 May 1768, n. 12.

8. *Joannis Rossi . . . Historia Regum Angliae*. Cole refers to the second edition, Oxford, 1745. The print of Rous is copied from that in Dugdale's *Antiquities of Warwickshire*, 1656, p. 184.

9. Hearne is quoting from ibid. 183, 185.

10. Robert Arden (d. 1643), of Park Hall, in Warwickshire, 'the chief seat of the Ardens for neer CCC. years last past' (ibid. 649). Dugdale was acquainted with Arden, and borrowed the roll from him in 1636 (see Dugdale to Sir Symon Archer, 18 Nov.

1636, in *The Life, Diary, and Correspondence of Sir William Dugdale*, ed. William Hamper, 1827, pp. 159–60).

11. Cole's interpolation. For 'another authority,' see Leland's *Itinerary*[2] iii. 80 n. The usual form of the name is Elias de Derham (see *Calendar of Patent Rolls, 1232–1247*, pp. 166, 180).

12. Second edn, 9 vols, Oxford, 1744–5. Cole's quotation is not exact. The reference in the third paragraph following is to the same edition.

13. John Alcock (1430–1500), Bp of Rochester 1472, of Worcester 1476, and of

pointed him Comptroller of all his works and buildings, and particularly those at Richmond.—Parker's *History of Cambridge,* p. 119.[14]

Pretty account of Gothic or Saracenic architecture in the *Annual Register for 1767,* p. 148.[15]

Hearne, in his preface to vol. 8, p. xxv, of Leland's *Itinerary,* mentions a MS[16] formerly belonging to Dean Aldrich,[17] of Walter de Millemet, in which are the portraits of King Edward III and his Queen Philippa.

Scrope House over against St Andrew's Church in Holborn, belonging to Sir John Scrope, Lord Scrope of Bolton,[18] 9 Henry VII.—*Collection of Curious Discourses,* published by Hearne, p. 125.[19]

Clifford's Inn belonged to Isabelle, Lady Clifford,[20] *temp.* Edward III.—Ibid., p. 111.

Furnival's Inn, to Lord Furnival,[21] *temp.* Richard II.—Ibid., p. 124.

Derby House given to the Heralds in Queen Mary's time.—Ibid., p. 244.

Richard Grey, Earl of Kent, died 1523, at his house in Lombard Street in London.—Brook's *Catalogue of Kings* etc., p. 196.[22]

Gilbert Talbot, Earl of Shrewsbury, died 1616, at his house in Broad Street, London.—Ibid., p. 293.

Barons' Coronets

In Fern's *Blazon of Gentry,* printed 1586, p. 125,[23] is this stuff relating to that subject.

Ely 1486; founder of Jesus College, Cambridge.

14. *The History and Antiquities of the University of Cambridge,* n.d. [1721], a translation of a Latin work by Richard Parker (1572–1629), written in 1622, but not published until 1715, when Thomas Hearne printed it in his addition to vol. v of Leland's *Collectanea.* It subsequently appeared in translation, as above.

15. The account is entitled 'Historical Remarks on Ancient Architecture. From the Grecian Orders of Architecture; by Stephen Riou, Esq.' (*Annual Register,* 1767, pp. 144–50). The part relating to Gothic architecture appears at 148–50.

16. Written in 1326.

17. Henry Aldrich (1647–1710), divine and scholar; Dean of Christ Church, Oxford, 1689–1710.

18. John Le Scrope (1435–98), 5th Bn Scrope of Bolton.

19. Oxford, 1720. The following references are to the same edition.

20. Isabel de Berkeley (d. 1362), dau. of Maurice de Berkeley, Lord Berkeley; m. (1) in 1328, Robert de Clifford (1305–44), Lord Clifford; (2) in 1345, Sir Thomas Musgrave.

21. William de Furnivall (1326–83), 4th Bn Furnivall.

22. Ralph Brooke (1553–1625), *A Catalogue and Succession of the Kings* [etc.] *of England,* first published in 1619. Cole refers to the second edition, 1622.

23. Sir John Ferne (d. 1610?), *The Blazon of Gentrie,* 1586. Cole's quotation, which is not exact, appears at p. 130 of the copy in the Yale University Library.

Barons are with us, as the Senatours were with the Romanes, being admitted into the Upper House and Secret Chamber of Parliament. When they go to that Assembly, they were [wear] long Robes or Kirtles of Scarlet colour, with Chapeaus set on their Heads, doubled or turned up with Ermine, according to the Fashion of the Romane Senatours, who wore, when they went to the Capitol, under their Robe, a little Kirtle of Purple with Studes, which they called *Laticlavium.*

In the same absurd book, pp. 166–7,[24] are two coats or shields of his patrons, as seems to me, one of Clifford Earl of Cumberland,[25] and close to it that of Edmond Lord Sheffield of Butterwick.[26] The first has an earl's coronet over it; the other has nothing above it to distinguish it from the coats of two knights' shields which are close to it.

In 1666, when Dugdale published his *Origines Juridiciales* for the first time, barons' coronets did not seem to be settled: at least not long before, for in a painted window in the Middle Temple Hall are several noblemen's coats, with their proper coronets over them, among the rest Edward Hyde Earl of Clarendon, who had not long enjoyed that title; this has an earl's coronet over it. William Knolles Viscount Wallingford has a viscount's coronet over his, and close to them are several barons' coats without any coronet at all over their shields: as Edward Lord Stafford, Edward Lord Windsor, John Lord Darcy, etc.—*Origines Juridiciales,* p. 224.

I have a print of Bishop Mountain[27] of London with *G. Y.*[28] *sculpsit 1659* and *Peter Stent,*[29] *excudit.*

I have another in folio of a fat clergyman in his gown and cassock and hood, with *Wm Reader*[30] *pinxit,* and *J. Collins sculpsit.*[31]

I herewith send you Jane Shore and a print of the Countess of Exeter by VanDyck.[32] If you should have met with one since I saw

24. P. 167 of the copy in the Yale University Library.

25. George Clifford (1558–1605), 3d E. of Cumberland.

26. Edmund Sheffield (1564?–1646), 3d Bn Sheffield of Butterwicke; cr. 5 Feb. 1626 E. of Mulgrave.

27. George Montaigne or Mountain (1569–1628), Bp of London 1621–8.

28. George Yeates (see *Granger*[5] ii. 49).

29. (fl. 1650–62) an engraver or print-seller (see *Engravers, Works* iv. 29–30).

30. (fl. 1680), best known for his portrait of John Blow (1648–1708) the composer.

31. John Collins (fl. 1680), mentioned in *Engravers, Works* iv. 81–2.

32. Frances Brydges (1580–1663), dau. of William Brydges, 4th Bn Chandos of Sudeley; m. (1) Sir Thomas Smith (d. 1609) and (2) as his second wife, Thomas Cecil (1542–1623), 1st E. of Exeter. 'This is one of Faithorne's best portraits, and very scarce. The original, which represents her aged, and in mourning, is in the gallery at Strawberry Hill' (*Granger*[1] i. 548). This print, 'most brilliant and extremely rare,' was sold London vi. 766.

you, you may return it. I value it no more than any other print of equal goodness, whereas you have two reasons to value it, as she is an ancestress,[33] and as you have the original.[34] I am, dear Sir,

Your ever faithful servant,

Wm Cole

To Cole, Saturday 20 August 1768

Add MS 5952, ff. 63–4.

Address: To the Reverend Mr Cole at Waterbeche, Cambridgeshire.
Postmark: Isleworth 20 AV.

Strawberry Hill, Aug. 20, 1768.

YOU are always heaping so many kindnesses on me, dear Sir, that I think I must break off all acquaintance with you, unless I can find some way of returning them. The print of the Countess of Exeter is the greatest present to me in the world: I have been trying for years to no purpose to get one. Reynolds the painter promised to beg one for me of a person he knows, but I have never had it. I wanted it for four different purposes; as a grandmother (-in-law, by the Cranes and Allingtons); for my collection of heads; for the volumes of prints after pieces in my own collection; and above all, for my collection of Faithornes, which though so fine, wanted such a capital print—and to this last I have preferred it. I give you unbounded thanks for it; and yet I feel exceedingly ashamed to rob you. The print of Jane Shore I had;[1] but as I have such various uses for prints, I easily bestowed it. It is inserted in my *Anecdotes* where her picture is mentioned.[2]

Thank you too for all your notices. I intend next summer to set about the last volume of my *Anecdotes,* and to make still further additions to the former volumes, in which these notes will find their place. I am going to reprint all my pieces together, and to my shame

33. See following letter.
34. It was sold SH xxi. 66. For HW's description of it, see *Description of SH, Works* ii. 463.

1. It seems more likely that HW is thinking of his mezzotint of her by Faber (see *ante* 6 June 1768).

2. HW first mentioned her portrait (in the Provost's Lodge, King's College, Cambridge) in *Anecdotes*[2] i. 47 n. The print is so inserted in HW's copy of *Anecdotes*[1] now in the possession of Lord Derby at Knowsley.

be it spoken, find they will make at least two large quartos.[3] You, I
know, will be partial enough to give them a place on a shelf; but as
I doubt many persons will not be favourable, I only think of leaving
the edition behind me.

Methinks I should like for your amusement and my own, that you
settled at Ely; yet I value your health so much beyond either, that I
must advise Milton; Ely being, I believe, a very damp, and consequently a very unwholesome situation. Pray let me know on which
you fix; and if you do fix this summer, remember the hopes you have
given me of a visit. My summer, that is, my fixed residence here, lasts
till November. My gallery is not only finished,[4] but I am going on
with the round chamber at the end of it;[5] and am besides playing
with the little garden on the other side of the road,[6] which was old
Franklin's and by his death come into my hands. When the round
tower[7] is finished, I propose to draw up a description and catalogue
of the whole house and collection,[8] and I think you will not dislike
lending me your assistance.

Mr Granger of Shiplake is printing his laborious and curious catalogue of English heads,[9] with an accurate though succinct account of
almost all the persons. It will be a very valuable and useful work, and
I heartily wish may succeed, though I have some fears. There are of
late a small number of persons who collect English heads, but not
enough to encourage such a work; I hope the anecdotic part will
make it more known and tasted. It is essential to us, who shall love
the performance, that it should sell; for he prints no farther at first,
than to the end of Charles the First and if this part does not sell well,
the bookseller[10] will not purchase the remainder of the copy, though

3. HW began to print the proposed edition of his works 24 Aug. 1768. The project
was abandoned in 1787, after one volume
and part of another had been printed (see
Jour. Print. Off. 13, 20, 51–2).

4. The Gallery was almost finished, but
not furnished, when Cole was at SH in
Oct. 1763 (cf. *SH Accounts* 108–11).

5. The Round Room, or Round Draw-
ing-Room, as it is called in *Description of
SH* (*Works* ii. 468–70).

6. Later known as the Cottage Garden
or Flower Garden. 'The area of this piece
of ground, which was on the north side of
the road from Twickenham to Hampton
Court, is given on the estate plan as two

acres, sixteen poles' (*SH Accounts* 132; see
also 11, 131 and 'Genesis of SH' 87–8).

7. Projected in 1758, it was not finished
until 1771 (*SH Accounts* 106–7).

8. *A Description of the Villa of Horace
Walpole . . . at Strawberry Hill,* SH, 1774.
An undated, abridged edition for the use
of the servants showing the house, was
printed apparently in the same year, and
the third, with additions, in 1784 (see *Jour.
Print. Off., passim*).

9. *A Biographical History of England.*

10. Thomas Davies (1712?–85), who introduced Boswell to Johnson. His correspondence with Granger is printed in
Granger, *Correspondence* 22 ff.

he gives but an hundred pounds for this half: and good Mr Granger is not in circumstances to afford printing it himself.[11] I do not compare it with Dr Robertson's[12] writings, who has an excellent genius with admirable style and manner; and yet I cannot help thinking that there is a good deal of Scotch puffing and partiality, when the booksellers have given the Doctor three thousand pounds for his life of Charles V,[13] for composing which he does not pretend to have obtained any new materials.[14]

I am going into Warwickshire,[15] and I think shall go on to Lord Strafford's;[16] but propose returning before the end of September.[17]

Yours ever,

H. W.

From Cole, Wednesday 5 October 1768

VA, Forster MS 110, ff. 58–60. Cole's copy, Add MS 5824, ff. 184v, 185v, 186.
Address: [From Cole's copy.] For the Honourable Horace Walpole Esq. at Strawberry Hill in [Twickenham in] Middlesex.

Horseth Hall, Oct. 5, 1768.

Dear Sir,

A S I have been on a long visit[1] at this place, where is an excellent library, I have usually employed my mornings in it, and was

11. It appears from Granger's letter to 'Mr Ryder,' 28 Nov. 1771, that his *Biographical History* had brought in at that time 'above 400*l.*' (see N&Q, 11 July 1857, 2d Ser., vol. 4, p. 22).

12. William Robertson (1721–93), the historian, and HW's occasional correspondent.

13. Boswell wrote to Temple, 14 May 1768: 'Dr Robertson is come up [to London] loaden with his *Charles the V*. Three large quartos; he has been offered 3,000 guineas for it. To what a price has literature risen!' (*Letters of James Boswell*, ed. Chauncey B. Tinker, 2 vols, Oxford, 1924, i. 160–1.) The work was published in 3 vols, 1769, as *The History of the Reign of the Emperor Charles V.*

14. Cf. Robertson's preface to his *Charles V.*

15. For HW's account of his tour in

Warwickshire, Leicestershire, Derbyshire, Yorkshire and Nottinghamshire, see *Country Seats*, pp. 62–7. His account is dated 2 Sept. 1768.

16. Wentworth Castle, Yorks, near Barnsley.

17. He returned to SH 19 Sept. (see HW to Thomas Warton 20 Sept. 1768).

———

1. The first paragraph of Cole's copy reads: 'I received your last favour at Horseth, where I have been on a long visit for these last six weeks, and am likely to continue all my life if I agree to my Lord Montfort's obliging proposals to me; who gives me the choice of three of his own houses, all on the edge of his park and none more distant from his house than a quarter, or the farthest, half a mile from his own house: these he will repair for me, find me materials for building me a large

much pleased to fall upon the following precept, which I here transcribe for your use from Rymer's *Foedera*,[2] vol. 5, p. 670:

De Pictoribus eligendis.

Rex Universis & singulis Vicecomitibus, Majoribus, Ballivis, Ministris, & aliis Fidelibus suis, tam infra Libertates, quam extra, ad quos &c. Salutem.

Sciatis quod assignavimus dilectum nobis, Hugonem de Sancto Albano, Magistrum Pictorum, pro Operationibus, in Capella nostra in Palatio nostro Westmonasteriensi faciendis, assignatorum, ad capiendum & eligendum tot Pictores & alios Operarios, quot pro Operationibus illis faciendis necessarii fuerint, in locis ubi expedire viderit, tam infra Libertates, quam extra, in Comitatibus Kantiæ, Middlesexiæ, Essexiæ, Surriæ & Sussexiæ, & ad Operarios illos usque Palatium nostrum prædictum venire faciendum, ibidem in Obsequio nostro, ad Vadia nostra, quamdiu necesse fuerit, moraturos.

Et ideo vobis mandamus quod eidem Hugoni, in præmissis faciendis & exequendis, Intendentes sitis, Consulentes, & Auxiliantes quotiens, & prout, super hoc, per ipsum Hugonem, ex parte nostra, fueritis præmuniti.

In cujus &c.

Teste Rege apud Westmonasterium, decimo octavo die Martii.

Per Billam Thesaurariæ.

Pat. 24. Edw. 3. (1350) p. 1. m. 26.

Eodem modo assignantur subscripti, ad hujusmodi Pictores, in Comitatibus subscriptis, eligendum & capiendum, sub eadem Data; videlicet,

Johannes Athelard in Comitatibus
Linc', North', Oxon', Warr' & Leyc'.
Benedictus Nightegale in Comitatibus
Cantebr', Hunt', Norff' & Suff'.

Per eandem Billam.

room for my books, will take no rent of me, and give me a lease of 21 years: a term sufficient to put a period to my life, now just past 54. However, I am doubtful and hesitate much whether to accept it, as too near a neighbourhood to so great a neighbour may be attended with difficulties, especially to a person who loves to be his own master, both of his time and amusements. He talks of going to London, as he has just now made a new purchase, and is obliged to sign writings sometime next month, and will carry me with him in his chaise and bring me back again. I will then do myself the honour of spending a few days with you at Strawberry Hill. In my Lord's library are Rymer's *Foedera*. In looking over it t'other day, I met with the following curious precept which I think has escaped your researches, and therefore transcribed it for your use. It is in vol. 5, p. 670.'

2. Thomas Rymer (1641–1713), editor of *Foedera, Conventiones, et cujuscunque generis Acta Publica*, 20 vols, 1703–35. HW did not use Cole's note.

May not this Hugh de St Alban be properly enough styled the King's sergeant painter, and as such appear as the senior on that list? It appears to me a curiosity in that way in which you have so much obliged the world, and more especially as it preserves the names of three artists employed by that great English monarch and hero, King Edward III.

At the same time I can't help transcribing a passage for your use also out of [an] author now much in fashion, which I don't love for his too Whiggish principles, but as it illustrates and vindicates an argument you have lately pursued, I will e'en give it you for your sake, and not out of regard for Francis Osborn, who, in his *Advice to a Son*,[3] printed among his *Works,* seventh edition, London, octavo, 1673, p. 227, speaking of moderation and how unsafe it is to ascend a throne by spilling much blood, thus writes:

Now where this *moderation* is observed, and all *Liberties, Honours, and Immunities* religiously preserved, I apprehend no more cause of *grief* than the *English* had occasion for *Joy,* when they exchanged King *Richard* the third for *Henry* the seventh: It remaining indubitable, that however *the first* might be a *Murderer,* he did not with the *second, oppress* the people: wherefore such as call him *Tyrant,* offer violence to a number of *good Laws* he *made;* and *shew too much partiality,* if they esteem *him* the better Prince that *brake* them: *Kings* that succeed by *birth,* acknowledging no obligation to any but their *Ancestors:* whereas *Richard* endeavoured to gain the *Love* of the Nation, and did so far prevail, as to have *an Army* appear for him against *the Duke of Lancaster,* in those days *the Darling of the Commons,* and wherein were divers *of quality;* a strong presumption of a juster and milder temper in Government, than the ignorant and partial *Historians* of those times are found to record; So as though *he* may be reckoned amongst the *worst of Men,* his *Laws* will recover *him* a place with the *best of Kings* . . .

You will observe that he mistakes in this place the Duke of Lancaster for the Earl of Richmond, the head of the Lancastrian interest.[4]

I am very glad the print of the old Countess of Exeter was so acceptable, and more so to find you engaged in so good a work as collecting all your pieces together. I shall be happy and much honoured

3. Francis Osborne (1593–1659), whose *Advice to a Son* was published in 1656. The passage quoted by Cole appears in the second part, section 45. HW did not use the note.

4. 'the title of Duke of Lancaster sinking into the Crown ever since Henry IV's time' (addition in Cole's copy).

in having them in my study, where no books are so often turned over as those with your name in them.

On Monday last I agreed with the Bursar of King's College for the house at Milton,[5] but as the season is so far advanced, nothing can be done this year, and if I get into it by midsummer next it will be as much as I am apt to suppose I shall be able to do.

I long to take a walk in your gallery and give a peep into the round chamber. I shall then more than ever fancy I am in some castle in King Edward III's time. Whenever you are disposed to draw up a description and catalogue of your whole house and collection, I shall be not only at your service, but greatly obliged in giving you any assistance you will please to impose on me.

I find[6] Mr Granger does not publish his book by subscription. I shall be much pleased to see it out, as it is on a subject I much admire. As I am not sure you have seen a book in this way, which I saw t'other day at Cambridge, and published since you left Paris, I will give you the title of it. Perhaps it may be of use to you in the article of engravers: *Dictionnaire des Graveurs anciens & modernes, depuis l'Origine de la Graveur; avec une Notice des principales Estampes qu'ils ont gravées; suivi des Catalogues des Oeuvres de Jacques Jordans et de Corneille Visscher.* Par F. Basan, Graveur. 3 tomes, Paris, octavo, 1767.[7]

As I write at a place where I have not your book of *Engravers,* I can't tell whether you mention among Faithorne's works a fine half-length print of Dr Henry More, aet. 61, sitting in his cassock only under a tree, with a river and landscape at a distance.[8] I met with it in the collection of one Mr Barnard,[9] rector of Withersfield in Suffolk, and King's Chaplain, who has a curious collection of books, prints,

5. 'On Monday last [3 Oct.] the Bursar of King's College [Edward Betham] dined with me, with whom I came to a full determination to take a twenty-year lease of the house at Milton, but as I cannot enter till next Lady Day, and the year so far advanced that no repairs can be set about at present, I don't apprehend I shall be able to inhabit it till midsummer' (addition in Cole's copy). The house was not ready until late in Dec. 1769.

6. 'by a letter from Mr Granger' (addition in Cole's copy). The letter is not in Granger's *Correspondence,* but Cole's letter to Granger, 8 Sept. 1768, offering his subscription and assistance in the work, is pp. 320–1.

7. HW did not mention this book in *Engravers.* He later bought the second edition, 2 vols, Paris, 1789, which was sold London ix. 1145.

8. HW had listed it in *Engravers*[2] p. 68 (it was not in *Engravers*[1]). Henry More (1614–87) was one of the Cambridge Platonists.

9. 'formerly of St John's College in Cambridge' (addition in Cole's copy). Thomas Barnard (1719–81), Chaplain to the King, 1762; rector of Withersfield, Suffolk, 1765–81 (see *Alumni Cantab.*). For a brief ac-

Roman urns and other antiquities, many of which were found in his parish.

In the *Catalogue of the Harleian Manuscripts* in the British Museum I took notice of these articles for you:

No. 433. 2215: Warrant to Aid & Assist Anthony Lambeson whom the King had Commaunded to take up Peynters (as welle within Franchises, as without) for Peynting within the Castelle of Windesore. Yeven 31 Maii, 1 Edw. 5 (1483), fo. 225b.

No. 433. Art. 2310: Litteræ R. Ricardi 3. Fratri Leonardo de Prato, Equiti Hierosolomitano, ipsius Religionis in Angliam & Hiberniam Commissario. Dat. apud Westm. 5 Decembris 1485. Fo. 272b.

No. 433. Art. 2378: Letter of K. Richard III. (perhaps to the Bishop of London)[10] commanding him to dehort Thomas Lynom his (the King's) Sollicitor from marrying with Jane Shore, late the wife of William Shore, now being in Ludgate. Fo. 340b.

No. 1052. Art. 322: Concessio Augmentationis ac Cristæ, Armis D. Johannis Walpole Equitis Aurati, per D. Edwardum Walker, Garterium. Dat. 1 Junii, 1646. Fo. 211.

No. 1107. Art 37 and 43: Descent of the family of Walpole.

No. 1408. Art. 57: Descent of Walpole. Fo. 62b; and Art. 103, fo. 90b.

I remain, dear Sir,

Your ever obliged and faithful servant,

Wm Cole

To Cole, Saturday 27 May 1769

Add MS 5952, ff. 65–6.

Address: To the Reverend Mr Cole at Waterbeach near Cambridge.
Postmark: 27 MA.

Arlington Street, May 27, 1769.

I HAVE not heard from you this century, nor knew where you had fixed your staff. Mr Gray tells me you are still at Waterbeach.[1] Mr Granger has published his catalogue of prints and lives down to the

count of his collection of antiquities, see Cole to Gough, 24 July 1779, la i. 681.

10. The letter was written to John Russell, Bishop of Lincoln, and Lord Chancellor under Richard III. The date is probably 1484 (see DNB *sub* Jane Shore). Cole

had forgotten that HW printed the letter in *Historic Doubts*[1] (pp. 118–9).

1. 'Old Cole lives at Water-Beach near the road from Cambridge to Ely' (Gray to HW 26 May 1769).

Revolution,[2] and as the work sells well, I believe, nay, do not doubt but we shall have the rest.[3] There are a few copies printed but on one side of the leaf.[4] As I know you love scribbling in such books as well as I do, I beg you will give me leave to make you a present of one set. I shall send it in about a week to Mr Gray, and have desired him, as soon as he has turned it over, to convey it to you. I have found a few mistakes, and you will find more. To my mortification, though I have four thousand heads, I find upon a rough calculation that I still shall want three or four hundred.

Pray give me some account of yourself, how you do, and whether you are fixed. I thought you rather inclined to Ely. Are we never to <hav>e the history of that cathedral? I wish you would tell me that you have any thoughts of coming this way; or that you would make me a visit this summer. I shall be little from home this summer till August, when I think of going to Paris for six weeks.[5]

To be sure you have seen the *History of British Topography*,[6] which was published this winter and is a delightful book in our way.[7] Adieu! dear Sir,

Yours ever,

H. Walpole

From Cole, Monday 29 May 1769

VA, Forster MS 110, f. 61. Cole kept no copy.
Address: For the Honourable Horace Walpole in Arlington Street, London.

Fulburne,[1] May 29, 1769.

Dear Sir,

I SHALL never, was I to live ever so long, be out of your debt. I called on Mr Gray this morning, who tells me that the books[2] are expected next week. Whenever they come I shall forever value them

2. *A Biographical History of England* was published 16 May 1769 (see Granger, *Correspondence* 25). It is dedicated to HW, whose annotated copy is now in the Princeton University Library.

3. Granger died before he completed his design, but in 1806 Mark Noble published a continuation, *A Biographical History of England, from the Revolution to the End of George I's Reign,* 3 vols, 'the materials being supplied by the manuscripts left by Mr Granger, and the collections of the editor.'

4. Cf. Boswell, *Johnson* iii. 91, 484–5. HW doubtless had a set, but it does not appear in MS Cat. or Sale Cat.

5. HW left London for Paris 16 Aug. and returned 11 Oct. (see *Paris Jour.*).

6. *Anecdotes of British Topography,* published anonymously, 1768, by Richard

the more as coming from you, and may I say it, for your polishing part of them,[3] for I am pretty clear I see your pencil in some parts of them, having run through them to my great satisfaction last week. I made a few observations on them, and though I have heard some difficult people criticize them, yet for my own part I never read a book that pleased my taste better, except those from Strawberry Hill. I write this on a particular occasion from a friend's house[4] where I dine, and send it in a cover with another to Sir Robert Ladbrook.[5]

A gentleman of my acquaintance has long teased me to get him an admission to see your house at Twickenham, and last night sent his servant over to me to let me know that he was going to London to-day, and would be obliged to me for a note of introduction. I know you don't love interruption, and did not know but you might be there yourself, and knew so much of him, that if you was there, he might probably ask to see you himself, so I begged to be excused as well as I could. However, as I necessarily was obliged to return you my most humble thanks for Mr Granger's book, I thought I would ask this favour for him at the same time: that you would give him a permit to see the house. He is a Doctor of Law, a man of good fortune, and acts as Justice of Peace for town and county of Cambridge. His name is Dr Ewin,[6] is a man of virtu, has a taste for antiquity, loves Gothic work, painted glass, and has a large collection of prints. You will greatly oblige him by a sight of your house, and at the same time

Your most assured servant,

WM COLE

Gough (1735–1809), the correspondent of Cole and HW.

7. 'Vide vol. 25, p. 190 [of Cole's MSS], for a different opinion about it' (Cole's note on his copy of HW's letter, Add MS 5824, f. 132v). He refers to his copy of HW's letter to him 19 May 1780. See also Cole to HW 24 May 1780. HW's change of opinion may be explained by his dislike of Gough, a friend of Masters and Milles, adverse critics of *Historic Doubts*. Still later, however, he corresponded with Gough on friendly terms.

1. Fulbourn, Cambs, four miles SE of Cambridge. Cole was visiting his friend William Greaves (see *ante* 16 May 1762).

2. Granger's *Biographical History*. Cole already had bought an ordinary set (*Waterbeach Diary* 166).

3. HW read the work in MS and offered various suggestions to Granger, but there is nothing to indicate the specific passages to which Cole refers (see Granger, *Correspondence* 15–6; *Granger*[1] i. verso of sig. b).

4. William Greaves's.

5. Sir Robert Ladbroke (1712–73), Kt; alderman and Lord Mayor (1747) of London; M.P. for London, 1754–73; President of Christ's Hospital (see James P. Malcolm, *Londinium Redivivum*, 1803, iii. 388–9).

6. William Howell Ewin (1731?–1804), who was suspended from his degrees for usury in 1778, but was restored in the following year. Cole's MSS contain numerous references to him. For Cole's reception of Ewin's letter, see *Waterbeach Diary* 165.

From COLE, Tuesday 6 June 1769

VA, Forster MS 110, ff. 62–5. COLE's copy, Add MS 5824, ff. 132v, 133v.
Address: To the Honourable Horace Walpole, Strawberry Hill, Twickenham,
Middlesex. Free Wm Burrell. *Postmark:* Cambridge 9 IV.

Waterbeche, June 6, 1769.

Dear Sir,

ONCE more my sincerest thanks for your kind present,[1] which
Mr Gray brought me yesterday, and dined with me.[2] I love
scribbling in books as much as anyone, and I make no doubt but I
shall employ it in the service you recommend: whatever the fruits be,
you are entitled to them, as well as good Mr Granger, who was so
kind to send me a copy, utterly unexpected, as I had contributed so
little or nothing to the usefulness of his book.[3]

I wish I knew what were the heads you want: if I have them, you
shall not be without them. If it is possible, I will do myself the honour of seeing you at Strawberry Hill for a day or two in July, though
I hope to be so fully employed as to have my hands full. I am still at
Waterbeche, but am preparing to fit up and repair my old house at
Milton next week, in order to be able to get into it before Christmas,
for was you to see the place that I now inhabit, you would not wonder at my impatience to get away[4] from it.

You are so kind to ask after me and my present employment. At
the end of February I fell ill of a fever which hardly left me of two
months, and indeed I take the bark still, but my comfort in my illness
was two MSS[5] which I copied and greatly amused me. When I was
getting better, and for these last six weeks, I have been backwards and
forwards to Cambridge and Ely, at which last place I have been much
entertained, as they are now making great alterations and improvements. But church work is slow, and *that* the writer of the *Antiqui-*

---

1. Granger's *Biographical History*, printed on one side of the paper only. See also *Waterbeach Diary* 169.

2. 'for the first time since I returned into Cambridgeshire' (addition in Cole's copy).

3. 'which I had indeed purchased at Cambridge the first week of its publication, and as the *Registrum Roffense* by Dr Thorpe costs the same price of two guineas, and is just now advertised, the booksellers

will take Mr Granger's present in lieu of that' (addition in Cole's copy). John Thorpe (1682–1750), M.D., collected the materials which were published by his son John Thorpe (1715–92) under the title *Registrum Roffense*, 1769 (see DNB).

4. 'but at my perseverance to stay in it so long' (addition in Cole's copy).

5. 'of good antiquity, relating to Cambridgeshire' (addition in Cole's copy).

ties of that cathedral very fully evinces.[6] However, he promises to let the world have the benefit of his lucubrations before the end of the year, yet as I know his natural slowness, I am apt to doubt it. We made a curious discovery there about three weeks ago. An old wall being to be taken down behind the choir, on which were painted seven figures of six Saxon bishops and a Duke, as he is called, of Northumberland, one Brythnoth:[7] which painting I take to be as ancient as any we had in England; therefore I was very desirous to have a copy of it taken before it was destroyed, and spoke to one of the prebendaries[8] about it, who ordered it to be left till myself and a gentleman of Benet,[9] an excellent draughtsman, went over to Ely. I guessed by seven arches in the wall below the figures that the bones of these seven benefactors to the old Saxon conventual church were reposited in the wall under them, and accordingly we found seven separate holes, all of them full of the remains of the said persons which had been removed from the old church when that was deserted and the new one erected. Mr Tyson has taken an exact copy of the picture, which Mr Bentham designs to add to his book: a contributor to the plate is wanting,[10] but I imagine he will find one for it. I wish, for the credit of that book, that your name was to one of the threescore plates which it will be ornamented with, though I guess this plate now wanting won't be less than ten guineas. This I mention, not with any design, for it never entered my head till I came to the line I wrote it on: the propriety of inscribing such a plate to one who has wrote so inimitably on our old painters and painting gave me the thought above, and though I know your generosity on all occasions where proper, yet at the same time I am aware of your continual expense to oblige the public,[11] who, on these private occasions, may very well find encouragers elsewhere.

6. James Bentham published his *Ely* in 1771, about twenty years after he began it.

7. For the names and a brief account of these bishops and Duke Brithnoth (hero of the Fight at Maldon), see Bentham, *Ely*[2] pp. 83–5, 285–6, Addenda, p. 23; DNB.

8. Probably Dr John Gooch, Cole's intimate friend.

9. Michael Tyson (see following note).

10. The plate does not appear in Bentham's *Ely*. The figures were engraved in Gough's *Sepulchral Monuments*, vol. 1, pt 1, opp. p. clvi, where Gough says: 'The oldest original paintings of bishops in their

habits of ceremony may be supposed those in the north wall of the old choir at Ely, built in the reign of Edward III which, before the removal of the choir to its present situation, were copied by Mr Tyson, 1769, who gave them, 1778, to Mr Cole. From the last of these gentlemen I received them, for the purpose of having them engraved for this work.' A copy of the plate (reduced) is in William Stevenson's *Supplement to . . . Bentham's Ely*, Norwich, 1817, opp. p. 69.

11. 'but if you will give me leave, and you should decline it, I should be much

When I have a clean house at Milton, and fit to receive you, how happy will you make me to come there for a few days! Ely will much amuse you, and the new chapel at Clare Hall[12] and other daily improvements at Cambridge, where a spirit of embellishment prevails, will equally please you.

The *English Topography* I bought on its first appearance, and it highly delighted me. The author, one Mr Gough, educated at Benet College in my time, lives in London: a most retired man, and quite unknown while in the University.

I long to see you at Strawberry Hill[13] and will come to thank you for civilities to Dr Ewin and Mr Rawlinson,[14] who are in raptures about it.[15] The impertinences of such visits I know you abominate,[16] yet did you know the happiness you conveyed to Dr Ewin, I think your humanity would easily sacrifice a little to give so much pleasure.

I am, dear Sir,

Your ever faithful and most obliged servant,

WM COLE

obliged to you for your interest with another encourager of the arts: I mean the Duke or Duchess of Northumberland, to whom the plate might be inscribed with equal propriety. If you would oblige me in either case, I will send you the draught by Mr Tyson, who is busy in collecting specimens of Gothic architecture, in order to reduce it to a regular system' (addition in Cole's copy). HW declined the opportunity to pay for the plate (see following letter). For this passage as Cole sent it to HW, see the third paragraph after Cole's signature.

12. Begun in 1764 and finished in 1769, it was consecrated 5 July 1769. Sir James Burrough, Master of Caius College, designed it, and after his death in 1764, the work was superintended by James Essex (see *Clare College 1326–1926*, 2 vols, 1928–30, i. 115).

13. 'the gallery was not finished when I was there last. I will come there in July, if it is only to thank you for your civilities to Dr Ewin and Mr Rawlinson, who was with him' (addition in Cole's copy).

14. 'lately a Fellow Commoner of Trinity College, and since married to one of Sir Robert Ladbrook's daughters' (addition in Cole's copy). Walter Rawlinson (1735–1805), only son of Sir Thomas Rawlinson, Kt; knighted 4 March 1774; M.P. for Queensborough, 1774–84; for Huntingdon, 1784–90; a partner in the firm of Ladbroke, Rawlinson and Co., bankers, Bank Building, at the time of his death (see *Admissions to Trinity College, Cambridge, 1701–1800* p. 170; Musgrave, *Obituary*).

15. 'Dr. Ewin was with me on Sunday, and in raptures, both from your politeness to him and the elegances of your habitation. I told you in my last letter from Mr Greaves's at Fulburn a little relating to the Doctor, who is much disposed towards virtu. He has brought from London with him all the apparatus for painting on glass. He has a forge, colours—in short, everything but the skill how to make use of them' (addition in Cole's copy).

16. 'but I knew not how to extricate you from this: if I had not given you a line I am satisfied a certain forwardness of behaviour would have thrown him in your way, perhaps in a more disagreeable manner' (addition in Cole's copy).

Meeting Dr Burrell[17] at Horseth last year, I got two franks from him, among many others, to you.

When I was at Ely last month at Mrs Greene's[18] house, I saw three or four pictures or drawings by a black lead pencil, exquisitely and most softly finished by her late husband, Bishop Greene of Ely: one of Archbishop Tennison;[19] a second of Bishop Trimnell.[20] This ascertains the Bishop of Ely mentioned in your *Anecdotes*.[21]

I wish the Duke or Duchess of Northumberland[22] knew of Duke Brithnoth, and his want of a con<tri>butor to his plate; perhaps, as encouragers of <the> arts, they might contribute the plate, as it would with great propriety be inscribed to them. What was singular, in every other hole in the wall there were evident marks or pieces of the skull; in three or four they were quite whole; not the least sign of any in the Duke's, and history informs us[23] that he was beheaded by the Danes and his head sent away. His limbs, viz., leg and thigh bones, of an enormous size, and very perfect. An apothecary standing by at the taking them out, said he could not be much short of seven feet high.

17. William Burrell (1732–96), LL.D.; afterwards Sir William Burrell, 2d Bt, of West Grinstead Park, Sussex; Cole's 'friend and acquaintance, and Member of the House of Commons. . . . An active, stirring man; a good antiquary. He is rather low, and squints a little; but very ingenious, and scholar-like. The first time I was acquainted with him was meeting him at Paris, at Mr Horace Walpole's [25 Oct. 1765; see *Jour. to Paris* 56]. I often met him since at Lord Montfort's at Horseheath' (Cole, quoted in Brydges, *Restituta* iii. 48). He bequeathed his collections for the history of the county of Sussex to the British Museum.

18. 'who lives in her son's prebendal house, the present Dean of Salisbury, and is a fine old lady of 87 years of age, cheerful and hearty, and plays at cards every afternoon' (Cole's copy). She was Mrs Catharine Greene, widow of Thomas Greene (1658–1738), Bp of Ely; and mother of Thomas Greene (d. 1780, Dean of Salisbury 1757–80, and Prebendary of Ely 1737–80); she died 20 March 1770, and a monumental inscription to her memory was placed in the south aisle of the choir of Ely Cathedral (see Bentham, *Ely*[2], Appendix, p. 48).

19. Thomas Tenison (1636–1715), Abp of Canterbury.

20. Charles Trimnell (1663–1723), successively Bp of Norwich and Winchester.

21. HW had identified 'the bishop of Ely,' mentioned by Vertue as an artist, as Simon Patrick or Thomas Greene (see *Anecdotes*[2] iii. 147). The passage remains unchanged in later editions.

After this passage, Cole's copy continues: 'As I have mentioned old Mrs Green, I will, for the honour of the situation, just tell you that there is at the same place now living and hearty an old Mr Aungier of 98 years of age; one Mrs Bringhurst of 87, whom I see every day in the Cathedral; and the Bishop of the same age.'

22. Sir Hugh Smithson (1715–86), 4th Bt; m. (1740) Elizabeth Seymour, dau. and heir of Algernon Seymour, D. of Somerset; suc. (1750), in right of his wife, to earldom of Northumberland, and changed his name to Percy; cr. (1766) 1st D. of Northumberland of the 3d creation.

23. See Bentham, *Ely*[2] pp. 83–5, 285.

FROM COLE 6 JUNE 1769

I will beg the favour to let your servant put Mr Granger's letter[24]
into the postoffice, which I have taken the liberty to put into your
cover, as I thought it would lessen the expense and be a double letter
to him.[25]

To COLE, Wednesday 14 June 1769

Add MS 5952, ff. 67–8.

Address: [From COLE's copy, Add MS 5824, f. 134v.] To the Rev. Mr Cole at
Waterbeche near Cambridge.

Strawberry Hill, June 14, 1769.

Dear Sir,

AMONG many agreeable passages in your last, there is nothing I
like so well as the hope you give me of seeing you here in July.
I will return that visit immediately—don't be afraid, I do not mean
to incommode you at Waterbeach, but if you will come, I promise I
will accompany you back as far as Cambridge; nay, carry you on to
Ely, for thither I am bound. The Bishop has sent a Dr Nichols[1] to me
to desire I would assist him in a plan for the east window of his cathedral, which he intends to *benefactorate* with painted glass. The window is the most untractable of all Saxon uncouthnesses; nor can I
conceive what to do with it, but by taking off the bottoms for arms
and mosaic, splitting the crucifixion into three compartments, and
filling the five lights at top with prophets, saints, martyrs or such-like,
after shortening the windows like the great ones. This I shall propose; however, I choose to see the spot myself, as it will be a proper
attention to the Bishop after his civility, and I really would give the
best advice I could. The Bishop, like Alexander VIII,[2] feels that the

24. This letter, dated 6 June 1769, is
printed in Granger, *Correspondence* 323–6.

25. The expense would be less because
the distance was less. The rates for a *single*
letter follow: Not exceeding one Post stage,
1d.; above one but not two Post stages, 2d.;
above two stages but not exceeding 80
miles, 3d.; above 80 miles, 4d. A *single* letter (a sheet of paper without any enclosure)
could be sent for half the sum required for
a *double* letter (one containing an enclosure of any kind; or one indited to two different people, although written on a single
sheet of paper); see John G. Hendy, *The*

*History of the Early Postmarks of the Brit-
ish Isles,* 1905, pp. 184–5.

1. John Nicols (d. 1774), fellow of Merton; 'many years resident Chaplain to the
English merchants settled at Oporto in
Portugal'; Prebendary of Ely 1748–74 (Bentham, *Ely*[2] p. 247 and Addenda, p. 17).

2. Pope Alexander VIII (Pietro Otto-
boni) (1610–91), who became Pope (1689)
in extreme old age. See also HW to Cole
19 Dec. 1780, and to William Beloe 28
Oct. 1793.

clock has struck half an hour past eleven, and is impatient to be let depart in peace after his eyes shall have seen his vitrification;3 at least he is impatient to give his eyes that treat—and yet it will be pity to precipitate the work. If you can come to me first, I shall be happy; if not, I must come to you, that is, will meet you at Cambridge. Let me know your mind, for I would not press you unseasonably. I am enough obliged to you already, though by mistake you think it is you that are obliged to me. I do not mean to plunder you of any more prints; but shall employ a little collector4 to get me all that are *gettable;* the rest, the greatest collectors of us all must want.

I am very sorry for the fever you have had; but Goodman Frog, if you will live in the fens, do you expect to be as healthy as if you were a fat Dominican at Naples? You and your MSS will all grow mouldy. When our climate is subject to no sign but Aquarius and Pisces, would one choose the dampest county under the heavens? I do not expect to persuade you, and so I will say no more. I wish you joy of the treasure you have discovered. Six Saxon bishops and a Duke of Northumberland! You have had fine sport this season. Thank you much for wishing to see my name on a plate in the history—but seriously I have no such vanity. I did my utmost to dissuade Mr Granger from the dedication, and took especial pains to get *my virtues* left out of the question; till I found he would be quite hurt if I did not let him express his gratitude as he called it; so to satisfy him, I was forced to accept of *his present,* for I doubt I have few virtues but what he has presented me with; and in a dedication you know one is permitted to have as many as the author can afford to bestow. I really have another objection to the plate, which is, the ten guineas. I have so many draughts on my extravagance for trifles that I like better than vanity, that I should not care to be at that expense. But I should think either the Duke or Duchess of Northumberland would rejoice at such opportunity of buying incense—and I will tell you what you shall do. Write to Mr Percy,5 and vaunt the discovery of Duke Brythnoth's bones, and ask him to move their Graces to contribute a plate.

3. Bishop Mawson died before the window was completed (see *post* 15 Dec. 1770).

4. A man named Jackson, who proved unsatisfactory as a print-collector. His connection with HW apparently terminated at the end of this year (see *post* 18, 21 Dec. 1769).

5. Rev. Thomas Percy (1729–1811), afterwards (1782) Bp of Dromore; editor of the *Reliques.* He was at this time Chaplain to the Duke of Northumberland.

They could not be so unnatural as to refuse—especially if the Duchess knew the size of his thigh-bone.

I was very happy to show civilities to your friends, and should have asked them to stay and dine, but unluckily expected other company. Dr Ewin seems a very good sort of man and Mr Rawlinson a very agreeable one. Pray do not think it was any trouble to me to pay respect to your recommendation.

I have been eagerly reading Mr Shenstone's letters,[6] which though containing nothing but trifles, amused me extremely, as they mention so many persons I know, particularly myself.[7] I found there what I did not know, and what I believe Mr Gray himself never knew, that his ode on my cat was written to ridicule Lord Lyttelton's monody.[8] It is just as true, as that the latter will survive and the former be forgotten. There is another anecdote equally vulgar and void of truth: that my father, *sitting in George's Coffee-house* (I suppose Mr Shenstone thought that after he quitted his place, he went to coffee-houses to learn news) was asked to contribute to a figure of himself that was to be beheaded by the mob.[9] I do remember something like it, but it happened to myself. I met a mob, just after my father was out, in Hanover Square, and drove up to it to know what was the matter. They were carrying about a figure of my sister.[10] This probably gave rise to the other story. That on my uncle[11] I never heard, but it is a good story and not at all improbable. I felt great pity on reading

---

6. William Shenstone (1714–63), the poet. His letters formed vol. iii of his *Works* (vols i and ii, 1764; vol. iii, 1769). The MS Cat. lists only the first two volumes (K.9.50–1), but three volumes were sold SH iii. 115.

7. See especially Shenstone's letter to Richard Graves, 20 Nov. 1762, where HW is characterized as 'a lively and ingenious writer; not always accurate in his determinations, and much less so in his language; too often led away by a desire of routing prejudices and destroying giants: and yet there is no province wherein he appears to more advantage, in *general*, than in throwing new light upon characters in British history' (William Shenstone, *Works*[1], 1764–9, iii. 381).

8. 'I heard . . . it [Lord Lyttelton's *Monody*] was burlesqued under the title of "An Elegy on the Death of a Favourite Cat;" but the burlesque will die, and the

poem will survive' (Shenstone to Graves 17 Sept. 1751, ibid. 213). George Lyttelton (1709–73), 1st Bn Lyttelton, wrote his best poem, *To the memory of a lady lately deceased. A Monody*, 1747, on the death of his first wife, Lucy Fortescue.

9. 'The people that were carrying Lord Orford in effigy, to behead him on Tower-Hill, came into the box where he was, accidentally, at George's, to beg money of him, amongst others' (Shenstone to Richard Jago, 1741, Shenstone, op. cit. 37).

10. Lady Maria, or Mary, Walpole (d. 1801), natural dau. of Sir Robert Walpole by Maria Skerrett; m. (1746) Charles Churchill. When Sir Robert Walpole became Earl of Orford, he obtained for her the rank of an earl's daughter. (See HW to Mann 8 April 1742.)

11. Horatio Walpole (1678–1757), 1st Bn Walpole of Wolterton; HW's uncle and namesake. The anecdote to which HW re-

these letters for the narrow circumstances of the author, and the passion for fame that he was tormented with; and yet he had much more fame than his talents entitled him to. Poor man, he wanted to have all the world talk of him for the pretty place he had made,[12] and which he seems to have made only that it might be talked of. The first time a company came to see my house, I felt his joy. I am now so tired of it, that I shudder when the bell rings at the gate. It is as bad as keeping an inn, and I am often tempted to deny its being shown, if it would not be ill-natured to those that come, and to my housekeeper. I own, I was one day too cross. I had been plagued all the week with staring crowds. At last it rained a deluge. Well! said I, at least nobody will come today. The words were scarce uttered, before the bell rang; a company desired to see the house—I replied, tell them they cannot possibly see the house, but they are very welcome to walk in the garden.

Observe: nothing above alludes to Dr Ewin and Mr Rawlinson; I was not only much pleased with them, but quite glad to show them how entirely you command my house and your most sincere friend and servant,

Hor. Walpole

From Cole, Saturday 17 June 1769

VA, Forster MS 110, ff. 66–7. Cole's copy, Add MS 5824, ff. 134v, 136v–140v.
Address: For the honourable Mr Horace Walpole at Strawberry Hill in Twickenham, Middlesex. *Postmark:* Cambridge 23 IV.

June 17, 1769, Waterbeche.

Dear Sir,

YOU must remember Mr Smith[1] of King's College while you was a member there, and possibly his great formality and exactness. At least I do very well, who continued there so many years after you

---

fers is told in one of Shenstone's letters to Reynolds, 1740 (William Shenstone, *Works*[1] iii. 29).

12. The Leasowes, Worcs. See *Gray's Corr.* iii. 1067 for a similar comment by Gray.

---

1. John Smith (1705–75), eminent for his

knowledge of civil law and algebra; Fellow of King's 1726–70; HW's tutor (see *post* 26 June 1769). Cole's account of him is printed in LI viii. 583–4. In 1768 Smith was Senior Bursar of King's, and had been, Cole says, 'these many years.' He inherited a large fortune and retired to his estate near St Albans (see *Eton Coll. Reg. 1698–1752*).

left it. He is still Fellow and Bursar, and the College is much indebted to him for adjusting their accounts and managing their estates, but much more for the excellent example he has always set them, and pity it is they so little regard it. I have from under his hand the following corrections[2] in your first volume of *Anecdotes,* wholly relating to the indentures for building and glazing the Chapel, most of which are very material and worthy your notice.

P. 106, line 18: for *c £.* read *c s.*
    22: for *ryfaats, gabletts* read *ryfant gabletts.*
    Appendix.
No. 1, p. 1, lines 8, 11, 17, etc.: for *Severick* read *Semerk.*
    line 20: for *sound* read *sand.*
    p. 2, line 7: for *And on that the seid John Wastell* read *And over that the seid Provost, Scolers & Surveyor graunten that the seid John Wastell* etc.
    line 15: for *the Time* read *the Terme.*
No. 2, p. 1, lines 17, 18: for *And that* read *And over that* etc.
    p. 2, line 11: for *40* read *60.*
    25: for *every Severy at 100£.* read *every Severy 100s.* *Sum 100£.*
No. 3, p. 2, line 8: for *ryfaat Gabbletts* read *ryfant Gabletts.*
No. 5, p. 2, line 28: for *Twenty Foot* read *Every Foot.*
    p. 3, line 2: for *Eightene* read *Sixtene.*

June 21, 1769.

Since I wrote the former part,[3] I received on Monday last your most entertaining letter, which met me on my road to Cambridge. The contents gave me double pleasure, as it informed me of your design for Ely, and as it was most seasonable to revive my spirits at that time much depressed by fears and apprehensions of inundations over my estate,[4] great part of which has been drowned these two years, and is now getting dry again. However, I hope I am safe, bating the

2. HW did not make the corrections. The errors remain in *Works* iii. 88–9; iv. 156–64.
3. Cole's copy reads: 'Your entertaining letter met me on the road to Cambridge to meet Mr Gray at Mr Tyson's chamber in Benet College to dinner.'
4. In Haddenham and Aldreth, in the Isle of Ely, Cambs. Cole's copy of an abstract, dated 5 April 1770, of his title to the estate, prepared by Thomas Lombe, his attorney, is Add MS 5810, ff. 174–9. He copied it into the volume 8 April 1770. The estate was a legacy from his father, and Cole apparently sold it for an annuity of £200 (see Palmer, *William Cole* 18). Cole's father paid £5250 for it.

fright. This parish which I now inhabit was not so lucky. On Monday night[5] the bank of the river[6] blew up and has overflown a vast tract of country in this neighbourhood. I was all yesterday on the water to see their operations, but they will hardly be able to stop it in three or four days.[7] This mischief was occasioned by the rain on Sunday last. Longer rains I often remember, but never any so violent for the time it lasted, which was from Saturday night at ten o'clock till Sunday afternoon about three or four. All this part of the country is now covered with water, and the poor people of this parish utterly ruined.[8] I am determined to sell my estate in this county: every shower puts me on the rack, and I have suffered exceedingly for these last four or five years, besides the continual uneasiness it occasions.

I will wait on you at Strawberry Hill about Thursday or Friday, July 6 or 7, in hopes that you will convey me back again to Ely. I will stay with you two days, or more, as will be agreeable, and if it could be compassed, should be glad to pay a dining visit to Mr Granger, if his house is not at too great a distance from you.

We are going to be full of company and gaiety at Cambridge, where the oratorios and music begin on Thursday next, the new Chancellor[9] installed on Saturday, and the noise and riot not over till Wednesday, July 5.[10] I think you would not like Cambridge at such a time. If you should, I can accommodate you with my bed at a clean new house where you might be as quiet as you pleased, for I can easily get another. Mr Gray's ode on the occasion[11] is to be performed on Saturday. I am told it is much liked both as to the poetry and music. He leaves Cambridge for Cumberland immediately after the Com-

5. 19 June.
6. 'broke, and now is overflowing a vast tract of low country in three parishes, before this accident full of cattle of all sorts, and now all removed, to the infinite damage of this neighbourhood' (addition in Cole's copy). See also *Waterbeach Diary* 173-4.
7. 'though the breach is not above thirty or forty feet' (addition in Cole's copy).
8. 'I was much alarmed for my own property, which I thought in equal danger, till one of my tenants called on me last night to fetch out some young cattle which I had given him leave to put into our common in this parish, which was three feet up in water, and which I sent to my new habitation at Milton, where the floods have not reached. This I mention to show you that I am going into a better situation. My own estate has been drowned in great part these three years, but I hope [is] getting dry. It would have been a grievous mortification to have suffered a third inundation, just on the point of selling it, for sell it I am determined. Every shower gives me an alarm, and this last flood [has] shown the situation of such estates in all their horror' (addition in Cole's copy).
9. The Duke of Grafton.
10. For an account of the installation, etc., see Cooper, *Annals* iv. 356-60.
11. *Ode Performed in the Senate-House at Cambridge, July 1, 1769*, Cambridge, 1769. It was set to music by John Randall (1715-99), Professor of Music at Cambridge.

graver is George.* Mountain. To be fold at the Globe over the Exchange. I fuppofe this plate was copied from that of Pafs. †

Another print recorded by Vertue contains in a half fheet the king and queen of Bohemia and four of their children. Will. Pafs fecit ad vivum figurator 1621. About twenty Englifh verfes in two columns at bottom.

I have a very valuable print of the Palatine family on a large fheet, broadways, but without any name of engraver. By the manner I fhould take it for Sadeler. The king of Bohemia, aged, fat, and me-lancholy, is fitting with Elizabeth under fome trees. One of their fons, in appearance between twenty and thirty, ftands by the queen. On the other fide are three young children, the leaft playing with a rabbit. Two greyhounds, a pidgeon, a toad, and feveral animals are difpofed about the landfcape, which is rich, and graved with much freedom. The infcription is in French.

Of William Pafs I find thefe other works;

Robert earl of Leicefter, head in oval, good, two Latin verfes, ^P_W fe.

Frances duchefs of Richmond and Lenox, half-length, extremely neat, her arms in a fhield, on a table lies a book with thefe words, Conftantia coronat. Over her a ftate. Anno 1625 infculptum à Guilh. Paffeo Londinum. This print, which is in my poffeffion, refembles very much a whole-length (I believe by Mare Garrard) of the fame great lady, which I bought from the collection of the late earl of Pomfret.

I have it.

* I find but one other print with his name, and that a poor one; it is of Francis White, dean of Carlifle.

† This print, exceedingly inferior to the former, is now in the collection of fir William Mufgrave, who bought it, with many other fcarce portraits, from Thorefby's Mufeum in 1764. *I have this Print. Wm Cole.*

The Picture at Narford called Mary de Medicis is certainly nother, but the Duchefs of Richmond: it is a whole Length in Black. On one of the Gloves is F.R.I. which are the Initials of her Name certainly, & not a Painter's Mark. She ftands on a Carpet, & was probably painted by Mytens. Mr Tyson CCCC v. Anecdotes of Painting Vol: 2. p. 4.

FROM COLE'S COPY OF "ENGRAVERS"
VOLUME TWO

mencement is over, whither he goes with his friend Mr Mason[11a] for the summer.[11b] I shall see him tomorrow if my cold and sore throat which I caught on the water yesterday does not prevent me.

I don't know whether you are in jest or earnest in respect to Mr Percy, but I design seriously to write to him, but take no notice from whence I had the hint. I am prevented writing any further by the visit of a friend, and am, dear Sir,

Your ever faithful and obliged servant,

Wm Cole

[The following passage, containing Tyson's notes on the second edition of *Anecdotes,* volumes i and ii, and *Engravers,* appears in Cole's copy of this letter, after the phrase 'from whence I had the hint,' in the last paragraph. HW did not mention Tyson's notes, however, until 11 August, which would indicate that Cole possibly sent the notes with his next letter.]

I have so many notes to send you, communicated by Mr Tyson, who desires me to put a *T.* at the end of each, if I transcribe them into your book,[12] that it reminds me of Mr Shenstone's appetite for fame. These notes the gentleman desires me to communicate to you, and I wish for my own sake, who have troubled you with reams of the same sort, that you may not be surfeited with them. He is an ingenious man, and a great lover of antiquity.[12a]

Vol. 1, p. 36:[13] *In my possession is a remarkable piece,* etc.

Note: At the Red Lion in Newmarket is remaining an ancient piece of tapestry which came originally from Cheveley. The design is very nearly the same with this remarkable picture of Mr Walpole.[13a] The King, the Queen[14] and Kemp[15] the Archbishop are represented without any variation. The Gothic architecture over the figures,

11a. The Rev. William Mason (1724–97), HW's correspondent.

11b. Gray did not accompany Mason to Cumberland to spend the summer; he was in London 8–16 July, in York 18–23 July, and at Old Park, near Darlington, Durham (with excursion to Hartlepool), 23 July–29 Sept. (*Gray's Corr.* iii. p. xxxi).

12. Cole has conscientiously done this in his copy of *Engravers*[2] (now wsl), and pre-

sumably did it also in his copy of *Anecdotes*[2].

12a. HW used none of Tyson's notes.

13. *Works* iii. 37. The italicized phrases are from *Anecdotes*[2].

13a. Gray had already forwarded this note to HW (Gray to HW 14 Feb. 1768).

14. Henry VI and Margaret of Anjou.

15. John Kemp (1380?–1454), Abp of York and of Canterbury, and Cardinal.

nearly the same. There are many other personages introduced, which are not in the painting.

P. 68:[16] *At Lord Folkstone's,* etc.

Lord Folkstone[17] gave 110*l*. 5*s*. 0*d*. for Erasmus and 95*l*. 11*s*. 0*d*. for Aegidius.

P. 78:[18] *Our Painter undoubtedly had no hand in it. Vide* Warton on Spencer, vol. 2, p. 117. London, 1762.

P. 98:[19] *On the death of Sir T. Wyatt.* Republished by Hearne at the end of the first volume of Leland's *Itinerary,* from a corrected copy of Leland. There is an imitation of the woodcut by Holbein, at the back of the title page by M. Burgers,[20] badly executed.

P. 165:[21] Added at the bottom.[21a]

> Prince Henry by Isaac Oliver sold for . . . . 20. 0. 0.
> Ben Johnson by P. Oliver . . . . 21. 0. 0.
> Queen Elizabeth and Earl of Essex . . . . 40. 0. 0.
> Mary Queen of Scots, Henry VIII, [by] Isaac
> Oliver, and Sir P. Sidney by Isaac Oliver . . . . . . 140. 0. 0.

P. 172:[22] The house at Babraham was destroyed in 1767.[23] The chimney-piece was sold for about 12*l*. The most costly part is plainly of a much later date than Palavacini's time. It is a very rude work of white marble. The Scaevola in it is a medallion, or a kind of altar placed on the chimney. The arms are carved upon clunch stone, which is plainly the old work. The marble is modern, and indeed has the date 1616. Under the Scaevola is *Quid majus potuit?* "I[24] take leave to dissent from Mr Tyson in supposing this chimney-piece to have been erected at different times. It was put up by Sir Toby Palavicini, as his initials *T. P.* are upon it. It was sold by Mr Austin of Fulburn,[25] who gave 600*l*. for the whole house, in May, 1769, to Sir

16. *Works* iii. 60 n.

17. William Bouverie (1725–76), 1st E. of Radnor.

18. *Works* iii. 67. The painter is Holbein.

19. *Works* iii. 82.

20. Michael Burghers (1653?–1727), engraver.

21. *Works* iii. 131.

21a. That is, as a footnote.

22. *Works* iii. 136–7. Tyson's note is on a note which Cole sent to HW, concerning

Sir Horatio Palavicini (see *ante* 16 May 1762).

23. Cf. LA v. 255.

24. Cole places his remarks within quotation marks to distinguish them from Tyson's.

25. Richard Gough refers to him as 'one Austin, a carpenter at Fulburn' (*Short Genealogical View of the Family of Oliver Cromwell,* 1785, p. 45. This work is No. 31 of John Nichols's *Bibliotheca Topographica Britannica*).

Thomas Gage,[26] who removed it into Suffolk, and who gave about 12*l.* for it."

Vol. 2, p. 123:[27] *His own head is at Earl Paulet's,*[28] and at Narford,[29] equal to the head of Vanderdort[30] at Houghton. At Narford are also several pictures by Holbein. A lady as large as life. A small head in the picture closet wonderfully animated, and a very curious picture of the interview of Henry VIII with Anna Bullein. There are eight figures around a table, on which are spread music books and fruit.

Vol. 3, p. 19:[31] At Mr Bertie's at Uffington[32] is a picture of Lely, a philosopher studying, called by the family, Plato. At the same place is a portrait of the Earl of Lindsey,[33] engraved among the *Illustrious Heads.*[34]

P. 35:[35] Mr Greaves of Fulburne has two pieces by Varelst.

P. 43:[36] There is at Sir John Cotton's[37] at Madingley a portrait with *Ritus fecit* upon it.

P. 81:[38] She painted Archbishop Tenison, engraved by Vandrebanck,[39] 1695.

P. 90:[40] *adorned with his foliage,* and both spoiled by gilding.

P. 147:[41] Dr Thomas Green. Several drawings of his are in the possession of the family. They were done with a black lead pencil upon vellum, in the manner of Loggan,[42] from whom it is possible he might

26. Sir Thomas Rookwood Gage (1720?–96), 5th Bt, of Hengrave Suffolk, and Coldham Hall, Suffolk.

27. *Works* iii. 237. The first part of the note refers to William Dobson (1610–46), the portrait-painter.

28. At Hinton St George, Somerset, or at Buckland, Dorset, the chief seats of Vere Poulett (1710–88), 3d E. Poulett.

29. In Norfolk, the seat of Brigg Price Fountaine (d. 1825), great-nephew and heir to Sir Andrew Fountaine (1676–1753); see LA v. 253–5; Burke, *Landed Gentry*, 1879.

30. Abraham Van Der Dort (d. 1640) (see *Works* iii. 186).

31. *Works* iii. 292–3.

32. Uffington in Lincolnshire, seat of Charles Bertie (1734–80), grandson of Charles, youngest son of 2d E. Lindsey (see Collins, *Peerage*, 1812, ii. 19–20).

33. Robert Bertie (1582–1642), 1st E. of Lindsey.

34. See *The Heads of Illustrious Persons*

of Great Britain . . . with their Lives and Characters by Thomas Birch, 1813, p. 85.

35. *Works* iii. 302–4.

36. *Works* iii. 310 n, the article on John Michael Wright (1625?–1700).

37. Sir John Hinde Cotton (d. 1795), 4th Bt, of Madingley, Cambs; M.P. for St Germains, 1741–7; for Marlborough, 1752–61; for Cambridgeshire, 1764–80. He was Cole's intimate friend, and is frequently mentioned in later letters to HW.

38. *Works* iii. 337–8, the article on Mrs Mary Beale.

39. Peter Vanderbanck (1649–97).

40. *Works* iii. 343, the article on Grinling Gibbons: 'At Houghton two chimneys are adorned with his foliage.'

41. *Works* iii. 382–3. HW had described him merely as 'the Bishop of Ely.' See *ante* 6 June 1769, n. 21.

42. David Loggan (1635–1700?), engraver (see *Works* iv. 71–5).

have had some instructions. A full account of him in Masters's *History of C.C.C.C.,* p. 177.

P. 165:[43] After Castle Howard, etc., Earl of Carlisle's.[44]

        Eastbury, late Lord Melcombe's.[45]

        King's Weston, Mr Southwell's.[46]

        Easton-Neston, Earl of Pomfret's.[47]

        Grimsthorp in Lincolnshire, Duke of Ancaster's.[48]

Engravers.

P. 11:[49] I find I. B. prefixed to the frontispiece of *Aelfredi Regis Gestae,* published by Archbishop Parker, and printed by John Day, 1574. In the middle is the figure of Alfred, and round him, in different compartments, the emblems of the sciences, etc. Probably this I. B. did most of the woodcuts belonging to the Archbishop's editions of the monkish historians, which are in general not badly executed.

At the end of vol. 3, p. 167:[50] Henry Aldrich was born in London in 1647, educated at Westminster School. On 15 February was installed Canon of Christ Church; was made Dean 17 June 1689. 'A great deal of its present lustre and beauty it owes to his skilful and ingenious hand: for it was he that designed the beautiful square called Peckwater Quadrangle, which is esteemed a regular and complete piece of architecture.' He died at Christ Church, Dec. 14, 1710. *Biographia Britannica,* vol. 1, p. 96.

Engravers.

P. 9:[51] View of London.[52] Sold at Dr Meade's auction[53] for 14*l*. 0*s*. 0*d*.

43. *Works* iii. 396, a list of buildings designed by Sir John Vanbrugh.

44. In Yorks, the seat of Frederick Howard (1748–1825), 5th E. of Carlisle.

45. In Dorset, the seat of George Bubb Dodington (1691–1762), 1st Bn Melcombe. HW referred to it as 'that pile of ugliness' (to Mann 26 Sept. 1762).

46. In Glos, the seat of Edward Southwell, afterwards (1776) 20th Bn de Clifford.

47. Near Towcester, Northants; the seat of George Fermor (1722–85), 2d E. of Pomfret.

48. Near Edenham; seat of Peregrine Bertie (1714–78), 3d D. of Ancaster.

49. *Works* iv. 8–9, John Bettes (d. 1570?). Cole has written this and nearly all of Tyson's other notes in his copy of *Engravers*² and has added 'M. Tyson of C.C.C.C,' as directed.

50. Of *Anecdotes*². Tyson wrote in this account of Aldrich, who was not mentioned by HW.

51. *Works* iv. 7–8.

52. By Ralph Aggas.

53. The library of Dr Richard Mead (1673–1754) was sold by Samuel Baker 18 Nov. 1754 and 7 April 1755, the prints and drawings by Langford, 13 Jan. 1755. In the 71 sessions of the sale no item answers HW's description and no item sold for £14. The item which most resembles it was sold the first day of the prints, lot 66 'A Plan of London in 1560, unbound,' for 14s.

Dr Cunningham's book[54] finely printed and dedicated to Robert Lord Dudley,[55] whose arms are quartered at the beginning, has a very curious design of the sciences about the title-page. The Doctor's head in his 28th year, with these letters about the oval,

Η ΜΕΓΆ ΛΗ ΕΥ ΔΑΙΜΟΝΊΑ ΟΥΔΕΝΙ ΦΘΟΝΕΙΝ

and a large map of the city of Norwich, with several other cuts, some of which are done by himself. It contains 202 pages exclusive of the preface, contents and Queen's licence at the end.

P. 18:[56] *Volume containing the heads, etc.* This refers to Elstrack, not Holland. *Florus Britannicus* by Mat. Stevenson, printed by M. S. Sold by T. Jenner, 1662. With the Heads of the Kings of England by Elstrack.

P. 25:[57] This print of James's[58] family, and that of the three Colignis[59] are in the Pepys Library.

P. 26:[60] Frances Duchess of Richmond. The picture at Narford called Mary de Medici's is certainly not her, but the Duchess of Richmond. It is a whole-length in black. On one of the gloves is F. R. L., which are certainly the initials of her name, and not a painter's mark. She stands on a carpet, and was probably painted by Mytens.

P. 27:[61] At the end of this article, add: Lodovicus XIII.

P. 35:[62] Drayton's *Polyolbion*. With a pike: the same figure that is engraved in Holland's *Heroologia*, probably from Isaac Oliver. See Charles I, Catalogue.[63]

P. 39:[64] After *Sir H. remains,* in the first note, add: and much superior to that by Dolle.[65]

54. The *Cosmographicall Glasse,* 1559, by Dr William Cuningham or Keningham (b. 1531).

55. Robert Dudley (1532?–88), afterwards E. of Leicester.

56. *Works* iv. 14.

57. *Works* iv. 19, the first paragraph of the article on William Pass (1598?–1637?).

58. James I's.

59. A print by William Pass, of three brothers: Odetus, Gaspar and Franciscus Coligni (see *Works* iii. 131 n).

60. *Works* iv. 20, William Pass's print of Frances Howard, Duchess of Richmond and Lennox. See illustration.

61. *Works* iv. 21.

62. *Works* iv. 27, the print of Henry Prince of Wales, mentioned in the account of William Hole or Holle (fl. 1600–30).

63. *A Catalogue and Description of King Charles the First's Capital Collection of Pictures, Statues, Bronzes, Medals, &c.,* 1757. The catalogue was made by Abraham Van Der Dort, keeper of Charles I's collections, prepared for the press by George Vertue, and published with an advertisement by HW (*Works* i. 234–7).

64. *Works* iv. 30 n, the print of Sir Henry Wotton (1568–1639) by Peter Lombart (1620?–81).

65. William Dolle (fl. 1670–80) (*Works* iv. 30).

P. 40:[66] Bib. Harl. 38.[67] Majesty's sacred monument erected by A. D. V. Darcie, in memory of King James, Queen Anne and the nobility that died between these two apparitions (viz., a comet and a star in the moon). 'Tis a print of a tomb or mausoleum in memory of King James I, and came out (as Sir Simon D'Ewes[68] has noted at the top) in June, 1625, engraven by Robert Vaughan.

P. 41:[69] After *T. Fairfax*, add: with the handwriting, sign manual and medal of O. C.

P. 43:[70] at the bottom. Marshall engraved the frontispiece to a book entitled *A Boulster Lecture.*[71] This is neatly executed. It represents a man and his wife in bed: the husband turns from her, and she is represented as starting up with violence. On a label from her mouth is written, *Dum loquar ista, taces?* from his, *Surdo canis.* The motto to the book is, *O nox longa!*

P. 48:[72] Hollar. At the bottom of his own portrait, etched by himself, is annexed the following inscription: WENCELAUS HOLLAR, gentilhomme, né a Prage, l'an 1607, a esté de nature fort inclin pour l'art de miniature, principalement pour esclaircir, mais beaucoup retardé par son père: l'an 1627 il est partis de Prage, ayant demeuré en divers lieux en Allemaigne, il s'est addonné pour peu de temps à esclaircir et appliquer l'eau forte: estant partis de Coloigne avec le Comte d'Arondel vers Vienne et a dillée par Prage vers L'Angleterre, ou ayant esté serviteur domestique du Duc de York, il est retiré de la cause de la guerre à Anvers, ou il reside encores.

P. 78:[73] Izaak Walton in 1653 published in a very elegant manner his *Compleat Angler,* in small 12mo, adorned with exquisite cuts of most of the fish mentioned in it. The artist who engraved them has been so modest as to conceal his name, but there is great reason to suppose them the work of Lombart,[74] who is mentioned in the *Sculptura* of Evelyn. *Vide* Evelyn, p. 77, Hawkins's edition.

66. *Works* iv. 31–2. The note is an addition to the article on Robert Vaughan (d. ca 1667).

67. Tyson's note is a quotation (with minor changes) from *A Catalogue of the Harleian Collection of Manuscripts,* 2 vols, 1759, i. No. 38.

68. Sir Simonds D'Ewes (1602–50), Kt (1626) and 1st Bt (1641).

69. *Works* iv. 32.

70. *Works* iv. 33. The note is an addition to the article on William Marshall.

71. *Ar't Asleep Husband? A Boulster Lecture,* 1640, by Richard Brathwaite (1588?–1673). HW's copy (H.4.9) was sold SH iii. 14.

72. *Works* iv. 37–8.

73. *Works* iv. 60–2. This note of Tyson's is an addition to the article on Peter Lombart.

74. 'The engraver is unknown, but Pierre Lombart . . . and also Faithorne and Vaughan are possible candidates for the honour' (Thomas Westwood and

P. 84:[75] *No name to it.* This is a mistake. In the University Library is a mezzotinto of a Magdalen from M. Merian, at the bottom of which is the following inscription: *Rupertus D.G.C.P.D.B. Princeps Imperii, Animi Gratia lusit.*

P. 111:[76] At the house of Winstanley, a bookseller in Saffron-Walden, is preserved a portrait of Hamlet Winstanley, who was of the same family, said to be executed by himself. It is a head painted with spirit.[77]

P. 117:[78] Robson's Catalogue, 1768.[79] Smith's mezzotintos, containing 500 plates on miscellaneous subjects, painted by himself, the whole exceeding scarce, bound in three volumes gilt, etc., 21*l.*

P. 124:[80] Daniel King drew and engraved also the plates in Gunton's *Church History of Peterborough,* 1686.

P. 135:[81] H. Gravelot also invented the ornaments for the *Illustrious Heads.*

P. 136:[82] *Gentleman in Norfolk.* Sir Edward Astley.[83]

Vol. 1,[84] p. 25: *Itinerarium Fratris Simonis Simeonis et Hugonis Illuminatoris,* A. D. 1322, MS. C.C.C.C.—Et eidem monasterio quasi immediate conjungitur illud famosissimum palatium Regum Anglorum, in equo est illa vulgata camera, in cujus parietibus sunt omnes Historiæ bellicæ tocius Bibliæ ineffabiliter depictæ, atque in Gallico completissime et perfectissime conscriptæ in non modica intuentium admiratione et maxima regali magnificentia.

Vol. 4, at the end:[85] John Langton was born in the parish of St George in Stamford, 1671. The date of his fine specimen of writing at Burleigh is July 18, 1713. He designed and engraved the remains

---

Thomas Satchell, *Bibliotheca Piscatoria,* 1883, p. 217).

75. *Works* iv. 66, the article on Prince Rupert as an engraver.

76. *Works* iv. 95–6, the article on Hamlet Winstanley (1698–1756).

77. Cole added the following to Tyson's note in his copy of *Engravers*[2] (now WSL): 'I went with Mr Tyson to his shop at Walden, and would have purchased the picture, but he refused to part with it in 1771.'

78. *Works* iv. 99–100, the article on John Smith (1652?–1742).

79. That is, in a catalogue issued by James Robson (1733–1806), a bookseller of New Bond Street (see LA iii. 661; v. 323–5).

80. *Works* iv. 105, article on George King

(fl. 1740; Michael Bryan, *Dictionary of Painters and Engravers,* 1903).

81. *Works* iv. 112–3.

82. *Works* iv. 113, the article on Arthur Pond.

83. (1729–1802), 4th Bt, of Melton Constable, Norfolk.

84. Of *Anecdotes*[2]. Cf. *Works* iii. 29. This MS was published as, *Itineraria Symonis Simeonis et Willelmis de Worcestre,* ed. J. Nasmith, Cambridge 1778. This passage occurs on pp. 5–6.

85. That is, at the end of *Engravers*[2]. The account of Langton in Cole's hand at the end of his copy of *Engravers*[2] differs slightly from that given here. See also *ante* 30 Sept. 1763.

of the priory of St Leonard, prefixed to the history of it in Peck's *Annals of Stamford*.[86] But he deserves a place in the *Anecdotes* upon more accounts than one. He practised with success the art of staining glass. In the east window of St George's Church in Stamford is a copy by him of the Consecration of the Bread by Carlo Dolci at Burleigh. The colours are much better than the drawing. At his own house was one entire window of his own staining, consisting of various small figures, well executed. It was purchased some years after his death by the late Judge Noel,[87] and is now in a small temple in his garden at Stamford. He was by profession a writing master, and very eminent. A fine piece of writing upon vellum was presented to Queen Anne, for which he was rewarded with a golden pen. There is a duplicate of it at Burleigh. He published a copy-book with an engraving of his own head, and dying at Stamford on the 8th of May, 1724, was buried in the north aisle of St George's Church. There is a head of him, engraved by Bickham,[88] prefixed to one of his copy-books. This scarce print is in my possession. "Thus far Mr Tyson."

I am, dear Sir,

Your ever faithful servant,

WM COLE

To COLE, Monday 26 June 1769

Add MS 5952, ff. 71–2.
Address: To the Reverend Mr Cole at Waterbeach, Cambridgeshire.
Postmark: Isleworth 27 IV.

Strawberry Hill, Monday, June 26, 1769.

OH! yes, yes, I shall like Thursday or Friday 6th or 7th exceedingly. I shall like your staying with me two days exceeding*ly*er;

---

86. *Academia tertia Anglicana; or, the Antiquarian Annals of Stamford in Lincoln, Rutland, and Northampton Shires . . . In XIV. Books*. Compiled by Francis Peck, Rector of Godeby by Melton in Leicestershire, 1727. In HW's large-paper copy of this work (E.1.17, sold SH ii. 102, now WSL), the print ('The Remains of the Priory Church of S. Leonard by Stamford.

John Langton delin. et Sculp.') appears in Book III, opp. p. 8.

87. William Noel (1695–1762), M.P. for Stamford 1722–47; Justice of the Common Pleas, 1757.

88. Probably George Bickham (d. 1769) the elder. His MS notes are now in the British Museum.

and longer exceedingly*est;* and I will carry you back to Cambridge on
our pilgrimage to Ely. But I should not at all like to be catched in the
glories of an installation, and find myself a Doctor, before I knew
where I was. It will be much more agreeable to find the whole *caput*[1]
asleep, digesting turtle, dreaming of bishoprics, and humming old
catches of Anacreon and scraps of Corelli. I wish Mr Gray may not be
set out for the north, which is rather the case, than setting out for the
summer. We have no summers, I think, but what we raise like pine-
apples by fire. My hay is an absolute water-soochy,[2] and teaches me
how to feel for you. You are quite in the right to sell your fief in
Marshland. I should be glad you would take one step more and *quit*
Marshland. We live at least on *terra firma* in this part of the world,
and can saunter out without stilts. Then we do not wade into pools
and call it going upon the water, and get sore throats. I trust yours is
better; but I recollect this is not the first you have complained of.
Pray be not incorrigible, but come to shore.

Be so good as to thank Mr Smith, my old tutor, for his corrections.
If ever the *Anecdotes* are reprinted, I will certainly profit of them.

I joked it is true about Joscelin de Louvain and his Duchess,[3] but
not at all in advising you to make Mr P.[4] pimp for the plate. On the
contrary I wish you success, and think this an infallible method of
obtaining the benefaction. It is right to lay vanity under contribution, for then both sides are pleased.

It will not be easy for you to dine with Mr Granger from hence
and return at night. It cannot be less than six- or seven-and-twenty
miles to Shiplake. But I go to Park Place tomorrow which is within
two miles of him, and I will try if I can tempt him to meet you here.[5]
Adieu!

Dear Sir, Yours most sincerely,

Hor. Walpole

1. A council of six, including the Vice-
Chancellor, who passed upon graces sub-
mitted to the University Senate. (See Denys
A. Winstanley, *Unreformed Cambridge,*
Cambridge, 1935, pp. 26–7.)

2. 'A sodden mass' (OED; HW is quoted
as authority).

3. The Duke and Duchess of Northumberland. The Duke when Sir Hugh Smithson, like Joscelin de Louvain, married the
lineal heiress and descendant, and assumed
the name and arms of the Percy family.

4. Thomas Percy.

5. Granger was at SH when Cole arrived
there, 7 July (*Waterbeach Diary* 181).

To Cole, Saturday 15 July 1769

Add MS 5952, ff. 69–70.
Address: To the Reverend Mr Cole at Waterbeach near Cambridge.
Postmark: IW [Isleworth] 15 IY.

Strawberry Hill, July 15, 1769.

YOUR fellow-travellers, Rosette[1] and I, got home safe, perfectly contented with our expedition,[2] and wonderfully obliged to you. Pray receive our thanks and barkings, and pray say and bark a great deal for us to Mr and Mrs Bentham[3] and all that good family.

After gratitude, you know, always comes a little self-interest, for who would be at the trouble of being grateful, if he had no farther expectations? *Imprimis* then, here are the directions for Mr Essex[4] for the piers of my gates.[5] Bishop Luda[6] must not be offended at my converting his tomb into a gateway.[7] Many a saint and confessor, I doubt, will be glad soon to be *passed through,* as it will at least secure his being *passed over.* When I was directing the east window at Ely, I recollected the lines of Prior,[8]

> How unlucky were Nature and Art to poor Nel!
> She was painting her cheeks at the time her nose fell.

1. HW's dog, 'a tanned black spaniel' (HW to Mann 23 March 1770). On her death in 1773, HW wrote her epitaph (see HW to Nuneham 6 Nov. 1773).

2. After Cole's visit to HW, 7–9 July (*Waterbeach Diary* 181) they went to Ely, where HW, at the request of Bishop Mawson, gave advice concerning the east window of the Cathedral and the removal of the organ to a side door (ibid. 182–3).

3. Joseph Bentham (1710–78), alderman and mayor of Cambridge, and printer to the University; brother of James Bentham, author of *Ely;* married Ann Reste or Riste (d. 1781), sister and heiress of George Reste (see LA viii. 451; Bentham, *Ely*[2], 'Memoirs,' p. 2; *St James's Chronicle,* 6–8 Sept. 1781). HW was the guest of Mr and Mrs Bentham during his visit to Cole, 10–12 July (*Waterbeach Diary* 183), as Cole had no accommodations for guests at Waterbeach (see *post* 21 Dec. 1769).

4. James Essex (1722–84), architect and builder; designer of the Beauclerc Tower and the Offices at SH.

5. The gate is engraved in *Description of SH, Works* ii. 507, with the title 'Garden Gate.' Its position at this time is not en-

tirely clear. A 'Plan of the Estate' made about 1790 and pasted into HW's extra-illustrated copy of the 1784 *Description of SH* (now WSL) shows a 'Gothic Gate' on the southeast boundary, and is almost certainly the gate discussed here. There was also an 'Iron Gate' which opened (theoretically) upon the road to Hampton Court on the western boundary. The confusion probably arises from the Gothic Gate's having iron doors. Later this gate appears to have been moved to the immediate neighbourhood of the Chapel in the garden (see *A Catalogue of the Excellent Furniture . . . at Strawberry Hill,* 12 July 1842, lot 285* and Rowlandson's 'Temple at Strawberry Hill,' 1822, Stradler aquatinta). See illustration.

6. William de Luda (d. 1298), Bp of Ely 1290–8 (see Bentham, *Ely*[2] pp. 152–3).

7. The piers of the gate are copied from Luda's tomb, which was engraved at Cole's expense in Bentham's *Ely* (see 2d edn, Plate XVII, opp. p. 152).

8. 'A Critical Moment.' The first line should read: 'How capricious were Nature and Art to poor Nell?'

GATE AT STRAWBERRY-HILL

GATE AT STRAWBERRY HILL DESIGNED FROM
BISHOP LUDA'S TOMB

Adorning cathedrals when the religion itself totters, is very like poor Nel's mishap—but to come to Mr Essex.

The width of the iron gates is six feet two, and they are seven feet ten high. Each pilaster is one foot one wide: the whole width with the interstices, is eight feet ten. The ornament over the gates is four feet four to the point. Perhaps you will understand me from this scrawl. The piers should certainly, I think, be a little, and not much higher than the ornament over the gates, but Mr Essex will judge best of the proper proportion. I would not have any bas relief or figures in the bases. The tops to be in this manner—nothing over the gates themselves. (I have drawn these piers too wide.)

My next job is a list of some heads which I beg you will give to Mr Jackson; at his leisure he will try if he can pick them up for me.

Frances Bridges Countess of Exeter (You will think me very gluttonous about this.)

Duke of Buckingham by Faithorne in the manner of Mellan.[9]

Sir John Hoskins[10]	Mrs Cooper[18]	Lady Rooke[26]
Sir Robert Viner[11]	Sleidan[19]	Frontispiece to Academy of Eloquence[27]
Lady Paston[12]	Sir Bevil Granville[20]	
Hannah Wooley[13]	Prince Eugene, young[21]	Do. to Hist. of Ch. I by H. L.[28]
Lady Harrington[14]	Duke of Ormond, Do.[22]	
Venner[15]	Mrs Wellers[23]	Hen. Maria before the Queen's closet opened.[29]
Glanville[16]	Gouge[24]	
Wharton[17]	Maria Langham[25]	Do. See Granger vol. 1. p. 2. p. 335.[30]

9. George Villiers (1592–1628), 1st D. of Buckingham, 'engraved by Faithorne, without hatching, in the manner of Mellan' (*Granger*[1] i. 351). Claude Mellan (1598–1688) was a French engraver.

10. Sir John Hoskins or Hoskyns (1634–1705), 2d Bt, by Faithorne and R. White; barrister, Middle Temple; P.R.S. 1682–3 (see *Granger*[1] ii. 537–8; EBP).

11. (1631–88), 1st Bt; Lord Mayor of London; goldsmith and banker. Granger describes the print: 'long hair, black cap, cloak, etc., by Faithorne; without inscription; h. sh., very scarce' (1st edn ii. 286–7; see also DNB).

12. Margaret Hewitt, sister of Sir George Hewitt, m., as his 2d wife, Sir William Paston (1610?–63), 1st Bt, after whose death she m. George Strode (see GEC). The print is dated 1659 (see *Granger*[5] iv. 88; EBP). HW's copy ('materially damaged') was sold London vi. 784.

13. Mrs Hannah Woolley or Wolley (fl. 1670), afterwards Mrs Challinor. She published works on cookery 1661–75. The first impressions have the name of Mrs Sarah Gilly (d. 1659) (see DNB *sub* Woolley; also *Granger*[5] v. 308–9). HW in *Engravers* lists the print: 'Mrs. Sarah Gilly, small head in oval. This plate is sometimes inscribed

Charles II, Sheldon and Shaftsbury before old editions of Chamberlain's *Present State*.³¹ Q. Eliz., Burleigh and Walsingham, frontispiece

Hannah Wooley, but the best impressions have the name of Gilly' (*Works* iv. 54). HW's copy with the name of Gilly was sold London vi. 769.

14. Katherine Harrington (1617–75), wife of Sir James Harrington (1607–80), by Faithorne. The print, which shows her at the age of 36, is a plate to Sir James's *Horae Consecratae*, 1682 (see *Granger*¹ ii. 103–4; EBP). HW's copy was bought (London vi. 772) by the British Museum.

15. Tobias Venner (1577–1660), physician and medical writer who practised at Petherton and Bath. The print is dated 1660 (see *Granger*¹ ii. 58–9). HW's copy was sold London vi. 798.

16. Joseph Glanvill (1636–80), divine; author of *The Vanity of Dogmatizing*, 1661, and controversial works (see *Granger*¹ ii. 191–2).

17. Sir George Wharton (1617–81), 1st Bt, author of almanacs, works on astronomy, and a chronological history of England after 1600 (*Granger*¹ ii. 89).

18. Elizabeth Cooper; the print is engraved by William Faithorne, Jr, after the portrait by Sir Peter Lely; 'a child . . . seated, full face, a black boy offering her fruit' (EBP; see also *Granger*¹ ii. 446).

19. Johann Sleidan (1506–56), German historian. The print appears in the English translation of his *History of the Reformation in Germany*, for which Faithorne engraved five other plates (see *Granger*⁵ i. 156; there is no account of the print in *Granger*¹).

20. Sir Bevil Granville or Grenville (1596–1643), royalist; killed in battle of Lansdowne, near Bath. 'Aet. 39, 1640. By Faithorne, but without his name; 4to. Before the Oxford Verses on his Death' (*Granger*⁵ iii. 39; *Granger*¹ contains no account of this print; see also DNB and Falconer Madan, *Oxford Books*, Oxford, ii (1912). 286).

21. Francis Eugene (1663–1736), Prince of Savoy-Carignan, the famous general.

22. James Butler (1665–1745), 2d D. of Ormonde; general; engraved by Faithorne after the portrait by Sir Godfrey Kneller (see EBP; *Granger*¹,⁵ contain no account of this print).

23. 'Mr [not Mrs] —— Wellers; scarce, sm. mez. Faithorne, jun. sc. Mr. Bromley [Henry Bromley, *Catalogue of Engraved British Portraits*, 1793, p. 217] has placed this person amongst the gentry, but I question whether he was of that class. He is supposed by Mr Granger to have been an author' (Mark Noble, *Biographical History* [1688–1725], 3 vols, 1806, i. 389–90). 'This may have been a bookplate' (John Chaloner Smith, *British Mezzotinto Portraits*, 4 vols, 1884, ii. 476).

24. William Gouge (1578–1653), Puritan divine; author of *Commentary on the Epistle to the Hebrews*, 1655, to which the print, with eight English verses, was frontispiece (see *Granger*¹ i. 401).

25. Mary Alston (d. 1660), dau. of Sir Edward Alston; m. Sir James Langham. The print appears 'before her "Funeral Sermon," by Dr Edward Reynolds, rector of Braunston in Northamptonshire, and afterwards Bishop of Norwich. Scarce.' (*Granger*⁵ v. 380). It was sold London vi. 738, where it was described as one of five known impressions.

26. Mary Luttrell (d. 1702), second wife of Sir George Rooke (1650–1709), the admiral (see EBP).

27. *The Academie of Eloquence*, 1654, by Thomas Blount; often reprinted. The frontispiece contained small oval portraits of Bacon and Sir Philip Sidney; HW's copy of the print was sold London vi. 742.

28. 'Charles I in an oval; above is the Church of England, represented as a matron at the point of death, with an inscription, in Greek, signifying that many physicians have killed her. Faithorne sc. It is the title to the "History of King Charles," by H. L. (Hamon l'Estrange), Esq.' (*Granger*⁵ ii. 243–4; the print is not described in *Granger*¹).

29. Henrietta Maria (1609–69), Queen Consort of Charles I. The print appears 'before "The Queen's Closet opened," 1655' (*Granger*¹ ii. 3).

30. 'Henrietta Maria; richly adorned; Van Dyck p. Faithorne sc. . . . fine' (*Granger*¹ i. 335).

31. 'Charles II sitting in a chair of state; Abp Sheldon [Gilbert Sheldon (1598–1677),

to Sir Dudley Digges's *Compleat Embassador*.[32] N.B. All the above are by Faithorne, or by his son in mezzotinto. I shall not mind paying for books to get the prints. Here are a few others.

Sir Thomas Armstrong in a print with other heads.[33] Lady Mary Airmine.[34] Catherine Boleyn.[35] Charles Blount Lord Mountjoy.[36] George Earl of Berkeley.[37] Lord Brounker.[38] Mary Duchess of Beaufort.[39] Madam Sophia Bulkeley.[40] Lady Brandon.[41] Arthur Lord Chichester.[42] Giovanni Dudley Duca di Northumberland.[43] Lady Anastasia Digby.[44] Lord Dartmouth.[45] Lady Falconberg.[46] Humphrey Duke

Abp of Canterbury] and the Earl of Shaftsbury [Anthony Ashley Cooper (1621–83), 1st E. of Shaftesbury] standing by him. . . . Before several of the early editions of Chamberlayne's "Present State of England" ' (*Granger*[1] ii. 115).

32. 'Elizabeth, sitting under a canopy, Lord Burleigh on her right hand, and Sir F. Walsingham on her left.—Title to Sir Dudley Digg's "Compleat Ambassador," 1655, fol.' (*Granger*[1] i. 130).

33. Sir Thomas Armstrong (1624?–84). The print, engraved by John Savage (fl. 1690–1700), is in a large half-sheet with seven other heads (see *Granger*[1] ii. 289–90; EBP v. 73).

34. Mary Talbot (d. 1676), m. (2) Sir William Armine or Armyne (1593–1651) (see DNB). The print, engraved by F. H. Van Hove, is in Samuel Clarke's *Lives* (see *Granger*[5] v. 376).

35. 'Aunt and governess of the Princess [afterwards Queen] Elizabeth' (*Granger*[5] i. 148). The print appears in Gregorio Leti's *Historia overo Vita di Elisabetta* . . . Amsterdam, 1703, as figure 8 of part 1. It is not listed in EBP, and is probably false (see *post* 11 Aug. 1769).

36. HW is following *Granger*[1] i. 144–5, where the subject of this print is identified as Charles Blount (1563–1606), E. of Devonshire and 8th Bn Mountjoy; the print represents his natural son, Mountjoy Blount (1597?–1666), 1st E. of Newport (see *Granger*[5] ii. 303; EBP). It is engraved by Martin Droeshout (fl. 1620–51).

37. George Berkeley (1628–98), 1st E. of Berkeley; the print is engraved by David Loggan (1635–1700?) (see *Granger*[5] iv. 190).

38. William Brounker or Brouncker (1620?–84), 2d Vct Brouncker of Castle Lyons; mathematician and first president

of the Royal Society; the print, engraved by Hollar, is 'a small head in the frontispiece to [Thomas] Sprat's "History of the Royal Society," ' 1667 (*Granger*[1] ii. 363).

39. Mary Capel (1630–1715), 'daughter to Arthur, Lord Capel, murdered by the rebels in 1648' (*Granger*[1] ii. 426); m. (1) Henry Lord Beauchamp and (2) Henry Somerset (1629–1700), 1st D. of Beaufort. The print is engraved by Joseph Nutting after the portrait by Robert Walker (see Collins, *Peerage*, 1768, i. 212).

40. Sophia Stuart (d. ca 1716), 'daughter of Walter Stuart, Esq., third son of Lord Blantyre, and sister to Frances, Duchess of Richmond' (*Granger*[5] v. 386–7); a court beauty; lady of the bedchamber to Queen Mary Beatrice; m. Henry Bulkeley, Master of the Household to Charles II. Her print is from the portrait by Henry Gascar (see EBP).

41. Anne Mason (1668–1753), dau. of Sir Richard Mason of Whitehall and Sutton in Surrey; m. (1) in 1683, Charles Gerard (1659?–1701), 2d Bn Gerard of Brandon and 2d E. of Macclesfield and (2) Col. Henry Brett; reputed mother of the poet Savage. Granger lists two mezzotinto prints of her, both after the portrait by Willem Wissing (1656–87) (see *Granger*[1] ii. 556; EBP).

42. Arthur Chichester (1563–1625), Bn Chichester of Belfast; Lord Deputy and Lord High Treasurer of Ireland; the print is anonymous and rare (see *Granger*[5] ii. 98).

43. John Dudley (1502?–53) D. of Northumberland; executed for resisting the succession of Queen Mary to the throne. The print appears as figure 25 in part 1 of Leti's *Historia overo Vita di Elisabetta*, Amsterdam, 1703 (see *Granger*[1] i. 94).

44. Venetia Anastasia Stanley (1600–33),

of Gloster.[47] Countess of Hertford.[48] Sir John Hotham.[49] *Jacob Hall.*[50] Theoph. Earl of Huntingdon.[51] Eliz. Countess of Kent.[52] Louisa Princess Palatine.[53] Duke and Duchess of Newcastle and children at table by Diepenbecke.[54] Sir John Perrot.[55] Percy gunpowder conspirator.[56] Tobias Rustat.[57] Alex. Earl of Stirling.[58] Eliz. Countess of Southampton.[59] Lady Eliz. Shirley by Hollar.[60] Earl of Tyrconnel.[61] Lady

dau. of Sir Edward Stanley; m. (1625) Sir Kenelm Digby. The print is by Hollar, dated 1646 (see *Granger*[5] iii. 230–1).

45. George Legge (1648–91), 1st Bn Dartmouth; the print (which Granger says is 'very scarce') was engraved by Peter Vanderbank or Vandrebanc (1649–97) (see *Granger*[5] vi. 64).

46. Mary Cromwell (d. 1713), 3d dau. of Oliver Cromwell; m. (1657), as his second wife, Thomas Belasyse (1627–1700), E. Fauconberg, a supporter of Cromwell and later a Privy Councillor of Charles II. The print, engraved by George King, appears in Francis Peck's *Life of Cromwell* (see *Granger*[1] ii. 101–2).

47. Humphrey (1391–1447), Duke of Gloucester. The print is 'a head-piece in the Catalogue of the Bodleian Library, over the letter K' (*Granger*[5] i. 23).

48. Frances Howard (ca 1573–1639), afterwards Duchess of Richmond; see *Granger*[5] ii. 171; EBP; cf. *ante* 19 Aug. 1762.

49. (d. 1645), 1st Bt; parliamentarian and governor of Hull; executed for his negotiations with the royalists with a view to rejoining them. The print is anonymous (see *Granger*[1] i. 429; EBP).

50. (fl. 1668), 'a famous rope-dancer; cap, his own hair, comb. This print is very scarce' (*Granger*[1] ii. 461). It was engraved by P. de Brune after the portrait by J. van Oost (see *Granger*[5] vi. 13). 'This plate has been accepted as a portrait of Hall, without any authority' (EBP).

51. Theophilus Hastings (1650–1701), 7th E. of Huntingdon. The print, dated 1687, was engraved by R. Williams after the portrait by Kneller (see *Granger*[1] ii. 501; EBP).

52. Elizabeth Talbot (1581–1651), 2d dau. and coheir of Gilbert Talbot, 7th E. of Shrewsbury; m. Henry Grey, 7th E. of Kent. The only print of her listed in *Granger*[1] (i. 543–4) is the frontispiece to her *Secrets in Physick*, 1656, but HW may refer to another (see *Granger*[5] iii. 209; EBP).

53. Louise Hollandina (1622–1709), Princess Palatine, niece of Charles I; painter (pupil of Gerard Honthorst) and engraver. She is mentioned as a painter in *Granger*[1] i. 346, 531, but no print of her is listed. Cf. *Anecdotes*, ed. Wornum, iii. 204 n.

54. William Cavendish (1592–1676), D. of Newcastle; m. (1645), as his second wife, Margaret Lucas (1624?–74), youngest child of Sir Thomas Lucas. The print, engraved by P. Clouwet after A. van Diepenbeke, represents the Duke and Duchess with ten children in a room in which a fire is burning (see *Granger*[5] iii. 308–9; EBP v. 49).

55. (1527?–92), Kt; Lord Deputy of Ireland; commonly reputed to be a son of Henry VIII by Mary Berkley (afterwards wife of Thomas Perrot). The print, dated 1584, 'is prefixed to an anonymous "History of his Government in Ireland," 1626' (*Granger*[1] i. 143; see also DNB).

56. Thomas Percy (1560–1605), organizer of the 'Gunpowder Plot'; mortally wounded while resisting capture. The print is engraved by Crispin van de Pass (see *Granger*[1] i. 317).

57. (1606?–94), Yeoman of Robes to Charles II, 1650–85; benefactor of Oxford and Cambridge Universities; the print is anonymous (see *Granger*[1] ii. 302; DNB). The British Museum copy is 'the only impression known' (EBP).

58. William Alexander (1567?–1640), 1st E. of Stirling; poet and statesman. The print, by William Marshall, is the frontispiece to Stirling's *Recreations with the Muses*, 1637, and 'is very scarce, as it is rarely found in any of the copies: it is one of Marshall's best performances' (*Granger*[1] i. 500; see also EBP).

59. Elizabeth Leigh, dau. of Francis Leigh, E. of Chichester; 2d wife of Thomas Wriothesley (1607–67), 4th E. of Southampton. The print is after the portrait by Van Dyck (see *Granger*[1] i. 544; EBP).

60. Teresia (d. 1668), dau. of Ismael Khan, a noble Circassian; m. (before 1607)

Mary Vere.[62] Sir H. Vane *the elder*.[63] Sir Thomas Wyat.[64] Edw. Earl of Warwick.[65] I will trouble you with no more at present but to get from Mr Lort[66] the name of the Norfolk monster,[67] and to give it to Jackson. Don't forget the list of English heads in Dr Ewin's book[68] for Mr Granger, particularly the Duchess of Chevreuse.[69] I will now release you, only adding my compliments to Dr Ewin, Mr Tyson, Mr Lort, Mr Essex, and once more to the Benthams. Adieu! Dear Sir

Yours ever,

H. W.

Remember to ask me for acacias, and anything else with which I can pay some of my debts to you.

Robert Shirley or Sherley (1581?–1628), called Sir Robert or Count Shirley. The print has the incorrect title, 'Lady Elizabeth Sherley'; it is by Hollar after the portrait by Van Dyck (see DNB; *Granger*⁵ iii. 228–9; EBP).

61. Richard Talbot (1630–91), E. and titular D. of Tyrconnel. It is not clear which print of him HW had in mind (see *Granger*¹ ii. 497 and *Granger*⁵ vi. 68–70).

62. Mary Tracy (1581–1671), m. (1) William Hoby and (2) Horace Vere (1565–1635), Bn Vere of Tilbury. The print, by F. Van Hove, appears in Clarke's *Lives*, 1683 (see *Granger*⁵ ii. 180; EBP).

63. Sir Henry Vane (1589–1655), Kt; Secretary of State 1640–1. The print is by R. Cooper from an original drawing (*Granger*⁵ iii. 6).

64. Sir Thomas Wyatt (1503?–42), Kt; the poet; 'a wooden print, after a painting of [attributed to] Hans Holbein. Frontispiece to the book of verses on his death, entitled "Naenia," published by Leland' (*Granger*¹ i. 81).

65. Edward Rich (1673–1701), 6th E. of Warwick and 3d E. of Holland; his widow m. Addison. The print, dated 1684, is by John Smith after the portrait by Willem Wissing (see *Granger*¹ ii. 142).

66. Michael Lort (1725–90), antiquary; F.S.A., 1755; F.R.S., 1766; Regius Professor of Greek at Cambridge, 1759–71; D.D. and Librarian at Lambeth, 1785. His antiquarian interests brought him in contact with Cole and HW, with both of whom he corresponded.

67. Francis Bell (b. 1704), of Walsingham, Norfolk. His anonymous print represents him at the age of 66 (see EBP; *post* 30 May 1771).

68. A book of prints which he afterwards sold to Lord Mount-Stuart (see *post* 19 Sept. 1776).

69. Marie de Rohan (1600–79), Duchesse de Chevreuse, 'in the first class of the gay and gallant ladies of France' (*Granger*⁵ iii. 283). She visited England at least twice, in 1625 and in 1638, and on one occasion swam across the Thames (see Francis G. Waldron, *The Biographical Mirrour*, 3 vols, i (1795). 94–7).

From Cole, Thursday 3 August 1769

Cole's copy, Add MS 5824, ff. 142v–144v.
Address: [From Cole's copy.] For the Honourable Horace Walpole at Strawberry Hill in Twickenham, Middlesex.

[Water]Beche, Aug. 3, 1769.

Dear Sir,

THIS day I received from Mr Essex the plan of your gateway. With it I shall send a few prints not in your collection, and Jackson will do his best endeavours to get the remainder. I also send you with them Sir John Finett's *Philoxenis,* or his *Observations on the Reception of Embassadors Temp. Jac. I & Car. I,*[1] in which I think you will meet with many curious things to please you. If you have the book, I may have it again on some opportunity: I think it a scarce one—at least I never met with it till very lately. I have made a short index at the end of it, of a few things which struck me, for the index printed is good for nothing. Another reason why you should have the book is that he was your townsman, and had a country house at Twittenham.

Mr Essex bids me tell you that he has done no design for the iron gates,[2] on a presumption that you had prepared them yourself. If it is not so, on any notice to me or him, he will do these also. He desires me to tell you that he has some thoughts of putting all his collections towards a regular treatise on Gothic architecture together,[3] in order to bring it into a system on that subject, but should be infinitely obliged to you to sketch out a little plan for him, which he will pursue according to your method. I suppose he is as well qualified for such an undertaking as anyone I know, having made it his study for many years. If you will favour him or me with your thoughts on this design, I will convey them to him.

Your very apposite application of Mr Prior's distich on poor Nell, I hope will be long in fulfilling, though am too apt to think with

1. *Finetti Philoxenis: some choice Observations, touching the Reception, Precedence, &c. of forren Ambassadors in England,* 1656. Sir John Finett (1571–1641) was Master of the Ceremonies. HW had a copy of the first edition (E.6.48, sold SH ii. 32), which he had just received (see *post* 11 Aug. 1769).

2. HW had them (see *post* 11 Aug. 1769). *SH Accounts,* under 15 July 1769, shows that they cost ten guineas.

3. These collections, which were never published, are now in the British Museum (see DNB).

you, and that on too many accounts. The Chapter, since you left Ely, have been much divided in their opinions about placing the organ, and have also found out a more ancient picture in glass of St Etheldreda, which, because it is in more gaudy colours, they are disposed to think will look better than the other which you saw in the window at the palace, dressed only in black and white, as an abbess. The other, in a window of one of the prebendal houses, has been taken down and sent to Mr Tyson at College, for him to take a drawing of it, which he has done very exactly, and has given it to me in a frame, as, upon a view of both, the Bishop is most inclined to the former one, dressed as an abbess. The affair of the organ has made more stir. Those that were for its position on one side under an arch of the north aisle, in order to strengthen their cause, made use of your name, as the adviser of it. I, who knew how little concerned you was about it, took the liberty to tell Dr Gooch and others, who disapprove of that scheme, that I was well assured that you was no further concerned in it, than barely giving your opinion, when both plans were proposed, that you thought Mr Essex's[4] was very light, airy and advantageous to the view of the whole church, which you thought the organ over a screen at the west end of the choir would obstruct.

Since I had the pleasure of seeing you, I have been but once at Cambridge, and that was to meet my Lord Montfort and Mr Cadogan[5] at a corporation dinner, and went back with his Lordship to Horseth in the evening, and returned this day. Indeed, I have not been quite well all this hot weather, and have had no disposition for writing, which must be my excuse for delaying my thanks for your kind reception at Strawberry Hill and in Arlington Street. I have done nothing but read since I saw you: among other things, that bundle of papers which a gentleman of Benet College[6] sent to me for my perusal, while you was with me at Mr Bentham's at Cambridge, containing an account of the contents of several of their MS volumes in

---

4. He proposed to place the organ at the eastern end of the choir on the grounds that it would 'conceal much cold unornamented wall!' (*Handbook to the Cathedral Church at Ely*, Ely, 13th edn [1887], p. 117.)

5. Charles Sloane Cadogan (1728–1807), 3d Bn Cadogan (1776), cr. Vct Chelsea and E. Cadogan (1800); m. (1) in 1747, Frances Bromley (d. 1768), dau. of 1st Bn Montfort, and (2), in 1777, Mary Churchill, dau. of Charles Churchill by Lady Mary Walpole (dau. of Sir Robert Walpole), from whom he was divorced in 1796.

6. James Nasmith (1740–1808), antiquary, who arranged and catalogued the MSS which Archbishop Parker gave to Corpus Christi College and published *Catalogus Librorum Manuscriptorum quos Collegio Corporis Christi . . . legavit . . . Matthaeus Parker,* Cambridge, 1777. Cole's MS life of Nasmith is in Add MS 5886 (see DNB).

their College Library. Among them I met with one something similar to the subject of your *Mysterious Mother*.[7] It is in Class C, Miscellanea Q, No. 10, and is thus titled, at p. 325:[8]

De Sancto Albano.

Fabulosa hæc historia, male scripta, et abbreviationibus ubique scatens, in quinque paginis enarrat vitam nescio cujus Albani, qui ex incesto thalamo procreatus, et in Hungariam deportatus, ibique expositus regi deferturque ab eodem in filium adoptatur. Deinde inscienter propriam matrem ducit in uxorem. Re autem comperta, deliciis mundi renuens, reliquam vitam anachoretice agit.

Another book [that] has fallen in my way is *Les Négotiations de Monsieur de Noailles*,[9] published in five octavo volumes, 1763. Two things, which if you have not the book, you will be pleased with. Speaking of the Earl of Surrey,[10] vol. 1, pp. 87–8, he thus proceeds:

. . . mais ce qui acheva de déterminer Henri[11] à les[12] perdre, ce fut un tableau que le comte de Hartfort[13] eut l'adresse de faire voir au roi, & dans lequel le comte de Surrey, fier de sa haute naissance, s'étoit fait peindre appuyé sur une colonne brisée; ses armes & celles d'Angleterre étoient représentées au pied, & on lisoit auteur du fût de cette colonne (*ce qui reste suffit*), comme si par cette colonne brisée il eût voulu faire allusion au mauvais état de la famille royale, & marquer en même temps, par ses armes jointes à celles d'Angleterre, qu'il se regardoit comme l'espérance prochaine de la nation.

At bottom, in a note, is added:

J'ai vu l'an 1637, chez le comte d'Arundel,[14] arrière-fils[15] de ce comte de Surrey, l'original de ce tableau.

Loigny, *ann. d'Angl.* Paris, chez Recolet 1647,[16] p. 286.

7. The subject is a double incest. In a contemporary MS copy of this play (now wsl) is 'Rev. Mr Cole's MS note in his copy of this play: It may be difficult to determine which passions the lively and ingenious author has laboured most to excite, either those of terror and pity or an envenomed spite and hatred against all Churchmen; a passion most glaring and outré in this play and more or less in every one of his productions. It seems to be an enthusiasm at all times and carried to an excess in this work.'

8. The classification of this MS differs slightly in Nasmith's *Catalogus* 65: 'C.9. De Sancto Albano, p. 365.'

9. *Ambassades de Messieurs de Noailles*

en Angleterre. Rédigées par feu M. l'Abbé [René Aubert] de Vertot, Leyden.

10. Henry Howard (1517?–47), E. of Surrey; the poet.

11. Henry VIII.

12. That is, the D. of Norfolk and his son, the E. of Surrey, who were too powerful.

13. Edward Seymour (1506?–52), 1st E. of Hertford and D. of Somerset.

14. Arundel House, the seat of Thomas Howard (1586–1646), 2d E. of Arundel; great-grandson of the E. of Surrey; formed the first considerable art collection in England. See following letter, n. 13.

15. Read *arrière-petit-fils*.

16. That is, the French translation by de

In a letter from M. de Noailles to his Prince, dated Nov. 14, 1553, he tells him of a painter in Queen Mary's service,

nommé Nicolas, qui est né vostre subject, & a demouré par-deçà l'espace de 32 ans, tousjours bien traicté des roys Henry & Edouard, & à present de cestedicte royne . . .

—Tome 2, p. 255.

I suppose this was Nicolas Lysard, mentioned in your *Anecdotes*,[17] vol. 1, p. 136.

I have not yet had time to do anything for Mr Granger: my workmen, with a listlessness for writing, totally prevent me at present.

Since I wrote the former I have read more of the *Négotiations de Noailles,* and find more about Nicolas Lysarde. On the marriage of Queen Mary to Philip of Spain, the French ambassador at our court did all in his power to make the nation uneasy, and jealous of the Spaniards, by propagating all sorts of lies and stories against the Queen and her ministry, being ready to inflame and even excite the people to an insurrection. This is evident throughout the whole of these *Négotiations*. On 16 Dec. 1554, the French minister sent an express to his master of such reports as were then current, as that Philip was going to draw both men and money out of the kingdom to aid and assist his father Charles V against the French, and then adds as follows:

Et à ce propoz, ung painctre François, nommé Nicolas, qui sert de longtemps d'advertisseur aux ambassadeurs qui sont par deçà, a donné advis que le filz dudict millord Thresorier luy avoit tenu mesme langaige, & que cest esté ne passeroit sans desclairation de guerre de leur cousté.

—Tome 4, p. 61.

And at p. 155 of the same volume, his chief employ in England is sufficiently described in a letter dated 20 Jan. 1554, from the ambassador, giving an account that the war was so near being declared that the standards were already prepared.

Ce que j'ay faict tesmoigner à mon frere depuis qu'il est icy, & mesme par un painctre François nommé Nicolas, qui a faict les susdicts estandartz & enseignes, & lequel doibt estre pensionnaire du roy de six vingt escus, que

---

Loigny, *Annales des choses plus mémorables arrivées, tant en Angleterre qu'ailleurs, sous les regnes de Henry VIII, Edouard VI et Marie,* from the Latin work,

Annales Rerum Anglicarum, 1616, by Francis Godwin.

17. Cole refers to the second edition. HW did not use Cole's notes on Lysard (see *Works* iii. 110).

je vous diray à ce propoz qu'il demande fort, & dont il n'a esté payé des-
puis le temps que M. de Bois-Daulphin s'en alla. Il est Poictevin, habitant
en ce pays il y a quarante ans, ou environ, & bien traicté de ceste royne de
plus de quatre cens livres de nostre monnoye d'estat par chascun an, & est
celluy mesme qui me donna des premiers advis comme ladicte dame
faisoit faire à luy & à d'aultres plusieurs painctures & devises de ce roy
avecques les siennes, quand leur mariaige fust au commencement ainsy
secrettement accordé, & a de grandes intelligences & moyenz en la maison
du millord Thresorier, lequel, comme ledict painctre m'a souvent asseuré,
s'attendoit bien à l'ouverture de la guerre . . .

At the bottom of the page is this note, which shows his integrity to
great advantage:

Lysarde, il étoit aussi pensionnaire de la reine d'Angleterre, comme on le
peut voir par le brevet inséré dans le 15e. tome du recueil de Rymer, pag.
433.

When you was at Cambridge you wanted to get Mr Gray's *Ode*,[18]
which was not to be had. There is a second edition, and I have sent a
copy of it to you.

The prints I have sent you out of my collection are Serjeant Bar-
nardiston;[19] Maria Lady Langham; Elizabeth Countess of Kent; Mrs
Hannah Woolley; Caterina Bolena, Zia e Governatrice di Elizabetta;
Henry Malden, King's College Chapel Clerk;[20] A Plan for a Music
Room at Cambridge in 1768, which proved abortive;[21] Dr Billing-
ford's Tomb;[22] Count Bryan of Bury;[23] Queen Charlotte with Scrip-

---

18. *Ode Performed in the Senate-House*,
1769. The second edition appeared in the
same year.

19. Thomas Barnardiston (1706–52),
serjeant-at-law and legal reporter. The
print was engraved by George Bickham, Jr,
ad vivum (see EBP; Richard Almack, 'Kedington, *alias* Ketton, and the Barnardiston
Family,' *Suffolk Institute of Archaeology
and Natural History* iv (1874). 155). HW's
copy of the print was sold London iv. 545.

20. He died 27 Aug. 1769, and was buried in the churchyard of the Church of St
Edward, Cambridge (see Cooper, *Memorials* iii. 281). The print, by Thomas Orde,
was the frontispiece to *An Account of
King's College Chapel, in Cambridge*,
Cambridge, 1769. Malden's name appears
on the title-page as the author of this
work, but it was really written by Thomas

James (1748–1804), then an undergraduate
at Cambridge (see DNB).

21. 'A plan for an amphitheatre for pub-
lic lectures and music in the University of
Cambridge, engraved 1768, by [Thomas]
Major [(1720–99) (see DNB)], des[igned] by
Dr [Sir James] Marriot' (Gough, *British
Topography*² i. 250*; *Gray's Corr.* iii. 1050;
Cooper, *Annals* iv. 352).

22. Richard Billingford (d. 1432), D.D.;
Chancellor of Cambridge, 1400, 1402, 1409,
1413; Master of Corpus Christi College,
1398–1432. The print appeared in Masters's *History of the College of Corpus
Christi, Cambridge,* Cambridge, 1753, plate
2, opp. p. 39. As Cole was responsible for
the discovery of the tomb, the plate was inscribed to him (see *Blecheley Diary* 57;
Masters, ibid.,² Cambridge, 1831, pp. 45–7).

23. Not identified. See *post* 16 June 1771.

ture Sentences; Jacob Butler; and Sir Thomas Wyatt.[24] The first, I suppose, is a curiosity and not easily met with. I had it given me by one of the family.[25] He was a lunatic and the next in entail to the Downing estate.[26]

If I hear no more of you before you leave England, I heartily wish you a good journey to Paris, and a safe back again to your own more delightful habitation, and am,

Your most obliged and faithful servant,

WM COLE

To COLE, Friday 11 August 1769

Add MS 5952, ff. 73–4.
HW erroneously dated this letter Aug. 12; the postmark is clearly 11 AV.
Cole received this and the following letter 15 August (*Waterbeach Diary* 191).
Address: To the Reverend Mr Cole at Waterbeche near Cambridge.
Postmark: Isleworth 11 AV.

Strawberry Hill, Aug. 12 [11], 1769.

I WAS in town yesterday and found the parcel arrived very safe. I give you a thousand thanks, dear Sir, for all the contents, but when I sent you the list of heads I wanted, it was for Mr Jackson, not at all meaning to rob you: but your generosity much outruns my prudence, and I must be upon my guard with you. The Catherine Bolen was particularly welcome; I had never seen it; it is a treasure, though I am persuaded not genuine, but taken from a French print of the Queen of Scots, which I have. I wish you could tell me whence it was taken, I mean from what book;[1] I imagine the same in which are two

24. Probably the print by Tyson, copied from the frontispiece to John Leland's *Naenia* (see *post* 22 June 1772; cf. *ante* 15 July 1769).

25. Probably John Barnardiston (1718–78), Master of Corpus Christi College, 1764–78 (see Robert Masters, *History of the College of Corpus Christi, Cambridge,* 1831, pp. 251–2), who was Cole's intimate friend.

26. Serjeant Barnardiston was the son of Thomas Barnardiston of Wyverston and Bury St Edmunds in Suffolk, by Mary Downing, daughter of Sir George Down-

ing, Bt. 'He [Serjeant Barnardiston] died unmarried, 1752, which ended this male line, and deprived the Barnardiston family of the great Downing estate entailed on Serjeant Barnardiston' (Richard Almack, 'Kedington, *alias* Ketton, and the Barnardiston Family,' *Suffolk Institute of Archaeology and Natural History* iv (1874). 155).

1. From Gregorio Leti's *Historia overo Vita di Elisabetta,* Amsterdam, 1703 (see *ante* 15 July 1769).

prints which Mr Granger mentions and has himself (with Italian inscriptions too) of a Duke of Northumberland,[2] and an Earl of Arundel.[3] Mr Barnadiston I never saw before, and do not know in what reign he lived, I suppose lately; nor do I know the era of the master of Bennet.[4] When I come back,[5] I must beg you to satisfy these questions. The Countess of Kent[6] is very curious too; I have lately got a very dirty one, so that I shall return yours again. Mrs Wooley I could not get high nor low—but there is no end of thanking you—and yet I must for Sir J. Finett,[7] though Mr Hawkins[8] gave me a copy a fortnight ago. I must delay sending them till I come back. Be so good as to thank Mr Tyson for his prints and notes; the latter I have not had time to look over, I am so hurried with my journey, but I am sure they will be very useful to me. I hope he will not forget me in October. It will be a good opportunity of sending you some young acacias, or anything you want from hence—I am sure you ought to ask me for anything in my power, so much I am in your debt. I must beg to be a little more, by intreating you to pay Mr Essex whatever he asks for his drawing,[9] which is just what I wished. The iron gates I have.

With regard to a history of Gothic architecture,[10] in which he desires my advice, the plan I think should lie in a very simple compass. Was I to execute it, it should be thus. I would give a series of plates even from the conclusion of Saxon architecture, beginning with the round Roman arch, and going on to show how they plastered and zigzagged it, and then how better ornaments crept in, till the beautiful Gothic was arrived at its perfection; then how it deceased in Henry the Eighth's reign, Archbishop Warham's tomb[11] at Canterbury being

2. John Dudley (1502?–53), D. of Northumberland (see *ante* 15 July 1769).

3. Henry Fitzalan (1511?–80), 12th E. of Arundel; godson of Henry VIII. The print described by Granger ('in armour; half length, round cap, ruff. The inscription is in manuscript.') is figure 22, part one, in Leti's *Historia* (see *Granger*[1] i. 139).

4. Richard Billingford (d. 1432) (see preceding letter).

5. From Paris. HW left 16 Aug. and returned 11 Oct. 1769 (see *Paris Jour.*).

6. Elizabeth Talbot (1581–1651), Countess of Kent.

7. A copy of his *Philoxenis* (see *ante* 3 Aug. 1769).

8. John Hawkins (1719–89), knighted in 1772; friend and biographer of Johnson and neighbour of HW at Twickenham. His *General History of Music*, 1776, was written at HW's suggestion.

9. A design for the pillars of the gate to the garden at SH (see *ante* 15 July 1769).

10. The three paragraphs following were published, with changes and omissions, in Gough's *Sepulchral Monuments*, 1786, vol. i, part 1, Preface, pp. 2–3. Cole communicated the extract to Gough when the latter was planning the work in 1781–2. Cf. HW to Gough 21 June 1786.

11. William Warham (1450?–1532), Abp of Canterbury; for a print of his tomb, see

I believe the last example of unbastardized Gothic. A very few plates more would demonstrate its change. Holbein embroidered it with some morsels of true architecture; in Queen Elizabeth's reign there was scarce any architecture at all; I mean no pillars, or seldom; buildings then becoming quite plain. Under James a barbarous composition succeeded. A single plate of something of Inigo Jones, in his heaviest and worst style should terminate the work, for he soon stepped into the true and perfect Grecian.

The next part Mr Essex can do better than anybody, and is perhaps the only person who can do it. This should consist of observations on the art, proportions and method of building, and the reasons observed by the Gothic architects for what they did. This would show what great men they were, and how they raised such aerial or stupendous masses, though unassisted by half the lights now enjoyed by their successors. The prices, and the wages of workmen, and the comparative value of money and provisions at the several periods, should be stated, as far as it is possible to get materials.

The last part, (I don't know whether it should not be first part) nobody can do so well as yourself. This must be to ascertain the chronologic period of each building—and not only of each building, but of each tomb, that shall be exhibited, for you know the great delicacy and richness of Gothic ornaments was exhausted on small chapels, oratories and tombs. For my own part I should wish to have added detached samples of the various patterns of ornaments, which would not be a great many, as excepting pinnacles, there is scarce one which does not branch from the trefoil; quatrefoils, cinquefoils, etc., being but various modifications of it. I believe almost all the ramifications of windows are so: and of them there should be samples too. This work, you see, could not be executed by one hand. Mr Tyson could give great assistance. I wish the plan was drawn out, and better digested. This is a very rude sketch and first thought. I should be very glad to contribute what little I know, and to the expense too, which would be considerable: but I am sure we could get assistance: and it had better not be undertaken, than executed superficially. Mr Tyson's history of fashions and dresses,[12] would make a valuable part of the work, as in elder times especially much must be depended on

John Dart, *History and Antiquities of the Cathedral Church of Canterbury*, 1726, p. 167. HW translated the tomb into a chimney-piece in the Holbein Chamber at SH (see *Works* ii. 454; 'Genesis of SH' 70).

12. This work was never completed.

tombs for dresses. I have a notion the King might be inclined to encourage such a work; and if a proper plan was drawn out, for which I have not time now, I would endeavour to get it laid before him, and his *patronage* solicited. Pray talk this over with Mr Tyson and Mr Essex. It is an idea worth pursuing.

You was very kind to take me out of the scrape about the organ, and yet if my insignificant name could carry it to one side, I would not scruple to lend it. Thank you too for St Alban and Noailles. The very picture the latter describes was in my father's collection[13] and is now at Worksop.[14] I have scarce room to crowd in my compliments to the good house of Bentham and to say yours ever

H. WALPOLE

To Cole, Thursday 14 December 1769

COLE's copy, Add MS 5824, f. 146v. The original is missing.
Cole received this letter 16 Dec. (*Waterbeach Diary*, Add MS 5835, f. 225v).
Address: [From COLE's copy.] To the Rev. Mr Cole at Milton, Cambridgeshire.

Arlington Street, Dec. 14, 1769.

Dear Sir,

THIS is merely a line to feel my way, and to know how to direct to you. Mr Granger thinks you are established at Milton, and thither I address it. If it reaches you, you will be so good as to let me know, and I will write again soon.

Yours ever,

H. W.

From Cole, Monday 18 December 1769

VA, Forster MS 110, ff. 68–9. COLE's copy, Add MS 5824, ff. 146v–147v.

COLE's copy is dated 'Milton, Sunday, Dec. 17, 1769'. In his *Waterbeach Diary*,

13. The picture 'was purchased in 1720, at the sale of the Arundel collection at Stafford-house, near Buckingham-gate, for Sir Robert Walpole, who made a present of it to the late Edward, Duke of Norfolk' (*Anecdotes*, ed. Ralph N. Wornum, 1876, i. 138).

14. In Notts, then the seat of Edward Howard (1686–1777), 8th D. of Norfolk. The picture was later removed to Arundel Castle (loc. cit.).

Add MS 5835, f. 225, Cole says he wrote to HW 17 Dec. to send him Jackson's
letter on HW's prints, which apparently cost 15s.

Address: [From COLE's copy.] For the Honourable Mr Horace Walpole in Arlington Street, London.

Milton, Dec. 18, 1769.

Dear Sir,

I AM not wholly settled at Milton, but am there every day seeing
the reparations go forward, nor do I think I shall be quite fixed
there till about May. Great part of the house is dry enough to get into
it with safety to myself, but hardly so for my servants, and though I
much long to remove myself from this nasty place, yet it will not be
prudent to do so till the March winds have blown about every part of
the house and made it safe to inhabit there.

I hope your last journey to Paris was quite agreeable to you, and
that the journey and change of air will lay you in a stock of health till
you can repeat the remedy.

I mentioned to Mr Essex what you was pleased to say to me about
gratifying him for his plan of the gateway, and would have paid him
for it, but he would accept of nothing, and begged me to make his
compliments to you and that you would do him honour to accept it.

I last week only received the enclosed letter from Jackson,[1] though
it is dated Nov. 26. I design in a day or two to pay him his 12s. 6d.,
and add half a crown more to it, which will make 15s., which you may
pay me when I have the honour of seeing you next. I dined yesterday[2] with Mr Tyson at Emanuel College, where Mr Percy was entered to take his Doctor's degree. On consultation with Mr Tyson, we
thought half a crown very sufficient for his trouble.

Mr Tyson has been etching three or four small heads,[3] which I
would send you, but I apprehend he had rather do so himself.[4] Mr
Gray is in London, but is about now expected at college.

1. Cole received the letter (which is missing) 9 Dec. In it Jackson said he had
bought some prints for HW (*Waterbeach
Diary*, Add MS 5835, f. 215).

2. 'I dined yesterday at Emanuel with
Dr Percy, who took his degree with us this
last week, and spent the whole day and
evening with him, and was much entertained with his company. We made no
small lodge of antiquaries, and spent the
day very cheerfully: Mr Farmer of Emanuel, Mr Tyson and Mr Nasmith, both of
Benet, Professor Martin of Sidney, etc. Dr

Percy had his wife with him, who is a very
handsome and agreeable woman' (addition
in Cole's copy). Percy's wife, whom he married in 1759, was Anne Gutteridge or
Goodriche (d. 1806), dau. of Barton Gutteridge of Desborough, Northants.

3. These were prints of Abp Parker,
Michael Dalton (author of *The Countrey
Justice*, 1618), and the Rev. Henry Etough
(see Tyson to Granger 19 Feb. 1770, Grang-
er, *Correspondence* 152–3, and Cole to
Granger 11 Dec. 1769, ibid., 331).

4. 'Jackson or Gaxon has not sent me

If you pursue your plan you once mentioned[5] of London Streets, etc., the two notes below[6] will be acceptable to you:

Lord St John,[7] in a letter to Archbishop Parker (the original now in Benet College Library), dated from his house in Fewter Lane, 28 Oct. 1566, desires a dispensation of non-residence for Sir William Tatham, parson of Aspley in Bedfordshire.

Sir Robert Sidney,[8] in a letter to the same Archbishop, desires a dispensation for his son Philip to eat flesh in Lent. Dated from Durham House, 3 March 1567.

I met in a clever French book of voyages, published this year in eight volumes octavo, into Italy, by one de la Lande,[9] this article relating to French painting on glass, vol. 2, p. 573:

Guillaume Marzille, François, l'un des plus grands maîtres pour l'art de peindre les vitres.
    —*Voyages d'un Français en Italie,* etc.

My Lord Montfort's servant calling on me this afternoon, I made him stay for this letter, as it will be a double one, and take it with him to Horseth.[10]

I will take the liberty to put you in mind about February to beg a bundle of your Strawberry Hill shrubs to adorn my Milton garden, and never am more rejoiced than when I meet with a letter under your hand. In the meantime [I] beg leave to subscribe myself, dear Sir,

Your ever faithful and obliged servant,

WM COLE

the prints. When I get them, you shall soon have them' (addition in Cole's copy).

5. See *ante* 16 April 1768 n. 9.

6. Cf. James Nasmith, *Catalogus Librorum Manuscriptorum,* Cambridge, 1777, CXIV, articles 93, 104, pp. 146–7. Cole probably took these notes from the MSS which Nasmith had sent to him for inspection (see *ante* 3 Aug. 1769).

7. Oliver St John (d. 1582), first Bn St John of Bletso in Bedfordshire.

8. *Read* Sir Henry Sidney (1529–86). This letter has been attributed to the E. of Leicester, but see Mona Wilson, *Sir Philip Sidney,* 1931, pp. 39, 289.

9. Joseph Jérôme le Français de Lalande (1732–1807), astronomer and author; Cole refers to his *Voyage en Italie.*

10. To be franked by Lord Montfort. 'His Lordship's letter was to advertise me of Lord Farnham [Robert Maxwell (d. 1779), 2d Bn and 1st E. of Farnham], Mr Vernon [Richard Vernon (1726–1800), 'father of the turf' (see DNB)] and his Miss [i.e., his mistress; see OED], and a party of the same sort from Newmarket, coming to him tomorrow for three days, as his Lordship had sent the week before to desire me to come over, he rightly judged how disagreeable such a party must have been to me, and sent over to warn me of it' (addition in Cole's copy).

I have a gentleman of St John's College, Mr Ashby, now with me, who was so kind to bring me the two plates enclosed of Cardinal Wolsey and Oliver Cromwell, from plates in his own possession, and were never sold, or will be. As I was going to put up this letter, he desired me to send them to your collection, and promises me two others.

To Cole, Thursday 21 December 1769

Add MS 5952, f. 75.

Arlington Street, Dec. 21, 1769.

Dear Sir,

I AM very grateful for all your communications and for the trouble you are so good as to take for me. I am glad you have paid Jackson, though he is not only dear, (for the prints he has got for me are very common) but they are not what I wanted, and I do not believe were mentioned in my list. However as paying him dear for what I do *not* want, may encourage him to hunt for what I *do* want, I am very well content he should cheat me a little. I take the liberty of troubling you with a list I have printed[1] (to avoid copying it several times) and beg you will be so good as to give it to him, telling him, these are exactly what I do want and no others. I will pay him well for any of these, especially those marked thus x: and still more for those with double or treble marks. The print I want most is the *Jacob Hall.*[2] I do not know whether it is not one of the London cries, but he must be very sure it is the right. I will let you know certainly when Mr West comes to town, who has one.

I shall be very happy to contribute to your garden; and if you will let me have exact notice in February how to send the shrubs, they shall not fail you; nor anything else by which I can pay you any part of my debts. I am much pleased with the Wolsey and Cromwell,

1. The list is missing. It is mentioned in a letter from the Hon. Mrs Robert Cholmondeley to HW 13 Jan. [1770]. It is one of the rarest of the detached pieces printed at SH, and is not included in Baker's *Catalogue* or in Lowndes. There is a copy in Richard Bull's collection of SH detached pieces at the Huntington Library. It is a broadside printed on both sides, and contains 223 names arranged alphabetically.

2. See *ante* 15 July 1769, n. 50.

and beg to thank you and the gentleman from whom they came. Mr Tyson's etchings will be particularly acceptable. I did hope to have seen or heard of him in October. Pray tell him he is a visit in my debt, and that I will trust him no longer than to next summer. Mr Bentham I find one must trust and trust without end. It is pity so good a sort of man should be so faithless.[3] Make my best compliments however to him and to my kind host and hostess.[4]

I found my dear old blind friend[5] at Paris perfectly well, and am returned so myself. London is very sickly, and full of bilious fevers, that have proved fatal to several persons, and in my Lord Gower's family[6] have even seemed contagious. The weather is uncommonly hot, and we want frost to purify the air.

I need not say I suppose that the names scratched out in my list are of such prints as I have got since I printed it, and therefore what I no longer want. If Mr Jackson only stays at Cambridge, till the prints drop into his mouth, I shall never have them. If he would take the trouble of going to Bury, Norwich, Ely, Huntingdon and such great towns, nay, look about in inns, I do not doubt but he would find at least some of them. He should be no loser by taking pains for me; but I doubt he chooses to be a great gainer without taking any. I shall not pay for any that are not in my list—but I ought not to trouble you, dear Sir, with these particulars. It is a little your own fault, for you have spoiled me.

Mr Essex distresses me by his civility. I certainly would not have given him that trouble, if I had thought he would not let me pay him. Be so good to thank him for me, and to let me know if there is any other way I could return the obligation. I hope at least he will make me a visit at Strawberry Hill, whenever he comes westward. I shall be very impatient to see you, dear Sir, both there and at Milton.

Your faithful humble servant,

Hor. Walpole

3. HW refers to James Bentham's delay in publishing his *Ely* and failure to accept an invitation to SH.

4. Mr and Mrs Joseph Bentham of Cambridge.

5. Mme du Deffand.

6. Granville Leveson-Gower (1721–1803), 2d E. Gower; cr. (1786) M. of Stafford. His family at this time consisted of a son and three daughters by his second wife, his third wife, Lady Susanna Stewart, and an infant daughter, none of whom died of this illness (see Collins, *Peerage*, 1812, ii. 451–2).

From COLE, Friday 5 January 1770

VA, Forster MS 110, ff. 70–1. Cole kept no copy.

Horseth Hall, Friday, Jan. 5, 1770.

Dear Sir,

I TAKE the opportunity of one of my Lord Montfort's servants calling on you with this packet, which I am quite ashamed to send to you, considering what I gave for it to Jackson, who would not be pacified without a crown for his trouble in getting you five prints at 12s. 6d., which probably he makes you pay double for besides. As I found him so unreasonable in his demands and by no means alert in his expressions about procuring you those in the list you sent to him, with such advantageous proposals to one in his way, I thought proper to take that catalogue[1] away from him, and design giving it to another person[2] in Cambridge, who, I daresay, will do all in his power to procure them, and not make that unreasonable profit [which Jackson] seems to have set his mind on.

Mr Tyson desires his compliments to you and purposes to send up to you next week a few of his own etchings, and will wait on you certainly in the summer. Mr Essex bids me tell you that he is extremely happy that you will accept his design, and proposes a great deal of pleasure in seeing Strawberry Hill and its beauties.

I have taken the liberty to add a print of Trusty Dick Pendrell[3] to the other prints. It was lately engraved at Cambridge. Among your wants in the catalogue I observe many in my possession, which I won't send now, as you may not be willing to have them thence, but as I know you have multitudes that I have not, one is well as another for my purpose, and we may exchange.

I am, Sir,

Your most obedient servant,

WM COLE

When I came to roll up the five prints, I found that Pendrell's was not among them, so suppose I left it at Cambridge. I won't forget it in another packet.

1. HW's printed list of desired prints (see preceding letter).
2. Not identified.
3. Richard Penderel (d. 1672), royalist who assisted Charles II to escape after the battle of Worcester. The print, engraved by P. S. Lamborn of Cambridge, is false (see EBP; *Granger*[5] vi. 1).

To Cole, Thursday 15 November 1770

Cole's copy, Add MS 5823, f. 142v. The original is missing.
Address: [From Cole's copy.] To the Rev. Mr Cole at Milton near Cambridge.

Arlington Street, Nov. 15, 1770.

Dear Sir,

IF you have not engaged your interest in Cambridgeshire, you would oblige me much by bestowing it on young Mr Brand,[1] the son of my particular acquaintance, and our old schoolfellow.[2] I am very unapt to trouble my head about elections, but wish success to this.

If you see Bannerman, I should be glad you would tell him that I am going to print the last volume of my *Painters,* and should like to employ him again for some of the heads, if he cares to undertake them:[3] though there will be a little trouble, as he does not reside in London. I am in a hurry, and am forced to be brief, but am always glad to hear of you, and from you.

Yours most sincerely,

Hor. Walpole

Mr Tyson promised me all his etchings, but has forgot me.[4]

1. Thomas Brand (1749–94), son of Thomas Brand (d. 1770) of The Hoo, Herts; M.P. for Arundel, 1774–80; entered Trinity College, Cambridge, 1765, as fellow commoner, but did not graduate (*Admissions to Trinity College, Cambridge, 1701–1800,* ed. W. W. Rouse Ball and J. A. Venn, 1911, pp. 206–7). In 1771 he married the Hon. Gertrude Roper, who succeeded her brother in 1794 as Baroness Dacre.

2. Thomas Brand senior was one form below HW and Cole (Eton List, 1728). He was famous for laughing (see HW to Brand 26 Oct. 1760).

3. Alexander Bannerman (fl. 1762–72), engraver. HW was not pleased with his work for the fourth volume, but accepted several of the prints (HW to Gray 25 March 1771).

4. At the end of his copy, Cole notes: 'Had I received this sooner, as Mr Cadogan was out of the question, I should have given my vote and interest to Mr Brand, but I had engaged myself early to my Lord Montfort, and not an hour before I left Cambridge had told Messrs Moore of Whittlesy and Gotobed of Ely, Sir Sampson Gideon's and Lord Hardwicke's agent, who came to me, and told me that my tenants had refused them both their votes, as they did not know how I would have them act: I told Mr Gotobed to write to them from me, to act with my Lord Hardwicke's tenants: so I had put it out of my power to serve Mr Brand, whose father I remember at Eton School, and was both a worthy and ingenious man: he was member for Okehampton, and lived near Hitchin in Hertfordshire. When Mr Brand was admitted of Trinity College, he spent so much money in a little time, that his father took him from thence, and put him under the care of Mr [William] Barford, Public Orator [1761–8], formerly of King's College, and now one of the prebendaries of Canterbury, who then lived in the town, which he quitted about 1767.'

From Cole, Thursday 15 November 1770

VA, Forster MS 110, f. 72. Cole kept no copy.
Address: For the Honourable Mr Horace Walpole in Arlington Street, London.

Milton near Cambridge, Nov. 15, 1770.

Dear Sir,

A NEIGHBOUR of mine,[1] a farmer in this parish, who serves you with Cotenham cheese, as he tells me, offers to leave this in Arlington Street. I could not resist asking after your health, which, I have been informed, has not been as I could wish. I hope this will find you either well or mending.

I have promised Mr Tyson to get him a cover in order to send you a little essay he has just printed, on a miniature or illumination in a MS in his college library.[2] I would have sent one by this bearer, but know his de<sign>, and therefore dare not do it.

We are all in confusion in this county on the death of the Marquis of Granby.[3] The seat was offered to Sir Joseph[4] and Mr John[5] Yorke: both refused it at first, but it was understood that Mr John Yorke had accepted it. However, on the morning of the nomination day, when the gentlemen were all met, Lord Hardwicke[6] informed them that his brother's ill health did not allow him to accept the offer. This occasioned no small confusion, as no one was thought of besides, so the mee<ting> adjourned to that day sennight, Nov. 16. In this interval <Lord> Montfort produced his nephew, Captain Charles Cadogan;[7] Sir Samp<son Gide>on[8] offered himself; as also a young gentleman,

---

1. Not identified.

2. *An Account of an Illuminated Manuscript in the Library of Corpus Christi College, Cambridge,* 1770 (see also *post* 19 March 1773). It was reprinted in *Archaeologia* ii (1773). 194–7.

3. John Manners (1721–70), M. of Granby; eld. son of John Manners, 3d D. of Rutland; M.P. for Cambs 1754–70; d. 19 Oct. 1770 (Collins, *Peerage,* 1812, i. 486–7).

4. Hon. Sir Joseph Yorke (1724–92), K.B., cr. Baron Dover, 1788; 3d son of the 1st E. of Hardwicke; Minister at The Hague 1751–61; Ambassador there 1761–80; M.P. for Dover 1761–74; for Grampound 1774–80.

5. (1728–1801), 4th son of the 1st E. of Hardwicke; M.P. for Reigate, 1768–84;

F.R.S. (see GM Sept. 1801, lxxi. 862b; Albinia Lucy Cust, *Chronicles of Erthig on the Dyke,* 2 vols, 1914, ii. 254).

6. Philip Yorke (1720–90), 2d E. of Hardwicke; M.P. for Reigate 1741–7; for Cambs 1747–64; F.R.S. 1741; F.S.A. 1744; Lord Lieutenant of Cambs 1757–90; High Steward of the University of Cambridge 1764–90.

7. Hon. Charles Henry Sloan Cadogan (1749–1833), eld. son of Charles Sloane Cadogan, 1st E. Cadogan, by Frances Bromley, dau. of 1st Bn Montfort; sometime an officer in the army; suc. (1807) as 2d E. Cadogan; insane for more than 25 years before his death.

8. Sir Sampson Gideon (1745–1824), 1st Bt; in 1789 he took (by royal license) the

one Mr Brand; and Mr Panton's son of Newmarket.⁹ In case Mr Cadogan does not proceed, Sir Sampson has Lord Hardwicke's, Lord
Montfort's and the Bishop of Ely's interest; Mr Brand has that of the
Duke of Bedford;¹⁰ and the county is now getting drunk in every
quarter of it. Thank God it can't be long in dispute.

I am settled in my new habitation, which I like much, but the incessant rains threaten to keep me in as low and humble a state as ever.
I am not recovered of a six or seven years' inundation, and now,
probably, am going to be as bad as ever. I hardly ever <re>member
such heavy and severe rains as we have had for these last ten days or a
fortnight.

Mr Essex and I promise ourselves a day's pleasure of visiting you at
Strawberry Hill next year. I hope soon to hear of your good health,
which will give infinite pleasure to, dear Sir,

Your ever faithful and obliged servant,

WM COLE

To COLE, Tuesday 20 November 1770

Add MS 5952, ff. 76–7.

Address: To the Reverend Mr Cole at Milton, Cambridgeshire.
Postmark: EK 20 NO.

Arlington Street, Nov. 20, 1770.

I BELIEVE our letters crossed one another without knowing it.
Mine, it seems, was quite unnecessary, for I find Mr Brand has
given up the election. Yours was very kind and obliging as they always are. Pray be so good as to thank Mr Tyson for me a thousand
times; I am vastly pleased with his work, and hope he will give me
another of the plates for my volume of heads (for I shall bind up his
present) and I by no means relinquish his promise of a complete set
of his etchings, and of a visit to Strawberry Hill. Why should it not
be with you and Mr Essex, whom I shall be very glad to see—but

name of Eardley and was cr. Bn Eardley of
Spalding; M.P. for Cambs 1770–80.

9. Thomas Panton (1731–1808), son of
Thomas Panton (1697–1782), Master of the
King's Running Horses at Newmarket (see
DNB; Frank Siltzer, *Newmarket*, 1923, p.

229 *et passim*). He appears as 'The Sport-
ing Rover' in the notorious *Tête-à-Tête*
series in the *Town and Country Magazine,*
ix (1777). 569–72.

10. John Russell (1710–71), 4th D. of
Bedford.

what do you talk of a single day? Is that all you allow me in two years?

I rejoice to see Mr Bentham's advertisement[1] at last. I depend on you, dear Sir, for procuring me his book the instant it is possible to have it. Pray make my compliments to all that good family.

I am enraged and almost in despair, at Pearson the glass-painter,[2] he is so idle and dissolute—he has done very little of the window, though what he has done is glorious, and approaches very nearly to Price.[3]

My last volume of *Painters* begins to be printed this week, but as the plates are not begun, I doubt it will be long before the whole is ready. I mentioned to you in my last Thursday's letter a hint about Bannerman the engraver. Adieu! Dear Sir,

Yours most sincerely,

HOR. WALPOLE

From COLE, Wednesday 28 November 1770

VA, Forster MS 110, ff. 73–4. Cole kept no copy.
Address: For the Hon. Horace Walpole in Arlington Street, London.
Postmark: Cambridge 29 NO.

Milton, Nov. 28, 1770.

Dear Sir,

I WAS at Cambridge at Mr Bentham's all last week, both on account of the election[1] and that I might not be left to myself on such repeated misfortunes as befall me. This is the third time within

1. The following advertisement appeared in *Lloyd's Evening Post* 14–16 Nov., and in *The London Chronicle* 15–17 Nov.: 'ANTIQUITIES OF ELY. The Reverend Mr James Bentham having sent to the press the last sheet of his *History of Ely Cathedral*, etc., desires that all those who have honoured him with their subscriptions, or intend to subscribe, will send their names to him, at Ely; or to Mr Bathurst, Bookseller, in Fleet Street, London; or Mr Merril, or Mr Woodyer, at Cambridge, before the 1st of December, in order to their being inserted in the List of Subscribers.'

2. James Pearson (d. 1805), who had been engaged to paint the glass in the east window of Ely Cathedral. He also painted

some of the glass at SH (see *SH Accounts* 160–1).

3. William Price (d. 1765), the younger, 'whose colours are fine, whose drawing good, and whose taste in ornaments and mosaic is far superior to any of his predecessors', is equal to the antique, to the good Italian masters, and only surpassed by his own singular modesty' (*Anecdotes, Works* iii. 159). He painted some of the glass at SH (see *SH Accounts, passim*), Westminster Abbey, Winchester College and New College, Oxford (see DNB).

1. 'Thursday, Nov. 22, in as vile a day as ever was remembered, it raining without cease all the day, Sir Sampson Gideon was

six years that my estate has been drowned, and now worse than ever.[2] Indeed I expected it could be no other from such incessant rain and bad weather. When things are at the worst, it is to be hoped they will mend.

Mr Brand left his friends in the lurch without ever taking leave of them, so left the field open to Sir Sampson Gideon. I knew neither of the gentlemen, but was so far engaged with my Lord Montfort, on his nephew Captain Cadogan's account, who was first proposed, that I am very happy there was no further contest, as it would have been impossible for me to have obliged you, though I had no kind of regard for Mr Brand's opponent and a great one for himself, both as your friend, son to our schoolfellow, and a very worthy young gentleman, as by his friends' report.

<M>r Tyson tells me by letter that he has sent you a packet. I got a cover for him of Mr Jenyns[3] for that purp<ose,> and though I was a week at Cambridge, I saw neither him or anyone else, but he dines at Milton tomorrow, and I will communicate the contents of your last kind letter.

Mr Bentham's book will certainly appear in January.[4] I was, and indeed have been long, very busy in pressing it forward last week.

elected without any opposition, but from a few old women and some of the discontented mob who were vexed there was no further opposition, and that their drunken licentiousness was at an end' (Cole MSS, Add MS 5823, f. 143v).

2. 'This shocking weather, and the consequences of having my estate again drowned and four feet under water for the fourth time within these six years, and receiving no rent, or little, of course, of my tenants, determined me to part with my estate at Hadenham and Aldreth' (loc. cit.).

3. Soame Jenyns (1704–87), poetaster, M.P. for Cambs, 1742–54 and 1760–80; for Dunwich, 1754–60. Cole describes him in his 'Athenae Cantabrigienses' (LI viii. 575): 'The first performance in the poetical way which appeared was his "Essay on Dancing," which is well esteemed of in its way: and indeed one would wonder that it should be otherwise, inasmuch as the author seems calculated in nature, person, and manner to excel in that exercise; and if a person who did not know him was to be asked, on seeing him dressed, what was his profession, I think it is ten to one but that he would say he was a dancing-master. He has the misfortune to be extremely short-sighted, a circumstance not unusual with eyes formed as his are, which are very projecting; and, though he has a large wen on his neck, which a grave and even no very large wig would cover or hide, yet the predominancy of dress is such, that a small, little bag pig-tail wig is preferred, by which means the aforesaid blemish is visible to every one. Mr. Jenyns is a man of a lively fancy and pleasant turn of wit; very sparkling in conversation, and full of many conceits and agreeable drollery, which is heightened by his particular inarticulate manner of speaking through his broken teeth; and all this is mixed with the utmost good nature and humanity, having hardly ever heard him severe upon any one, and by no means satirical in his mirth and good humour.'

4. *Ely* was not published until June 1771 (see *Lloyd's Evening Post* 12–14 and 14–17 June 1771).

The index is quite finished, and nothing remains to go to the press but the preface, which is also finished as to the composition. The Bishop's death[5] will probably retard it a few days. I wish it may not put a stop to his good works at Ely. I am vastly concerned that the window was not done before he had blessed his eyes with it:[6] I am only afraid it now never will be done. You may depend upon my getting you Mr Bentham's book the instant it is published.

It pleases me beyond measure that you are going on with the last volume of *Painters*. I suppose Bannerman wrote to you, as he said he designed, when I sent to him on the receipt of your first letter. He seemed much pleased to be employed by you, and thought the difficulty of his residence at Cambridge not much, as the conveyance was daily all the year through. I will be ready to do everything you will please to commission me, in order to forward so good a work.

I think you will be pleased with Mr Bentham's book. I hear the Dean of Exeter has used you scurvily.[7] I have not had leisure to read the book,[8] and indeed never saw the outside of it but at Mr Tyson's chamber when it first came out. I only sent for it last week, and let Mr Essex have it, where it now is, before it comes to, dear Sir,

Your ever faithful and obliged servant,

WM COLE

From COLE, Saturday 15 December 1770

VA, Forster MS 110, ff. 75–6. Cole kept no copy.
Address: For the Honourable Horace Walpole in Arlington Street, London.
Postmark: Cambridge 19 DE.

Milton, Dec. 15, 1770.

Dear Sir,

IT gave me great pleasure to see your last letter to Mr Tyson,[1] with your zeal and plan towards executing a work[2] every lover of antiquities must rejoice to see forwarded by one of your taste and abili-

---

5. Matthias Mawson, Bp of Ely, d. 23 Nov. 1770.

6. See *ante* 14 June 1769.

7. Jeremiah Milles (1714–84), antiquary; F.S.A. 1741; F.R.S. 1742; P.S.A. 1768–84; Dean of Exeter 1762–84. He used HW 'scurvily' by replying to part of *Historic Doubts* in *Observations on the Wardrobe*

Account for the Year 1483, read at the Society of Antiquaries 8 March 1770, and published in *Archaeologia* i (1770). 361–83.

8. The first volume of *Archaeologia*.

1. Missing.

2. The proposed history of Gothic architecture.

ties. The letter you wrote to me on that subject,[3] which was a long one, I gave to Mr Tyson and Mr Essex, who, I know, both copied it. If Mr Tyson has not preserved his copy, I will furnish him with your original letter, but *entre nous,* I then apprehended, as I do at present, that if Mr Essex stays till Mr Tyson gets his materials ready for this excellent design, I am afraid it will never appear while I am in being. The truth of the case is this: Mr Essex has all his materials ready, and every measurement on paper, relating to every part of Gothic architecture, in which he really wants the assistance of no person except yourself to revise and put in method his own designs, yet if Mr Tyson would <fin?>ally and in earnest set about this affair with him, his help would be very agreeable to him, and his undertaking the dresses and fashions, with his skill in drawing, would be not only a most useful but entertaining addition to the work. I am ready to lend all the assistance in my power, in case it is wanted, and desire nothing so much as to see the work go forward under your auspices, and I know this to be the sentiment of Mr Essex also, who wants Mr Tyson to accompany him to town for one day only in order to talk the matter over with you, for till that is done, I see no hopes of beginning.

I was at the poor Bishop of Ely's funeral last week at Ely, and everyone regretted his loss. The window, I am afraid, will not go forward so cheerfully now he is gone, though I am told he has provided by will for the finishing it.[4] You will be surprised and pleased with the beauty of that church since the alterations last year. I hope you'll look at it from Milton, where is a bed at your service, and you'll much honour, dear Sir,

Your most faithful servant,

WM COLE

I shall see Mr Tyson next Friday, and will carry your former letter with me for fear he may have mislaid the copy.

3. 11 Aug. 1769.

4. 'Bishop Mawson had formed a design of filling this [the east] window (for it is generally considered as one window of eight lights), with stained glass, and selected an artist to carry it into effect. The work, however, was not then finished. A figure of S. Peter, with the arms of the Bishop and of contemporary members of the Chapter, originally a part of this design, is now placed in the easternmost window of the north triforium of the nave. Two other heads, one of S. Paul and the other of S. Etheldreda, which were also parts of this design, are preserved in the windows of the Deanery dining room. The east window was completed by the liberality of Bishop [Bowyer Edward] Sparke [1760–1836], who gave in his lifetime a large sum for that purpose' (Charles William Stubbs, *Ely Cathedral Handbook,* 21st edn, Ely, 1904, pp. 147–8).

I should be very glad if you would assist in getting Mr Granger's name put in the list of the Antiquarian Society.[5] I promised him to help in this affair in the summer.

Mr Bentham's book will be out in January.

Since I wrote my letter I accidentally met with the original resignation of a scholarship in King's College by your father, all wrote in his own fair hand except the witness's name. As it may be a curiosity to you, I send it.

May ye 19, 1698.

The days of my leave of absence from the college being near expir'd, and my father holding his resolutions that I shall not any more reside there, I do hereby resign my scholarship of King's College in Cambridge. Witness my hand the day and year above written,

Robert Walpole

Signed in the presence of
Hen. Hare.[6]

To Cole, Thursday 20 December 1770

Add MS 5952, ff. 78–9.

Cole's copy of his letter to HW, 18 April 1771, follows HW's signature in the MS.

Address: To the Reverend Mr Cole at Milton, Cambridgeshire.
Postmark: EK 20 DE.

Arlington Street, Dec. 20, 1770.

Dear Sir,

I AM very zealous, as you know, for the work,[1] but I agree with you in expecting very little success from the plan. Activity is the best implement in such undertakings, and that seems to be wanting; and without that, it were vain to think of who would be at the expense. I do not know whether it were not best that Mr Essex should publish his remarks as simply as he can.[2] For my own part, I can do no more

5. Granger never became a member of the Society of Antiquaries.

6. Possibly a mistake for Francis Hare (1671–1740), afterwards (1731–40) Bp of Chichester, who was tutor of Sir Robert Walpole at King's, and his life-long friend. Mr John Saltmarsh, of King's, and Mr J. W. Goodison, of the Fitzwilliam Museum, write (1936) that this letter does not appear to be extant.

1. The proposed history of Gothic architecture.

2. Essex never published a history of Gothic architecture, but he contributed to *Archaeologia* several papers connected with that subject: 'Remarks on the Antiquity and the different Modes of Brick and Stone Buildings in England' (iv. 73–109); 'Some Observations on Lincoln Cathedral' (iv. 149–59); and at the close of another

than I have done, sketch out the plan. I grow too old and am grown too indolent to engage in any more works; nor have I time. I wish to finish some things I have by me, and to have done. The last volume of my *Anecdotes,* of which I was tired, is completed,[3] and with them I shall take my leave of publications. The last years of one's life are fit for nothing but idleness and quiet, and I am as indifferent to fame as to politics.

I can be of as little use to Mr Granger in recommending him to the Antiquarian Society. I dropped my attendance there four or five years ago from being sick of their ignorance and stupidity, and have not been three times amongst them since.[4] They have chosen to expose their dullness to the world, and crowned it with Dean Milles's nonsense.[5] I have written a little answer to the last,[6] which you shall see, and there wash my hands of them.

To say the truth I have no very sanguine expectation about the Ely window. The glass-painter,[7] though admirable, proves a very idle worthless fellow, and has yet scarce done anything of consequence. I gave Dr Nichols[8] notice of his character, but found him apprised of it; the Doctor however does not despair, but pursues him warmly. I wish it may succeed!

If you go over to Cambridge, be so good as to ask Mr Gray when he proposes being in town: he talked of last month. I must beg you too to thank Mr Tyson for his last letter.[9] I can say no more to the plan than I have said. If he and Mr Essex should like to come to town, I shall be very willing to talk it over with them, but I can by no means think of engaging in any part of the composition.

paper, 'Observations on the Origin and Antiquity of Round Churches,' read before the Society of Antiquaries 24 May 1781, he mentions the design of 'a work purposely intended to explain what relates to the various styles of architecture which come under the general denomination of Gothic;—if I should live to complete it' (*Archaeologia* vi. 178). See also Tyson to Gough 4 Dec. 1779, and Gough to Tyson 11 Dec. 1779 (LA viii. 655–7).

3. That is, the writing was completed; the printing was finished 13 April 1771, but publication was deferred until 9 Oct. 1780 (*Jour. Print. Off.* 16, 19).

4. HW had his name taken from the books of the Society late in July 1772 (*post* 28 July 1772; 'Short Notes,' 1772).

5. Milles's *Observations* is the last article in *Archaeologia* vol. i.

6. *A Reply to the Observations of the Rev. Dr. Milles . . . on the Wardrobe Account,* dated 28 Aug. 1770, of which only six copies were printed (George Baker, *Catalogue of Books . . . Printed at Strawberry Hill,* privately printed 1810; Wm T. Lowndes, *Bibliographer's Manual*). It is reprinted in *Works* ii. 221*–44*. Cole read Gray's copy (*post* 10 Jan. 1771; 18 April 1771).

7. James Pearson.

8. Dr John Nicols.

9. Missing.

These holidays I hope to have time to range my drawings and give Bannerman some employment towards my book[10]—but I am in no hurry to have it appear, as it speaks of times so recent; for though I have been very tender of not hurting any living relations of the artists, the latter were in general so indifferent, that I doubt their families will not be very well content with the coldness of the praises I have been able to bestow. This reason, with my unwillingness to finish the work, and the long interval between the composition of this and the other volumes, have I doubt made the greatest part a very indifferent performance. An author, like other mechanics, never does well, when he is tired of his profession.

I have been told, that, besides Mr Tyson, there are two other gentlemen engravers at Cambridge. I think their names are Sharpe or Shaw,[11] and Cobbe,[12] but I am not at all sure of either. I should be glad however if I could procure any of their portraits—and I do not forget that I am already in your debt. Boydell is going to recommence a suite of illustrious heads,[13] and I am to give him a list of indubitable portraits of remarkable persons that have never been engraved; but I have protested against his receiving two sorts; the one, any old head of a family, when the person was moderately considerable; the other, spurious or doubtful heads; both sorts, apt to be sent in by families who wish to crowd their own names into the work; as was the case more than once in Houbraken's set,[14] and of which honest Vertue often complained to me.[15] The Duke of Buckingham,[16]

10. *Anecdotes* vol. iv.

11. Christopher Sharpe (1722–97), a turner and frame-maker of Cambridge; he engraved several prints (see EBP; Granger, *Correspondence* 306–9).

12. HW's mistake for *Orde:* Thomas Orde (1746–1807), afterwards (1795) Orde-Powlett, cr. 1st Bn Bolton, 1797; Eton and King's (B.A. 1770). While at Cambridge he etched portraits of local celebrities (EBP; Granger, *Correspondence* 87–8).

13. John Boydell (1719–1804), engraver and print-publisher, began to issue in 1769 a *Collection of Prints, engraved after the most capital Paintings in England . . . with a Description of each Picture in English and French.* The entire work, in 9 volumes atlas folio, containing 571 prints, is extremely rare. HW had only the first two volumes, containing 115 prints, which were sold London ix. 1204. Cole, apropos of

Boydell's design, wrote to Granger, 28 Dec. 1770: 'I heard last week from Mr Walpole, who mentioned the design on foot with Boydell: we here all wish it success' (Granger, *Correspondence* 341–3. The original letter is now WSL).

14. Jacob Houbraken (1698–1780) and George Vertue engraved the portraits for *The Heads of Illustrious Persons of Great Britain . . . with their Lives and Characters by Thomas Birch,* 1743. Later editions appeared in 1747–52, 1756, 1813. HW's large-paper copy of the first edition, 2 vols bound in one, was sold London iv. 595.

15. Cf. extract from Vertue's letter to Maurice Johnson, ca 1737, LA vi. 117–8.

16. Henry Stafford (1455–83), 2d D. of Buckingham. The error is noted in *Granger*[5] i. 42 n: 'This is Edward Duke of Buckingham: the inscription on Houbraken's print is erroneous.' See also EBP. The print

Carr Earl of Somerset,[17] and Thurloe,[18] in that list, are absolutely not genuine—the first is John Digby Earl of Bristol.[19]

I am, Dear Sir, Yours most sincerely,

Hor. Walpole

From Cole, Thursday 3 January 1771

VA, Forster MS 110, ff. 77–8. Cole kept no copy.

Milton, Jan. 3, 1771.

Dear Sir,

THE reason why I did not answer your last earlier was that Mr Gray told me he should be in town and call on you very shortly. My present reason for troubling you is a report[1] that Mr Essex has heard that Mr Sandby[2] was at Cambridge about a fortnight ago, employed by his Majesty to take draughts of King's College Chapel, and was to return again in about a month or two to take other measurements, with a design for publication. As Mr Essex, so long ago as 1756, printed proposals for such a design, has all his drawings ready, and is excellently skilled in the theory as well as practice of Gothic architecture, as appears by his having already erected altar-pieces in the Cathedrals of Lincoln and Ely, and now actually putting up one in King's College Chapel[3] in the same style and not in the motley manner of those usually given for Gothic even by some of the best

is Edward Stafford (1478–1521), 3d D. of Buckingham, founder of Magdalene College, Cambridge; executed for treason.

17. Robert Carr or Ker (1587?–1645), E. of Somerset; favourite of James I. 'This portrait [in *Illustrious Heads*], which represents him as a black robust man, is not genuine' (*Granger*[1] i. 224; see also Thomas Pennant, *Tour in Scotland, 1769*[3] p. 62). The authenticity of the print is not questioned in EBP.

18. John Thurloe (1616–68), Secretary of State. 'This head is, with good reason, supposed to have been done for some other person' (*Granger*[1] ii. 38). EBP agrees, but does not identify it.

19. John Digby (1586–1653), 1st E. of Bristol. HW is apparently mistaken (see n. 16 above).

1. It was not true (see following letter).

2. Thomas Sandby (1721–98), draughtsman and architect; first Professor of Architecture to the Royal Academy (1770), of which he was an original member; joint architect with James Adam of H. M. Office of Works, 1777.

3. Several changes under Essex's direction were made in King's College Chapel between 1770 and 1776: among others, the paving of the ante-chapel was completed, the lectern was moved to the library in the side chapel, and a new altar designed by Essex was erected. HW was pleased with the alterations (*post* 22 May 1777), but 'a later generation . . . has not scrupled to condemn and undo Essex's work' (Augustus Austen-Leigh, *King's College*, 1899, p. 203).

modern architects, it is pity this design should go out of the hands of a person so well qualified for it, and who seems to have a sort of title to it. He therefore desires me to mention to you with what propriety his treatise on that kind of architecture would come into a description of that royal chapel, and how ready and willing he is to set about it immediately, if his plans and designs could be laid before the King by your or any other mediation. He will at any warning come up to town and bring his papers and drafts with him, that you may judge whether they are worthy of such a patronage. Whoever attempts to give an account of the Chapel can never hope to do it with the accuracy of Mr Essex, who sent me the following account of what he has already done in this affair:

In the year 1756, etc., scaffolds being erected to the highest points of the four angular towers of King's College Chapel, which were completely repaired under my inspection, I used that opportunity of taking dimensions of all the parts of them, and have made a perfect elevation, section and plans of the several parts. The like opportunities have been taken to make an exact section of the great vault, and taking all other necessary measures for describing every other part of it. I have likewise the exact measures of the east, west and side windows, the general plan of the whole building and vaulting, the finials and all the principal parts, not to be measured without scaffolding; and if any parts remain not taken, they are within reach.

I have a fair drawing of:

The vault and its plan.

A tower or one of the angular turrets, an elevation, section and plans of it.

A plan and elevation of the basement of a tower, with the mouldings at large.

The east end, with a design for a new altar.

The measures for drawing all the other parts, which should be described at large.

Mr Essex, I know, is in earnest, and has long wanted to prosecute this work. How it has been retarded so long is not my business to inquire.

I don't love to be thus troublesome, but my regard to Mr Essex and love to Gothic architecture, which I think will thrive well in his hands, has made me get over my usual scrupulousness in these matters.

I was at Cambridge to dinner on Tuesday, where I met a gentleman of Trinity College who has promised me to ask Mr Topham,[4] a fellow commoner of that college and an etcher, for his prints, and will bring them to me when he gets them. I have an access by a friend to Mr Orde of King's College, and hope to procure those of his etching. Sharpe, an ingenious tradesman of Cambridge, has etched a few, and I will assuredly get them for you and make you up a packet, and send them together. I don't recollect whether you are curious about Roman antiquities: however that may be, a gentleman of my acquaintance at Cambridge brought me hither last week three prints of an old stone urn, if such it be, found at Chesterford,[5] near us. It was etched by a clergyman, a Dr Gower,[6] who is a physician at Chelmsford in Essex, one of which is appropriated to you.

Boydell's design, under your inspection, will be admirable. I long to see it, but am fearful that it will be too expensive for common folks, for engravers are now so saucy they know not what to ask. I have lived so long to see a shilling print now advanced to five. I hope Bannerman has wrote to you his readiness to undertake anything you will please to employ him about: that[7] is the work I most long to see.

Mr Bentham's book advances with a slow and solemn pace: church works, especially such great cathedrals, are never quick in their execution, but, when finished, surprise by their majesty and grandeur. If the book won't run a parallel on all fours with this comparison, I dare presume to say it will not disgust the reader by its subject or the manner of treating it, but I must needs say that he is one of the slowest of mortals. Everything is ready, and yet it is put off from week to week. I suppose about Lady Day it will appear. I am, dear Sir,

Your most obliged and faithful servant,

WM COLE

---

4. Edward Topham (1751–1820), journalist, man of fashion and dramatist; Eton and Trinity College, Cambridge; largely responsible for *The World*, a newspaper, 1787–94 (*Eton Coll. Reg. 1753–1790*). Like Thomas Orde, he seems to have been interested chiefly in humorous subjects for his prints (see BM *Cat. of Prints and Drawings: Satires* iv. 702; Christopher Wordsworth, *Social Life at the English Universi-ties in the Eighteenth Century*, 1874, p. 409).

5. Great Chesterford, Essex, ten miles SE of Cambridge.

6. Foote Gower (1726?–80), M.D., rector of Chignall St James, Essex, 1761–7; collected materials for histories of Cheshire and Essex.

7. *Anecdotes* iv.

To Cole, Thursday 10 January 1771

Add MS 5952, ff. 80–1.

Cole wrote the following note on the cover: 'In Dr Parson's *Remains of Japhet*,[1] London, 4to, 1767, p. 250, it is said that the Gomerian name for a dog, *canis*, is *kene*, as the Magogian *chana*. No wonder Bishop Keene[2] has a dog or talbot in his arms.'

In spite of the address 'near Peterborough,' the letter apparently reached Cole without difficulty.

Address: To the Reverend Mr Cole at Milton near Peterborough.
Postmark: 10 IA.

Arlington Street, Jan. 10, 1771.

AS I am acquainted with Mr Paul Sandby,[3] the brother of the architect, I asked him if there was a design, as I had heard, of making a print or prints of King's College Chapel by the King's order? He answered directly, by no means. His brother made a general sketch of the Chapel for the use of the lectures he reads on architecture at the Royal Academy. Thus, dear Sir, Mr Essex may be perfectly easy that there is no intention of interfering with his work. I then mentioned to Mr Sandby Mr Essex's plan, which he much approved, but said the plates would cost a great sum. The King, he thought, would be inclined to patronize the work; but I own I do not know how to get it laid before him. His own artists[4] would probably discourage any scheme that might intrench on their own advantages.[5] Mr Thomas Sandby the architect is the only one of them I am acquainted with, and Mr Essex must think whether he would like to let him into any participation of the work. If I can get any other person to mention it to his Majesty, I will; but you know me, and that I have always kept clear of connections with courts and ministers, and have no interest with either, and perhaps my recommendation might do as much hurt as good, especially as the artists in

1. James Parsons (1705–70), M.D., author of *Remains of Japhet: being Historical Enquiries into the Affinity and Origin of the European Languages*.

2. Edmund Keene (1714–81), Bp of Chester (1752–71) and of Ely (1771–81). His arms were: 'Argent, a talbot sable, collared or, on a chief indented azure 3 cross-crosslets or' (Bentham, *Ely*[2] Appendix, p. *47).

3. (1725–1809), watercolour-painter; original member of the Royal Academy; introduced into England the 'aquatint' process

of engraving. He made several drawings of SH which were engraved (see *SH Accounts, passim*).

4. The thirty-six members nominated by George III to the recently (10 December 1768) formed Royal Academy of Arts, which the King called 'My Academy' (John E. Hodgson and Fred A. Eaton, *The Royal Academy and Its Members 1768–1830*, New York, 1905, pp. 12–13).

5. For these see op. cit., Appendix I.

favour might be jealous of one who understands a little of their professions and is apt to say what he thinks. In truth there is another danger, which is, that they might not assist Mr Essex without views of profiting of his labours. I am slightly acquainted with Mr Chambers the architect,[6] and have a good opinion of him; if Mr Essex approves my communicating his plan to him or Mr Sandby, I should think it more likely to succeed by their intervention, than by any lord of the court, for at last, the King would certainly take the opinion of his artists. When you have talked this over with Mr Essex, let me know the result. Till he has determined, there can be no use in Mr Essex's coming to town.

I am much obliged to you as I am continually, for the trouble you have taken to procure me Mr Orde's, Mr Topham's and Mr Sharpe's prints, and shall be very thankful for them. As to Roman antiquities, I do not collect prints of them, having engaged in too many other branches already.

Mr Gray will bring down some of my drawings to Bannerman, and when you go over to Cambridge, I will beg you now and then to supervise him. For Mr Bentham's book, I rather despair of it; and should it ever appear, he will have made people expect it too long, which will be of no service to it, though I do not doubt of its merit. Mr Gray will show you my answer to Dr Milles.[7]

I am, Dear Sir, Your ever obliged humble servant,

HOR. WALPOLE

From COLE, Thursday 18 April 1771

VA, Forster MS 110, ff. 79–80. COLE's copy is written on the last page and cover of HW's letter of 20 December 1770, Add MS 5952, ff. 79, 80v.

Address: For the Honourable Horace Walpole in Arlington Street, London.
Postmark: 22 AP.

Milton, April 18, 1771.

<D>ear and ever honoured Sir,

THAT I have never answered your letter of many months past must be accounted for by my untoward and unlucky situation. Ever since I had the honour of attending you a tour in Northamp-

6. William Chambers (1726–96), became a Swedish knight, 1771; author of *Treatise of Civil Architecture*, 1759, and *Dissertation on Oriental Gardening*, 1772, for which he was satirized in Mason's *Heroic Epistle*, 1773.

7. HW's letter to Gray about it is miss-

tonshire,[1] etc., we have had nothing but wet seasons, one following another, and I have been a continual sufferer, but never so bad as by last November's floods, which totally drowned all our county, and when it will be dry again God knows. This has been a constant damp upon my mind, and every shower put me on the rack. Thank God, I have got rid of this plague and anxiety by parting with my estate[2] which, instead of being of service, was a continual uneasiness to me, and of no great advantage. Within these two months, in consequence of these calamities, one tenant[3] broke, by whom I lose above £400. I am sorry I have wrote so much on a disagreeable subject and which, I know, will give you pain. My reason for it was in order to disculpate myself in not writing to you, but in good truth my mind was never at ease enough to sit down to write to my friends. I yesterday finished a very long letter of queries to Mr Granger, which I had begun on 6 March,[4] and could never get myself into a disposition to finish.

I believe near two months ago Mr Tyson brought me two small heads of the old Marquis of Winchester, Paulet,[5] <who> was Lord Treasurer under Henry VIII, Edward VI, Queen Mary and Elizabeth. It is etched by <him> from a painting on board in the possession of Dr Glynn,[6] Vice-Provost of King's College and M.D. I have also for you several other small prints from Mr Topham of Trinity College, and Sharp of Cambridge. Mr Ord of King's is in France and has been these twelve months, so his can't be got till his return. I only wait for a convenient opportunity of sending them to you.

I am glad to hear you was no great sufferer by your house being broke open.[7]

Mr Gray, by your permission, some three months ago lent me your answer to Dr Milles. I never took more ill-natured pleasure in seeing an impertinent and unnecessary meddler chastised than in your per-

ing, and there is no mention of Milles in *Gray's Corr.*

---

1. In the summer of 1763.

2. See *ante* 28 Nov. 1770.

3. Not identified.

4. For an incomplete copy of this letter, see Granger, *Correspondence* 347–52.

5. Sir William Pawlet or Poulet (1485?–1572), 1st M. of Winchester.

6. Robert Glynn (1719–1800); Eton and King's; took the name of Clobery late in life on inheriting property from an uncle. His firm belief in the authenticity of Chatterton's Rowley poems ended his friendship with Cole and HW.

7. HW's house in Arlington Street was broken open on the night of 17 March, but nothing was taken (see HW to Mann 22–6 March 1771; to Gray 25 March 1771). Cole probably received his information from newspapers or from Gray.

formance, which is equally masterly, convincing and severe. I hope
I shall never deserve to come under your hands in the same way. He
richly deserves all your sneer, contempt and sarcasm.

The Master of Magdalen College, Dr Sandby,[8] some two or three
months ago, desired me to give his compliments to you, and gave me
a note or two which I have mislaid,[9] relating to a royal author which
he conceives you have omitted: it is Charles II, whose account of his
escape after the Battle of Worcester, by himself, is printed lately by
—— Dalrimple, from a MS in his College library.[10]

I much wish to see you at Milton this summer, that we may go together to Ely, which, by Mr Essex's skill, is now made one of the
noblest, grandest and finest things of the sort in England. It is, in
short, like no one cathedral besides, and is a singularity you will not
repent the trouble of a journey on purpose to see. The east window
would make it glorious, and it is a most lamentable thing to have
fallen into such hands as Pearson, who has skill and abilities, had he
application equal to them.

I will trouble you no more, and wishing you all earthly felicity,
am, dear Sir,

Your ever faithful and most obliged servant,

WM COLE

Mr Bentham's book has been finished these two months, and it is
amazing what can retard the publication at so critical a juncture.

To COLE, Wednesday 29 May 1771

Add MS 5952, ff. 82–3.

Cole wrote, 'June 13, 1771, at Milton,' before his copy of HW's letter: 'I received the following letter from my most worthy and ingenious friend, the Hon-

8. George Sandby (1717–1807), 'a cheerful agreeable man'; D.D. 1760; Master of
Magdalene 1760–74; Vice-Chancellor of
Cambridge 1760; Chancellor of the Diocese
of Norwich 1768–1807 (see Cole's account
in Brydges, *Restituta* iii. 245–7; LA ix. 667).

9. See *post* 16 June 1771 n. 17.

10. *An Account of the Preservation of
King Charles II after the Battle of Worces-*

ter, drawn up by himself, 1766. In the
preface, which is signed 'Dav. Dalrymple,'
is this sentence: 'Dr Sandby, Master of
Magdalen College, communicated this
manuscript to me; and, in the most obliging manner, gave me permission to print
it' (p. vi). Sir David Dalrymple (1726–92),
Lord Hailes, was the editor; friend and
correspondent of HW and Boswell.

ourable Mr Horace Walpole, youngest son to the Right Honourable Robert Walpole, Earl of Orford, Knight of the Garter, in June 1771' (Add MS 5845, f. 4).

Address: To the Reverend Mr Cole.
Postmark: None [Essex conveyed the letter to Cole].

Arlington Street, May 29, 1771.

Dear Sir,

I HAVE but time to write you a line, that I may not detain Mr Essex, who is so good as to take charge of this note, and of a box that I am sure will give you pleasure, and I beg may give you a little trouble. It contains the very valuable seven letters of Edward the Sixth to Barnaby Fitzpatrick.[1] Lord Ossory,[2] to whom they belong, has lent them to me to print,[3] but to facilitate that, and to prevent their being rubbed or hurt by the printer, I must entreat your exactness to copy them, and return them with the copies. I need not desire your particular care, for you value these things as much as I do, and will be able to make them out better than I can do, from being so much versed in old writing. Forgive my taking this liberty with you, which I flatter myself will not be disagreeable.[4] Mr Essex and Mr Tyson dined with me at Strawberry Hill, but could not stay so long as I wished. The party would have been still more agreeable if you had made a fourth. Adieu! Dear Sir.

Yours ever,

H. Walpole

PS. I am rejoiced you are delivered from the dread of inundations.

1. Sir Barnaby Fitzpatrick (1535?–81), 2d Bn of Upper Ossory; educated at court with Prince Edward (afterwards Edward VI); corresponded with him while in France; resided in Ireland, where he killed the rebel Rory O'More.

2. John Fitzpatrick (1745–1818), 2d E. of Upper Ossory; m. (1769) HW's intimate friend and correspondent, Hon. Anne Liddell, divorced wife of the 3d D. of Grafton.

3. The letters were printed at SH 1–13 June 1772, with the title *Copies of Seven Original Letters from King Edward VI. to Barnaby Fitzpatrick.* Two hundred copies were printed, half for HW and half for Lord Ossory (*Jour. Print. Off.* 17, 58). The present whereabouts of the letters is unknown.

4. Cole notes after his copy of HW's letter: 'By some means or other the box did not reach me till June 9, when I also heard of Mr Walpole's preparing for a journey to Paris, for about six weeks: on which account I immediately wrote to him, to desire to know whether he was in any hurry to have them returned, or whether I might defer sending them till his return from France. An answer, dated June 11, informed me that he did not set out for Paris till July 7, and that he should not want them till about a week before that time. After having transcribed them, I returned them by the Cambridge coach, with the following letter [June 16, 1771].' (Add MS 5845, f. 4.)

From COLE, Thursday 30 May 1771

VA, Forster MS 110, f. 81. Cole kept no copy.

Milton, May 30, 1771.

Dear Sir,

A NEIGHBOUR of mine who serves your family with Cotenham and soft cheese calling on me this morning with an offer to convey any little packet to town, I embraced the opportunity of sending the following prints by him, which ought indeed to have been with you months ago. In my last I gave some reasons why I have been so tardy and so silent.

Two of the Marquis of Winchester: present from Mr Tyson.

A small head of Mr Evely,[1] by Christopher Sharp of Cambridge.

Joane Cromwell,[2] by the same Sharp, a turner at Cambridge.

Francis Bell, the Norfolk monster.

Jedediah Buxton,[3] the mathematician, and three others by Mr Topham of Trinity College.

Mr Ord of King's College, who has done some things of this sort, has been in France these twelve months. When he returns I will get them and send them.

At last, dear Sir, you are likely to have Mr Bentham's book. He is now in town, and may have probably called on you. I know he went there on purpose to present it to the Bishop last week: this I heard at Ely yesterday, where I dined with his brother,[4] who showed me the book, ready to be published as soon as he returns, which is expected this week.

I know Mr Essex and Mr Tyson are, or have been, in town. Possibly you may have seen them.

After long waiting, thank God, we have had this morning a most grateful shower. I was yesterday almost choked with dust and wind in going to Ely. How much more must you have suffered about London! The lilacs and every flower rejoices in the rain of this morning:

1. Not identified.

2. Probably Elizabeth Bourchier (d. 1665) wife of the Protector whose parsimony earned her the nickname 'Joan' (see N&Q, 10, 17 Aug. 1935, vol. 169, pp. 101, 124). For Ewin's good opinion of this print, see Granger, *Correspondence* 307, 309–10.

3. (1707–72), illiterate calculating genius; exhibited in London 1754; the print shows him at the age of 63 (EBP).

4. Jeffery Bentham (1719–92), 'Minister of Trinity Parish' in the city of Ely (see Bentham, *Ely*² pp. 2, 281, Addenda, p. 21).

jonquils, polyanthuses, tulips, etc., from their first appearance to this time have drooped and gone off without any beauty or enjoyment, from the continuance of the cold, dry and windy weather.

I will detain you no longer, and am, dear Sir,

Your ever obliged and faithful servant,

WM COLE

From COLE, Sunday 9 June 1771

VA, Forster MS 110, f. 82. Cole kept no copy.
Address: For the Honourable Mr Horace Walpole in Arlington Street, London.
Postmark: Ca[mbridge] 11 IV.

Milton, Sunday, June 9, 1771.

Dear Sir,

SENDING my servant yesterday to Cambridge to ask Mr Essex and his family[1] to dine with me here today, he sent me your letter enclosed in the box with King Edward's seven letters. This is only to beg a line or two from you merely to inform me whether you want them back this week, or whether you are in no immediate occasion for them, as Mr Tyson, who called here yesterday evening, told me you was going to Paris for a few weeks. If you would have them transcribed and sent to you directly, I will do it, as it is most probable that by the time I have your answer I shall have done them, for they are not long, and easy to be read. If I hear not from you, still I heartily wish you a good journey and safe return.

I must tell you one piece of news I heard yesterday from Mr T[yson]. He told me that a very near neighbour of mine in this county, the author of the *History of C.C.C.C.*, has been fool enough to imitate Dr Milles's example, and read a paper at the Antiquary Society[2] about some most trifling mistake, if it is one, relating to a Duchess of Norfolk, mentioned in your *Richard III*.[3] He is a most singular char-

1. Essex's family consisted of his wife and daughter: his wife was Elizabeth Thurlborne or Thurlbourne (1731–90), daughter of a bookseller at Cambridge (LA ix. 671), and his daughter was Milicent (1757–87), who m., after Essex's death, John Hammond (d. 1830), Fellow of Queens' College

(see Cooper, *Memorials* iii. 259; LI vi. 309, 893).

2. *Some Remarks on Mr. Walpole's Historic Doubts,* read at the Society of Antiquaries 7 and 14 Jan. 1771. It was published in *Archaeologia* ii. 198–215.

3. HW mentions no Duchess of Norfolk

acter: one whom I have great reason to avoid any connections with, and have had none since I returned into Cambridgeshire, except that he has extorted from me for the use of his house[4] about £40, when the house itself was not worth that sum. I may be peevish about such a wretch: it may be so: but I long to see you trim the dull fellow in the way of his predecessor.

I am in a great hurry and hope you'll excuse this scrawl from, Sir,

Your ever faithful and most obliged servant,

WM COLE

To COLE, Tuesday 11 June 1771

Add MS 5952, ff. 84–5.

Cole wrote at the end of the letter: 'In my letter to Mr Walpole of Sunday, June 9, of which I kept no copy, I wanted to be informed whether he would have the letters[1] returned directly, or stay till his return from Paris, whither Mr Tyson informed me, June 8, Saturday, that he was going for about six weeks. Mr Tyson had also at the same time informed me that Mr Masters had lately read a paper at the Antiquarian Society against some mistake, if it is true it is one, in Mr Walpole's *Richard III,* about a Duchess of Norfolk. This I informed him of in my letter, and said something to him of his extortion in making me pay £40 towards the repairing his vicarage house at Waterbech, which he pretended he had fitted up for my reception.'

Address: To the Reverend Mr Cole at Milton near Cambridge.
Postmark: 11 IV.

Arlington Street, June 11, 1771.

YOU are very kind, dear Sir, and I ought to be, nay, what is more, I am, ashamed of giving you so much trouble; but I am in no hurry for the letters. I shall not set out till the 7th of next month, and it will be sufficient if I receive them a week before I set out.

Mr C. C. C. C. is very welcome to attack me about a Duchess of Norfolk. He is even welcome to be in the right; to the edification I hope of all the matrons at the Antiquarian Society, who I trust will insert his criticism in the next volume of their *Archaeologia* or *Old*

in *Historic Doubts,* nor does Masters, who, however, attempts to catch HW out on the genealogy of Lady Eleanor Butler (*Archaeologia* ii. 206). HW successfully answers him in *Short Observations on the Remarks of Mr. Masters, Works* ii. *248.

4. At Waterbeach.

1. From Edward VI to Barnaby Fitzpatrick.

Women's Logic; but indeed I cannot bestow my time on any more of them, nor employ myself in detecting witches for vomiting pins. When they turn extortioners like Mr Masters, the law should punish them, not only for roguery, but for exceeding their province, which our ancestors limited to killing their neighbour's cow, or crucifying dolls of wax. For my own part, I am so far from being out of charity with him, that I would give him a nag or new broom whenever he has a mind to ride to the Antiquarian Sabbat, and preach against me. Though you have more cause to be angry, laugh at him as I do. One has not life enough to throw away on all the fools and knaves that come 'cross one. I have often been attacked and never replied but to Mr Hume and Dr Milles[2]—to the first because he had a name; to the second, because he had a mind to have one—and yet I was in the wrong, for it was the only way he could attain one. In truth it is being too self-interested, to expose only one's private antagonists, when one lets worse men pass unmolested. Does a booby hurt me by an attack on me more than by any other foolish thing he does? Does not he tease me more by anything he says to me without attacking me, than by anything he says against me behind my back? I shall therefore most certainly never inquire after or read Mr C. C. C. C.'s criticism,[3] but leave him to oblivion with her Grace of Norfolk and our wise Society. As I doubt my own writings will soon be forgotten, I need not fear that those of my answerers will be remembered.

I am, Dear Sir, Yours most sincerely,

Hor. Walpole

From Cole, Sunday 16 June 1771

VA, Forster MS 110, ff. 83–6. Cole's copy, Add MS 5845, ff. 4–9.
Address and Postmark: None. [The letter was sent with the letters of Edward VI; see following letter.]

Milton, Sunday, June 16, 1771.

Dear Sir,

I HEREWITH return your seven original letters of King Edward VI to Mr Barnaby Fitz-Patrick, together with my copies of them.

2. That is, not publicly. His *Supplement to the Historic Doubts,* in which he answers several minor critics, is dated 6 Aug. 1769. It was not published until 1798 in *Works* ii. 185–220.

3. HW later wrote an answer to Masters, *Short Observations,* first printed in *Works* ii. 245*–251*.

I found no difficulty in transcribing them, as they are all written in that large schoolboy's hand which it is easy to decipher. Two of the letters have suffered a little damage in two or three lines, by means of the softness of the paper on which they are written, for being doubled or folded up and often unfolded, the paper is cracked and the words quite worn away; one line is also lapped and pasted over another line and so become illegible. However, as good luck has ordered it, Dr Fuller, in his *Church History*,[1] Book VII, p. 409 and 413, has printed one whole letter and part of a second, and by so doing one of the illegible lines is recovered: the other would have been preserved had he printed the whole letter. If you consult his book, you will find him a very faithful transcriber, except that he has not followed the original orthography, in which I am scrupulously exact as well as in the abbreviations. Otherwise he has made very few mistakes, and was of use to me in my copying one of the letters in more places than one.

At p. 411 of his book he has also preserved the King's private instructions to his favourite in what manner to behave at the French court.

At p. 408 he mentions a circumstance curious enough, was it authentic, relating to the Lord Rich's[2] resignation of the seals on account of a mistake he had made in sending a letter to the Duke of Norfolk,[3] which was intended for the Duke of Somerset.[4] *To the Duke* seems to be rather too concise an address for so formal and circumstantial a method used in that age. The King in one of these letters says that on account of the Lord Rich's sickness, the seals were given to Goodrich Bishop of Ely,[5] to hold during the session. This seems to contradict the *affirmed story*, told by Dr Fuller. It is certain the King seems to know nothing of it by the tenor of his letter.

Strype, in his second volume of *Memorials*,[6] p. 287 and 331, mentions these letters and the subject of them, but I suspect only as from Fuller.

1. Thomas Fuller (1608–61), historian and divine. His *Church-History of Britain* was published in 1655. Cole's reference should read pp. 409–10, 412–13.

2. Sir Richard Rich (1496?–1567), 1st Bn Rich; Lord Chancellor 1548–51. He resigned the Great Seal 21 Dec. 1551 because of illness.

3. Thomas Howard (1473–1554), 3d D. of Norfolk of the Howard House. He was confined in the Tower at the time to which Fuller refers, 1551.

4. Edward Seymour (1506?–52), 1st D. of Somerset; the Protector.

5. Thomas Goodrich (d. 1554), Bp of Ely; appointed Lord Chancellor 19 Jan. 1552.

6. John Strype (1643–1737), ecclesiastical historian and biographer; author of *Ecclesiastical Memorials*, 3 vols, 1721.

I have exactly transcribed also what was written on the outsides of these letters, but have carefully marked what I thought written by the King, and what appears to be in another handwriting.

I wish to see these papers printed by you who have the art to enliven subjects seemingly the most barren—not that I think these letters come under that notion. The seeming coldness and indifference of the young King's narrative concerning his own uncle's[7] trial and execution, manifestly shows in whose hands he then was,[8] how insensible he was to the ruin of his own blood and family, and how little reason there is in Fuller's conceit, p. 425, that King Edward's *consumption* was occasioned by his *grief* for the death of his uncle. His scruples concerning the mass seem to have taken a more intimate hold of his conscience.

I have, to spare you some trouble, slightly looked over *King Edward's Journal,* which is printed in the Appendix to the second volume of Burnet's *History of the Reformation,* p. 32, in order to find whether he mentions any circumstance relating to Mr Fitz-Patrick, and only see his name recorded at pp. 36, 62, to which I refer you.

Fuller, p. 412, says that Barnaby Fitz-Patrick, on his return to England, was created by the King, Baron of Upper Ossory, and that he died a most excellent Protestant. No wonder! Two religious houses added to his own patrimony was a most infallible argument to confirm his faith in the doctrine of Calvin.

If you find no better motto for the title-page, this remark of honest Fuller, p. 424, may serve.

If Papists superstitiously preserve the Fingers, Teeth, yea, Locks of Haire of their pretended Saints, wonder not if I prize the smallest Reliques of this gracious Prince.[9]

The similarity of the subject has made me subjoin copies of two or three letters which I transcribed from the originals in Benet College Library. Two of them from a Princess Cecily in the reign of Queen Elizabeth, which, though the subjects of them are of no consequence, yet they are curious in this respect, I suppose, as coming from a daughter of King Edward IV, who must have been very an-

---

7. Edward Seymour, D. of Somerset.

8. John Dudley (1502?–53), 1st D. of Northumberland, who procured the execution of Somerset.

9. HW quotes this passage and acknowledges his indebtedness to Cole for it in the conclusion of his 'Advertisement' to *Letters of King Edward VI.*

cient in 1567. I take her to have been Viscountess Welles,[10] but not
having Sandford,[11] am not sure of my fact. If I am not right, I know
of no one who can set me so, so well as yourself. The other is no less
a curiosity, being a letter from the famous Earl of Leicester, and
shows the hospitality, popularity and manners of the Queen in the
beginning of her reign. They are all three addressed to Archbishop
Parker.

I heartily wish you a good journey and a safe return, and I hope
the exercise and change of air will be of use to you. When you are
returned to Strawberry Hill in the autumn, Mr Essex and I have a
design to spend two or three days with you. He is quite in raptures
with your place, as is Mr Tyson.

Your description of my late Jew landlord[12] gave me no small entertainment. It is wonderful that so dull, so clumsy-headed a fellow
should ever think of writing anything in the way that Dr Mills has
thought fit to do. It is probable he had an ambition to contradict
you, and so be thought somebody, and presumed upon your never
troubling yourself to answer such blockheads.

I hope you received a little roll of prints I sent you about a fortnight ago. In the box with the letters are enclosed a few more from,
dear Sir,

Your ever faithful and most obliged servant,

WM COLE

PS. I think I have ranged King Edward's letters in the order of time.

I have sent you a print just published at Cambridge by Mr Lam-
bourn,[13] designed as a frontispiece to a little book describing the
plants in our Botanic Garden,[14] of the late Dr Walker,[15] Vice-Master
of Trinity, whom you may possibly recollect by the print, it is so

10. Cecily Plantagenet (1469–1507), 3d
dau. of Edward IV; m. (1) before Dec. 1487,
John Welles (d. 1499), 1st Vct Welles, and
(2) about 1503, Thomas Kymbe or Kyme of
the Isle of Wight (see Mary Anne Everest
Green, *Lives of the Princesses of England,*
6 vols, 1849–55, iii. 404–36). As she died in
1507, Cole is mistaken in assigning the letters to her; it is not known who wrote them
(see Montague Rhodes James, *A Descriptive Catalogue of the Manuscripts in the*
*Library of Corpus Christi College, Cam-
bridge,* 2 vols, Cambridge, 1912, i. 258).

11. Francis Sandford (1630–94), herald.
Cole refers to his *Genealogical History of
Kings of England,* 1677.

12. Robert Masters.

13. Peter Spendelowe Lamborn (1722–74).

14. Thomas Martyn, *Catalogus Horti
Botanici Cantabrigiensis,* Cambridge, 1771.

15. Richard Walker (1679–1764), founder
of the University Botanical Garden, 1762.

like him. Mr Martyn of Sidney, Professor of Botany, publishes the book for the benefit of the garden, which he generously takes care of gratis, as the revenue to support it falls very short. Dr Gooch begged the print of Mr Martyn two or three days ago, but I imagine I shall easily get another.

I accidentally met with the print of Mr Brian of Bury, designed by Mr Kent,[16] in a cottage at Linton.[17]

Copies of three original letters bound up in a MS volume in Benet College Library in Cambridge. Miscellany J.CXIV.

To the most hoñable & my singuler goode L. my L. th'archebysshop of Canterbury his goode Grace:

My goode Lorde,
A Servaunte of myne, Simon Bowier, one of my Gentlemen, hathe desired my Lres of Requeste to yr L. for the next Advowson of the Vycaradge of Blagbourne[18] in Lankyshire, now in the Occupacon of one John Hilton,[19] whose simple Peticon as I could be contented in a greater matter to advaunce, so in this I maye not reasonably denye: desiringe yr L. to further his Sute in suche Sorte, as he may finde himselfe gratefied, & I by yr Gentlenes towardes him bownde to requyte yr good L. with the Lyke as Occasyone hereafter may serve.

Cecilia.

The letter does not seem to be written by the same hand as the signature, which is large, black, and seemingly not straight, as if wrote by an infirm and shaking hand. The seal is an antique of a woman's head. It is at p. 347.—W. C.

16. William Kent (1684–1748), the architect and landscape-gardener.

17. On the Granta, about ten miles SE of Cambridge. Cole's copy continues: 'Looking among some loose papers, I found this memorandum for you which I made last winter and forgot to send to you [see *ante* 18 April 1771]. Dr Sandby, the Master of Magdalen, who desired his compliments to you, prayed me to give you these two additions to your *Royal and Noble Authors.*

'King Charles II penned himself an account of his escape after the battle of Worcester: the MS is in Magdalen College Library, from whence Dr Sandby transcribed it about four or five years ago for Sir David Dalrymple, who published it in an octavo volume. Mr Carte printed part of it [in *A General History of England,* 4 vols, 1747–55, iv. 639–51], but says not from [whence] he had it.

'*Character of King Charles* by the Marquis of Normanby, a MS also in the library of Magdalen College, which Mr Carte likewise mentions, though conceals from whence he had it.'

18. Blackburn.

19. Or Hulton (d. 1582). He was Vicar of Blackburn from 18 June 1562 to 10 Nov. 1580, when he resigned and was succeeded by Edward Walsh (*Victoria History of Lancaster* vi. 241).

My verie goode Lorde,

Yr late Courtesie shewed to one of my Gentlemen, enforceth me to thanke you hartelie therefore, & might have stayed me any farther to trouble you, but that my Chapplen John Willms[20] (whose Sinceritie I dare by Proofe comend unto yr L.) moveth me sumewhat in his Behalf yet ones againe to requeste yr Gentlenes towardes me: that yt maye please yr L. at the Instaunce of thes my Lres, to graunte unto him yr favorable Lres for th'obteyninge of the Personage of Abchurche[21] in London, in the Gyfte of the Quene's Ma:tie, who useth not to passe any suche Graunte wthowt yr L. Assente (as I am enfourmed) wherein yf it maye please yr L. to further him with yr beste Favour, I shall thinke myself dooble bownde unto you, & as Occasyon shall serve endevour to requyte you.

Ffrom Arundell Howse the viiith of Februarii 1563.

Cecilia.

There is no direction remaining to this original letter. The date seems to me to be 1563. Perhaps it may be 1567, the only year when that living was vacant, according to Newcourt,[22] from 1560 to that year.—Wm Cole.

To the right honõable & my singuler good Lorde my L. of Cantrbies Grace, geve these:

My L.,

The Q. Ma:tie being abroad hunting Yesterday in the Forrest, and having had veary good Happ, beside great Sport, she hath thought good to remember yr Grace wt pt of her Pray, and so comaunded me to send you frõ her Highnes a great & a fatt Stagge killed wt her owen Bowe Hand. Wch bycause the Wether was woght, and the Dere somwhat chafed, and daungerous to be caryed so farre wtout some Helpe, I caused him to be p[ar]boyled in this Sort, for the better pservacon of him, wch I dowbt not butt shall cause him to com unto you as I wold be glad he shuld. So having no other Matter at this psent to trouble yr Grace wtall, I wyll comytt you to th'almighty, and with my most harty Comendacyons take my Leave in Hast, at Wyndsor this iiiith of September.

Yr G. assured

R Duddeley.[23]

20. John Williams. He did not get the living requested of Archbishop Parker.

21. The rectory of St Mary Abchurch.

22. See Richard Newcourt (d. 1716), *Repertorium Ecclesiasticum*, 2 vols, 1708–10, i. 430–2.

23. This letter was printed in the *Antiquarian Repertory*, 2d edn, 4 vols, 1807–9, iii. 179.

From Cole, Tuesday 18 June 1771

VA, Forster MS 110, f. 87. Cole kept no copy.
Address: For the Honourable Mr Horace Walpole in Arlington Street, London.
Postmark: Cambridge 19 IV.

Monday, Milton, June 18, 1771.[1]

Dear Sir,

I AM sending my servant to Cambridge this afternoon with this letter to be put into the post office this evening, in order to advertise you that your box of seven letters, together with the copies of them for the printer, and a letter of mine enclosed, will set off on Thursday[2] by the Cambridge coach,[3] and get into town that afternoon. I have sent a line to the master of the coach to take particular care of the box, with orders to send a porter with it to Arlington Street the moment it gets in.

I am, dear Sir,

Your ever faithful and most obliged servant,

Wm Cole

To Cole, Saturday 22 June 1771

Add MS 5952, ff. 86–7.
Cole made four sketches of the proposed cross on the cover of the letter.
Address: To the Reverend Mr Cole at Milton near Cambridge.
Postmark: EK 22 IV.

Arlington Street, June 22, 1771.

I JUST write you a line, dear Sir, to acknowledge the receipt of the box of papers, which is come very safe, and to give you a thousand thanks for the trouble you have taken. As you promise me another letter, I will wait to answer it.

At present I will only beg another favour, and with less shame, as it is of a kind you will like to grant. I have lately been at Lord Os-

1. Cole originally wrote 'Monday, Milton, June 17, 1771,' which is correct; he then changed the date to June 18 without changing the day to Tuesday.
2. Cole originally wrote 'tomorrow.'
3. 'The London and Cambridge Diligence, which carries three passengers at 13s.

6d. each, sets out from the Sun Inn opposite Trinity College at 8 o'clock every morning . . . and gets to the White Horse, Fetter Lane, at 4 o'clock the same afternoon' (*Cantabrigia Depicta,* Cambridge [1776], p. 112; Cooper, *Annals* iv. 331).

sory's at Ampthill.[1] You know Catherine of Arragon lived some time there. Nothing remains of the castle, nor any marks of residence but  a very small bit of her garden. I proposed to Lord Ossory to erect a cross to her memory on the spot, and he will. I wish therefore you could from your collections or books or memory pick out an authentic form of a cross, of a better appearance than the common run. It must be raised on two or three steps, and if they were octagon, would not it be handsomer? Her arms must be hung, like an order, upon it. Here is something of my idea: the shield appendant to a collar. We will have some inscription to mark the cause of erection. Adieu!

Your most obliged,

Hor. Walpole[2]

1. HW was at Ampthill for three days about the middle of June (see HW to Conway 17 June 1771), at which time he wrote the following account of it: 'Ampthill, the seat of John Fitzpatrick Earl of Ossory, whose father Lord Gowran first Earl of Upper Ossory, bought it of the Lord Viscount Fitzwilliam. It is a very large handsome house of 25 windows in front, including the fronts of the wings. The present Earl is greatly improving the seat, under the direction of Mr Chambers, and the park, by the advice of Mr Brown. At the extremity of the park stood the castle, in which Queen Catherine of Arragon resided [in 1533] during the progress of her divorce at Dunstable. Some small indications of the garden still appear: and not long ago a pewter plate with her cypher was dug up there' (*Country Seats* 69–70).

2. Following his copy of HW's letter Cole has written: 'As I knew my own inability to draw out a proper cross for this purpose, I applied to Mr Essex, architect, who was thoroughly skilled in these affairs, for his assistance, who sent me, after the Commencement at Cambridge was over, the following letter, with an admirable neat drawing in Indian ink, which I shall disgrace by my copy on the opposite page:

"To the Rev. Mr Cole at Milton
                    Cambridge, July 3, 1771.
Dear Sir,

I have enclosed the sketch of a cross: the style is suited to the age of Henry VIII, but as near as possible to Mr Walpole's design. I have made it as simple as possible without making it too mean for the person it is intended to commemorate. I have made no scale to the drawing, not knowing the height it is intended to make it, but when a height is determined, the person who executes it may make a scale to the given height, which will serve to measure all the other parts. I should recommend the keeping exactly to the proportions in the drawing, as they are set out agreeable to the principles of Gothic architecture. I think the whole height, including the steps, should not be less than sixteen feet.

I beg you will present my respects to Mr Walpole, and compliments to Miss Cole, and am, Sir,

Your obedient humble servant,

Jam: Essex." '

(Add MS 5845, f. 9v. Cole's copy of the drawing appears at f. 10.)

To Cole, Monday 24 June 1771

Add MS 5952, ff. 88–9.
Address: To the Reverend Mr Cole at Milton near Cambridge.
Postmark: 25 IV.

Strawberry Hill, June 24, 1771.

WHEN I wrote to you t'other day, I had not opened the box of letters, and consequently had not found yours, for which and the prints I give you a thousand thanks, though Count Bryan I have,[1] and will return to you. Old Walker[2] is very like, and is valuable for being mentioned in the *Dunciad;*[3] and a curiosity, from being mentioned there without abuse.

Your notes are very judicious, and your informations most useful to me in drawing up some little preface to the letters, which however I shall not have time now to do before my journey, as I shall set out on Sunday sennight. I like your motto much. The Lady Cecilia's letters are, as you say, more curious for the writer than the matter. We know very little of those daughters of Edward IV, yet she and her sister Devonshire[4] lived to be old, especially Cecily, who was married to Lord Wells, and I have found why: he was first cousin to Henry VII[5] who, I suppose thought it the safest match for her. I wish I knew all she and her sisters knew of their brothers and their uncle Richard III. Much good may it do my Lord of Canterbury with his parboiled stag![6] Sure there must be many more curiosities in Bennet library!

Though your letter is so entertaining and useful to me, the passage I like best is the promise of a visit you make me in the autumn with Mr Essex. Pray put him in mind of it, as I shall you. It would

1. Cole sent him a print of Count Bryan in 1769 (see *ante* 3 Aug. 1769).
2. See *ante* 16 June 1771 n. 15.
3. 'His [Bentley's] hat, which never vail'd to human pride,
Walker with rev'rence took, and laid aside.'
—*The Dunciad,* Book IV, ll. 205–6.
'[Bentley:] "Walker! our hat"—nor more he deign'd to say,
But stern as Ajax' spectre, strode away.'
—ibid., ll. 273–4.

See also Pope, *Works,* ed. Elwin and Courthope, iv. 357, 360.
4. Katherine Plantagenet (1479–1527), 6th dau. of Edward IV; m. (1495) William Courtenay (ca 1475–1511), E. of Devonshire.
5. John Welles (d. 1499), 1st Vct Welles, was half-uncle to Henry VII, being half-brother to Margaret Countess of Richmond, Henry VII's mother.
6. See *ante* 16 June 1771.

add much to the obligation, if you would bring two or three of your MSS volumes of collections with you. Adieu, dear Sir!

Yours with the utmost gratitude,

H. WALPOLE

TO COLE, Monday 12 August 1771

Add MS 5952, ff. 90–1.

Cole wrote before his copy of the letter (Add MS 5833, f. 14v): 'On Wednesday, Aug. 21, I received the following affecting letter from Mr Walpole, then at Paris.'

Address: To the Reverend Mr Cole at Milton near Cambridge, Angleterre. *Postmark:* P 19 AV.

Paris, Aug. 12, 1771.

Dear Sir,

I AM excessively shocked at reading in the papers that Mr Gray is dead![1] I wish to God you may be able to tell me it is not true! Yet in this painful uncertainty I must rest some days! None of my acquaintance are in London—I do not know to whom to apply but to you—alas! I fear in vain! Too many circumstances speak it true— the detail is exact, a second paper arrived by the same post, and does not contradict it—and what is worse, I saw him but four or five days before I came hither;[2] he had been to Kensington for the air, complained of the gout flying about him, of sensations of it in his stomach, and indeed I thought him changed and that he looked ill—still I had not the least idea of his being in danger—I started up from my chair when I read the paragraph—a cannon-ball would not have sur-

1. HW read the account (he noted the fact in *Paris Jour.* 11 Aug.) in 'the *Chronicle*' (to Mason 9 Sept. 1771), that is, either in the *Morning Chronicle* or in the *London Chronicle:* in the latter, 1–3 Aug. 1771, is the following account: 'On Tuesday evening [30 July] died of the gout in his stomach, at his rooms in Pembroke College, Cambridge, Thomas Gray, L.L.B. Professor of Modern History and Languages in that University; a gentleman well known in the literary world as author of the 'Elegy in a Country Church Yard,' and many other much admired pieces. The professorship, worth upwards of 400 l. a year, is in the gift of the crown.'

2. This statement illustrates HW's unreliability in the matter of dates: in his letter to Conway 11 Aug., he says he saw Gray 'two or three days before I came hither,' and to Mason 9 Sept., he says, 'I saw him the day before I left England.'

prised me more! The shock but ceased to give way to my concern, and my hopes are too ill-founded to mitigate it! If nobody has the charity to write to me, my anxiety must continue till the end of the month, for I shall set out on my return on the 26th,[3] and unless you receive this time enough for your answer to leave London on the 20th in the evening, I cannot meet it till I find it in Arlington Street, whither I beg you to direct it.

If the event is but too true, pray add to this melancholy service that of telling me any circumstances you know of his death. Our long, very long friendship and his genius must endear to me everything that relates to him. What writings has he left? Who are his executors[4]—I should earnestly wish, if he has destined anything to the public, to print it at my press[5]—it would do me honour and would give me an opportunity of expressing what I feel for him. Methinks as we grow old, our only business here is to adorn the graves of our friends or to dig our own! Adieu! dear Sir,

Yours ever,

Hor. Walpole

PS. I heard this unhappy news but last night, and have just been told that Lord Edward Bentinck[6] goes in haste tomorrow to England, so that you will receive this much sooner than I expected. Still I must desire you to direct to Arlington Street, as by the surest conveyance to me.[7]

---

3. HW's departure from Paris was delayed by the weather, and he did not reach London until 6 Sept. (*Paris Jour.*).

4. They were James Brown and William Mason.

5. The only MS HW printed was Gray's transcript of Sir Thomas Wyatt the elder's *Defence* (*Jour. Print. Off.* 59).

6. Lord Edward Charles Cavendish Bentinck (1744–1819), 2d son of 2d D. of Portland; m. (1782) Elizabeth Cumberland, eld. dau. of Richard Cumberland the dramatist. HW calls him 'an idle and worthless younger brother' who helped to bring his brother, the 3d D. of Portland, into financial straits (*Last Journals* ii. 448;

see also Elizabeth Duchess of Northumberland, *Diaries*, ed. James Greig, 1926, pp. 89, 133; *Paris Jour. passim*).

7. Cole wrote at the end of his copy of HW's letter: 'I immediately returned an answer and sent my servant to Cambridge with it in order to save this night's post, though except it would get some other conveyance to him, it would remain in London till Mr Walpole's arrival from Paris. My letter was as follows, but the detail of Mr Gray's death I shall omit here, as it is the same with what I have said above.' An abridged copy of Cole's letter to HW 21 Aug. 1771, follows in the MS.

From COLE, Wednesday 21 August 1771

VA, Forster MS 110, ff. 88–9. COLE's copy (abridged), Add MS 5833, f. 15v.

Address: For the Honourable Horace Walpole in Arlington Street, London.

Postmark: Cambridge 22 AV.

Milton, Wednesday, Aug. 21, 1771.

Dear Sir,

THE news you have received is but too true, yet you must have the uneasy situation of uncertainty for some days longer. At least my letter will not be in London time enough to set off for Paris and get to you there before you leave it, for your letter dated from thence Aug. 12, this moment was left here by the Ely postman, at four o'clock, and I am writing this answer while my servant is getting ready to go with it to Cambridge, in order to set out this evening.[1] But at all events, as you leave Paris the 26th, this can't meet you anywhere but in Arlington Street, whither it is directed.

Poor Mr Gray had been complaining some time of the gout flying about him, but had been much out of order with it in his stomach for a week or thereabouts before his death. I heard nothing of his being ill till the morning of the day he died, when Mr Essex, in his way to Ely, called on me to acquaint me with it, and of his danger. In the evening I sent my servant to Cambridge to know how he was, but he was then dying and no messages could be delivered. This was on Tuesday, July 30, and he died that evening about seven or eight o'clock. He desired to be buried very early in the morning at Stoke Poges,[2] so he was enclosed in a leaden coffin, and on the Sunday morning following was carried in an hearse from college, which was to lie at Hodsdon[3] that night and the next at Salt Hill,[4] in order to be near Stoke the next morning. He made the new Master of Pembroke Hall, his particular friend (Mr Browne),[5] his executor, who attended him to the grave, with a cousin who lives at Cambridge (Miss Antrobus),[6] and a young gentleman of Christ's College[7] with

1. But see postmark on this letter.

2. For Gray's will see *Gray's Corr.*, Appendix X, iii. 1283–6.

3. Hoddesdon, in Herts, about 34 miles from Cambridge.

4. In Bucks, about two miles from Stoke Poges, and about 38 miles from Hoddesdon, via the London road.

5. James Brown (1704–84), Master of Pembroke College 1770–84; Vice-Chancellor of Cambridge 1771–2 (see *Alumni Cantab.*; GM Oct. 1784, liv. 798a).

6. Mary Antrobus (b. 1732), Gray's cousin and one of his principal legatees (see *Gray's Corr.* iii. 1284).

7. Not identified.

whom he was very intimate, but whose name I am ignorant of: these, with the husband of another Miss Antrobus,[8] attended the hearse to Stoke. What fortunes he has left behind him he has divided between these two ladies. How much that is I know not: at fir<st it w>as reported £8000 be<tween> them; it is since much lessened, and indeed I s<uppose it> hardly possible for him <to> have saved so much. His books and MSS ar<e all left b>y him to his friend Mr Mason, with a discretionary power to print <or not> as he pleases. Some few days before his death he sent an express to Mr Stonehewer,[9] whom I suppose you know, to beg he would come down to Cambridge, and as Dr Gisburne[10] was accidentally with him when the messenger arrived, he prevailed with that physician to go down with him. This was the more necessary as the Professor here[11] had been sent to, and because it was in the night, refused to attend. But it was too late for advice, and all that could be done was to make his exit as easy as possible.

There is a circumstance, though I have scarce time, which I must relate to you, as it appeared striking to me. The last time I saw him was at the funeral of Dr Long,[12] the late Master of Pembroke. You wrote to me next day, with a desire I would mention something to Mr Gray which I forget:[13] however, I sent my servant with your letter, and in mine,[14] by way of joke, took notice to him of some indecencies and slovenliness I thought I observed in the solemnity for so good a master and benefactor. His answer[15] was in jest also, that they knew no better, having had no funeral in their chapel in anyone's remembrance: that when the next happened, they would apply to me for my advice, which, however, said he, I hope won't yet

8. Richard Comings or Comyns (d. 1799), described at his death as 'a merchant agent to the Sun Fire-Office, and a commissioner under the Income Act' at Cambridge, m. Dorothy Antrobus (b. 1734), sister of Mary Antrobus (see GM July 1799, lxix. 622a).

9. Richard Stonehewer (1728?–1809), tutor and afterwards private secretary of 3d D. of Grafton; obtained for Gray the professorship at Cambridge; inherited from Mason, Gray's library and MSS.

10. Thomas Gisborne (d. 1806), Fellow of St John's College, Cambridge; President of the College of Physicians 1791, 1794, 1796–1803.

11. Russell Plumptre (1709–93), M.D.; Regius Professor of Physic at Cambridge 1741–93.

12. Roger Long (1680–1770), divine and astronomer; Master of Pembroke Hall 1733–70. He died 16 Dec. and was buried 21 Dec. in a vault of Pembroke College Chapel.

13. See ante 20 Dec. 1770.

14. For a fuller account of this letter, the original of which apparently has not survived, see Gray's Corr. iii. 1154–5.

15. Gray's Corr. iii. 1155.

be these forty years. Poor man, I little thought then that his would be the next, and so soon, too!

I can write no more for time, and will be glad, very glad to hear of your safe arrival to England, and shall then wait with impatience to hear from you. The circle of one's nearest and dearest friends draws every day smaller and smaller.

I have a nice cross for the gardens of Lord Ossory, which Mr Essex drew out just when you set out for Paris, and which I will send to you on your arrival. In the meantime, pray God give you a safe and happy voyage, and I am, Sir,

Your most obliged and faithful servant,

WM COLE

From COLE, Saturday 24 August 1771

VA, Forster MS 110, ff. 90–1. COLE's copy, Add MS 5833, ff. 15v, 21v, 22v. *Address:* [From COLE's copy.] For the Honourable Horace Walpole in Arlington Street, London. *Postmark:* None [cf. last paragraph of this letter].

Milton, Saturday, Aug. 24, 1771.

Dear Sir,

NOT being satisfied with my late hasty answer to your letter from Paris,[1] I drank my tea yesterday with the Master of Pembroke, that I might from the fountain-head give you a more authentic account of the subject of your letter, which I gave him to peruse. He was very obliging and communicative, showed me Mr Gray's will,[2] executed July 2, 1770, in which, after desiring to be put into a coffin of well-seasoned oak, without lining either within or withoutside, and to be buried in a vault contiguous to his dear mother in the churchyard of Stoke Poges, and attended to his grave by one of his executors, if anyways convenient, he leaves £500 to Mr Stonehewer, the like to the Master of Pembroke, and the same sum to Mr Mason, precentor of York, to whom he also leaves all his books, MSS, coins, medals, music books both printed and MS, with a discretionary power to do with his papers what he thinks proper. To his two

1. 'after dining yesterday at our County Club' (addition in Cole's copy).

2. 'on a skin of parchment' (addition in Cole's copy).

cousins Antrobus[3] of Cambridge, as well as I can recollect, he leaves each a £1000 and to his servant £50.[4] These, I think, are the most considerable legacies, and, as far as I can judge, he died worth about £6000,[5] having sold his paternal property,[6] not being made for tenants and repairs, placing the money in the Funds, and with part buying an annuity, as I was informed, in order to have a fuller income.[7] The Master and Mr Mason are left residuary legatees. The latter was lately at Cambridge, and, as the Master told me, talked with him about the propriety of sending you an account of the affair, as the long friendship between you and Mr Gray seemed to require it, but as Mr Mason was acquainted with you, the Master put it upon him to do so, but he added that when Mr Mason left Cambridge, where this business took up all his thoughts and time, he went to his residence at York where the hurrying time of the races were beginning,[8] and where Lord John Cavendish[9] was to take up his lodgings with him, so that he doubted whether he had yet wrote to you from his multiplicity of business, but made not the least doubt but you would soon hear from him, and on my expressing a desire that he should be acquainted with the contents of your truly affecting letter, he promised to mention the purport of it in his first letter to him, which would be soon.

All his furniture he divided between his cousins here, who, on the Master's representation, sent back a pianoforte which had been given to him by Mr Stonehewer, but, as the Master said, Mr Gray had accepted of it reluctantly, not liking to put his friend to such an expense, he thought it right that Mr Stonehewer should have it again. On the same principle Mr Mason designs to return an antique seal representing the figure of Justice, which was forced upon him by

3. Mary Antrobus and Mrs Richard Comings. Cole overstates the amounts of all Gray's legacies (see *Gray's Corr.* Appendix X, iii. 1283–6).

4. Stephen Hempsted, afterwards Butler of Pembroke College (see *Universal British Directory*, 5 vols, 1791–8?, ii. 492). Gray also left him 'all my wearing apparel and linen.'

5. Cole noted in his copy of Mason's *Gray* that Gray's property at the time of his death amounted to about £7000 (John Mitford, *Works of Thomas Gray*, 5 vols, 1835–43, i. p. cvii).

6. 'in houses' (addition in Cole's copy).

7. 'Cole was probably misinformed as to Gray's having purchased an annuity for himself. He had done so for Mrs Olliffe' (*Gray's Corr.* iii. 1278 n. 6).

8. The races were held at York 19–24 Aug. (Monday–Saturday) of this year (see *London Chronicle* 22–4, 27–9, 29–31 Aug. 1771).

9. (1732–96), 4th son of the 3d D. of Devonshire; twice Chancellor of the Exchequer, in 1782 and 1783.

Mr Bedingfield,[10] a brother of the baronet,[11] and a great admirer of Mr Gray, who had been delicately scrupulous in receiving it, and knew not how to refuse it with good manners.

By a memorandum the Master lately found, it appears that he was near fifty-five years of age, being born Dec. 26, 1716. He went off pretty easily, considering the nature of his disorder, the gout in his stomach, which occasioned a sickness and loss of appetite; neither would anything stay in his stomach. He complained also for want of proper evacuations, and it was not till the Friday before he died that he had any convulsions, at which time he was seized with the first, and then had them occasionally till his death on the Tuesday night following, though not to any great degree, the Master sitting with him till within half an hour of his exit. He retained the use of his senses to the last, but gave proof of their decay a day or two before his death, which was not unexpected, as he told one of his cousins, 'Molly, I shall die!' The decay I mentioned was this: seeing the Master sitting by him, he said, 'Oh, Sir! Let Dr Hallifax[12] or Dr Heberden[13] be sent to!' He certainly meant for physical assistance: now Dr Hallifax, the King's Professor of Law,[14] and his acquaintance, is a divine and no physician. He gave another proof some few days before his death of his apprehensions of it, for being on his couch when Professor Plumptre and Dr Glynn were consulting about him in the room, giving the Master the keys of his bureau, he told him where to find his purse and to bring him some gold to fee the physicians, which he did with his own hands, and very cheerfully asked them, 'Well, gentlemen! What must this complaint of mine be called, after all?' 'Certainly,' answered the Professor, 'the gout in the stomach, but however,' added he, 'don't be uneasy, as we make

10. 'a Roman Catholic gentleman' (addition in Cole's copy). Edward Bedingfield (1730–18–), son of Sir Henry Arundell Bedingfield (d. 1760), 3d Bt of Oxburgh, Norfolk; friend and correspondent of Gray (see *Gray's Corr.* i. 446–7, ii. 474–5, *et passim*).

11. Sir Richard Bedingfield (1726–95), 4th Bt.

12. Robert Hallifax (1735–1810), apothecary to the King's household and to the Prince of Wales; cr. (1783) Doctor of Medicine by the Archbishop of Canterbury (see William Munk, *Roll of the Royal College of Physicians*, 2d edn, 2 vols, 1878, ii. 336).

13. William Heberden (1710–1801), the elder, practised medicine in Cambridge for several years before removing to London (1748), where he ultimately reached the top of his profession (see Munk, ibid. ii. 159–64). For Cole's account of him, see Brydges, *Restituta* iii. 227–9.

14. Samuel Hallifax (1733–90), D.D., brother of Dr Robert Hallifax; Professor of Arabic, Cambridge, 1768–70; Regius Professor of Civil Law, 1770–82; Bp of Gloucester 1781–9, and of St Asaph 1789–90. Cole is mistaken in assuming that Gray referred to him (see *Gray's Corr.* iii. 1279 n. 10).

no doubt to drive it from thence.' When he told the Master where
to find the purse, he said, 'And Master, if there should be any occasion for it, you will find something else in the same drawer,' meaning his will, which was all that he said on this melancholy subject. I
have been thus minute and particular as I guess you would like to
know the most trifling circumstances and features, that out of the
whole a more striking likeness may be formed.

As it was warm weather and the distance considerable, it was impossible to comply with that part of his will relating to his coffin,
which was wrapped in lead.

Mr Tyson, seeing me pass by in Free School Lane in my way yesterday to Pembroke, called to me out of the window, begging me to
come into his chamber to look at a drawing he had just finished of
Mr Gray, which I have a notion he intends either to send to you or,
if he etches it, to inscribe to you, for I did not well understand him.
It is very like him, but I think not more so than the etching by Mr
Mason, which no doubt you have, and which he would persuade me
is very unlike, though in my opinion his own is copied from it.

As my sister goes to Bath on Monday, having paid me a two-
months visit, I shall take the opportunity of sending this by her,
together with Mr Essex's plan of the stone cross and his letter about
it to me,[15] and wishing you once more a safe and happy arrival, I remain, dear Sir,

Your ever obliged and faithful servant,

Wm Cole

To Cole, Tuesday 10 September 1771

Add MS 5952, ff. 92–3.

Address: To the Reverend Mr Cole at Milton near Cambridge.
Postmark: [Isleworth?] 12 SE.

Strawberry Hill, Sept. 10, 1771.

HOWEVER melancholy the occasion is, I can but give you a
thousand thanks, dear Sir, for the kind trouble you have taken
and the information you have given me about poor Mr Gray. I received your first letter at Paris; the last I found at my house in town,

---

15. This drawing has not been located.
The cross is engraved in Camden's *Britan-*   *nia,* ed. Richard Gough, 3 vols, 1789, i. opp.
329.

where I arrived only on Friday last.[1] The circumstance of the Professor[2] refusing to rise in the night and visit him, adds to the shock. Who is that true Professor of Physic? Jesus! is their absence to murder as well as their presence?

I have not heard from Mr Mason, but I have written to him.[3] Be so good as to tell the Master of Pembroke, though I have not the honour of knowing him, how sensible I am of his proposed attention to me, and how much I feel for him in losing a friend of so excellent a genius. Nothing will allay my own concern like seeing any of his compositions that I have not yet seen. It is buying even them too dear—but when the author is irreparably lost, the produce of his mind is the next best possession. I have offered my press to Mr Mason, and hope it will be accepted.

Many thanks for the cross, dear Sir; it is precisely what I wished. I hope you and Mr Essex preserve your resolution of passing a few days here between this and Christmas. Just at present I am not my own master, having stepped into the middle of a sudden match in my own family. Lord Hertford is going to marry his third daughter to Lord Villiers,[4] son of Lady Grandison,[5] the present wife of Sir Charles Montagu. We are all felicity, and in a round of dinners—I am this minute returned from Beaumont Lodge at Old Windsor,[6] where Sir Charles *Grandison*[7] lives. I will let you know, if the papers do not, when our festivities are subsided.

I shall receive with gratitude from Mr Tyson either drawing or etching of our departed friend,[8] but wish not to have it inscribed to me, as it is an honour more justly due to Mr Stonehewer. If the Mas-

1. 6 Sept.

2. Russell Plumptre; see *ante* 21 Aug. 1771 n. 11.

3. See HW to Mason 9 Sept. 1771.

4. Lady Gertrude Seymour Conway (1750–93), m. (10 Feb. 1772) George Mason-Villiers (1751–1800), 2d E. Grandison. HW's opinion of the couple is given to Mann 9 Sept. 1771.

5. Elizabeth Villiers (d. 1782), only dau. and surviving child of John Fitzgerald (otherwise Villiers), 1st E. Grandison; cr. (1746) Viscountess Grandison of Dromana and (1767) Viscountess Villiers and Countess Grandison; m. (1) Aland John Mason, of Waterford and (2) in 1763, Lt-Gen. Sir Charles Montagu (d. 1777), K.B., younger

brother to George Montagu, HW's correspondent.

6. Sir Charles Montagu occupied Beaumont Lodge from 1768 to about 1774, when he sold it to Thomas Watts, Esq. Warren Hastings purchased it in 1786 (Thomas Eustace Harwood, *Windsor Old and New*, 1929, pp. 187–98).

7. 'Mr Walpole calls Sir Charles Montagu in this letter jocosely *Sir Charles Grandison*, in allusion to a favourite romance of this name, which is the more apropos as Sir Charles Montagu married Lady Grandison' (Cole's note, following his copy of HW's letter, Add MS 5833, f. 22v).

8. Gray.

ter of Pembroke will accept a copy of a small picture I have of Mr
Gray,[9] painted soon after the publication of the Ode on Eton,[10] it
shall be at his service—and after his death I will beg it may be bequeathed to his college.[11] Adieu! Dear Sir,

Yours most sincerely,

Hor. Walpole

From Cole, Monday 16 September 1771

VA, Forster MS 110, ff. 92–3. Cole's copy, Add MS 5833, ff. 23v–25v.[1]
Address: For the Honourable Mr Horace Walpole in Arlington Street, London.
Postmark: 18 SE.

Milton, Sept. 16, 1771. Monday.

Dear Sir,

I SENT my servant to Cambridge with your letter on Saturday to
the Master of Pembroke, being disabled to stir myself out of my
chair, with a sudden weakness in my knee: a complaint I have been

9. By John Giles Eccardt. The original
is now in the National Portrait Gallery.

10. Gray's *Ode on a Distant Prospect of
Eton College* was published at HW's suggestion in the summer of 1747.

11. The portrait still hangs in the Master's Lodge at Pembroke.

---

1. Cole's copy reads: 'I herewith send
you the Master of Pembroke's note to me,
which I received yesterday by his servant.
As the Master will probably be Vice-Chancellor in a month or two, I could wish
your designed present [the portrait of
Gray] could be sent him before he is out
of his office.

'I give you joy of your cousin's marriage,
and hope it will be happy on all sides. The
prospect of happiness, if we may judge
from the number of divorces and elope-
ments within these two or three last years
among the nobility, is very casual, but I
make no doubt of the prudence of the
young lady from the great virtue and strict
morality of her father. I dread the consequences of a match in agitation that more
nearly affects me, as I am somewhat allied,
and have always been as one of the family

of my Lord Montfort, who is now upon
the point of matrimony with Miss Blake,
whose brother Patrick Blake married Sir
Charles Bunbury's sister. I heartily wish
the young lady, who is not quite of age,
success and happiness, but I really see no
great probability of it. I must needs say I
wonder at her courage, which must be
great. She has known my Lord and his
ways of [sic] some time, so must thank
herself if she throws herself away for a
title and very fine place, for such is
Horseth. Her fortune is about £12,000, and
her figure gentile [sic]. My Lord told me
of this two or three months ago, but I did
not believe him, upon the presumption
that no woman of fashion would take such
a step. As it is to be in November [the marriage took place 29 Feb. 1772], when the
lady comes of age, I pray God a new manner of living may take place, than was the
practice from last November, the election
of Sir Sampson Gideon for the county, on
the Marquis of Granby's death, for many
months following. Such a constant. succession of drunkenness would have dis-
patched any other but one of his Lordship's constitution, which nothing seems

frequently subject to. Thank God, today I find myself on the mending hand, after having been laid up for about a fortnight. The Master yesterday sent his servant over with the following note, which I would have enclosed but for the double postage:

Mr Brown presents his respectful compliments, and wishes to hear a better account of Mr Cole's health. He desires the favour of Mr Cole to express, in his name, to Mr Walpole his best thanks for the intention Mr Walpole entertains of giving him a copy of the picture of Mr Gray. He will be very glad of preserving such a memorial of Mr Gray before his eyes as long as he lives, and at his death will leave it to the College. He trusts the Society will be ever sensible how honourable to the College was Mr Gray's relation to it, and that they will think Mr Walpole's present one of their best ornaments.

Pembroke Hall, Sept. 15, 1771.

I give you joy of your cousin's marriage, and hope it will be happy on all sides.

I have not seen Mr Essex since I received <your> last favour, but if I am well enough, will most readily <accom>pany him to Strawberry Hill before Christmas. I know he has set his heart on that journey, as he has mentioned it to me more <than> once.

I can't help relating to you a most shocking accident that happened in this county this week: the family I am much acquainted with, and the poor unhappy gentleman[2] was a fellow commoner, I

to hurt. Sir John Cotton called upon me the other day and proposed to me to endeavour to persuade him to throw up the colonelcy of the Cambridgeshire militia, which brings him into very low company, and is the occasion of his Lordship's annually exposing himself for a month together, in May, to the whole University, where his conduct is so void of all decency and behaviour, that one would suppose he contrived every method he could invent to demean himself and make himself low and despicable to all the county. It seems a madness, and is unaccountable, considering his excellent parts and capacity. I told Sir John that surely he must know Lord Montfort better than to think that even an angel who would attempt to persuade him to anything, even though he did not disapprove it, could have any hopes of success. I know Sir John wants

his son to take his Lordship's place, and won't submit to have him rank beneath the others, for the officers are some of the lowest people of the county.

'From one melancholy subject, if matrimony may be called so, give me leave to go on to another still more unhappy. It happened the last week at a place called Kneesworth, the seat of the Nightingales of this county, in the parish of Bassingbourn. I am much acquainted . . .' [for continuation, see fourth paragraph of the letter].

2. Edward Nightingale (1726–82), 8th Bt (but never assumed title) of Kneesworth, Cambs; admitted pensioner, Peterhouse, Cambridge, 1744; d. at Town Malling, Kent (see Thomas Alfred Walker, *Admissions to Peterhouse*, Cambridge, 1912, p. 283; Betham, *Baronetage* ii. 3).

think in your time or soon after, of Peterhouse, from whence his
father[3] took him after two or three years' stay, to the Inns of Court,
and sent him abroad on his travels. The young man was a remarkable handsome person and a great favourite of his parents, who were
of the chief families of this county, with an estate of about £1500 per
annum. The father, Mr Nightingale, was a very sensible man, and
an acting Justice of the Peace, but violent, and for some time before
his death thought to be disordered in his intellects. The son was
confined in a madhouse for some years before his father's decease, I
suppose these twenty years, but on the death, the beginning of this
year, of the second brother,[4] who had the management of the
estate, Mrs Nightingale, the mother, a very worthy woman, and who
had a pique against her third son,[5] who had married[6] against her in-
clinations, in order to deprive him of the benefit of looking after the
estate, determined to send for her eldest son out of the madhouse,
probably thinking that by her care of him, he would behave with
some sort of propriety. Accordingly he was sent for home, and occasionally went to market to Royston now and then, and paid bills,
etc. However, this week a mad fit overtook him, and going into the
yard, he ordered the servant who used to attend him to get him his
horse immediately; the man told him he had not breakfasted, but
that he would go in and get it and wait on him forthwith: this did
not satisfy him, but, swearing at him, ordered him to get the horse
directly. The fellow, foreseeing that all things were not right, runs
into the parlour to Mrs Nightingale, who came out and told her son
that if he went on at this rate he must be sent up to London again,
upon which he immediately knocked her down with his fist, and
getting a stake, beat the poor woman so, breaking three of her ribs
and her skull in two places, that she died on Thursday.[7] Mr Hop-

3. Edward Nightingale (1696–1750), 7th
Bt (but never assumed title); m. Eleanor
Ethelston (1700–71), dau. of Charles Ethelston, by whom he had six sons and five
daughters (ibid.).

4. Geoffrey Nightingale, died in May
1771 (ibid.).

5. Gamaliel Nightingale (1731–91), 9th
Bt (but never assumed title); Captain R.N.;
m. Maria Clossen (1739–89), 'dau. of Peter
Clossen, a merchant at Hamburgh, but a
native of Mechlenburgh Schwerin' (ibid.).
He 'had the command of a twenty-gun

ship in the Royal Navy' (addition in Cole's
copy).

6. 'an innkeeper's daughter of the name
of Classen, at Hamburgh, and thereupon
on ill terms with the mother, though Captain Gamaliel's wife is a very prudent and
accomplished woman' (addition in Cole's
copy).

7. The Thursday preceding the date of
Cole's letter was 12 Sept., but Mrs Nightingale died Saturday, 14 Sept. (Betham,
Baronetage, loc. cit.). Cole, however, in his
copy of the letter, says specifically that she

kins,[8] the surgeon of Cambridge who attended her the two or three days she survived, asked him if he meant to kill his mother. He answered, 'God forbid,' but said he meant to kill the servant. I am much concerned, as I have long been acquainted with the family.

I must abruptly bid you adieu, etc.,

WM COLE

Lord Montfort is going to be married to Miss Blake,[9] sister to Mr Blake[10] who married Sir Charles Bunbury's sister. Most people think the lady has good courage.

To COLE, Saturday 12 October 1771

Add MS 5952, ff. 94–5.

Address: To the Reverend Mr Cole at Milton near Cambridge.
Postmark: 12 OC.

Strawberry Hill, Oct. 12, 1771.

Dear Sir,

AS our wedding will not be so soon as I expected, and as I should be unwilling to have you take a journey in bad weather, I wish it may be convenient to you and Mr Essex to come hither on the 25th of this present month. If one can depend on any season, it is upon the chill suns of October, which, like an elderly beauty, are less capricious than spring or summer. Our old-fashioned October, you know, reached eleven days into modern November, and I still depend upon that reckoning when I have a mind to protract the year.

Lord Ossory is charmed with Mr Essex's cross, and wishes much to consult him on the proportions. Lord Ossory has taken a small

died 'Thursday, Sept. 12: that is, two or three days after the fact.'

8. Allen Hopkins (d. 1777). At this time he was one of the three surgeons who attended Addenbrooke's Hospital gratis (see 'The State of Addenbrooke's Hospital' 1771, p. 7, appended to T. Rutherforth's *A Sermon preached before the President and Governors of Addenbrooke's Hospital on Thursday, June 27, 1771*, Cambridge, 1771; *Register of . . . St. Michael's Parish, Cambridge, 1538–1837*, ed. John Venn,

Cambridge, printed for Cambridge Antiquarian Society, 1891, p. 156a).

9. Mary Anne Blake (d. ca 1830), dau. of Andrew Blake of St Kitts and Montserrat in the West Indies, by Marcella French; m. (29 Feb. 1772) Thomas Bromley, 2d Bn Montfort.

10. Patrick Blake (ca 1730–84), M.P. for Sudbury, 1768–84; became (1772) 1st Bt, of Langham, Suffolk; m. (ca 1765) Annabella Bunbury (b. 1745), sister of Sir Thomas Charles Bunbury (1740–1821), 6th Bt.

house very near mine,[1] is now and will be here again after Newmarket.[2] He is determined to erect it at Ampthill, and I have written the following lines to record the reason;

> In days of old here Ampthill's tow'rs were seen,
> The mournful refuge of an injur'd queen.
> Here flow'd her pure, but unavailing tears;
> Here blinded zeal sustain'd her sinking years.
> Yet Freedom hence her radiant banners wav'd,
> And Love aveng'd a realm by priests enslav'd.
> From Cath'rine's wrongs a nation's bliss was spread,
> And Luther's light from Henry's lawless bed.[3]

I hope the satire on Henry VIII will make you excuse the compliment to Luther, which like most poetic compliments does not come
from my heart—I only like him better than Henry, Calvin, and the
Church of Rome, who were bloody persecutors. Calvin was an exe-
crable villain and the worst of all, for he copied those whom he pretended to correct. Luther was as jovial as Wilkes, and served the
cause of liberty, without canting.

Yours most sincerely,

HOR. WALPOLE

From Cole, Saturday 19 October 1771

VA, Forster MS 110, ff. 94–5. Cole kept no copy.

Address: <For the Hono>urable Mr Horace Walpole in Arlington Street,
London. *Postmark:* Cambridge [The date is missing. It probably was on the
square which HW cut out of the MS (see n. 4 below)].

Milton, Oct. 19, 1771.

Dear Sir,

YOUR most agreeable and entertaining letter found me with a
little touch of the gout or rheumatism or some other weakness
in my knee that confined me absolutely to my chair for a fortnight.

---

1. Not identified.
2. The second October meeting ended
26 Oct. Lord Ossory raced several horses
(see *Bailey's Racing Register*, 3 vols, 1845,
i. 346–7).
3. These verses were reprinted in the
London Magazine, Oct. 1773, p. 514; in

Camden's *Britannia*, ed. Gough, 1789, i.
329; in LI vi. 287; and in GM Feb., 1819,
lxxxix. 104, where the question is raised if
they were by Fitzpatrick. This is answered
ibid. 197. The cross was engraved by
Schnebbelie in *Antiquaries' Museum*.

I am now, thank God, as well as usual, yet with rheumatic complaints flying about me.

You are so kind to mention 25th of this month for Mr Essex and my waiting on you at Strawberry Hill for a day or two, and am sorry the objection comes from myself. My servant that very day sets out for Buckinghamshire[1] with two of his sisters[2] who are here with me, and won't return to me till about five or six days after, and I am so very helpless that I can't well do without him on a journey. So that except a day or two in the first week in November would suit you, I must beg you to excuse my visit till next summer, but as Mr Essex will necessarily be in town about the end of October and stay there above a fortnight, he will certainly call on you at any day you will fix, and by that means see Lord Ossory and yourself.

I am very glad that the cross pleases and is likely to be erected. The verses are admirable, and every line conveys an history. The arms should be England and France quarterly impaling Castile and Leon quarterly, which probably may be sufficient, though in a window of Thorney Abbey[3] her arms accurately are thus blazoned: England and France quarterly for Henry VIII, impales quarterly first and fourth quarterly, gules, a tower, or, for Castile; second and third, argent, a lion rampant, gules, for Leon; second, or, four pallets gules for Arragon, impaling Arragon on two flaunches argent, as many eaglets displayed, sable, beaked, gules, for Sicily; third as the second; fourth as the first.

I thought I would mention this as so inconsiderable a circumstance might pass by unnoticed. I will just give a sketch of both[4] and conclude myself, dear Sir,

Your ever faithful and obliged servant,

WM COLE

1. That is, Bletchley, where the Wood family lived, and where Cole was living when Tom entered his service (see *Blecheley Diary, passim*).

2. One of these was probably Molly Wood, who is mentioned in the *Blecheley Diary* as being Cole's cook for a month and helping in the kitchen on various occasions. She wished to go with Cole to Waterbeach as his servant (ibid., *passim*). The name of the other sister is not known.

3. In Cambs, seven miles NE of Peter-

borough. Cole visited the Abbey, 7 July 1744, wrote a description of the arms, and made a drawing of them (see Palmer, *Monumental Inscriptions* 170, Plate XIII).

4. Only the drawing of the arms as they appeared in Thorney Abbey remains in the MS; the other drawing has been cut out: it probably was used as a model for the stone-cutter in making the cross. HW evidently considered the arms in Thorney Abbey too complicated for his purpose.

I would have answered your letter before, but was in daily and hourly expectation of seeing people to settle an affair which I had much on my mind,5 and they never came till the day before yesterday. Till I had seen them I was not master of my own motions.

To Cole, Wednesday 23 October 1771

Add MS 5952, ff. 96–7.

Address: To the Reverend Mr Cole at Milton near Cambridge.
Postmark: [Isleworth?] 23 OC.

Strawberry Hill, Oct. 23, 1771.

I AM sorry, dear Sir, that I cannot say your answer is as agreeable and entertaining as you flatter me my letter was; but consider, you are prevented coming to me, and have flying pains of rheumatism—either were sufficient to spoil your letter.

I am sure of being here till tomorrow sennight the last of this month: consequently I may hope to see Mr Essex here on Monday, Tuesday, or Wednesday next. After that I cannot answer for myself on account of our wedding, which depends on the return of a courier from Ireland. If I can command any days certain in November, I will give you notice; and yet I shall have a scruple of dragging you so far from home at such a season. I will leave it to your option; only begging you to be assured that I shall always be most happy to see you.

I am making a very curious purchase at Paris, the complete armour of Francis the First.1 It is gilt in relief, and is very rich and beautiful. It comes out of the Crozat collection.2 I am building a

---

5. Presumably the 'affair' was connected with the sale of Cole's estate at Haddenham and Aldreth, or with arrangements for an annuity which he purchased with the money.

---

1. HW paid £52.10.0 for the armour, in the purchase of which Mme du Deffand acted as his agent. The armour was sold SH xix. 77, for £320.5.0, and is now (1936) on loan in the Stuyvesant Collection in the Metropolitan Museum of Art, New York. The armour is no longer believed to have been Francis I's, but is assigned to

the late sixteenth century, and is believed to be of German origin. Only the upper half of the suit survives (see Bashford Dean, *The Collection of Arms and Armor of Rutherfurd Stuyvesant,* Privately Printed, [New York] 1914). HW describes the armour more fully in *Description of SH, Works* ii. 439. See also *Walpoliana* ii. 83 and *SH Accounts* 138–45.

2. It was formed by Pierre Crozat (1661–1740), secretary to the King, who acquired a magnificent collection of pictures and *objets d'art,* which, at his death, descended to his three nephews: Louis-François (d.

small chapel too in my garden[3] to receive two valuable pieces of antiquity, and which have been presents singularly lucky for me. They are the window from Bexhill with the portraits of Henry III and his Queen,[4] procured for me by Lord Ashburnham.[5] The other, great part of the tomb of Capoccio,[6] mentioned likewise in my *Anecdotes of Painting*[7] on the subject of the Confessor's shrine, and sent to me from Rome by Mr Hamilton[8] our minister at Naples. It is very extraordinary that I should happen to be master of these curiosities. After next summer, by which time my castle and collection will be complete (for if I buy more, I must build another castle for another collection)[9] I propose to form the catalogue and description,[10] and shall take the liberty to call on you for your assistance. In the meantime there is enough new to divert you at present.

I am, Dear Sir, Yours most sincerely,

HOR. WALPOLE

1750), Joseph-Antoine (d. 1750), and Louis-Antoine (1700–70). The last added to the collection, which was dispersed after his death (see *Grande Encyclopédie*).

3. For HW's description and a plate of the chapel, see *Description of SH, Works* ii. 507. Apparently the building of the chapel had not begun at this time, for HW to Mason 9 May 1772 says: 'The foundations of the chapel in the garden are to be dug on Monday.' It was not completed until May 1774 (see *SH Accounts* 151–4).

4. 'The window was brought from the church of Bexhill in Sussex. The two principal figures are King Henry III and Eleanor of Provence his queen, the only portraits of them extant. King Henry died in 1272, and we know of no painted glass more ancient than the reign of his father King John. These portraits have been engraved for the frontispiece to the [1st volume of] *Anecdotes of Painting*' (Inscription over the door of the chapel, *Description of SH, Works* ii. 508). The window was sold SH xxiv. 84.

5. John Ashburnham (1724–1812), 2d E. of Ashburnham.

6. 'The shrine in front [of the chapel] was brought in the year 1768 from the church of Santa Maria Maggiore in Rome, when the new pavement was laid there. This shrine was erected in the year 1256 over the bodies of the holy martyrs Simplicius, Faustina, and Beatrix, by John James Capoccio and Vinia his wife; and was the work of Peter Cavalini, who made the tomb of Edward the Confessor in Westminster Abbey' (Inscription over the door of the chapel, *Description of SH, Works* ii. 508). It was sold SH xxiv. 85. Cavalini's authorship of the tomb is open to doubt (*Anecdotes*, ed. Wornum, i. 17).

7. See *Works* iii. 25–6.

8. William Hamilton (1730–1803), M.P. for Midhurst, 1761–4; knighted 1772; plenipotentiary at Naples 1764–1800. He married, as his second wife, the celebrated Emma Harte, Lady Hamilton.

9. Nevertheless, as the *Accounts* and *Description of SH* show, HW continued to add to SH (see *SH Accounts* 16, 18, 165–7, 175–6; 'Genesis of SH').

10. *A Description of the Villa of Horace Walpole . . . at Strawberry Hill*, of which HW printed 100 copies (six on large paper) in 1774 (see *Jour. Print. Off.* 60).

From Cole, Sunday 3 November 1771

VA, Forster MS 110, f. 96. Cole kept no copy.
Address: For the Honourable Mr Horace Walpole in Arlington Street, London.
Postmark: None [Essex conveyed the letter to HW; see below].

Milton, Nov. 3, 1771.

Dear Sir,

I AM very sorry my own situation prevented my waiting on you on 25 October, but I was then in the very midst of settling my own affairs which I hope to finish tomorrow in good part, and though not much to my mind, yet necessity has no law. After which time I shall be more at leisure, yet as you are so kind to excuse my stirring this winter, shall, with infinite pleasure, wait on you next summer at Strawberry Hill and lend my assistance in any employ you will please to put me to. I long much to see that place again, as I am told it has received great embellishments since I was there. Francis I's armour complete, with the window from Bexhill, are such acquisitions, with Capoccio's altar or tomb, that one would wonder how they possibly could meet altogether at Strawberry Hill in such a short space.

Mr Essex sets out for London on Tuesday, where he stays about three weeks. He proposes carrying this to Arlington Street, and will call on you at any time you will appoint.

I have a favour to beg of you. A relation of mine, a considerable tradesman in the City, one Mr Mawdesley,[1] has a great desire to see your house at Strawberry Hill. If you will be pleased to indulge him and two or three friends with him at any <tim>e, for I don't know that he is in any hurry, you will add a new obligation to the many already conferred on, dear Sir,

Your ever faithful and obliged servant,

WM COLE

1. Roger Mawdesley, a cheesemonger of London, partner of Abraham Daking, 'they being the most considerable cheesemongers in London, or England'; a nephew of Hector Mawdesley, Cole's brother-in-law (Cole, *Jour. to Paris* 3–4). In a *List of* . . . *Liverymen of London,* 1792, p. 92, he is listed as a wholesale cheesemonger, a member of the Clothworkers Company, and his residence is given as 60 Bishopsgate Street.

From COLE, Friday 17 January 1772

VA, Forster MS 110, f. 97. Cole kept no copy.
Address: For the Honourable Horace Walpole in Arlington Street, London.
Postmark: Penny Post Paid. [See last paragraph.]

Milton, Jan. 17, 1772.

Dear Sir,

NOTHING but sheer idleness has kept me from writing to you
these six months,[1] but as I hear nothing from you, I begin to
long to know that you are well. My indolence is the more inexcus-
able as two months ago Mr Bannerman sent me in a letter two of
his proposals, one of which only is enclosed.[2] Probably he meant one
for me, though I shall hardly subscribe for it. Indeed I am to blame,
as possibly he may accuse you for my neglect; and yet I thought of
writing every week, and still might have delayed it but for a passage
I met with in reading Mr Anstis's[3] *Observations Introductory to an
Historical Essay upon the Knighthood of the Bath,* London, quarto,
1725. At p. 53 he mentions a summons for persons to receive that order at the coronation of King Edward V, on 22 June, the order being
dated the 5th of that month; in the Appendix, p. 34, No. 54, is the
list of the designed Knights, with the order, taken from Rymer,[4] vol.
12, p. 185.

The reason of my sending this, which possibly you may have overlooked, is that I think Dr Mill[e]s somewhere <o>r other seems
to make a doubt whether there ever was su<ch a> design.[5] This
proves it even without your roll.[6]

I hope you'll excuse this hasty scrawl, being going to Cambridge,
and will get Mr Lort to put this into the penny post from, dear Sir,

Your ever faithful and obliged servant,

WM COLE

1. A *façon de parler;* Cole's last letter was written only ten weeks before.
2. The proposal is missing. Bannerman probably wished to publish a series of plates by subscription.
3. John Anstis (1669–1744), the elder, Garter King-of-Arms and author of several heraldic works.
4. That is, his *Foedera.*

5. Cole refers to Dean Milles's *Observations on the Wardrobe Account (Archaeologia* i. 361–83), particularly to pp. 364–5. Masters states the 'doubt' more clearly in his *Some Remarks (Archaeologia* ii. 209).
6. The coronation roll or wardrobe account for 1483, which was the bone of contention between Milles and HW.

To Cole, Tuesday 28 January 1772

Add MS 5952, ff. 98–9.
Address: To the Reverend Mr Cole at Milton near Cambridge.
Postmark: EK 28 IA.

Arlington Street, Jan. 28, 1772.

IT is long indeed, dear Sir, since we corresponded. I should not have been silent if I had had anything worth telling you in your way—but I grow such an antiquity myself, that I think I am less fond of what remains of our predecessors.

Thank you for Bannerman's proposal, I mean, for taking the trouble to send it, for I am not at all disposed to subscribe. Thank you more for the notes on King Edward; I mean too for your friendship in thinking of me. Of Dean Milles I cannot trouble myself to think any more. His piece is at Strawberry; perhaps I may look at it for the sake of your note. The bad weather keeps me in town, and a good deal at home, which I find very comfortable, literally practising what so many persons pretend they intend, being quiet and enjoying my fireside in my elderly days.

Mr Mason has shown me the relics of poor Mr Gray. I am sadly disappointed at finding them so very inconsiderable. He always persisted, when I inquired about his writings, that he had nothing by him. I own I doubted. I am grieved he was so very near exact—I speak of my own satisfaction; as to his genius, what he published during his life will establish his fame as long as our language lasts, and there is a man of genius left. There is a silly fellow, I do not know who, that has published a volume of letters on the English nation, with characters of our modern authors.[1] He has talked such nonsense on Mr Gray,[2] that I have no patience with the compliments he has paid me.[3] He must have an excellent taste! and gives me a

1. *Letters Concerning the Present State of England. Particularly respecting the politics, arts, manners, and literature of the times,* 1772. The author has not been identified.

2. The anonymous writer considers Gray 'the strongest instance in the world of what little avail learning is of to a poet; and yet more so, that plainness and simplicity are more sure of pleasing than the most laboured exertions. I do not mean, that this writer is of genuine simplicity in any of his works, but the *Country Churchyard* is a beautiful poem; and, compared with his Pindaric odes, simplicity itself. It will be read and admired when the latter are forgotten; an affected obscurity, and a broken composition of fits and starts, did well in the Greek, but are vile in English' (ibid. 360).

3. HW is 'one of the most agreeable, spirited and lively writers that this age has produced: with him, the *Gentleman* is never lost in the author: his *Royal and*

woeful opinion of my own trifles, when he likes them, and cannot see the beauties of a poet that ought to be ranked in the first line. I am more humbled by any applause in the present age, than by hosts of such critics as Dr Milles. Is not Garrick reckoned a tolerable author, though he has proved how little sense is necessary to form a great actor? His *Cymon*,[4] his prologues and epilogues and forty such pieces of trash are below mediocrity, and yet delight the mob in the boxes as well as in the footman's gallery. I do not mention the things written in his praise, because he writes most of them himself. But you know any one popular merit can confer all merit: two women talking of Wilkes, one said he squinted—t'other replied—'Squints!— Well, if he does, it is not more than a man should squint.' For my part, I can see how extremely well Garrick acts, without thinking him six feet high. It is said Shakespeare was a bad actor; why do not his divine plays make our wise judges conclude that he was a good one? They have not a proof of the contrary, as they have in Garrick's works—but what is it to you or me what he is. We may see him act with pleasure, and nothing obliges us to read his writings. Adieu! Dear Sir,

Yours most sincerely,

HOR. WALPOLE

To COLE, Tuesday 9 June 1772

Add MS 5952, ff. 100–1.

Cole noted on his copy of the letter: 'Wednesday, June 10, 1772, I received the following letter from the honourable Mr Horace Walpole, with the following queries on the former part of the letter, in another hand' (Add MS 5844, f. 28).

Address: To the Reverend Mr Cole at Milton near Cambridge.
Postmark: EK 9 IV.

[Enclosure.]

A gentleman abroad[1] who is making a collection of all the books and

Noble Authors is the best of his works, and is full of ingenuity and penetration: his *Historic Doubts* show what a thorough master he is of the English history' (ibid. 399–400).

4. *Cymon. A Dramatic Romance . . .*

the music by Mr Arne, 1767. It is founded on Dryden's fable of *Cymon and Iphigenia*, which in turn is taken from Boccaccio's *Decameron* v. i.

1. Not identified.

manuscripts in every language which treat of the Order of Malta, whether historical, political, descriptive, etc., etc.,—in a word, of all books which regard in any respect that order, or even of such as have been written by any of the Knights, has applied to a person in England to procure him any books or manuscripts in the English language, which fall under the above description. He particularly names three to him, as the only ones he has as yet been able to hear of, and the titles of which he has extracted from the Catalogue of the Bodley Library.[2] They are:

1. d'Aubusson, Pet.,[3] Master of Rhodes, *His Life,* London, 1679, 8vo.
2. Favyn, André,[4] *Le Théâtre d'Honneur et de Chevalerie, ou l'histoire des ordres militaires traduit en Anglois,* London, 1623.
3. Malta.[5] Desperate Assault and Surprising of Two Castles of the Turks. London, 1603, 4to.

He farther adds that in the histories of the Order of Malta frequent mention is made of an English gentleman, a Knight of that Order, by name Oliver Starquei (Starkey)[6] who lived about 1555, as of a distinguished scholar in polite literature and an elegant poet. He was created *Commendator* of Muennington (Mannington).[7] The gentleman who is making this collection is very desirous to know whether any of his works are extant, and are to be come at.

It would be considered as a singular favour, if Mr Walpole would be so obliging as to communicate any lights he may have upon this subject. If he could point out any *books,* a farther favour would be asked of him, which is, to recommend some bookseller, or other fit person, who would

2. *Catalogus impressorum Librorum Bibliothecae Bodleianae in Academia Oxoniensi,* 2 vols, Oxford, 1738.

3. Pierre d'Aubusson (1423–1503), French cardinal; Grand Master of the Order of St John of Jerusalem, 1476; defended Rhodes against the Turks (1479) and compelled them to raise the siege, 27 July 1480. The book mentioned here is *The Life of the renowned Peter d'Aubusson, Grand Master of Rhodes,* translated from the French of Dominique Bouhours.

4. André Favyn (b. ca 1560), *The theater of honour and knighthood. Or, A compendious chronicle and historie of the whole Christian world . . . with all the ancient and moderne military orders of knighthood in euery kingdome,* translated from the French, 1623.

5. *Newes from Malta, written by a gentleman of that iland, to a friend of his in Fraunce; shewing the desperate assault and surprising of two castles of the Turkes by the Italian forces.*

6. (d. 1588), Commander of Quenyngton; lieutenant-Turcopolier; Bailiff of Aquila, 1569; Secretary to John de la Valette (d. 1568), Grand Master of the Knights of Malta; present at siege of Malta; 'buried in the vault of the Grand-Masters in the coventual church of St John, the only knight of the Order so distinguished' (Whitworth Porter, *A History of the Knights of Malta,* rev. edn, 1883, p. 730; see also p. 424).

7. An error; see preceding note.

make it his business afterwards to find *them,* and who would be well rewarded for his trouble.

Arlington Street, June 9, 1772.

Dear Sir,

THE preceding paper was given me by a gentleman,[8] who has a better opinion of my bookhood than I deserve. I could give him no satisfaction, but told him I would get inquiry made at Cambridge for the pieces he wants. If you can give me any assistance in this chase, I am sure you will; and as it will be trouble enough, I will not make my letter longer.

Yours ever,
H. W.

From Cole, Thursday 11 June 1772

VA, Forster MS 110, ff. 102–4. Cole's copy, Add MS 5844, ff. 28–9.

Address: For the Honourable Mr Horace Walpole in Arlington Street, London. Single Sheet. *Postmark:* Cambridge 13 IV.

Bale's account[1] of Oliver Starkey, from Grimoaldus,[2] is this, [part 2] p. 74, Cent. 11:

Oliverus Starkey, licet homo sit mihi tantum ex nomine notus, locum nihilominus in nostrorum scriptorum catalogo, justissimo jure poscit, quum opuscula quædam, multa eruditione referta, scriptor et ipse secum adferat. Ita enim ille a primis studiorum annis, ut ex scriptis apparet, doctis assuevit artibus, ut maximarum rerum noticiam inde non infeliciter hauserit. Unde inter cætera condidit eloquenter ac nitide,

Rhythmos in Ecclesiasten, Lib. I.
Discursum in Sallustium, Lib. I.

Num alia præter hæc scripserit, affirmare adhuc non possum. Claruisse fertur anno salutis humanæ 1550, Edwardo sexto regnante.

Pitts's account[3] of him is as follows, p. 739:

Oliverius Starcaius, natione Anglus, vir a varia multiplicique doctrina

---

8. Not identified.

1. John Bale, *Scriptorum Illustrium Maioris Britanniae,* 2 pts, Basle, 1557–9. Cole has modernized the spelling of a few words in the quotation.

2. Nicholas Grimald (1519–62), chaplain to Bp Ridley.

3. John Pits or Pitseus (1560–1616), Roman Catholic priest; biographer; author of *Relationum Historicarum de Rebus Anglicis Tomus primus quatuor Partes complec-*

multum commendatus, quique potissimum, ab elegantia Latini sermonis, magnam commeruit laudem. Diversa de diversis materiis opuscula scripsit omni eruditionis genere referta, quibus etiam stylus comptus et tersus non parum addidit decoris. Ex ejus autem lucubrationibus adhuc extare ferunt, ut inter alios testis est Grimoaldus,

> *Rithmos in Ecclesiastem, Librum unum.*
> *Discursum in Salustium, Librum unum.*

Aliorum operum titulos hactenus non invenio. Claruit anno postquam Dei Filius in carne apparuit 1550, regnante in Anglia Edwardo sexto.

In neither of these writers is the least mention of his being a Knight of Malta. This might be ascertained probably by his pedigree, which no doubt is in the Cheshire visitations, many of which are in the British Museum. The family was seated at Over in Cheshire, and gave for arms, argent, a stork, sable. Hugh Starkey of Over, Esq., Gentleman Usher to King Henry VII, died 1500, and is buried in that parish church, where many of the family lie buried, as in my vol. 29,[4] pp. 54–5, etc., they are entered, being there in 1757. They came from the adjoining parish[5] of Olton,[6] the heiress of which name they married, and quarter Olton with their own arms.

In the *Harleian Catalogue*,[7] No. 139, [Art.] 100, is:

Notes of the families of Olton and Starkey, which Mr Bostoke found in the Church of Over (but thinks are wrong in some particulars). Fo. 26b.

These notes are probably such as I have mentioned, viz., epitaphs of the families of Starkey and Olton in Over Church, which might be more numerous and perfect in Mr Bostock's time than when I visited it in 1757, passing through the parish to Vale Royal Abbey.

In the same catalogue, vol. 2, No. 6794, [Art.] 1, is this tract:

Discorso sopra la Fratella di Malta.

This is probably some reflections upon the *Discorso* which, from the title, seems to be some ludicrous story concerning the order.

I have a small book written by two enthusiastic Quaker women

---

tens, Paris, 1619. The work is usually known by its running title, *De Illustribus Angliae Scriptoribus*.

4. Add MS 5830.

5. Cole first wrote 'the neighbouring.'

6. Oulton Low, a township in the parish of Over, not a parish itself (see Lysons, *Mag. Brit.* iii. 719).

7. *A Catalogue of the Harleian Collection of Manuscripts . . . in the British Museum*, 2 vols, 1759.

who were inspired to travel into Italy to convert the Pope and other popish princes. Its title is:

A true account of the great trials and cruel sufferings undergone by those two faithfull servants of God, Katherine Evans and Sarah Cheevers, in the time of their above three years and a half's confinement in the Island of Malta. London, 8vo, 1663. Pages 292.

with

A brief discovery of God's eternal truth, etc. Written in the Inquisition of Malta by a servant of the Most High, called Katherine Evans. London, 8vo, 1663. Pages 101.

In the *Catalogue of the MSS in the Harleian Library,* vol. 1, No. 1386, [Art.] 28, is:

A note (i.e. the arms) of certen Knights of the Rhodes, or of St John of Hierusalem. Fo. 48b.

In the same catalogue, vol. 2, No. 2009, [Arts.] 98, 99, 100, are the three following tracts relating to the order:

98. Tract of Peter Leicester, Esq., concerning the institution of Knights Templars and Knights Hospitallers of St John of Hierusalem, with the charters of priviledges granted to the said Hospitallers: applicable to the townshippe of Nether-Tabley in Com. Cestr. (which was of their fee) and wherein himself and his tenants were concerned. p. 326.

This was transcribed from the original (which was written 1649) by the second Randal Holme, A. D. 1650.

99. Carta qua Frater Nicholaus Valens Magister Domus Hospitalis Jerusalem in Com' Cestr' recepit Symonem filium Mar. de Bertumley in defensione sua et custodia. p. 333.

100. Instrumentum quo Frater Georgius Sutton, Miles, et Magister de Burton S. Lazari Jerusalem in Anglia, et ejusdem loci confratres, innotescunt se in eorum confraternitatem recepisse Dnm' Willelmum Browne, suorumque privilegiorum, indulgentiarum, ac aliorum pietatis operum participem in omnibus fecisse. Dat' 10 Junii A° Dni' 1486 (Cum absolutionis formula). p. 335.

Dear Sir,   Milton, June 11, 1772.

I RECEIVED your commission yesterday, and wish it was more in my power to assist the gentleman than I am afraid I shall be able. The time of writing at all began, in a manner, when these valiant knights, who besides, I suppose, seldom troubled themselves with literary amusements, were no more in this island. Therefore I should guess very few materials of this sort especially relating to the English Knights of Malta are to be met with. As there were no commanderies to invite them, it is very possible that few of our Catholic gentry thought much of a military order which could yield them no emoluments and besides might give more umbrage to a government always jealous of their power. Other orders, besides religious zeal, had occasional establishments either in gentlemen's families at home or in their convents abroad, and often had prelatures conferred upon them in France, Italy and Spain.

I have Favine's *Theater of Honour* in folio, 1623. It is too common a book to make an offer of it to you, as it is easily had in any shop: the Quaker book and Favine are, however, much at the gentleman's service if they are worth his acceptance.

Our schoolfellow Mr Bryant's book in quarto to prove, among other things, that the Island of Malta was not the Melita on which St Paul landed,[8] is a subject too nice to be transmitted to that island, though, by the learned, it is agreed that he had proved his point: a subject, it seems, that was treated of before by a learned abbé,[9] though unknown to Mr Bryant till within this last year.

I have the names, arms and epitaphs of several of the commendators or preceptors of Shengay and Wendy[10] in Cambridgeshire, but as these seem too minute to fall under the description in your letter, I will not trouble you with them. They may be had, if desired, on sending me word.

I am concerned that I can assist the gentleman no farther. I should have a double pleasure in doing so, was it in my power: by obliging you, and forwarding an undertaking that I am pleased with.

8. Jacob Bryant (1715–1804), classical scholar and antiquary; at Eton and King's with HW and Cole. His 'book in quarto' was *Observations and Inquiries relating to various parts of ancient history; containing dissertations on the wind Euroclydon, and on the island Melite*, Cambridge, 1767.

9. 'In the year 1730 there was published, at Venice, in a quarto volume, of 300 pages, a Latin dissertation, entitled, *D. Paulus Apostolus in mari quod nunc Venetus sinus dicitur naufragus, et Melitae Dalmatensis insulae post naufragium hospes, &c.*, i.e. "An essay in which it is proved that the shipwreck of St Paul, mentioned in the 27th and 28th chapters of the *Acts*,

happened on the coasts of the island of Méléda, in Dalmatia, and not on the coasts of the isle of Malta. By Ignatio Giorgi, a Benedictine of the congregation of Méléda." ' (Letter from *Crito*, GM, Supp. for 1775, xlv. 633.)

10. About five miles NW of Royston. The remains of the preceptory of Shingay, founded in 1140, were torn down about 1794. Both Shingay and Wendy were formerly the seats of preceptories of the Knights Hospitallers of the Order of St John of Jerusalem (see Lysons, *Mag. Brit.* ii. 251, 275). Cole's collections for Shingay and Wendy, to which he refers, are in Add MS 5810, ff. 111, 115; 5812, f. 214.

My visit to Strawberry Hill was prevented last autumn by various accidents. I hope I shall be luckier another time, for I want much to revisit a place which has been much improved, and that I thought impossible since I was there last time. I grieve for the loss you sustained by the explosion of the powder mills at Hounslow.[11] I took an exact account of all the arms in every window of your house.[12]

Mr Gough is going to give an additional volume to his *Topography*.[13] If you have any memoranda[14] to add or correct anything in the book, he will, I am sure, be much obliged to you for them.

I am, dear Sir,

Your ever obliged and faithful servant,

WM COLE

I am going to Cambridge to dinner, and will ask a friend of mine, Mr Farmer of Emmanuel College, whether he knows anything more of this matter than I do.

To COLE, Wednesday 17 June 1772

Add MS 5952, ff. 102–3.

Cole received the letter Friday, 19 June (see following letter).

Address: To the Reverend Mr Cole at Milton near Cambridge.

Postmark: Isleworth 18 IV.

Strawberry Hill, June 17, 1772.
Dear Sir,

YOU are a mine that answers beyond those of Peru. I have given the treasures you sent me to the gentleman from whom I had the queries. He is vastly obliged to you, and I am sure so am I, for

11. Eight painted-glass windows at SH were broken by the explosion of three powder mills at Hounslow, 6 Jan. 1772 (see HW to Lady Ossory 5 [6] Jan.; to Conway 7 Jan. 1772. Cf. *Lloyd's Evening Post* 3–6 Jan. 1772, a reprint of which Cole doubtless saw in the *Cambridge Chronicle*.

12. Cole's account (Add MS 5841, ff. 78–84), which contains numerous drawings of the arms he describes, is dated 3 Sept. and 29 Oct. 1762. In Cole's copy (Add MS 5844, f. 29) this sentence reads: 'I took an exact account of all the arms in every window of your enchanting castle at Strawberry Hill about ten years ago.'

13. The second edition of Gough's *Anecdotes of British Topography*, 1768, was published in two volumes, 1780, with the title *British Topography. Or, An Historical Account of what has been done for illustrating the Topographical Antiquities of Great Britain and Ireland*.

14. Cole notes on this passage: 'In my letter to Mr Walpole of June 11, in a postscript [*sic*], though I have omitted transcribing it, I desired him, if he had any notes on Mr Gough's *British Topography*, to communicate them, as he was going to give a new edition. I had then forgotten that I had myself taken a copy of all that

the trouble you have given yourself—and *therefore* I am going to give you more. *King Edward's Letters* are printed;[1] shall I keep them for you, or send them, and how? I intend you four copies; shall you want more? Lord Ossory takes an hundred, and I have as many; but none will be sold.

I am out of materials for my press. I am thinking of printing some numbers of miscellaneous MSS from my own and Mr Gray's collections. If you have any among your stores that are historic, new, and curious, and like to have them printed, I shall be glad of them. Among Gray's, are letters of Sir Thomas Wyat the elder.[2] I am sure you must have a thousand hints about him. If you will send them to me, I will do you justice,[3] as you will see I have in *King Edward's Letters*.[4] Do you know anything of his son the insurgent[5] in Queen Mary's reign?

I do not know whether it was not to Payne the bookseller,[6] but I am sure I gave somebody a very few notes to the *British Topography*. They were indeed of very little consequence.

I have got today and am reading with entertainment[7] two volumes in octavo, *The Lives of Leland, Hearne and Antony Wood*.[8] I do not know the author,[9] but he is of Oxford. I think you should add that of your friend Brown Willis. There is a queer piece on freemasonry in one of the volumes, said to be written, on very slender

he had written on the margins of his book on that subject' (Add MS 5844, f. 29v). HW's copies (both edns) were sold SH i. 57, v. 16.

---

1. The printing was completed 13 June 1772 (*Jour. Print. Off.* 17).

2. HW printed in *Miscellaneous Antiquities, Number II*, 1772, Gray's transcript of 'Sir Thomas Wyat's Defence.' HW wrote in the introduction: 'The following papers of Sir Thomas Wyat were copied by Mr Gray from the originals in the Harleian Collection, now in the British Museum. . . . What Mr Gray thought worth copying, who will not think worth reading?' (p. 3).

3. HW makes no acknowledgment of the information he received from Cole concerning Sir Thomas Wyatt.

4. Cole's notes are there signed with his initials, 'W.C.'

5. Sir Thomas Wyatt (1521?–54), the younger, who took part in the insurrection to prevent the marriage of Queen Mary with Philip of Spain, and was executed for high treason.

6. Thomas Payne (1719–99), bookseller in The Strand, London; known as 'Honest Tom Payne.' He was one of the booksellers who published Gough's *British Topography*.

7. Cf. HW to Conway 22 June 1772.

8. *The Lives of those eminent Antiquaries, John Leland, Thomas Hearne, and Anthony à Wood*, 2 vols, Oxford, 1772. HW's copy was sold SH v. 124.

9. William Huddesford (1732–72), Keeper of the Ashmolean Library 1755–72, was the author of the life of Leland and editor of the work. Joseph Pote, the bookseller at Eton, apparently enlisted Huddesford's aid (see DNB *sub* Huddesford and Pote). HW had written Huddesford at least one letter (19 Feb. 1771).

authority, by Henry VI with notes by Mr Locke[10]—a very odd conjunction! It says that arts were brought from the East by *Peter Gower*.[11] As I am sure you will not find an account of this singular person in all your collections, be it known to you, that Peter Gower was commonly called Pythagoras. I remember our newspapers insisting that Thomas Kouli Khan[12] was an Irishman, and that his true name was Thomas Collaghan.

On reading over my letter, I find I am no sceptic, having affirmed no less than four times that *I am sure*. Though this is extremely awkward, *I am sure* I will not write my letter over again, so pray excuse or burn my tautology.

Yours ever,

H. W.

PS. I had like to have forgotten the most obliging and to me most interesting part of your letter, your kind offer of coming hither. I accept it most gladly, but for reasons I will tell you, wish it may be deferred a little. I am going to Park Place, then to Ampthill and then to Goodwood,[13] and the beginning of August to Wentworth Castle,[14] [so] that I shall not be at all settled here till the end of the latter month. But I have a stronger reason. By that time will be finished a delightful chapel I am building in my garden, to contain the shrine of Capoccio and the window with Henry III and his Queen. My new bedchamber[15] will be finished too, which is now all in litter—and besides September is a quiet month; visits to make or receive are over, and the troublesome go to shoot partridges. If that time suits you, pray assure me I shall see you the first of September.

From COLE, Sunday 21 June 1772

VA, Forster MS 110, ff. 98–9. COLE's copy, Add MS 5844, ff. 29v, 30.

Cole enclosed this letter and the following in one packet, which he entrusted

10. Op. cit. i. 67–8. Appendix No. vii. 96–103.

11. Ibid. i. 98–9 nn.

12. Nâdir Shâh, or Thamas Kouli Khân (1688–1747), celebrated Persian conqueror, of Turkish extraction; King of Persia, 1736–47 (see Joseph Thomas, *Universal Pronouncing Dictionary*, 5th edn [1930]).

13. In Sussex, three miles NE of Chichester; seat of the Dukes of Richmond.

14. In Yorkshire, near Barnsley; seat of William Wentworth, 2d E. of Strafford. For an account of this part of HW's tour, see *Country Seats* 71–5.

15. The Great North Bedchamber, or State Bedchamber, the most elaborate bedroom in the house (see 'Genesis of SH'; *SH Accounts* 12–3; *Works* ii. 494–503).

to Gough. The latter carried it to London and mailed it in the Penny Post (see three following letters).

Address: For the Honourable Mr Horace Walpole at Strawberry Hill in Twickenham, Middlesex. *Postmark:* 27 IV.

Milton, Sunday, June 21, 1772.

Dear Sir,

YOUR most obliging letter came on Friday, and yesterday was too hot to do anything but read some cool book.[1] I am very glad the slender account I sent met with so fair reception. Since I wrote that letter my friend Mr Farmer of Emmanuel, who wrote an ingenious book on *The Learning of Shakespeare,*[2] has sent me to this place a most curious and scarce book, being *Statuta Hospitalis Hierusalem.*[3] It is in folio, printed at Rome in 1588, full of fine prints, containing the heads of all the masters to Cardinal Hugh de Loubenx Verdala,[4] whose head is twice elegantly engraved, and various prints of him in different situations throughout the book, representing the functions of the knights: the first is a representation of Hugo de Loubenx on his knees before Pope Sixtus V,[5] who is putting the Cardinal's hat on his head. There is a neat map of the island and a plan of the city of Valetta. As Mr Farmer has written the following notes on a blank leaf, I will transcribe them, especially as it is possible from the scarcity of the book that it may not readily be met with:

This is a curious and scarce work, says Dr Rawlinson in his *Fresnoy,* vol. 2, p. 81.[6] He does not, however, appear to have seen it, as he gives 1584 for the date. The Pope's licence is dated 1586.

'The reason, I apprehend, why he gives 1584 for the year of printing is from the last leaf of the book, where is Master Hugh de Loubenx Ver-

1. 'in the shadiest part of my garden' (addition in Cole's copy).

2. *An Essay on the Learning of Shakespeare,* of which the first and second editions were published at Cambridge, 1767.

3. Edited by J. B. Rondinellus, 'Index . . . per P. Veltronium . . . nuper adjectus' (*BM Cat.* 1586 edn). In 1798, at the sale of Farmer's Library (7 May and 35 days following) this book was sold (7th day, lot 1896) (see *Bibliotheca Farmeriana,* 1798).

4. Hugh Loubenx de Verdala (d. 1595),

Grand Master of the Knights of Malta, 1581–95 (see Whitworth Porter, *A History of the Knights of Malta,* rev. edn, 1883, pp. 504–6).

5. Felice Peretti (1521–90), elected Pope 24 April 1585.

6. Richard Rawlinson (1690–1755), *A New Method of Studying History,* 2 vols, 1728; 2d edn, 1730. Translated from the French of Nicolas Lenglet du Fresnoy (1674–1755). The title as given by Rawlinson ii. 81, is *Statuta Ordinis S. Joannis Hierosolymitani.*

dala's confirmation of these statutes: "Datum Melitæ in Conventu nostro durantibus Retentionibus Capituli Generalis die 23 Mensis Julii 1584."— W. Cole.'

In Vogt's *Catal. Libr. Curios.*, p. 705,[7] we have the following account: 'Ptolomæi Veltronii, Statuta Ordinis Hospitalis S. Johannis Hiersolymitani. Romæ, cum Privilegio, in fol., 1588, e Fig. Liber eximiæ Raritatis, a paucissimis allegatus, & vix centesimo visus. Struvii, Bibl. Antiq., an. 1706, p. 225.[8] Gerdes, Florileg., p. 115.'[9]

Thus far Mr Farmer: but as antiquaries in such a chase, as you are pleased to express it, are apt to follow the scent wherever it will lead them, so in these researches the least hint may be useful or agreeable to a gentleman who is making collections for an history of Maltese antiquities. At the last page, therefore, of this book, in the writing of an Italian, nearly as old as the book itself, as I guess, is this written:

Gio. Batta Vinto,[10] melo[11] che sia esalto nella virtù sua così eccellente essendo Persona assai meritevole.

If anything more was added, it is cut off by the binder. If he was one of the Knights of Malta (and if he was not I see no reason for this being wrote here) it is a little scrap of an anecdote relating to him.

While this our nation was connected with this noble order, the chief officer was entitled *turcopoliero*. This title is thus defined in the nineteenth chapter, *De Verborum Significatione*, p. 201 of this curious book:

Turcopolerius Baiulivus [Bailivus][12] Conventualis venerandæ Linguæ Angliæ dicitur a Turcopolis, qui, ut in Historiis Bellorum a Christianis in Syria gestorum habetur, Equites erant levis Armaturæ.

Dr Rawlinson, in his *New Method of Studying History*, vol. 1, p. 200, mentions several particulars relating to the Maltese historians. This is a translation from Langlet du Fresnoy, and in the second vol-

7. Johann Vogt (1695–1765), *Catalogus Historico-Criticus Librorum Rariorum*. Farmer's edition of this work (Hamburg, 1753) was sold in his sale (see n. 3 above), 1st day, lot 84.

8. Burkhard Gotthelf Struve (1671–1738), *Bibliotheca Antiqua*, Jena, 2 vols, 1705–6.

9. Daniel Gerdes (1698–1765), *Florilegium Historico-Criticum Librorum Rariorum*, Groningen, 1740.

10. Not identified.

11. This word is deleted in the MS.

12. Cole's interpolation.

ume, p. 81, is a catalogue of all the writers upon the subject of the military orders, which may be useful to consult.

In Hall's *History of England*,[13] fo. cciii b, cciiii a, b, is a curious account of the taking of Modon by the Prior of Rome and Turcuplyar of England with sixty knights, six of which were English. It is the more curious and authentic as it was sent by the Grand Master of Rhodes to the Lord Prior of St John's in England.

I am sorry for it, but I see I must make this only a cover to another part of my letter in answer to your last, or rather send my other packet by another post. However, will just mention a circumstance and conclude this epistle.

Some day in the last week our Vice-Provost, Dr Glyn, whom you probably remember when at school and afterwards at college, came over to me here to beg that I would intercede with you for leave to see your house at Strawberry Hill, and this very morning, as soon as college chapel was over, he was with me again on the same errand. As he is the most practising physician in the University, and on that account can't often leave Cambridge, from whence he has not stirred these four years, and has a call on his private affairs to London in about a week, he is very desirous before he returns to College to see your house. If, therefore, on his calling at Strawberry Hill and giving his name, in your absence, that favour might be shown him, you will oblige him and me very singularly. I will give him a line when he comes,[14] as a passport to you, which you will excuse, I hope, in, dear Sir,

Your ever obliged and faithful servant,

Wm Cole

On St George's Day,[15] three or four antiquaries in the University, with myself, were invited by our brother Mr Farmer of Emmanuel College, to dine with him in his chambers, when we agreed upon a little party, one of which was Dr Glyn, to make an excursion to town for two days, one of which was dedicated to this same scheme of seeing your house. However, it did not take effect.

---

13. Edward Hall (d. 1547), author of a chronicle (usually called 'Hall's Chronicle'), *The Union of the two Noble and Illustre Famelies of Lancastre and York;* 1548.

14. Cole's introduction is missing.
15. 23 April. Cole's copy continues: 'in honour of our Society [of Antiquaries], and in imitation also.'

From COLE, Monday 22 June 1772

VA, Forster MS 110, ff. 100–1. COLE's copy, Add MS 5844, ff. 30v, 31.
Address and Postmark: See introductory note to preceding letter.

Dear Sir,   Milton, June 22, 1772.

YOUR kind offer of four copies of *King Edward's Letters* is too luxurious a treat to me not to be desirous of having them as soon as may be. I shall therefore be greatly obliged to you if they could be sent to me by the Cambridge coach or wagon,[1] and directed to be left for me at Mr Bentham's at Cambridge. If it would not be impertinent in me after so bountiful a present, I would beg one for the present Vice-Chancellor, Dr Browne, Master of Pembroke Hall. My reason for it is this. About six weeks ago he called upon and made me a present, very genteelly, of a silver box in which Mr Gray used to keep his seals and other trinkets, as a memorial of him: being a present from him and Mr Mason, as joint executors.[2]

Mr Mason has lately had a very elegant and most like print taken of him.[3] He gave the Vice-Chancellor ten, which he disposed of to his friends, and as he promised to send for ten more in order to give me one, I begged him to let me also have one for you. He said, No, because he meant to make you the present himself. When it comes, I will take care of it for you.

The proposal you make me flatters my vanity and does me the greatest honour possible, yet I doubt I have nothing among my trash that is worthy of appearing in such good company: my materials, like the collector of them, are fit only to live in obscurity, yet if, upon a search among them, I should discover anything that will not dis-

1. See n. 21 below.

2. 'Wednesday, May 13, 1772, the Vice-Chancellor, Dr Brown, came to me at Milton, and in his and Mr Mason's name desired my acceptance of a large silver embossed snuff box, or more in shape and size of what people use for a tobacco box, by its ornamented figures, seemingly made in China, as a memorial of Mr Gray. The Vice-Chancellor told me that they designed this elegant agate seal of arms and curious bloodstone as a present to Mr Walpole, who has long since sent the College the picture of Mr Gray which he desired their ac-

ceptance of. In 1774 I gave this silver box to my brother Apthorp, who is a great smoker of tobacco, which I never could conquer' (Cole's note, Add MS 5833, f. 25v). Brown delivered the bloodstone and seal to HW 25 Aug. 1772 (see Brown to HW that date).

3. That is, of Mason himself, not of Gray. HW understood that Cole meant the print was of Gray (see HW to Mason 21 July 1772). This print is not in EBP. It was from a sketch by Mason's servant Charles Carter (information from Mr Leonard Whibley).

credit the company they will keep, I will certainly submit them to your judgment to reject or retain them as you see proper. In the meantime I herewith send you all the notices relating to Sir Thomas Wyat, father and son, that have fallen in my way.

In Ascham's *Scholemaster,* by Upton, edit. 1711, p. 184, Sir Thomas Wyat (the elder) is mentioned as one of the best translators of the Latin poets of the age he lived in.[4]

See Mr Dod's *Catholic Church History of England,* vol. 1, p. 191,[5] where is an abridged account of his life, but nothing more than what is to be found in Wood's *Ath. Oxon.,* vol. 1, p. 49,[6] which is reprinted in the second volume of Leland's *Itinerary,* and some notes added by the editor Tom Hearne, Preface, p. iii, iv, etc., at which place is a wooden cut of Sir Thomas Wyat, with verses on his death, entitled *Næniæ in Mortem Thomæ Viati Equitis incomparabilis, Joanne Lelando Antiquario Auctore.*[7] Mr Tyson etched a copy of this cut some three or four years ago, which you have.[8]

In the glossary, p. 641, at the end of Peter Langtoft's *Chronicle,* vol. 2,[9] mention is made of an history in MS by Dr Nicholas Harpsfield,[10] where, among other passages of secret history, it is said that Sir Thomas Wyat confessed to Henry VIII that he had debauched Anne Bullen before the King had any thoughts of espousing her, and therefore dissuaded him from that purpose.[11]

I suppose the 'Master Wyat who hathe now bought the Lordeshipe of Ailesford in Kent,' mentioned by Leland in his *Itinerary,* vol. 8, p. 92, was the father of the elder Sir Thomas Wyat; if not, Sir Thomas himself.

In Leland's *Collectanea,* vol. 5, is prefixed his *Encomia illustrium*

4. HW printed this sentence almost *verbatim* in *Miscellaneous Antiquities, No. II* 8.

5. Charles Dodd (1672–1743), Roman Catholic divine, whose real name was Hugh Tootel; author of *The Church History of England, from . . . 1500, to . . . 1688,* 3 vols, Brussels, 1737–42.

6. Cole refers to the first edition, 2 vols, 1691–2. HW printed the reference to the second edition, i. 56, in *Miscellaneous Antiquities, No. II* 4.

7. Cole refers to the second edition, 9 vols, Oxford, 1744–5, to which he was a subscriber.

8. HW condensed this passage: 'It is called *Naenia* . . . Mr Tyson, of Bennet

College Cambridge, has copied it' (*Miscellaneous Antiquities, No. II* 9 n).

9. *Peter Langtoft's Chronicle . . . Transcrib'd and now first publish'd, from a MS in the Inner-Temple Library by Thomas Hearne,* 2 vols, Oxford, 1725.

10. Nicholas Harpsfield (1519?–75), historian and theologian. Cole refers to Harpsfield's *A Treatise on the Pretended Divorce between Henry VIII and Catharine of Aragon,* edited by Nicholas Pocock for the Camden Society in 1878. Cole quotes the passage in question to HW *post* 9 July 1772.

11. This paragraph was printed *verbatim* by HW in *Miscellaneous Antiquities, No. II* 12.

Virorum, where, at p. 116,[12] is a copy of Latin verses *Ad Thomam Viatum, Equitem clarissimum.*

In Bale's *Scriptores Angliae illustres, Pars secunda,* pp. 103–4,[13] is his account of the elder Sir Thomas Wyat, whom probably he knew personally.

In the *Sylloge Epistolarum,* at the end of *Titi Livii Foro-Juliensis Vita Henrici Quinti,* published by Hearne, p. 155,[14] is Queen Mary's proclamation against Sir Thomas Wyat the younger.

Before Hearne's edition of *Camdeni Annales Elizabethae* is a preface by the editor, who, at p. lxxiii and following,[15] exculpates the Princess Elizabeth from having any concern in Sir Thomas Wyat's rebellion under her sister, and in proof thereof produces an original letter of that Princess to the Queen, in which she utterly disavows, with a good round oath, any knowledge of it. This letter is quoted by Mr Warton in his *Life of Sir Thomas Pope,* p. 67, just now published, in which work, at pp. 44, 45, 65, 79,[16] the younger Sir Thomas Wyat is occasionally mentioned, but nothing particularly worth sending for it if not by you.[17]

Sir Thomas Wyat the elder, High Sheriff for Kent, 28 Henry VIII. . . . . . . the younger, High Sheriff for Kent, 4 Edward VI. (Fuller's *Worthies,* p. 93.)[18]

An account of Sir Thomas the father in Fuller's *Worthies in Kent,* pp. 81–2.

In Weever's *Fun. Monuments,* pp. 852–3, is some account of Sir Thomas the elder, which is chiefly transcribed into Fuller aforesaid.

In Strype's *Memorials,* vol. 3, pp. 86–9, 97–8, is an account of Sir Thomas Wyat's rebellion in Queen Mary's reign, taken from MSS and other authorities.

These are all the hints I can furnish you with relating to these

---

12. *Joannis Lelandi Antiquarii De Rebus Britannicis Collectanea. Ex Autographis descripsit ediditque Tho. Hearnius,* 6 vols, Oxford, 1715. Cf. *Miscellaneous Antiquities, No. II* 9.

13. HW quotes from this passage, *Miscellaneous Antiquities, No. II* 4, and refers to Bale again at p. 8.

14. HW did not use this note.

15. *Guilielmi Camdeni Annales Rerum Anglicarum et Hibernicarum Regnante Elizabetha . . . Eruit ediditque Tho. Hearnius,* 3 vols, Oxford, 1717.

16. Thomas Warton (1728–90). *The Life of Sir Thomas Pope, Founder of Trinity College Oxford,* Oxford, 1772.

17. HW made no use of this paragraph and does not seem to have had the book.

18. Thomas Fuller, *Worthies of England,* 1662. Cole's reference (to the section on Kent) was quoted by HW in *Miscellaneous Antiquities, No. II* 11.

gentlemen, yet if you will employ me in any further researches, I will cheerfully execute your orders.

Until I received your last letter I had utterly forgot that when I was last at Strawberry Hill, with your leave I transcribed all your notes from the margins of the *British Topography*. This paper I laid aside with others when I came home, and from my constant occupation with workmen, never thought more of it. On your mention of having given these notes to Payne or somebody, I recollected the circumstance and readily recovered the paper, which I send this post, in the state I first took it, to Mr Gough. There are some corrections and observations that he ought to be much beholden to you for, and which it would have been a pity he should have been deprived of. Possibly you may have given them to Payne.

There is a paltry sketch of a life of Mr Browne Willis by Dr Ducarel, which I think is inserted in the *Biographia*.[19]

It was a pleasant mistake to christianize Pythagoras. The etymology now found out, I am afraid, will prove another fatal argument against the high antiquity of our University, and the founder of Pythagoras's School at the back of St John's College[19a] be reduced to some obscure Peter Gore of the fourteenth or fifteenth century.

I long much to pay my devotions in your chapel, and shall as impatiently wait for the first of September as sportsmen of another cast do to destroy partridges.

I am, dear Sir,

Your most obliged and faithful servant,

Wm Cole

The Cambridge fly puts up in Gray's Inn Lane,[20] and the Cambridge wagon by Mr Salmon in Bishopsgate Street.[21]

19. Andrew Coltee Ducarel, *Some Account of Browne Willis, Esq.*, read at the Society of Antiquaries, 22 May and 12 June 1760. It is a pamphlet of eight pages. The account in the *Biographia Britannica*, to which Cole refers, is said to be 'taken chiefly' from Ducarel's account.

19a. See *post* 3 Feb. 1781.

20. 'The fly for four passengers at 12s. each, which goes to London every day by Chesterford, Hockerill, and Epping, sets out at 8 o'clock from the Rose, in the Marketplace, and gets to the Queen's Head,

Gray's Inn Lane, at 5 o'clock the same evening; from whence another fly sets out every morning for Cambridge' (*Cantabrigia Depicta*, Cambridge [1776], p. 112). In 1763 the fly left at 7 o'clock in the morning, one more hour being required for the journey than in 1776 (see Cooper, *Annals* iv. 331).

21. 'James Salmon, Cambridge carrier, has wagons set out from his warehouse in Cambridge, every Monday and Tuesday, and get in at the Green Dragon Inn in Bishopsgate Street, London, every Tuesday and Thursday; return from thence every

Monday, eight o'clock in the evening: Mr Gough, Mr Tyson, Mr Essex and another London antiquary[22] just now having been to see Ely, called here in their way, and as he goes to London[23] on Thursday, I thought it would be as well to send all my packets together.

To Cole, Sunday 28 June 1772

Cole's copy, Add MS 5841, f. 31. The original is missing.

Address: [From Cole's copy.] To the Reverend Mr Cole at Milton near Cambridge.

[Strawberry Hill,] June 28, 1772.

Dear Sir,

AS I am getting into my chaise I received your packet,[1] for which I have only time to give you a thousand thanks. I have sent you six copies,[2] and have left orders for Dr Glynn and his friends to see my house; but I fear it will be to great disadvantage; for my housekeeper[3] is very ill, and there will only be a maid that can tell them nothing.

Yours ever,

H. W.

To Cole, Tuesday 7 July 1772

Add MS 5952, ff. 104–5.

Address: To the Reverend Mr Cole at Milton near Cambridge. *Postmark:* Isleworth 7 IY.

Strawberry Hill, July 7, 1772.

Dear Sir,

I SENT you last week by the Cambridge fly, that puts up in Gray's Inn Lane, six copies of *King Edward's Letters,* but fear I forgot to

Wednesday, Thursday, and Friday; get into Cambridge every Friday, Saturday, and Monday' (*Cantabrigia Depicta,* Cambridge [1776], p. 114). Cf. Cooper, *Annals* iv. 332; *post* 28 May 1777.

22. Edward Haistwell (1736–83), Gough's friend and contemporary at Corpus Christi College, Cambridge, on whose marriage Gough wrote an epithalamium (see LA vi. 338, 615–6); F.S.A.; Director of the South

Sea Company (see Cole's brief account of him, Add MS 5886, f. 27).

23. Cole presumably refers to Gough.

———

1. Cole's letters of 21 and 22 June, which Gough had carried to London, and mailed the preceding day in the Penny Post.

2. Of *King Edward's Letters.*

3. Margaret Young.

direct their being left at Mr Bentham's, by which neglect perhaps you have not yet got them; so that I have been very blameable, while I thought I was very expeditious; and it was not till reading your letter[1] again just now that I discovered my carelessness. I have not heard of Dr Glynn and Co., but the housekeeper has orders to receive them.

Thank you a thousand times for the Maltese notes, which I have given to the gentleman; and for the Wyattiana: I am going to work on the latter.

I have not yet seen Mr Gray's print,[2] but am glad it is so like. I expected Mr Mason would have sent me one early; but I suppose he keeps it for me, as I shall call on him in my way to Lord Strafford's.[3]

Mr West, one of our brother antiquaries, is dead.[4] He had a very curious collection of old pictures, English coins, English prints, and MSS, but he was so rich, that I take for granted nothing will be sold.[5] I could wish for his family-pictures of Henry V and Henry VIII.[6] Foote, in his new comedy of *The Nabob*,[7] has lashed Master Doctor Milles and our Society very deservedly for the nonsensical discussion they had this winter about Whittington and his cat[8]—I am not sorry for it: few of them are fit for anything better than such researches.

Poor Mr Granger has been very ill, but is almost recovered; I intend to invite him to meet you in September. It is a party I shall be very impatient for; you know how sincerely I am,

Dear Sir, Your obliged and obedient humble servant,

HOR. WALPOLE

1. Of 22 June 1772.
2. HW misunderstood Cole's statement in his letter of 22 June. The print was of Mason, not of Gray.
3. HW changed his plan, and first visited Lord Strafford at Wentworth Castle. On Monday 17 Aug. he 'went to Mr Mason's at Aston Melton near Kiveton. He has built himself a very good new parsonage-house and laid out his ground prettily' (*Country Seats* 74).
4. He died 2 July 1772; see *ante* 16 May 1762, n. 49.
5. HW was mistaken. See *post* 18 Feb. and 7 April 1773.

6. HW bought these pictures at West's sale (see *post* 7 April 1773).
7. Samuel Foote (1720–77), dramatist and actor. *The Nabob* was first performed at the Haymarket 29 June 1772, and ran for twenty-four performances in its first year (see Mary Megie Belden, *The Dramatic Work of Samuel Foote*, New Haven, 1929, p. 195).
8. This was led by Samuel Pegge (1704–96). 'Mr Pegge gave us next the history of Whittington, but could make nothing at all of his cat,' Gough to Tyson 27 Dec. 1771 (LA viii. 575). In his copy of *The Nabob*, 1778 (now WSL), HW has written in the

PS. Pray tell me who *the Cardinal*[9] was, whose lectures Ant. Wood says Sir T. Wyat went to Oxford to hear. In my edition the column is 56, not *51*, as in your letter.[10] I have not Hearne's Langtoft: if there is any fact in Hearne's notes relating to Sir Thomas, be so good as to transcribe it.[11]

From COLE, Thursday 9 July 1772

VA, Forster MS 110, ff. 105–6. COLE's copy, Add MS 5844, ff. 31v, 32.

Address: For the Honourable Horace Walpole at Strawberry Hill in Twickenham, Middlesex. Single Sheet.

Postmark: None. [The letter, as appears by Cole's postscript, was franked by Sir John Cotton, but the frank is missing. Cole wrote the above address before Sir John's arrival, and a fresh sheet was used for the cover.]

Milton, July 9, 1772.

Dear Sir,

MANY thanks for your bountiful present of *King Edward's Letters,* which came very safe, and I dare say directed to Mr Bentham's, as they were sent to me from thence. I should certainly have acknowledged the receipt of them and thanked you for them but for the note which came with them, signifying your just then getting into your carriage, which I ignorantly supposed meant your setting out on your intended journey mentioned in a former letter.

I should have liked your book better had there been more of your own and less of mine in it. I wish your preface had been longer, though, short as it is, you have lengthened my credit and done me an honour I have great reason to be proud of.

I have not seen the Vice-Chancellor[1] since I received your present,

middle of the scene, Act iii, p. 55, 'This was literally discussed at the Antiquarian Society.' Foote's ridicule gave HW a good excuse to resign from the Society of Antiquaries, which he did late in this month. The real reason for his withdrawal was his pique at the attacks upon his *Historic Doubts,* by the president (Milles) and a fellow (Masters): see 'Short Notes' for 1772; *Works* ii. 251* n.

9. Cardinal Wolsey (see following letter).

10. HW's edition of *Athenae Oxoniensis,* was the second, 1721. It is now WSL. Cole's

reference to the first edition, 1691–2, was vol. 1, col. 49, not 51. HW is evidently writing from memory after a hasty glance at Cole's letter.

11. See following letter.

1. This paragraph is considerably enlarged in Cole's copy: 'I have not seen the Vice-Chancellor [James Brown] since I received them, for though the last week or ten days is the gayest time we have at Cambridge, and the last more particularly so, as the Miss Lindleys [see end of note] from

though at Cambridge for this last fortnight there has been little else but oratorios, music and balls, but the weather was too hot for me to go among them, so that I have seen no one all this time except the squire of the parish,[2] as they call him here, a rich clergyman, who called on me yesterday morning. This gentleman, having about five years ago purchased the chief part of the parish, has, to my no small mortification, taken it into his head to like the situation and is now actually building a good house to reside in. When I made choice of this place for my residence, one of its recommendations was its privacy and solitude.

If I said in my letter that a new print of *Mr Gray* was very like him, I made a mistake or expressed myself improperly. The print I meant to speak of was of *Mr Mason* himself, sitting in a chair, and is a striking likeness.

I had not heard of Mr West's death, but Foote's ridicule on the Society I heard much of, for Mr Gough the topographer, with whom I am but slightly acquainted, with a Mr Haistwell, another of the London antiquaries, being on a visit to Mr Tyson and Mr Nasmith, both antiquaries of Benet College, where the two former also received their education, made a party to dine here one day. Mr Nasmith is going to print two volumes in the nature of Hearne's publications, containing three or four old historians in that college Library.[3] One of the Whittingtonians, guessing my real sentiments,

Bath and the best music from town that could be procured to perform at St Mary's the oratorio of Sampson [by Handel], and other grand concertos, for two whole days together, morning and evening, yet the weather was so hot, I had no disposition to mix in the crowd. This was the week before, on account of the County Hospital [Addenbrooke's Hospital], and the commencement this week had no charms for me to draw me to Cambridge, though invited on Sunday to dine in Trinity College Hall, and on Tuesday elsewhere; so that I have seen no one all this time except the Squire of the Parish [Samuel Knight (see n. 2 below)], as they call him here, a rich clergyman who, having lately purchased almost the whole property there, has, to my no small mortification, taken it into his head to like the situation, and is actually building a good house in order to reside here. When I made choice of this village, one of its recommendations was its being void of company, and its rural and private situation not interrupted by an air of dissipation and gaiety I have no relish for.' [Elizabeth Ann Linley (1754–92), afterwards married to Richard Brinsley Sheridan; and Mary Linley (1758–87). For Elizabeth Ann's account of her stay at Cambridge on this occasion, see W. Fraser Rae, *Sheridan, a Biography*, 2 vols, New York, 1896, i. 193–6.]

2. Samuel Knight (d. 1790), son of Samuel Knight (1675–1746); purchased the manor of Milton from the Pembertons in 1767 (see LA v. 360–3; Lysons, *Mag. Brit.* ii. 237).

3. Nasmith's only publication that fits this description is *Itineraria Simonis Simeonis et Willelmi de Worcestre, quibus accedit tractatus de Metro*, Cambridge, 1778. His *Catalogus Librorum Manuscriptorum quos Collegio Corporis Christi . . .*

had yet an inclination to be further satisfied, and asked my opinion concerning your great stumbling-block to the President, *Richard III*, which he said had been answered two or three times. I told him I thought your book was one of the most ingenious that had appeared; that the title of it showed that you meant not arbitrarily to establish your doubts in certainties, which yet would be no easy task to contradict; and that if your book was answered, it was news to me, who had never heard of such answers. A London antiquary, whose name and performance I have forgot (so conclude he was no very redoubtable antagonist),4 was mentioned, together with Dr Milles and the paper which Mr Masters read last winter at the Society, and which it seems is to appear in the second *Archaeologia*.5 The mention of this man reminds me of what Mr Knight, the rich clergyman mentioned above, told me yesterday in my garden. On some occasion his name being brought up, Mr Knight asked me if I had not heard of an affair relating to him which happened the week before last. I told him, No, for I had seen no one from Cambridge since the Commencement. He said that this man was much suspected and talked of at Cambridge as having defrauded, stolen from or cheated the County Hospital of some paltry sum, out of one of the basins in which he collected the money on that occasion (the oratorio) for the use of the Hospital. I said they deserved to be so cheated (as his dirty character was universally known) for trusting him to finger any part of their money, which would naturally stick to his fingers like birdlime. What the particulars are, I have not yet heard, not being curious to inquire about it too much, as my former connections with him might give occasion to think I was too much delighted to hear anything to his discredit. I must own one loves to have such adversaries.

legavit . . . Matthaeus Parker, Cambridge, 1777, and his edition of Tanner's *Notitia Monastica,* Cambridge, 1787, may be in Cole's mind, but it is likely that Nasmith's original plan was changed, and the *Itineraria* was the result.

4. *An Answer to Mr Horace Walpole's late work, entitled Historic Doubts . . . or, an Attempt to confute him from his own arguments.* By F. W. G[uydickens or Guidickins] of the Middle Temple, 1768. HW dismisses him as 'a very civil gentleman, who did me the honour of answering

my doubts in a volume as large as my own. He paid me so many compliments, that I beg he will draw upon me for the full debt, whenever he has occasion for the like number' ('Supplement to the Historic Doubts,' *Works* ii. 191). HW mistakenly attributed this pamphlet to William Guthrie (see HW to Montagu 12 March 1768).

5. 'What so clumsy-headed a mortal has to advance, besides his mistake, as he pretends, about a Duchess of Norfolk, is to me astonishing: how he got through his

I am glad to hear Mr Granger is getting better.[6] I am so bad a correspondent, except to yourself and two or three other very particular friends that I don't often hear from my other acquaintance. I shall be very glad to give him the meeting, but I hope you won't appoint him for a certainty. I am so subject to sore throats and colds that I can never answer for myself long together. I know I fully purpose being with you at the time appointed, but God knows when the time comes whether I shall be able.

I take it that Anthony Wood means no more at p. 56 than that Sir Thomas Wyat went to Oxford to hear the lectures which Cardinal Wolsey had lately founded in that University, though the fact to me is very doubtful, especially as Mr Baker, in a note upon the passage, on the margin of his copy, has these words:

One Sir Tho. Wyat, Knt., was of St John's Coll. Cambridge, but whether this Sir Thomas or his son, I am not sure. It must be the father.

These notes of Mr Baker I many years ago copied from his book into my own. The reason, I apprehend, why Mr Baker made such an observation (as Wood owns that Sir Thomas was of St John's College) was that it was not unusual for Anthony thus to filch eminent Cambridge men and engraft them at Oxford, where perhaps they spent no part of their time. Yet we have great obligation to honest Anthony for preserving and producing many curious materials for the lives of Cambridge men, which would not so easily have been met with without him.

The Cardinal founded his seven lectures at Oxford about 1520, some time before his great foundations at Christ Church, as it is now styled.

The passage in the glossary at the end of Peter Langtoft's *Chronicle*, p. 641, relating to Sir Thomas Wyat is as follows, taken from a MS of Dr Nicholas Harpsfield, Archdeacon of Canterbury, in New College Library, bearing this title: *A Treatise of Dr Nicholas Harpsfield's Concerninge Marriage, Occasioned by the Pretended Divorce*

Benet College History I can better account for' (addition in Cole's copy). For Masters's paper, see *Archaeologia* ii. 198–215.

6. 'I am glad to hear Mr Granger is getting better. I am so bad a correspondent, except to yourself and two or three other particular friends, that I avoid much letter-writing as much as I can, and have not wrote to Mr Granger these two years, but shall be very glad to meet him. He corresponds with a Mr [George] Ashby of St John's College, often, and by him I hear of his welfare now and then' (addition in Cole's copy).

between King Henry VIII and Queen Catherine. The author, reciting Queen Catharine's virtues, thus proceeds:

I have credibly also heard, that att a Time, when one of her Gentlewomen began to curse the Ladie Anne Bull: [with whom Sir Thomas Wyatt the elder had had carnal pleasure before the King married her, as Sir Thomas himself told the King when he endeavoured to disswade his Majesty from the match, because her conversation had been very loose and base, if you will believe what this Author observes in another place],[7] she answered, 'Hold your peace, curse her not, but pray for her; for the time will come shortly when you shall have much neede to pittie and lament her case.' And so it chanced indeed.

But I will trouble you with no more at present, but assuring you that I am, dear Sir,

Your most obliged and faithful servant,

[WM COLE][8]

Sir John Cotton calling here this afternoon will frank it.

To COLE, Tuesday 28 July 1772

Add MS 5952, ff. 106–7.
Cole received the letter Wednesday 29 July (see following letter).
Address: To the Reverend Mr Cole at Milton near Cambridge.
Postmark: Isleworth 28 IY.

Strawberry Hill, July 28, 1772.

I AM anew obliged to you, as I am perpetually, for the notice you give me of another intended publication against me in the *Archaeologia,* or *Old Women's Logic*. By your account the author[1] will add much credit to their society! For my part I shall take no notice of any of his *handy-crafts*. However as there seems to be a willingness to carp at me, and as gnats may on a sudden provoke one to give a slap, I choose to be at liberty to say what I think of the learned Society, and therefore have taken leave of them, having so good an occasion presented as their council on Whittington and his cat, and the ridicule that Foote has thrown on them. They are welcome to

7. The brackets are in Hearne's edition   1. Robert Masters.
of the *Chronicle,* 1725.
8. Name cut away in MS.

say anything of my writings, but that they are the works of a Fellow of so foolish a Society.

I am at work on the life of Sir Thomas Wyat, but it does not please me, nor will be entertaining, though you have contributed so many materials towards it. You must take one trouble more: it is to inquire and search for a book that I want extremely to see. It is called, *The Pilgrim,* was written by William Thomas, who was executed in Queen Mary's time, but the book was printed under, and dedicated to Edward VI.[2] I have only an imperfect memorandum of it, and cannot possibly recall to mind from whence I made it. All I think I remember is, that the book was in the King's library.[3] I have sent to the Museum[4] to inquire after it: but I cannot find it mentioned in Ames's *History of English Printers*.[5] Be so good to ask all your antiquarian friends, if they know such a work.

Amidst all your kindness, you have added one very disagreeable paragraph—I mean your doubt about coming hither in September. Fear of a sore throat would be a reason for your never coming. It is one of the distempers in the world the least to be foreseen, and September, a dry month, one of the least likely months to bring it. I do not like your recurring to so very ill-founded an excuse, and positively will not accept it, unless you wish I should not be so much as I am,

Dear Sir, Your most faithful humble servant,

Hor. Walpole[6]

2. William Thomas (d. 1554), Italian scholar and Clerk of the Council to Edward VI. His *Il Pellegrino Inglese ne'l quale si defende l'innocente, & la sincera vita de'l pio & religioso re d'Inghliterra Henrico ottauo* was published in 1552. He also wrote, but did not publish, an English version, with dedication to Pietro Aretino, of which a copy is preserved in the Cottonian MSS at the British Museum: HW quoted this version in his *Miscellaneous Antiquities, No. II* 55–62. Other transcripts are preserved in the Harleian Collection and at the Bodleian. The English version was first published in entirety in 1774, in *The Works of William Thomas.*

3. 'In 1757, King George II presented the Library of his predecessors [the Old Royal Library] . . . to . . . the British Museum' (Edward Edwards, *Libraries and Founders of Libraries,* New York, 1865, pp. 177–8).

4. The British Museum.

5. Joseph Ames, *Typographical Antiquities,* 1749. HW's copy (B.3.27) was sold SH i. 118.

6. Under HW's signature Cole added: 'To enquire whether in the third volume of Browne's *Fasciculus,* this *Pilgrim* is translated into Latin and remitted therein.' Edward Brown, rector of Sundridge, Kent, edited Ortwin Gratius's *Fasciculus Rerum expetendarum et fugiendarum,* 2 vols, 1690. The third volume was never published.

On the cover of this letter Cole wrote: 'In Henry Foulis's *History of Romish Treasons,* p. 408, printed at London, folio, 1671, it is said expressly that it [*The Pilgrim*] was never printed.'

From Cole, Thursday 30 July 1772

Forster MS 110, f. 107. Cole's copy, Add MS 5844, ff. 32v, 33.

Address: For the Honourable Mr Horace Walpole at Strawberry Hill in Twickenham, Middlesex. *Postmark:* Cambridge 31 IY.

Milton, Thursday, 30 July 1772.

Dear Sir,

I RECEIVED yours of 28th last night, and for answer think that William Thomas's *Pilgrim* was never printed. However, I will make such inquiries on Wednesday next,[1] when I dine at Cambridge, that if there is such a printed book in any of our libraries there, you shall be sure to have it if it may be procured. My reason for thinking it never was printed is that Bishop Tanner, in his *Bibliotheca Britannico-Hibernica*, p. 710,[2] gives the following account of this book among that author's other publications, which may assist you in your inquiries after the MS:

Le Peregrynne, sive Defensionem Henrici 8, ad Aretinum Poetam Italum. MS Cotton. Vespasian. D.XVIII. Pr. Prol. ad Aretin: 'Lyke as many Tymes the wyld.' Pr. Lib.: 'Constrayned by Misfortune.' MS Bibl. Bodl. NE.B.2.7. Bibl. Simon D'Ewes.

This is all that is said of this work. The Bishop adds:

ineunte Regno Mariae, tanquam laesae Majestatis reus, ut pote qui Rebellionem Wiati adjuvit, Poenas dedit apud Patibulum Tiburnense 18 Maii 1554.

But what puts this out of dispute that it never was published is this quotation from Anthony Wood, vol. 1, p. 91,[3] giving an account of his publications:

Le Peregrynne, written at Bologna la grassa. 'Tis a MS in Bodley Library, qu. D.23. Th. fol. 71. The beginning of it is this, 'Constrained by Misfortune to habandon the Place of my Nativity &c.' This book, called Le Peregrynne, is about to be translated into Latin <with> a Design to be

---

1. 5 August, 'when I dine at our Corporation annual Venison Club' (addition in Cole's copy).

2. Thomas Tanner (1674–1735), Bp of St Asaph; his *Bibliotheca Britannico-Hiber-* *nica* was published in 1748. HW's copy (F. 1.24) was sold SH ii. 171.

3. *Athenae Oxonienses.* Cole is here quoting from the second (1721) edition.

remitted in the third tome of Fascic<ulus>, collected by Edward Brown of Christ's College [it should be Clare Hall][4] in Cambridge.

As I have not Brown's *Fasciculus* I can't say whether this design took effect.

In Strype's *Life of Grindal*, p. 5,[5] it looks as [if] Bishop Ridley,[6] the Protestant martyr, had no great opinion in 1550 of the character of William Thomas, whom Father Persons the Jesuit[7] accuses of a design to kill Queen Mary, but Bishop Bale of Ossory[8] says that the reason of his execution was a design upon the life of Bishop Gardiner[9] (Cent. [16], vol. 2, p. 110). In either case it shows the violence of his principles. Bale's words are these:

Cum in Stephanum Wintoniensem violentas Manus injicere statuisset, supplicio affectus est A. D. 1554.[10]

If I can be of any further use, please to command me.

Last year, about October,[11] I begged the favour of you to give a relation of mine, Mr Mawdsley, a considerable tradesman in London, leave to see your house at Strawberry Hill. I don't remember you ever gave me any answer to it, through inadvertency, I make no doubt. As his servants keep Sturbridge Fair,[12] I shall see him again probably at the end of September, and shall be glad to tell him that he may have that liberty.

I take your reprehension very kindly. I am sure I have inclination enough to come to Strawberry Hill, and wish my excuse concerning it may not be too real, and allow me that pleasure, but my sore throats are so sudden, frequent and troublesome, that I can never

4. Cole's interpolation.

5. John Strype, *The History of the Life and Acts of . . . Edmund Grindal,* 1710. The passage to which Cole refers is a quotation from a letter of Bishop Ridley to Sir John Cheke.

6. Nicholas Ridley (1500?–55), successively Bishop of Rochester and London.

7. Robert Parsons or Persons (1546–1610), Jesuit missionary and controversialist; author of more than thirty works.

8. In his *Scriptorum Illustrium Maioris Britanniae,* 1557–9. In his copy of this letter, Cole calls Bale 'foul-mouthed Bale, the protestant Bishop of Ossory.'

9. Stephen Gardiner (1483?–1555), Bp of Winchester.

10. Cole has slightly modernized the spelling. The following addition appears in his copy: 'We may reasonably conclude he [Thomas] deserved to be hanged, or Bale, of whose fiery spirit he seems to partake, would have made some apology for him.'

11. See *ante* 3 Nov. 1771.

12. The fair began 7 Sept. and continued for three weeks (see *Bibliotheca Topographica Britannica,* No. 38: *The History and Antiquities of Barnwell Abbey, and of Sturbridge Fair,* 1786, p. 80).

answer for myself. At this present I have such a swimming in my
head I can hardly finish this letter, and subscribe myself, dear Sir,

Your ever obliged and faithful servant,

WM COLE

From COLE, Thursday 6 August 1772

VA, Forster MS 110, f. 108. Cole kept no copy.

Cole wrote in one of his MS volumes: 'Mr Lort dined with me on Thursday,
Aug. 6, and assured me that there was only two volumes of the *Fasciculus*, in
neither of which was the *Pilgrim:* accordingly I wrote to Mr Walpole' (Add MS
5844, f. 33).

Address: For the Honourable Horace Walpole at Strawberry Hill in Twickenham, Middlesex.

Dear Sir,   Milton, Thursday evening, Aug. 6, 1772.

I COULD meet with nobody at home yesterday, but today Mr Lort
calling upon me, assures me that *Le Peleryne* cannot have been
published in the third volume of the *Fasciculus,* as there never was
but two volumes published, and it is in neither of them. Possibly
that work did not take, and the design dropped.

As I promised to write on this account, I now fulfill my engagement, and if I can be of any farther use, please to command me, who
am never better pleased than in executing any commissions from
you, and am, dear Sir,

Your ever faithful and most obliged servant,

WM COLE

To COLE, Tuesday 25 August 1772

Add MS 5952, ff. 108–9.

Cole received the letter 27 Aug. (see following letter).

Address: [From COLE's copy, Add MS 5844, f. 33v.] To the Reverend Mr Cole
at Milton near Cambridge. Free H. S. Conway.

Arlington Street, Aug. 25, 1772.

I THANK you for your notices, dear Sir, and will deliver you from
the trouble of any farther pursuit of the *Peleryne* of Thomas: I

have discovered him among the Cottonian MSS in the Museum,[1] and am to see him.

If Dr Browne[2] is returned to Cambridge, may I beg you to give him a thousand thanks for a present he left for me at my house, a goastone and a seal that belonged to Mr Gray? I shall lay them up in my cabinet at Strawberry among my most valuables.[3] Dr Browne however was not quite kind to me, for he left no direction where I might find him in town, so that I could not wait on him, nor invite him to Strawberry Hill, as I much wished to do. Do not those words *invite him to Strawberry* make your ears tingle? September is at hand, and you must have no sore throat. The new chapel in the garden is almost finished, and you must come to the dedication.

I have seen Lincoln and York,[4] and to say truth prefer the former in some respects. In truth I was scandalized in the latter. William of Hatfield's tomb and figure[5] is thrown aside into a hole; and yet the Chapter possess an estate that his mother[6] gave them. I have charged Mr Mason with my anathema, unless they do justice.[7] I saw Roche Abbey[8] too, which is hid in such a venerable chasm, that you might lie concealed there even from a squire-parson of the parish. Lord Scarborough,[9] to whom it belongs, and who lives at next door,[10] neglects it as much as if he was afraid of ghosts. I believe Montesino's

1. For HW's use of Thomas's *Pilgrim*, see *Miscellaneous Antiquities, No. II* 58–62.

2. He called twice in Arlington Street while HW was in Yorkshire (see HW to Mason 24 Aug. 1772; Brown to HW 25 Aug. 1772).

3. HW listed in *Description of SH,* among the 'curiosities in the glass closet in the great bedchamber,' 'an agate puncheon with the arms of Mr Gray the poet, and a goa stone; given to Mr Walpole by Doctor Browne and Mr W. Mason, Mr Gray's executors' (*Works* ii. 499). They were sold SH xvi. 56.

4. HW saw Lincoln 6 Aug. and York 11 Aug. 1772 (see *Country Seats* 71–2).

5. William of Hatfield (d. 1344), second son of Edward III. For a print of the figure, see Francis Drake, *Eboracum: or the History and Antiquities of the City of York,* 1736, p. 491. See *post* 22 May 1777.

6. Philippa of Hainault (1314?–69),

queen of Edward III, and dau. of William the Good.

7. See HW to Mason 24 Aug. 1772. Apparently through their efforts, the figure was placed in its present position 'in the westernmost bay of the north aisle. . . . The effigy of the prince is fine, though much damaged. . . . The statue appears to have been removed from its proper place, and neglected for a long time' (Arthur Clutton-Brock, *The Cathedral Church of York* . . . revised by the Rev. F. Harrison, 1931, pp. 129–30; see p. 129 of that work for a picture of the tomb). See also in this connection, *post* 22 May 1777.

8. On Tuesday, 18 Aug. (see *Country Seats* 74). The Abbey was founded by the Cistercians about 1147, and its ruins may still be visited.

9. Richard Lumley-Saunderson (1725–82), 4th E. of Scarborough.

10. At Sandbeck Park, three miles SW of Tickhill, in the West Riding of Yorkshire.

cave[11] lay in just such a solemn thicket, which is now so overgrown, that when one finds the spot, one can scarce find the ruins.

I forgot to tell you that in the screen of York Minster there are most curious statues of the Kings of England from the Conqueror to Henry VI,[12] very singular, evidently by two different hands, the one better than the other, and most of them, I am persuaded, very authentic; Richard II, Henry III, and Henry V, I am sure are; and Henry IV, though unlike the common portrait at Hampton Court in Herefordshire,[13] the most singular and villainous countenance I ever saw. I intend to try to get them well engraved.[14] That old fool James I is crowded in, in the place of Henry VI, that was taken away to make room for this piece of flattery—for the Chapter did not slight live princes.

Yours ever,
H. W.

From Cole, Tuesday 25 August 1772

VA, Forster MS 110, ff. 109–10. Cole's copy, Add MS 5844, f. 33.
Address: For the Honourable Mr Horace Walpole at Strawberry Hill in Twickenham, Middlesex. *Postmark:* 28 AV.

Milton, Aug. 25, 1772.

Dear Sir,

MY harvest not being yet got in, though very near it, makes it impossible to stir from home at present. I talk in the style of a farmer, yet am very little concerned in the transactions about farming,[1] yet I find it necessary to be on the spot while the winding up of the year is in hand. I have this year eight loads of wheat, four of oats, one of barley, and I hope four or five of peas and beans, and

---

11. Montesinos was a character of medieval romance who retired to a cave in La Mancha. Don Quixote visited the cave and had a vision of Montesinos and other heroes.

12. HW gives a similar, though shorter, account of the statues, which he saw 11 Aug., in *Country Seats* 72.

13. HW mentions this portrait in *Anecdotes, Works* iii. 31, 34; see also *Anecdotes*, ed. Wornum, 1876, i. 29–30 nn.

14. HW made at least two unsuccessful efforts to get drawings or casts of the statues of Henry IV and Richard III. Finally he abandoned the project (see HW to Mason 29 July 1773, 11 March 1776, [14]–16 April 1776).

---

1. 'so little that I never saw my own arable lands, and don't even know where they lie, except two or three acres next the turnpike road' (addition in Cole's copy).

thank God, all in perfection, as I am told. Therefore it is to be expected from the general good crops that the poor will find the benefit of it, and that it will contribute to the lowering the price of provisions.

When I reflect on the advantage you offer me of entertaining me at Strawberry Hill, an opportunity that most would catch at, I stand amazed at myself for my not doing so too, but I will be sincere with you, Sir, who have ever patronized me from my early youth: I am grown so indolent and inactive that I hardly ever stir farther than Cambridge—there very seldom. I had not been at Horseth these fifteen months, though repeatedly solicited, till last week for two days, when it was <im>possible to refuse it: nor at Sir John Cotton's[2] these two years, though <h>e has been here three or four times. The only chance I have of seeing Strawberry Hill will be my taking an opportunity[3] of going to town with Lord Montfort for two or three days, and then coming to you.

I hope my excuses, though very lame ones, will meet with indulgence. In the world there is not a person to whom I would sooner go, was it convenient, than to yourself. Pray excuse me: I can hardly do so myself, and will therefore say no more about it till I am in a better disposition.

I am, dear Sir,

Your ever obliged and faithful servant,

WM COLE

I this moment (Wednesday [Thursday] evening, Aug. 27) received your most agreeable, polite, entertaining and lively letter, of the same date as this, which my unconquerable indolence has let me keep two days by me sealed up, for want of sending it to the turnpike two or three stone's cast from my door. My ears really do tingle at the words, which I dare not repeat. I am really ashamed of myself, and begin to fear that I must beg it as a singular favour to be admitted at Strawberry Hill: indeed that is saying nothing, as I ever did and shall always esteem it such.

Much obliged am I for your observations at York. When you take

2. Madingley Hall, Cambs.

3. 'of Lord Montfort's coach when next my Lady goes to town for four or five days, and then coming to you' (addition in Cole's copy).

journeys the public is ever the better for them: of this I needed not your lively account of York and Roche Abbey.[4]

I will make it my business in a day or two to call on the Vice-Chancellor,[5] whom I have not seen since he kindly called here and made me a present of the silver box to keep in memory of Mr Gray, to whom it belonged.

I believe in all my epistles I have never told you how strangely I have spent all this spring and summer. I accidentally met with the two folio registers of Croyland Abbey and Spalding Priory. I have thought them so curious that I have almost transcribed them both,[6] and though I have worked like an horse at a mill from morning to night, and rarely going out, yet I assure you I am not tired of my employment, though, thank God, I am drawing to a conclusion, to the benefit of my eyes.

Your mention of the statues at York puts me in mind of a circumstance of which I forgot to send you an account. Last year in repairing Bishop Alcok's Chapel at Ely, among the rubbish, very carefully concealed, was found a most elegant small statue in marble of King Henry VII. Mr Bentham drew up an account of it, and Mr Tyson copied the figure, and though it is judged by all who ever saw it to

4. 'as I once (and I remember it with pleasure) had the honour to be your fellow-traveller to Burleigh House, etc.' (addition in Cole's copy).

5. Cole wrote to James Brown instead (Cole's copy, Add MS 5844, f. 34). Addressed 'For the Rev. Mr Vice-Chancellor at Pembroke Hall, Cambridge.'

'Milton, Aug. 25 [27], 1772.
Dear Sir,

I received the enclosed letter this evening from Mr Walpole, who desires me to call on you with his thanks for the present you was pleased to make him: but as I am never in an hurry to stir from home, I thought Mr Walpole's own letter would be as satisfactory.

About six weeks ago Mr Walpole sent me a few copies of the enclosed publication, if that may be called so which is not to be sold, which I ought to have sent to you before now: as I desired him, by letter, to send me one extraordinary for that purpose.

I am ashamed I have not yet called upon you, but intend myself that pleasure very

shortly, and am in the meantime, dear Mr Vice-Chancellor,
    Your much obliged and faithful servant,
        Wm Cole.'

For Brown's reply, see *post* 3 Oct. 1772.

6. Michael Tyson wrote to Richard Gough, 8 Feb. 1772: 'Cole has got two immense folios: the Leiger-books of Crowland and Spalding Monasteries [both in Lincolnshire], which he is busy in transcribing. He had them from Commissary Greaves; they belong to the Wingfield family, to whom Greaves is nearly related—

"Amidst them all he in a chaire is sett,
    Tossing and turning them withouten end;
But for he was unable them to fett,
    A little boy did on him still attend,"
etc.

This admirable Portrait of an Antiquary one would think was drawn from the *very Milton Hearne* himself. His *lameness,* his employments, admirably answer.—Pray turn to your Spenser, Book II, Canto 9.' (LA viii. 581.) Cole's copies of these registers are in Add MSS 5844–5.

be a most striking resemblance of that King, and the place or tomb where found would in a manner ascertain it to be no one else, yet the Antiquary Society, to whom both were sent, from the shape or fashion of the crown only, unanimously determined it not to be a statue of Henry VII,[7] and took very little or no notice of it, to the no small mortification and disappointment both of Mr Bentham and Mr Tyson.

To COLE, Friday 28 August 1772

Add MS 5952, f. 110.

Address: [From COLE's copy, Add MS 5844, f. 34.] To the Reverend Mr Cole at Milton near Cambridge.

Strawberry Hill, Aug. 28, 1772.

YOUR repentance is much more agreeable than your sin, and will cancel it whenever you please. Still I have a fellow-feeling for the indolence of age, and have myself been writing an excuse this instant for not accepting an invitation above threescore miles off.[1] One's limbs, when they grow old, will not go anywhere when they do not like it. If yours should find themselves in a more pliant humour, you are always sure of being welcome here, let the fit of motion come when it will.

Pray what is become of that figure you mention of Henry VII,[2] which the destroyers, not the builders, have rejected? and which the antiquaries, who know a man by his crown better than by his face, have rejected likewise? The latter put me in mind of characters in comedies, in which a woman disguised in a man's habit and whose features her very lover does not know, is immediately acknowledged by pulling off her hat and letting down her hair, which her lover had never seen before. I should be glad to ask Dr Milles if he thinks the Crown of England was always made like a quart-pot by Win-

---

7. For a full discussion of the merits of the statue and the attitude of the Society of Antiquaries, see the correspondence between Tyson and Gough, LA viii. 588–91, 595. Tyson apparently never made an etching of the statue. There is a print of it in William Stevenson's *Supplement to Bentham's Ely,* Norwich, 1817, facing p. 69.

1. This letter (addressee unknown) is missing.

2. James Bentham deposited the statue in the Deanery at Ely (see William Stevenson, *Supplement to Bentham's Ely,* Norwich, 1817, p. 69). See also following letter.

chester measure?[3] If Mr Tyson has made a print from that little statue, I trust he will give me one; and if he or Mr Essex or both will accompany you hither, I shall be glad to see them.

At Buckden[4] in the Bishop's palace[5] I saw a print of Mrs Newcome,[6] I suppose the late mistress of St John's. Can you tell me where I can procure one? Mind, I insist that you do not serve me as you have often done, and send me your own if you have one—I seriously will not accept it, nor ever trust you again. On the staircase in the same palace there is a picture of two young men in the manner of Van Dyck, not at all ill done; do you know who they are, or does anybody? There is a worse picture in a large room of some lads, which too the house-maid did not know.[7] Adieu!

Dear Sir, Yours ever,
H. W.

From Cole, Saturday 3 October 1772

VA, Forster MS 110, ff. 111–12. Cole's copy, Add MS 5844, ff. 34v, 35. The latter is dated Oct. 4, 1772.

Address: For the honourable Mr Horace Walpole at Strawberry Hill in Twickenham, Middlesex. *Postmark:* Cambridge 6 OC.

Milton, Oct. 3, 1772.

Dear Sir,

I AM afraid you will think my long silence, ever since August 28, the date of your last letter, very ill-mannerly, but I was unwilling to multiply letters upon you unnecessarily, and I could not before today give you a satisfactory answer to some queries in it. On my receipt of it I accidentally, the day after, fell into company with the

3. 'Dry and liquid measures, the standards of which were originally deposited at Winchester' (OED).

4. In Huntingdonshire three miles SW of Huntingdon, where HW spent the night of 19 Aug. 1772: he arrived in Buckden at 8 P.M., and set out for London at 10 the following morning. He probably visited the Palace at this time (*Country Seats* 74).

5. Buckden Palace, formerly the episcopal mansion of the Bishops of Lincoln. The Bishop of Lincoln in 1772 was John Green (1706?–79), an acquaintance of Johnson and Garrick.

6. —— Squire (d. 1763), second wife of Dr John Newcome (1683–1765), Dean of Rochester and Master of St John's, Cambridge. Cole called her 'a woman of excellent parts and abilities; of sound sense and masculine judgment,' and compared her with Mme de Maintenon (LA i. 559; also quoted in Baker's *History of St John's College* ii. 1026; see also EBP; GM March 1763, xxxiii. 146a).

7. See following letter for replies to these queries.

Bishop of Lincoln's chaplain,[1] who was going to Bugden[2] and promised to give me all the information he could pick up relating to the two pictures you inquire after.

The picture on the staircase of two young men, after the manner of Vandyck, is of a Duke of Florence and his secretary.[3] The other in a large room of some lads, and damaged, belongs to the family of Howard Earl of Stafford,[4] the Popish family. This is the information I had from Dr Gordon yesterday.

The very day I received your letter Mr Lort,[5] late Greek Professor, happened to call on me, and asking where I could procure a print of Mrs Newcome (who was wife to the late Dr N., Master of St John's College and Dean of Rochester), he told me I could not have applied better, for that he actually was employed in getting it engraved for the Master, and that he had one at your service, which he sent hither in a day or two, and which I would have sent before had I found a proper conveyance. It won't be <lon>g ere you have it, but to give two shillings for the carriage of a common mezzotinto print, which used to be only a shilling price, I thought too much. Although there is no engraver's name on the plate, which is only to be had from the family, it was done by Watson,[6] as Mr Lort has wrote on it,[7] for he was with him on this account.

1. John Gordon (1725–93), of Peterhouse and Emmanuel, became chaplain to the Bishop of Lincoln in 1765 (see Thomas Alfred Walker, *Admissions to Peterhouse*, Cambridge, 1912, p. 285). Cole had no high opinion of Gordon, whom he describes as a tall thin man, priggish and fulsome, and contemptuously refers to him as 'his pragmatical Reverence' (*Blecheley Diary* 33–5, 220, *et passim*).

2. A variant of Buckden.

3. Not identified.

4. John Paul Stafford-Howard (1700–62), 4th E. of Stafford, the last of this line.

5. 'of Trinity College happened to walk over to dine with me' (addition in Cole's copy). Lort was Regius Professor of Greek at Cambridge 1759–71, and at this time was rector of St Matthew, Friday Street, London.

6. Presumably Thomas Watson (1743–81) or James Watson (1739?–90). The print is not listed among their works in Gordon Goodwin, *British Mezzotinters: Thomas Watson, James Watson, Elizabeth Judkins*, 1904. It is listed in John Chaloner Smith,

British Mezzotinto Portraits iv. 1740, but the name of the artist is not given, nor is it in Charles E. Russell, *English Mezzotint Portraits*, 2 vols, 1926.

7. Cole gives the following history of the plate: 'Mr Lort told me, that he [Dr Newcome] employed him, after her death, to get an engraving of her picture: accordingly, a large mezzotinto is taken from a picture of her, which, I think, does not do her justice. As only *Mrs Newcome* is wrote under it, being a private plate, it is in danger of being soon utterly forgot, for whom it was engraved. Mr Beadon [a near relation to Mrs Newcome] was so kind to give me one of them, which I sent to my honoured friend the Honourable Mr Horace Walpole, to be reposited among his choice, valuable and numerous collection of English portraits, designed by him for a public library, but which particularly, I am not at liberty to declare, where it will be safe, and known for whom it was designed, as I have written under it' (quoted in LA i. 559–60 and in Baker's *History of St John's College* ii. 1026–7).

The figure of Henry VII at Ely, in possession of the Dean,[8] as I suppose, I have not seen, having not been there since it was found about fifteen months ago. Mr Tyson has a drawing of it which he sent to the Society, and calling upon him in hopes he would have given me the sketch or copied one for me to send to you, he told me that he designed soon to make an etching of it, so I said no more about it. He has repeated the same design to me since. He and everyone that has seen it speak much in its praise as an elegant performance. When it is etched you may depend upon a copy. I communicated your kind invitation to him and Mr Essex, who both desired me to make their acknowledgments to you, and will take an opportunity of waiting on you.

I don't know whether you have seen it, but I saw t'other day a good mezzotinto folio print of the famous Mr Mudge the watchmaker.[9] It is a private plate, and if you have no access to him, who, I am told, has left off business and retired into the west, I will do my endeavour to get you one. I am acquainted with a friend[10] of his to whom the print was sent. Count Bruhl[11] was the occasion of its being engraved.

I have enclosed with Mrs Newcome's print a little etching by Mr Tyson of a remarkable ear of Italian wheat, sent by the Dean of Glocester, Dr Tucker,[12] to Mr Commissary Greaves, as also another etching by him of a fish which was exhibited to the Royal Society this year, an account of which, with the drawing, is in their *Transactions* for this year, Part 1.[13]

Though I gave you no account of it, immediately on your letter of August 25, I waited on[14] Dr Browne the Vice-Chancellor with your message of thanks to him, and said all that was proper on the occasion. I should have informed you of this, with his answer in a

---

The public library which HW was at this time considering for his collection was Eton. 'Mr Walpole's collection at Strawberry Hill, which he told me ten years ago that he designed for Eton College Library' (Cole to Granger 21 Oct. 1774, Add MS 5825, f. 151v).

8. Hugh Thomas.

9. Thomas Mudge (1717–94), partner of William Dutton; retired to Plymouth in 1771 to devote himself to improvement of maritime chronometers; King's watchmaker, 1776.

10. Not identified.

11. John Maurice (1736–1809), Count of Brühl; diplomatist and astronomer; Saxon ambassador to London, 1764–1809.

12. Josiah Tucker (1712–99), Dean of Gloucester 1758–99; author of economic, political and religious works.

13. See *Philosophical Transactions*, vol. 61, for 1771, pt 2, pp. 247–9, and the plate, fig. 8, opp. p. 245.

14. A white lie: Cole sent a letter to Brown (see *ante* Cole to HW 25 Aug. 1772, n. 5, and note below).

letter of September 1, on my sending him one of *King Edward's Letters* as from you. His words are:[15]

I am much obliged to you, etc.

Mr Walpole, we knew, would set a value upon any relics of his friend, which induced Mr Mason and myself to think of the present[16] Mr Walpole so kindly accepts. I will desire the favour of you to return him my particular thanks for the honour he had intended me. I thank you much for the *Letters of Edward VI,* and it is with some satisfaction I observe that for this present I am obliged to you both: to you for making the request; to Mr Walpole for his compliance.

This is the whole of his letter, which I would enclose but for making it double. My reason for sending *Edward VI's Letters* in my own name, though begged for him, was that in your letter to me I had no direction from you to send it in yours. What occasions my confusion in this affair is this: On Thursday I dined with the Master of Benet[17] and the Vice-Chancellor was there; he told me he had lately received a very kind letter from you[18] on this subject, and I could find by what he said to me that had I done as I ought, you might not have been put to the trouble of a second letter. I beg pardon for my negligence and will amend if I can. In good truth, my real reason for not writing sooner, and is my best excuse, was the daily expectation of seeing Dr Gordon from Buckden.

On Thursday I was told at Benet College by Mr William Cole of Ely[19] that his brother Mr Charles Cole,[20] a counsellor and Recorder of Cambridge, who lately this year gave a new edition of that scarce book of Sir William Dugdale, *The History of the Fens,*[21] is now going to give us a new edition of the *Baronage* also.[22] I shall be very glad of it, as it is a book I have long wanted, but found it too ex-

15. Brown's letter (Cole's copy, Add MS 5844, f. 34v) is addressed 'To the Rev. Mr Cole at Milton near Cambridge' and is dated 'Pembroke Hall, Sept. 1, 1772.' It begins: 'I am much obliged to you for the favour of your letter, and for the sight of that which you sent me enclosed.' The second paragraph follows, as given by Cole.

16. Gray's seal and goa stone.

17. John Barnardiston.

18. Missing.

19. (1722–93), Rector of Aldborough, Norfolk; m. Mary (1722–87) eld. dau. of Zachary Grey (*Alumni Cantab.;* Bentham, *Ely*², Addenda, p. 22).

20. Charles Nalson Cole (1723–1804), lawyer and editor; m. 22 Oct. 1770 Anne Hester Abdy, sister of Sir Anthony [Thomas] Abdy, 5th Bt (*London Magazine,* Oct. 1770, xxxix. 536a).

21. *The History of Imbanking and Draining of Divers Fens and Marshes,* 2d edn, revised and corrected by Charles Nalson Cole. Printed by W. Bowyer and J. Nichols, at the expense of Richard Geast, 1772.

22. This did not happen (see following note). The only edition of this work is the first, 1675–6, 3 vols folio, in 2 vols, 7 guineas in boards.

pensive to purchase. One Mr Guest[23] is to be at the expense of it, as he was of the other.[24]

Adieu, dear Sir, and believe me,

Your most faithful and obliged servant,

WM COLE

From COLE, Saturday 24 October 1772

VA, Forster MS 110, f. 113. COLE's copy. Add MS 5844, f. 35.
Address: For the Honourable Mr Horace Walpole in Arlington Street, London.
Postmark: None. [Essex delivered the letter to Arlington Street; see letter below and HW's reply.]

Dear Sir,   Milton, Oct. 24, 1772.

I HOPE you received Mrs Newcome's print, which I got a friend[1] to leave at your house: together with a letter by the post about a fortnight since.

Mr Essex called on me yesterday and desired me to give him a let-

23. Richard Geast (d. 1806), of Blythe Hall, in Warwickshire; lineally descended by the maternal line from Sir William Dugdale; assumed in 1799 the surname and arms of Dugdale (Burke, *Commoners*, 1833, i. 490). When asked for his permission to publish a new edition of the book, he readily undertook to publish it at his own expense (Dugdale, *History of Imbanking*[2] p. iv). 'It was Mr Geast's intention to have proceeded with the other parts of his learned ancestor's works; but the restraint laid upon literary property has effectually diverted his thoughts from an expense which a period of *fourteen years* can never be expected to pay' (Gough, *British Topography*[2] i. 154).

24. Cole's copy continues as follows: 'I wish they may do justice to it, but neither of the brothers seem to me to have a right taste for such a work. Mr William Cole, who is a clergyman, and married one of the late Dr Zachary Grey's daughters, corrected the press for the former work, and thought proper to correct Sir William Dugdale's spelling: if he does so in the *Baronage* it will be horrible. I told him of the impropriety of altering the spelling in the Fen Book at his first setting out, but he did not seem to enter into my argument. He told me t'other day that

he was so tired of that work that he would not enter into the other. Both the brothers were of St John's, and their uncle, Mr Cole of Ely, dying two or three years ago, left a large fortune to them. The younger brother is an eminent counsellor, but from a paralytic stroke has had ill health for these four or five years, yet married about two years ago a sister of Sir Anthony [Thomas] Abdy. If this work goes forward, it is pity that he has not all the assistance possible, with what corrections may be come at. I have a book by Mr [Charles] Hornby [probably *A small specimen of the many mistakes in Sir W. Dugdale's Baronage*, 1730, or *Three letters containing remarks on some of the numberless errors and defects in Dugdale's Baronage*, 1738.] which promises much: whether he performed as much I know not. But it is time to subscribe myself, dear Sir,

Your most obliged and faithful servant,

Wm Cole.

'Since I wrote my letter I have met with a conveyance for Mrs Newcome's print by Mr Martyn, the botanic professor, who sets off from Cambridge on Tuesday morning. About a fortnight ago I received a noble present from my Lord Montfort of 26 volumes in folio, finely bound and gilt, of the ter to you. He is now actually determined to prosecute alone the design of giving the world some information about Gothic architecture, but dares not of himself, without you will be so kind to look over his plan and some of his drafts of windows, doors, pillars, etc., which he brings with him, prosecute an undertaking which he may be apprehensive may be too mighty both for his skill and purse, except you will aid him with your advice, direction and patronage. He means, as I guess, not that you are to be at expense in plates, etc., but only to promote his design with your interest and influence, as, to make it worthy of the subject and public, it will be attended with great expense from the number of plates: as also, if it will not interfere with your own avocations, to give his papers your correction, as he means to consult no other person on the subject but yourself.[2]

Mr Essex means to bring this to town with him, setting off <from C>ambridge on Monday next, and to deliver it into your hands, when he will <have> an opportunity to explain more at large what he has to propose on this subject, so will detain you no longer, but by assuring you of the constant esteem and regard of, dear Sir,

Your ever devoted and faithful servant,

WM COLE

To Cole, Saturday 7 November 1772

Add MS 5952, ff. 111–12. Cole did not receive the letter until 19 November (see next letter).

Address: To the Reverend Mr Cole at Milton near Cambridge.
Postmark: Isleworth 7 NO.

Strawberry Hill, Nov. 7, 1772.

Dear Sir,

I DID receive the print of Mrs Newcome, for which I am extremely obliged to you with a thousand other favours; and should certainly have thanked you for it long ago, but I was then and am now confined to my bed with the gout in every limb, and in almost every joint. I have not been out of my bedchamber these five weeks today, and last night the pain returned violently into one of my feet, so that

---

Journals of the House of Commons to the death of Queen Anne. Three of them contain a MS index to the whole.'

1. Thomas Martyn.
2. This (unpublished) work was doubtless inspired by HW to Cole 11 Aug. 1769.

I am now writing to you in a most uneasy posture, which will oblige me to be very short.

Your letter, which I suppose Mr Essex left at my house in Arlington Street was brought to me this morning. I am exceedingly sorry for his disappointment, and for his coming without writing first, in which case I might have prevented his journey. I do not know even whither to send to him, to tell him how impossible it is for me just now in my present painful and helpless situation to be of any use to him. I am so weak and faint that I do not see even my nearest relations, and God knows how long it will be before I am able to bear company, much less application. I have some thoughts, as soon as I am able, of removing to Bath,[1] so that I cannot guess when it will be in my power to consider duly Mr Essex's plan with him. I shall undoubtedly, if ever I am capable of it, be ready to give him my advice, such as it is, or to look over his papers, and even to correct them, if his modesty thinks me more able to polish them than he is himself. At the same time I must own I think he will run too great a risk by the expense. The engravers in London are now arrived at such a pitch of exorbitant imposition, that for my own part I have laid aside all thoughts of having a single plate more done.[2]

Dear Sir, pray tell Mr Essex how concerned I am for this mischance, and for the total impossibility I am under of seeing him now. I can write no more, but shall be glad to hear from you on his return to Cambridge; and when I am recovered, you may be assured how glad I shall be to talk his plan over with him. I am his and your obliged humble servant,

Hor. Walpole

From Cole, Friday 20 November 1772

VA, Forster MS 110, ff. 114–5. Cole's copy, Add MS 5844, ff. 35v, 36.

Address: For the Honourable Mr Horace Walpole at Strawberry Hill in Twickenham, Middlesex. *Postmark:* Cambridge 23 NO.

Dear Sir,   Milton, Nov. 20, 1772.

I WISH I could as easily give you relief as compassionate your present situation, but patience and warmth, I hope, will alleviate your pains, and a journey to Bath quite set you up again. I don't

1. He did not go.
2. Nevertheless, HW had several plates engraved for the 1784 edition of the *Description of SH.*

know whether you ever tried those waters. I long to have you there, and that you may not take cold on the road in this uncomfortable month.

I did not receive your letter of the 7th instant[1] till yesterday, having been at Lord Montfort's for ten or twelve days, where I had the pleasure of finding a very agreeable young lady whom, I believe, you know, and a neighbour at Hampton, Miss Sophia Thomas.[2] She has spent some time with my Lady, and I left her there on Tuesday.

My reason for writing now is to relieve a pain in your mind: I wish I could as easily do so for your body. I know the thoughts of giving anyone uneasiness distresses your humanity, but Mr Essex's journey to town was not solely on the account of his plan. He has other business that frequently calls him there, and being to stay there a fortnight or three weeks, he desired me to write the former letter. Whether he is returned to Cambridge as yet I know not, not stopping at his house as I returned from Horseth. However, I will acquaint him with the contents of your <let>ter in a day or two at furthest—perhaps today.

<In> my way home through Trumpinton[3] yesterday, I accidentally called on a friend,[4] <where> I met with a neighbour of yours, a Mr Gulston of Ealing.[5] He knew something of me, and a proposal to see my prints ensued. Accordingly, he breakfasted here today, and on

1. MS reads *instance,* but Cole's copy reads *instant.*

2. 'niece [first cousin] to the late Lord Albemarle [George Keppel (1724–72), 3d E. of Albemarle, who d. 13 Oct. 1772], and for whom she went out of mourning while I was there. She has spent some time with Lady Montfort, and I left them together on Tuesday with a promise to go again, but as my Lord is of the party, I rather think I shall stay at Milton' (addition in Cole's copy). Sophia Thomas was a daughter of Gen. John Thomas, by Lady Sophia Keppel (1711–73), only daughter of 1st E. of Albemarle (see Collins, *Peerage,* 1812, iii. 733). HW was acquainted with Lady Sophia Thomas, and undoubtedly with her daughter (see, e.g., HW to Montagu 23 Aug. 1765).

3. Two miles south of Cambridge.

4. 'Mr Pemberton,' as appears from Cole's reference below. Probably Jeremiah Pemberton (1711?–1800), of Emmanuel College; Lord of the Manor of Trumpington; or it may have been Jeremiah's brother

Christopher (1727–1809), Fellow of St Catharine Hall (1751–61), who married in 1760, Ann Stevenson, the daughter of Cole's friend John Stevenson (see *Alumni Cantab.;* Palmer, *Monumental Inscriptions,* pp. xiii, xiv, 177, 258).

5. Joseph Gulston (1745–86), M.P. for Poole, Dorset, 1780–4; a famous collector of books and prints, in the collection of which he spent a large fortune; he was obliged to sell his books in 1784, and his prints (the sale lasted forty days) in 1786, a few months before his death (see DNB). In HW's notes on Collectors of English Portrait-Prints in his 1771 MS Book of Materials, p. 2, now in the Folger Library, he says: 'Richard Bull and Mr Gulston, who were indefatigable, and the former especially, in little more than a year amassed a most prodigious collection. These two gentlemen spared no expense, and thence raised the prices so exceedingly, that heads which used to be sold for sixpence or less, were advanced to five shillings. They both have given five guineas for a scarce single print that two

a very slight offer of accommodating him with such prints or heads as he had not, he absolutely has taken 187 of my favourite and most valuable heads, such as he had not, and most of which he had never seen, and all this with as much ease and familiarity as if we had been old acquaintance. I must do him the justice to say that I really did offer him at Mr Pemberton's to take such as he had not, but this I thought would not have exceeded a dozen or thereabouts. He has absolutely gutted and garbled my collection of all my choice old heads of the greatest scarcity and curiosity, and I never more shall have any chance of meeting with the same again. My natural modesty (may I call it so) prevented my putting a stop to his voraciousness, and so he took all that struck him. My grief is that all this destruction is for a person with whom I am noways acquainted and probably shall never see again. What he means to give me in return I know not: he talked of some books, but in my own mind he can scarce make me an equivalent. When he was gone I could not but recollect the infinite difference of your delicate scrupulosity in even not too long looking at any head you might wish to have, for fear of an offer of it. But so much does one man differ from another! As I may thank myself for not putting a stop to his garbling my prints, so I must e'en make the best of a foolish bargain and say nothing of it but to yourself. He wanted me to come to Ealing to him this next week for a few days, but I am sure if I go not to Strawberry Hill I shall hardly think of any other place. I wish this recital of my folly may make you less sensible of your own pains, and if it occasions the forgetfulness of a single twinge of your gout, my loss will be made much lighter to, dear Sir, with the sincerest wishes for your speedy recovery,

Your most obliged and faithful servant,

WM COLE

Mr Gulston had a person with him, a little man of Oxford, whom he called Jack—probably the clergyman of the parish.[6]

years before would not have fetched two shillings. But the greatest mischief they did was in cutting books to pieces for a single print or two.' Richard Bull of Ongar, Essex (1725–1806), M.P. for Newport, Cornwall, 1754–80 (see L[ewis] B. Namier, *Structure of Politics at the Accession of George III*, 1929, 2 vols, esp. ii. 571 n).

6. Probably (see *post* 6 Jan. 1773 n. 5), John Higgate (1737–88), son of John Higgate of St James, Westminster; rector of Slapton, Bucks, 1765–88 (*Alumni Oxon*). There is no record that he was the vicar of Ealing (see Thomas Faulkner, *The History and Antiquities of Brentford, Ealing, & Chiswick*, 1845, p. 178).

To Cole, Tuesday 15 December 1772

Add MS 5952, ff. 113–4.

Cole has endorsed the letter; 'Received Wednesday, December 16, 1772.'

Address: To the Reverend Mr Cole at Milton near Cambridge.

Postmark: 15 DE.

[Strawberry Hill, Dec. 15, 1772.]

I HAVE had a relapse and not been able to use my hand, or I should have lamented with you on the plunder of your prints by that Algerine hog.[1] I pity you, dear Sir, and feel for your awkwardness, that was struck dumb at his rapaciousness—the beast has no sort of taste neither—and in a twelvemonth will sell them again. I regret particularly one print, which I dare to say he seized, that I gave you, Gertrude More;[2] I thought I had another and had not; and as you liked it, I never told you so. This Muley Moloch[3] used to buy books, and now sells them. He has hurt his fortune, and ruined himself to have a collection, without any choice of what it should be composed. It is the most underbred swine I ever saw, but I did not know it was so ravenous—I wish you may get paid anyhow. You see by my writing, how difficult it is to me,[4] and therefore will excuse my being short.

Yours ever,

H. W.

From Cole, Wednesday 6 January 1773

VA, Forster MS 110, ff. 116–7. Cole kept no copy.

Address: To the Honourable Hor. Walpole Esq., Arlington Street, London. Free Montfort. *Postmark:* Saffron Walden 8 IA.

Horseth Hall, Jan. 6, 1773.

Dear Sir,

I WAS desirous, very desirous, to know how you fared in mind and body with your shocking companion the gout before I sent you

1. Joseph Gulston; his father was 'head of the first mercantile house in the British factory at Lisbon' (see LI v. 2–3). Gulston's corpulence warranted the epithet 'hog' (see a print of him in op. cit., frontispiece to vol. v).

2. Helen More (1606–33), dau. of Cresacre More, and great-granddaughter of

Sir Thomas More. In 1623 she took the veil as 'Gertrude' and became a nun of Cambray (see DNB). The print is probably that described in *Granger*[1] ii. 105–6: a 12mo, R. Lochon sc., *Magnes Amoris Amor*, but see also *Granger*[5] iii. 145.

3. Abd el Malek, or Muley Moloch (d. 1578), King of Morocco 1576–8. HW prob-

this letter, but not hearing from you, and as you have no reason to write to me directly, I despaired of a letter from you very soon to inform me of your present situation in that respect. I was unwilling to add vexation of the most minute sort to your too many already complaints, but am not capable of holding out longer on a subject possibly you may still be ignorant of, as the book is not published, and may expect very naturally from my friendship to be informed of it. Know then, that the formidable, threatening author of the *Benet College History* has produced his nothing of twenty pages in quarto[1] about a fortnight ago, for on Dec. 24, dining at the Master of Pembroke's, who is his neighbour rector in the country,[2] but no otherwise connected with him, while I was with him, his blue paper pamphlet came in as a present. Mr Tyson was there also, and by him I could find out, though I believe he did not mean that I should hear him, that the author of the *Topography*, who is, I think, a director and manager at the Antiquary Society,[3] had them printed, as I guess, at the Society's expense, with an intention, as I suppose, to make a part of the second volume of the *Archaeologia*, and sent him down thirty copies to Cambridge, where the answerer always is for a week or ten days at Caius College in order to guttle among the colleges that will receive him this festival time. These were to be distributed by him among his acquaintance; accordingly, going from Pembroke to Tyson's room at Benet College, I found two on his table, one for himself, the other <for> Mr Nasmith,[4] then at Norwich. I carried one home with me, and in my life never read such <a> heap of rubbish, and in his unpolished style is of the true blackguard stamp. Trifles of objections which you will never give yourself the trouble to think of. I do not know how to send you one: possibly they are to be met with at the Society or among the members, but if difficult for you to come at in this unpublished state, I will do my

ably is thinking of him as he appears in Dryden's *Don Sebastian, King of Portugal,* not as an historical personage.

4. The writing is very cramped.

---

1. Robert Masters's *Some Remarks on Mr Walpole's Historic Doubts.*

2. James Brown was rector of Stretham, Cambridgeshire (see GM Oct. 1784, liv. 798).

3. Richard Gough, author of *Anecdotes*

of *British Topography,* 1768, 'was, on the death of Dr Gregory Sharpe, Master of the Temple, nominated Director of the same Society, 1771; which office he held till Dec. 12, 1797, when he quitted the Society altogether' (LA vi. 271).

4. HW has written 'Mr Nasmith' above the passage in Cole's letter, where the writing is blurred.

endeavour to get one from the Master of Pembroke, who I dare say will lend me his. He desired me to make his particular compliments to you. I am sorry to see a society abet the impertinence of their president, but am glad they have employed the dullest fellow among them. Envy and jealousy will always attend superior parts and abilities, and it is a tax you must not expect to be exempted from with such a fund as you have.

Pray let me hear from you as soon as is convenient to you. All I have heard speak of this stupid production are of the same opinion with me.

I am glad to inform you Gertrude More is destined to Strawberry Hill. I was sorry to hear of your politeness, and would never have taken it had I known all circumstances, but by good fortune I have it, and you are its real proprietor. I had a letter t'other day from Ealing, very polite, with an invitation to stay there two or three months, which was singular on such an acquaintance.[5] What is more to the purpose, he acquiesces in my proposal of half a crown a head, one with the other, which comes to just £25 within a trifle, and I am to have books in lieu.[6]

Mr Gray's head is elegantly engraved in the same size and copied from Mr Mason's print by one Henshaw,[7] an extraordinary genius for engraving which arose at Cambridge without anyone's taking any notice of him till just now. I gave him Mr Mason's etching and have gotten leave for him to copy two or three capital pictures at Lord Montfort's, particularly one of Chancellor Bromley,[8] of whom there is no print, which made me desirous of his engraving it.

But I will tire you no longer with this scrawl, not having a suit-

5. The letter was written by John Higgate, 31 Dec. 1772, for Gulston, who was suffering from the gout. In the postscript is this passage: 'Mr Gulston desires me to add, that if you will come to town in about a fortnight's time, he will send his carriage to meet you in London any day you will fix; and further hopes you will come and stay two or three months with him' (Add MS 5992, f. 207; Cole's copy, ibid. 5844, f. 37).

6. Writing to Gulston, 20 Dec. 1772, Cole listed some of the books he wished in exchange: 'a good Paris edition of Moreri's Dictionary, Comte Caylus's works, with Lodge's *Peerage of Ireland*,' and Anthony à Wood's *Historia & Antiquitates Oxon.* (Cole's copy, Add MS ibid.) It is not known which books he finally received.

7. William Henshaw (1753–75), son of John Henshaw, a gunsmith of Cambridge and pupil of Bartolozzi. It was printed in two states, black and red. See W. S. Lewis, *A Selection of the Letters of Horace Walpole*, New York and London, 1926, 2 vols, i. 17. See *post* 24 Dec. 1775 n. 19.

8. Sir Thomas Bromley (1530–87), who became Lord Chancellor, 1579, and presided over the trial of Mary Queen of Scots, 1586. He was Montfort's ancestor.

able pen, and take my leave, praying God to grant you many happy
and healthful returns of this season, and am, dear Sir,

Your ever obliged and faithful servant,

WM COLE

I wish this trumpery fellow's more trumpery performance may
provoke you to publish the answer[9] to Dr Milles's first absurd attack.

To Cole, Friday 8 January 1773

Add MS 5952, ff. 115–6.
Address: [From COLE's copy, Add MS 5844, f. 37.] To the Reverend Mr Cole,
Milton near Cambridge. Free Geo. Selwyn.

Arlington Street, Jan. 8, 1773.

IN return to your very kind inquiries, dear Sir, I can let you know
that I am quite free from pain, and walk a little about my room
even without a stick; nay, have been four times to take the air in the
park. Indeed, after fourteen weeks, this is not saying much—but it
is a worse reflection, that when one is subject to the gout, and far
from young, one's worst account will probably be better than that
after the next fit. I neither flatter myself on one hand, nor am impatient on the other—for will either do one any good? One must
bear one's lot[1] whatever it be.

I rejoice Mr G. has justice though he had no bowels. How Gertrude More escaped him I do not guess. It will be wrong to rob you
of her after she has come to you through so many hazards—nor would
I hear of it, either if you have a mind to keep her, or have not given
up all thoughts of a collection since you have been visited by a Visi-
goth.

I am much more impatient to see Mr Gray's print, than Mr What-
d'ye-call-him's[2] answer to my *Historic Doubts*. He may have made
himself very angry, but I doubt whether he will make me at all so.
I love antiquities, but I scarce ever knew an antiquary who knew
how to write upon them. Their understandings seem as much in

9. It was not published until 1798, in
Works ii. 221*–*244.

1. MS reads *one lot's*.
2. Robert Masters's *Some Remarks*.

ruins as the things they describe. For the Antiquarian Society, I shall leave them in peace with Whittington and his cat. As my contempt for them has not however made me disgusted with what they do not understand, antiquities, I have published two numbers of *Miscellanies,* and they are very welcome to mumble them with their toothless gums. I want to send you these—not their gums, but my pieces, and a Grammont,[3] of which I have printed only an hundred copies, and which will be extremely scarce, for twenty-five copies are gone to France. Tell me how I shall convey them safely.

Another thing you must tell me, if you can, is, if you know anything ancient of the freemasons. Governor Pownal,[4] a Whittingtonion,[5] has a mind they should have been a corporation erected by the popes. As you see what a good creature I am and return good for evil, I am engaged to pick up what I can for him to support this system, in which I believe no more than in the Pope; and the work is to appear in a volume of the Society's pieces.[6] I am very willing to oblige him; and turn my cheek that they may smite that also—Lord help them, I am sorry they are such numskulls, that they make me almost think myself something!—but there are great authors enough to bring me to my senses again. Posterity I fear will class me with the writers of this age, or forget me with them, not rank me with any names that deserve remembrance. If I cannot survive the Milleses, the What-d'ye-call-hims, and the compilers of catalogues of topography,[7] it would comfort me very little to confute them. I should be as little proud of success, as if I had carried a contest for churchwarden.

3. *Mémoires du Comte de Grammont, par Monsieur le Comte Antoine Hamilton. Nouvelle Edition, Augmentée de Notes & d'Eclaircissemens necessaires, Par M. Horace Walpole.* Strawberry Hill. MDCCLXII. The book was dedicated, but not by name, to Mme du Deffand, who assisted with the introduction and dedication. HW records that at the end of May, 1772, he 'finished the *Mémoires de Grammont,* which had been delayed by various accidents' (*Jour. Print. Off.* 16).

4. Thomas Pownall (1722–1805), politician and antiquary; lieutenant-governor of New Jersey 1753; governor of Massachusetts 1757–9; and of South Carolina 1759–60; M.P. for Tregony, 1767–74; for Mine-

head, 1774–80; author of *The Administration of the Colonies,* 1764, and numerous other publications. He was HW's occasional correspondent, and wrote an account of Sir Robert Walpole which was printed in William Coxe, *Memoirs of Walpole,* 1798, iii. 615–20.

5. That is, a member of the Society of Antiquaries.

6. 'Observations on the Origin and Progress of Gothic Architecture, and on the Corporation of Free Masons supposed to be the Establishers of it as a regular Order,' read before the Society of Antiquaries, 14 and 21 Feb. 1788, and published in *Archaeologia* ix (1789). 110–26.

7. Richard Gough.

Not being able to return to Strawberry Hill, where all my books and papers are, and my printer[8] lying fallow, I want some short bits to print. Have you anything you wish printed? I can either print a few to amuse ourselves, or if very curious and not too dry, could make a third number of *Miscellaneous Antiquities*.[9]

I am not in any eagerness to see Mr What-d'ye-call-him's pamphlet against me; therefore pray give yourself no trouble to get it for me. The specimens I have seen of his writing,[10] take off all edge from curiosity. A print of Mr Gray will be a real present. Would not it be dreadful to be commended by an age that had not taste enough to admire his Odes?[11] Is not it too great a compliment to me to be abused too? I am ashamed! Indeed our antiquaries ought to like me; I am but too much on a par with them. Does not Mr Henshaw come to London? Is he a professor, or only a lover of engraving? If the former, and he were to settle in town, I would willingly lend him heads to copy.

Adieu! dear Sir. Believe me,

Ever most faithfully yours,

Hor. Walpole[12]

8. Thomas Kirgate (1734–1810), HW's printer and secretary for nearly thirty years: 18 March–24 Aug. 1765 and 6 April 1768 to HW's death in 1797 (see *Jour. Print. Off.*, *passim*; W. S. Lewis, *The Forlorn Printer; being Notes on Horace Walpole's Alleged Neglect of Thomas Kirgate*, Farmington, Conn., Privately Printed, 1931).

9. Nothing came of this proposal.

10. HW probably refers to Masters's *History of Corpus Christi College, Cambridge*.

11. Cf. *ante* 28 Jan. 1772.

12. On the verso of the last page of HW's letter, Cole has written the following notes for his reply: 'Dame G. More, Henshaw, Mr Gray's print, Lord Ossory's cross.'

At the end of his copy of this letter Cole wrote: 'This sprightly answer to my letter wrote from my Lord Montfort's at Horseth Hall on Jan. 7 [6], three days before, may want explanation in some parts, but as I wrote it from home, I kept no copy of my letter, which informed him of Mas-

ters's pamphlet, printed at the Antiquary Society's expense, and to make a part of their next or second volume of *Archaeologia*, thirty copies of which were sent to him by Mr Gough during Mr Walpole's dangerous sickness, and which Masters distributed as presents to his friends at Cambridge during the Christmas holidays. I mentioned to him also young Henshaw's surprising genius, without much of a master except some instructions in Yorkshire for about nine months from his uncle, Mr Stevens [William Stephens, engraver and printseller], late engraver at Cambridge. His father [John Henshaw (fl. 1773–91); see *Universal British Directory*, 5 vols, 1791–8?, ii. 492] is a gunsmith at Cambridge. I got my Lord Montfort to let him copy a small madonna by Carlo Maratti, a picture of Chancellor Bromley, and lent him a head of Mr Gray which he had given me, etched by Mr Mason and amended by Mr Mason with a black lead pencil, and which he admirably finished. I wrote also to Mr Gulston from Horseth, but kept no copy.'

From COLE, Wednesday 13 January 1773

VA, Forster MS 110, ff. 118–9. COLE's copy, Add MS 5844, f. 38.
Address: For the Honourable Mr Horace Walpole in Arlington Street, Westminster. *Postmark:* Cambridge 14 IA.

Milton, Jan. 13, 1773.

Dear Sir,

NOT a more refreshing letter could I possibly receive than your last, giving me an account of your recovery. May every day add fresh strength to you, and so far from apprehending every new attack will make greater havoc, I am apt to believe the contrary, and think the venom spends itself as it grows older. However that be, your rule is a very good one, not to be impatient about what we can't avoid.

I returned[1] here on Friday, and have been laid up with a cold[2] ever since, and was to have dined today at Emmanuel with a party of[3] antiquaries, but was forced to send yesterday to make my excuse. I wrote to my two most intelligent friends, Messrs Lort of Trinity and Farmer of Emmanuel about the freemasons, but neither could give me any account of their so early institution. The earliest account I ever saw of them is what you pointed out to me last summer in *Leland's Life,* where mention is made of Peter Gower.[4] I wish I could help you in this matter, but I know your forces, and am glad to have the chance of a brilliant in our next *Archaeologia,*[5] though it may utterly extinguish the glare of the false stones from our Whittingtonians.

I long vastly to have your two numbers of *Miscellaneous Antiquities* and the edition of Grammont, and think myself greatly obliged to you for remembering me for one when your number is so small. I ever esteemed the book, and shall so doubly from the press it comes. Please to send it to me by the Cambridge fly in Gray's Inn Lane, Holborne, and to be left at Mr Alderman Bentham's. When I see your *Miscellaneous Antiquities* I shall be a better judge of what

1. 'from Lord Montfort's' (addition in Cole's copy).

2. 'and its constant attendant, a sore throat' (addition in Cole's copy).

3. 'eight or nine antiquaries, summoned on my account, which makes my disorder more uneasy to me' (addition in Cole's copy).

4. See *ante* 17 June 1772.

5. Pownall's article on the freemasons was not printed in *Archaeologia* until 1789 (see preceding letter).

sort you compose them, and whether I have anything worthy your notice, which I much doubt. I know I shall esteem it as the greatest honour I can have done me to have even a mere trifle printed at a press that will ever be distinguished <as the> most capital one for taste and delicacy. I will run over my volumes and see whe<ther I> have anything that won't discredit your book, but think I have none.

The truth of the case is, Mr Gulston did take Dame Gertrude More, but in my letter to him about the price he was to give me for his depredations I first of all set out that that print was none of my own, and that I insisted upon its being returned: this he has promised.[6] I did not mention your name in any shape, so he has no idea to whom it belongs, and shall not know it. When I have it, which I suppose will be soon, with my books, you shall have it, with Mr Gray's print, which is only a copy from one done by Mr Mason and a little touched up by him with a black lead pencil, and by Mr Gray given to me about four years ago. This I lent to Mr Henshaw. Since that, there is another print of Mr Gray by one Sharp[7] of Cambridge, but a very bad one, from the same original print by Mr Mason. Mr Henshaw is a young engraver at Cambridge, son to a gunsmith there, and nephew to one Mr Stevens, an engraver and printseller at Cambridge in your time, whom you possibly may remember. He had a good fortune left him in Yorkshire,[8] and his nephew was with him for about eight or nine months, which is all the instruction he has had, but it is great pity he has not the advantage of a London or Paris education, which would make him one of the greatest of his profession. I will, the next time I go to Cambridge, inform him of what you say.

Mr Essex has had orders from Lord Ossory to see the cross finished at Cambridge and to send it from thence to Ampthill. I suppose I may let him have the eight verses which you sent to me some time ago, to be inscribed under it. He has asked about them.

I am sending my servant to Lord Montfort's, and will get him to

6. Cole wrote to Gulston, 20 Dec. 1772: 'There is one head which I must beg to be returned at all events, as it cannot properly be called my own: Dame Gertrude More. I did not observe that you laid it aside, or should have mentioned it. Since I saw you, it is reclaimed by the person who has a better title to it than myself, and I shall be uneasy if I do not replace it where it ought to go' (Cole's copy, Add MS 5844, f. 37). John Higgate, writing for Gulston, 31 Dec. 1772, replied: 'The Gertrude More will be returned in due time' (Cole's copy, loc. cit.).

7. Christopher Sharpe, 'a frame-maker of Cambridge' (addition in Cole's copy).

8. 'whither he is retired' (addition in Cole's copy).

frank this.⁹ I am in no small hurry, and hope you'll excuse this scrawl. My reason for sending is this: This morning a discovery was made by his brother¹⁰ to me, that my boy,¹¹ for he is not above eighteen, though he has lived with me above ten years, has a child ready to be sworn to him. The lad is frightened out of his wits, and is going to fly the neighbourhood. I wish him a good settlement as a groom. I will be answerable to anyone for his honesty, integrity, fidelity and every good quality a servant can have, and as for understanding horses and driving a coach and keeping horses, harness and coach clean, it is his passion, but I must say that he understands little else. The stable is his delight, and there he lives, but very awkward about anything else. If it should lie in your way to recommend him to any gentleman who wants a faithful servant whom I regret to part with, you will add to the infinite obligations I have already received from you, and am, dear Sir,

Yours most faithfully,

WM COLE

From COLE, Friday 12 February 1773

VA, Forster MS 110, f. 120. COLE's copy, Add MS 5844, f. 38v.
Address: For the Honourable Mr Horace Walpole in Arlington Street, London.
Postmark: Cambridge 15 FE.

Milton, February 12, 1773.

Dear Sir,

I HAVE waited and waited till I am out of all patience, in expectation of receiving Dame Gertrude More, and though it is above six weeks that I desired it might be returned to me, with some books I named, yet I have heard nothing of them. It was in this expectation that I deferred thanking you for your most kind and entertaining presents,¹ which, as they deserve, I ever value more than any books in my study.

I have a design of coming to town about April for a few days, and

9. The letter is not franked, and the address is in Cole's hand.
10. Thomas Wood, 'who has lived with me sixteen years' (addition in Cole's copy).
11. James or 'Jem' Wood.

1. *Miscellaneous Antiquities, Nos. I and II,* and *Mémoires du Comte de Grammont* (see *ante* 8 Jan. 1773).

shall then take an opportunity of calling on you and talking over what you was so kind to mention in relation to any curious tracts which may have fallen in my way. I should and meant to have sent Mr Gray's print with the other, but Mr Henshawe calling on me on Sunday sennight, informed me that he has given one to Dr Ewin, who was going to town, and intended calling at Arlington Street. When you see more of this young engraver's performances, I think your opinion of him will improve. He designs doing himself the honour to wait on you when he goes to town, and I dare say his modest and engaging behaviour will contribute to raise his merit with you as an artist, who are generally such coxcombs as to make themselves troublesome.

I had a letter from Mr Lort today, dated February 6, in which he tells me of his having had a card from you,[2] and of his intention of waiting on you, as last week. I hope he will be civiller to you than he was to me when I asked him if he knew anything of the freemasons' institution. As he knew for whom I requested the information, he told me very bluntly, in his manner, that what he knew of that matter he should communicate to Governor Pownall, who had spoke to him of it. I said no more, and have only asked him and Mr Farmer, as being the only two that I am acquainted with whom I thought likely to know anything relating to it. I wish I could be more useful.

I hope this will find you quite recovered, and that you procured at Mr West's sale[2a] such prints as wanted. I hear they sold very dear.

I am sorry to inform you that Lord Orford[3] has been and continues[4] to be dangerously ill at Chesterford, where Dr Batty[5] from London, and the Pro<fes>sor[6] and Dr Glynn from Cambridge, attend him constantly. He was apprehensive, by an eruption on his hands, that he had got some cutaneous distemper, and was advised to take Maredant's drops,[7] which struck the humour inwards and occa-

2. The card is missing. Lort's reply is dated 4 Feb. 1773.

2a. See *ante* 16 May 1762.

3. George Walpole (1730–91), 3d E. of Orford; HW's nephew.

4. 'confined at Gardiner's at Chesterford' (addition in Cole's copy).

5. William Battie (1704–76), physician; delivered lectures at Cambridge, which HW attended while at the University; practised at Cambridge, Uxbridge, and

London; proprietor of a large private asylum; practice limited almost exclusively to insanity. He again attended Lord Orford in 1777 (see HW to Sir Edward Walpole 25 April 1777).

6. Russell Plumptre, Regius Professor of Physic at Cambridge.

7. A 'celebrated antiscorbutic' of undetermined content invented by 'Surgeon Norton' (Sir Ambrose Heal, N&Q 21 Sept. 1935, clxix. 209).

sioned a delirium, which possesses him now. They talk of moving him to London as soon as possible.

Lord Ossory has sent to Mr Essex to have the cross made at Cambridge and from thence to be sent to Ampthill.

I am, dear Sir,

Your ever obliged and faithful servant,

WM COLE

People that write as you do have little to fear or care about the Grub Street of Messrs Milles, What-d'ye-call-'em or the Compilers of Topography. When the Society is in such hands, there can be little credit to be called a member of it. Mr Lort writes me word that the great print of the Camp Drap d'Or[8] is to be out by Lady Day.

I dare say you was surprised when the Master of Catharine's Hall's book[9] came to you. He heard that I was at the Rose Tavern at dinner last Friday,[10] and he came to me there, and gave me his book, and sat down with the company, who were all strangers to him. He afterwards followed me to Mr Bentham's, where I drank tea,[11] and there I found out that in honour to your father's memory and in regard to your own literary merit, he had sent a copy not only to you, but to Sir Edward Walpole, whom I dare say he never saw in his life. Poor man! his bodily infirmities, which have been and are very great, with stone or gravel, have shattered his intellects in such a manner that it is hardly fit he should be suffered to wander about the town as he does.[12] But he is not to be contradicted, it seems, at home, and therefore does as he pleases. This therefore must be his excuse.

8. 'Le Champ de Drap d'Or. The Interview of Henry VIII, King of England, and the French King Francis I, between Guines and Ardres, in the Month of June 1520. From the original picture, twelve feet one inch in length, and six feet five inches in height, preserved in the private apartments in Windsor Castle. Drawn from the original by E. Edwards. Engrav'd by James Basire. Publish'd . . . Nov. 10, 1774.' It was published by the Society of Antiquaries, and sold, with 'an Historical Description thereof in Letter Press,' for £2.2.0 (see 'List of Works Published by the Society of Antiquaries' at end of *Archaeologia* iii, 1775).

9. Kenrick Prescot (1702–79), Master of St Catharine's College, Cambridge, 1741–79 (see *Alumni Cantab.*; George Forrest Browne, *St. Catharine's College*, 1902, pp. 206–8). The book mentioned is his *Letters concerning Homer the Sleeper in Horace: with additional classic amusements*, Cambridge, 1773. HW's copy was sold SH v. 147.

10. 'at the County Club' (addition in Cole's copy).

11. Cole's copy reads *coffee*.

12. 'and be so much his own master as to expose himself by writing and acting as if he was *compos mentis*' (addition in Cole's copy).

To Cole, Thursday 18 February 1773

Add MS 5952, ff. 117–8.

Cole wrote the following note for his reply on the cover: 'To tell Mr. W. from Mr Ashby, President of St John's, that "butter the rooks nests," etc., must infallibly be a mistake for "battre or batter" them, agreeable to Knox's principles and position, to pull down entirely all churches and monasteries, that the monks might have no prospect of ever returning again.' The note refers to a passage in *Miscellaneous Antiquities, No. II* 19.

Address: To the Reverend Mr Cole at Milton near Cambridge.
Postmark: 18 FE.

Arlington Street, Feb. 18, 1773.

THE most agreeable ingredient of your last, dear Sir, is the paragraph that tells me you shall be in town in April, when I depend on the pleasure of seeing you; but to be certain, wish you would give me a few days' law,[1] and let me know too where you lodge. Pray bring your books, though the continuation of the *Miscellaneous Antiquities* is uncertain. I thought the affectation of loving veteran anecdotes[2] was so vigorous, that I ventured to print 500 copies. 130 only are sold—I cannot afford to make the town perpetual presents, though I find people exceedingly eager to obtain them when I do: and if they will not buy them, it is a sign of such indifference, that I shall neither bestow my time or my cost to no purpose. All I desire is to pay the expenses, which I can afford much less than my idle moments. Not but the operations of my press have often turned against myself in many shapes. I have told people many things they did not know, and from fashion they have bought a thousand things out of my hands, which they do not understand, and only love *en passant*. At Mr West's sale I got literally nothing; his prints sold for the frantic sum of fourteen hundred and ninety-five pounds ten shillings. Your and my good friend Mr Gulston threw away above two hundred pounds there.

I am not sorry Mr Lort has recourse to the fountain-head: Mr Pownal's system of freemasonry is so absurd and groundless that I am glad to be rid of intervention. I have seen the former[3] once: he

---

1. Notice, leeway (see OED sb. iv. Sport).
2. HW introduced the first number of *Miscellaneous Antiquities* with 'The taste for anecdotes and historic papers, for ancient letters that record affairs of state, illustrate characters of remarkable persons, or preserve the memory of former manners

and customs, was never more general than at present' (p. [iii]).
3. Gulston: Lort was not a print-collector on a large scale, and furthermore HW had been acquainted with him since 1769 (see *ante* 15 July 1769). Mrs Gulston, writing to Granger, 4 Feb. 1772, says: 'he [Gul-

told me he was willing to sell his prints as the value of them is so increased—for that very reason I did not want to purchase them.

Paul Sandby promised me ten days ago to show Mr Henshaw's engravings (which I received from Dr Ewin) to Bartolozzi,[4] and ask his terms, thinking he would delight in so very promising a scholar; but I have heard nothing since, and therefore fear there is no success. Let me however see the young man when he comes, and I will try if there is any other way of serving him.

What shall I say to you, dear Sir, about Dr Prescot? or what shall I say to him? It hurts me not to be very civil, especially as any respect to my father's memory touches me much more than any attention to myself, which I cannot hold to be a quarter so well founded. Yet how dare I write to a poor man, who may do, as I have lately seen done by a Scotch woman that wrote a play, and printed Lord Chesterfield's and Lord Lyttelton's letters to her, as *testimonia autorum*.[5] I will therefore beg *you* to make my compliments and thanks to the Master, and to make them as grateful as you please, provided I am dispensed with giving any certificate under my hand. You may plead my illness, which though the fifth month ended yesterday, is far from being at an end. My relapses have been endless; I cannot yet walk a step; and a great cold has added an ague in my cheek for which I am just going to begin the bark. The prospect for the rest of my days is gloomy. The case of my poor nephew still more deplorable: he arrived in town last night, and bore his journey tolerably—but his head is in much more danger of not recovering, than his health, though they give us hopes of both—but the evils of life are not good subjects for letters—why afflict one's friends? Why make commonplace reflections? Adieu!

Yours ever,

H. W.

ston] has been with Mr Walpole' (LI v. 58), which may be the meeting to which HW refers.

4. Francesco Bartolozzi (1727–1815), engraver; born at Florence; came to England as engraver to the King, 1764; original member of Royal Academy, 1769. He later accepted Henshaw as his pupil.

5. Cole notes on this passage: '*Vide Critical Review* for March 1773, pp. 231–3 [230–2].—*Sir Harry Gaylove; or Comedy in Embryo*. In Five Acts. London. 8vo.' (Add MS 5844, f. 39). The author of the play, Mrs Jane Marshall or Marishall (fl. 1765),

dramatist and imitator of Richardson, first published it by subscription in Edinburgh, 1773. The title-page of the play reads 1772, but HW corrected his copy (now WSL) to 1773, and wrote beneath, 'Jan. 5.' Mrs Marshall gives an account in the preface of her unsuccessful efforts to have the play acted: Garrick, Colman and Foote refused it. In hope of receiving encouragement from higher quarters, she sent the play to Lord Chesterfield and Lord Lyttelton, whose letters in reply she quotes at the conclusion of the preface.

From COLE, Friday 19 March 1773

VA, Forster MS 110, f. 121. COLE's copy, Add MS 5844, f. 39.
Address: For the Honourable Mr Horace Walpole in Arlington Street, Westminster. *Postmark:* [Cambridge] 20 MR.

Milton, March 19, 1773.

Dear Sir,

I WAS unwilling to trouble you with a letter till I had fully executed your commission at Catharine Hall, for though I sent such a letter as I think you would have approved,[1] yet as I received no answer in return, I thought it best to call in person, which I did yesterday, and drank tea there. The Master said he loved the Walpoles, and that was all that he said on the subject and seemed to be well satisfied with the apology I had made in my letter to him for you, after which I had nothing from him but scraps out of the Latin and Greek poets and a vast deal about the cock in Shakespeare, with other things in his book, by which I found that he thought of little else, and was wholly occupied by the subject.

I hear the *Archaeologia* is come out. Nay, indeed I saw it on Mr Tyson's table, into whose chamber I went for a few minutes after my dining[2] in their hall, and before I went to Catharine Hall. Among the rest of the publications he pointed out to me a little dissertation which I wrote out for him about three years ago,[3] in half an hour, and which he soon after printed,[4] with a small historical

1. Cole wrote Prescot 19 Feb. 1773: 'I this moment received a letter from Mr Horace Walpole, commissioning me to make his most grateful thanks and acknowledgments to you for the kind present of your book, and to make excuses at the same time for not writing himself. The truth is, he is so ill at this time, with continual relapses, added to the concern he is now in for his nephew's situation (who got to town but the night before last) that I am assured (from his letter to me) he is in no condition or spirits for writing. He says, "Lord Orford bore his journey tolerably, but his head is in much more danger of not recovering than his health, though they give us hopes of both. But the evils of life are not good subjects for letters—why afflict one's friends?" I will take Mr Wal-

pole's hint, and not repeat a more melancholy part of his letter. What I have already quoted will be his excuse for an omission which, had he been in better health and spirits, would not have happened' (Cole's copy, Add MSS 5844, f. 39).
2. 'with the Society on their first commemoration feast of Bishop Mawson' (addition in Cole's copy).
3. *An Account of an Illuminated Manuscript in the Library of Corpus Christi College, Cambridge,* printed in *Archaeologia* ii. 194–7. Cole presumably is 'a learned friend to whom I am much obliged for many hints' mentioned at p. 195.
4. 'in a meagre quarto book of two or three pages' (addition in Cole's copy). Tyson sent HW a copy of it (see *ante* 15 and 28 Nov. 1770).

print with an author offering a book to Henry V, etc.—a little trumpery performance, and which he seems to value himself on much, and though he knows he had it from me, yet he never once mentioned it. Perhaps he has forgot it.[5]

You amazed me at the price of Mr West's prints. One would wonder where people found the money to throw it away in such handfuls. Mr Gulston has neither sent me my books I desired to have three months ago, with Dame Gertrude More, which he promised and I shall insist on. I believe a journey to him for a day or two will be necessary, though I have a much more necessary affair[6] that should carry me to town, and yet I doubt my indolence and dislike of moving will still keep me in the country. If I stir next month I will write a line to you a week before.

<I>[7] have a commission to you from the President of St John's, Mr Ashby,[8] a very learned <but> singularly talkative man. He desired me to make his compliments and tell you that the <p>roverb made use of by Sir Thomas Wyat,[9] of 'Butter the rooks nests, etc.' must certainly be a mistake or false reading for 'Abattre' or 'Batter the rooks nests,' that is, pull them down <and> destroy them, which was agreeable to Knox the Scotch reformer's position and princi<ple to> entirely demolish all religious houses and monasteries, that the monks might have <no pros>pect of ever returning to inhabit them again. It seems to me a very reaso<nable in>terpretation.

<I h>ope you mend every day, and that this very fine, though cold, season is in your favour: <a piece o>f intelligence which will give great pleasure to, dear Sir,

Your ever faithful and obliged servant,

WM COLE

5. Cole afterwards gave a different account of this affair. In a passage written after Tyson's death, he says: 'I drew up the account of this illumination, and gave it to Mr Tyson. It is not worth reclaiming: but I think he alludes to it in the paper [see note 3 above]. Had he not done so, I should not have mentioned it; he being always very free to own from whom he received it, and it was my desire that he should say nothing further about it, being an insignificant trifle, drawn up at his chambers, when I looked at the MS' (LA viii. 206–7).

6. Probably connected with his annuity, which he purchased with the money he received for his estate at Haddenham and Aldreth.

7. This and the following passages in brackets are supplied from Cole's copy.

8. 'a very learned, ingenious, but singularly talkative and opinionative man' (addition in Cole's copy).

9. See *Miscellaneous Antiquities, No. II* 19.

To Cole, Wednesday 7 April 1773

Add MS 5952, ff. 119–20.

Address: To the Reverend Mr Cole at Milton near Cambridge.
Postmark: EK 7 AP.

Arlington Street, April 7, 1773.

I HAVE now seen the second volume of the *Archaeologia* or *Old Women's Logic,* with Mr Masters's answer to me. If he had not taken such pains to declare it was written against my *Doubts,* I should have thought it was a defence of them, for the few facts he quotes make for my arguments, and confute himself; particularly in the case of the Lady Eleanor Butler;[1] whom by the way he makes marry her own nephew, and not descend from her own family, because she was descended from her grandfather.[2] This Mr Masters is an excellent Sanco Panca to such a Don Quixote as Dean Milles!—but enough of such goosecaps!

Pray thank Mr Ashby for his admirable correction of Sir Thomas Wyat's *bon mot;* it is right beyond all doubt, and I will quote it, if ever the piece is reprinted.[3]

Mr Tyson surprises me by usurping your dissertation.[4] It seems all is fish that comes into the net of the Society. Mercy on us! What a cart-load of brick and rubbish and Roman ruins they have piled together! I have found nothing tolerable in the volume but the dissertation of Mr Maseres,[5] which is followed by an answer,[6] that, like Masters's, contradicts him without disproving anything.

1. Lady Eleanor Talbot (d. ca 1468), dau. of the famous John Talbot, 1st E. of Shrewsbury; m. Sir Thomas Boteler, son of Sir Ralph Boteler (d. 1473), 6th Bn Sudeley. For HW's erroneous account of her, see *Works* ii. 133.

2. For Masters's involved argument, see *Some Remarks, Archaeologia* ii. 206. HW's reply is in *Works* ii. *248.

3. It was not reprinted. In J. W. Croker's copy of *Miscellaneous Antiquities* (now wsl) Croker has written: 'I wrote to Mr Lockhart to ask Miss Berry why these tracts were not published in her father's edition of Walpole's *Works*—this was his answer.' Lockhart's letter is pasted below: 'May 23 1849. Dear Croker: Miss Berry says "Nothing was included in Ld Orford's *Works,* 4to, but such miscellaneous papers as he himself had left for publication—among which the tracts alluded to by Mr

C. were *not:* nor did I ever know of their existence till found among other printed papers upon his death. So that I have no idea why they were never continued beyond 2 or 3 numbers (I forget which) and why never published. This I regret as much as Mr Croker as I remember thinking them very entertaining." '

4. This passage is obliterated in the original MS. Cole's copy (Add MS 5844, f. 39v) reads as above.

5. 'A View of the ancient Constitution of the English Parliament. By Francis Maseres, Esquire, of the Inner Temple,' printed in *Archaeologia* ii. 301–40. Francis Maseres (1731–1824), mathematician, historian and reformer, lawyer; of Clare College, Cambridge. Wright, Cunningham and Toynbee incorrectly print 'Masters.'

6. 'Observations on Mr. Maseres's View of the ancient Constitution of the English

Mr West's books are selling outrageously.[7] His family will make a fortune by what he collected from stalls and Morefields.[8] But I must not blame the *virtuosi,* having surpassed them. In short, I have bought his two pictures of Henry V[9] and Henry VIII[10] and their families, the first of which is engraved in my *Anecdotes,* or as the catalogue says *engraved by Mr H. Walpole,*[11] and the second described there. The first cost me £38[12] and the last, 84; though I knew Mr West bought it for six guineas. But in fact, these two with my marriages of Henry VI and VII[13] compose such a suite of the House of Lancaster, and enrich my Gothic house so completely, that I would not deny myself. The Henry VII cost me as much, and is less curious; the price of antiquities is so exceedingly risen too at present, that I expected to have paid more. I have bought much cheaper at the same sale a picture of Henry VIII and Charles V in one piece,[14] both much younger than ever I saw any portrait of either. I hope

Parliament, by Charles Mellish, Esquire,' printed in *Archaeologia* ii. 341–52. Charles Mellish (d. 1797), lawyer, F.S.A., Recorder of Newark, Commissioner of Stamps (see John Raine, *The History and Antiquities of the Parish of Blyth,* Westminster, 1860, p. 84; H. Askew, N&Q 24 Aug. 1935, clxix. 140).

7. West's books were sold 29 March 1773 and 23 days following, for £2,927.1.0, a very large sum for the time (see DNB). They were chiefly bought by the great book collectors of the day: George III purchased the most important (see Seymour de Ricci, *English Collectors of Books & Manuscripts, 1530–1930,* Cambridge, 1930, pp. 51, 55).

8. 'How contemptibly . . . looks . . . a well-grown Paul's Church-yard bookseller upon one of the trade that sells second-hand books under the trees in Morefields' (Thomas Brown, *Works . . . in Prose and Verse, serious, moral, and comical,* 4 vols, 1707–11, iv. 12).

9. The picture is fully described in *Anecdotes, Works* iii. 35–6; the engraving, by Charles Grignion (or Grignon) (1717–1810) the elder, appears opp. p. 36. In the *Catalogue of the . . . Collection of Pictures . . . of James West* it was 1st day, lot 68, where it was described as 'A most curious historical picture, *the oldest extant in oil,* of *Henry* V, his Queen and family; *vide* Walpole's *Anecdotes.*' Opposite this in his copy of the catalogue (now WSL), HW wrote 'bought by Mr Walpole—35-0-0.' It

was sold SH xxi. 26 to Forster (for Earl Waldegrave) for £131.5.0.

10. For HW's description of this picture, see *Anecdotes, Works* iii. 115 n, and letter to Gough, 27 June 1789. In West's sale it was 3d day, lot 66. HW noted opposite it, 'bought by Mr Walpole—84-0-0,' and he drew a line through the name of the artist to whom it was attributed, Sir Antonio More. It hung over the chimney in the Great North Bedchamber at SH (see *Description of SH, Works* ii. 494), and was sold SH xx. 86 to J. P. Bevan, Esq., for £220.10.0.

11. HW is quoting from memory, and confuses this description with that of lot 16, 1st day: 'Two of Henry V's family, from the celebrated picture engraved by Mr Walpole.' HW did not buy this lot.

12. Probably £35, the figure in HW's catalogue of the sale, is correct (see n. 9 above).

13. Both pictures are described and engraved in *Anecdotes* (*Works* iii. 37–9; 50–1). The 'Marriage of Henry VI' was sold SH xx. 25 to the Duke of Sutherland for £84; it is now in the Toledo [Ohio] Museum of Art. See illustration and Appendix for the 'Marriage of Henry VII,' and *ante* 13 Nov. 1762.

14. This lot is not printed in the West sale catalogue, but at the end of the second day, HW has written in his copy, 'Bought by Mr Walpole—Henry VIII and Charles V—7-7-0.' It hung on the staircase at SH:

your pilgrimage to St *Gulaston's*[15] this month will take place, and that you will come and see them. Adieu! Dear Sir,

> Yours ever,
>
> H. W.[16]

From Cole, Friday 16 April 1773

VA, Forster MS 110, f. 122. Cole kept no copy.
Address: For the Honourable Mr Horace Walpole in Arlington Street.

Queen's Head, Gray's Inn Lane, Friday, April 16, 1773.
Dear Sir,

THIS is merely to inform you that I got to town last night and am gone this morning into the City about the affair that called me hither.[1] What time I shall get back I know not, but shall be glad

'Henry VIII, aged 29, and Charles V, aged 20. . . . Behind Charles V are two figures, probably designed for his grandfather and father, the Emperor Maximilian, and Philip' (*Description of SH, Works* ii. 439). It was sold SH xxi. 27 to James Roberts-West (1811–82), Esq., of Alscot Park, Glos, great-grandson of James West. The artist is not known. It was copied by G. P. Harding and engraved by J. Brown for *Ancient Historical Pictures, No. 1,* 1844 (not in EBP).

15. By *Gulaston*, HW apparently means 'the swallowing thing' or monster, alluding to Gulston's gluttony in taking so many of Cole's prints.

16. Cole has the following note at the end of his copy of this letter (Add MS 5844, ff. 39v, 40): 'Soon after this I paid a visit to Mr Walpole, who carried me down to Strawberry Hill, where I stayed a day or two, then went to Mr Gulston's at Ealing, who paid me very honourably for my prints: and calling again on Mr Walpole in Arlington Street to take leave of him, he told me that Mr Bartolozzi had just left him, was going in a few weeks for Italy to stay a month or two, and would take Mr Henshaw with him, but desired to know what his father would advance with him, and to inform him as soon as might be. I went also to dinner on St George's Day with the Antiquary Society, where the President, Dean Milles, did me the honour to desire Mr Lort to introduce him to me. [This was the first meeting Cole had attended in many years—twenty, he says; see his letter to Gough 9 April 1773, LA i. 674]. As I sat by Mr Lort, the Bishop of Peterborough [John Hinchliffe (1731–94), Bp of Peterborough 1769–94, and Master of Trinity College, Cambridge, 1768–88] and others, the President was giving an account to them of some new discovery in Rastal's *Chronicle* [*The Pastyme of People,* 1529] relating to the murder of Edward V. At the same meeting Mr Gough, the Director, gave me some distant hint that he should like to be introduced to the acquaintance of Mr Walpole, to which I made no other answer than that Mr Walpole no doubt would be proud of the opportunity, and immediately dropped the conversation. However, my friendship from a child with Mr Walpole made me give him notice of both these circumstances by a letter which I wrote in London [24 April 1773] and sent by Mr Essex, who was going to call upon him. The day after I got to Milton I received this letter' [dated 27 April 1773. Cole kept no copy of the two following letters].

1. Probably connected with his annuity (see *ante* 19 March 1773).

to be informed if you are in town or going to Strawberry Hill, or when it will be most convenient for you to see me, and to beg that you will not put yourself out of your way on my account in the least tittle, for if I have not the pleasure of seeing you now, I will take some other opportunity as may be more suitable to you, whom I will not in any manner be troublesome to.[2]

I purpose to go to Mr Gulston's for two days, from whom I had not heard these four months, except Wednesday afternoon, when I received a letter to tell me he should be glad to see me as soon as I came to town, in answer to one of mine to him on that subject. Friday next I mean to celebrate St George's Day at the anniversary meeting of the Society, and return to Milton on the day following.

I am, dear Sir,

Your ever obliged and faithful servant,

WM COLE

From COLE, Saturday 24 April 1773

VA, Forster MS 110, f. 123. Cole kept no copy.
Address: For the Honourable Mr Horace Walpole in Arlington Street, Westminster. [Essex carried the letter to HW.]

[London,] April 24, 1773.

Dear Sir,

MR Essex and myself dining this day in the City with the gentleman to whom you was so kind to give me the ticket of admission to your house at Strawberry Hill,[1] my sister, Mrs Cole, was importunate with me to get her such another, or for four or five in the whole. If it will not be too impertinent, I beg the favour of you to grant me this request, and Mr Essex will take charge of it.

I spent the day yesterday for the last time with the antiquaries at their annual celebration of St George. I never was in such a mob—

2. Cole went to SH, as appears from N&Q 3d S. viii. 379, 4 Nov. 1865, where W.C.B. states that he has Cole's copy of R. Hurd, *Select Works of Mr A. Cowley*, 2 vols, 1772, in which Cole has noted: 'E Libris Guli. Cole ex Donis hon: Viri Hor. Walpole, apud Strawberry Hill, Apr. 18

1773. Dr. Hurd sent this copy as a present to Mr Walpole, who before had purchased it: so he gave it to me.' HW's note inviting Cole to SH is missing.

1. Roger Mawdesley. See *ante* 3 Nov. 1771, 30 July 1772.

hardly able to hear one another speak. The President-Dean,[2] though unknown to me, did me the honour to come and introduce himself to me. Before dinner, and before he knew what he was,[2a] I heard him in deep conversation with people whom I did not know, talking about a discovery from Rastal's *History,* I think, for I did not listen too attentively, bought, as I take it, at Mr West's sale, that made some discoveries concerning the murder of Edward V.[3] I can only just hint this to you, as I heard nothing very distinctly. Mr Gough came to me and seemed to express a wish to me as if he wanted to be introduced to you.

I was fatigued to death yesterday with my walking, and am far from well today, and want sadly to be down at my own little place. I have just sent my servant for my portmanteau and things to be placed at the Queen's Head in Gray's Inn Lane, for the hours at Seymour Place[4] quite kill me.

I am, Sir,

Your most obliged and faithful servant,

WM COLE

To COLE, Tuesday 27 April 1773

Add MS 5952, ff. 121–2.

For Cole's introduction to this letter, see final note on HW to Cole 7 April 1773. Cole received it Friday 30 April (see next letter).

Address: To the Reverend Mr Cole at Milton near Cambridge.
Postmark: RB 28 AP.

Arlington Street, April 27, 1773.

I HAD not time this morning to answer your letter by Mr Essex, but I gave him the card[1] you desired. You know, I hope, how happy I am to obey any orders of yours.

In the paper I showed you in answer to Masters, you saw I was apprised of Rastel's *Chronicle,*[2] but pray do not mention my knowing of it, because I draw so much from it, that I lie in wait, hoping

2. Jeremiah Milles.
2a. Possibly Cole has omitted *about.*
3. Rastell's *Chronicle* was sold 22 April 1773, lot 4094, £19, for George III. It is now in the British Museum. The West catalogue's description of the book quotes West's note referring to the murder of Edward V.

4. Where Lord Montfort lived at this time (see *post* 3 May 1773).

———

1. Of admission to SH for Cole's sister Catherine.
2. HW refers to it in support of his thesis that Sir Thomas More is not a reli-

that Milles or Masters or some of their fools will produce it against me, and then I shall have another word to say to them which they do not expect, since they think Rastel makes for them.

Mr Gough wants to be introduced to me! Indeed! I would see him as he has been midwife to Masters,[3] but he is so dull that he would only be troublesome—and besides you know I shun authors, and would never have been one myself, if it obliged me to keep such bad company. They are always in earnest, and think their profession serious, and dwell upon trifles, and reverence learning. I laugh at all those things, and write only to laugh at them and divert myself. None of us are authors of any consequence, and it is the most ridiculous of all vanities to be vain of being mediocre. A page in a great author humbles me to the dust, and the conversation of those that are not superior to myself reminds me of what will be thought of myself. I blush to flatter them or to be flattered by them, and should dread letters being published sometime or other, in which they should relate our interviews, and we should appear like those puny conceited witlings in Shenstone's[4] and Hughes's Correspondence,[5] who give themselves airs from being in possession of the soil of Parnassus for the time being, as peers are proud because they enjoy the estates of great men who went before them. Mr Gough is very welcome to see Strawberry Hill, or I would help him to any scraps in my possession that would assist his publications,[6] though he is one of those industrious who are only reburying the dead—but I cannot be acquainted with him. It is contrary to my system and my humour; and besides I know nothing of barrows, and Danish entrenchments, and Saxon barbarisms, and Phoenician characters—in short I know nothing of those ages that knew nothing—then how should I be of

able authority: More and Rastell give conflicting accounts of the death of Edward V and his brother (see *Works* ii. *246–7*).

3. Gough, as Director of the Society of Antiquaries, sent thirty copies of Masters's *Short Remarks* to Cambridge (see *ante* 6, 8 Jan. 1773).

4. See *ante* 14 June 1769. In his letters to Graves and Jago, Shenstone praises Whitehead, 'Cotswouldia,' Robert Dodsley and 'a Miss Wheatly of Walsall: many of the pieces written in an excellent and truly classical style; simple, sentimental, harmonious, and more correct than I almost ever saw written by a lady' (*The Works in Verse and Prose of William Shenstone*, 3d

edn, 1773, iii. 152, 283, 300–1, 331 *et passim*).

5. John Hughes (1677–1720). His 'Correspondence' is *Letters by Several Eminent Persons Deceased, including the Correspondence of John Hughes, Esq.*, published from the originals, with notes by John Duncombe, 3 vols, 1772. A second edition appeared in 1773. Two volumes of Hughes's *Letters* were sold SH v. 130. SH v. 141 included 'Duncombe's Letters,' which probably is the third volume. In these letters Jabez Hughes, Glover, Hammond and Duncombe are praised.

6. HW later furnished some of the materials for Gough's *Sepulchral Monuments*.

use to modern *literati?* All the Scotch metaphysicians have sent me their works. I did not read one of them, because I do not understand what is not understood by those that write about it, and I did not get acquainted with one of the writers. I should like to be intimate with Mr Anstey,[7] even though he wrote *Lord Buckhorse*,[8] or with the author of the *Heroic Epistle*[9]—I have no thirst to know the rest of my cotemporaries, from the absurd bombast of Dr Johnson[10] down to the silly Dr Goldsmith, though the latter changeling has had bright gleams of parts, and the former had sense till he changed it for words and sold it for a pension. Don't think me scornful. Recollect that I have seen Pope, and lived with Gray. Adieu!

Yours ever,

H. WALPOLE

PS. Mr Essex has shown me a charming drawing from a charming round window at Lincoln. It has revived all my eagerness to have him continue his plan.

From COLE, Monday 3 May 1773

VA, Forster MS 110, ff. 124–5. COLE's copy, Add MS 5844, ff. 40–41.

Address: For the Honourable Mr Horace Walpole in Arlington Street, Westminster. *Postmark:* Cambridge 4 MA.

Dear Sir,   Milton, Monday, May 3, 1773.

YOUR most sensible and agreeable letter found me at this place on Friday, when I was far from well.[1] Thank God! I am much mended since that time, and enjoy myself and my garden (though

---

7. Christopher Anstey (1724–1805), author of *The New Bath Guide,* 1766, which HW greatly admired (see HW to Montagu 20 June 1766).

8. *The Patriot: a Pindaric Epistle, addressed to Lord Buckhorse,* a burlesque 'written at the close of the Duke of Newcastle's administration, and first published in the year 1767' (John Anstey, *The Poetical Works of the late Christopher Anstey,* 1808, p. 137) 'Lord Buckhorse' whose real name was John Smith (d. 1772) was 'the most noted bruiser of his time' (ibid., p. xxvi; see also Musgrave, *Obituary*).

9. William Mason. HW's reputed co-authorship of the poem was not completely dispelled until the publication of *Satirical Poems Published Anonymously by William Mason, with Notes by Horace Walpole,* ed. Paget Toynbee, Oxford, 1926. HW knew the secret from the beginning, but pretended ignorance to all his correspondents except Mason (ibid. 11–16).

10. See HW's 'General Criticism on Dr. Johnson's Writings,' *Works* iv. 361–2.

---

1. 'yet surrounded by company' (addition in Cole's copy).

too cold still) with much higher relish after the fatigue of so much stirring and bustle one necessarily falls into in town.[2]

Many thanks for the card you was so obliging to give Mr Essex for me, but I am sorry to say that he was the occasion of its being lost at the inn before I saw it. He sent it up to me before I was stirring, and my boy[3] laid it on some papers in the room, which I took all together, and in my passage to the coach it was dropped, for I searched for it the moment I got in, but to no purpose. In passing through Hackney I advertised my sister of the mischance, and she sent away forthwith to the inn in hopes to recover it.[4]

As you lie in wait, I hope the gudgeons will bite, that you may catch them in your snare. They heartily deserve your lash, and will be pitied by no one of taste or understanding.

I entirely agree with you in your notions of Mr Gough. Mr Farmer of Emmanuel, a most sensible, reasonable man, told me three or four months ago that he thought the worse of the Society for making him the Director, who, he said, was noways equal to such a task. I thought as he did, and assure you I never met with a poorer creature or duller mortal. How they came to pitch on such an animal is inconceivable,[5] and yet his book is entertaining and useful. As he said in a slight way to me what I related to you, I thought proper on

2. 'which I hardly ever quitted without bringing back with me a bad cold. My garden gives a proof of the uncertainty of your system that jonquils don't thrive kindly out of Middlesex, for never was such a profusion of the finest sort as actually in this garden, except at Strawberry Hill' (addition in Cole's copy).

3. Cole's copy reads *my servant*, meaning Thomas Wood. James Wood, whom Cole usually calls 'my boy,' had left Milton (see *ante* 13 Jan. 1773).

4. The following paragraph is added in Cole's copy: 'I was forced to quit my excellent lodging in Seymour Place two or three days before I left town, and go to the inn in Gray's Inn Lane on account of my cold and sore throat, for both Lord and Lady Montfort loving to sit up till two or three o'clock, and my bedchamber going out of their dining room, I could not possibly go to bed till they did, and such hours are death to me, even when I am well, much more when out of order. One morning at four or five o'clock his Lord-

ship was standing by my bedside in his masquerade habit, and candle in his hand, which waked me, just as he came from the masquerade at the Pantheon. They both carried me to Ealing and fetched me back again, and if it had not been that her Ladyship was on the eve of falling to pieces, we should have troubled you for a card to have had admittance to see Strawberry Hill, which they threaten to see.' Henry Bromley, afterwards 3d Bn Montfort, was born 14 May 1773.

5. 'except from his plodding industry, of which he seems to be master, which accounts for the usefulness of his book [*British Topography*[1]], though it does not for its entertaining qualifications, for I will do him the justice to say that I have not been better pleased with any modern publication than with his, bating some exceptions in it, and of which I gave him my opinion. I almost doubt whether this is not an actual condemnation of it with persons of a more refined taste' (addition in Cole's copy).

all accounts to <i>nform you of it, and then you were to act as you pleased.[6] I <plan> to write to him soon, but shall not take the least notice of having said a word to you. He claimed a promise of me, which I had utterly <forgotten,> to send him an account of the paintings in Ashridge College.[7]

It gives me great pleasure to inform you of the honourable amende our Univer<sity> made you last week by the Public Orator,[8] after the envious and detracting behaviour of Mr What-d'ye-call-'em and his fautors. One day last week when Mr Beadon the Orator, a most polite and ingenious man, according to form, presented Mr Walpole[9] to the Vice-Chancellor[10] for his honorary degree, he took occasion first to mention your father with all due honour, and then dwelt on your subject for more time than usual, and in such a manner as gave great satisfaction[11] to the members present.[12] This I had from three or four Benedictines[13] who dined with me on Friday, one of whom said that he was not able to get through half of your last

6. 'It is probable they think they have gone too far, especially as the fen parson's publication is such a disgrace to them, and want to make up in private for their public rudeness. I am to write him [Gough] soon, but shall avoid giving the least hint of my having delivered his compliment, which can indeed hardly be called one, as he did not desire me to say so, only in general said he should be glad to be introduced to you' (addition in Cole's copy).

7. Cole wrote to Gough 9 April 1773, apologizing for his forgetfulness, and promised the 'account' when he came to London, 23 April (see LA i. 673–4). It is now Add MS 5840, ff. 196–209. That he did not send the account until about the middle of May appears from an incomplete copy of his letter to Gough 8 May 1773, in which he says Colman will carry the letter for him 'on Friday next,' 14 May (see Add MS 5844, f. 42). Gough wanted the account for his edition of Camden's *Britannia* (1789), but he greatly condensed it: 'The cloisters were . . . beautifully painted, in water colours, the history of our Saviour, in 40 compartments; of which 12 were in 1767 entirely defaced' (Camden, *Britannia*², 4 vols, 1806, ii. 41; see also Henry J. Todd, *The History of the College of Bonhommes at Ashridge*, 1823, pp. 58–9). The College was founded as a monastery in 1283, and later Princess (afterwards Queen) Elizabeth

resided there for some time. A vast mansion, which is now the Bonar Law Memorial College of the Conservative party, was built there in 1808. Nothing remains of the monastery but the crypt (*The Blue Guides: 70 Miles around London*, ed. Findlay Muirhead, 1930, p. 184).

8. Richard Beadon (1737–1824), Public Orator 1768–78; Bp of Gloucester (1789) and of Bath and Wells (1802).

9. Hon. Horatio Walpole (1752–1822), eld. son of Horatio Walpole, 2d Bn Walpole of Wolterton; Eton and Trinity College, Cambridge. He m., 27 July 1781, his distant cousin, Sophia Churchill (d. 1797), dau. of Charles Churchill by Lady Mary Walpole, HW's half-sister; suc. his father in 1809 as 2d E. of Orford of the 3d creation (see *Eton Coll. Reg. 1753–90*).

10. William Cooke (1711–97), Cole's contemporary at Eton and Kings. Provost of King's 1772; Vice-Chancellor 1772–3; Dean of Ely 1780. Cole's opinion of him was most unfavourable (see *post passim*).

11. The Public Orator's remarks are not extant (from Mr Leonard Whibley).

12. 'to the University, and would have burst the President [Milles], Director [Gough] and parson [Masters] had they been present' (addition in Cole's copy).

13. That is, members of Benet, or Corpus.

answerer's stupid performance.[14] Another of them, Mr Colman,[15] the President of the College, a very learned, decent, modest and amiable man, will carry the apostle's spoon[16] to town with him in about a week and leave it with your porter.

I called a second time, with Mr Lort, on Bretherton,[17] but had the same success as before, though I was importunate to see his wife,[18] in order to beg her husband would make haste and finish the copy[19] of Dame Gertrude More, that you might have the original.[20]

I will take the liberty to remind you of the root of the yellow

14. 'which I thought a thorough condemnation, as he is a fast friend of Gough, and visits at Landbeche' (addition in Cole's copy). The work in question is Masters's *Some Remarks*.

15. William Colman (1728–94), Master of Corpus 1778–94; Vice-Chancellor 1778–9, 1793–4 (see Masters, *History of CCCC*, 1831, pp. 253–7). He was Cole's intimate friend (see Brydges, *Restituta* iv. 258–9).

16. On his recent visit to HW, Cole apparently had offered him an apostle-spoon for his collection. HW describes it: 'A silver gilt apostle-spoon. Addison, in *The Drummer*, mentions apostle-spoons; and so do Beaumont and Fletcher in one of their plays. It was an ancient fashion to have a little figure at the end of a spoon's handle, as this has. It was a present from the Reverend Mr W. Cole' (*Description of SH, Works* ii. 500). It was among the curiosities in the glass closet in the Great North Bedchamber, and was sold SH xvi. 67.

17. James Bretherton or Brotherton (d. 1806), an engraver and printseller of Cambridge who had moved to London. He resided at 134 New Bond Street until a short time before his death, when he moved to Michael's Grove, Brompton. He engraved four plates for *Anecdotes*[1] vol. iv; his son, Charles Bretherton (d. 1783), also engraved plates for the same work (see GM May 1806, lxxvi. 484a; Musgrave, *Obituary;* Redgrave, *Dict. of Artists; Universal British Directory*, 5 vols, 1791–8?, i. 84).

18. Sarah —— (fl. 1762–73) m. (before 1762) James Bretherton (see *The Register of . . . St Michael's Parish, Cambridge,* ed. John Venn, Cambridge, 1891, p. 50a *et passim*).

19. The copy was for either Cole or Gulston.

20. Cole's copy continues: 'Your cousin Lord Beauchamp and Lord Mount-Stuart were to dine with Mr Gulston on Saturday was sennight: the last, a great collector; the former, if not for himself, at least for Mr Gulston, who told me so. Indeed, while I was with him a print came from his Lordship to Ealing. I forgot to ask you about poor Lord Orford.

'After I saw you I spent a whole day with Mr Lort in his new lodgings in Old Bond Street. After breakfast the Marquis of Granby came in to pay Mr Lort for a parcel of books which he had commissioned him to buy for him two or three days before at the conclusion of Mr West's sale. I was glad to see with what eagerness he looked at his purchases and thought it a good sign for a young nobleman of his rank, fashion and figure to set out with such a taste as must give a relish to his future enjoyments. We then went to look over Mr Bull's collection, which is delicate and choice. It was the day [2 April] Wilkes went to the House to demand his seat, as both Mr Bull and Mr Benet his son-in-law, [Richard Henry Alexander Bennett (1744–1814), Bull's stepson, son of his wife by a former marriage to Bennet Alexander Bennett (d. 1745); M.P. for Newport 1770–4 (see N&Q, 11th Series, i. 238, 311, 370–2)] left us about two, to go to the House, and we stayed an hour after they were gone. I thought it wrong, but Mr Lort overruled me. Dr Percy spent the evening with us. Mr Lort changed his lodgings, as I apprehend, to be near the Duke of Devonshire, who has appointed him to take care of his medals, etc., and while I was with him, a message came from his Grace to desire him to be with him next day at such an hour, as the Marquis of Rockingham had appointed to come and look over his medals.'

martagon or Crown Imperial,[21] now it is out of blow. You have two of them in one plat on the left hand going to your cottage from the house.[22]

I sent a letter[23] to Young Henshaw with what you mentioned[24] relating to Bartolozzi. Yesterday morning at six o'clock his father was in my stable with my servant with the following letter, and went away directly. The son came by dinner and seemed to be much concerned for his father's absurdity, wants to go to Italy with Mr Bartolozzi exceedingly, burst into tears at his father's behaviour, said he would willingly and could give him £100,[25] if that would be accepted. I promised to inform you of what he said, but am not willing myself to be further concerned in the affair, and choose to write no more about it, yet I thought it necessary to give you a true account of the whole transaction, which I leave with you. It is cruel when a gentleman puts himself to the trouble and inconvenience of endeavouring to serve other people, to find abuse instead of thanks. But I will say no more; such is the world and mankind! and am, with the greatest regard, dear Sir,

Your ever faithful servant,

WM COLE

For the Rev. Mr Cole at Milton.

Sir,

My son showed me the letter you sent him. I was greatly surprised. I think he is very well settled if he knows when he is. He shall never have my consent to go abroad to lose all his business; neither would I advance a shilling, and as he is not at age to judge for himself, I think it my duty to judge for him. I have done great things for him, considering my capacity. I know where the scheme was laid and for what reason.

I am, Sir,

Your most obedient humble servant,

Jno. Henshaw

Cambridge, May 1, 1773.

21. *Fritillaria imperialis.*
22. 'I had one of them once, but have lost it' (addition in Cole's copy).
23. Missing.
24. In conversation with Cole at SH the latter part of April.

25. Bartolozzi afterwards accepted Henshaw as a pupil on the payment of eighty guineas (see *post* 13 June 1773).

My answer to the son was as follows:

To Mr Henshaw, Junior, in Cambridge.

Sir,

I have this day sent a copy of your father's letter to Mr W., and if I have any answer which it is necessary you should be informed of, you may depend upon my letting you hear it. As to my own share, I am sorry to inform you that I choose no longer to meddle in an affair where so wrong-headed and impertinent a man as your father is so nearly concerned. Both Mr W. and myself thought we were doing a service, but if we were mistaken, we still deserved thanks. But it is absurd to reason with mad folks, and your father's letter has strong symptoms of the sort.

Please to send the pencils by my servant, and I am,

Your very humble servant,

Wm Cole

Milton, May 3, 1773.
Monday.

To Cole, Tuesday 4 May 1773

Add MS 5952, ff. 123–4. The enclosure is from Cole's copy, Add MS 5844, f. 41v.

Address: To the Reverend Mr Cole at Milton near Cambridge.

Postmark: RB[?] 4 MA.

Arlington Street, May 4, 1773.

I SHOULD not have hurried to answer your letter, dear Sir, the moment I receive it, but to send you another ticket[1] for your sister, in case she should not have recovered the other, and I think you said she was to stay but a fortnight in town.[2] I would have sent it to her, if I had known whither: and I have made it for *five* persons,[3] in case she should have a mind to carry so many.

I am sorry for the young engraver, but I can by no means meddle with his going abroad without the father's consent; it would be very wrong, and might hurt the young man essentially if the father has anything to leave. In any case I certainly would not be accessory to

1. See end of letter.
2. HW is mistaken (see next letter).
3. HW seldom relaxed his rule of admitting only four guests to see SH at one

time, but Cole's sister had asked for 'four or five,' and Cole's recent gift of the apostle-spoon would have made refusal awkward.

sending away the son against his father's will. The father is an impertinent fool—but that you and I cannot help.

Pray be not uneasy about Gertrude More; I shall get the original or at least a copy. Tell me how I shall send you martagons by the safest conveyance, or anything else you want. I am always in your debt, and the apostle-spoon will make the debtor side in my book of gratitude run over.

Your public orator has done me too much honour by far—especially as he named me with my father, to whom I am so infinitely inferior, both in parts and virtues. Though I have been abused undeservedly, I feel I have more title to censure than praise, and will subscribe to the former sooner than the latter. Would not it be prudent to look upon the encomium as a funeral oration, and consider myself as dead—I have always dreaded outliving myself, and writing after what small talents I have, should be decayed. Except the last volume of the *Anecdotes of Painting,* which have been finished and printed so long, and which, appear when they may, will still come too late for many reasons, I am disposed never to publish any more of my own myself—but I do not say so positively, lest my breaking my intention should be but another folly. The gout has however made me so indolent and inactive, that if my head does not inform me how old I grow, at least my mind and my feet will—and can one have too many monitors of one's weakness? I am sorry you think yourself so much inconvenienced by stirring from home. That is an incommodity by which your friends will suffer more than yourself, and nobody more sensibly than,

Yours most sincerely,

Hor. Walpole

[Enclosure.]

To Mr Walpole's Housekeeper at Strawberry Hill.

Any day between twelve and three you may show my house to Mrs Cole, and four more, on their delivering this ticket to you.

Hor. Walpole

From Cole, Thursday 13 May 1773

VA, Forster MS 110, ff. 126–7. Cole's copy, Add MS 5844, f. 42.
Address: For the Hon. Horace Walpole in Arlington Street, Westminster.
Postmark: None. [William Colman carried the letter to HW; see below.]

Milton, May 13, 1773.

Dear Sir,

IN your last letter of May 4 you mentioned your last volume of *Anecdotes of Painting* being finished and printed long ago. I am sorry for it, for I have got a most curious anecdote to have inserted in your appendix.[1] Perhaps you never heard of one Marlibrunus, a Jew, the most skilful painter in the whole world, who dwelt at Bilinsgate in the time of Edward I. That he was so eminent in his art we have not only divine authority, but the oath of King Edward I before Adrian, Bishop of the Tartars, and the Pope's legate,[2] 1291. No doubt you have so common a book as Newcourt's *Repertorium*.[3] The whole story, which is not a little curious, may be seen there at p. 765 of volume 1. If you have not the book I will transcribe the passage and send it to you. A Jew painter of portraits is singular enough.

Many thanks for the first and second ticket, which I will convey to my sister by the same gentleman[4] who conveys the apostle-spoon. If I said she was in town for a fortnight only, I made a mistake, as she lives altogether at Hackney.

Mr Colman of Benet, who brings this, tells me he will leave his place where he lodges with your porter.[5] He stays in town about a fortnight, and will bring me the martagon root and, if you can easily spare them, a few of your fine jonquil roots.

I am much concerned for the latter part of your letter, in which you seem to give up all thoughts of future publications. I hope you

1. 'and indeed your work will be imperfect without it. It seems very odd that a person of your inquisitiveness into these matters should be a perfect stranger to the fame of the most accomplished painter this island ever produced. Be astonished when I inform you that Marlibrunus . . . dwelt . . .' (addition in Cole's copy). HW did not add Marlibrunus to later editions.

2. Mr K. B. McFarlane suggests that he

may have been in England about the Tartar embassy sponsored by the Pope in 1291 (see *Foedera,* ed. Thomas Rymer *sub anno* 1291, *passim*).

3. *Repertorium Ecclesiasticum Parochiale Londinense,* by Richard Newcourt, 2 vols, 1708–10.

4. William Colman (see next paragraph).

5. Cole's copy reads: 'he will leave his place of abode with your porter.'

will change your mind, and I will venture to prophesy that you will be guilty of no folly in so doing.

I dined at Benet yesterday, where Mr Tyson put the enclosed paper into my hand, with an intimation it was for you. It is taken from their Foundation Book. Whether it makes for your argument[6] or against it, I never inquired, not caring to trouble or perplex you more about a subject you are master of. However, as it was his request, I send it, and am, dear Sir,

Your ever faithful and obedient servant,

WM COLE

I must own my ignorance in not being able to make sense out of the pedigree enclosed. I told him so: he said it is as in their Book.

[Enclosure.][7]

Famosa ac Deo deuota Eleanora Botelar, quondam uxor Thomæ Botelar Militis filii et heredis Radulphi Botelar domini de Sudeley jam defunct[i], ac filia Johannis nup[er] comit[is] Salop[iæ], et *Margaret,* uxoris dict[i] Comit[is], primogenite filie et unius hered[is], ac quondam uxor Thome Buttelar Militis filii et hered[is][8] Radulphi Buttelar domini de Sudeley, Benefactrix, etc. etc.

Fundatio unius Socii et biblioth[ecæ] per Ducissam Norf[olcæ] et Soror[em] Eleanor Botelar.
Dated May 20, 1495.

To COLE, Saturday 29 May 1773

Add MS 5952, f. 125.

Address: [From COLE's copy, Add MS 5844, f. 42v.] To the Reverend Mr Cole at Milton near Cambridge.

Arlington Street, May 29, 1773.

Dear Sir,

I HAVE been so much taken up of late with poor Lord Orford's affairs, that I have not had, and scarce have now, time to write you a line, and thank you for all your kindnesses, informations and

---

6. In *Historic Doubts* (see *ante* 7 April 1773).

7. In Tyson's hand.
8. MS reads *heered.*

apostle-spoon. I have not Newcourt's *Repertorium* and shall be obliged to you for the transcript, not as doubting, but to confirm what Heaven, King Edward I and the Bishop of the Tartars, have deposed in favour of Marlibrunus, the Jew-painter's, abilities—I should sooner have suspected that Mr Masters would have produced such witnesses to condemn Richard III. The note relating to Lady Boteler does not relate to her marriage.

I send you[1] two martagon roots and some jonquils: and have added some prints, two enamelled pictures[2] and three medals: one of Oliver[3] by Simon,[4] a fine one of a pope,[5] and a scarce one of the Seven Bishops.[6] I hope the two latter will atone for the first. As I shall never be out of your debt, pray draw on me for any more other roots, or anything that will be agreeable to you; and excuse me at present.

Yours most assuredly,

H. Walpole

From Cole, Sunday 13 June 1773

VA, Forster MS 110, ff. 128–30. Cole's copy, Add MS 5844, ff. 42v, 43.
Address: For the Honourable Mr Horace Walpole in Arlington Street, Westminster. *Postmark:* Penny Post Paid 6 SA [Henshaw carried the letter to London; see below].

Milton, Sunday, June 13, 1773.

Dear Sir,

AT p. 105 of your *Richard III* you say, 'could we recover the register of the births of her [Duchess Cecily][1] children,' etc. I have recovered such a register, and send you the following extracts from it. It is in William Botoner *alias* Willielmi de Wyrcester *Annales*

1. Probably by William Colman.
2. Not identified.
3. Cole gave the medal to his friend Dr Glynn in 1779 (see *post* 1 March 1780).
4. Thomas Simon (1623?–65), medallist and seal engraver under Cromwell and Charles II (see Redgrave, *Dict. of Artists*).
5. Pope Clement X (Emilio Altieri) (1590–1676). See next letter.
6. The seven bishops, headed by William Sancroft (1617–93), Abp of Canterbury, who refused to read James II's declaration of liberty of conscience, and signed a petition protesting against it (see DNB *sub* Sancroft).

___

1. Cole's interpolation. Cicely Neville (1415–95) dau. of Ralph Neville, 1st E. of Westmorland; m. (1424) when she was nine years of age, to Richard (1411–60), 3d D. of York (see DNB *sub* Richard).

Rerum Anglicarum, printed at the end of Hearne's edition of *Liber Niger Scaccarii,* edit. 2, in 1771.[2]

1439. Apud Fodryngay nata est Anna,[3] Ducissa Excestriæ, filia Ricardi Ducis Eboraci, & Ceciliæ uxoris ejus, X die Augusti, inter horam 5[tam] & 6[tam] in mane diei Martis. p. 460.

1441. Natus est Henricus,[4] primogenitus Ricardi, Ducis Eboraci, apud Hattefeld X die Februarii hora 5ta in mane diei Veneris. p. 461.

1442. Natus est Edwardus, filius secundus Ricardi, Ducis Eboraci, & heres, Rex Angliæ & Franciæ, XXVIII[o] die Aprilis, hora 2 post mediam noctem in mane diei Lune, apud Rothomagum, qui conceptus est in camera proxima capellæ palacii de Hatfeld. p. 462.

1443. Natus est Edmundus,[5] 3[tius] filius Ricardi, ducis Eboraci, hora septima post merediem diei Lunæ, XVII die Maii, apud Rothomagum. p. 462.

1444. Nata est Elizabeth,[6] 2da filia Ricardi, ducis Eboraci, XXII die Aprilis, hora 2da in mane diei Martis, apud Rothomagum. p. 462.

1446. Nata est Margareta,[7] filia tercia Ricardi, ducis Eboraci, tercio die Maii in die Martis apud Fodryngay. p. 463.

1447. Natus est Willelmus,[8] quartus filius Ricardi ducis, VII die Julii apud Fodryngay. p. 464.

1448. Natus est Johannes,[9] V[tus] filius Ricardi, ducis Eboraci, VII die Novembris, apud Neyte juxta Westmonasterium. p. 465.

1449. Natus est Georgius,[10] VI[tus] filius Ricardi ducis, 21 die Octobris in meredie diei Martis in Hibernia. p. 465.

1452. Natus est Ricardus[11] apud Fodryngay 2do die Octobris die Lunæ. p. 477.

1455. Nata est Ursula,[12] filia Ricardi ducis Eboraci, apud —— XX Julii die Sanctæ Margaretæ. p. 477.

Unluckily Thomas[13] is the only son unregistered or unnoticed in these annals, the author of which, by his punctuality, seems to have

2. William Botoner or Worcester (1415–82?), chronicler and traveller. His *Annales Rerum Anglicarum* was first published in 1728 at the end of Hearne's *Liber Niger Scaccarii;* reprinted in the editions of 1771, 1774, and by Rev. Joseph Stevenson, 1864.

3. Ann Plantagenet (1439–76), m. (1) (ca 1447), Henry Holand (1430–75), D. of Exeter, from whom she was divorced in 1472; (2) Sir Thomas St Leger (see *ante* 14 May 1768; *post* 26 March 1780).

4. Henry Plantagenet d. in infancy.

5. Edmund Plantagenet (1443–60), known as E. of Rutland.

6. Elizabeth Plantagenet (1444–1503?), m. (ca 1460) John de la Pole (1442–91), D. of Suffolk.

7. Margaret Plantagenet (1446–1503), m. (1468) Charles (the Bold), D. of Burgundy.

8. Died young.

9. Died young.

10. George (1449–78), D. of Clarence.

11. Afterwards Richard III.

12. Died young.

13. Died young. He was born ca 1450 or 1451.

been a domestic chaplain or in some other office in the family.[14] But by the birth of Richard in 1452, in October, it is plain he was but a little turned of 33 years of age at his death.

At p. 525 is a second registry of their births, with some differences, in which none are named after George Duke of Clarence.

Thus far was written, though not dated, above three weeks ago, but as I don't love to trouble you more than necessary, I thought it time enough to send it when I should have more to say, and now you have given me such ample occasion that I could defer it no longer. However, I stayed a few days, that Mr Henshaw,[15] who is going to Mr Bartolozzi, might take it to town. He is much obliged to you for your kind interposition in this affair.

And now how can I thank you sufficiently for all your presents! which are most acceptable. Archbishop Sancroft[16] alone would have atoned, had there been occasion, without the Pope,[17] for old Oliver's face: it is a fine medal, and for your sake I shall preserve it choicely. The other two need only my own predilection in their favour. The pictures and prints please me much and greatly ornament my room.[18] Many thanks for your multiplied favours, and I am sorry to be so troublesome.

Poor Lord Orford's misfortune concerns me greatly, as well on his own, as your account.[19]

The following is the extract relating to Marlibrunus: *totius mundi sapientior picturæ artifex apud Billingsgate, London, com-*

14. There is no foundation for Cole's conjecture.

15. 'might convey it as far as London. He sets off tomorrow to go to Mr Bartolozzi for a year, and is to give him 80 guineas for his instructions during that time' (addition in Cole's copy).

16. In the medal of the Seven Bishops.

17. Cole's copy reads: 'Pope Clement X.'

18. 'I am sorry I have no more old spoons to send to bear company with your three owls at Strawberry Hill, especially as they turn to so good an account' (addition in Cole's copy). The three owls are not mentioned in *Description of SH*, but two pairs of 'curious silver owls, formerly used as calls by the nobility and gentry, previous to the introduction of bells,' were sold SH xvi. 107–8. See also Dudley Costello, 'Strawberry Hill Re-Visited,' *Ainsworth's Magazine* i (1842). 174.

19. Cole's copy reads: 'I am extremely concerned for poor Lord Orford. His misfortune is of that nature that will probably continue for many years. I attend the funeral tomorrow at St Clement's Church in Cambridge of my aunt Tuer, who has been confined [for insanity] at Chelsea and Hackney these fifty years, and died last week at the age of 87. I scarcely think it a compliment to wish you to live so long to enjoy a title, which could give you no additional honour, and would not be worth having at that time of life. But let me not omit giving you joy on the birth of the princess, your niece [Princess Sophia Matilda of Gloucester (1773–1844), dau. of William Henry, D. of Gloucester by HW's niece, Maria Walpole], which I hope will be the means of reconciliation between the King and her father.'

morans. Methinks it is no small impeachment of your sagacity in being unacquainted with the merits and character of so singular an ornament and artist of our island, especially as you have professed treating[20] about them.

I went to the stone-cutter's[21] the last week to see the cross Lord Ossory is going to erect to good Queen Catharine, and I dare say he will be pleased with the elegance of every part of it.

I am, dear Sir,

Your most obliged and faithful servant,

WM COLE

An Indulgence[22] of 40 Days Pardon to such as shall pay their Devotions to the Image of our Lady of Barking [near the Tower].[23]

Universis sanctæ Matris Ecclesiæ filiis, præsentes Literas inspecturis. Nos miseratione divina. . . . . . . et *Adrianus,* Tartarorum Episcopi, Domini Papæ Legati, salutem in Domino sempiternam. Quia datum est nobis intelligi per illustrissimum Regem *Angliæ, Edvardum* filium Regis *Henrici,* quod Capella in cœmiterio de *Berking-Chirch, London,* situata, per strenuum *Richardum* quondam Regem *Angliæ* mirabiliter extiterat fundata, ac etiam qualiter *Wallenses Angliam* invaserunt cavente dicto *Henrico,* et patriam undique devastarunt, homines ac mulieres, ac infantes in cunabulis occiderunt, et quod auditu horrendum est, mulieres in puerperio decubantes gladio trucidaverunt, et ulterius *Insulam de Ely,* hostiliter ceperunt et illam per unum annum manu forti custodierunt, et finaliter indempnes, cum tempus sibi placuerit, *Walliam* redierunt. Idem *Edvardus,* tunc temporis juvenis tot damna cernens, injuria et opprobria in exhæreditationem patris sui et destructionem totius *Angliæ* flevit amariter, et tantam doloris tristitiam acerbi, cordisque mœrorem præsertim suo corpori ministravit, ut lecto recumbens pœnitus semivivo relicto nullam se credidit sanitatem recuperare. Quadam vero nocte Dei genitricis *Mariæ* auxilio postulans piam ejus clementiam devotè imploravit, ut ipsum ex divina revelatione nocturna visione inspiraret, quomodo de *Wallensibus* Anglici possent citissimè vindicari. Ut factum est autem eo dormiente, virgo venustissima, etc., ipsi apparuit dicens, O *Edvarde,* amice Dei, quid clamas? Ecce adsum. Scias pro certo, quod vivente patre tuo, non possunt *Wallenses* ab Anglicis totaliter opprimi aut subjugari; et hoc est ob patris tui vile peccatum, ac nimias extortiones; sed vade cras mane ad

20. MS reads *treated.*
21. Not identified.
22. Taken from Richard Newcourt, *Re-*

pertorium Ecclesiasticum 1708–10, i. 765–6 (see *ante* 13 May 1773).
23. Cole's interpolation.

quendam *Judæum* nomine *Marlibrunum* totius mundi sapientiorem picturæ artificem apud *Billinsgate, London,* commorantem, et eum tibi facere imaginem constringas sub tali forma quam nunc me vides, qui ex divina inspiratione duas in ipsa perficiet facies, unam filio meo Jesu valdè similem, alteram mihi in cunctis consimilem perornabit, ut nulla deformitas possit ab aliquo veraciter enarrari. Ipsam imaginem sic plenè compositam Capellæ in cœmiterio de *Berking-Chirch* juxta turrim *London* situatæ, quam citius destinare studeas, et ibidem ex parte aquilonari decenter ornari facias, unde majora tibi mirabilia scias veraciter protinus eminere. Nam tam cito, quam facierum vultus dictus *Marlibrunus* infra ipsam Capellam diligenter inspexerit, mox in amorem cœlestem affectabitur, ut ad Fidem Catholicam, una cum uxore sua *Judæa* convertetur, qui postmodum tibi multa *Judæorum* secreta est revelaturus, unde puniendi sunt. Et tu, *Edvarde,* cum hoc miraculum videris, Omnipotenti Deo votum tuum vove, quod te vivente, et in *Anglia* existente quolibet anno quinquies dictam imaginem sub honore matris Christi visitabis, eandemque Capellam quotiescunque opus fuerit reparabis, et sustentabis. Nam ille locus verè esse laudandus, qui cum hoc votum genuflectendo feceris, super omnes gentes semper victoriosissimus atque insuperabilis eris, et mortuo patre tuo, tu es Rex *Angliæ* subjugator *Walliæ,* et oppressor totius *Scotiæ* futurus. Et crede mihi, quod quilibet justus *Angliæ* Monarchus, seu forte alius, qui hoc votum devote voverit, & juxta suum posse firmiter adimpleverit super *Wallenses* et *Scotos* semper sine dubio victoriosissimus, atque insuperabilis erit, et his dictis evanuit. Ut ergo evigilans, et sui sompnum commemoravit velut raptus penè spiritu cœpit admirari. Verumtamen totum implevit quemadmodum per sompnum in mandatis præhabuit. Insuper coram nobis in præsentia multorum magnatum tam *Angliæ,* quam *Scotiæ* dictus *Edvardus* sponte præstitit juramentum: Quod omnia per sompnum sibi ostensa, ut prædictum est, huc usque invenit veracissima. Nos igitur cupientes, ut dicta Capella congruis honoribus frequentetur, et à Christi fidelibus jugiter veneretur, omnibus verè pœnitentibus et confessis, qui ad ipsam Capellam causa devotionis et orationis accesserint, et qui ad luminaria, reparamenta, et ornamenta manus suas porrexerint adjutrices: necnon et qui pro animabus nobilis *Richardi* quondam Regis *Angliæ,* cujus cor in eadem Capella sub summo Altari requiescit humatum: et omnium fidelium defunctorum in Christo quiescentium, orationem dominicam cum salutatione Angelica quotiescunque et quandocunque pia mente dixerint de Omnipotentis Dei misericordia, et beatorum *Petri* et *Pauli* Apostolorum ejus meritis et authoritate confisi singuli singulas quadragenas dierum de injunctis eis pœnitentiis misericorditer in Domino relaxamus, dum tamen loci Diocesanus hanc nostram ratam habuerit indulgentiam. In quorum omnium Testimonium præsentes Literas nostris Sigillis duximus roborandas. Dat' apud *Northampton* existente Parliamento tam *Angliæ* quam *Scotiæ* vicesimo die *Maii,* Anno Domini millesimo ducentesimo nonagesimo primo.

Such evidence as this is irresistible. There can be no room for doubting here, where a great king, voluntarily, before the Bishop of the Tartars and some other nameless prelate, both apostolical legates, makes oath of the veracity of the fact. If this is called in question, adieu all reliance on history!

I am, dear Sir, once more and forever,

Your most obliged and faithful servant,

WM COLE

Milton, Sunday night,
June 13, 1773.

To COLE, Wednesday 4 May 1774

Add MS 5952, ff. 126–7.

Address: To the Reverend Mr Cole at Milton near Cambridge.
Postmark: 4 MA.

Arlington Street, May 4, 1774.

Dear Sir,

WE have dropped one another, as if we were not antiquaries, but people of this world—or do you disclaim me, because I have quitted the Society? I could give you but too sad reasons for my silence. The gout kept entire possession of me for six months; and before it released me, Lord Orford's illness and affairs engrossed me totally. I have been twice in Norfolk since you heard from me.[1] I am now at liberty again—what is your account of yourself? To ask you to come above ground, even so far as to see me, I know is in vain— or I certainly would ask it. You impose Carthusian shackles on yourself, will not quit your cell, nor will speak above once a week. I am glad even to hear of you and to see your hand, though you make that as much like print as you can. If you were to be tempted abroad,

1. HW went to Houghton in the latter part of Aug. 1773 (see his letter to Conway 30 Aug., and to Mason 3 Sept.), and again (with Lord Orford after his recovery) for a fortnight in March 1774 (see HW to Mason 19 and 23 March).

it would be by a pilgrimage, and I can lure you even with that. My chapel[2] is finished, and the shrine[3] will actually be placed in less than a fortnight. My father is said to have said that every man had his price:[4] you are a *beatus* indeed if you resist a shrine. Why should not you add to your cloistral virtues that of a peregrination to Strawberry? You will find me quite alone in July. Consider, Strawberry is almost the last monastery left, at least in England. Poor Mr Bateman's[5] is despoiled: Lord Bateman[6] has stripped and plundered it; has sequestered the best things, has advertised the site, and is dirtily selling by auction,[7] what he neither would keep, nor can sell for a sum that is worth while. I was hurt to see half the ornaments of the chapel, and the *reliquaires,* and in short a thousand trifles exposed to sneers. I am buying a few to keep for the founder's sake.[8] Surely it is very indecent for a favourite relation, who is rich, to show so little remembrance and affection—I suppose Strawberry Hill will have the same fate! It has already happened to two of my friends. Lord Bristol[9] got his mother's house[10] from his brother[11] by persuading her he was in love with it. He let it in a month after she

2. In the garden at SH. It was begun in 1772 (see *ante* 23 Oct. 1771).

3. See *ante* 23 Oct. 1771.

4. 'I never heard him say, that all men have their prices; and I believe no such expression ever came from his mouth' (*Walpoliana* i. 88).

5. Richard Bateman's seat at Old Windsor. It had a number of Gothic rooms, the original drawings for which, by J. H. Müntz, 1761–2, are now WSL.

6. John Bateman (1721–1802), 2d Vct Bateman, nephew and heir of Richard Bateman.

7. The first auction, which included only 'a few of the Old Windsor articles,' was held at Christie's '3 May 1774, and the six following days;' the second, at which HW bought 'a cargo of ancient chairs,' was held at Old Windsor July 1775 (see Thomas Eustace Harwood, *Windsor Old and New,* 1929, pp. 331–3; HW to Lady Ossory 23 July 1775).

8. HW mentions in *Description,* 'a crucifix inlaid with mother-of-pearl, bought at the sale of the Honourable Richard Bateman in 1774,' which he placed in the Chapel at SH (*Works* ii. 508); it was sold SH xxiv. 91. 'Fourteen more [draughtsmen of boxwood], bought at Mr Bateman's sale,' (*Works* ii. 500) perhaps were purchased in this year, but eight other purchases probably belong to the second sale, 1775 (see *Works* ii. 402, 453, 506–7, 509–10).

9. George William Hervey (1721–75), 2d E. of Bristol.

10. His mother was HW's correspondent, Mary Lepell, Lady Hervey. Her house was in St James's Place, overlooking the Green Park.

11. Augustus John Hervey (1724–79), 3d E. of Bristol. On the occasion of his mother's death, he wrote to his friend Grenville 5 Sept. 1768: 'My mother *has left her house, plate, furniture, etc., and all her jewels, to my brother Bristol and his son;* then to me and mine; and then to brother William forever, cutting out the Bishop. . . . There were two wills, the one of 1763 that left all to me, and this of last May in the manner I tell you. Some small legacies to . . . Mr Walpole, etc., whom (between you and I) I believe have in some degree influenced that opinion which may have occasioned the unexpected change' (*Grenville Papers,* ed. Wm James Smith, 4 vols, 1852–3, iv. 357–8). There is no evidence that the charge against HW is true.

was dead[12]—and all her favourite pictures and ornaments, which she had ordered not to be removed, are mouldering in a garret! You are in the right to care so little for a world, where there is no measure but avoirdupois. Adieu!

Yours sincerely,

H. W.[13]

From COLE, Thursday 19 May 1774

VA, Forster MS 110, ff. 131–2. Cole kept no copy.

Address: For the Honourable Mr Horace Walpole in Arlington Street, London.

Milton, May 19, 1774.

Dear Sir,

YOUR most obliging, kind and entertaining letter gave me more than ordinary pleasure, as it informed me of your health and made such friendly inquiries after mine. Thank God! I continue to rub on as usual, and with my books, garden and love of antiquities, the longest day appears too short, even when I am by myself, which is chiefly the case, for though Cambridge is so near, I am seldom there, and few people resort to so old-fashioned a person. Just at Christmas I had two slight fits of the gout. It left me for about three weeks and then returned for about ten days more. I think I find myself much better in my complaints of my stomach since these attacks. I hope it has the same effect upon you, and though you are a very great martyr to its malignity, yet I make no doubt but it will clear you of all other complaints. I am sure it ought to do so. It gives me great pleasure to hear Lord Orford is about again. He was at Ely and laid there some few weeks ago, and I was informed seemed perfectly well.

12. To Frederick Howard, 4th E. of Carlisle. Lady Hervey died 2 Sept. 1768, and George Selwyn was 'empowered to take' the house for Lord Carlisle in October 1768 (see John H. Jesse, *Selwyn,* ii. 332, 336).

13. Cole notes in his copy: 'In my answer to this letter [19 May 1774] I accidentally mentioned my having written two letters of no inconsiderable length to Mr Gough, and at the interval of near a year after each of them, [he] had the manners to write to me and hardly thank me for the trouble I had been at [Cole refers to his letter concerning the paintings at Ashridge College]: but though Mr Walpole is so polite to say that he will not receive his visits on my account, yet probably the true reason may be seen at p. 75 of this volume [the page containing Cole's copy of HW's letter, 27 April 1773], etc.' (Add MS 5844, f. 43v).

The real and only occasion of my long silence of nine or ten months was my fear of interrupting you. I know your politeness will not suffer you to be in debt without <urg>ent reasons, and I had no mind, even for my own gratification, to put you to the trouble of answering my unnecessary letters.

Your quitting a society I am a member of may and does concern me, as it is deprived of an honour and credit not to be repaired. The Director, Mr Gough, is one of the rudest mortals I ever corresponded with. At his request I sent him some year and half ago a letter of observations, etc., of about four whole sheets of paper. He never had the civility of thanking me for them till near a twelvemonth after, when he wanted a fresh information,[1] which I sent him, and cost me some trouble about Christmas, and have heard nothing of him since that time. I think I shall hardly give myself any farther trouble about him.

You certainly judge right that a shrine is an irresistible temptation, especially one at Strawberry Hill, and I hope to pay my devotions there for a day or two in July, when it will be most convenient to you to receive the pilgrim. I never wished for money more than at this instant, to enable me to have purchased St Anthony or St Francis over the door at Mr Bateman's, with some other of his relics, and particularly Caducanus the Welsh bishop.[2] I hope your reflections on the fate of collections may not be wholly true. I am sure the very thoughts of such a collection as you are master of, being dispersed, makes one shudder.

I hope you received no further damage from the late explosion at Hounslow Heath.[3] I once felt a small shock at your house on a similar occasion, which did no mischief, and I hope this will prove as friendly.

1. Not known.

2. The tomb of Caducanus or Cadwgan (d. 1241), Bp of Bangor 1215–36, which Bateman removed from the Abbey of Dore in Herefordshire and placed in a small mausoleum on the grounds of his estate at Old Windsor. 'Upon the altar lay a mitre, a crozier, and a copy of the bishop's work, *The Looking-Glass for Christians*' (Thomas Eustace Harwood, *Windsor Old and New*, 1929, p. 324). The tomb was sold in 1775 (ibid. 332).

3. 'Yesterday [Sunday 24 April] between twelve and one o'clock, a powder mill on Hounslow-Heath blew up; a few minutes after which two others likewise blew up, occasioned by the explosion of the first. Two men lost their lives by the above accident' (*Lloyd's Evening Post* 22–5 April 1774). 'The above happening during the time of divine service, the congregation in Isleworth church were so terrified, imagining the church was falling, that they hurried out with the greatest precipitation; however, happily, no other mischief ensued than being greatly frightened' (*London Chronicle* 23–6 April 1774).

I have been long (ever since 1765) in expectation of the living of Burnham near Eton. My brother quits it for Warplesden near Guilford, and I am told I am now to have it, yet I have met with so many disappointments of the sort that I don't think myself certain of it till I am in possession, and that I hope will be ab<out> July, or not at all.

With abundance of thanks for all favours, I am, dear Sir,

Your ever obliged and faithful servant,

WM COLE

To Cole, Saturday 28 May 1774

Add MS 5952, ff. 128–9.

Address: [From COLE's copy, Add MS 5844, f. 43v.] To the Reverend Mr Cole at Milton, near Cambridge. Free Hertford.

Strawberry Hill, May 28, 1774.

NOTHING will be more agreeable to me, dear Sir, than a visit from you in July. I will try to persuade Mr Granger to meet you; and if you had any such thing as summer in the fens, I would desire you to bring a bag with you. We are almost freezing here in the midst of beautiful verdure with a profusion of blossoms and flowers: but I keep good fires, and seem to feel warm weather while I look through the window, for the way to insure summer in England, is to have it framed and glazed in a comfortable room.

I shall be still more glad to hear you are settled in your living. Burnham is almost in my neighbourhood, and its being in that of Eton and Windsor, will more than console you I hope for leaving Ely and Cambridge. Pray let me know the moment you are certain. It would now be a disappointment to me as well as you. You shall be inaugurated in my chapel, which is much more venerable than your parish church, and has the genuine air of antiquity. I bought very little at poor Mr Bateman's. His nephew disposed of little that was worth house-room, and yet pulled the whole to pieces.

Mr Pennant[1] has published a new tour to Scotland and the Heb-

---

1. Thomas Pennant (1726–98), traveller and naturalist; friend of Gilbert White, and occasional correspondent of HW and Cole. Johnson had a high opinion of him as a traveller (Boswell, *Johnson* iii. 271 *et passim*).

rides,[2] and though he has endeavoured to paint their dismal isles and rocks in glowing colours, they will not be satisfied, for he seems no bigot about Ossian, at least in some passages,[3] and is free in others, which their intolerating spirit will resent. I cannot say the book is very entertaining to me, as it is more a book of rates than of antiquities.[4] The most amusing part was communicated to him by Mr Banks,[5] who found whole islands that bear nothing but columns, as other places do grass and barley.[6] There is a beautiful cave called Fingal's,[7] which proves that Nature loves Gothic architecture. Mr Pennant has given a new edition of his former *Tour*[8] with more cuts. Among others is the vulgar head[9] called the Countess of Desmond.[10] I told him I had discovered and proved past contradiction that it is Rembrandt's mother;[11] he owned it and said he would correct it by a note—but he has not.[12] This is a brave way of being an antiquary:

2. *A Tour in Scotland, and Voyage to the Hebrides, 1772,* Chester, 1774. Pennant's first 'tour,' *A Tour in Scotland, 1769* (Chester, 1771), attracted other tourists to the highlands, and gained for him the reputation of a lively and entertaining writer. The first three editions (D. 5) were sold SH iv. 6.

3. Ossian is mentioned at pp. 181, 287, 363; and at p. 263 Pennant quotes from Banks's description of Fingal's Cave in the 'Account of Staffa' (see n. 5): 'how fortunate that we should meet with the remembrance of that chief [Fingal], whose existence, as well as that of the whole epic poem, is almost doubted in England.'

4. HW has confused two passages in Pennant's *Tour in Scotland, 1769*[3], pp. 60, 161 n, in which Pennant lists the prices of provisions at Edinburgh and Inverness.

5. Joseph Banks (1743–1820), cr. (1781) 1st Bt, of Revesby Abbey, Lincs; P.R.S. 1778–1820; accompanied Cook in his expedition around the world. He contributed the 'Account of Staffa,' to Pennant's *Tour in . . . 1772,* pp. 261–9, and Pennant dedicated the work to him.

6. The islands of Booshala and Staffa. See Plates XXIX and XXX.

7. See ibid., Plate XXVIII.

8. *A Tour in Scotland, 1769*[3], Warrington, 1774.

9. See ibid. 73–4, and Plate VI.

10. Catherine Fitzgerald, who m., as his second wife, Thomas Fitzthomas Fitzgerald, 11th E. of Desmond. The account of her longevity in HW's *Fugitive Pieces* (*Works* i. 210–7) is not now accepted: she is said to have died in '1604, aged 140 years as generally reported, but more probably about 95' (GEC).

11. HW discovered the original at Windsor with 'The Mother of Rembrandt, given by Sir Robert Carr' written on the back. He proved this to be the picture given to Charles I by Sir Robert Kerr, E. of Ancram, and printed a note to this effect on an unpaged leaf which he had inserted in his remaining copies of his *Fugitive Pieces,* 1758 (*Works* i. 217). When Pennant called at this time HW gave him a copy of *Fugitive Pieces,* 1758, which is now WSL. Pennant has noted 'The Gift of the Author, April 14th 1774,' in it, but this copy lacks the inserted leaf.

12. The account of the Countess of Desmond, with her portrait, appeared unchanged in the fourth edition of Pennant's *Tour,* 1776, pp. 85–6, for the reason revealed in a letter of Pennant's to an unidentified correspondent. '21 Oct. 1774 . . . I have examined the Countess of Desmond's picture at Windsor; not a word is there on the back of its being Rembrandt's mother: whose print I have now seen, and am convinced that you and I are right *malgré* M. Walpole' (Guildhall Library, MS 367, letter 48).

as if there could be any merit in giving for genuine what one knows is spurious. He is indeed a superficial man, and knows little of history or antiquity[13]—but he has a violent rage for being an author. He set out with ornithology and a little natural history,[14] and picks up his knowledge as he rides.[15] I have a still lower idea of Mr Gough, for Mr Pennant at least is very civil. The other is a hog. Mr Fenn,[16] another smatterer in antiquity, but a very good sort of man, told me Mr Gough desired to be introduced to me—but as he has been such a bear to you, he shall not come. The Society of Antiquaries put me in mind of what the old Lord Pembroke[17] said to Anstis the herald:[18] 'Thou, silly fellow, thou dost not know thy own silly business.'[19] If they went beyond taste by poking into barbarous ages when there was no taste, one could forgive them—but they catch at the first ugly thing they see, and take it for old because it is new to them, and then usher it pompously into the world as if they had made a discovery, though they have not yet cleared up a single point that is of the least importance, or that tends to settle any obscure passage in history.

I will not condole with you on having had the gout, since you find it has removed other complaints. Besides as it begins late, you are never likely to have it severely. I shall be in terrors in two or three months, having had the four last fits periodically and biennially. Indeed the two last were so long and severe, that my remaining and shattered strength could ill support such. I must repeat how glad I shall be to have you at Burnham. When people grow old as you and I do, they should get together. Others do not care for us, but we seem wiser to one another by finding fault with them—not that I am apt to dislike young folks, whom I think everything becomes; but it is a kind of self-defence to live in a body. I dare to say that monks never find out that they grow old fools. Their age gives them authority and nobody contradicts them. In the world one cannot help

13. In later years HW changed his opinion. Pinkerton reports him as saying: 'Mr Pennant is a most ingenious and pleasing writer. His *Tours* display a great variety of knowledge, expressed in an engaging way' (*Walpoliana* i. 139).

14. HW refers to Pennant's earlier works, *British Zoology*, 1766, and *Genera of Birds*, Edinburgh, 1773.

15. Cf. *post* 28 July 1776, 18 June 1782.

16. John Fenn (1739–94), knighted in 1787; first editor of the *Paston Letters*; HW's occasional correspondent.

17. Thomas Herbert (1656–1733), 8th E.; P.R.S.

18. John Anstis (1669–1744), the elder; Garter King-of-Arms 1714–5, 1718–44.

19. According to Lord Dover, this was said by Chesterfield (see *Letters of HW to Horace Mann*, 3 vols, 1833, ii. 412 n).

perceiving one is out of fashion. Women play at cards with women of their own standing, and censure others between the deals, and thence conclude themselves Gamaliels. I who see many young men with better parts than myself, submit with a good grace, or retreat hither to my castle, where I am satisfied with what I have done and am always in good humour; but I like to have one or two old friends with me—I do not much invite the juvenile, who think my castle and me of equal antiquity, for no wonder if they suppose that George I lived in the time of the Crusades. Adieu! my good Sir, and pray let Burnham Wood and Dunsinane be good neighbours.

Yours ever,

Hor. Walpole

From Cole, Thursday 2 June 1774

VA, Forster MS 110, ff. 133–4. Cole's copy, Add MS 5844, ff. 44–45.

Address: [From Cole's copy.] For the Honourable Horace Walpole at Strawberry Hill in Twickenham, Middlesex.

Dear Sir,   Milton, June 2, 1774. Thursday.

YOUR extreme politeness and kindness in interesting yourself so much about my success in the living of Burnham obliges me to write this now, for fear I should have no time when I am absent. I set off for London tomorrow in order to get to Eton or Burnham next day,[1] but am now going to Cambridge and shall carry this letter myself to town, where I shall hardly have time to call at Arlington Street. I shall be obliged soon, if I really get presented to it, to make another journey for induction, but as things of this world are uncertain till actual possession, I must beg leave to postpone fixing any positive time for my visit to you till I am clearer about my title to the living. Yet I had a letter last week from Dr Apthorp to inform me that this very day I was to be nominated by the College, and he made no doubt but with success.[2] However, I have met with so many

1. 'and am going to Cambridge this evening when my dining visitors leave me' (addition in Cole's copy).

2. 'He himself has left Burnham, and goes on Monday to his new great living of Warplesdon near Guilford' (addition in Cole's copy). The living of Worplesdon was worth about £400 per annum (see Cole, *Jour. to Paris* 56).

disappointments about it that I can't bring myself to be so sure about it as he seems to be till I am absolutely invested. Whenever I come I will endeavour to catch a bag of the finest weather this uncertain climate will produce, but am very indifferent about it, especially as it is always had in perfection, framed and glazed, nowhere so completely and comfortably as at Strawberry Hill. For want of your precaution in those three or four vile and detestable days last week, and not being contented to stand at my window and view the garden from thence, I caught a bad cold by being constantly in it and am far from well, though obliged[3] to take a journey. The thoughts of my situation at Burnham giving me an opportunity of seeing a friend of your cast and disposition occasionally is an addition of no small value to the benefice, and according to the canons I may very legally be inaugurated to your chapel and hold it in commendam with the vicarage, as the distance is within the law.

Mr Lort, some two months ago, wrote to me that Mr Pennant was come to town to print his new *Tour*. He informed him of your doubts and proof relating to the Countess of Desmond, and of your dissertation in the *Fugitive Pieces* concerning her, on which account he got an introduction to you and came back very blank, as Mr Lort said, on his being convinced that your information destroyed the originality and authority of his print, taken from a picture in Scotland,[4] but this dejection lasted but a short time, for Mr Lort, who is keeper of the Duke of Devonshire's medals, carried him in a day or two, as he wrote word to me, to Devonshire House, and in a garret showed him an old picture exactly resembling his print, and on it the Countess's name.[5] This, I suppose, determined him to publish it in his book, but I rather wonder that after the civilities received from you on the occasion he did not acquaint you with his alteration of his plan.

I remember I told you about this time twelvemonth[6] that Mr Gough made an innuendo to me of his desire to be introduced to

3. 'by my brother [Apthorpe] unnecessarily to take a journey, for it would have been time enough for me to have gone when my presentation, if I am to have one, was made out' (addition in Cole's copy).

4. At Dupplin, the seat of the E. of Kinnoul (see Pennant, *Tour in Scotland, 1769*[2], pp. 72–4).

5. In his copy of *Fugitive Pieces* (now in the Percival Merritt Collection, Harvard College Library), Cole notes on the unpaged sheet opposite p. 216 which relates to the Countess of Desmond, that Lort wrote him 15 April 1774 and continues almost exactly as above. He concludes, 'I remember a tolerable good old picture of her at Mr Dicey's, Prebendary of Bristol, at Walton in Bucks.' See illustration.

6. See *ante* 24 April 1773.

and that She died in 1612, two years before the
publication of Sir Walter Raleigh's history,
She will then have been no less than * one
hundred and forty five years of age, a particu-
larity singular enough to excite, and I hope,
to excuse this Inquiry.

* Lord Bacon, says Fuller, computed her age to
be one hundred and forty at least; and added, that
She three times had a new set of teeth; for so I
understand, ter vices dentisse, not that She recovered them three times after casting them, as
Fuller translates it, which is giving her four sets
of teeth.

Worthies in Northumb. p. 310.

Being at Strawberry Hill in Apr: 1773, I saw
there a Copy of the Picture, comonly attributed to
the old Countess of Desmond: but mr. Walpole
told me, that there is sufficient Proof, that it
is a Painter's Mother: I think ~~Titiers. Rem~~
~~brants~~. However, by a Lr. from
mr. Lort Apr: 15. 1774, he assures me, that on mr.
Pennant's calling at Strawberry Hill to see this Picture he was much chagrined at having a Print of it
engraved for his Book, till mr. Lort revived him
by carrying him to a Garret in Devonshire House
where was a Picture of this same Countess, with
her Name on it, exactly corresponding to his
engraved Print. I remember a tolerable good
old Picture of her at mr. Diesy's Bohemdean
Bristol, at Walton in Bucks.

COLE ON THE COUNTESS OF DESMOND

you, and I thought it behoved me to inform you of it, as I dare say he expected it, yet I thought it very singular that a person who had taken so much pains to usher Masters's production into the University before it appeared by his means in the *Archaeologia* should think of it.

I have not yet seen Mr Pennant's book, nor the *History of Dorsetshire*,[7] though a subscriber for it. Mr Warton's *History of English Poetry*[8] has much pleased and amused me.

It was in 1765, when I was setting off for Paris, that my brother proposed my taking the living of Burnham on his going to Warplesdon, as he guessed he should. However, at that time Dr Burton stepped in before him, though a very old man and had a large living sweetly seated on the Thames at Mapledurham, and not two months ago Dr Roberts,[9] one of the fellows of Eton College, made a declaration that in case Dr Apthorp took Warplesdon he would claim Burnham. However, it seems, on other views, he has since declined it. As I never made application for this, any more than any other preferment, it ought not much to affect me which way soever it turns out, yet it has been so constantly held out to me of late that I shall begin to think it a disappointment if I miss it: not that I think I shall ever make it the place of my residence except I be obliged to it, but only part of the year. Had it come when it was first proposed to me and before I resigned Blecheley, I should have gone thither with pleasure and with an intention to have fixed my tent there for life, but as I have laid out five or six hundred pounds upon an house, fitted it up exactly to my own taste, settled myself and books and furniture about me, I own I shall be loth, however odd it may appear to you, to quit the fens of Ely and Cambridge for the politer scene of Eton and Windsor. My time of life is more calculated for such a retreat than a change now into a more gay and embellished circle.

I have the honour to be, dear Sir,

Your ever obliged and most faithful servant,

WM COLE

7. *The History and Antiquities of the County of Dorset*, vols i, ii, 1774, by John Hutchins (1698–1773).

8. The first volume of Thomas Warton's *History of English Poetry* appeared in this year.

9. William Hayward Roberts (1734–91), Eton and King's (became fellow of Eton 1771; provost 1781–91).

Some eight or nine months ago I was wrote to by Mr Gulston to know if I would part with my whole collection of prints. My servant was then dying, as I apprehended, and [I] not in a condition to look after them: I neglected saying anything about it, but about six weeks ago, on a second letter, I made a catalogue and sent it to him. I understand the purchase is for Lord Mount-Steward.

From COLE, Monday 18 July 1774

VA, Forster MS 110, f. 135. Cole kept no copy, but he gives the following account of the letter: 'After my institution to Burnham by the Bishop of Lincoln, June 10, 1774, I returned to my house at Milton near Cambridge, with a bad cold which I imagine I increased by being driven out several evenings together till past nine at night, in an open phaeton, by Lady Montfort at Horseth, where I soon after my return went for a week or ten days, and returned to Milton with a great hoarseness, cough and defluction on my breast, attended by a fever, which still is in possession of me: on which account I wrote an excuse [that is, the following letter] to Mr Walpole for not waiting on him in July as was agreed on: to which he returned me this answer [of 21 July 1774].' (Add MS 5844, f. 45.)

Address: For the Honourable Horace Walpole at Strawberry Hill in Twickenham, Middlesex. *Postmark:* Cambridge.

Milton, July 18, 1774.

<D>ear Sir,

IT is high time that I give you some account of myself. I wish I could give a good one: however, I will give a true one, and I hope your indulgence will acquit me of a rudeness which my silence may seem to burden me with.

I have all along amused myself with the imaginary pleasure of waiting upon you at Strawberry Hill sometime this month, but I see no prospect of it at present. I called upon you in June, about the 10th, in Arlington Street, but you was just gone to your Tusculum.[1] On coming into the country I was seized by a violent cough, defluction on my breast, attended with a fever, and though I did not regard it much the first week, it has made me more observant for this month, during which time I have not been able to stir out and am now as bad as ever with my cough and hoarseness. I don't know how I shall come off with my superiors, but my mandate for induc-

1. Cicero's villa at Tusculum was about the same distance from Rome as SH was from London.

tion into the living of Burnham expires this day, but I suppose illness is a legal excuse, and had it not thus happened I firmly purposed to have been with you either in going thither or on my return, as would best have suited you to have seen me.

I have read very lately (last week) Mr Pennant's *Tour* in two volumes quarto,[2] and fully subscribe to your opinion concerning the book, which I think as trumpery an one as I have read, and wonder at myself how my former reading of his first volume[3] could have so much deceived me. Mr Banks's account of the Isle of Staffa is very different from the rest of the book.

Whenever I shall have the pleasure of seeing you I must be a beggar for two or three of your portraits,[4] though I own you have repeatedly given them to me already, but I am eternally pestered by three people of Cambridge to get them a print of you, and I have told them I would endeavour to oblige them. In short, I cannot say No, and that has cost me several you have already bestowed on me.[5] The last I gave away was one framed in my house, and it was begged to hang up in the parlour at King's College, and there I sent it a year or two ago.[6] I will trouble you no farther at present, as my hand is quite unsteady, and am, dear Sir,

Your ever faithful and most obliged servant,

WM COLE

To COLE, Thursday 21 July 1774

Add MS 5952, ff. 130–1.
Address: To the Reverend Mr Cole at Milton near Cambridge.
Postmark: 21 IY.

Strawberry Hill, July 21, 1774.

YOUR illness, dear Sir, is the worst excuse you could make me; and the worse as you may be well in a night, if you will, by

2. The first volume was the third edition of *Tour in Scotland, 1769,* Warrington, 1774. The second volume was the first edition of *Tour in Scotland . . . 1772,* Chester, 1774. The volumes had a uniform format.

3. That is, his *Tour in Scotland, 1769,* which Cole read in the first (Chester, 1771) or the second (London, 1772) edition.

4. That is, the print by McArdell after Reynolds.

5. Only two are mentioned in the correspondence (see *ante* 18 July 1764, 27 Dec. 1767).

6. Mr John Saltmarsh reports (1936) that it is no longer there, nor is its location known.

taking six grains of James's powder.[1] He cannot cure death; but he can most complaints that are not mortal, or chronical. He could cure you so soon of colds, that he would cure you of another distemper, to which I doubt you are a little subject, the fear of them. I hope you was certain that illness is a legal plea for missing induction, or you will have nursed a cough and hoarseness with too much tenderness, as they certainly could bear a journey. Never see my face again, if you are not rector of Burnham.[2] How can you be so bigoted to *Milton*—I should have thought the very name would have prejudiced you against the place, as the name is all that could approach towards reconciling me to the fens.[3] I shall be very glad to see you here, whenever you have resolution enough to quit your cell—but since Burnham and the neighbourhood of Windsor and Eton have no charms for you, can I expect that Strawberry Hill should have any? Methinks when one grows old, one's contemporary friends should be our best amusement, for younger people are soon tired of us and our old stories; but I have found the contrary in some of mine. For your part, you care for conversing with none but the dead, for I reckon the unborn for whom you are writing, as much dead, as those from whom you collect.

You certainly ask no favour, dear Sir, when you want prints of me. They are at anybody's service that thinks them worth having. The owner sets very little value on them, since he sets very little indeed on himself; as a man, a very faulty one, and as an author, a very middling one; which whoever thinks a comfortable rank is not at all of my opinion. Pray convince me that you think I mean sincerely, by not answering me with a compliment. It is very weak to be pleased with flattery; the stupidest of all delusions to beg it. From you I

1. Robert James (1705–76), inventor of the famous fever powder; friend of Johnson; grandfather of G. P. R. James, the novelist. The powder, composed of antimony and phosphate of lime, was widely used: HW was a 'fanatic believer in its efficacy.' For a discussion of its effect upon Goldsmith, see Frederick A. Pottle, 'James's Powders,' N&Q 4 July 1925, cxlix. 11–12; and see Sir D'Arcy Power, 'Medicine,' *Johnson's England* ii. 276, and the references there cited.

2. Cole was vicar, not rector, of Burnham.

3. Cole wrote on this passage: 'In my last letter I had told Mr Walpole that my illness had even obliged me to omit going for induction on the day appointed in the Archdeacon's mandate, viz., on July 18. I believe he thinks I have no desire to get into possession of the living. However noble Milton's poetry may be, yet his political and religious principles are my aversion: not Mr Walpole's, whose verses on Queen Catherine's cross may be seen, with a plan of the cross itself, in my vol. — p. —' (Add MS 5844, f. 45v). For Cole's reference in the last sentence, see *ante* 12 Oct. 1771, 22 June 1771, and illustrations.

should take it ill. We have known one another almost fifty years—to very little purpose indeed, if any ceremony is necessary, or downright sincerity not established between us. Only tell me that you are recovered, and that I shall see you sometime or other. I have finished the catalogue of my collection, but you shall never have it without fetching,[4] nor, though a less punishment, the prints you desire. I propose in time to have plates of my house added to the catalogue,[5] yet I cannot afford them unless by degrees. Engravers are grown so much dearer without my growing richer, that I must have patience; a quality I seldom have *but* when I must. Adieu!

Yours ever,

H. W.

PS. I have lately been at Ampthill, and saw Queen Catherine's cross. It is not near large enough for the situation, and would be fitter for a garden than a park: but it is executed in the truest and best taste. Lord Ossory is quite satisfied,[6] as well as I, and designs Mr Essex a present of some guineas. If ever I am richer, I shall consult the same honest man about building my offices,[7] for which I have a plan; but if I have no more money ever, I will not run in debt and distress myself; and therefore remit my designs to chance and a little economy.

From Cole, Monday 25 July 1774

VA, Forster MS 110, ff. 136–7. Cole's copy, Add MS 5844, ff. 45v, 46.

Address: For the Honourable Horace Walpole at Strawberry Hill in Twickenham, Middlesex. *Postmark:* 27 IY.

Monday, July 25, 1774.

Dear Sir,

I WRITE now with the fever on me, and am much disposed to follow your prescription of James's Powder, for I have swallowed a load of bark, and all to no purpose. I am sorry to say that your

4. *A Description of the Villa of Horace Walpole . . . at Strawberry Hill*, SH, 1774. Cole's large-paper copy (one of six printed) is in Lord Waldegrave's collection at Chewton Priory. HW gave it to him when Cole was at SH 29 Oct. 1774 (*Jour. Print. Off.* 60–1).

5. The enlarged edition (1784) of the *Description of SH* contained 33 plates, in-

cluding the frontispiece and five folding plates, whereas the first edition (1774) had only a vignette on the half-title, and in a few copies one folding plate.

6. Cole notes that 'this cross cost Lord Ossory considerably above an £100' (Add MS 5845, f. 10).

7. In 1777 HW paid 'To Mr Essex the architect for the Beauclerc Tower and de-

sagacity lets nothing escape you: I own I am apt to fear colds, and may have nursed myself more than was necessary for them. However, I am convinced that no one can be a perfect judge of another person's constitution. Who, for instance, with your delicate frame of body, could at all conceive that in November, slip-shod in thin slippers on the wet grass, without greatcoat, without hat or other covering for your head than the hair on it, you could walk about your garden as unconcerned as in July? Such an experiment I am certain would utterly demolish me, notwithstanding my seemingly robust make. The least cold gives me a sore throat and fever, and I am laid up for a month or two. I was in great hopes yesterday,[1] from a sudden tendency in the evening to a breathing sweat, most unusual with me, and which I promoted by going to bed and taking whey, that my fever would have left me, but I flattered myself in vain, as it is come again today without being wished for.

At present it is impossible to move to Burnham, was I well enough, as I am in the midst of all my hay and the harvest threatens to follow apace. When they are got in I hope I shall be able to move there and call at Strawberry Hill, the very thoughts of which I hope will contribute to my recovery. I wish to see your *Catalogue,* but dare say no more about it.

Mr Pennant, as I apprehend, will say what he has to say about the Countess's picture when he prints his appendix or third volume,[2] for that he means to give another volume is evident by promising things in the former of which he afterwards takes no notice.

I am, dear Sir,

Your ever obliged and most faithful servant,

WM COLE

Mr Essex drank tea here on Saturday. I showed him your letter, and he is much pleased that the cross is approved of. He has left some papers here, which I read over yesterday, about freemasons,

signing the Offices, etc.,' £31.10.0 (*SH Accounts* 16). Essex died in 1784, but the Offices were built in 1790 from his designs (see ibid. 18, 175–6).

———

1. 'afternoon after tea, on taking an airing in my chaise to Denney Abbey [about three miles from Milton], from a sudden

tendency to a gentle perspiration' (addition in Cole's copy).

2. In *A Tour in Scotland, 1772, Part II,* 1776, pp. 87–8, Pennant mentions five portraits of the Countess of Desmond and rejects, without mentioning his name, HW's theory that the portrait is of Rembrandt's mother.

manner of building in England, and something of Gothic architecture.[3] I can't say it satisfies me: it seems a bundle of collections from Vitruvius, etc., ill patched together.[4] When he comes to treat professedly of Gothic architecture, I am in better hopes of him. The new altar-piece, by his plan, is partly erected, and, as I am told, pleases everyone but the Provost, Dr Cook, who affects to be pleased with nothing but what comes from himself.

To COLE, Monday 15 August 1774

Add MS 5952, ff. 132–3

Address: [From COLE's copy, Add MS 5844, f. 46.] To the Reverend Mr Cole at Milton near Cambridge.

Matson near Gloucester,[1] Aug. 15, 1774.

Dear Sir,

A S I am your disciple in antiquities, for you studied them when I was but a scoffer, I think it my duty to give you some account of my journeyings in the good cause. You will not dislike my date:

3. Essex read a paper before the Society of Antiquaries 8 Dec. 1774 (printed in *Archaeologia* iv. 73–109): 'Remarks on the Antiquity and the different Modes of Brick and Stone Buildings in England.' It probably is the paper, or one of the papers, to which Cole refers.

4. 'with a parade of learning, with which he is totally unacquainted: so much so, that I have corrected at least an hundred false spellings in his own language. When he comes to treat professedly of Gothic architecture, which he understands, and leaves Latin, Greek, Italian, French and Saxon, which he knows nothing of, I am in better hopes of him. The new altar-piece, under his direction, in King's College Chapel, is partly erected, and, as I am informed, pleases everyone [cf. *post* 22 May 1777] but the Provost, Dr Cook [William Cooke (1711–97)], who affects to be pleased with nothing but what comes from himself. He is the merest pedant, pedagogue and scholar that ever existed. His master George [William George (1697–1756), headmaster (1728–43) of Eton; provost of King's 1743–56], to whom he was pimp and lick-

spittle, and whose manner he imitates, was a gentleman to him. He dined here about a fortnight ago, when he took occasion to speak slightingly of antiquaries. In order to please him, I showed him that part of one of your late letters respecting the Society. In a day or two after, he was one of the auditors, with Dr Ewin, at the Conservators' [of the River Cam] meeting in Cambridge, where in speaking of the same fraternity, he expressed himself exactly in your words. This I mention as a compliment to you and none to himself. Dr Ewin, who is going a tour into Scotland this week, drank tea here on Friday and told me the story, which it is time to finish, by assuring you that I am, dear Sir,

Your most faithful and obliged servant,
Wm Cole'

(Addition in Cole's copy.)

1. The seat of George Selwyn, about a mile SE of Gloucester, on Robin Wood's Hill. Selwyn wrote Lord Carlisle 13 Aug. 1774: 'At night [Friday, 12 Aug.] I heard that Mr Walpole is here; I was then at

I am in the very mansion where King Charles I and his two eldest sons[2] lay during the siege,[3] and there are marks of the last's hacking with his hanger on a window, as he told Mr Selwyn's grandfather afterwards.[4] The present master has done due honour to the royal residence, and erected a good marble bust of the Martyr in a little gallery. In a window is a shield in painted glass with that King's and his Queen's arms which I gave him,—so you see I am not a rebel, when Alma Mater Antiquity stands godmother.

I went again to the Cathedral,[5] and on seeing the monument of Edward II,[6] a new *historic doubt* started, which I pray you to solve. His Majesty has a longish beard, and such were certainly worn at that time. Who is the *first* historian that tells the story of his being shaven with cold water from a ditch, and weeping to supply warm, as he was carried to Berkeley Castle? Is not this apocryphal? The house whence Bishop Hooper[7] was carried to the stake is still standing *tale quale*. I made a visit to his actual successor, Warburton,[8] who is very infirm, speaks with much hesitation, and they say, begins to lose his memory. They have destroyed the beautiful cross; the two battered heads of Henry III and Edward III are in the postmaster's garden.[9]

Gloucester; so I hurried home, and have now some person to converse with who speaks my own language. He came yesterday from Lady Ailesbury's, and stays with me till Tuesday, and then I hope we shall return to London together. I am to have the satisfaction of another festival on Monday, on which day Mr Walpole proposes to go and see Berkley and Thornbury Castles' (Edward S. Roscoe and Helen Clergue, *George Selwyn, his Letters and his Life*, 1899, p. 87).

2. Charles Prince of Wales (afterward Charles II) and James Duke of York (afterward James II).

3. Of Gloucester, undertaken by Charles I in 1643.

4. Brig.-Gen. William Selwyn (d. 1702) (see S. Parnell Kerr, *George Selwyn and the Wits*, [1909], p. 13). Sir Nathaniel Wraxall, on George Selwyn's authority, tells practically the same story in *Historical and Posthumous Memoirs*, ed. Henry B. Wheatley, ii. 288; see also HW to Bentley Sept. 1753.

5. Gloucester Cathedral, which HW had seen in 1753 (see HW to Bentley Sept. 1753).

6. 'King Edward II's tomb is very light and in good repair' (HW to Bentley Sept. 1753).

7. John Hooper (d. 1555), Bp of Gloucester and Worcester; opposed Queen Mary; sentenced for heresy and burned at Gloucester. 'As I am a Protestant Goth, I was glad to worship Bishop Hooper's room, from whence he was led to the stake' (HW to Bentley Sept. 1753). See also *Country Seats* 75.

8. A somewhat surprising visit, in view of Warburton's attack on HW (see Arthur William Evans, *Warburton and the Warburtonians*, Oxford, 1932, p. 232 *et passim*).

9. The High Cross at Gloucester, 34 feet six inches in height, raised on octagonal steps, stood on elevated ground at the meeting of Northgate, Southgate and Westgate Streets. The ground and second story dated from about 1320; the third from the sixteenth century. At the time of its demolition about 1750, it contained statues of King John, Henry III, Queen

Yesterday I made a jaunt four miles hence that pleased me exceedingly, to Prinknash,[10] the individual villa of the abbots of Gloucester
—I wished you there with their mitre on. It stands on a glorious but
impracticable hill, in the midst of a little forest of beech, and commanding Elysium. The house is small but has good rooms, and
though modernized here and there, not extravagantly. On the ceiling of the hall is Edward IV's jovial device, *à Fau-con serrure*.[11] The
chapel is low and small, but antique, and with painted glass with
many angels in their coronation robes, i. e., wings and crowns. Henry
VIII and Jane Seymour lay here;[12] in the dining room are their arms
in glass, and of Catherine of Arragon,[13] and of Bray and Bridges.[14]
Under a window a barbarous bas relief head of Harry,[15] young; as it
is still on a sign at an ale-house on the descent of the hill. Think of
my amazement, when they showed me the chapel plate,[16] and I found
on it, on four pieces, my own arms, quartering my mother-in-law
Skerret's,[17] and in a shield of pretence, those of Fortescue, certainly
by mistake for those of my sister-in-law, as the barony of Clinton
was in abeyance between her and Fortescue Lord Clinton.[18] The

Eleanor, Edward III, Richard II and III,
Queen Elizabeth and Charles I (see Aymer
Vallance, *Old Crosses and Lychgates* [1920]
108–10; Kippis, *Vetusta Monumenta*, 1789,
ii. Plate 8; Thomas Dudley Fosbrooke, *An
Original History of the City of Gloucester*,
1819, pp. 132–3).

10. Prinknash Park, then the seat of
John Howell, Esq., who had purchased it
in 1770 (see *Country Seats* 75 and n). See
also Rev. William Bazeley, 'History of
Prinknash Park,' *Transactions of the Bristol and Gloucestershire Archaeological Society* for 1882–3, vii. 267–306; this and the
following paragraph are quoted at pp.
301–2.

11. Cf. *Country Seats* 58, where HW calls
the falcon-and-fetterlock device a 'bawdy
invention of Edward 4th'; and ibid. 75,
where he terms it 'a quibble, à Faux Con,
serrure.'

12. Anne Boleyn, not Jane Seymour, accompanied Henry VIII on his visit to
Prinknash in 1535. 'It is well known where
he held his court on each day during the
brief married life of Jane Seymour' (Bazeley, op. cit. 283).

13. See ibid. 275, 279–80.

14. Edmund Brydges (d. 1573), 2d Bn

Chandos, eldest surviving son of Sir John
Brydges, m. Dorothy Bray (d. 1605), dau.
of Sir Edmund Bray. Henry VIII granted
Prinknash Park to them 'in consideration
of the marriage to be contracted and sol-
emnized between' them. Their arms are
given ibid. 279–80, and on Plate XXVIII.

15. Ibid. 276, and Plate XXVI, Fig. 2.
Another print of it is in GM Nov. 1794,
lxiv. 980, Plate II.

16. Thomas Jones Howell (d. 1858) sold
Prinknash to James Ackers in 1847, and at
the same time sold the plate to another
person (see Bazeley, op. cit. 301 and n).

17. Maria Skerrett (1702–38), second wife
of Sir Robert Walpole; HW's stepmother.

18. Margaret Rolle (1709–81), Baroness
of Clinton and Countess of Orford; wife of
Robert Walpole (1701–51), 2d E. of Orford. From 1751 (on the death of Hugh
Fortescue, Earl Clinton) to 1760 the barony
of Clinton was in abeyance between her
and Margaret Fortescue (d. 1760); on the
death of the latter the abeyance was terminated in favour of the Countess of Orford.
She and Lord Orford separated in 1746,
and he settled £1,500 a year on her. She m.
in 1751, Hon. Sewallis Shirley, son of 1st E.
Ferrers, and separated from him.

whole is modern and blundered, for Skerret should be impaled not quartered, and instead of our crest, are two spears tied together in a ducal coronet, and no coronet for my brother, in whose time this plate must have been made, and at whose sale it was probably bought, as he finished the repairs of the church at Houghton, for which I suppose this decoration was intended—but the silversmith was no herald, you see.

As I descended the hill, I found in a wretched cottage a child in an ancient oaken cradle, exactly in the form of that lately published from the cradle of Edward II—I purchased it for five shillings, but don't know whether I shall have fortitude enough to transport it to Strawberry Hill—people would conclude me in my second child-hood.[19]

Today I have been at Berkeley[20] and Thornbury Castles.[21] The first disappointed me much, though very entire. It is much smaller than I expected, but very entire, except a small part burnt two years ago, while the present Earl[22] was in the house. The fire began in the housekeeper's room, who never appeared more; but as she was strict over the servants, and not a bone of her was found, it was supposed that she was murdered and the body conveyed away. The situation is not elevated nor beautiful, and little improvements made of late but some silly ones *à la chinoise* by the present Dowager.[23] In good sooth I can give you but a very imperfect account, for instead of the Lord's being gone to dine with the Mayor of Gloucester[24] as I expected, I found him in the midst of all his captains of the militia. I am so sillily shy of strangers and youngsters that I hurried through the chambers and looked for nothing but the way out of every room. I just observed that there were many bad portraits of the family, but

19. He did not take it to SH (see HW to Mary Berry 28 Aug. 1795). The print of Edward II's cradle did not appear in *The Gentleman's Magazine*, as HW there states, but in the *London Magazine*, March 1774, xliii. opp. p. 133, with a full description on pp. 135–6.

20. Berkeley Castle, about 12 miles SW of Gloucester. HW gives a similar account of his visit in *Country Seats* 75.

21. About seven miles SW of Berkeley Castle; see also *Country Seats* 75–6.

22. Frederick Augustus Berkeley (1745–1810), 5th E. of Berkeley. HW apparently was not acquainted with him (HW to

Mann 11 Feb. 1765, and to Conway 7 Sept. 1774).

23. Elizabeth Drax (1720–92), m. (1) in 1744, Augustus Berkeley (1716–55), 4th E. of Berkeley, and (2) in 1757, as his third wife, Robert Nugent (d. 1788), 1st E. Nugent. HW wrote to Mann 16 Nov. 1778, 'There is nothing so black of which she is not capable. Her gallantries are the whitest specks about her.'

24. John Jefferis. He was Mayor in 1769, and again in 1774 (see Thomas Dudley Fosbrooke, *An Original History of the City of Gloucester*, 1819, p. 420).

none ancient, as if the Berkeleys had been commissaries and raised themselves in the last war. There is a plentiful addition of those of Lord Berkeley of Stratton;[25] but no Knights Templars, or barons as old as Edward I. Yet are there three beds on which there may have been as frisky doings three centuries ago, as there probably have been within these ten years. The room shown for the murder of Edward II, and *the shrieks of an agonizing King,*[26] I verily believe to be genuine: it is a dismal chamber almost at top of the house, quite detached, and to be approached only by a kind of foot-bridge and from that descends a large flight of steps that terminate on strong gates; exactly a situation for a *corps de garde.* In that room they show you a cast of a face in plaster, and tell you it was taken from Edward's. I was not quite so easy of faith about that, for it is evidently the face of Charles I. The steeple of the church, lately rebuilt handsomely, stands some paces from the body: in the latter are three tombs of old Berkeleys with cumbent figures. The wife of the Lord Berkeley,[27] who was supposed to be privy to the murder has a curious head-gear:[28] it is like a long horseshoe quilted in quatrefoils, and like Lord Foppington's wig,[29] allows no more than the breadth of a half crown to be discovered of the face—Stay, I think I mistake:[30] the husband was a conspirator against Richard II, not Edward; but in those days, loyalty was not so rife as at present.

From Berkeley Castle, I went to Thornbury, of which the ruins are half ruined. It would have been glorious, if finished[31]—I wish the Lords of Berkeley had retained the spirit of deposing till Harry the VIII's time! The situation is fine, though that was not the fashion, for all the windows of the great apartment look into the inner court

25. John Berkeley (1697?–1773), 5th Bn Berkeley of Stratton, dying without issue, left his estates to his distant cousin the E. of Berkeley and his heirs male.

26. Gray, 'The Bard,' l. 56.

27. Thomas de Berkeley (1292?–1361), 3d Bn Berkeley; tried as an accessory to the murder of Edward II, but acquitted; m., as his second wife, in 1347, Catherine Clivedon (d. 1385), widow of Sir Piers le Veel of Tortworth, Glos; both buried in Berkeley Church.

28. HW made a rough drawing of it in his notebook (see *Country Seats* 76 n).

29. See Vanbrugh's *The Relapse, or Virtue in Danger,* 1696, Act i, sc. 3. Lord Foppington and his periwig-maker, Mr. Foretop:

'*Fore.* Heaven bless my eye-sight. . . . Sure I look through the wrong end of the perspective; for by my faith, an't please your honour, the broadest place I see in your face does not seem to me to be two inches diameter.

'*Lord Fop.* If it did, it would be just two inches too broad; for a periwig to a man should be like a mask to a woman, nothing should be seen but his eyes.'

30. HW did not mistake.

31. It was begun by Edward Stafford (1478–1521), 3d D. of Buckingham, who was convicted on false charges of disloyalty to Henry VIII, and executed for high treason. HW copied a tower there for his own Beauclerc Tower in 1776 (see HW to Lady Ossory 9 Oct. 1776).

—the prospect was left to the servants. Here I had two adventures. I could find nobody to show me about. I saw a paltry house that I took for the sexton's at the corner of the close, and bade my footman[32] ring and ask who could show me the castle. A voice in a passion flew from a casement, and issued from a divine—'What! was it *his* business to show the castle? Go look for somebody else! What did the fellow ring for, as if the house was on fire!' The poor Swiss came back in a fright and said the Doctor had sworn at him. Well! we scrambled over a stone stile, saw a room or two glazed near the gate and rung at it. A damsel came forth and satisfied our curiosity. When we [had] done seeing, I said, 'Child, we don't know our way, and want to be directed into the London road: I see the Duke's steward yonder at the window; pray desire him to come to me that I may consult him.' She went, he stood staring at us at the window—and sent his footman. I do not think courtesy is resident at Thornbury. As I returned through the close, the divine came running out of breath and without his beaver or bands, and calls out, 'Sir, I am come to justify myself; your servant says I swore at him, I am no swearer— Lord bless me (dropping his voice) is it Mr Walpole?' 'Yes, Sir, and I think you was Lord Beauchamp's tutor at Oxford, but I have forgot your name.'—'Holwell, Sir.'[33] 'Oh yes'—and then I comforted him, and laid the ill breeding on my footman's being a foreigner, but could not help saying, I really had taken his house for the sexton's—'Yes, Sir, it is not very good without, won't you please to walk in?' I did, and found the inside ten times worse, and a lean wife suckling a child. He was making an index to Homer, is going to publish the chief beauties,[34] and I believe had just been reading some of the delicate civilities that pass between Agamemnon and Achilles, and that what my servant took for oaths, were only Greek compliments. Adieu! You see I have not a line more of paper.

Yours ever,

H. W.

32. Probably David Monnerat, a Swiss.

33. William Holwell (1726–98); tutor of Christ Church and proctor (1758); vicar of Thornbury; chaplain in ordinary to George III. HW visited Lord Beauchamp at Oxford in July 1760 (HW to Conway 28 June 1760 and Beauchamp to HW 9 July 1760).

34. *The Beauties of Homer, selected from the Iliad*, Oxford, 1775. As this work has an unusually fine index for the time, it is likely that Holwell was working upon it rather than upon an index to all Homer. Holwell also published *Extracts from Mr. Pope's Translation, corresponding with the Beauties of Homer*, 1776.

From Cole, Wednesday 5 October 1774

VA, Forster MS 110, f. 138. Cole kept no copy.
Address: For the Honourable Mr Horace Walpole at Strawberry Hill in
Twickenham, Middlesex. *Postmark:* 6 OC.

Milton, Oct. 5, 1774.

Dear Sir,

I PRESUME that you are got home by this time from your tour
in the west. My uncertainty on this head was the occasion of my
not answering your most obliging and entertaining last letter from
Matson. Your kind wishes at Prinknash gave me great pleasure, and
among the multitude of various religious opinions abounding in this
isle, a mitred abbot in such a church as Glocester would exhibit a
show and occasion more concourse to that city than to Bath or any
of the watering places, now so frequented. Your rencounters at
Thornbury were really comic, and Mr Holwell's development of
himself after so much bearishness must have been a very laughable
scene. I wish I could satisfy your inquiries about Edward II, relating
to the story of his being shaved with cold water. The representation
of him on his tomb, which would infallibly be af<ter> the mode of
the age in which he lived, seems to me more authentic than any idle
story vamped up after his death.

We are at Cambridge in the very centre of riot and confusion. Mr
Cadogan and Mr Jenyns, who have served[1] for the town with appro-
bation, seem to have tired the mob and a factious party (who can
allege nothing against them) by their mere long continuance in that
service. Two people, without ever being heard of three months ago,
one of them named Meek,[2] a timber merchant from Lambeth, and
the other a Mr Byde[3] of Hertfordshire, people utterly unknown and
unconnected with any of the corporation or county, have been
searched out and brought to Cambridge to stir up an opposition. It
seems to me as if they would shake the old interest, if not carry the
day, which, happily, is on Saturday:[4] otherwise, had not the late

1. Charles Sloane Cadogan was M.P. for
the town of Cambridge 1749–54, 1755–76,
and Soame Jenyns 1758–80.
2. Samuel Meeke (Cooper, *Annals* iv.
372).
3. Thomas Plumer Byde (1720–89), of
Ware Park, Herts; d. at Naples 26 May

1789 (see Musgrave, *Obituary;* Cooper,
Annals iv. 372).
4. 'The poll was taken on [Saturday] the
8th of October, when the votes were
Jenyns 92; Cadogan 89; Byde 63; Meeke
60' (loc. cit.).

measure been adopted, of dissolving the Parliament,[5] there would have been the same riot and mobbing for four or five months longer.

I propose going to Burnham about the last week of this month and calling on you for a day or two if it will be convenient: otherwise can now make it more convenient occasionally, as I shall possibly have frequent occasions of coming to town. I will call at Arlington Street, where I may get intelligence if I have not the favour of hearing from you, as you may possibly be still on your rambles.

Dr Bernardiston, Master of Benet College, calling here yesterday, came out of Norfolk last week where he had paid a visit with Dr Hammond[6] at Houghton, where almost all that part of the county were on a dining visit, and found Lord Orford cheerful, easy and perfectly well.

I am, dear Sir,

Your ever obliged and faithful servant,

WM COLE

To COLE, Tuesday 11 October 1774

Add MS 5952, ff. 134–5.

Address: To the Reverend Mr Cole at Milton near Cambridge.
Postmark: EK 11 OC.

Strawberry Hill, Oct. 11, 1774.

Dear Sir,

I ANSWER yours immediately, as one pays a shilling to clench a bargain when one suspects the seller. I accept your visit in the last week of this month, and will prosecute you if you do not execute.

I have nothing to say about elections, but that I congratulate myself every time I feel I have nothing to do with them. By my nephew's strange conduct about his boroughs,[1] and by many other

---

5. Parliament was dissolved 30 Sept. 1774, 'six months before its natural death, and without the design being known but the Tuesday before, and that by very few persons' (HW to Mann 6 Oct. 1774; see also *Last Journals* i. 375–9; 388).

6. Horace Hammond or Hamond (d. 1786), of Corpus Christi College, Cambridge (D.D. 1755); rector of Harpley and

Great Bircham, Norfolk 1744–86 (see *Alumni Cantab.*).

---

1. 'Bob [Robert Macreth, afterwards knighted], formerly a waiter at White's, was set up by my nephew for two boroughs, and actually is returned for Castle Rising with Mr Wedderburn' (HW to Mason Oct. 1774). HW was also concerned at Lord Or-

reasons, I doubt whether he is so well as he seemed to Dr Bernard-iston—It is a subject I do not love to talk on, but I know I tremble every time the bell rings at my gate at an unusual hour.

Have you seen Mr Granger's *Supplement?*[2] Methinks it grows too diffuse. I have hinted to him that fewer panegyrics from funeral sermons would not hurt it.[3] Adieu!

Yours ever,

H. W.

From Cole, Friday 18 November 1774

Edited from Toynbee, *Supp.* iii. 234–5. The original was lot 109 in the Waller Sale at Sotheby's, 5 Dec. 1921. Its present whereabouts is not known. Cole's copy of his letter (Add MS 5847, f. 204) is greatly abridged, but his copy of Nell Gwyn's letter (Add MS 5847, ff. 203v, 204) is complete.

Address: For the Honourable Mr Horace Walpole at Strawberry Hill in Twickenham, Middlesex. *Postmark:* 19 NO.

Burnham, near Maidenhead, Berks, Friday, Nov. 18, 1774.

Dear Sir,

MANY thanks for your kind hospitality at Strawberry Hill[1] and for every favour there. I continued with Dr Apthorp[2] for three or four days, all which time I was quite as lame and out of sorts as when with you, which made my journey and visits very irksome and tedious. However, as great good luck would have it, as I fell lame the very day I left Cambridge, so the day I left my brother I found myself as suddenly recovered, and, thank God, continue as well as usual, and if I grow no worse shall esteem myself very happy. I stay here about ten days longer, and then get, I hope, to my own fireside at Milton.

As my brother came to Eton College this week, I called upon him, and there saw an original letter, given him last year by Mrs Pitt[3] of

ford's conduct about his mother's boroughs (see HW to Mann 6 Oct. 1774).

2. *A Supplement . . . to a Biographical History of England . . . and a List of Curious Portraits of Eminent Persons not yet Engraved, Communicated, by the Honourable Horace Walpole,* 1774.

3. HW's letter is missing. HW exaggerates the number of funeral panegyrics.

———

1. See Appendix 6 for Cole's account of his visit at SH 29–31 Oct. 1774.

2. 'in Surrey' (addition in Cole's copy).

3. Not identified.

Maddox Street, from Nel Gwyn to a Mrs Jennings.[4] As the contents
of it show her character and give a little insight into a court with
whom you are as much acquainted as anyone can be at this distance,
I thought a transcript of it might be agreeable to you. It is written
on a thin, fine gilt paper in a neat Italian hand,[5] the seal small of
black wax, but the impression, whatever it was, is lost. I would have
procured the original, but on feeling gently about it, found the Doctor would not part with it to me. I thank you for the honour you have
done me in recording my poor name in your *Catalogue*,[6] which I did
not discover till I got here. But I shall leave no room for the letter,
and therefore take leave in haste, and am

Your most obliged faithful servant,

WM COLE

[Enclosure.][7]

These
    For Madam Jennings
        over against the Tub Tavern
            in Jermin Street   Windsor.
                London.   Burford House,[8]
                                                  Aprill 14
                                                    1684.

Madam.

I have receiv'd y[r] Letter, & I desire y[u] would speake to my Ladie Williams[9] to send me the gold Stuffe, & a Note with it, because I must sign it,

---

4. Not identified.
5. 'Not Nell Gwyn's, as she could not
write' (Toynbee).
6. Cole is twice mentioned in *Description of SH*, 1774, at p. 109, as the donor of
'a silver gilt apostle-spoon,' and of 'a box
with ancient round trenchers, with scrip-
tural mottoes' (*Works* ii. 500).
7. Printed literally from Cole's copy,
which he introduces as follows: 'Calling
upon my brother Apthorp, Vice-Provost
of Eton, at his apartments in that college,
Wednesday, Nov. 16, 1774, in order to go
together from thence to dine with our
learned friend Jacob Bryant, Esq., at Cip-
penham, he showed me an original letter
of Mrs Eleanor Gwyn, possibly to the great
Sarah Duchess of Marlborough, as she
afterwards was, though of this I am uncertain, as I have not my books to consult,

when that lady married John Churchill,
the future fortunate general. As it is a
curiosity to us at this time to recover any
part of the correspondence of such memorable characters, I carried it with me to
Burnham, and copied it out here that
evening, that my brother might have the
original again as soon as I saw him next.
It does not mean the Duchess, as is evident
by many marks.
'It is written on a sheet of gilt paper,
very thin, in a neat Italian hand, and was
sealed with a small seal of black wax, but
the impression is lost. It was given to Dr
Apthorp, as by a note in his hand on the
cover which enclosed it, by Mrs Pitt, Maddox Street, London, July 9, 1773.'
The letter apparently was first printed
(incomplete), from Cole's letter to HW, in
Peter Cunningham's 'The Story of Nell

then she shall have her Money yᵉ next Day of Mr. Trant; pray tell her
Ladieship, that I will send her a Note of what Quantity of Things I'le have
bought, if her Ladieship will put herselfe to yᵉ Trouble to buy them;
when they are bought I will sign a Note for her to be payd. Pray Madam,
let yᵉ Man goe on with my Sedan, & send Potvin[10] & Mr. Coker[11] down to
me, for I want them both. The Bill is very dear to boyle the Plate; but
Necessity hath noe Law. I am afraid Mᵐ you have forgott my Mantle,
which you were to line with Musk Colour Sattin, & all my other Things,
for you send me noe Patterns nor Answer. Monsieur Lainey[12] is going
away. Pray send me Word about your Son Griffin,[13] for his Majestie is
mighty well pleasd that he will goe along with my Lord Duke.[14] I am
afraid you are soe much taken up with your owne House, that you forgett
my Businesse. My Service to dear Lord Kildare,[15] & tell him I love him
with all my Heart. Pray Mᵐ see that Potvin brings now all my Things
with him: my Lord Duke's Bed &c. if he hath not made them all up, he
may doe that here for if I doe not get my Things out of his Hands now, I
shall not have them untill this Time Twelvemonth. The Duke brought
me down with him my Crochet of Diamonds; & I love it the better because he brought it. Mr Lumley,[16] & everie Body else will tell you that it
is the finest Thing that ever was seen. Good Mᵐ speake to Mr. Beaver[17]
to come down too, that I may bespeake a Ring for the Duke of Grafton[18]
before he goes into France.

I have continued extream ill[19] ever since you leaft me, & I am soe still.
I have sent to London for a Dr. I believe I shall die. My Service to the
Dutchesse of Norfolk,[20] & tell her, I am as sick as her Grace, but doe not

Gwyn,' GM July 1851, xxxvi (n.s.). 37. It has
been reprinted several times.

8. By a deed dated 13 and 14 Sept. 1680,
Charles II conveyed Burford House to the
E. of Dorset and others, in trust for Nell
Gwyn, and, afterwards, for her son Charles
E. of Burford, afterwards D. of St Albans
(see Thomas Eustace Harwood, Windsor
Old and New 122).

9. 'Perhaps the Mrs Williams, also called
Lady Williams, mistress of Lord Brouncker, frequently mentioned by Pepys' (Toynbee).

10. John Potvin or Poietevin was an up-
holsterer (see Peter Cunningham, The
Story of Nell Gwyn, New York, 1891, p.
104 n).

11. The MS perhaps should read Cokes:
Nell Gwyn bought much of her silver from
John Coques or Cooqus, a silversmith (see
ibid. 167–9).

12. Perhaps 'Lany, the Frenchman,' mentioned by Pepys in his Diary, 17 Jan. 1662.

13. Not identified; perhaps Mrs Jennings's son-in-law.

14. Charles Beauclerk (1670–1726), 1st D.
of St Albans, natural son of Charles II by
Nell Gwyn.

15. John FitzGerald (1661–1707), 18th E.
of Kildare.

16. Not identified.

17. Not identified.

18. Henry Fitzroy (1663–90), 1st D. of
Grafton, natural son of Charles II by the
Duchess of Cleveland.

19. For a discussion of the cause of her
illness, see Clifford Bax, Pretty Witty Nell,
New York, 1933, pp. 269–72.

20. Jane Bickerton (1644–93), second
wife of Henry Howard (1628–84), 6th D.
of Norfolk.

know what I ayle, although shee does, which I am overjoyed that shee goes on with her great Belly.[21]

Pray tell my Ladie Williams, that the King's Mistresses are accounted ill-pay-Masters, but shee shall have her Money the next Day after I have the Stuffe.

Here is a sad Slaughter at Windsor, the young Men's taking y[r] [their] Leaves & going to France, & although they are none of my Lovers, yet I am loath to part with the Men. Mrs. Jennings I love you with all my Heart, & soe good b'y.

Let me have an Answer to this Letter.

E. G.[22]

To Cole, Monday 9 January 1775

Add MS 5952, ff. 136–7.

Cole wrote a note on the cover, then marked through it: 'Rob. Br. Wigorn [Hon. Brownlow North (1741–1820), Bp of Worcester 1774–81] Jan. 11, '75, Rel. [reluctant?] to offer himself as a Found[er's] Kinsm[an] at All Soul's' [North was elected fellow of All Soul's, 1763, on the grounds that he was founder's kin.] Cole did not use the note in his letters to HW.

Address: To the Reverend Mr Cole at Milton near Cambridge.
Postmark: EK[9?] IA.

Arlington Street Jan. 9, 1775.

I EVERY day intended to thank you for the copy of Nel Gwyn's letter, till it was too late; the gout came, and made me moult my goosequill. The letter is very curious, and I am as well content as with the original.

It is lucky you do not care for news more recent than the Reformation. I should have none to tell you; nay nor earlier neither. Mr Strut's second volume[1] I suppose you have seen. He showed me two or three much better drawings from pictures in the possession of Mr

---

21. Frederick Howard (1684–1727) was born in Sept. (Collins, *Peerage*, 1812, i. 135).
22. Cole notes at the end of the letter: 'If I had read any part of the letter but the address or superscription, I could not have made the mistake in supposing it to have been written to Sarah Duchess of Marlborough.'

1. Joseph Strutt (1749–1802), antiquary and artist. HW refers to his *Compleat View*

of the *Manners, Customs, Arms, Habits, &c. of the Inhabitants of England*, 3 vols, 1775–6, which avowedly followed the plan 'of the celebrated Montfaucon's *Monarchie Françoise*' (i. p. ii). The second volume brought the history down to the end of the reign of Henry VIII. HW's copy, 3 vols bound in 2, green morocco, with HW's arms on the side, was sold London 1073 (SH vii. 130).

Ives.[2] One of them made me very happy: it is a genuine portrait of Humphrey Duke of Gloucester,[3] and is the individual same face as that I guessed to be his in my Marriage of Henry VI. They are infinitely more like each other than any two modern portraits of one person by different painters. I have been laughed at[4] for thinking the skull of Duke Humphrey at St Alban's[5] proved my guess; and yet it certainly does, and is the more like, as the two portraits represent him very bald, with only a ringlet of hair, as monks have. Mr Strut is going to engrave his drawings.[6]

Yours faithfully,

H. W.

From COLE, Sunday 9 April 1775

VA, Forster MS 110, ff. 139–40. Cole kept no copy.
Address: For the Honourable Mr Horace Walpole in Arlington Street, London.
Postmark: Cambridge 10 AP.

Milton, April 9, 1775.

Dear Sir,

IT is so long since I heard from you, and then you was far from well, that I should be glad, if it was only two lines, to be informed that you are in tolerable health and that this severe, penetrating weather agrees with you. Thank God! I hardly ever passed a better winter, but writing and transcribing has been totally neglected, though I have an hundred things ready before me. Yet a certain indisposition to write in my volumes has seized me and I have absolutely done nothing that way these six months. Reading has taken place, and seems still to fascinate me, yet I hope soon to get loose and repair to my old trade—the only one I seem fit for.

2. John Ives (1751–76), antiquary, herald and collector.

3. HW afterwards bought this portrait (see *post* 20 Feb. 1777), and described it in *Description of SH, Works* ii. 507–8.

4. By Henry Fox (see *post* 20 Feb. 1777).

5. Duke Humphrey's body 'was discovered by accidentally opening the vault 1703, and found lying in pickle in a leaden and wooden coffin: but has been so rudely handled by inquisitive persons ever since, that only the broken skeleton remains (the skull without the teeth)' (Gough, *Sepulchral Monuments* ii. 142–3). See also Mrs Maude C. Knight, 'Humphrey, Duke of Gloucester,' *St. Albans and Herts Architectural and Archaeological Society, Transactions,* 1903–4, vol. 2, pt 1, pp. 82–3.

6. Apparently he did not.

No doubt Mr Mason has sent you Mr Gray's *Life*.[1] I purchased it, and was sorry to get to the end of it, yet methinks there are some particular circumstances that are omitted which would <have d>one no discredit to the subject. Why he omits Mr Gray's great benefaction to himself is rather singular: that a person whom he represents throughout as in very strait circumstances should yet be able to bequeath to him to the amount of £1500 or £2000, without doing injustice to his own relations, with several other friendly benefactions, would have done credit to his friend's character, though it might have contradicted his insinuations of poverty, which was never the fact: £200 per annum, which Mr Gray was always, I believe, in possession of, was surely more than enough to exempt him from that assertion. Mr Mason had £500, all his vast collection of books, two or three rooms full over his own apartment, all his medals, MSS, musical instruments and music, etc., was a great benefaction to Mr Mason, who just hints in one place that his books were bequeathed to him.[2] Why could he not tell us where he was buried,[3] and several other particulars which a curious person is always pleased to be acquainted with? But great geniuses must be singular and not go on in the beaten track. However, altogether it has amused me much and impressed an higher idea of Mr Gray's worth, abilities and humanity than I was aware of, though so long acquainted with him.

I design the week after Easter to send you three or four or more curious portraits, by Mr Lort, who wrote to me yesterday that he is coming to Cambridge for the Easter holidays, and returns to town immediately after. One is a print of Gertrude More, whose print, about a month ago, I found in an imperfect life of her[4] which I bought in Moorfields some five years since, and which, with other

1. *The Poems of Mr. Gray. To which are prefixed Memoirs of his Life and Writings*, York, 1775. The work was published the end of March (see advertisements in *The London Chronicle* 28–30 March, 30 March–1 April 1775; *Lloyd's Evening Post* 27–9, 29–31 March 1775), and the second edition appeared early in June (see *The London Chronicle* 6–8, 8–10 June 1775; *Lloyd's Evening Post* 7–9 June 1775).

2. 'Amongst the books, which his friendship bequeathed to me' (ibid. 336).

3. 'I was then on the eastern side of Yorkshire, at a distance from the direct post, and therefore did not receive the melancholy intelligence soon enough to be able to reach Cambridge before his corpse had been carried to the place he had, by will, appointed for its interment' (ibid. 400). Cole overlooked Mason's note on Gray's aunt, Mrs Mary Antrobus, who died in 1749, 'and was buried in a vault in Stoke church-yard near the chancel door, in which also his mother and himself (according to the direction in his will) were afterwards buried' (p. 207). HW refers to this passage in his next letter.

4. Possibly *The Spiritual Exercises of the Most Virtuous and Religious D. Gertrude More*, Paris, 1658 (see DNB).

my books, I was looking into and never knew before that I had the print, which was placed in the middle of the book and was the occasion of my oversight. You may judge how eagerly I plucked it out in order to send it to you, as I never could recover that which your generosity had given to me and which, unknowingly, Mr Gulston took from me. Some two months ago I parted with my whole collection to him for £140,[5] which I am to be paid for some time hence. However, I have reserved two or three for you which I know he has not. One of them is a small print of Mr Crawford of Queen's,[6] a person who made a great noise at Cambridge some two years ago, and in town, by his disputes, etc., with a Mr Lovell.[7] With these I mean to send you one of myself, a drawing by Mr Gooch,[8] a son of Sir Thomas, and which I have an ambition to have placed in your last volume of modern and unknown heads. I would have sent them in this, but was unwilling Gertrude More should be creased. I am informed that you have a new and great acquisition of miniatures of the Digby family.[9] I hope it is true and that they are as fine as the best of your former set.

I am, dear Sir,

Your ever faithful and most obliged servant,

WM COLE

5. Gulston bought the collection for Lord Mountstuart (see *ante* 2 June 1774, and *post* 24 Feb. 1782).

6. Charles Crawford, fellow-commoner of Queens', 1768, whose riotous and blasphemous conduct engaged the College authorities for seven years (see Cooper, *Annals* iv. 363–4, 378; Denys A. Winstanley, *Unreformed Cambridge*, 1935, p. 218). Cole habitually follows the eighteenth century practice of spelling Queens' 'Queen's.'

7. Michael Lovell was a London merchant who was active in opposition to Wilkes in the election for Lord Mayor in 1773. A dispute with Crawford was utilized by Wilkes to forward his own candidacy. A long account of the quarrel appears in *The Whitehall Evening Post* 5–7, 12–14 Oct. 1773; a shorter account in GM Oct. 1773, xliii. 517. For a description of a satirical print (published in the *Macaroni Magazine* 1 Nov. 1773), in which Crawford, Lovell and Wilkes figure, see Mary Dorothy George, *Catalogue of Political and Personal Satires . . . in the British Museum, 1771–83*, 1935, v. 126.

8. HW inserted this drawing in his copy of the *Description of SH*, 1774, now in the Spencer Collection in the New York Public Library. The following inscription in Cole's hand appears on the verso: 'Wm. Cole de Milton juxta Cantabrigiam, A: M: Vicarius de Burnham juxta Windesoriam, 1775. Johan. Gooch Arm: Aedis Christi apud Oxon, Filius Domini Thomæ Gooch Baronetti, fecit 1771.' There is another copy of this drawing in the British Museum (see George J. Gray, *Index to the . . . Cole Manuscripts*, Cambridge, 1912, p. vii). John Gooch (1752–1823), of Christ Church, Oxford (B.A. 1773); rector of Saxlingham, Norfolk, and of Benacre, Suffolk; archdeacon of Sudbury; prebendary of Wells (see *Alumni Oxon*). See *post* [20] April 1775.

9. See following letter.

About two years ago I lent Mr Tyson the very beautiful print of the Earl of Cumberland,[10] which you had given to me, in order, as he said, to copy it. I had asked him for it several times, and was always told he could not find it, but as I had put it into the catalogue of my prints which I had sent to Mr Gulston when I sent the collection itself, I wrote to him and told him the case, and that Mr Tyson had promised to hunt after it. His answer was that he expected that print particularly, so I showed his letter to Mr Tyson, which produced the print about a month ago. However, I have never heard more of Mr Gulston since, and as I had intimated my fears that I never should recover it, it is likely he may never think more of it. Indeed he has no right to it, as I told him my doubts about it before I made or concluded my bargain with him, and in truth, was it not so, he is in my debt for that Gertrude More which I never sold him and which he took away without my knowledge and promised me to return but never did, so that I make no scruple to retain this and not to let him know that I have recovered it. All this preamble is to inform you that you may have that print also, if you please, at the same time as the others come.

To COLE, Tuesday 11 April 1775

Add MS 5952, ff. 138–9.

Address: [From COLE's copy, Add MS 5824, f. 82v.] To the Reverend Mr Cole at Milton near Cambridge. Free Hertford.

Arlington Street, April 11, 1775.

I THANK you, dear Sir, for your kind letter and the good account you give of yourself—nor can I blame your change from writing—that is, transcribing, to reading—sure you ought to divert yourself rather than others—though I should not say so, if your pen had not confined itself to transcripts.

I am perfectly well, and heed not the weather; though I wish the

10. A print of George Clifford (1558–1605), 3d E. of Cumberland, by Robert White. The Earl is 'dressed as for a tournament; a beautiful print' (*Engravers, Works* iv. 85). HW had at least four prints of him, including this one, which were sold in the London sale i. 48–9. Cole noted in his copy of *Engravers*[2] (now WSL) p. 103, opposite HW's account of this print: 'Mr Walpole gave one of them to me, which I gave to Mr Tyson, as he seemed much to admire it.'

seasons came a little oftener into their own places instead of each others'. From November till a fortnight ago we had warmth that I should often be glad of in summer—and since we are not sure of it then, was rejoiced when I could get it. For myself, I am a kind of delicate Hercules: and though made of paper, have, by temperance, by using as much cold water inwardly and outwardly as I can, and by taking no precautions against catching cold, and braving all weathers, become capable of suffering by none. My biennial visitant the gout has yielded to the bootikins,[1] and stayed with me this last time but five weeks in lieu of five months. Stronger men perhaps would kill themselves by my practice, but it has done so long with me, I shall trust to it.

I intended writing to you on Gray's *Life* if you had not prevented me. I am charmed with it, and prefer it to all the biography I ever saw. The style is excellent, simple, unaffected: the method, admirable, artful and judicious. He has *framed* the fragments (as a person[2] said) so well, that they are fine drawings if not finished pictures. For my part, I am so interested in it, that I shall certainly read it over and over. I do not find that is likely to be the case with many *yet*. Never was a book, which people pretended to expect so much with impatience, less devoured[3]—at least in London, where quartos are not of quick digestion. Faults are found, I hear, at Eton with the Latin poems for false quantities—no matter—they are equal to the English—and can one say more?

At Cambridge I should think the book would both offend much, and please—at least if they are as sensible to humour as to ill humour. And there is orthodoxy enough to wash down a camel. The Scotch and the reviewers will be still more angry, and the latter have not a syllable to pacify them—so they who wait for their decisions will probably miss of reading the most entertaining book in the world—a punishment, which they, who trust to such wretched judges deserve, for who are more contemptible than such judges, but they who pin their faith on them?

In answer to you yourself, my good Sir, I shall not subscribe to your censure of Mr Mason, whom I love and admire, and who has

---

1. 'A soft boot or mitten made of wool and oiled silk, worn as a cure for the gout' (OED; see also N&Q, 1st Ser. iv. 232). The earliest quotation in OED is from HW to Montagu 31 July 1767. HW describes their use, *post* 25 April 1775.

2. Not identified.

3. Cf. HW to Mason 14 April 1775.

shown the greatest taste possible in the execution of this work. Surely he has *said* enough in gratitude, and *done* far beyond what gratitude could demand. It seems delicacy in not expatiating on the legacy; particularizing more gratitude would have lessened the evidence of friendship, and made the justice done to Gray's character look more like a debt. He speaks of him in slender circumstances, not as distressed—and so he was till after the deaths of his parents and aunts, and even then, surely not rich. I think he does somewhere say that he meant to be buried with his mother, and not specifying any other place, confirms it. In short, Mr Mason shall never know your criticisms; he has a good heart and would feel them, though certainly not apprised that he could merit them. A man who has so called out all his friend's virtues could not want them himself.

I shall be much obliged to you for the prints you destine for me. The Earl of Cumberland I have, and will not rob you of. I wish you had been as successful with Mr G. as with Mr T.[4] I mean if you are not yet paid—now is the time, for he has sold his house to the Duke of Marlborough[5]—I suppose he will not keep his prints long:[6] he changes his pursuits continually and extravagantly—and then sells to indulge new fancies.

I have had a piece of luck within these two days. I have long lamented our having no certain piece written by Anne Boleyn's brother Lord Rochford.[7] I have found a very pretty copy of verses by him in the new published second volume of the *Nugae Antiquae*,[8] though by mistake he is called Earl of, instead of Viscount Rochford. They are taken from a MS dated 28 years after the author's death, and are much in the manner of Lord Surry's and Sir T. Wyat's

4. 'Mr G. [Gulston] as with Mr T. [Tyson]' (addition in Cole's copy). The square brackets are Cole's.

5. Joseph Gulston (d. 1766), M.P. for Tregoney, 1737–41 and for Poole, 1741–66 and the father of the collector, purchased Ealing Grove in 1755. His son converted it into an Italian villa, spent £30,000 on it, but was obliged, after dissipating the greater part of a vast fortune, to sell it to George Spencer (1739–1817), 4th D. of Marlborough, for £12,000 (see LI v. 26–8; GEC).

6. Gulston was obliged to sell his prints in 1786, a few months before his death (see DNB).

7. George Boleyn (d. 1536), Vct Rochford, accused of incest and high treason, and executed two days before his sister.

8. Sir John Harington (1561–1612), *Nugae Antiquae: being a Miscellaneous Collection of Original Papers*, ed. by Henry Harington (1755–91), 2 vols, 1769–75. HW apparently had two copies of the work. One (D.6), in 3 vols, 1779, in boards, was sold SH i. 83, and another, 3 vols, 1779, in morocco, was sold London vii. 995. In this edition Lord Rochford's verses appear at iii. 286.

poems. I should at first have doubted if they were not counterfeited, on reading my *Noble Authors;*[9] but then the blunder of *Earl* for *Viscount* would hardly have been committed. A little modernized and softened in the cadence, they would be very pretty.[10]

I have got the rest of the Digby pictures, but at a very high rate.[11] There is one very large[12] of Sir Kenelm, his wife and two sons,[13] in exquisite preservation, though the heads of him and his wife, not so highly finished as those I have—yet the boys and draperies are so amazing, that together with the size, it is certainly the most capital miniature in the world[14]—there are a few more, very fine too. I shall be happy to show them to you, whenever you Burnhamize—I mean before August, when I propose making my dear old blind friend[15] a visit at Paris—nothing else would carry me thither. I am too old to seek diversions, and too indolent to remove to a distance by choice, though not so immovable as you to much less distance. Adieu! pray tell me what you hear is said of Gray's *Life* at Cambridge.

Yours ever,

H. W.

From Cole, Thursday [20] April 1775

VA, Forster MS 110, ff. 141–2. Cole's copy, Add MS 5824, ff. 83v, 84v, 85v.

Cole erroneously dated the letter 'Thursday, April 18, 1775.' Thursday was 20 April, and Cole states that he has been confined with the gout for four days, since Sunday.

HW, who received the letter 25 April, made the following notes on f. 141: 'Green Dragon & Bull [crossed through]. Bp Hinch[liffe?, Bishop of Peterbor-

9. See *Works* i. 294–5.

10. HW modernized the lines and added an account of them in *Roy. & Nob. Authors, Works* i. 527–9. See also HW to Percy 18 Sept. 1792 and LI viii. 292. It has been questioned whether the modernization is an improvement (*Nugae Antiquae*, ed. Thomas Park, 2 vols, 1804, ii. 400 n).

11. HW already owned nine miniatures of the Digby family, all of which he purchased in 1771 (see *Description of SH, Works* ii. 421–2; Granger, *Correspondence* 308). In 1775 he purchased seven others from 'the lady who shared them with the other heir' (*Description of SH, Works* ii. 423, 426), which were sold SH xi. 42–3, 54–6.

12. It was sold SH xi. 56, to Farrer for Miss Burdett-Coutts, for £241.10.0.

13. Probably Kenelm (1625–48), and John (b. 1627), the eldest sons of Sir Kenelm and Lady Digby; they had two other sons, Everard and George, who died young.

14. HW had already described the portrait of Lady Lucy Percy, the mother of Venetia Lady Digby, as 'perhaps the finest and most perfect miniature in the world' (*Description of SH, Works* ii. 422).

15. Madame du Deffand. HW left on his last visit to Paris 16 Aug. and returned to London 17 Oct. (*Paris Jour.*).

ough?] Queen's head Gray's Inn Lane machine.' The explanation of 'Bp Hinch'
does not appear, but 'Queen's head . . . machine' is to remind HW to send the
bootikins (see following letter).

   Address: [From Cole's copy.] For Horace Walpole, Esq., in Arlington Street,
London. [Lort conveyed the letter to London; see below.]

Milton, Thursday, April 18[20], 1775.

Dear Sir,

ALTHOUGH your last favour is a complete censure and refuta-
tion of my absurd opinion relating to the execution of some
part of Mr Gray's *Life,* it is yet so just, so able, so demonstrative,
that one must be obstinate beyond measure not to be convinced. I
assure you I am thoroughly, and though I may retain the vulgar
prejudices of antiquarianism in wishing to see minutiae and things
not worthy public notice, having been all my lifetime collecting
such scraps, yet your most sensible stricture on that part of the letter, as well as respecting Mr Mason's gratitude, is set in a light so
convincing and full that a man must be lost to all sense and feeling
not to subscribe to it. I find the University people much divided
about it. The seniors think his reflections on their method of education unnecessary sarcasm on poor Dr Waterland,[1] and general disgust at a place he chose for his constant residence might as well have
been omitted, but all concur in admiring his poetry, descriptions
and letters. I am surprised at what you mention relating to the slow
sale in London: in Cambridge, above a fortnight ago, Mr Woodyer[2]
had sold forty copies and Merrill[3] as many, and had they more, could
have disposed of them, and I am told that a new edition[4] is already
at the press. This looks as if the first impression was all vended.[4a]

---

1. Daniel Waterland (1683–1740), theologian; Master of Magdalene 1713–40. For
Gray's contempt for Cambridge, see Wm
Mason, *Life of Gray*[1] pp. 12–14; at p. 182
Gray refers to the 'stupidity' of Waterland.
   2. John Woodyer (1720–1804), 'a man of
extensive knowledge, placid disposition,
and great probity;' 'a liveryman of the
Company of Stationers.' He afterwards
moved to London, where he died (LI viii.
472).
   3. Joseph Merrill (1735–1805), Cole's
friend and bookseller; brother of John
Merrill, alderman and mayor of Cambridge (see LA ix. 647). His father, Thomas

Merrill (1703–81) was also his partner in
the business, but Cole's dealings apparently were with the son (see GM June 1781,
li. 294b). Cf. *post* 24 Dec. 1775.
   4. The second edition appeared early in
June (see *ante* 9 April 1775 n. 1).
   4a. 'At the end of Mason's work Mr.
Cole wrote the following memorandum:
"I am by no means satisfied with this *Life;*
it has too much the affectation of classical
shortness to please me. More circumstances
would have suited my taste better; besides,
I think the biographer had a mind to revenge himself of the sneerings Mr Gray
put upon him, though he left him, I guess,

I am heartily glad your bootikins have been so useful to you, and that you have passed so good a winter and spring. I believe I must beg to know how I can procure the same sort of clothing. I went to church on Easter Sunday seemingly very well, and in the afternoon a fit of the gout seized me, made me pull off my shoe, and has confined me to my chamber[5] ever since. Last night I suffered great pain and got no rest, and this morning, though easy in my chair, am very feverish, as you may perceive by the badness of my writing.

Mr Lort was to come to Cambridge on Monday, and I had engaged to dine with him one day this week, as he returns to town on Saturday to be in readiness to celebrate St George's Day on Monday.[6] I was forced to send to him and excuse myself. I expect he will call this day,[7] and so am willing to get my letter ready that he may take it with the few prints. O. Cromwell is from the original at Sidney College, sent thither by the late Mr Hollis.[8] I am not paid for my prints, but have a note of hand from Mr Gulston and Mr Bretherton jointly to pay me in fifteen weeks from the date, about a month or six weeks ago. I have not yet heard anything from him requiring the Earl of Cumberland, and as you won't have it, I shall not scruple to keep it myself, as he certainly is in my debt for the Gertrude More.

I am glad you have got that noble miniature of the Digby family to complete your collection. I shall be happy to call on you to see it in my way to Burnham: but probably after your return from Paris. It was very lucky, as I once had a design, that I did not go to Burnham this Easter: to have been laid up with the gout in that house without furniture, attendance or conveniences, would have been doubly unfortunate.

above a thousand pounds, which is slightly hinted at only; yet Mr Walpole was quite satisfied with the work when I made my objection." ' (*Letters of HW*, ed. Wright, 6 vols, 1840, v. 413 n.) The whereabouts of Cole's copy of Mason's *Life of Gray* is not known.

5. 'now four days' (addition in Cole's copy).

6. As St George's Day fell on Sunday this year, the Society of Antiquaries had their annual meeting 24 April. 'The Society then dined together, according to annual custom, at the Mitre, in Fleet Street, where an elegant entertainment was provided on the occasion' (*Lloyd's Evening Post* 24–6 April 1775). Cf. *ante* 16 and 24 April 1773.

7. 'as it is so very fine, and he always chooses to walk, if the weather allows it' (addition in Cole's copy).

8. Thomas Hollis (1720–74), 'republican'; benefactor of Sidney Sussex, and Trinity, Cambridge, and Harvard College. He sent the portrait to Sidney Sussex College 15 Jan. 1766. There is an etching of it by P. S. Lamborn, as well as the print mentioned by Cole (engraved by Sharpe) below (see Francis Blackburn, *Memoirs of Thomas Hollis*, 2 vols, 1780, i. 298).

Pray do you know anything of a pamphlet I have seen advertised, called *A Peep into the Gardens of Twickenham,*[9] etc.? I took it for a catchpenny thing and so never sent for it.

Have you looked into the *History of Manchester*?[10] It is written with great spirit. The author is a Drawcansir:[11] Mr Carte, Mr Hume[12] and many other respectable names meet with no quarter at his hands. But I must put an end to my writing, as I fear you will hardly be able to read it, and subscribe myself, dear Sir,

Your ever faithful and most obliged servant,

WM COLE

Pray are you satisfied with Mr Gray's print?[13] I am by no means. It gives him a sharpness, a snappishness, a fierceness that was not his common feature, though it might occasionally be so. The little etching of him by Mr Mason, since copied by Henshaw, conveys a much stronger idea of him to me.

[Enclosure, from Cole's copy.]

Explanation of the prints I send you by Mr Lort:

1. Mr Purkis[14] of Magdalen College, Proctor in 1773, to whom some wag advertised him by letter that a basket of game was coming to him by the Cambridge coach, which turned out to be dead dogs and cats, etc. It is an handsome likeness of him. He stands in the attitude

9. *A Peep into the Principal Seats and Gardens in and about Twickenham.* By a Lady of Distinction, in the Republic of Letters. 1775. The author was Mrs Robert Hampden Pye (see following letter).

10. *The History of Manchester. In Four Books.* Book I, 'Containing the Roman and Roman-British Period,' 1771; Book II, 'Containing the Saxon Period,' 1775. Books III–IV were not published, but a transcript of the continuation is in the Chetham Library, Manchester. The author was John Whitaker (1735–1808), friend of Johnson and Gibbon, and author of historical, antiquarian and religious writings.

11. A blustering, bragging character in Villiers's burlesque, *The Rehearsal,* who in the last scene is made to enter a battle and to kill all the combatants on both sides.

12. Whitaker, in addition to corrections in the text, devotes 72 pages (vol. 2, Appendix 1, 499–570) to a discussion of the mistakes in the histories of Hume and Carte. See also his *Principal Corrections made in the History of Manchester, Book I,* 1773, pp. 124–62.

13. Prefixed to Mason's *Life:* 'W. Mason & B. Wilson Vivi memores delineavere. Engrav'd by James Basire.'

14. William Purkis (d. 1791), of Magdalene (A.B. 1756; D.D. 1786; Fellow and Tutor at the time of his death); F.S.A. 1774; rector of Carlby and of Anderby, Lincs (see GM Feb. 1791, lxi. 281a). For a description of the print, entitled 'Venus Turn'd Proctor,' see Mary Dorothy George, *Catalogue of Political and Personal Satires . . . in the British Museum, 1771–83,* 1935, v. 145–6.

of the Venus de Medici, in which posture he would frequently place himself before his friends. Indeed he is a most consummate vain coxcomb, always talking of uniting the gentleman and the scholar, which gained him the name of Mr Union. Though people thought it wrong thus to expose a worthy man, for he was no ways vicious, but a good tutor and no bad scholar, yet others thought his vanity deserved it.

2. Dr Halifax, the present law professor, commonly called Louse Hallifax, from his affectation of always getting among the heads of colleges, and consorting with them. He wrote and preached excellently in defense of subscription to articles, and against the clerical petitioners, than whom none was more violent and vehement than Mr Barker,[15] a fat fellow of Queen's College, and warm republican. The figures represent them very well: Barker particularly; the insignificant mean figure of Dr Halifax is very well hit off.

3. The Hon. Mr Stanley,[16] brother to Lord Stanley,[17] and Fellow Commoner of Trinity College, is spitting in Dr Ewen's face. The likenesses are tolerably well preserved. Dr Ewen does not squint enough.[18] He cast Mr Stanley, on a trial in Westminster Hall, made him[19] pay, and ask pardon.

4. Oliver Cromwell. Done by Sharpe of Cambridge from the original sent by the late Mr Hollis to Sidney College.

5. Michael Dalton.[20] Original at Mr Greaves's at Fulburn, which he

---

15. Robert Barker (d. 1796), of Queens', Cambridge (B.A. 1758, B.D. 1770, Fellow and Tutor); vicar of Youlgreave, Derbyshire, 1770–96; rector of Hickling, Notts (in the gift of Queens' College) at the time of his death (see GM Dec. 1796, lxvi. 1095b; John Charles Cox, *Notes on the Churches of Derbyshire*, 4 vols, Chesterfield, London and Derby, 1875–9, iv. 512). Cole records that on 25 April 1768 'I went with the Mayor [Joseph Bentham] to the Town Hall to dinner at their audit feast. Mr Barker . . . and I had a dispute about Government; he was a violent republican and bitter against James I, Charles I and II, and wished for another such as Cromwell; so I could not contain myself' (Palmer, *William Cole* 52). For a description of the print, entitled 'The Bear, the Louse, and Religion, a Fable,' see Mary Dorothy George, op. cit., v. 144–5.

16. Hon. Thomas Smith Stanley (1753–79), 2d son of James Smith Stanley, Bn Strange; Eton and Trinity; M.P. for Lancashire 1776–9; d. Jamaica (see *Eton Coll. Reg. 1753–90*).

17. Edward Smith Stanley (1752–1834), 12th E. of Derby.

18. Ewin was known as 'Dr Squintum' (see DNB). For a description of the print, entitled 'The Justice in the Suds,' see Mary Dorothy George, op. cit., v. 143–4.

19. MS reads *his*.

20. (d. 1648?), author of *The Countrey Justice*, 1618. In his 'Short Account of such Antiquaries as have received their education in Corpus Christi College, Cambridge,' Cole writes: 'Among the list of his [Mi-

bought of my sister Pole,[21] a near relation of the family. It is a proof plate by Mr Tyson.

6. A full-length neat print of Charles Crawford, Esq., Fellow Commoner of Queen's College, from whence he was expelled in 1773. It was drawn and engraved by Mr Henshaw, but never published.

7. Mrs Hopkins, wife to a surgeon at Cambridge,[22] and one of the daughters of the celebrated Cooper Thornhill,[23] who kept an inn at Stilton, and won a wager by riding to London in a certain time. Mr Speiss,[24] a Swiss dancing master at Cambridge, had been *valet de chambre* to Lord Sandwich, and is much like him. It was etched, 1771, by one Mr Ellis of Ely,[25] an apprentice to a draper at Cambridge. Mr Beverley, the bedel, married her sister.[26] The poor woman has been since confined for lunacy.

8. Mrs Lagden[27] of Bournbridge, who keeps the inn and turnpike there: a woman of a very singular appearance and character, educated a Quaker at Ashdon in Essex in the neighbourhood of Horseth, first a servant, then a kept mistress to Captain William Bromley,[28] uncle to the late Lord Montfort, who lived in a house opposite the parsonage. She then married Mr Lagden[29] and they were placed in a hut at Bournbridge to keep the turnpike, where from little be-

chael Tyson's] etchings, one of his best he had done me the honour to inscribe to my name: it is of Michael Dalton, the author of the famous book called *The Country Justice.* I told him of the original picture, which is an admirable one, by Cornelius de Neve [fl. 1637–64], and came out of my family, it being the property of my sister Pole, a descendant of the Daltons, who obliged Mr Commissary Greaves with it, who was most eager to have it, as he had purchased the family seat of the Daltons at Fulburne. Nothing can be more like than the print is to the original painting. Mr Granger, in his *Supplement*, p. 137, describing the etching, says it is in the possession of G. Greaves, Esq. His name is William' (Add MS 5886, f. 26; see also LA viii. 207).

21. Anne Cole, Cole's half-sister (by his father's first marriage), married Ralph Pole of Buntingford, Herts. She was dead before 1742, when Cole refers to her as Pole's 'late wife.' She was buried 'on the right hand of my father just before the altar on the steps in the chancel' of Babraham Church

(Palmer, *Monumental Inscriptions* 4; Add MS 5811, f. 50).

22. Mrs Allen Hopkins, née Mary Thornhill (*The Register of . . . St Michael's Parish, Cambridge, 1538–1837*, ed. John Venn, Cambridge, 1891, p. 49b *et passim*).

23. Cooper or Cowper Thornhill (d. 1759), master of the Bell Inn, Stilton, Hunts, who died possessed of an estate of £600 per annum (see GM March 1759, xxix. 146a). His ride from Stilton to London took place in 1745.

24. Not further identified.

25. Not identified.

26. John Beverley (1743–1827), esquire bedell 1770–1827; m., 5 April 1767, Susannah Thornhill (*The Register of . . . St Michael's*, etc., 92a).

27. (b. 1698). Tyson made two etchings of her, aged 74 and 76 (EBP).

28. Died 1729 at Horseheath Hall (see Musgrave, *Obituary*).

29. Died before 1775.

ginnings they throve very well, and built on the waste, by consent of Mr Western of Abington,[30] a very good house. The husband was a meek, quiet, inoffensive man, whom she made no scruple to cuckold before his face. Their son, Mr Jeremiah Lagden,[31] is at this time steward to the present Lord Montfort, under whose ill conduct he has throve marvellously. He was first his footboy at Eton School, then travelled with him as a footman, and is now married to one of the nieces[32] of the late Dr Conyers Middleton,[33] with whom he became acquainted when his Lordship boarded in the Doctor's family at Cambridge for education. Mrs Middleton,[34] the Doctor's widow, told me that she was a natural daughter of the Doctor's brother.[35] She lived for some time as housekeeper at Horseth Hall. The drawing is done by Mr Tyson, who gave it me November 26, 1769. *O qualis facies, et quali digna tabella!*[36] It is very like, as you must be sensible. She is now very old, yet dressed out like an old bawd, and very active. I dined at her house this year and saw no alteration in her.

9. Dr Muncey,[37] M.D., of Chelsea Hospital, a great friend and acquaintance of Francis, late Earl of Godolphin,[38] and very like him. It was given to me Jan. 19, 1770, by Mr Tyson.

10. Mr Purkis of Magdalen College, Proctor in 1772. It is an *outré*, rough likeness, and etched by Mr Riddel,[39] A. B. of Trinity College,

30. Thomas Western (1695–1754), of Great Abington, Cambs, Cole's 'old friend . . . who died at Bath . . . of a gradual decay,' and was buried in the churchyard of Great Abington Church (Palmer, *Monumental Inscriptions* 2). He was one of the pallbearers at the funeral of Cole's father in 1735 (see Charlotte Fell Smith, 'The Western Family of Rivenhall,' *Essex Review*, Jan. 1901, x. 10).

31. Probably the Jeremiah Lagden of Wentworth near Ely who d. 3 Feb. 1804, 'at Abington, co. Cambridge, in a very advanced age' (GM Feb. 1804, lxxiv. 187a).

32. Not identified.

33. (1683–1750), divine and controversialist; friend and correspondent of HW and Cole.

34. Anne Powell (d. 1760), dau. of John Powell of Boughrood near Radnor, who m. Middleton not long before his death, as his third wife (Musgrave, *Obituary*).

35. Probably William Middleton, half-brother to Conyers Middleton, who is said to have been extravagant, 'proved graceless, and died poor' (LA v. 405). He is almost certainly the 'unfortunate brother' of whom Middleton wrote in 1741, that he 'had nothing else to leave' but two daughters, and those it was his duty to care for (see DNB).

36. Juvenal, *Satires* x. 157.

37. Messenger Monsey (1693–1788), physician to Chelsea Hospital. In gratitude for a cure which he effected on him, Godolphin secured the appointment for him, and introduced him to the leading Whig politicians. Monsey was noted as an eccentric.

38. Francis Godolphin (1678–1766), 2d E. of Godolphin.

39. George Riddell (1752–74), son of Andrew Riddell of Enfield, Middlesex.

who died 1774. Mr Richard Reynolds,[40] butler of Caius College, gave it to me July 23, 1773.

11. A lady. Inscribed by Mr Hutchinson[41] of Sidney College, since dead, to Lady Henrietta Roper.[42] Query, if not Queen Henrietta Maria? Given to me by Mr Christopher Sharpe, Jan. 13, 1774.

12. Dame Gertrude More. *Magnes amoris amor.* R. Lachon *sculpsit.*

13. My own picture by Mr John Gooch, son of Sir Thomas Gooch, student of Christ Church, 1771. He took it while he was at dinner with me at Milton with his uncle, Dr Gooch, and family. It is drawn as I sat, in a red silk cap, gown and cassock and band, in an oval and profile, and is thought to be like.[43]

Wm Cole de Milton
juxta Cantabrigiam,
A: M: Vicarius de
Burnham juxta Win-
desoriam. 1775
    Johan. Gooch Arm: Ædis
Christi apud Oxon, Filius
Dñi Thomæ Gooch Baro-
netti, fecit 1771.

40. He was still Butler of Caius College in 1791 or 1792 (see *Universal British Directory,* 5 vols, 1791–8?, ii. 493). See also *post* 26 March 1776.

41. Rev. Julius Hutchinson (A.B. 1765);

d. Hartfield, Herts (see GM Oct. 1771, xli. 475a).

42. Not identified.

43. See illustration, from HW's copy of the *Description of SH,* 1774, in the Spencer Collection, New York Public Library.

To Cole, Tuesday 25 April 1775

Add MS 5952, ff. 140–1.

Address: [From Cole's copy, Add MS 5824, f. 85v.] To the Reverend Mr Cole at Milton near Cambridge.

Arlington Street, April 25, 1775.

THE least I can do, dear Sir, in gratitude for the cargo of prints I have received today from you, is to send you a medicine. A pair of bootikins will set out tomorrow morning in the machine that goes from the Queen's Head in Gray's Inn Lane. To be certain, you had better send for them where the machine inns, lest they should neglect delivering them at Milton. My not losing a moment, shows my zeal—but if you can bear a little pain, I should not press you to use them. I have suffered so dreadfully, that I constantly wear them to diminish the stock of gout in my constitution; but as your fit is very slight, and will not last, and as you are pretty sure by its beginning so late, that you will never have much; and as the gout certainly carries off other complaints, had not you better endure a little, when it is rather a remedy than a disease? I do not desire to be entirely delivered from the gout, for all reformations do but make room for some new grievance; and in my opinion, a disorder that requires no physician is preferable to any that does. However I have put relief in your power and you will judge for yourself. You must tie them as tight as you can bear, the flannel next to the flesh; and when you take them off, it should be in bed. Rub your feet with a warm cloth, and put on warm stockings, for fear of catching cold while the pores are open. It would kill anybody but me, who am of adamant, to walk out into the dew in winter in my slippers in half an hour after pulling off the bootikins. A physician sent me word good-naturedly that there was danger of catching cold after the bootikins, unless one was careful. I thanked him, but told him my precaution was, never taking any. All the winter I pass five days in a week without walking out, and sit often by the fireside till seven in the evening. When I do go out, whatever the weather is, I go with both glasses of the coach down, and so I do at midnight out of the hottest room. I have not had a single cold however slight, these two years.

You are too candid in submitting at once to my defence of Mr Mason. It is true I am more charmed with his book than I almost ever was with one. I find more people like the grave letters than those of humour, and some think the latter a little affected, which is as wrong a judgment as they could make, for Gray never wrote anything easily but things of humour. Humour was his natural and original turn—and though from his child[1][hood] he was grave, and reserved, his genius led him to see things ludicrously and satirically; and though his health and dissatisfaction gave him low spirits, his melancholy turn was much more affected than his pleasantry in writing. You knew him enough to know I am in the right—but the world in general always wants to be told how to think as well as what to think. The print, I agree with you, though like, is a very disagreeable likeness, and the worst likeness of him. It gives the primness he had when under constraint; and there is a blackness in the countenance which was like him only the last time I ever saw him, when I was much struck with it; and though I did not apprehend him in danger, it left an impression on me that was uneasy and almost prophetic of what I heard but too soon after leaving him. Wilson[2] drew the picture under much such impression, and I could not bear it in my room;[3] Mr Mason altered it a little,[3a] but still it is not well, nor gives any idea of the determined virtues of his heart. It just serves to help the reader to an image of the person, whose genius and integrity they must admire, if they are so happy as to have a taste for either.

The *Peep into the Gardens at Twickenham* is a silly little book, of which a few little copies were printed some years ago for presents,[4] and which now sets up for itself as a vendible book. It is a most inaccurate, superficial, blundering account of Twickenham and other places, drawn up by a Jewess, who has married twice and turned Christian, poetess and authoress.[5] She has printed her poems too,[6]

1. MS reads *child*. Possibly, HW intended to write 'from a child.'

2. Benjamin Wilson (1721–88), painter and man of science, friend and correspondent of Mason.

3. Cf. HW to Mason 23 March 1774.

3a. Cf. LA ix. 718.

4. It was privately printed in 1760 under the title *A Short Account of the Principal Seats*, and in 1767 as *A Short View*. HW probably refers to the latter, as Mrs Pye's *Poems*, mentioned below, were apparently distributed with the former.

5. Jael Mendez (d. 1782), of Red Lion Street, Holborn, m. (1), in 1762, John Neil Campbell, of Milton Ernest, Beds, and (2), in 1766, Robert Hampden Pye, an officer in the Foot Guards, and brother to Henry James Pye, Poet Laureate (see *London Chronicle* 23–5 Feb. 1762, 21–3 Oct. 1766; GM Feb. 1762, xxxii. 93; Oct. 1766, xxxvi. 494). Mrs Pye was commonly known as Mrs Hampden Pye, and she called herself Joel (not Jael) Henrietta Pye.

6. *Poems*. By a Lady. Privately printed, 1767. The volume is 'most affectionately

and one complimentary copy of mine[7] which in good breeding I could not help sending her in return for violent compliments in verse to me.[8] I do not remember that hers were good; mine I know were very bad, and certainly never intended for the press.

I bought the first volume of Manchester,[9] but could not read it; it was much too learned for me; and seemed rather an account of Babel than Manchester, I mean in point of antiquity. To be sure it is very kind in an author to promise one the history of a country town, and give one a circumstantial account of the antediluvian world into the bargain. But I am simple and ignorant, and desire no more than I pay for. And then for my progenitors Noah and the Saxons, I have no curiosity about them. Bishop Lyttelton used to plague me to death with barrows and tumuli and Roman camps, and all those bumps in the ground that do not amount to a most imperfect ichnography; but in good truth I am content with all arts when perfected, nor inquire how ingeniously people contrived to do without them—and I care still less for remains of arts that retain no vestiges of art. Mr Bryant, who is sublime in unknown knowledge, diverted me more, yet I have not finished his work,[10] no more than he has. There is a great ingenuity in discovering all history (though it has never been written) by etymologies. Nay he convinced me that the Greeks had totally mistaken all they went to learn in Egypt, etc., by doing, as the French do still, judge wrong by the ear—but as I have been trying now and then for above forty years to learn something, I have not time to unlearn it all again, though I allow this is our best sort of knowledge. If I should die when I am not clear in the history of the world below its first three thousand years, I should be at a sad loss on meeting with Homer and Hesiod or any of those *moderns* in the Elysian fields, before I knew what I ought to think of them.

Pray do not betray my ignorance: the reviewers and such *literati* have called me *a learned and ingenious gentleman*. I am sorry they ever heard my name, but don't let them know how irreverently I

inscribed to Henry James Pye, Esquire, by his sister, friend, and servant, the author.'

7. 'To the Authoress of some Lines on Strawberry Hill,' at p. 11 of her *Poems*. Cf. HW's *Fugitive Verses*, ed. W. S. Lewis, New York and London, 1931, p. 186.

8. 'On Mr. Walpole's House, at Strawberry Hill,' *Poems* 9–10.

9. Only vol. 1 of Whitaker's *History of Manchester* was sold SH v. 53.

10. *A New System, or Analysis of Ancient Mythology*, 3 vols, 1774–6. See also HW to Mason 23 March and 7 April 1774. HW's copy was sold SH v. 39.

speak of the erudite, whom I dare to say they admire. These wasps, I suppose, will be very angry at the just contempt Mr Gray had for them,[11] and will, as insects do, attempt to sting, in hopes that their twelvepenny readers will suck a little venom from the momentary tumor they raise—but good-night—and once more thank you for the prints.

Yours ever,

H. W.

From Cole, Saturday 29 April 1775

VA, Forster MS 110, ff. 143–4. Cole kept no copy.
Address: For the Honourable Mr Horace Walpole in Arlington Street, London.
Postmark: Cambridge 1 MA.

Milton, April 29, 1775.

Dear Sir,

MANY thanks for your kind present and attention in sending the bootikins, which came very safely, yet I rather choose to follow your opinion and bear a little present pain than use myself to a remedy that may be necessary hereafter. I have the gout in both my feet and have very uneasy, restless nights, yet my days are cheerful, and I get up to a very pleasant window that commands my garden and yard: appetite good, and no other complaint prevailing, but pain on nights, no sleep or very little, and an utter incapacity of moving an inch without help. These slight inconveniences I consider as trifles when I reflect how severely you have been handled with this disorder and for so many months.

Your criticism on *Manchester* is admirable, such as no one could make but yourself: it is literally true. I am told within this fortnight, I think by Mr Lort, that it is supposed that his intellects are a little deranged.[1] Perhaps it may be so, and that <his> second volume may have amused me the more for it. I wish <we> had less of the Romans and more of Manchester.

---

11. See Gray's letter to Mason 25 July 1756 (Wm Mason, *Gray*[1] p. 246), in which the reviewers are called 'Man-midwives and Presbyterian parsons,' whose 'impertinence' 'we must all swallow.'

1. This report was without foundation (see DNB).

I am sorry to find you rather disposed to banter the sublimity of Mr Bryant's learning. For my part, who never pretended to much more than was sufficient to make me spell my own language right, I never aimed to understand it, but because I saw Dr Apthorp and other pedagogues at Eton and Cambridge perfectly idolize the book and its author, I implicitly subscribed to what I took for granted and did not understand—which in general is no bad method. I read part of the book and wondered at his learning, yet even I had my doubts which I knew not how to solve. But, in short, as you observe, if one was to go on in this manner, the one half of life would be spent in learning and the other half in unlearning, and in this case the block-head is a more rational creature than the greatest scholar. By the by, when I was at Burnham[2] I saw Mr Bryant several times. He is very civil, and was remarkably kind and obliging to me, and (I mention it as a secret to you) he mentioned your name several times to me, was much disposed to call on you, said he had unluckily failed wait-ing on you for some time, but meant to call at Arlington Street. Whether he has done so or not, I am ignorant. He was then, I know, in the very crisis of authorial flattery, and whether he wished to have your sanction, to me seemed probable. I am sorry to find so good, so exquisite a judge[3] at one blow knock down all the puffs of the re-viewers. These last are a race of mortals I know nothing of, no more than they do of me: I only have learned to hold them in the same contempt that you do, for many years. I am one of the twelvepenny readers, as I find it useful to know new publications, but their judg-ments I rely on as you do. Neither they nor Mr Bryant shall know what has passed on their score. I am only concerned to find that the greatest of all scholars is likely to dwindle into a doubtful etymolo-gist.[4] You see what a loss my *Athenae Cantabrigienses* is like to suffer.

I wish you may be able to read my scrawl, on a book on one knee, with a tremulous hand, but I would not omit my duty and grati-tude to my worthiest and kindest friend, and wishing you all earthly blessings, I am, dear Sir,

Your ever faithful and most obliged servant,

Wm Cole

2. See *ante* 18 Nov. 1774 n. 7.
3. That is, HW.
4. Professor Pottle points out that Milla-mant in *The Way of the World* tells Mira-bel that she may finally 'dwindle into a wife.'

From COLE, Friday 2 June 1775

VA, Forster MS 110, ff. 145–6. COLE's copy, Add MS 5824, ff. 86v, 87v.

Address: [From COLE's copy.] For the Honourable Horace Walpole at Strawberry Hill in Twickenham, Middlesex.

Milton, June 2, 1775.

Dear Sir,

I AM still chained to my chair, and, having had a respite from pain and insomnia, was again attacked a week ago with both for several nights. Thank God! they seem to have left me again, as the third night is passed without either. I have hardly ever lost my appetite, and never my spirits, though I had the fever on Monday and Tuesday pretty severely and sent for a doctor[1] from Cambridge. I took the bark freely, and, supposing I had caught a cold, from a pain in my back, which continues, and prevents my lying easily on either side, I made no hesitations about it. Yesterday Dr Glynn, the most practising physician at Cambridge, in a friendly manner called to see me and utterly forbade the use of bark while anything of the gout was upon me, and that it is still on me is visible by my puffed-up foot, and which has never had a shoe on these seven weeks. All this preamble is to show your wisdom in having no recourse to the faculty at all. I have been often, before this, much puzzled which to follow of two discordant opinions, and perhaps to have followed neither would have been wisest. Yesterday I was alarmed and still continue rather perplexed at Mr Essex's report to me: he has been often over to see me during my confinement, and yesterday he brought word from his brother-in-law, Mr Hales,[2] the chief surgeon of Cambridge, that a new-painted room would bring on the gout, and actually did so some time ago to a Mr Mortlock[3] of Cambridge, who died of it there about a month ago. Now I have not only had *a* room, but *every* room in my house,[4] passages, windows and every part of it, painted double and treble times over since I have been laid up, having no objection to the smell of fresh paint, and my hall

---

1. 'an apothecary from Cambridge, for the first time since my confinement' (addition in Cole's copy).

2. Richard Hayles (1714–81) m. Essex's sister, Martha Essex (1721–99). He was one of the surgeons who attended free at Addenbrooke's Hospital. Their 4th dau., Sophia, m. Thomas Kerrich (see Cooper,

Memorials iii. 259; *The State of Addenbrooke's Hospital* [Cambridge], 1771, p. 7).

3. Not identified.

4. 'painted over, the upper rooms treble times, nay, five times over, as I have lately new wainscoted them, since my confinement' (addition in Cole's copy).

is actually finishing at this instant. Last night, waking early, this news got into my head, and the smell then was so disagreeable to me, through my fears, that I shall proceed no further. But I am ashamed of so much talk of myself and complaints. I hope I am better and that I shall soon be released. I hope also this malady flies you and your bootikins, and ever will do so. To have it at any time is an evil, but to have been deprived of the progress of this remarkable fine spring, flowers, etc., in one's garden, is a double misfortune.

The two immediate occasions of my troubling you at all at this time are the following note on a slip of paper which I lately met with, and knew not whether I ever communicated to you, for whom it was noted: In the life of Dr John North,[5] by Roger North, Esq., p. 237, mention is made of one Mr Blemwell,[6] a painter of Bury, an acquaintance of Sir Peter Lely. The second reason of writing is on Dr Glynn's account, and I hope you will not take it amiss of me in doing what I can't avoid. You was so kind, on my intercession, two years ago to give him admittance to see Strawberry Hill. He has ever since talked of it in raptures, and now desires me to renew my application to you for a second view of it, and to give leave, if you should not be at home, to give orders for his admittance when he calls, to your servants.[7]

Since my confinement I have taken the pains to make an entire and minute index to your *Catalogue* of furniture, paintings and curiosities at Strawberry Hill.[8] If you have the least desire to have a copy, I can do it in half a day, and will do it with pleasure and satisfaction, and as I am good at these low, humble things, wish you would employ me in your service for anything of that sort, which I will do with grateful satisfaction.

5. *The Life of . . . Sir Dudley North . . . and of Dr. John North* [(1645–83) (see DNB)], 1744, by Roger North (1653–1734), lawyer and historian.

6. MS and Cole's copy read *Slemwell*, but in the work cited above he is called 'one Mr Blemwell, a picture-drawer' of Bury, 'an early friend and acquaintance of Sir Peter Lely,' who allowed Blemwell 'to have had a very good judgment in the art of picture, but his performances were not equal to his skill.'

7. 'He is a worthy man, though an oddity' (addition in Cole's copy).

8. 'and to Mr Gray's *Life*. The least intimation that a copy of either or both [will be acceptable to you], will be so far from a trouble, that it will be an amusement to me to do them for you' (addition in Cole's copy). Cole's index to Mason's *Gray*, 1775, is bound into the Isaac Reed–George Daniel–Sir William Fraser copy and is now (1937) in the Yale University Library. Cole noted at the end: 'Wm Cole. May 16. 1775. in a fit of the gout.'

I wish you are able to read my scrawl, but I am in an habit of writing so fast that my ideas are lost if I stay to correct my pen. Adieu, dear Sir, and Heaven protect you to be an ornament to the age we live in. I am, Sir,

Your most obliged and faithful servant,

Wm Cole

To Cole, Monday 5 June 1775

Add MS 5952, ff. 142-3.

Address: To the Reverend Mr Cole at Milton near Cambridge.
Postmark: 6 IV.

Strawberry Hill, June 5, 1775.

I AM extremely concerned, dear Sir, to hear you have been so long confined by the gout. The painting of your house may from the damp have given you cold—I don't conceive that paint can affect one otherwise, if it does not make one sick, as it does me of all things. Dr Heberden, as every physician to make himself talked of, will set up some new hypothesis, pretends that a damp house and even damp sheets, which have ever been reckoned fatal, are wholesome; to prove his faith he went into his own new house totally unaired, and survived it. At Malverne they certainly put patients into sheets just dipped in the spring—however I am glad you have a better proof, that dampness is not mortal: and it is better to be too cautious, than too rash. I am perfectly well and expect to be so for a year and half— I desire no more of the bootikins than to curtail my fits.

Thank you for the note from North's *Life,* though having reprinted my *Painters,* I shall never have an opportunity of using it. I am still more obliged to you for the offer of an index to my catalogue—but as I myself know exactly where to find everything in it, as I dare to say nobody else will want it, I shall certainly not put you to that trouble.

Dr Glynn will certainly be most welcome to see my house, and shall, if I am not at home. Still I had rather know a few days before, because else he may happen to come when I have company, as I have often at this time of the year, and then it is impossible to let it be seen, as I cannot ask my company, who may have come to see it too, to go out, that somebody else may see it, and I should be very sorry to have the Doctor disappointed. These difficulties, which have happened more than once, have obliged me to give every ticket for a particular day; therefore if Dr Glynn will be so good as to advertise me of the day he intends to come here, with a direction, I will send him word what day he can see it.

I have just run through the two vast folios of Hutchins's *Dorsetshire.*[1] He has taken infinite pains; indeed all but those that would make it entertaining.

Pray can you tell me anything of some relations of my own, the Burwells?[2] My grandfather married Sir Jeffery Burwell's daughter of Rougham in Suffolk.[3] Sir Jeffery's mother I imagine was daughter of a Jeffery Pitman of Suffolk;[4] at least I know there was such a man as the latter, and that we quarter the arms of Pitman. But I cannot find who Lady Burwell, Sir Jeffery's wife,[5] was. Edmondson has searched in vain in the Herald's office; and I have outlived all the ancient of my family so long that I know not of whom to inquire, but you of the neighbourhood. There is an old walk in the park at Houghton called Sir Jeffery's walk, where the old gentleman used to teach my father Sir Robert his book. Those very old trees encouraged my father to plant at Houghton, when people used to try to persuade him nothing would grow there. He said, why will not other trees grow as well as those in Sir Jeffery's walk?—Other trees have grown to some purpose! Did I ever tell you that my father was descended from Lord Burleigh? The latter's grand-daughter by his son Exeter married Sir Giles Allington,[6] whose daughter married Sir Robert Crane, father of Sir Edward Walpole's wife.[7] I want but Lady

---

1. HW's copy (A. 1) was sold SH i. 75.

2. See following letter.

3. Robert Walpole (1650–1700), of Houghton, Norfolk, m. Mary Burwell (d. 1711), dau. and coheir of Sir Jeffery Burwell (d. 1684) (see LeNeve, *Knights* 166; Collins, *Peerage*, 1812, v. 651–2; Walter A. Copinger, *The Manors of Suffolk*, 7 vols, Privately Printed, London and Manchester, 1905–11, vi. 322).

4. Sir Jeffery's father, Edmund or Edward Burwell (d. 1652), of Woodbridge, Suffolk, m. Mary Pitman, dau. of Jeffery Pitman, also of Woodbridge (see Le Neve, *Knights* 165; W. A. Copinger, loc. cit.).

5. Sir Jeffery Burwell m. Elizabeth Dere-

haugh (d. 1678), only dau. of Thomas Derehaugh (d. 1619) of Colston Hall, Suffolk (see LeNeve, *Knights* 166; Copinger, ibid. iv. 11; following letter).

6. Dorothy Cecil (d. 1613), 7th dau. of Thomas Cecil, 1st E. of Exeter (see *ante* 1 Dec. 1763).

7. Susan Allington (1605–81), 3d dau. of Sir Giles Allington, m., as his 2d wife, Sir Robert Crane (1585–1643), 1st Bt, of Chilton, Suffolk, whose 3d dau. and coheir, Susan Crane (1632–67), m., in 1649, Sir Edward Walpole (1621–68), K.B. (HW's greatgrandfather) (see LeNeve, *Knights* 19; *The Topographer for 1790*, vol. 2, 1790, p. 377; Collins, *Peerage*, 1812, v. 650).

Burwell's name to make my genealogic tree shoot out stems every way. I have recovered a barony in fee, which has no defect but in being antecedent to any summons to Parliament, that of the Fitz Osberts;[8] and on my mother's side it has mounted the Lord knows whither, by the Philipps's to Henry VIII and has sucked in Dryden for a great-uncle; and by Lady Philipps's mother Darcy to Edward III, and there I stop for brevity's sake—especially as Edward III[9] is a second Adam; who almost is not descended from Edward? as posterity will be from Charles II, and all the princes in Europe from James I. I am the first antiquary of my race—people don't know how entertaining a study it is. Who begot whom is a most amusing kind of hunting; one recovers a grandfather instead of breaking one's own neck—and then one grows so pious to the memory of a thousand persons one never heard of before. One finds how Christian names came into a family, with a world of other delectable erudition. You cannot imagine how vexed I was that Blomfield died before he arrived at Houghton[10]—I had promised myself a whole crop of notable ancestors—but I think I have pretty well unkennelled them myself. Adieu, Dear Sir,

Yours ever,

H. W.

8. 'Sir Henry de Walpole married Isabel, dau. of Sir Peter Fitz-Osbert, and heir to her brother, Sir Roger Fitz-Osbert, summoned to Parliament among the Barons of the realm, in 22 Edward I. Which Isabel, surviving the said Sir Henry, was married, secondly, to Sir Walter Jernegan. . . . She deceased about 1311' (Collins, *Peerage*, 1812, v. 636). HW exaggerates the importance of his 'recovery,' for the above account appeared in Collins's *Peerage* as early as the 3d edn, 1756, iii. 582–3, the last edition published under Collins's superintendence.

9. Sir John Philipps (d. 1629), 1st Bt, of Picton Castle, Pembroke, m. Anne Perrot (d. ca 1610), dau. and coheir of Sir John Perrot (1527?–92), commonly reputed to be a son of Henry VIII by Mary Berkley (afterwards wife of Thomas Perrot). Their son, Sir Richard Philipps (d. ca 1648), 2d Bt, m. Elizabeth Dryden, dau. of Sir Erasmus Dryden, first Bt, and aunt of John Dryden the poet (who was son of Erasmus Dryden, 3d son of Sir Erasmus). Their son and heir, Sir Erasmus Philipps (ca 1623–97), 3d Bt, m. (1660), as his 2d wife, Catharine Darcy (1641–1713?), dau. and coheir of Hon. Edward Darcy, by Elizabeth, dau. of Philip Stanhope, 1st E. of Chesterfield. Sir Erasmus, HW's great-grandfather, was thus a first cousin of Dryden and HW was only a first cousin thrice removed. The descent from Edward III came through the mother of the 1st E. of Chesterfield, Cordell Allington, granddaughter of Sir Giles Allington, who 'married Dorothy, dau. of Thomas Cecil, E. of Exeter, and Dorothy, his wife, daughter and coheiress of Neville Lord Latimer, a marriage which brought the blood of John of Gaunt, and of Thomas of Woodstock, and consequently of Edward the Third, to the succeeding generations of Alingtons' (Arthur Hervey, 'Horseheath and the Alingtons,' *Suffolk Institute of Archaeology and Natural History*, vol. 4, 1874, p. 114).

10. See *ante* 2 Sept. 1764. HW's remark was probably suggested by the publication (in this year) of the last two volumes of Blomefield's *Norfolk*.

PS. I found a family of Whaplode in Lincolnshire who give our arms, and have persuaded myself that Whaplode is a corruption of Walpole, and came from a branch when we lived at Walpole in Lincolnshire.[11]

From Cole, Friday 9 June 1775

VA, Forster MS 110, ff. 147–8. Cole's copy, Add MS 5824, ff. 88v, 89v.

On the cover of the original HW made a rough drawing of the arms of the Derehaugh family, wrote above it 'Derehaugh' and at the side 'or, on a bend cotised sable 3 martlets or.'

Address: For the Honourable Mr Horace Walpole at Strawberry Hill in Twickenham, Middlesex. *Postmark:* Cambridge.

Milton, June 9, 1775.

Dear Sir,

MY gout is chiefly left me, but pains in my back, sore throat, fever, still make this excessive hot weather very troublesome. Dr Heberden's hypothesis of the wholesomeness of damp seems, however, to be confirmed by one circumstance, and that a very material one. In France they hardly know what it is to put on an aired shirt or a dry pair of sheets. I have had sheets brought to lay on my bed that might almost have been wrung, and was told it was never otherwise.

I am much obliged to you for your civility to Dr Glynn, whom I have not seen since I wrote last, but will communicate the contents of yours.

I am very happy to be able to inform you that Sir Jeffery Burwell's wife was daughter and sole heiress of Thomas Derehaugh, Esq., of Colton Hall[1] in Badingham in Suffolk,[2] whose family had been possessed of the manors of Gedgrave and Trayford,[3] 6 Edward VI; of Burstonhaugh,[4] Badingham and Wicklowes, with lands in Peasing-

---

11. For an account of the Walpoles of Whaplode in Lincolnshire, descendants of Thomas Walpole (d. 1514), whose second son Henry married Margaret Holtofte of Whaplode, see Collins's *Peerage,* 1812, v. 642. The last of the branch died about 1748. 'Walpole' in the last clause of this sentence is apparently HW's slip for 'Whaplode.'

1. A mistake for Colston or Coulston Hall (see *post* 9 Sept. 1776).

2. Unless otherwise noted, the places mentioned in this and the following paragraph are in Suffolk.

3. Or Treyford, in Sussex.

4. Burton Haugh.

hall, Sibton and Heveningham, 8 and 13 Elizabeth; and gave for arms, which you ought to quarter, or, on a bend cotised sable, three martlets, or.

The family of Burrell or Burwell was of knight's degree, and seated first at Colton Hall in Badingham in Hoxon Hundred, by marriage with Derehaugh, and afterwards removed to Rougham in Thedwestre Hundred. They bear argent, a saltire gules, between four oak leaves vert, on a chief azure a lion's head erased between two Danish axes or. These are somewhat different from those in your windows, but the green leaves show them to be the same in effect. In King Charles II's time Sir Jeffery Burwell sold Rougham to Robert Davers, Esq.[5]

It is a double pleasure I have in thus being able to send you <t>he name of your great-grandmother, Lady Burwell, especially after a fruitless disquisition by a King-at-Arms.[6] I should be excessively vain, and plume myself prodigiously upon such an advantage, did I not owe my knowledge to a little MS containing the antiquities of the Suffolk families, by a Sir Richard Gipps,[7] a good antiquary of that county in the last century. It was lent to me many years ago[8] by Mr Soame of Thurlow,[9] who had it as a present from Lady Barnardiston.[10] I have copied the MS into my 28th volume, and if you have an eager desire to see it, though intermixed with an hundred out-of-the-way rubbish of my own, I will send you the volume, and you [are] the only person I would send it to, as I know your nicety of honour in not communicating or showing it to anyone else. Lady Burwell's Christian name is unluckily omitted.[11]

I am glad Antiquity has such an advocate as you. Whether in joke or earnest, I have been amused and entertained with the study of it

5. Sir Robert Davers (ca 1620–84), 1st Bt, of Rougham, Suffolk. He bought the manor of Rougham between 1680 and 12 May 1682 (when he was made a baronet).

6. Joseph Edmondson.

7. *Antiquitates Suffolcienses, or an Essay towards recovering some account of the Ancient Familys in the County of Suffolk,* by Sir Richard Gipps (1659–1708), Kt. It is printed, with introductory notes by the Rev. Francis Haslewood in *Suffolk Institute of Archaeology and Natural History,* viii (1894). 121–214, from the original in the British Museum (Add MS 20,695). 'This note is found at the beginning of the Index

of Names: "Copied this into my 28 Vol. Jul. 3, 1757. Wm Cole" ' (Gipps, ibid. 214).

8. In 1757.

9. Stephen Soame (1709–64), of Little Thurlow, Suffolk; of Sidney College; admitted to the Middle Temple, 1727 (see *Alumni Cantab.*).

10. 'of Kedington' (addition in Cole's copy). Catharine Winn (1708–57), wife of Sir Samuel Barnardiston (1681–1736), 5th Bt, of Kedington (Ketton), Suffolk.

11. It was Elizabeth (see preceding letter). Cole has added in his copy: 'That might easily be recovered, I apprehend, from the parish register of Badingham.'

all my life. How much more amusing must it be to you who have ancestry than to me who have none, is too obvious to remark. But even to me, the tracing connections is very entertaining.

I rather think your confounding Walpole and Whaplode is a mistake. Whaplode, or Quaplode, as it is called in ancient deeds, is a very large village near Spalding in Lincolnshire, in Marshland, and at no great distance from Walpole in Norfolk. The family of Whaplode gave for arms, barry of six pieces, or and azure, over all a bend gules, which are quartered singly by Sir Nicholas Bacon,[12] Lord Keeper, and are over the door of Benet College Chapel to this day, he being a contributor to the building it. These are the same arms which are in your second window of the gallery at Strawberry Hill, which are the very same with those of Gilbert de Gaunt, Earl of Lincoln temp. Henry III,[13] who was a benefactor to Spalding Abbey near Whaplode, from whom, perhaps, as was not unusual, the family of Whaplode, from alliance or descent, might take the same bearing. However, if there is a family in Lincolnshire of the name of Whaplode who give the arms of Walpole, no doubt your reasoning is good.

Adieu, dear Sir, and believe me to be

Your most affectionate, obliged servant,

Wm Cole

To Cole, Sunday 10 December 1775

Add MS 5952, ff. 144–5.

Address: To the Reverend Mr Cole at Milton near Cambridge.
Postmark: RD 12 DE.

Strawberry Hill, Dec. 10, 1775.

I WAS very sorry to have been here, dear Sir, the day you called on me in town.[1] It is so difficult to uncloister you, that I regret not seeing you when you are out of your own *ambry*.

I have nothing new to tell you that is very old; but you can inform me of something within your own district. Who is the author,

12. (1509–79), Kt; Lord Keeper of the Great Seal, 1558.

13. Gilbert de Gant or Gaunt (d. ca 1242), called Earl of Lincoln.

1. See the first paragraph of the following letter.

E. B. G., of a version of Mr Gray's Latin Odes into English? and of an elegy on my wolf-devoured dog, poor Tory?[2]—a name you will marvel at in a dog of mine; but his godmother was the widow of Alderman Parsons,[3] who gave him at Paris to Lord Conway,[4] and he to me. The author is a poet, but makes me blush, for he calls Mr Gray and me, *congenial pair*.[5] Alas! I have no genius; and if any symptom of talent, so inferior to Gray's, that Milton and Quarles might as well be coupled together. We rode over the Alps in the same chaise, but Pegasus drew on his side and a cart-horse on mine. I am too jealous of his fame, to let us be coupled together.

This author says he has lately printed at Cambridge a Latin translation of the Bards; I should be much obliged to you for it.

I do not ask you if Cambridge has produced anything, for it never does. Have you made any discoveries? has Mr Lort? where is he? Does Mr Tyson engrave no more?

My plates for Strawberry[6] advance leisurely. I am about nothing. I grow old and lazy, and the present world cares for nothing but politics, and satisfies itself with writing in newspapers. If they are not bound up and preserved in libraries, posterity will imagine that the art of printing was gone out of use. Lord Hardwicke has indeed reprinted his heavy volume of Sir Dudley Carleton's *Dispatches*,[7] and

---

2. Edward Burnaby Greene (d. 1788), author of *The Latin Odes of Mr Gray, in English Verse, with an Ode on the Death of a favourite Spaniel*, 1775 (see DNB, and *post* 24 Dec. 1775). HW assumed that he was of Cambridge because Greene's 'Ode Pindarica pro Cambriae Vatibus Latino Carmine reddita,' was printed at Cambridge (Matthews, 1775).

3. Humphrey Parsons (1676?–1741), brewer of Aldgate, alderman of Portsoken (1721), Lord Mayor of London (1730, 1740), and an 'incorruptible Tory.' He m. Sarah Crowley or Crawley (d. 1759), dau. of Sir Ambrose Crowley. After the death of her husband, Mrs Parsons and her children lived much at Paris.

4. Francis Seymour Conway, afterwards 1st E. and M. of Hertford.

5. Greene prefaces his 'Ode V. on the Death of a Favorite Spaniel' with a long extract from Gray to his mother, 7 Nov. (n.s.) 1739 (Wm Mason, *Gray*[1] 63), which tells of Tory's death. The Ode begins:

'Where in lone grandeur to the sight
Alps heave o'er Alps, tremendous height,
The PAIR congenial roam.'

6. Which were used in the *Description of SH*, 1784. The plates done at this time were from Pars (whose drawings of SH were made in 1772) and from Bentley's designs of the chimney-pieces and shell bench (which were drawn about 1753).

7. *Letters from and to Sir Dudley Carleton, Knt during his Embassy in Holland*, 2d edn 'with large additions to the historical preface,' 1775. The 1st edn (only 20 copies) was privately printed in 1757, when Hardwicke was Lord Royston. He sent HW a copy (A.2.25), which was sold SH v. 25. HW noted in MS Cat.: 'A few only of these were printed for presents.' Sir Dudley Carleton (1573–1632), Vct Dorchester, was suspected of complicity in the Gunpowder Plot, but afterwards served as ambassador abroad.

says I was in the wrong to despise it.[8] I never met with anybody that thought otherwise. What signifies raising the dead so often, when they die the next minute? Adieu!

Yours ever,
H. W.

From COLE, Tuesday 12 December 1775

VA, Forster MS 110, ff. 149–50. COLE's copy, Add MS 5824, f. 89v. The enclosure (Gough to Cole, 27 Oct. 1775) is edited from Cole's copy, Add MS. 5834, ff. 72v, 73.

On the cover of Cole's letter, HW has drawn four coats of arms mentioned in Gough's letter to Cole, and noted:

'Sir Ch. Tufton of Twickenham.
v. Collins in Tufton.'

[Drawing: Barry of six pieces, 'or' and 'gules'.]

'Qu. if Savoy.'

'A Kt and five men, soldiers in red.'

'Cannot be Fr. 1st or Constable, for no fleurs de lis.'

'Tufton family Henry 7th.'

[Drawing: Paly of seven, 'or' and 'gules'.]

[Drawing (crossed through and marked 'sent'), Argent, a mullet 'gules or sable.' To the right of the drawing HW has written 'gallies' (galleys).]

[Drawing: 'Argent,' a crescent 'gules or sable.']

'Some ladies in town receiving messenger on his knees.'

'A soldier addressing a damsel on his knees.'

'Vide for this—& Jernegan & FitzOsbert.'

The last note refers to HW's pedigree (see *post* 14 Dec. 1775).
Address: For the Honourable Mr Horace Walpole in Arlington Street, London.
Postmark: 1[3?] DE.

---

8. See *Roy. & Nob. Authors, Works* i. 349–50. Hardwicke denied HW's criticism that the letters 'turned chiefly on the Synod of Dort,' and claimed 'a right to rank this correspondence amongst the materials for no uninteresting period of Civil History' (*Letters from and to Sir Dudley Carleton*[2], pp. xxxv–xxxvi). See *post* 24 Dec., n. 5.

Milton near Cambridge, Dec. 12, 1775.

Dear Sir,

IN my journey to Burnham[1] I called in Arlington Street, with little expectation of meeting you there, but only to know how you
did, but was informed that you arrived from Paris the Tuesday before,[2] and was not gone for Strawberry Hill an hour before I called.[3]
As one of my sisters was to go with me next day[4] to Dr Apthorp's
through Kingston, I could not call on you, and was vexed that I
could not.

I returned here from Burnham on Saturday, not well, having had
a slight touch of the gout while I was there, and now indisposed
with the common cold that still hangs upon me, with a cough. On
my table I found a letter which had been here six weeks, from Mr
Gough, giving a most minute account of a painting lately discovered
in London, and which it is probable you have either seen or had an
account of. However, for fear it may have escaped you, I send you
Mr Gough's letter, more especially as he seems to make a request to
you through me, both of your opinion about it and to know whether
Mr Vertue has taken any notice of it in his papers. I shall therefore
take it as a favour, if you have seen the painting, that you will be so
kind to give me your thoughts concerning it, if you do not choose to
do so to Mr Gough.

I hope you had your health well at Paris, and that the journey has
done you service.

I am a little doubtful whether you received my last letter to you,
some two months before you set off for France, as I generally know
you are punctual: it was relating to a query in your pedigree. If you
did not receive it, as I have your letter, I can easily send you a so-
lution.

I am, dear Sir,

Your ever obliged and faithful servant,

Wm Cole

1. 'two months ago' (addition in Cole's copy).

2. HW reached London at noon, Tuesday 17 Oct. 1775 (Paris Jour.).

3. 'I had been to call on Lord Montfort, who was just set out for Paris' (addition in Cole's copy).

4. 'to Warplesdon in Surrey' (addition in Cole's copy).

[Enclosure.]

Dear Sir,   Enfield, Oct. 27, 1775.

In taking down some old houses just without Temple Bar, whose
site was granted by Henry VII or VIII, to some of the Tufton family, and now belongs to the Earl of Thanet,[5] and was lately occupied
by the Rose Tavern, a very curious painting on the wall is come to
light. It seems of the sixteenth century, but the subject is not yet
ascertained. I shall give you the particulars, as I took them on a
leisure<ly> examination yesterday, and hope for your opinion of
them at your earliest leisure.

The principal figure is a knight whose horse is down, his battle-
axe on the ground, his head covered with a kind of network over
his hair; he is middle-aged, bearded, wears a collar and chain, his
shoulder-sleeves mail, and his skirts the same; his hat and feather on
the ground. On his harness, which is richly embroidered, are, in
rondeaux, two heads of warriors, one with a battle-axe. Four halberdiers wearing caps and feathers, slashed sleeves, breeches and
hose, and black vests, surround him in a wood; a fifth points to him,
while a sixth advances, carrying a large sword of state, the point
downwards, and extending his right hand to a horseman helmeted
and armed, riding upon a black horse, as if to receive the submis-
sion or surrender of the fallen knight, who, lifting up his face and
hands to heaven, says, *Pater noster, Quid me vis facere?* Behind the
fallen knight are a seventh halberdier, in a red coat like an officer,
talking to an eighth dressed as the others. These last are cut in two
by a small window about a foot square, which, with another, seem
coeval with the painting. Further on, in the same front line, is a
large party of horsemen trotting up, their lances erect, their skirts,
trumpets and banners charged with barry or and gules. Some have
helmets and mail, and a few are in red, as officers. Others on foot,
shouldering red muskets, march down from behind a wood, as of
the same party. On the back line rides a man on a white horse, with
a hat and feather, in a red-striped vest, followed by two halberdiers,
and preceded by two more at some little distance. A large corps de
reserve of foot-soldiers with lances, form a circle at the top to the
right corner. From them goes an officer in red, with a hat and
feather, on a black horse, to a battery of four cannon on carriages

5. Sackville Tufton (1733–86), 8th E. of Thanet.

of the modern form, which are firing on three galleys, whose sails
are charged with paly or and gules, and a building on the stern has
argent, a crescent sable or gules. These galleys carry eight or ten
guns, and on a long rostrum are two trumpeters, whose trumpet
flags have paly, as above. They are making towards a town fortified
by embattled walls and towers, and at the inner gate are some ladies
receiving a knight, or messenger, who kneels to them. Two channels
or harbors before this town are fortified by chains, and behind these
lie four more ships unrigged. In the front right corner, a soldier on
his knees is paying his addresses to a damsel, and behind him stands
a flagon and . . . [sic]. The side of the room on which this painting
is [is] about twenty feet long, and the front figures twenty-three
inches high.

The circumstances of the captive knight agree with the taking of
Francis I at the battle of Pavia, by five soldiers who knew him not
till he surrendered to the Viceroy Lanoy,[6] as Hollingshed,[7] or as
Montfaucon (*Mon. de la Mon. Fr.*),[8] to the Sieur de Pomperant,[9]
who caused the rest to retire. The galleys and their crescent seem to
make it a Turkish history, but I cannot help persuading myself it is
a true history, and something in which our countrymen were concerned. I am impatient to have your opinion on it. Perhaps if Mr
Walpole were applied to, he might find something in Vertue's London papers about this house at least.

I am,

Yours faithfully,

R. Gough

To Cole, Thursday 14 December 1775

Add MS 5952, ff. 146–7.

Address: To the Reverend Mr Cole at Milton near Cambridge.
Postmark: EK 14 DE.

Arlington Street, Dec. 14, 1775.

OUR letters probably passed by each other on the road, for I
wrote to you on Tuesday, and have this instant received one

6. Charles de Lannoy (ca 1470–1527),
Viceroy of Charles V at Naples (see *Biographie Universelle*).

7. See Raphael Holinshed, *Chronicles of
England*, 1586, iii. pt 2, p. 884.

8. 'Il [Francis I] se rendit enfin au Sieur
de Pomperant, qui avoit accompagné le
Duc de Bourbon quand il quitta la France
. . . Le Viceroi Lanoi vint ensuite, et le
roi lui donna sa foi' (Bernard de Mont-

from you, which I answer directly, to beg pardon for my incivility, nay ingratitude, in not thanking you for your present of a whole branch of most reputable ancestors the *Derehaughs*—why, the *Derehaughs* alone would make gentlemen of half the modern peers, English or Irish. I doubt my journey to France was got into my head, and left no room for an additional quarter—but I have given it to Edmondson, and ordered him to take care that I am born again from the *Derehaughs*. This Edmondson has got a ridiculous notion into his head that another, and much ancienter of my progenitors, Sir Henry Walpole, married his wife Isabella Fitz Osbert when she was widow to Sir Walter Jernegan; whereas all *the old testament* says Sir Walter married Sir Henry's widow.[1] Pray send me your authority to confound this gainsayer, if you know anything particular of the matter.

I had not heard of the painting you tell me of. As those boobies, the Society of Antiquaries, have gotten hold of it, I wonder their *piety* did not make them bury it again, as they did the clothes of Edward I.[2] I have some notion that in Vertue's MSS or somewhere else, I don't know where, I have read of some ancient painting at the Rose Tavern. This I will tell *you*—but Mr Gough is such a bear, that I shall not satisfy him about it. That Society, when they are puzzled, have recourse to me; and that would be so often, that I shall not encourage them. They may blunder as much as they please from their heavy president down to the pert Governor Pownall, who accounts for everything immediately, before the creation or since. Say only to Mr Gough, that I said I had not leisure now to examine Vertue's MSS.[3] If I find anything there, *you* shall know—but I have

faucon, *Les Monumens de la Monarchie Françoise*, 5 vols, Paris, 1729–33, iv. 254).

9. Not identified.

———

1. Sir Henry de Walpole, elder brother of Ralph de Walpole (d. 1302), Bp of Ely, m. 'Isabel, daughter of Sir Peter Fitz-Osbert . . . which Isabel, surviving the said Sir Henry, was married, secondly, to Sir Walter Jernegan. . . . She deceased about 1311' (Collins, *Peerage*, 1812, v. 636). See also the following letter. Later genealogists confirm the above statement.

2. See Sir Joseph Ayloffe, 'An Account of the Body of King Edward the First, as it appeared on opening his Tomb in the Year 1774,' *Archaeologia* iii. 376–413, especially the last paragraph, by which it appears that the Society of Antiquaries could not have removed anything from the tomb: the Dean of Westminster was present to see that nothing was molested from the time it was opened until it was closed with cement.

3. Cole followed HW's direction in his letter to Gough 24 Dec. 1775: 'As I told you in my last, [he says] I took the liberty of sending your letter to Mr Walpole, whose answer to me was this: "That he had not leisure now to examine Vertue's MSS." As his answer was so cold, I don't care to say anything further about it' (LA i. 675).

no longer any eagerness to communicate what I discover. When there was so little taste for MSS which Mr Gray thought worth transcribing, and which were so valuable,[4] would one offer more pearls?[5]

Boydel brought me this morning another number of the prints from the pictures at Houghton.[6] Two or three in particular are most admirably executed—but alas! it will be twenty years before the set is completed. That is too long to look forward at any age—and at mine!—nay, people will be tired in a quarter of the time. Boydel, who knows this country, and still more this town, thinks so too. Perhaps there will be newer, or at least more fashionable, ways of engraving, and the old will be despised—or which is still more likely, nobody will be able to afford the expense. Who would lay a plan for anything in an overgrown metropolis hurrying to its fall?

I will return you Mr Gough's letter when I get a frank. Adieu!

From COLE, Sunday 24 December 1775

VA, Forster MS 110, ff. 151–3. COLE'S copy, Add MS 5824, ff. 90v, 91v.

Address: For the Honourable Mr Horace Walpole in Arlington Street, London.

Postmark: None. [The letter apparently has not been through the post. Cole probably sent it in a packet with the books mentioned below.]

Milton, Dec. 24, 1775.

Dear Sir,

I HAVE two of your letters unanswered before me, but when I tell you I have not been once out of my house since I returned hither from Burnham, but have been, though not expressly ill, yet mawkish and indisposed by a cough, gout flying about me, I hope you will excuse my indisposition for writing.

I immediately sent for and got you the Latin translation of *The Bard,* printed at Cambridge. That and the translation of Mr Gray's

4. HW refers to the slow sale of *Miscellaneous Antiquities*, especially *No. II,* 'Sir Thomas Wyat's Defence,' printed from Gray's transcript of the original (see *ante* 17 June 1772 and n. 2; 18 Feb. 1773).

5. That is, more numbers of *Miscellaneous Antiquities.*

6. *The Houghton Gallery,* 2 vols, atlas folio, was published by Boydell in 1788. The prints were originally issued in numbers, ten plates to each number, at two guineas a number. Four numbers had been issued by 1780 (see Gough, *British Topography*[2] ii. 25). HW's copy of the complete work was sold London viii. 1125 (SH viii. 48).

Latin odes, etc., are the performance of one Mr Edward Burnaby Green, now a porter brewer in Westminster of great wealth, but formerly a fellow commoner of Benet College. He has translated Juvenal[1] and other things. When I sent to Cambridge for *The Bard,* I wrote to a friend or two to inquire after the translator, but could get no intelligence, but one of the College,[2] who knows him, happening to call here, he immediately, from the initials, hit it off. At the time I sent for *The Bard* to Mr Merrill my bookseller, he sent me another,[3] supposing it to be that I inquired after, with the enclosed note. I send you the book also, as it is another translation of *The Bard* at Chester.

Mr Lort is at Cambridge and has called here twice since my return. He could give me no account of *E. B. G.,* but there can be no doubt but Mr Colman of Benet's interpretation is a good reading. Mr Tyson has left off engraving for some time,[4] and I don't believe will ever resume it.

I am entirely of your mind in respect to Sir Dudley Carleton's *Letters.* I saw his Lordship was picqued at your sensible, lively and true observation. The index to the new edition,[5] as well as the place in the preface it refers to, is a proof of it.

Now to your second letter.

I am glad the house of your grandmother Derehaugh pleased you, but it would be too great a presumption to gainsay Mr Edmondson again in his own profession. It is more than sufficient that I was able to gratify your curiosity in a point which did not fall under his observation at the time. My authority in the present question corroborates Mr Edmondson's book, whether new or old.[6] In Sir Richard Gippes's *Antiquitates Suffolcienses,* a MS in my possession, is this account, where the name is not Fitz-Osbert.

1. *Satires of Juvenal paraphrastically imitated, and adapted to the Times,* 1763.

2. William Colman (see below).

3. *The Bard. A Pindaric Poem, by Mr Gray. Translated into Latin Verse. To which is prefixed a dedication to the genius of antient Britain,* Chester, 1775. The translation is by Rev. R. Williams, rector of Machynlleth, Montgomeryshire (see Clark Sutherland Northup, *A Bibliography of Thomas Gray,* 1917, p. 62).

4. 'ever since Mr Bretherton left Cambridge, and it is my opinion will not re-

sume it except Mr. B. should return again' (addition in Cole's copy).

5. The following entry appears in the index under *Walpole* (*Mr*): 'politely mentions the Editor of this volume in his account of noble authors, but is mistaken in the motives of the publication, pref. xxxv.' See *ante* 10 Dec., n. 8.

6. Cole probably means the old or new 'testament' (see preceding letter, n. 1). *Baronagium Genealogicum: or the Pedigrees of the English Peers,* by Sir William Segar, 'continued to the present time,' by Joseph

Fitz-Osburne. This most ancient family was seated at Somerley Town in Lothing Hundred, and descended from that famous Fitz-Osburne who was Marshal to the Conqueror, and conquered the Isle of Wight, of which island he was the first Lord,[7] and it continued in his family till they were dispossessed of it by an invasion of the French. From this great man, who was at last killed in Flanders, descended Sir Peter Fitz-Osburne[8] of Somerley Town, who left one son and two daughters, Robert, Alice and Isabella. Robert died without issue, and Alice, the eldest daughter and co-heir, married to Sir John Noyon;[9] and Isabella to Sir Walter Jernegan. They were lords of Somerley Town 9 Edward II, and bare gules, two gemels argent, a canton vert.

Sir Roger Fitz Owborne or Osborne[10] was a knight banneret in the time of Edward I. He bare gules, three bars gemels, or, a canton argent.

But here we seem to be all in the <wrong>, for the Fitz-Osberts' arms, whose coat you quarter, is quite different from t<hat of> Fitz-Osborn, who married Jernegan. Yet Camden[11] calls the Lord of the Isle <of Wig>ht Fitz-Osborn, and Ralph Brooke,[12] York Herald temp. Jac. I, says that William Fitz-Osborne, Earl of Bretevile[13] in Normandy, who was son of Osborne de Crepon by Albreda his wife, daughter of Ralph Earl of Ivery,[14] whose grandfather[15] Herfastus the Dane was brother to Gonora, wife of Richard the first Duke of Normandy,[16] great-grandmother to William the Conqueror. This William Fitz-Osborne came into England with the Conqueror, who made him Earl of Hereford in 1068,[17] and Marshal and Steward of England. His arms are gules, a bend argent, over all a fess or. I leave Mr Edmundson to reconcile these differences.

Edmondson, 6 vols [1764–84]. Cole refers to v. 483; see following letter.

7. William FitzOsbern (d. 1071), Seigneur de Breteuil in Normandy, and 1st E. of Hereford in England; son of Osbern the Seneschal by Emma, dau. of Ralph or Rudolf, Count of Ivry. Osbern was son of Herfast the Dane, whose sister Gunnor married Richard I, D. of Normandy.

8. Peter Fitz-Osbert (d. 1275) (see Walter A. Copinger, *The Manors of Suffolk* ii. 174; v. 62).

9. Sir John Noyoun (d. 1341?) (see ibid. ii. 175; v. 63).

10. Roger Fitz (Peter) Osbert (d. 1302?) (see ibid. ii. 174–5; v. 62).

11. See William Camden, *Britannia*, ed. R. Gough, 4 vols, 2d edn, 1806, i. 175–6.

12. In the remainder of this paragraph, Cole closely follows Ralph Brooke's *Catalogue and Succession of the Kings*, etc., 2d edn, 1622, p. 172.

13. That is, Breteuil.

14. See n. 7 above.

15. That is, the grandfather of William FitzOsbern.

16. Richard I (935–96), called 'The Fearless,' D. of Normandy, m. as his second wife, his mistress, Gonnar or Gunnor (see *Nouvelle Biographie Générale*).

17. The date is elsewhere said to be 1067 (see DNB; GEC).

I have not yet wrote to Mr Gough, but mean to do so this day.[18]

I am sorry Boydel's prints are too expensive for common folks, and that the time to finish them is so distant. I wish this excellent design don't end in the same way as Houbraken's did some twenty or thirty years ago, from the variable temper of our countrymen.

No doubt you have heard long ago, and lamented the death of poor Henshaw.[19] I had a great loss, as his gratitude for my introducing him to you, and you to Bartolozzi, made him inform me of everything new in the print way, which I now hear nothing of.

I am, dear Sir, your most faithful and obliged servant,

WM COLE

[Enclosure.]

Sir,

I know not the translator of *The Bard*. They were sent me from a bookseller of Chester who did not mention who did it—possibly by some young Welshman of St John's College.

Mr Gray's 'Elegy in a Country Churchyard' is just turned into Latin by a soph of Jesus College named Wakefield.[20]

Sir, your obedient,

J. Merrill

Cambridge, Dec. 14, 1775.[21]

18. The letter, dated 24 Dec. 1775, is printed in part in LA i. 675–7.

19. He died of a violent fever, in London, 18 Aug. 1775, aged 22 (see Add MS 5844, f. 47).

20. *An Elegy written in a country Church-yard. Elegia in caemeterio rustico scripta, numeris elegiacis latine reddita.*

Auctore *** Coll: Cant: Alumno. London. Printed for J. Nicholson in Cambridge, 1776. The translator was Gilbert Wakefield (1756–1801), of Jesus College (B.A. 1776), later well known as scholar and controversialist.

21. Added in Cole's hand.